T0212941

# Lecture Notes in Artificial Intelligence 13502

Subseries of Lecture Notes in Computer Science

More information about this subseries at https://link.springer.com/bookseries/1244

Petr Sojka · Aleš Horák · Ivan Kopeček ·
Karel Pala (Eds.)

# Text, Speech, and Dialogue

25th International Conference, TSD 2022
Brno, Czech Republic, September 6–9, 2022
Proceedings

 Springer

*Editors*
Petr Sojka
Faculty of Informatics
Masaryk University
Brno, Czech Republic

Aleš Horák
Faculty of Informatics
Masaryk University
Brno, Czech Republic

Ivan Kopeček
Faculty of Informatics
Masaryk University
Brno, Czech Republic

Karel Pala
Faculty of Informatics
Masaryk University
Brno, Czech Republic

ISSN 0302-9743          ISSN 1611-3349 (electronic)
Lecture Notes in Artificial Intelligence
ISBN 978-3-031-16269-5     ISBN 978-3-031-16270-1 (eBook)
https://doi.org/10.1007/978-3-031-16270-1

LNCS Sublibrary: SL7 – Artificial Intelligence

This Springer imprint is published by the registered company Springer Nature Switzerland AG
The registered company address is: Gewerbestrasse 11, 6330 Cham, Switzerland

# Preface

The annual International Conference on Text, Speech and Dialogue Conference (TSD), which originated in 1998, is continuing its third decade. In the course of time, thousands of authors from all over the world have contributed to the proceedings. TSD constitutes a recognized platform for the presentation and discussion of state-of-the-art technology and recent achievements in the field of natural language processing. It has become an interdisciplinary forum, interweaving the themes of speech technology and language processing. The conference attracts researchers not only from Central and Eastern Europe but also from other parts of the world. Indeed, one of its goals has always been to bring together NLP researchers with different interests from different parts of the world and to promote their mutual cooperation.

One of the declared goals of the conference has always been, as its title suggests, twofold: not only to deal with language processing and dialogue systems, but also to stimulate dialogue between researchers in the two areas of NLP, i.e., between text and speech researchers. In our view, the TSD conference was again successful in this respect in 2022. We had the pleasure of welcoming two prominent invited speakers this year: Eneko Agirre from the University of the Basque Country, Spain, and Anna Rogers from the University of Copenhagen, Denmark.

This volume contains the proceedings of the 25th TSD conference, held in Brno, Czech Republic, in September 2022. In the review process, 43 papers were accepted out of 94 submitted, based on three reviews per paper, giving an acceptance rate of 46%.

We would like to thank all the authors for the efforts they put into their submissions and the members of the Program Committee and reviewers who did a wonderful job selecting the best papers. We are also grateful to the invited speakers for their contributions. Their talks provided insight into important current issues, applications, and techniques related to the conference topics.

Special thanks are due to the members of Local Organizing Committee for their tireless effort in organizing the conference. The TEX pertise of Petr Sojka resulted in the production of the volume that you are holding in your hands.

We hope that the readers will benefit from the results of this event and disseminate the ideas of the TSD conference all over the world. Enjoy the proceedings!

July 2022

Aleš Horák
Ivan Kopeček
Karel Pala
Petr Sojka

# Organization

TSD 2022 was organized by the Faculty of Informatics, Masaryk University, in cooperation with the Faculty of Applied Sciences, University of West Bohemia in Plzeň. The conference webpage is located at https://www.tsdconference.org/tsd2022/.

## General Chair

Nöth, Elmar (General Chair)　　Friedrich-Alexander-Universität
　　　　　　　　　　　　　　　　Erlangen-Nürnberg, Germany

## Program Committee

| | |
|---|---|
| Agerri, Rodrigo | University of the Basque Country, Spain |
| Agirre, Eneko | University of the Basque Country, Spain |
| Benko, Vladimír | Slovak Academy of Sciences, Slovakia |
| Bhatia, Archna | Carnegie Mellon University, USA |
| Černocký, Jan | Brno University of Technology, Czech Republic |
| Dobrisek, Simon | University of Ljubljana, Slovenia |
| Ekstein, Kamil | University of West Bohemia, Czech Republic |
| Evgrafova, Karina | Saint-Petersburg State University, Russia |
| Fedorov, Yevhen | Cherkasy State Technological University, Ukraine |
| Fischer, Volker | EML Speech Technology GmbH, Germany |
| Fišer, Darja | Institute of Contemporary History, Slovenia |
| Flek, Lucie | Philipps-Universität Marburg, Germany |
| Gambäck, Björn | Norwegian University of Science and Technology, Norway |
| Garabík, Radovan | Slovak Academy of Sciences, Slovakia |
| Gelbukh, Alexander | Instituto Politécnico Nacional, Mexico |
| Guthrie, Louise | University of Texas at El Paso, USA |
| Haderlein, Tino | Friedrich-Alexander-Universität Erlangen-Nürnberg, Germany |
| Hajič, Jan | Charles University, Czech Republic |
| Hajičová, Eva | Charles University, Czech Republic |
| Haralambous, Yannis | IMT Atlantique, France |
| Hermansky, Hynek | Johns Hopkins University, USA |
| Hlaváčová, Jaroslava | Charles University, Czech Republic |
| Horák, Aleš | Masaryk University, Czech Republic |
| Hovy, Eduard | Carnegie Mellon University, USA |
| Jouvet, Denis | Inria, France |

| | |
|---|---|
| Khokhlova, Maria | Saint Petersburg State University, Russia |
| Khusainov, Aidar | Tatarstan Academy of Sciences, Russia |
| Kocharov, Daniil | Saint Petersburg State University, Russia |
| Konopík, Miloslav | University of West Bohemia, Czech Republic |
| Kopeček, Ivan | Masaryk University, Czech Republic |
| Kordoni, Valia | Humboldt University of Berlin, Germany |
| Kotelnikov, Evgeny | Vyatka State University, Russia |
| Král, Pavel | University of West Bohemia, Czech Republic |
| Kunzmann, Siegfried | Amazon Alexa Machine Learning, Germany |
| Ljubešić, Nikola | Jožef Stefan Institute, Slovenia |
| Loukachevitch, Natalija | Lomonosov Moscow State University, Russia |
| Magnini, Bernardo | Fondazione Bruno Kessler, Italy |
| Marchenko, Oleksandr | Taras Shevchenko National University of Kyiv, Ukraine |
| Matoušek, Václav | University of West Bohemia, Czech Republic |
| Mouček, Roman | University of West Bohemia, Czech Republic |
| Mykowiecka, Agnieszka | Polish Academy of Sciences, Poland |
| Ney, Hermann | RWTH Aachen University, Germany |
| Nivre, Joakim | Uppsala University, Sweden |
| Orozco-Arroyave, Juan Rafael | University of Antioquia, Colombia |
| Pala, Karel | Masaryk University, Czech Republic |
| Piasecki, Maciej | Wroclaw University of Science and Technology, Poland |
| Psutka, Josef | University of West Bohemia, Czech Republic |
| Pustejovsky, James | Brandeis University, USA |
| Rigau, German | University of the Basque Country, Spain |
| Rosso, Paolo | Universitat Politecnica de Valencia, Spain |
| Rothkrantz, Leon | Delft University of Technology, The Netherlands |
| Rumshisky, Anna | University of Massachusetts Lowell, USA |
| Rusko, Milan | Slovak Academy of Sciences, Slovakia |
| Rychlý, Pavel | Masaryk University, Czech Republic |
| Sazhok, Mykola | International Research and Training Center for Information Technologies and Systems, Ukraine |
| Scharenborg, Odette | Delft University of Technology, The Netherlands |
| Skrelin, Pavel | Saint Petersburg State University, Russia |
| Smrž, Pavel | Brno University of Technology, Czech Republic |
| Sojka, Petr | Masaryk University, Czech Republic |
| Stemmer, Georg | Intel Corp., Germany |
| Šikonja, Marko Robnik | University of Ljubljana, Slovenia |
| Tadić, Marko | University of Zagreb, Croatia |
| Trmal, Jan | Johns Hopkins University, USA |

| | |
|---|---|
| Varadi, Tamas | Hungarian Academy of Sciences, Hungary |
| Vetulani, Zygmunt | Adam Mickiewicz University, Poland |
| Wawer, Aleksander | Polish Academy of Sciences, Poland |
| Wiggers, Pascal | Amsterdam University of Applied Sciences, The Netherlands |
| Woliński, Marcin | Polish Academy of Sciences, Poland |
| Wróblewska, Alina | Polish Academy of Sciences, Poland |
| Zakharov, Victor | Saint Petersburg State University, Russia |
| Žganec Gros, Jerneja | Alpineon, Slovenia |

## Additional Referees

Dan Zeman
Pavel Pecina
Tanvina Patel
Andrej Žgank
Jakob Lenardič
Kaja Dobrovoljc
Rudolf Rosa
Zdenek Zabokrtsky
Milos Jakubicek
Vera Evdokimova
Zuzana Nevěřilová
Adam Rambousek
Nicolás Cortegoso Vissio

Jiří Mírovský
Gorka Azkune
Xabier Soto
Róbert Sabo
Volodymyr Kyrylov
Ondřej Pražák
Taja Kuzman
Matej Ulčar
Matej Klemen
Piotr Przybyła
Giulia Rizzi
Ipek Baris Schlicht
Somnath Banerjee

## Organizing Committee

Aleš Horák (Co-chair)
Ivan Kopeček
Karel Pala (Co-chair)
Adam Rambousek (Web System)
Pavel Rychlý
Petr Sojka (Proceedings)

## Sponsors and Support

The TSD conference is regularly supported by the International Speech Communication Association (ISCA). We would like to express our thanks to Lexical Computing Ltd., IBM Česká republika, spol. s r. o., and Amazon Alexa for their kind sponsor contributions to TSD 2022.

# Contents

**Speech**

**Dialogue**

**Text**

# Evaluating Attribution Methods
# for Explainable NLP with Transformers

Vojtěch Bartička[iD], Ondřej Pražák[(✉)][iD], Miloslav Konopík[iD],
and Jakub Sido[iD]

Department of Computer Science and Engineering, NTIS – New Technologies for the
Information Society, Faculty of Applied Sciences, University of West Bohemia,
Plzeň, Czech Republic
{barticka,ondfa,konopik,sidoj}@ntis.zcu.cz
http://www.nlp.kiv.zcu.cz

**Abstract.** This paper describes the experimental evaluation of several
attribution methods on two NLP tasks: Sentiment analysis and multi-
label document classification. Our motivation is to find the best method
to use with Transformers to interpret model decisions. For this purpose,
we introduce two new evaluation datasets. The first one is derived from
Stanford Sentiment Treebank, where the sentiment of individual words
is annotated along with the sentiment of the whole sentence. The second
dataset comes from Czech Text Document Corpus, where we added keyword information assigned to each category. The keywords were manually
assigned to each document and automatically propagated to categories
via PMI. We evaluate each attribution method on several models of different sizes. The evaluation results are reasonably consistent across all
models and both datasets. It indicates that both datasets with proposed
evaluation metrics are suitable for interpretability evaluation. We show
how the attribution methods behave concerning model size and task. We
also consider practical applications – we show that while some methods perform well, they can be replaced with slightly worse-performing
methods requiring significantly less time to compute.

**Keywords:** Explainable AI · Transformers · Document classification

## 1 Introduction

Interpretability in NLP is a large, fast-growing area. Its goal is to discover what
inputs mainly influence particular decisions of machine learning models. This
paper focuses on interpretability in transformer-based models, which are currently state of the art in the most common NLP tasks. We pay special interest
to post-hoc explanations where we focus on already trained models to produce
the explanations (i.e. we do not modify the training procedure).

In this work, we use two datasets for evaluating explanations. The first
dataset, Stanford Sentiment Treebank [14], is naturally ideal for evaluating

ⓒ Springer Nature Switzerland AG 2022
P. Sojka et al. (Eds.): TSD 2022, LNAI 13502, pp. 3–15, 2022.
https://doi.org/10.1007/978-3-031-16270-1_1

explanations since it provides sentiment annotation for both tokens and phrases. The second dataset is newly created from Czech Text Document Corpus [8]. Our main goal is to evaluate post-hoc explanations (specifically attribution methods) used with standard pretrained Transformer models.

## 2   Related Work

The simplest approaches for interpreting models are based solely on gradients. Such methods are called *Vanilla Gradients* methods. They compute gradients of logits of the predicted class with respect to input embeddings. These methods were first used for images in [12] and later for NLP in [4].

Authors of [10] proposed multiplying gradients with inputs (often referred as *gradient x input*). They proved the equivalence of *gradient x input* to *Layerwise Relevance Propagation* (LRP) [1] for piecewise linear activation functions while LRP being more computationally expensive. Gradient x input is better than vanilla gradients, because it leverages the sign and strength of the input [10].

Integrated Gradients [16] use baselines. A baseline is an input for which the model prediction is neutral, or which represents a lack of information. The need for baselines when explaining model decisions has been discussed prior to Integrated Gradients in [9]. The method then interpolates a linear path with evenly spaced points between the baseline and input. Gradients are computed for each point created this way. The method then integrates over the gradients, which yields the final attributions.

SmoothGrad [13] tackles the issue of noisy gradient attributions. The authors identify that the gradients sharply fluctuate with small changes to the input. They propose a simple method to suppress this phenomenon - create multiple samples by adding noise to the input, compute the sample gradients and average them. The authors show that the method successfully improves the visual coherence of attributions on images.

Chefer et al. [3] proposed relevance propagation method designed specifically for Transformers. This method has very good results but unlike other methods presented here, which are model-agnostic, this method uses specific operations for every layer. Therefore, if we change the architecture of the model[1], we need to modify the method.

Authors of ERASER [6] try to create a general evaluation framework for NLP models similar to GLUE [18]. They collected eight datasets with discrete explanations (rationales) annotated. Some of the datasets had been annotated on the token level in their original form; the rest were annotated for explanations evaluation in ERASER. Documents in all datasets in ERASER are very long, so for most of them, we cannot use pretrained BERT-like models in their standard form.

ERASER has quite a broad scope. It is meant to be used with both continuous and discrete explanations and both post-hoc explanations and models trained

---

[1] Different activation, slightly different layer operation.

specifically to provide good explanations. The authors use standard metrics to measure agreement with human annotations (F1 score for discrete rationales, AUPRC [15] for continuous). They also suggest new metrics to evaluate the faithfulness of the model.

## 3   Evaluation Datasets

As the first step, we build two datasets for evaluating explanations. One is derived from Stanford Sentiment Treebank, which is in English, and the other is from Czech Text Document Corpus.

### 3.1   Sentiment Analysis

To create this dataset, we slightly modify Stanford Sentiment Treebank (SST). The dataset contains continuous sentiment annotations (0–1) for all nodes of the syntactic tree of the sentence. Therefore, the dataset contains sentiment values for all phrases and all words in the sentence and a global sentence-level score. This makes the dataset ideal for evaluating explanations since we know how the sentiment of individual words contributes to the overall sentiment of a given sentence. This is quite strong assumption and it means we ignore some linguistic structures such as negation by assuming the sentiment of individual words is independent of the sentence. However, we believe this simplification does not have significant impact on the results. Since the annotations are continuous, we are able to compare how important are the individual tokens in the sentence.

One of the key changes we made is the removal of neutral sentences from train, validation, and test splits. We believe that it is counterproductive to perform attributions on neutral or unclear examples since it can be expected that the attributions will not make much sense. We consider a sentence to be neutral if its sentiment is between 0.4 and 0.6. Moreover, attribution methods such as Integrated Gradients, which use a neutral baseline as a reference, would be penalized by including the neutral sentences. We also do not evaluate the ability of the attribution methods to explain uncertain decisions of the models.

To create the test and validation splits, we use the original splits while removing neutral sentences as mentioned. We have expanded the training split compared to the original in a way similar to GLUE SST-2 dataset [18]. The original training split contains only whole sentences. We remove neutral sentences from the training split and add all non-neutral phrases (sequences of one or more tokens) that do not occur in any of the sentences from test and validation splits. We show the sizes of the splits in Table 1.

**Table 1.** Statistics of the splits of the sentiment dataset

| Split | Samples | Positive samples | Negative samples | Tokens |
|-------|---------|------------------|------------------|--------|
| Train | 83 710  | 45 068           | 38 642           | 878 901 |
| Val   | 872     | 444              | 428              | 17 046 |
| Test  | 1 821   | 909              | 912              | 35 023 |

## 3.2 Multi-label Document Classification

This dataset is derived from Czech Text Document Corpus (CTDC). CTDC is a corpus for multi-label document classification. It consists of news articles classified into 60 different categories. Statistical information such as word count and class count histograms are available in the original paper [8].

The original dataset does not contain any clues how to explain the assignment of labels to documents. However, we believe that manually annotated keywords should be sufficient explanation of the category assignments. Fortunately, the documents in the CTDC dataset come from journalists who include keywords in documents. Thus, the first step is to associate the documents with the keywords provided by journalists. However, we can not be certain that all the keywords really support the document categories. Moreover, we can not distinguish which keywords and categories associate to each other (the dataset contains multiple labels for each document). To solve both issues, we employ the *pointwise mutual information* (PMI), which tells us how much more likely is that a keyword $k$ and a class $c$ appear together than it would happen by chance (if $k$ and $c$ were independent). We take manually annotated keywords for the original news articles, and we compute PMI for each keyword with each class. The keywords with the largest PMI with a class are considered keywords for that class. We publish the PMI values to preserve soft rationales information, but in the experiments, we used hard rationales by setting the PMI threshold for class keywords.

We have 37 121 keywords and PMI values in total for all 60 classes in the original dataset, but some of the classes have only a few keywords. We consider as class keywords all those with PMI greater than 0 and occurring at least ten times in that class. If we consider all PMI values greater than 0, there are 568 keywords per class on average. The PMI values, however, are low in general. If we consider keywords with a PMI of at least log(5), we end up with an average of 135 keywords per class. The percentiles of PMI are shown in Table 2.

The keywords can be single words or phrases of up to three words. About 84% of the keywords are single words, 16% are two-word phrases, and less than 1% are three-word phrases.

The keywords are, in a sense, characteristic of their respective category. The PMI tells us how significant they are. We would expect the model to pay more attention to the keywords than to other words in the document when deciding whether or not the document belongs to a category. This enables us to measure the performance of attribution methods since we have a ground truth in terms of what should be important in the decision process of a model.

**Table 2.** Percentiles of PMI distribution

| Percentile | 0.1 | 0.2 | 0.3 | 0.4 | 0.5 | 0.6 | 0.7 | 0.8 | 0.9 |
|---|---|---|---|---|---|---|---|---|---|
| PMI | 1.20 | 1.46 | 1.76 | 2.15 | 2.66 | 3.34 | 4.43 | 6.46 | 12.80 |

## 4 Experiments

We design the set of experiments to evaluate two new datasets and to find the best attribution method for common NLP tasks with *Transformers*. We evaluate several methods on various models with different sizes (in terms of trainable parameters).

### 4.1 Attribution Methods

We choose multiple gradient-based attributions methods and one transformer-specific attribution method from Chefer et al. [3]. All of these methods allow us to get class-specific attributions.

For gradients, we use vanilla gradients [12] and *gradients × input* [10]. For SmoothGrad we replicate the reference implementation [13]. Afterwards we employ a noise with standard deviation of 0.15 (the reference implementation default). We used sample counts of 20, 50, and 100 examples. For each sample count, we multiply the resulting attributions by input.

For Integrated Gradients [16], we use the same sample counts as in Smooth-Grad.

For Chefer et al., we used their implementation of the method. In sentiment analysis, we evaluate this method on all models. However, for multi-label document classification, we only evaluate it on one model since our second model does not rely on the BERT architecture. The method only provides positive attributions. For this reason, we do not compare it with positive and negative attributions but only with absolute attributions.

Additionally, we compare these methods to randomly generated attributions.

### 4.2 Models

**Sentiment Analysis.** For sentiment analysis, we choose four BERT models of different sizes; base [5], medium, small and mini. All of these models are already pre-trained. The medium, small and mini models were pre-trained using knowledge distillation [17] and ported to HuggingFace in [2]. The base model is cased and the medium, small and mini models are uncased. All the models were trained for four epochs. Table 3 shows the model accuracies on the validation split.

Neutral baseline samples for Integrated Gradients are created by randomly generating embeddings which the model classifies as neutral. This was done for each of the five models.

**Multi-label Document Classification.** For multi-label document classification, we choose Czert [11], which is a BERT-base size model pre-trained on Czech data, and small-e-czech [7], which is Electra-small model pre-trained on Czech data. Czert is a cased model and small-e-czech is uncased.

For this task, we choose to use the same training procedure as the authors of the original dataset. We use five-fold cross-validation on the training split leaving one fold out as a test fold. After obtaining predictions for all the folds, we measure the model performance using micro F1 score on the whole training split. The results are shown in Table 3.

Neutral baseline samples for Integrated Gradients are created by adding a baseline class to the training data. The baseline class contains samples with empty documents (consisting of padding tokens, as suggested by the authors [16]).

## 4.3   Metrics

**Sentiment Analysis.** For the sentiment analysis task, we discard any sentence with an incorrect or neutral prediction (probability below 0.6). The rationale behind this decision is the same as with the dataset; we can expect the attributions to be of decreased quality. Therefore, each model is evaluated on a slightly different set of sentences. For a specific model, all methods are evaluated using the same sets of sentences, meaning that the method results are comparable.

**Table 3.** Training results for all models for both datasets. For sentiment analysis we show accuracy on the validation split. For multi-label classification we show micro F1 score on the training split.

| Sentiment | model | BERT-base | BERT-medium | BERT-small | BERT-mini |
|---|---|---|---|---|---|
| | Accuracy | 0.9232 | 0.9128 | 0.8945 | 0.8773 |
| **Document class.** | model | Czert | Small-e-czech | | |
| | Micro F1 | 0.8574 | 0.7597 | | |

As a metric, we choose to use the size of the intersection between top $k$ annotated tokens and top $k$ attributed tokens. We divide the size of the intersection by $k$, formally:

$$s_k = \frac{|top_k(gold) \cap top_k(pred)|}{k}, \tag{1}$$

where $top_k(gold)$, $top_k(pred)$ takes $k$ words with the highest annotated, and attributed values, respectively. We use $k = 1, 3, 5$. We choose to eliminate sentences with less than 12 words since sentences with a few words often contain neutral sentiment. This way, we can have more confidence that the k words with the highest sentiment are not neutral.

We evaluate the attributions in two ways; as absolute attributions and as positive or negative attributions. For the absolute attributions, we convert the sentiment annotations to absolute values as well and then match the top $k$ attributions and top $k$ annotations. For polarised attributions (positive and negative), we consider highest $k$ annotations for sentences with overall positive sentiment and lowest $k$ annotations for sentences with overall negative sentiment. In the tables below, we report these metrics as an average over all evaluated samples.

**Multi-label Document Classification.** For the multi-label document classification task, we first filter out documents that would not fit into the 512 token limit of our models. We treat every category the document belongs to as a single evaluation instance because we can get class-specific attributions for each category. As with the sentiment analysis dataset, we decided to discard incorrectly classified categories. We also discard categories, for which the prediction was uncertain, meaning lower than 0.6. We take into account only keywords with PMI of at least $\log(5)$ and consisting of a single word. Value $\log(5)$ was chosen to eliminate keywords with small significance to their respective class. The PMI of $\log(5)$ means that a keyword $k$ is five times more likely to occur in the document of class $c$ than it would be by chance. We do not evaluate categories that contain no keywords in a given document. During evaluation we stem the keywords and document words to account for slight differences in their form.

As a metric, we choose the size of intersection between top $k$ attributions and all keywords for a given category present in the document $n$. We divide the size of the intersection by $n$. Formally:

$$s_k = \frac{|keywords \cap top_k(pred)|}{|keywords|} \tag{2}$$

We have used $k = 5, 10, 15$. We use higher value of $k$ than in case of SST, because here the documents are much longer (on average). We choose to consider all keywords present during the evaluation. We know keywords with high PMI are relevant to the category. However, we do not believe that, past a certain threshold, a higher PMI should always correspond to a higher attribution.

As in the case of sentiment analysis, we evaluate the attributions as polarised (positive or negative) and as absolute. In both cases, we consider top $k$ positive attributions. Our annotations contain only positive rationales, as there are no "anti-keywords" that would indicate an absence of a category. In the tables below, we report these metrics as an average over all evaluated samples.

## 5   Results and Discussion

Results for the sentiment analysis dataset are in Tables 4 and 5. For the multi-label document classification dataset, see Table 6.

## 5.1   Gradients and *Gradients × Inputs*

Vanilla gradients are fast and perform well on larger models. However, their performance drops as the models get smaller (compared to other well-performing methods). With smaller models, the speed advantage of vanilla gradients becomes less significant, and other slower methods produce significantly better results. We can also see that vanilla gradients perform better if interpreted as absolute attributions. These findings are in agreement with the motivation behind multiplying gradients with inputs described in Related Work.

Multiplying gradients by inputs degrades performance, especially on larger models (see Table 4). On smaller models, the impact is not as significant. For BERT-small, the performance has improved considerably (see Table 5), which we consider an anomaly if we take into account the behavior observed in other models. We believe multiplying the gradients by inputs negatively affects the performance with larger models because we combine the noise from gradients and the noise from the token embeddings, which increases with model size.

## 5.2   SmoothGrad

SmoothGrad performs poorly across all models and datasets. In some cases, its performance is close to randomly assigned attributions (see Table 4). We believe this is caused by the datasets and metrics used. By adding noise to the input and then averaging the resulting gradients, we flatten out the distribution of attributions across all tokens. This means that we suppress extreme attribution values, distributing them among surrounding tokens. Since our metrics only operate with extreme attribution values, we penalize this attribution method, even though the attributions may be correct to some degree.

Multiplying SmoothGrad by input significantly improves the performance. This is because SmoothGrad by itself does not take into account the sign and size of the input (embedding). While SmoothGrad removes the noise usually present in vanilla gradients, multiplying it by inputs corrects the flattened distribution of the attributions. This makes the method viable, especially for smaller models (see Table 5), where it performs exceptionally, and the computational cost of multiple forward and backward passes is more acceptable compared to large models.

## 5.3   Integrated Gradients

Integrated Gradients perform consistently across all models and datasets. On the sentiment analysis dataset, Integrated Gradients show worse results than SmoothGrad multiplied by input (see Table 4). In multi-label classification, they slightly outperform or almost match SmoothGrad multiplied by input (see Table 6). We observe that for smaller models, a low number of interpolation steps is enough. For BERT-mini with 11.3M parameters, using more than 20 steps brings little to no performance. This behavior also seems to be task-dependent –

in multi-label document classification, the performance with Czert (110M parameters) saturates at 20 interpolation steps. Overall, Integrated Gradients perform above average in this task.

### 5.4    Chefer et al.

The method from Chefer et al. has, in many cases, outperformed the other methods (see Tables 4, 5 and 6). It proved to be especially useful on larger models, where other comparable methods require multiple gradient calculations. The gradient computation is a resource-intensive process, which makes methods that require multiple gradient calculations less practical with large model sizes. The method from Chefer et al. needs only one forward and two backward passes (see Table 7), which gives it a significant speed advantage. This speed advantage can be a factor in practical applications. The method only provides positive attributions, which we consider a limitation. Additionally, the implementation is architecture-specific, which makes it less portable than other methods.

### 5.5    Datasets

In both datasets, most of the methods performed consistently. We can see that our assumptions about the agreement of automatic rationales with human annotation are correct. The exception are Integrated Gradients, which show excellent results in the multi-label classification task. They matched SmoothGrad multiplied by input while requiring less gradient computations but were outperformed by Chefer et al. However, Integrated Gradients struggle in the sentiment analysis task, where they are consistently outperformed by both SmoothGrad multiplied by input and Chefer et al.

**Table 4.** Metrics on the sentiment analysis dataset for BERT-base and BERT-medium models. Note that for BERT-base we used SmoothGrad with noise size of 0.05.

| BERT-base | Pos / Neg | | | Absolute | | | BERT-medium | Pos / Neg | | | Absolute | | |
|---|---|---|---|---|---|---|---|---|---|---|---|---|---|
| method | top1 | top3 | top5 | top1 | top3 | top5 | method | top1 | top3 | top5 | top1 | top3 | top5 |
| grads | .147 | .266 | .372 | .202 | .351 | .465 | grads | .169 | .274 | .380 | .208 | .358 | .467 |
| grads x I | .108 | .212 | .330 | .145 | .280 | .405 | grads x I | .138 | .258 | .365 | .125 | .262 | .383 |
| ig 20 | .106 | .244 | .362 | .087 | .217 | .344 | ig 20 | .158 | .290 | .403 | .108 | .249 | .373 |
| ig 50 | .126 | .259 | .378 | .091 | .227 | .354 | ig 50 | .185 | .306 | .411 | .129 | .267 | .380 |
| ig 100 | .135 | .265 | .380 | .102 | .235 | .355 | ig 100 | .200 | .315 | .416 | .144 | .280 | .390 |
| sg 20 | .063 | .203 | .337 | .067 | .192 | .326 | sg 20 | .057 | .199 | .333 | .072 | .208 | .333 |
| sg 50 | .06 | .194 | .329 | .064 | .198 | .324 | sg 50 | .079 | .210 | .343 | .097 | .215 | .349 |
| sg 100 | .054 | .191 | .327 | .061 | .185 | .321 | sg 100 | .079 | .210 | .340 | .079 | .213 | .344 |
| sg 20 x I | .164 | .299 | .418 | .127 | .258 | .366 | sg 20 x I | .264 | .377 | .454 | .212 | .324 | .418 |
| sg 50 x I | .188 | .31 | .422 | .135 | .264 | .373 | sg 50 x I | .325 | .397 | .470 | .264 | .369 | .454 |
| sg 100 x I | .188 | .326 | .429 | .143 | .272 | .379 | sg 100 x I | .333 | .423 | .489 | .288 | .393 | .479 |
| Chefer et al. | - | - | - | .277 | .327 | .401 | Chefer et al. | - | - | - | .308 | .374 | .444 |
| random | .061 | .190 | .332 | .057 | .187 | .314 | random | .055 | .205 | .334 | .058 | .190 | .326 |

**Table 5.** Metrics on the sentiment analysis dataset for BERT-small and BERT-mini models.

| BERT-small | Pos / Neg | | | Absolute | | | BERT-mini | Pos / Neg | | | Absolute | | |
|---|---|---|---|---|---|---|---|---|---|---|---|---|---|
| method | top1 | top3 | top5 | top1 | top3 | top5 | method | top1 | top3 | top5 | top1 | top3 | top5 |
| grads | .157 | .279 | .383 | .211 | .360 | .471 | grads | .153 | .273 | .375 | .209 | .365 | .472 |
| grads x I | .215 | .312 | .400 | .206 | .358 | .463 | grads x I | .143 | .245 | .338 | .214 | .371 | .479 |
| ig 20 | .188 | .300 | .398 | .146 | .270 | .382 | ig 20 | .266 | .359 | .446 | .199 | .312 | .417 |
| ig 50 | .209 | .313 | .409 | .160 | .284 | .394 | ig 50 | .287 | .364 | .452 | .213 | .319 | .424 |
| ig 100 | .218 | .319 | .411 | .169 | .294 | .401 | ig 100 | .288 | .369 | .453 | .218 | .323 | .428 |
| sg 20 | .068 | .210 | .339 | .076 | .217 | .346 | sg 20 | .086 | .213 | .343 | .099 | .242 | .364 |
| sg 50 | .085 | .219 | .345 | .087 | .226 | .356 | sg 50 | .070 | .221 | .358 | .116 | .249 | .374 |
| sg 100 | .076 | .203 | .334 | .082 | .217 | .345 | sg 100 | .100 | .228 | .355 | .106 | .245 | .372 |
| sg 20 x I | .269 | .365 | .448 | .218 | .324 | .419 | sg 20 x I | .393 | .468 | .509 | .297 | .431 | .513 |
| sg 50 x I | .316 | .390 | .455 | .255 | .364 | .442 | sg 50 x I | .410 | .480 | .520 | .308 | .453 | .540 |
| sg 100 x I | <u>.343</u> | <u>.404</u> | <u>.462</u> | .283 | .379 | .455 | sg 100 x I | <u>.418</u> | <u>.486</u> | <u>.525</u> | <u>.312</u> | <u>.464</u> | <u>.550</u> |
| Chefer et al. | - | - | - | <u>.334</u> | <u>.428</u> | <u>.500</u> | Chefer et al. | - | - | - | .262 | .376 | .465 |
| random | .054 | .202 | .328 | .056 | .200 | .329 | random | .067 | .194 | .335 | .055 | .195 | .321 |

**Table 6.** Metrics on the multi-label classification dataset for Czert and Small-e-czech models.

| Czert | Pos / Neg | | | Absolute | | | Small-e-czech | Pos / Neg | | | Absolute | | |
|---|---|---|---|---|---|---|---|---|---|---|---|---|---|
| method | top5 | top10 | top15 | top5 | top10 | top15 | method | top5 | top10 | top15 | top5 | top10 | top15 |
| grads | .166 | .239 | .303 | .229 | .335 | .419 | grads | .157 | .225 | .273 | .233 | .326 | .392 |
| grads x I | .140 | .213 | .270 | .213 | .322 | .396 | grads x I | .151 | .228 | .285 | .207 | .320 | .386 |
| ig 20 | .308 | .405 | .472 | .289 | .378 | .447 | ig 20 | .314 | .428 | .483 | <u>.303</u> | .417 | .475 |
| ig 50 | <u>.309</u> | .405 | .473 | .291 | .380 | .447 | ig 50 | .311 | <u>.430</u> | .482 | .301 | .421 | <u>.478</u> |
| ig 100 | <u>.309</u> | .405 | .474 | .291 | .380 | .447 | ig 100 | .311 | <u>.430</u> | .482 | .301 | <u>.422</u> | <u>.478</u> |
| sg 20 | .113 | .182 | .253 | .114 | .215 | .299 | sg 20 | .108 | .177 | .246 | .123 | .218 | .303 |
| sg 50 | .116 | .194 | .265 | .121 | .213 | .295 | sg 50 | .127 | .196 | .254 | .151 | .257 | .342 |
| sg 100 | .107 | .181 | .242 | .118 | .213 | .297 | sg 100 | .134 | .207 | .258 | .157 | .260 | .342 |
| sg 20 x I | .254 | .356 | .428 | .206 | .316 | .397 | sg 20 x I | .232 | .342 | .414 | .180 | .301 | .385 |
| sg 50 x I | .292 | .416 | .481 | .268 | .391 | .470 | sg 50 x I | <u>.316</u> | .423 | <u>.494</u> | .285 | .398 | .471 |
| sg 100 x I | .303 | <u>.425</u> | <u>.490</u> | .279 | .406 | .478 | sg 100 x I | .315 | <u>.430</u> | .492 | .293 | .412 | <u>.478</u> |
| Chefer et al. | - | - | - | <u>.313</u> | <u>.417</u> | <u>.480</u> | Chefer et al. | - | - | - | - | - | - |
| random | .077 | .161 | .226 | .068 | .155 | .250 | random | .064 | .134 | .204 | .064 | .144 | .226 |

**Table 7.** Number of forward and backpropagations for each of the attribution methods.

|  | Forward propagations | Back propagations |
|---|---|---|
| grad | 1 | 1 |
| grad x I | 1 | 1 |
| ig 20 | 20 | 20 |
| ig 50 | 50 | 50 |
| ig 100 | 100 | 100 |
| sg 20 | 20 | 20 |
| sg 50 | 50 | 50 |
| sg 100 | 100 | 100 |
| sg x I 20 | 20 | 20 |
| sg x I 50 | 50 | 50 |
| sg x I 100 | 100 | 100 |
| Chefer et al. | 1 | 2 |

# 6   Conclusion

In this paper, we present two datasets for evaluating explainable methods for Transformers. We design the evaluation specifically for transformer architectures making it usable for a wide range of NLP tasks.

Our results show that vanilla gradients do not perform very well compared to other methods. Moreover, they tend to have wrong signs. Multiplying them by input worsens performance significantly on large models, while on smaller models, the impact is less pronounced. Integrated Gradients provide consistent performance but are outperformed by SmoothGrad in the sentiment analysis task. SmoothGrad does not perform well due to the tasks and metrics used. Multiplying SmoothGrad by inputs improves the results significantly. The method from Chefer et al. performs very well across tasks and models. It is inexpensive to compute, requiring to compute gradients only once, which gives it an edge over the other well-performing methods. The method, however, only provides positive attributions and is less portable between architectures.

Our evaluation datasets are publicly available along with the evaluation source codes[2].

**Acknowledgements.** This work has been supported by the Technology Agency of the Czech Republic within the ETA Programme - No. TL03000152 "Artificial Intelligence, Media, and Law", and by Grant No. SGS-2022-016 Advanced methods of data processing and analysis. Computational resources were supplied by the project "e-Infrastruktura CZ" (e-INFRA CZ LM2018140) supported by the Ministry of Education, Youth and Sports of the Czech Republic.

---

[2] https://github.com/aitakaitov/tsd-2022-attributions.

# References

1. Bach, S., Binder, A., Montavon, G., Klauschen, F., Müller, K.R., Samek, W.: On pixel-wise explanations for non-linear classifier decisions by layer-wise relevance propagation. PLoS ONE **10**(7), e0130140 (2015)
2. Bhargava, P., Drozd, A., Rogers, A.: Generalization in nli: Ways (not) to go beyond simple heuristics. In: Proceedings of the Second Workshop on Insights from Negative Results in NLP, pp. 125–135 (2021)
3. Chefer, H., Gur, S., Wolf, L.: Transformer interpretability beyond attention visualization, pp. 782–791 (2021)
4. Denil, M., Demiraj, A., Kalchbrenner, N., Blunsom, P., de Freitas, N.: Modelling, visualising and summarising documents with a single convolutional neural network. arXiv preprint arXiv:1406.3830 (2014)
5. Devlin, J., Chang, M.W., Lee, K., Toutanova, K.: BERT: Pre-training of deep bidirectional transformers for language understanding. In: Proceedings of the 2019 Conference of the North American Chapter of the Association for Computational Linguistics: Human Language Technologies, Volume 1 (Long and Short Papers), pp. 4171–4186. Association for Computational Linguistics, Minneapolis, Minnesota, June 2019. https://doi.org/10.18653/v1/N19-1423, https://aclanthology.org/N19-1423
6. DeYoung, J., Jain, S., Rajani, N.F., Lehman, E., Xiong, C., Socher, R., Wallace, B.C.: Eraser: a benchmark to evaluate rationalized nlp models. In: Proceedings of the 58th Annual Meeting of the Association for Computational Linguistics, pp. 4443–4458 (2020)
7. Kocián, M., Náplava, J., Štancl, D., Kadlec, V.: Siamese bert-based model for web search relevance ranking evaluated on a new czech dataset. arXiv preprint arXiv:2112.01810 (2021)
8. Kral, P., Lenc, L.: Czech text document corpus v 2.0. In: Proceedings of the Eleventh International Conference on Language Resources and Evaluation (LREC 2018). European Language Resources Association (ELRA), Paris, France, May 2018
9. Shrikumar, A., Greenside, P., Kundaje, A.: Learning important features through propagating activation differences. In: International Conference on Machine Learning, pp. 3145–3153. PMLR (2017)
10. Shrikumar, A., Greenside, P., Shcherbina, A., Kundaje, A.: Not just a black box: Learning important features through propagating activation differences. arXiv preprint arXiv:1605.01713 (2016)
11. Sido, J., Pražák, O., Přibáň, P., Pašek, J., Seják, M., Konopík, M.: Czert-czech bert-like model for language representation. In: Proceedings of the International Conference on Recent Advances in Natural Language Processing (RANLP 2021), pp. 1326–1338 (2021)
12. Simonyan, K., Vedaldi, A., Zisserman, A.: Deep inside convolutional networks: Visualising image classification models and saliency maps. arXiv preprint arXiv:1312.6034 (2013)
13. Smilkov, D., Thorat, N., Kim, B., Viégas, F., Wattenberg, M.: Smoothgrad: removing noise by adding noise. arXiv preprint arXiv:1706.03825 (2017)
14. Socher, R., et al.: Recursive deep models for semantic compositionality over a sentiment treebank. In: Proceedings of the 2013 Conference on Empirical Methods in Natural Language Processing, pp. 1631–1642 (2013)

15. Sofaer, H.R., Hoeting, J.A., Jarnevich, C.S.: The area under the precision-recall curve as a performance metric for rare binary events. Methods Ecol. Evol. **10**(4), 565–577 (2019)
16. Sundararajan, M., Taly, A., Yan, Q.: Axiomatic attribution for deep networks, pp. 3319–3328 (2017)
17. Turc, I., Chang, M.W., Lee, K., Toutanova, K.: Well-read students learn better: On the importance of pre-training compact models. arXiv preprint arXiv:1908.08962 (2019)
18. Wang, A., Singh, A., Michael, J., Hill, F., Levy, O., Bowman, S.R.: Glue: a multi-task benchmark and analysis platform for natural language understanding. In: 7th International Conference on Learning Representations, ICLR 2019 (2019)

# DaFNeGE: Dataset of French Newsletters with Graph Representation and Embedding

Alexis Blandin[1,2](✉) ⓘ, Farida Saïd[3], Jeanne Villaneau[2],
and Pierre-François Marteau[2]

[1] UNEEK-Kosmopolead, 44300 Nantes, France
[2] Université Bretagne Sud, IRISA, 56000 Vannes, France
{alexis.blandin,jeanne.villaneau,pierre-francois.marteau}@uni-ubs.fr
[3] Université Bretagne Sud, LMBA, Vannes, France
farida.said@uni-ubs.fr

**Abstract.** Natural language resources are essential for integrating linguistic engineering components into information processing suites. However, the resources available in French are scarce and do not cover all possible tasks, especially for specific business applications. In this context, we present a dataset of French newsletters and their use to predict their impact, good or bad, on readers. We propose an original representation of newsletters in the form of graphs that take into account the layout of the newsletters. We then evaluate the interest of such a representation in predicting a newsletter's performance in terms of open and click rates using graph convolution network models.

**Keywords:** Newsletter · Dataset · Multimodal resource · Graph embedding · Graph convolutional network

## 1 Introduction

Artificial intelligence is growing in many fields and is increasingly used to address business problems. However, the open-source data available to train machine learning models are often irrelevant to specific applications, such as marketing optimization and email campaigns. This problem is even more acute in French, where resources lack or are a poor translation of English resources.

To contribute to the development of resources dedicated to business issues in French language, we present in this paper **DaFNeGE**, a dataset of French newsletters extracted from a CRM platform (Customer Relationship Management) and a classification task dedicated to predict newsletters' impact on readers. This dataset is intended to build predictive models of newsletter performance. However, it can be used in a wider range of marketing applications, such as assisting an editor in designing their newsletter to improve its performance and prevent it, for example, from being considered as spam by the readers.

© Springer Nature Switzerland AG 2022
P. Sojka et al. (Eds.): TSD 2022, LNAI 13502, pp. 16–27, 2022.
https://doi.org/10.1007/978-3-031-16270-1_2

The DaFNeGE dataset is composed of multimodal newsletters (text, image) that we propose to represent as graphs to model the influence of the newsletter layout on the reader's perception. This representation is used in some recent convolutional graph network models to classify newsletters in different performance categories, for instance, "good" and "bad".

## 2    Context and Data Origin

### 2.1    Existing Resources

To investigate how the design of newsletters impacts their performance, in terms of opening rate for example, we need to use dedicated resources. Very few datasets are available in the French language, and they are often designed for specific tasks unrelated to email performance prediction. For example, FQUAD [4] is a French dataset designed like its English counterpart [20] to train and evaluate machine learning models on question-answering tasks. Besides, some of the resources available in French are mere translations of English resources, such as the dataset [1], which is an automatic translation of the EmoLex [17] lexicon validated by professional translators. This approach is generally satisfactory when the text is short, as in tweets, but in our case, the texts of the emails are much too long, and the translation is not good enough to capture all the subtleties of the original texts.

Emails are characterized by a subject line and content, and there is a lack of open-source resources for such data, especially emails between companies and their customers or subscribers, due to the strategic nature of this type of information. One of the best known open resources in the business world is the "Enron" dataset [12]. While interesting in many ways (relatively large, well labeled, Etc.), this dataset is in English and concerns email exchanges between employees, and not the B2C (Business to Customer) communications of interest in this study.

Many email optimization tools are also available, but they generally do not provide open-source data or models to replicate or compare results. They also focus on tasks other than ours, such as the detection of phishing emails [21].

In other NLP studies on French email data, specific datasets have been constructed [7,10]. Likewise, we built our data set from emails sent by Kosmopolead customers[1] to their subscribers/clients.

### 2.2    Presentation of Our Dataset

UNEEK is a French company that provides customer relationship management (CRM) platforms. Its customers are various organizations such as schools, companies, or associations that use mailing newsletters to manage their communities of contacts. These newsletters are of different types: event invitations, news reviews, monthly newsletters, meeting reports, Etc. Each client customizes their

---

[1] Kosmopolead is a UNEEK's trademark offering services such as CRM (https://www.kosmopolead.com/).

newsletters in content and form with a choice of layout, fonts, or colors. None of the newsletters are used for commercial purposes; this is a determining factor in measuring their performance.

Our dataset consists of 799 newsletters from CRMs of different organizations. The dataset is not balanced between customers (see Fig. 1). However, the newsletters are similar enough per type to consider them a consistent set.

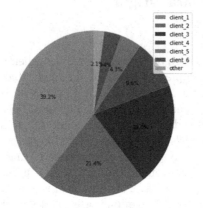

**Fig. 1.** Distribution of newsletters by client. *"other"* gathers clients with few data.

Following [2], we consider two categories of newsletters: "good" and "bad," corresponding to newsletters with satisfactory and unsatisfactory performance levels. Our task is to predict, before sending, the category of a newsletter from its textual and graphical features.

This task addresses UNEEK's intent to provide its clients with an editing tool that helps them optimize their interactions with their subscribers. Due to their non-commercial nature, the performance of the newsletters is not evaluated through the amount of money spent by the recipients as usually done in the newsletter and email impact analysis [3,13,16]. Instead, we use the open and click rates as performance indicators. They are calculated as the number of unique opens over the number of sends and the number of unique clicks over the number of unique opens, respectively. However, since the open rate can only be related to the email subject line, we only consider the newsletter click rate as a performance indicator if we analyze the email content.

Our task can be described as a multimodal document analysis: we use both graphical and textual features to represent the newsletters. To build our dataset, we used the open and click rates tracked and recorded by UNEEK and the *HTML* code of the newsletters. We took into account the layout of the newsletters through *.png* files from which we extracted graphical features. Our dataset is finally composed of a *.csv* file where each row corresponds to a newsletter described by its general features and a *.png* file for each newsletter.

# 3   Features Description

In [2], we used all text as raw material regardless of its location in the newsletter. However, giving the text in a button in the center of the newsletter as much weight as the small mandatory information text in the banner can result in a significant loss of information.

## 3.1   Features Extraction

We based our feature extraction on both *HTML* data and the image of the newsletters. To do so, we parsed the text of the *HTML* into paragraphs, and we segmented the image into text areas using a recent tool dedicated to layout parsing [24]. This tool uses a version of the Detectron2 model [27] to detect layout areas in a document automatically.

Using an OCR ensures less sensitivity to changes in the code and gives a better representation of what a human eye can see when opening the newsletter. However, this is not perfect, and some text areas or paragraphs may not be correctly detected.

Other multimodal analyses on emails, or filtering spams, attempt to compose the graphical and textual features by combining their vectors mathematically [23,28]. This study proposes an alternative approach where the textual features are directly enriched with graphical features obtained from the corresponding text area.

We aggregated the two sources of information to analyze the layout. To do this, we compared each recognized text from the OCR to each paragraph obtained from the *HTML* parsing. We then assigned each paragraph the text area containing the recognized text with the smallest Levenshtein distance from the source text.

However, some text-boxes may not be detected. In those cases, we still analyze the textual data, but without adding any graphical feature. Figure 2 shows the applied processes.

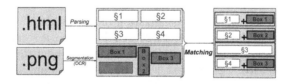

**Fig. 2.** Depiction of the matching of textual and graphical information

Thus, we have two categories of elements composing the newsletters:

– The text from the source detected by the OCR with the textual features obtained from the source, and the graphical features from the detected text-box.
– The undetected text with only the textual features obtained from the source text.

### 3.2 Textual Features

We analyzed the textual data by designing some features that seem to have an impact on the newsletter performance:

- **Sentimental features (dim 2):** In the literature the use of *sentimental* or *emotional* features may be confusing. We define here the sentimental features as the *polarity* and *subjectivity* features. We extracted them using the free NLP tool: *Python TextBlob for Natural Language Processing* [14].
- **Emotional features:** According to some marketing studies, emotion markers can have a negative impact on newsletter performance due to their mis-interpretation, mainly because of the lack of face-to-face communication. We consider the basic emotions defined by Paul Eckman [6] (joy, fear, sadness, anger, surprise, and disgust or love), using the two extraction techniques described in a previous work [2].
  - *FEEL (dim 6):* 6 features extracted using Feel lexicon (joy, fear, sadness, anger, surprise and disgust)
  - *T5-FR (dim 6):* 6 features extracted using an adaptation of the T5 model to detect emotions in French (joy, fear, sadness, anger, surprise and love)
- **Number of links (dim 1):** by detecting the regular expressions of URLs in the HTML text, one can tell if a paragraph is associated with one or more links.
- **Number of spam words (dim 1):** the use of spam words or phrases can be critical to email communication. Thus, we detect their number in a given text based on a list of French spam words mainly used in business.
- **Text length (dim 1):** the number of words in the text.
- **Syntactic depth (dim 1):** the mean depth of the syntactic tree of sentences in the given text. We get it by using the French language model from the Spacy python library [8].

### 3.3 Graphical Features

The impact of text location and visualization on the reader's reception of text has been confirmed in the literature [18,26,29]. Therefore, it seems interesting to improve the integration of texts by adding information about their visualization. To do so, we associate a given text with the corresponding text area in the newsletter image using OCR. From this image, we then extract the following graphical features:

- Coordinates (dim 4): we set the top-left corner of the image of the newsletter as the center of a Cartesian plane. All text-boxes in the image are rectangles that do not intersect. A rectangle is represented by the Cartesian coordinates of its top-left corner and its bottom-right corner in this order.
- Width, height (dim 2): based on the above coordinates, we calculate the width and height of every detected text-box. Its area is the product of these two values.

- Average color (R, G, B) (dim 3): we calculate the average pixel of a text-box as the average value of all its pixels (red, green, and blue). This value can inform on the visibility of the font used when associated with the previous graphical features. For instance, a bold *Impact* font leads to a darker average color in its box than a lighter font.
- Dominant color (R, G, B) (dim 3): we compute the dominant color of a text-box using K-Means[2] method. This feature is useful to determine for instance how a button can be flashy, while the average color is noised by the text font color.

## 4  Graphical Connections

### 4.1  Linkage Rule

Once all the parts of a newsletter have been extracted, we need to assemble them to reconstruct the newsletter's layout. For this purpose, we define rules to determine which text areas are connected. This approach is also used in document classification [15]. A first assumption is that the boxes do not intersect. If this happens during the OCR process, we merge the two boxes into a larger one before associating it with the text. While OCR focuses on detecting text characters, we expect these larger text boxes to contain whole paragraphs.

Next, we consider two boxes to be visually related if we can draw a line between their centers without crossing any other box. We state that a straight line passes through a box if it crosses one of its diagonals. The whole process is illustrated in Fig. 3.

**Fig. 3.** Illustration of the process used to determine if two boxes are connected. In the left sub-figure A and B are connected because their centers can be linked without crossing any box, while, in the right sub-figure, it crosses on the diagonals of C. (Color figure online)

### 4.2  Graph Representation of a Newsletter

The newsletter's layout is modeled by an undirected graph whose nodes are the textual elements of the newsletter linked according to the linking rules defined above. If the OCR does not detect some text, we connect it to the preceding and following text in the code *HTML*. The resulting graph is heterogeneous in the sense that texts that are isolated in the layout are located at the periphery

---

[2] With K set to 5, which here represents the number of colors to detect. It is rare to find more than 5 colors in the same portion of the image, and if it is the case, we only focus here on the dominant color.

of the graph. We shall note that the quality of the OCR tool strongly influences the resulting graph. Figure 4 illustrates the modeling process of the layout on real data and its resulting graph. One can observe that due to the poor quality of the OCR, the text contained in an image is not used. With this modeling, the graphical data can be seen as text embeddings supporting layout and visualization.

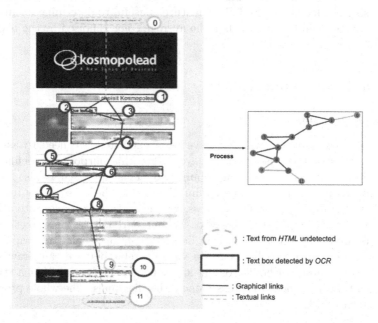

**Fig. 4.** Result obtained by our graph extraction algorithm on a real newsletter. We can see the two types of textual data, some with a visual text-box detected attached to it, and others, in yellow dotted lines, undetected by the OCR and considered as text. The abstract graph obtained after our process can be see on the right. (Color figure online)

## 5  Model

### 5.1  Relational Graph Convolutional Network

We evaluate this novel graphical representation of a newsletter in the performance categorization task. To take full advantage of the graphical connectivity of the data, we provide graph integration using graph convolution networks. We use a method inspired by the python library *DGL* [25] which consists in updating each node according to its neighboring data using a convolutional network of relational graphs, essentially an R-GCN model as defined in [22]. It is inspired by the GCN architecture [5,11], which applies a hidden representation for each node based on the information attached to its neighbors. An R-GCN can apply convolution on the graph elements according to their type (text detected by

OCR or not). In an R-GCN, edges can represent different relationships, which is helpful in our case to manage two types of edges: textual and graphical. Each node represents a different text-box, and is initialized with the feature extraction described previously. Missing features of undetected nodes are set to 0. This imputation method is intuitive [9]. The updates of the convolution filters allow us to assume that these imputations do not introduce significant bias. At the end of the convolution process, we obtain the representations of all the nodes that we aggregate into one representation for each graph. For this we apply a function $readout^3$. We finally use a linear classifier to perform the classification task. The complete architecture is shown in Fig. 5.

The classification task is performed with a simple linear classifier to evaluate the relevance of the proposed data representation and the addition of convolutional layers. More sophisticated methods can be considered to improve the classification.

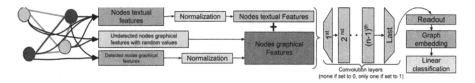

**Fig. 5.** Model architecture to perform the newsletter graph classification.

## 5.2   Results

To assess the relevance of the proposed representation in the task of predicting newsletters' performance, we trained several architectures by varying the number of convolutional layers, with the same dimension for all hidden layers. The number of hidden layers ranges from 0 to 6, which makes 7 architectures in total. 0 is our baseline, and only the nodes of the graph are read, while with six hops, the information reaches almost all graph nodes. More layers would make the aggregation less meaningful and the computation slower.

The models were trained to classify our data into two classes, *good* and *bad* newsletters. These classes are determined by splitting the dataset between the 50% newsletters with the lowest click rates and the 50% newsletters with the highest click rates. This method ensures the same number of newsletters in each class.

Next, we randomly split the dataset into three parts: 70% are used for learning, 15% as a validation set, and the remaining for testing. The size of the hidden layers was fixed at 128, and the models were trained on the training samples for 300 epochs. The classification task was performed 12 times on each of the seven architectures. The average learning curves are given by architecture in Fig. 6.

---

<sup>3</sup> As defined in [25].

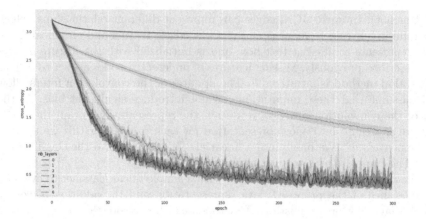

**Fig. 6.** Average learning curves per architecture.

It appears that the more convolution layers we add to the model, the faster it learns. However, this increases also the risk of over-fitting in the last epochs, where we can observe a lot of instability in the training. For this reason we tested the models not once the training has ended, but when the loss function reached a minimal value on the validation set. The efficiency of the models, depending on the number of hidden layers can be seen in Table 1

**Table 1.** F1-score statics on the performance prediction task when varying the number of convolutional layers, with 12 different learning/testing splits. The model with 0 graphical convolutional layer can be considered as a baseline.

| Layers | F1 Score mean | F1 Score std | F1 Score min | F1 Score max | F1 Score median |
|--------|---------------|--------------|--------------|--------------|-----------------|
| 0 | 0.54 | 0.07 | 0.44 | 0.66 | 0.54 |
| 1 | 0.51 | 0.01 | 0.32 | 0.65 | 0.53 |
| 2 | 0.59 | 0.09 | 0.46 | 0.72 | 0.63 |
| 3 | 0.65 | 0.06 | 0.51 | 0.73 | 0.66 |
| 4 | **0.67** | 0.06 | 0.57 | **0.78** | 0.66 |
| 5 | 0.66 | 0.05 | **0.60** | 0.73 | **0.67** |
| 6 | 0.66 | 0.06 | 0.56 | 0.75 | 0.65 |

We observe that, as expected, the more we add hidden convolutional layers in the model, the better seems to be the classification. However when we reach a certain number of convolutional layers, the results tend to stagnate, which may be correlated with the high instability of the learning process observed in Fig. 6. This limitation in the addition of convolutional layers is named as the *over-smoothing problem* and described by Oono and Suzuki [19]. That is why beyond 4 layers it is difficult to tell if adding more layers is a real benefit.

As pointed out before, our data is not evenly distributed among customers, so if all "good" newsletters come from the same set of customers, the model might learn to "recognize" a customer instead of predicting a click rate. We, therefore, checked the distribution of each performance class among the customers, which is given in Table 2.

**Table 2.** Proportion of good and bad newsletters among the CRM clients

| distribution | client-1 | client-2 | client-3 | client-4 | client-5 | client-6 | others |
|---|---|---|---|---|---|---|---|
| % of dataset | 39.2 | 21.4 | 20 | 9.6 | 4.3 | 3.4 | 2.1 |
| % of good | 54 | 68 | 29 | 26 | 74 | 21 | 0 |
| % of bad | 46 | 32 | 71 | 74 | 27 | 79 | 100 |

Furthermore, because of our approach by classification via the median, the "bad" newsletters which have an average click rate closer to the median seems to be tougher to classify properly.

If there is indeed a bias for some customers, it seems that for most of them, the distributions are relatively balanced. Moreover, as mentioned before, customers send newsletters with quite the same objectives and propose similar content (invitations to events, information reports, Etc.). If some clients tend to send "bad" or "good" newsletters, it may be related to their ability to design a newsletter rather than their content's specificity.

## 6 Conclusion

The main contribution of this paper is to present a new dataset of email graphs in French and a classification task aiming at predicting whether a newsletter will have a good impact on recipients. The dataset is extracted from a real context emailing campaign in customer relationship management, and it will be made available to the natural language processing community.

In addition, we propose an innovative graphical representation of the newsletters that considers the layout of the newsletters and the visual proximity of the text areas. However, this graphical representation is limited by the performance of the OCR tool used, but we hope that a better method will soon allow us to overcome this problem.

The proposed graphical representation was evaluated to predict the performance of newsletters. For this purpose, we constructed graph embeddings using sequences of convolution layers. Graphs are a helpful representation since adding convolution layers improves classification; however, due to over smoothing problems inherent to convolutional approaches, the results no longer improve beyond a certain number of convolution layers (3 in our experiment).

Our best result (F1 score of 0.78) is good enough to be used in a production environment. However, we must be cautious of over-fitting and consider an overall improvement of our models, especially by using more sophisticated classifiers than a simple linear classifier.

While these results are encouraging, many other model architectures are possible, and we hope the community will contribute to developing new models for this predictive task. Our newsletter dataset will be available for free very soon.

# References

1. Abdaoui, A., Azé, J., Bringay, S., Poncelet, P.: FEEL: a French expanded emotion Lexicon. Lang. Resources Eval. **51**(3), 833–855 (2017). https://doi.org/10.1007/s10579-016-9364-5. https://hal-lirmm.ccsd.cnrs.fr/lirmm-01348016
2. Blandin, A., Saïd, F., Villaneau, J., Marteau, P.F.: Automatic emotions analysis for french email campaigns optimization. In: CENTRIC 2021, Barcelone, Spain, October 2021. https://hal.archives-ouvertes.fr/hal-03424725
3. Bonfrer, A., Drèze, X.: Real-time evaluation of e-mail campaign performance. Marketing Science (2009)
4. d'Hoffschmidt, M., Belblidia, W., Brendlé, T., Heinrich, Q., Vidal, M.: Fquad: French question answering dataset (2020)
5. Duvenaud, D., et al.: Convolutional networks on graphs for learning molecular fingerprints. arXiv preprint arXiv:1509.09292 (2015)
6. Ekman, P.: Basic Emotions, chap. 3, pp. 45–60. John Wiley and Sons, Ltd (1999). https://doi.org/10.1002/0470013494.ch3. https://onlinelibrary.wiley.com/doi/abs/10.1002/0470013494.ch3
7. Guenoune, H., Cousot, K., Lafourcade, M., Mekaoui, M., Lopez, C.: A dataset for anaphora analysis in French emails. In: Proceedings of the Third Workshop on Computational Models of Reference, Anaphora and Coreference, pp. 165–175. Association for Computational Linguistics, Barcelona, Spain (online), December 2020. https://aclanthology.org/2020.crac-1.17
8. Honnibal, M., Montani, I.: spaCy 2: natural language understanding with Bloom embeddings, convolutional neural networks and incremental parsing (2017), to appear
9. Ipsen, N., Mattei, P.A., Frellsen, J.: How to deal with missing data in supervised deep learning? In: ICML Workshop on the Art of Learning with Missing Values (Artemiss) (2020)
10. Kalitvianski, R.: Traitements formels et sémantiques des échanges et des documents textuels liés à des activités collaboratives. Theses, Université Grenoble Alpes, March 2018. https://tel.archives-ouvertes.fr/tel-01893348
11. Kipf, T.N., Welling, M.: Semi-supervised classification with graph convolutional networks. arXiv preprint arXiv:1609.02907 (2016)
12. Klimt, B., Yang, Y.: The enron corpus: a new dataset for email classification research. In: Boulicaut, J.-F., Esposito, F., Giannotti, F., Pedreschi, D. (eds.) ECML 2004. LNCS (LNAI), vol. 3201, pp. 217–226. Springer, Heidelberg (2004). https://doi.org/10.1007/978-3-540-30115-8_22
13. Kumar, A.: An empirical examination of the effects of design elements of email newsletters on consumers' email responses and their purchase. J. Retailing Consumer Serv. **58**, 102349 (2021). https://doi.org/10.1016/j.jretconser.2020.102349. https://www.sciencedirect.com/science/article/pii/S0969698920313576

14. Loria, S.: textblob documentation. Release 0.15 2 (2018)
15. Mandivarapu, J.K., Bunch, E., You, Q., Fung, G.: Efficient document image classification using region-based graph neural network. CoRR abs/2106.13802 (2021). https://arxiv.org/abs/2106.13802
16. Miller, R., Charles, E.: A psychological based analysis of marketing email subject lines. In: 2016 Sixteenth International Conference on Advances in ICT for Emerging Regions (ICTer), pp. 58–65 (2016). https://doi.org/10.1109/ICTER.2016.7829899
17. Mohammad, S.M., Turney, P.D.: Crowdsourcing a word-emotion association lexicon. Comput. Intell. **29**(3), 436–465 (2013)
18. Olive, T., Barbier, M.L.: Processing time and cognitive effort of longhand note taking when reading and summarizing a structured or linear text. Writ. Commun. **34**(2), 224–246 (2017)
19. Oono, K., Suzuki, T.: Graph neural networks exponentially lose expressive power for node classification. arXiv preprint arXiv:1905.10947 (2019)
20. Rajpurkar, P., Jia, R., Liang, P.: Know what you don't know: unanswerable questions for squad (2018)
21. Salloum, S., Gaber, T., Vadera, S., Shaalan, K.: Phishing email detection using natural language processing techniques: a literature survey. Procedia Comput. Sci. **189**, 19–28 (2021). https://doi.org/10.1016/j.procs.2021.05.077
22. Schlichtkrull, M., Kipf, T.N., Bloem, P., van den Berg, R., Titov, I., Welling, M.: Modeling relational data with graph convolutional networks. In: Gangemi, A., Navigli, R., Vidal, M.-E., Hitzler, P., Troncy, R., Hollink, L., Tordai, A., Alam, M. (eds.) ESWC 2018. LNCS, vol. 10843, pp. 593–607. Springer, Cham (2018). https://doi.org/10.1007/978-3-319-93417-4_38
23. Seth, S., Biswas, S.: Multimodal spam classification using deep learning techniques. In: 2017 13th International Conference on Signal-Image Technology & Internet-Based Systems (SITIS), pp. 346–349. IEEE (2017)
24. Shen, Z., Zhang, R., Dell, M., Lee, B.C.G., Carlson, J., Li, W.: Layoutparser: a unified toolkit for deep learning based document image analysis. arXiv preprint arXiv:2103.15348 (2021)
25. Wang, M., et al.: Deep graph library: A graph-centric, highly-performant package for graph neural networks. arXiv preprint arXiv:1909.01315 (2019)
26. Wright, P.: The psychology of layout: Consequences of the visual structure of documents. American Association for Artificial Intelligence Technical Report FS-99-04, pp. 1–9 (1999)
27. Wu, Y., Kirillov, A., Massa, F., Lo, W.Y., Girshick, R.: Detectron2. https://github.com/facebookresearch/detectron2 (2019)
28. Yang, H., Liu, Q., Zhou, S., Luo, Y.: A spam filtering method based on multi-modal fusion. Appl. Sci. **9**(6), 1152 (2019)
29. Yesilada, Y., Jay, C., Stevens, R., Harper, S.: Validating the use and role of visual elements of web pages in navigation with an eye-tracking study. In: Proceedings of the 17th International Conference on World Wide Web, pp. 11–20 (2008)

# ANTILLES: An Open French Linguistically Enriched Part-of-Speech Corpus

Yanis Labrak[1]([⊠])(iD) and Richard Dufour[2]([⊠])(iD)

[1] LIA - Avignon University, 84911 Avignon, France
`yanis.labrak@univ-avignon.fr`
[2] LS2N - Nantes University, 44300 Nantes, France
`richard.dufour@univ-nantes.fr`

**Abstract.** Part-of-speech (POS) tagging is a classical natural language processing (NLP) task. Although many tools and corpora have been proposed, especially for the most widely spoken languages, these suffer from limitations concerning their user license, the size of their tagset, or even approaches no longer in the state-of-the-art. In this article, we propose ANTILLES, an extended version of an existing French corpus (UD French-GSD) comprising an original set of labels obtained with the aid of morphological characteristics (gender, number, tense, etc.). This extended version includes a set of 65 labels, against 16 in the initial version. We also implemented several POS tools for French from this corpus, incorporating the latest advances in the state-of-the-art in this area. The corpus as well as the POS labeling tools are fully open and freely available.

**Keywords:** Part-of-speech corpus · POS tagging · Open tools · Word embeddings · Bi-LSTM · CRF · Transformers

## 1 Introduction

For a few years now, several research areas have seen significant breakthroughs in both the arrival of big data and ways of exploiting it using deep learning based approaches. Then, various natural language processing (NLP) tasks reached a level of performance and maturity allowing them to be industrialized.

Among NLP field, part-of-speech (POS) tagging is a low-level grammatical task which consists in assigning, for each word of a sentence, its corresponding morphosyntactic category, such as verb (VERB), determinant (DET), adjective (ADJ) and much more (noun, auxiliary, etc.). This labeling is usually the root for more complex linguistic tasks such as named-entity recognition, text summarization, text generation, automatic speech recognition, spell checking, etc. In other words, many applications or research issues depend on the efficiency and quality of this labeling. While POS tagging problem was initially tackled with

© Springer Nature Switzerland AG 2022
P. Sojka et al. (Eds.): TSD 2022, LNAI 13502, pp. 28–38, 2022.
https://doi.org/10.1007/978-3-031-16270-1_3

rule-based approaches, supervised statistical learning now allows us to achieve the best performance [18,22].

French language has been relatively well studied for POS tagging. Nonetheless, for the sake of universality, the open multilingual corpora, and their derived tools, have mainly been designed with a limited number of tags across languages. To our knowledge, no open French corpus currently makes it possible to freely and easily train such a state-of-the-art POS tagging system with a sufficient level of tags granularity, allowing us to take into account this particular inflectional language.

We therefore propose in this article ANTILLES, an extended French corpus containing a set of linguistically enriched morphosyntactic tags. We then increase the capacities of the Universal Dependencies (UD) French GSD corpus [11] by extending its morphosyntactic information in single labels, from 16 to 63, thanks to the use of additional information present in the `Conll-U` format. This choice appears to be the most relevant since French GSD has been chosen for being one of the largest French manually annotated POS corpus, with a high level of granularity and a non-restrictive license of use. We also propose to evaluate different POS tagging systems using state-of-the-art neural network architectures. The corpus as well as the POS taggers are open and freely usable.

The paper is organized as follows. Section 2 presents an overview of the current resources (corpora and tools) available for French POS tagging. Then, Sect. 3 describes the proposed corpus and its inherent modifications. The experiments as well as the proposed POS tagging systems are detailed in Sect. 4. Finally, Sect. 5 concludes and opens new perspectives for the task.

# 2    Existing Resources for French POS Tagging

We propose, in this section, a detailed overview of the main resources in French, including the corpora (Sect. 2.1), as well as the available tools and their approaches (Sect. 2.2).

## 2.1    POS Corpora

Table 1 summarizes the most popular corpora annotated with morphosyntactic labels for the French language. For comparison, we provided the number of tokens (*i.e.* words, punctuation, ...), the number of POS tags (# Tags), the license of use and the nature of the documents in the corpus (Genre).

The corpora are detailed in the table under four parts: 1) those completely free to use (most UD corpora); 2) those free except for commercial use (TCOF-POS, UD French-ParTUT and French Treebank); 3) those that are not directly downloadable and with limited usage constraints (Valibel and Orféo); 4) those with a paid license, especially for commercial use (Crater). Among these corpora, we observe a great disparity in the number of tokens, with around 20k/30k tokens for the smallest and up to 10 millions for the largest. As we can see, most of the large corpora are distributed under a restricted license, requiring either to pay to be able to access the data, or to go through a registration form with acceptance (*Limited*).

Regarding the nature of the documents used, we can highlight two main types: those that are purely textual (news, wiki, blogs, etc.) and those that are speech-oriented, relying on speech transcriptions. The second is clearly less present in terms of number of corpus, and limited either in terms of annotated data or license of use.

**Table 1.** List of major French POS corpora, including the number of tag occurrences (# Tokens), the number of different tags (# Tags), their availability nature (License), and the genre of annotated documents (Genre).

| CORPUS | # TOKENS | # TAGS | LICENSE | GENRE |
|---|---|---|---|---|
| UD French-FQB [21] | 23,349 | 16 | LGPL-LR | nonfiction, news |
| UD French-PUD [24] | 24,131 | 15 | CC BY-SA 3.0 | wiki, news |
| UD French-ParisStories [12] | 29,438 | 15 | CC BY-SA 4.0 | spoken |
| UD French-Rhapsodie [13] | 43,700 | 15 | CC BY-SA 4.0 | spoken |
| UD French-Sequoia [6] | 68,596 | 16 | LGPL-LR | medical, nonfiction, wiki, news |
| UD French-GSD [11] | 400,399 | 16 | CC BY-SA 4.0 | blog, reviews, wiki, news |
| UD French-FTB [11] | 556,064 | 16 | LGPL-LR | news |
| TCOF-POS [4] | 22,240 | 62 | BY-NC-SA 2.0 | spoken |
| UD French-ParTUT [20] | 27,658 | 17 | CC BY-NC-SA 4.0 | legal, wiki, news |
| French Treebank [1] | 664,500 | 15 | CC-BY-NC-ND | news |
| Valibel [9] | 6 millions | 107 | Limited | spoken, thesis |
| Orféo [3] | 10 millions | 20 | Limited | interview, meeting, spoken |
| Crater 1 [15] | 1 million | 105 | Paying | telecommunication manuals |
| Crater 2 [17] | 1,5 millions | 105 | Paying | telecommunication manuals |

## 2.2   POS Taggers

As for the corpora, different morphosyntactic tagging tools specific to the French language have been proposed, each with its own specificities in terms of approaches and tags granularity. The list of the most popular POS taggers for the French language is detailed in Table 2.

**Table 2.** List of the most popular POS taggers for the French language.

|  | # Tags | License | Approach | Corpus |
|---|---|---|---|---|
| spaCy | 18 | MIT | Convolutional Neural Network | UD French Sequoia |
| Talismane | 27 | AGPL-3.0 | Support Vector Machine | French Treebank |
| MElt | 29 | LGPL-3.0 | Maximum-Entropy Markov models | French TreeBank |
| LGTagger | 29 | LGPL-LR | Conditional Random Fields | French Treebank |
| SoMeWeTa | 29 | GPL-3.0 | Brown clusters | French Treebank |
| MarMoT | 29 | GPL-3.0 | Conditional Random Field | French Treebank |
| gilf/french-postag-model | 29 | Unknown | bert-base-multilingual-cased | free-french-treebank |
| SEM | 30 | GNU | Hidden Markov Model | French Treebank |
| Stanford | 33 | GPL-3.0 | Cyclic Dependency Network | French TreeBank |
| TreeTagger | 33 | GPL-3.0 | Hidden Markov Model | French Treebank |
| Morfette | 33 | BSD-3-Clause | Logistic Regression | French TreeBank |
| NLTK | 33 | Apache-2.0 | Cyclic Dependency Network | French TreeBank |
| DisMo | 64 | GPL-3.0 | Conditional Random Field | PFC |
| LIA-Tagg | 103 | GPL-2.0 | Second-Order HMM | Private corpus |

We can first note that all POS taggers are based on statistical approaches and are, for the most part, trained on open corpora. Only LIA-Tagg relies on a private corpus, on which we found no description. Nevertheless, if we look at the open corpora, we see that French TreeBank is mostly used: its license being non-commercial (i.e. CC-BY-NC-ND, as seen in Table 1), only the spaCy tool, under a non-restrictive MIT license, is completely license free right of use.

spaCy however suffers from a limited number of tags (only 18). In general, the number of tags is very limited (between 18 and 33 tags). This is because most tools rely on corpora following the UD annotation guideline or [7] which sought to produce a set of labels that could apply to multiple languages.

The semi-free of use TCOF-POS corpus is nevertheless distinguished by its high number of tags (62). In reality, these additional tags are already an extension of the UD tags with morphosyntactic information (*e.g.* the ADJ tag is derived in 7 tags: demonstrative adjective, indefinite, etc.). Finally, note that although the UD corpora have a limited number of tags, morphosyntactic information exists, but is most often not used in the form of its own label.

In general, the sets of tags offered by the POS tools take little - or even no - account of the specificities of the French language, seeking to maintain their universality as much as possible. Only LIA-Tagg integrates a very complete set of tags, but suffers from an unavailable corpus and the use of an approach that is no longer in the state-of-the-art. Concretely, only spaCy and french-postag-model are maintained and implement state-of-the-art methods but on a restricted set of tags.

## 3   Extended Corpus Proposal

Each existing corpus for French language has interesting specificities, whether in relation to the size of the annotated data, their license free right of use, or the large number of labels offered, but no corpus combines all these advantages at the same time.

However, we found that although the associated tagset is often small, a lot of data related to linguistic information is available. This is particularly the case for UD corpora.

We have chosen to focus on the annotated French corpus UD French-GSD [11] because it includes all the necessary features to implement a linguistic enrichment of POS labels. Moreover, it is one of the few corpora completely free of use (see Sect. 2.1), allowing a complete redistribution of its improvements. It contains 16 POS tags and is composed of $16,341$ documents, for approximately 400k manually annotated word occurrences. It also offers data integrating the morphological characteristics of words (gender, number, tense, verbal form, person, etc.) which has been automatically annotated and then partially manually corrected.

The UD French-GSD corpus follows the standard UD [19] annotation scheme. The new annotation scheme that we propose follows the morphosyntactic tags proposed by the LIA-Tagg tagger, as they allow a complete and deep representation of the spelling as well as the grammar of French language. We achieve this enrichment by transforming the CoNLL-U tags (UPOS) and the features (FEATS) to our 65 new tags in order to give information on morphological characteristics such as the gender (feminine and masculine), number/person (first person, etc.), tense (past participle, etc.), types of pronouns (relative, indefinite, demonstrative, etc.) in a single label. The initial tags of the UD French-GSD corpus as well as the new tags of the ANTILLES extended corpus are detailed in Table 3. The ANTILLES corpus is freely accessible online[1] under CC-BY-SA 4.0 License.

---

[1] https://github.com/qanastek/ANTILLES.

**Table 3.** Labels of the initial corpus UD FRENCH-GSD and of the proposed extended corpus ANTILLES. The suffix **XX** at the end of a label corresponds to a declension among feminine singular (FS), feminine plural (FP), masculine singular (MS), masculine plural (MP).

| UD French-GSD | | ANTILLES | |
|---|---|---|---|
| ABBREVIATION | DESCRIPTION | ABBREVIATION | DESCRIPTION |
| ADP | Adposition | PREP | Preposition |
| | | PART | Demonstrative particle |
| SCONJ | Subordinating conjunction | COSUB | Subordinating conjunction |
| CCONJ | Coordinating Conjunction | COCO | Coordinating Conjunction |
| ADV | Adverb | ADV | Adverb |
| PROPN | Proper noun | PROPN | Proper noun |
| | | XFAMIL | Family name |
| NUM | Numerical Adjective | NUM | Numerical Adjective |
| | | CHIF | Number |
| AUX | Auxiliary Verb | AUX | Auxiliary Verb |
| VERB | Verb | VERB | Verb |
| | | VPP**XX** (x4) | FS/FP/MS/MP Past participle verb |
| | | VPPRE | Present participle verb |
| DET | Determinant | DET | Determinant |
| | | DET**XX** (x2) | FS/MS Determinant |
| | | ADJ | Adjective |
| ADJ | Adjective | ADJ**XX** (x4) | FS/FP/MS/MP Adjective |
| | | DINT**XX** (x2) | FS/MS Numerical adjectives |
| NOUN | Noun | NOUN | Noun |
| | | N**XX** (x4) | FS/FP/MS/MP Noun |
| | | PRON | Pronoun |
| | | PINT | FS Interrogative pronoun |
| | | PDEM**XX** (x4) | FS/FP/MS/MP Demonstrative pronoun |
| | | PIND**XX** (x4) | FS/FP/MS/MP Indefinite pronoun |
| | | PPOBJ**XX** (x4) | FS/FP/MS/MP Pronoun complements of objects |
| | | PPER1S | Personal pronoun - First person singular |
| | | PPER2S | Personal pronoun - Second person singular |
| PRON | Pronoun | PPER3**XX** (x4) | Personal Pronoun - Third Person FS/FP/MS/MP |
| | | PREFS | Reflexive pronoun - First person of singular |
| | | PREF | Reflexive pronoun - Third person of singular |
| | | PREFP | Reflexive pronoun - First/Second Person of plurial |
| | | PREL | Relative pronoun |
| | | PREL**XX** (x4) | FS/FP/MS/MP Relative pronoun |
| INTJ | Interjection | INTJ | Interjection |
| SYM | Symbol | SYM | Symbol |
| PUNCT | Punctuation | YPFOR | Final point |
| | | PUNCT | Punctuation |
| X | Other | MOTINC | Unknown word |
| | | X | Typos & Other |

# 4   Experiments

In addition to the extended corpus, we provide a comparison of several taggers using different approaches based on neural networks. In Sect. 4.1, we describe the implemented approaches. We then detail the results in Sect. 4.2.

## 4.1   Proposed Approaches

We implement three different state-of-the-art architectures to evaluate current performance on the POS tagging task by means of our extended French corpus:

1. Word embedding + Bi-LSTM-CRF. The first proposed system consists of a Bidirectional Long Short-Term Memory (Bi-LSTM) [10] with Conditional Random Field (CRF) [14] using, as inputs, different kinds of word embeddings. Our core system incorporates FastText embeddings [5] pre-trained specifically for French. Once this reference was obtained, we independently evaluated other state-of-the-art representations: Flair [2] and BERT [8] (here, CamemBERT [16] for the French).
2. Concatenation of word embeddings + Bi-LSTM-CRF. We propose to keep the same neural network, but train it here on the combination of several word embeddings concatenated at the input of the system. We explore all the possible concatenation combinations starting from the same word embeddings as before: FastText, Flair and CamemBERT.
3. CamemBERT Fine-Tuning. For the last system, rather than using the CamemBERT word embeddings as input to a Bi-LSTM-CRF as described in the previous architectures, we propose to directly perform a fine-tuning of the CamemBERT model by adding a linear layer dedicated to the POS labeling task after model outputs.

The complete training procedure was performed using the `Transformers` [23] library maintained by HuggingFace.

## 4.2   Results

Table 4 summarizes the results obtained by the three approaches proposed on the POS labeling task of the ANTILLES corpus test set. Overall, except for a few simple word embeddings (Bi-LSTM-CRF + FastText and Bi-LSTM-CRF + Flair), the performance obtained is quite similar regardless of the approach considered, from 95.24% to 97.97% for the success rate (Accuracy) and 95.19% to 97.98% for the F-measure (F1).

Our best performing model combines a Bi-LSTM-CRF architecture with a concatenation of two word embeddings Flair and Camembert as inputs (f-measure of 97.98%). The two word embeddings integrate quite different information, one coming from word sub-units (CamemBERT) and the other from characters (Flair), which could explain their complementary performances. It

**Table 4.** Results on the POS labeling task of the ANTILLES test set.

| MODEL | ACC. | PREC. | REC. | F1 | # PARAMS | INF. |
|---|---|---|---|---|---|---|
| *Simple Embeddings (Baseline)* | | | | | | |
| Bi-LSTM-CRF | | | | | | |
| + FastText | 95.24% | 95.26% | 95.24% | 95.19% | **1.27 M** | **34.91 s** |
| + Flair | 96.96% | 96.97% | 96.96% | 96.94% | 18.80 M | 320.42 s |
| + CamemBERT$_{oscar-4gb-base}$ | 97.77% | 97.80% | 97.77% | 97.75% | 113.35 M | 151.44 s |
| + CamemBERT$_{oscar-138gb-base}$ | 97.76% | 97.80% | 97.76% | 97.74% | 113.35 M | 147.37 s |
| *Multi-Embeddings* | | | | | | |
| Bi-LSTM-CRF | | | | | | |
| + FastText + Flair | 97.29% | 97.33% | 97.29% | 97.28% | 20.73 M | 337.46 s |
| + FastText + CamemBERT$_{oscar-138gb-base}$ | 97.88% | 97.90% | 97.88% | 97.85% | 114.52 M | 152.14 s |
| + Flair + CamemBERT$_{oscar-4gb-base}$ | 97.89% | 97.90% | 97.89% | 97.87% | 134.73 M | 411.77 s |
| + Flair + CamemBERT$_{oscar-138gb-base}$ | **97.97%** | **98.02%** | **97.97%** | **97.98%** | 134.73 M | 418.57 s |
| + Flair + CamemBERT$_{ccnet-135gb-large}$ | 97.87% | 97.92% | 97.87% | 97.87% | 362.80 M | 476.07 s |
| + Flair + FastText + CamemBERT$_{oscar-138gb-base}$ | 97.91% | 97.93% | 97.91% | 97.91% | 137.13 M | 439.95 s |
| *Fine-tuning* | | | | | | |
| CamemBERT$_{oscar-138gb-base}$ | 97.78% | 97.85% | 97.78% | 97.80% | 110.08 M | 53.94 s |

outperforms our benchmark based on a Bi-LSTM-CRF combined with FastText word embeddings by 2.73%.

Table 4 also integrates the size of the models (# Params) and their inference times (Inf.) to sequentially process 5,000 sentences with an RTX 2080 Ti graphics card. The performance gap between our least efficient system (Bi-LSTM-CRF + FastText) and the most efficient (Bi-LSTM-CRF + Flair + Camembert$_{OSCAR-138gb-base}$) appears small (difference in F1-score of 2.79%) considering the number of parameters as well as the inference time (12 times slower). Note that the large CamemBERT model trained on the CCNET corpus (*ccnet 135gb large*) is provided for information only in the table: we have not seen any improvement by using it, while its number of parameters is at least 2.5 times higher than any other model.

Finally, the fine-tuning approach of CamemBERT seems to be one of the best choices for this task compared to the Bi-LSTM-CRF, since it obtains results close to those obtained with the best system, but with an inference time at least 8 times faster (53.94s against ≈ 420s).

For information, we also compared our systems to one of the most widely used tool: spaCy. We used the POS tag and the morphological information given by spaCy to map their outputs to our tags and make the systems comparable with each other. Likewise, we also skipped the entities without annotation and represented in the test file as underscores to remove some noise in the metric.

This evaluation raised one big issue, which is the dissonance between the annotation guidelines of UD French GSD and UD French Sequoia v2.8, the first being used for training our systems and the second for training spaCy. For example, in UD French Sequoia corpus, and by extension spaCy:

– The symbols like €, $ and % are for most of the time unhandled but they are sometimes describe as NOUN, which us worse.

- Last names are not always tagged as proper nouns (PROPN) which make the mapping even more complicated.
- And last but not least, the biggest issue comes from the lack of information about the gender and number in the original annotation for the adjectives.
- Last names aren't all the time tagged as proper nouns (PROPN) which make the mapping more complicated.

Finally, to have a fair comparison, we removed from this evaluation the tags involved in the previously raised annotation issues. We then obtained an F1-score of 85.81% for the spaCy system and 91.29% for the proposed Flair one. To conclude, we can expect a performance increase using our systems compared to the existing annotation tools. Note that the choice of using Sequoia to train spaCy makes it less optimized for in-depth analysis of languages such as French. This difference in performance between the systems would surely be much lower if spaCy was trained on data with more consistent annotations like UD French GSD.

All developed taggers presented in this article are available and freely usable[2].

## 5  Conclusion and Perspectives

In this article, we proposed an extended corpus for POS tagging in the French language. This corpus fills the observed limitations of existing corpora, whether in terms of labels, user license or existing state-of-the-art tools.

This corpus, named ANTILLES, is an extended version of the free-to-use UD French-GSD corpus, integrating additional POS tags based on a set of associated morphological data. We have also implemented numerous POS tagging tools, then evaluated the performance of various state-of-the-art neural network architectures to give an idea of the current performance level in French POS tagging. ANTILLES as well as the associated POS labeling tools are freely distributed and can be used by academics or industrialists.

The corpus is intended to be enriched over time, by extending, in the same way, the other freely accessible corpora offered by the Universal Dependencies (UD) such as PUD, ParisStories, or Rhapsodie, using the same strategy and the same set of proposed labels. All the scripts necessary to perform this transformation are available on the GitHub repository[3], the models are also available on HuggingFace[4]. The extension to other languages can also be a possibility.

**Acknowledgements.** This work was financially supported by Zenidoc and the DIETS project financed by the Agence Nationale de la Recherche (ANR) under contract ANR-20-CE23-0005.

---

[2] https://huggingface.co/qanastek/pos-french-camembert.
[3] https://github.com/qanastek/ANTILLES.
[4] https://huggingface.co/qanastek.

# References

1. Abeillé, A., Clément, L., Toussenel, F.: Building a treebank for French. In: Abeillé, A. (ed.) Treebanks, vol. 30, pp. 165–187. Springer, Dordrecht (2003). https://doi.org/10.1007/978-94-010-0201-1_10
2. Akbik, A., Blythe, D., Vollgraf, R.: Contextual string embeddings for sequence labeling. In: COLING 2018, 27th International Conference on Computational Linguistics, pp. 1638–1649 (2018)
3. Benzitoun, C., Debaisieux, J.M., Deulofeu, H.J.: Le projet orféo: un corpus d'étude pour le français contemporain. Corpus (15) (2016)
4. Benzitoun, C., Fort, K., Sagot, B.: TCOF-POS: un corpus libre de français parlé annoté en morphosyntaxe. In: JEP-TALN 2012-Journées d'Études sur la Parole et conférence annuelle du Traitement Automatique des Langues Naturelles, pp. 99–112 (2012)
5. Bojanowski, P., Grave, E., Joulin, A., Mikolov, T.: Enriching word vectors with subword information. arXiv preprint arXiv:1607.04606 (2016)
6. Candito, M., Seddah, D.: Le corpus sequoia: annotation syntaxique et exploitation pour l'adaptation d'analyseur par pont lexical (the sequoia corpus : Syntactic annotation and use for a parser lexical domain adaptation method) [in French]. In: Proceedings of the Joint Conference JEP-TALN-RECITAL 2012, volume 2: TALN. pp. 321–334. ATALA/AFCP, Grenoble, France, June 2012. https://aclanthology.org/F12-2024
7. Crabbé, B., Candito, M.: Expériences d'analyse syntaxique statistique du français. In: 15ème conférence sur le Traitement Automatique des Langues Naturelles - TALN 2008, pp. 44–54. Avignon, France, June 2008. https://hal.archives-ouvertes.fr/hal-00341093
8. Devlin, J., Chang, M.W., Lee, K., Toutanova, K.: Bert: pre-training of deep bidirectional transformers for language understanding (2019)
9. Eshkol, I., Tellier, I., Samer, T., Billot, S.: Etiqueter un corpus oral par apprentissage automatique a l'aide de connaissances linguistiques. arXiv preprint arXiv:1003.5749 (2010)
10. Graves, A., rahman Mohamed, A., Hinton, G.: Speech recognition with deep recurrent neural networks (2013)
11. Guillaume, B., de Marneffe, M.C., Perrier, G.: Conversion et améliorations de corpus du français annotés en Universal Dependencies. Revue TAL **60**(2), 71–95 (2019). https://hal.inria.fr/hal-02267418
12. Kahane, S., et al.: Ud_french-parisstories (2021)
13. Lacheret, A., et al.: Rhapsodie: a prosodic-syntactic treebank for spoken French. In: LREC (2014)
14. Lafferty, J.D., McCallum, A., Pereira, F.C.N.: Conditional random fields: probabilistic models for segmenting and labeling sequence data. In: Proceedings of the Eighteenth International Conference on Machine Learning. ICML 2001, San Francisco, CA, USA, pp. 282–289. Morgan Kaufmann Publishers Inc. (2001)
15. Leech, G., McEnery, A., Oakes, M.: Multilingual corpus resources and tools developed in crater. In: Proceedings of SNLR: International Workshop on Sharable Natural Language Resources, Nara, Japan. Citeseer (1994)
16. Martin, L., et al.: Camembert: a tasty French language model. In: Proceedings of the 58th Annual Meeting of the Association for Computational Linguistics (2020). https://doi.org/10.18653/v1/2020.acl-main.645

17. McEnery, T., Wilson, A., SáNchez-LeóN, F., Nieto-Serrano, A.: Multilingual resources for European languages: Contributions of the crater project. Literary Linguistic Comput. **12**(4), 219–226 (1997). https://doi.org/10.1093/llc/12.4.219

18. Nguyen, D.Q., Verspoor, K.: An improved neural network model for joint POS tagging and dependency parsing. arXiv preprint arXiv:1807.03955 (2018)

19. Nivre, J., et al.: Universal dependencies v2: an evergrowing multilingual treebank collection (2020)

20. Sanguinetti, M., Bosco, C.: PartTUT: the Turin university parallel treebank. In: Basili, R., Bosco, C., Delmonte, R., Moschitti, A., Simi, M. (eds.) Harmonization and Development of Resources and Tools for Italian Natural Language Processing within the PARLI Project. SCI, vol. 589, pp. 51–69. Springer, Cham (2015). https://doi.org/10.1007/978-3-319-14206-7_3

21. Seddah, D., Candito, M.: Hard time parsing questions: building a question bank for French. In: Tenth International Conference on Language Resources and Evaluation (LREC 2016). Proceedings of the 10th edition of the Language Resources and Evaluation Conference (LREC 2016), Portorož, Slovenia, May 2016. https://hal.archives-ouvertes.fr/hal-01457184

22. Wang, P., Qian, Y., Soong, F.K., He, L., Zhao, H.: Part-of-speech tagging with bidirectional long short-term memory recurrent neural network. arXiv preprint arXiv:1510.06168 (2015)

23. Wolf, T., et al.: Huggingface's transformers: State-of-the-art natural language processing (2020)

24. Zeman, D., et al.: CoNLL 2017 shared task: multilingual parsing from raw text to Universal Dependencies. In: Proceedings of the CoNLL 2017 Shared Task: Multilingual Parsing from Raw Text to Universal Dependencies, pp. 1–19. Association for Computational Linguistics, Vancouver, Canada, August 2017. https://doi.org/10.18653/v1/K17-3001, https://aclanthology.org/K17-3001

# Statistical and Neural Methods
# for Cross-lingual Entity Label Mapping
# in Knowledge Graphs

Gabriel Amaral[1]([✉]) [ID], Mārcis Pinnis[2] [ID], Inguna Skadiņa[2] [ID],
Odinaldo Rodrigues[1] [ID], and Elena Simperl[1] [ID]

[1] King's College London, London WC2R 2LS, UK
{gabriel.amaral,odinaldo.rodrigues,elena.simperl}@kcl.ac.uk
[2] Tilde, 1004 Rīga, Latvia
{marcis.pinnis,inguna.skadina}@tilde.lv

**Abstract.** Knowledge bases such as Wikidata amass vast amounts of named entity information, such as multilingual labels, which can be extremely useful for various multilingual and cross-lingual applications. However, such labels are not guaranteed to match across languages from an information consistency standpoint, greatly compromising their usefulness for fields such as machine translation. In this work, we investigate the application of word and sentence alignment techniques coupled with a matching algorithm to align cross-lingual entity labels extracted from Wikidata in 10 languages. Our results indicate that mapping between Wikidata's main labels stands to be considerably improved (up to 20 points in F1-score) by any of the employed methods. We show how methods relying on sentence embeddings outperform all others, even across different scripts. We believe the application of such techniques to measure the similarity of label pairs, coupled with a knowledge base rich in high-quality entity labels, to be an excellent asset to machine translation.

**Keywords:** Entity Label Mapping · Knowledge Representation · Multilinguality · Data Quality

## 1 Introduction

Knowledge bases, such as Wikidata [33] and DBpedia [5], have amassed large amounts of multilingual information about various concepts. These include various named entities (e.g., persons, organisations, and locations) which can be useful for various language technologies, such as named entity recognition [8], multilingual dictionaries [31], and machine translation [23,25].

Most multilingual data stored in these knowledge bases has been crowd-sourced by non-professionals in linguistic aspects, let alone in aspects of multilinguality. This raises data quality concerns despite the existence of proper guidelines on creating appropriate labels,[1] as these are not always followed by

---

[1] https://www.wikidata.org/wiki/Help:Label.

© Springer Nature Switzerland AG 2022
P. Sojka et al. (Eds.): TSD 2022, LNAI 13502, pp. 39–51, 2022.
https://doi.org/10.1007/978-3-031-16270-1_4

editors. Additionally, linguistic, regional, and cultural factors contribute to main labels assigned to an entity across languages not being fully correct or cross-lingually equivalent. For instance, the Wikidata entry for Donald Trump has the main label *"Donald Trump"* in Lithuanian, however, the correct representation of the name in Lithuanian is *"Donaldas Trampas"*. The Wikidata entry for John F. Kennedy has the English label *"John F. Kennedy"* and the Latvian label *"Džons Kenedijs"* (without the initial of the middle name).

Besides main labels, Wikidata features also aliases, which are alternatives and variants that refer to that same entity. One entity's label in a certain language might correspond to an alias in another language. For instance, the American actor and politician Kane has the English label *"Kane"* and the French label *"Glenn Jacobs"*, however, both labels can be also found in the list of alternative labels of the other respective language. The main labels and the aliases are not in any way cross-lingually mapped, which hinders automated use of the multilingual data in use cases that rely on high-quality cross-lingual dictionaries.

Current neural machine translation (NMT) methods provide means for integration of term and named entity dictionaries in NMT systems thereby enforcing term and named entity translation consistency and correctness. E.g., the work by Bergmanis and Pinnis [6] allows integrating terms and named entities in dictionary/canonical forms in NMT for morphologically rich languages. For these methods to work properly, it is crucial that translation equivalents represent adequate translations such that no information is lost or added with respect to the source language. If we only used Wikidata's main labels as a dictionary for machine translation, we would often produce wrong translations. For instance, the main label for the American entertainment company Miramax in English is *"Miramax"* and in German – *"Miramax Films"*. Translating the English sentence *"Miramax Films released a new movie"* through a machine translation system that uses these main labels in its dictionary would yield *"Miramax Films Filme haben einen neuen Film veröffentlicht"*, with the word *"Films"* translated twice.

Therefore, the focus of this work is on how to cross-lingually map Wikidata labels (both main labels and aliases) such that it is possible to acquire linguistically and semantically correct parallel named entity dictionaries from Wikidata. Our contributions are as follows:

- We build and release a cross-lingual entity label mapping dataset based on Wikidata in order to aid research, ours and future, into improving entity label mapping.
- We apply and compare different cross-lingual word and sentence similarity metrics for the task of cross-lingual entity label mapping within Wikidata, demonstrating how sentence embedding techniques can greatly improve Wikidata's label mapping.
- We analyse the level of cross-lingual parallelism of main labels in Wikidata for 10 languages and show that cross-lingual data quality is a current issue in the knowledge base.

– We propose a method for cross-lingual mapping of labels that relies on similarity scores from cross-lingual word alignment methods and achieves a mapping accuracy of over 88% on our Wikidata dataset.

The paper is structured as follows: Sect. 2 describes related work on data quality in Wikidata and cross-lingual mapping of entities, Sect. 3 described our benchmark dataset used in the experiments, Sect. 4 describes our method for cross-lingual label mapping, Sect. 5 describes and discusses the results achieved, and finally Sect. 6 concludes the paper.

## 2   Related Work

The quality and reliability of crowdsourced data have been discussed a lot in recent years, with different dimensions and metrics proposed and analysed [1, 11,22]. However, few works analyse the quality of crowdsourced knowledge graph data, and only recent studies do so in a systematic way.

Most studies into measuring Wikidata's quality and identifying potential improvements ignore multilingual aspects [24,27,29]. For instance, Skenoy et al. [29] rely on language-agnostic editor behaviour and ontological properties to identify low-quality statements. Piscopo et al. [27] investigate the quality of information provenance for references only in English.

Some recent studies do address the multilinguality of Wikidata. Kaffee et al. [18] analyse language coverage in Wikidata, concluding that Wikidata knowledge is available in just a few languages, while many languages have almost no coverage. Amaral et al. [3] investigate provenance quality across different languages with distinct coverage, finding that quality did not correlate with coverage and varied significantly between languages. As far as we know, ours is the first work to measure an intrinsically multilingual quality dimension of Wikidata from a standpoint of applicability in downstream language tasks.

The task of mapping entity labels in Wikidata is closely related to cross-lingual terminology and named entity extraction and mapping in comparable [10,12,30] or parallel corpora [20]. Although these tasks are broader, involving the identification of words and phrases constituting terms and named entities in larger contexts, a crucial component in these tasks is the assessment of the cross-lingual parallelism of term and named entity phrases. Ştefănescu [30] proposed a term similarity metric that combines probabilistic dictionary and cognate-based similarity scores. While Ştefănescu analysed terms on word level, Pinnis [26] proposed to align subwords between source and target terms and assess parallelism using a Levenshtein distance [21] similarity metric. The subword-level nature of the method allows it to map compounds and complex multiword terms. Daille [10] assesses term co-occurrence statistics when calculating the parallelism of terms. Aker et al. [2] train a binary classifier that predicts the parallelism of terms given a set of features including dictionary-based and cognate-based features.

Since in our work, we try to address mapping in a use case without contextual information, we compare the context-independent term mapping method by Pinnis with more novel (state-of-the-art) text similarity assessment methods that rely on large pre-trained language models.

State-of-the-art methods usually rely on large, multilingual, pre-trained language models, such as BERT [13], XLM-R [9], and ALBERT [19]. For example, SimAlign word alignments obtained from such models demonstrated better results for English-German than traditional statistical alignment methods [15]. Pre-trained multilingual BERT models are also used for cross-lingual alignment of multilingual knowledge graphs [34]. Promising results have been demonstrated by sentence-level embedding methods, such as LaBSE [14] and LASER [4].

The complexity of entity linking is recognized also by the *Cross-lingual Challenge on Recognition, Normalization, Classification, and Linking of Named Entities across Slavic languages* [28]. The task involved recognizing named entity mentions in Web documents, name normalization, and cross-lingual linking for six languages (Bulgarian, Czech, Polish, Russian, Slovene, Ukrainian). While the best model for this task in terms of F-score reached 85.7% and performance for the named entity recognition task reached 90% F-score, results for cross-lingual entity linking were not so promising, reaching only an F-score of 50.4% for the best system [32] employing LaBSE sentence embeddings.

Finally, recent work by researchers from *Google* proposes one dual encoder architecture model for linking 104 languages against 20 million Wikidata entities [7]. While the authors demonstrate the feasibility of the proposed approach, the quality and reliability of Wikidata are not discussed.

## 3   Data Preparation

To properly assess the effectiveness of entity label mapping methods, we need to construct a benchmark dataset from Wikidata. We start by acquiring a full dump of the knowledge graph (as of November 2021). We identify the three main classes whose subclass trees will encompass our target entities: Person (Q215627), Organisation (Q43229), and Geographic Location (Q2221906). By following the paths defined by the graph's "subclass of" (P279) and "instance of" (P31) predicates, we identify and extract approximately 43K subclasses and 9.3M entities that are instances of Person, 27K subclasses and 3M instances of Organisation, and 29K subclasses and 10.3M instances of Place. In total, we extracted 21.6M distinct entities.

Our entity label dataset should not be too sparse, otherwise, our results would be unreasonably biased by dissimilar levels of label coverage between languages. Thus, we follow two approaches: keeping only languages with higher coverage of labels and aliases, as well as keeping only richly labelled entities. For each language $L$, we measure: its main label coverage, defined as the percentage of all entities that have a main label in $L$, its alias presence, defined by the percentage of all entities that have at least one alias in $L$, and the average quantity of aliases all entities have in $L$. We rank all languages according to these metrics, calculate the average rank, and pick the top 10 languages to compose our dataset. They are: Swedish ($SV$), German ($DE$), Spanish ($ES$), Russian ($RU$), French ($FR$), Italian($IT$), English ($EN$), Portuguese ($PT$), Chinese ($ZH$), and Dutch ($NL$).

**Table 1.** Small random sample from our benchmarking dataset. Each entry consists of a unique cross-lingual pair for a specific entity.

| entity_id | la_1 | lan_2 | label_1 | label_2 |
|---|---|---|---|---|
| Q152265 | FR | ZH | Zaher Shah | 穆罕默德·查希爾·沙阿 |
| Q1241726 | IT | PT | Rebecca Flanders | Donna Ball |
| Q1400802 | RU | EN | Иераполь Бамбика | Manbug |
| Q150652 | SV | DE | Vilhelm I av Tyskland | Kartätschenprinz |
| Q275715 | ES | NL | Estadio de Montjuïc | Olympisch Stadion |

We also filter entities based on their label coverage. To be kept, an entity must adhere to the following criteria: having a main label in at least 4 of the 10 selected languages and having at least 3 aliases in 3 of the 10 selected languages. These constraints are the highest values before label and alias coverage start to plateau. Out of 21.6M entities, only 33K (0.16%) adhere to this criteria.

As Wikidata is a collaborative effort, labels or aliases may be put under the wrong language either by mistake or intentionally. Thus, final filtering is performed on the 33K extracted entities. We ascertain the languages of labels with fastText's [16,17] language detection models, which calculate the probabilities of a label belonging to each supported language. Labels that do not have an ambiguous language (e.g., acronyms, personal names, etc.) and have a very low probability of being of the language they are assigned to get dropped.

We finish by reorganising the dataset so that each entry consists of a unique cross-lingual pairing of labels for a given entity, including both main labels and aliases. Table 1 shows a small random sample of the dataset. Our benchmark dataset consists of 8.9M cross-lingual label pairings extracted from 33K entities in the 10 selected languages and is available online[2]. The majority of entities extracted (67%) are Persons, followed by Organisations (22%) and Places (10%). For every selected language, entities with main labels far outnumber those without, with 5 out of 10 having over 90% coverage. The mean alias count is above 1 for all languages (and above 2.5 for 5), and the alias coverage is around or above 50% for all except *ZH* (37%). We perceive a moderate correlation (0.57) between the presence of *RU* and *ZH* labels, as well as between *SV* and *IT* (0.47).

## 4    Entity Label Mapping

We employ multiple methods to estimate the cross-lingual similarity of each entity label pair in our dataset and to solve the problem of entity label mapping. Then, we devise a greedy algorithm that transforms these scores into a set of high-similarity non-overlapping pairings of labels for each unique (*entity id*, *language 1*, *language 2*) tuple. Finally, we measure the performance of each method and its variations in identifying these optimal pairings of labels in our Wikidata

---

[2] https://doi.org/10.6084/m9.figshare.19582798.

benchmark dataset and compare them. Please note that all label pre-processing is done by the methods themselves.

### 4.1 Label Cross-Lingual Similarity Scoring Methods

MPAlligner [26] is a statistical cross-lingual terminology mapping tool that uses probabilistic dictionaries and Romanisation-based transliteration methods to identify reciprocal mappings between words and sub-word units of source and target terms. It scores each term pair by assessing the proportion of overlapping characters. Since MPAligner relies on the existence of large bilingual dictionaries or cognates that are shared between languages, its recall can be limited.

Simalign [15] is a word alignment method that does not require parallel data, relying instead on multilingual word embeddings created from monolingual data. It uses a multilingual BERT to retrieve sub-word embeddings and matches them across two sentences through a combination of cosine similarity and various matching strategies defined by the authors. We extract from Simalign the calculated similarity scores between sub-word units after being transformed by these matching strategies. Finally, we average out the pair's sub-word scores.

LASER [4] and LaBSE [14] are both sentence embedding methods. By embedding the entirety of each label, we acquire pairs of vectors to which we can directly apply similarity metrics. LASER embeds over 90 languages in a joint space by training an LSTM-based encoder-decoder neural network that is shared between all languages. LaBSE follows a similar approach but uses a multilingual BERT model fine-tuned on a translation ranking task. LaBSE establishes the current state-of-the-art results on multiple downstream multilingual tasks.

### 4.2 Best Match Algorithm

We aim to find the best cross-lingual mapping between entity labels. Thus, we devise a greedy algorithm that, given a list of cross-lingual label pairings and their respective similarity scores for a specific entity, provides us with a non-overlapping set of pairings deemed as the best matches. We apply this algorithm to the scores produced by each scoring method, compiling distinct lists of best matches, and comparing each to a manually annotated ground truth.

First, the algorithm divides the dataset into groups of scored cross-lingual label pairs, each indexed by a unique (*entity id, language 1, language 2*) tuple. On each group, it visits all pairs in descending order of similarity, declaring a pair as a best match only if no other pair in that same group containing either of this pair's labels was declared a best match before. This creates a one-to-one mapping between an entity's labels in a language $L1$ and language $L2$. If the entity does not have an equal amount of labels in both languages, some labels will remain without a match. This is expected and welcomed as not all labels have clear cross-lingual matches in Wikidata, and is better than perhaps forcing a match with dissimilar labels.

In addition to the aforementioned methods, we add two simple baselines: randomised and main label matching. The first declares best matches via a randomised walk through the dataset, rather than ordered by scores. The second declares all, and only, pairs of two main labels as best matches.

### 4.3   Ground Truth and Method Comparison

The best match selection algorithm assigns pairs a binary class, i.e. best match or not. Thus, these mappings can be compared to ground truth and have their performances measured through standard classification metrics. Elaborating such a ground truth is not trivial, as we first need to define what truly constitutes a label's best match.

We define a best match as a cross-lingual pairing of labels for the same entity wherein one neither adds information to nor removes information from the other. By information, we mean any data about an entity's identity, attributes, or qualities. An example of best matches in our ground truth can be seen in Table 2. This definition allows for potentially overlapping pairs, as Table 2 shows

**Table 2.** An example of pairings we consider best matches in our ground truth. For entity *Q398*, the second and third pairs introduce information, namely the official acronym and the fact Bahrain is a kingdom. For entity *Q311374*, pair 3 replaces the full first name with a generic nickname.

| Entity | Lan1 | Lan2 | Label1 | Label2 | Best |
|--------|------|------|--------|--------|------|
| Q398 | SV | EN | Bahrain | Bahrain | **Yes** |
| Q398 | SV | EN | Bahrain | BAH | No |
| Q398 | SV | EN | Bahrain | Kingdom of Bahrain | No |
| Q398 | SV | EN | Konungariket Bahrain | Kingdom of Bahrain | **Yes** |
| Q311374 | SV | FR | Aleksandr Ovetjkin | Aleksandr Ovetchkine | **Yes** |
| Q311374 | SV | FR | Aleksandr Ovetjkin | Alexander Ovechkin | **Yes** |
| Q311374 | SV | FR | Aleksandr Ovetjkin | Alex Ovechkin | No |

for entity *Q311374*, in the case of minor variations such as spelling of transliterated sub-words that are commonly found on natural text. This means that none of the tested mapping methods can achieve the maximum classification accuracy, but it still allows us to compare their performance to each other as they still benefit from selecting one of the ground truth best matches.

Our ground truth consists of a manually annotated representative sample from our benchmark dataset (95% confidence interval, 5% margin of error) rather than its totality due to annotation costs. This is obtained through a stratified sampling after a few processing steps to account for underlying aspects of the label distribution which might hinder comparison between methods. That is:

1. We remove from the benchmark dataset all entities with an outlier amount of labels pairs so that they do not bias the comparison. E.g., the entity *"Pope Adeodato I"*, has over 42 *PT-ZH* label pairs, over six times the average.

2. We remove all entities containing only one label pair for any language combination, as they are trivially solvable and do not contribute to the comparison.
3. We randomly reduce the number of entities with an identical pair (e.g. "Bahrain" and "Bahrain" in Table 2) by a factor of 50%, as they represent a much smaller challenge than entities with no identical pairs, yet compose half of all entities. This lets our comparison focus more on harder cases.

Then, we perform a stratified sampling so that languages are equally represented and carry similar weight. We manually annotate this sample according to our definition of best match to compose our ground truth.

## 5  Evaluation and Discussion

With our ground truth, we can measure the performance of each of the cross-lingual label similarity estimation methods and their variations. From the four methods described in Sect. 4, we devise and test nine variations, except for MPAligner, which is used as-is. For Simalign, we use each of its matching methods (Argmax, Match, and Itermax) to filter out scores of non-matching sub-word pairings and average those remaining. We also extract the sub-word embeddings used by the method and apply cosine similarity directly to them, extracting the mean. As for both LASER and LaBSE, we calculate cosine similarity and inverse Euclidean distance between pairs of label embeddings.

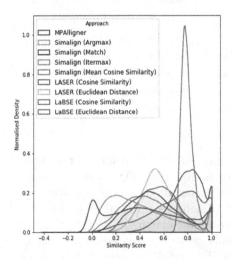 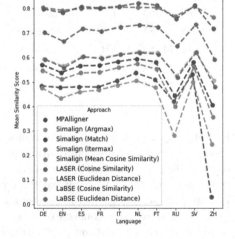

**Fig. 1.** Normalised probability density of the similarity scores calculated by each approach variation.

**Fig. 2.** The mean similarity scores per language as calculated by each approach variation.

Figure 1 shows the density distributions of similarity scores from each method. We can see how most methods have a bell-shaped curve between values

0 to 1, with a spike near 1, due to many pairs being nearly or truly identical. MPAlligner has a spike near 0; as it depends on constructed dictionaries, the lack of explicit equivalences means it will default to low values of similarity. The mean cosine similarity applied at Simalign embeddings has a narrow and tall curve centred in a high score, indicating these scores are either not very informative, or their domain is naturally restricted. All other methods follow expected distributions.

Figure 2 shows the mean similarity scores per language. All approaches seem to calculate similar scores regardless of language, except for the only two languages not using the Latin script: *RU* and *ZH*. This drop might be attributed to two factors. One is the natural lessened similarity between labels using different scripts, the other is the methods' inability to perceive cross-script similarities. This drop is bigger with the dictionary-based method (MPAlligner), lesser with sub-word embeddings, and minimal with sentence embeddings.

In Table 3, we show the accuracy obtained by all methods for all the data in the ground truth annotation, as well as broken down by language, including both baselines. Looking at the main-label baseline, we see how current Wikidata main labels can be significantly improved in terms of cross-lingual matching. For most languages tested, the gap in accuracy between depending on main labels and automated methods is very high, e.g., for *IT*, *FR*, *ES*, etc.

**Table 3.** Classification performance of different approaches as measured by accuracy across all languages and individually. *MPA* = MPAlligner; *SIM_A* = Simalign (Argmax); *SIM_M* = Simalign (Match); *SIM_I* = Simalign (Itermax); *SIM_C* = Simalign (Cosine); *LS_C* = LASER (Cosine); *LS_E* = LASER (Euclidean); *LB_C* = LaBSE (Cosine); *RAN* = Randomised Baseline; *ML* = Main Labels Baseline. LaBSE with Euclidean Similarity performs identically to LaBSE with Cosine Similarity.

| | ALL | DE | EN | ES | FR | IT | NL | PT | RU | SV | ZH |
|---|---|---|---|---|---|---|---|---|---|---|---|
| **MPA** | 0.832 | 0.846 | 0.840 | 0.830 | 0.816 | 0.867 | 0.880 | 0.833 | 0.865 | 0.813 | 0.679 |
| **SIM_A** | 0.827 | 0.826 | 0.844 | 0.798 | 0.844 | 0.857 | 0.880 | 0.860 | 0.865 | 0.801 | 0.649 |
| **SIM_M** | 0.808 | 0.851 | 0.831 | 0.807 | 0.844 | 0.814 | 0.817 | 0.827 | 0.806 | 0.832 | 0.582 |
| **SIM_I** | 0.810 | 0.841 | 0.844 | 0.798 | 0.844 | 0.809 | 0.805 | 0.838 | 0.822 | 0.819 | 0.619 |
| **SIM_C** | 0.807 | 0.831 | 0.836 | 0.816 | 0.816 | 0.835 | 0.828 | 0.822 | 0.822 | 0.795 | 0.597 |
| **LS_C** | 0.871 | 0.896 | **0.900** | **0.887** | 0.877 | 0.873 | **0.902** | 0.854 | **0.908** | 0.863 | 0.694 |
| **LS_E** | 0.867 | 0.891 | 0.896 | 0.873 | 0.883 | 0.873 | 0.880 | 0.870 | 0.892 | **0.869** | 0.686 |
| **LB_C** | **0.882** | **0.905** | 0.879 | **0.887** | **0.894** | **0.925** | 0.880 | **0.887** | 0.897 | 0.863 | **0.768** |
| **RAN** | 0.656 | 0.633 | 0.698 | 0.657 | 0.661 | 0.656 | 0.657 | 0.591 | 0.758 | 0.621 | 0.604 |
| **ML** | 0.776 | 0.787 | 0.784 | 0.765 | 0.755 | 0.735 | 0.788 | 0.779 | 0.844 | 0.819 | 0.679 |

We can see sentence-embedding models performing far better than other methods. MPAlligner generally outperforms sub-word embedding methods, which we find surprising, and indicates that approaching this task by looking at labels in their entirety rather than broken into units is beneficial. All methods are generally better than the baselines, except in the case of non-Latin script languages *RU* and *ZH*. For *RU*, most Simalign-based methods under-perform the main-label baseline, whereas for *ZH* that is all Simalign-based methods, some under-performing even the randomised baseline. Still, for *ZH*, LaBSE with cosine similarity is the only approach significantly outperforming the main-label baseline. These results point to LaBSE as the best-performing method for cross-lingual entity label mapping.

## 6  Conclusion

Cross-lingual mapping of entity labels such that information is properly preserved is an important challenge to be solved if we wish downstream tasks depending on such entities to improve. Resources such as Wikidata can greatly help, provided their labels have a higher quality of cross-lingual alignment. Through our contributions, we not only showcase the importance of such resources but suggest methods to improve such quality.

In this paper, we have presented the case of Wikidata by extracting and structuring a benchmark cross-lingual entity label mapping dataset from thousands of its entities. We have showcased a comparison between the performances of various text similarity estimation methods when applied to the task of cross-lingual entity label mapping. This comparison consists of adapting the various text similarity methods so that similarity scores are extracted for label pairs; devising an algorithm to select best matches based on similarity scores; developing a balanced and expressive ground truth dataset for the proper comparison of classification metrics.

We verified that Wikidata's main labels overall fail to match cross-lingual label pairings better than any of the text similarity estimation methods that were tested. We also ascertained that methods applied to labels as a whole tend to outperform those focused on their word and sub-word units. Furthermore, techniques based on sentence embeddings learned in a shared multilingual space have not only considerably outperformed other methods in same-script pairings, but also between distinct scripts. Finally, we have seen how many current and sophisticated word alignment techniques under-perform simplistic baselines at this task in specific languages. Our best match algorithm is based on comparisons between scores only, which is why we removed from our ground truth all entities with a single pairing on the basis of being trivially resolvable, even if that pairing is wrong. Using a threshold-sensitive approach would better treat these cases and is an interesting direction for future work.

**Acknowledgements.** This research received funding from the European Union's Horizon 2020 research and innovation programme under the Marie Skłodowska-Curie grant agreement no. 812997. The research has been supported by the European Regional Development Fund within the research project "AI Assistant for Multilingual Meeting Management" No. 1.1.1.1/19/A/082.

# References

1. Adler, B.T., de Alfaro, L., Mola-Velasco, S.M., Rosso, P., West, A.G.: Wikipedia vandalism detection: combining natural language, metadata, and reputation features. In: Gelbukh, A. (ed.) CICLing 2011. LNCS, vol. 6609, pp. 277–288. Springer, Heidelberg (2011). https://doi.org/10.1007/978-3-642-19437-5_23
2. Aker, A., Paramita, M.L., Gaizauskas, R.: Extracting bilingual terminologies from comparable corpora. In: Proceedings of the 51st Annual Meeting of the Association for Computational Linguistics (Volume 1: Long Papers), pp. 402–411 (2013)
3. Amaral, G., Piscopo, A., Kaffee, L.A., Rodrigues, O., Simperl, E.: Assessing the quality of sources in Wikidata across languages: a hybrid approach. J. Data Inf. Qual. 13(4), 1–35 (2021)
4. Artetxe, M., Schwenk, H.: Massively multilingual sentence embeddings for zero-shot cross-lingual transfer and beyond. Trans. Assoc. Comput. Linguist. 7, 597–610 (2019)
5. Auer, S., Bizer, C., Kobilarov, G., Lehmann, J., Cyganiak, R., Ives, Z.: DBpedia: a nucleus for a web of open data. In: Aberer, K., et al. (eds.) ASWC/ISWC -2007. LNCS, vol. 4825, pp. 722–735. Springer, Heidelberg (2007). https://doi.org/10.1007/978-3-540-76298-0_52
6. Bergmanis, T., Pinnis, M.: Facilitating terminology translation with target lemma annotations. In: Proceedings of the 16th Conference of the European Chapter of the Association for Computational Linguistics: Main Volume, pp. 3105–3111 (2021)
7. Botha, J.A., Shan, Z., Gillick, D.: Entity Linking in 100 Languages. In: Webber, B., Cohn, T., He, Y., Liu, Y. (eds.) Proceedings of the 2020 Conference on Empirical Methods in Natural Language Processing, EMNLP 2020, pp. 7833–7845 (2020)
8. Chen, B., Ma, J.Y., Qi, J., Guo, W., Ling, Z.H., Liu, Q.: USTC-NELSLIP at SemEval-2022 task 11: gazetteer-adapted integration network for multilingual complex named entity recognition. arXiv:2203.03216 (2022)
9. Conneau, A., et al.: Unsupervised cross-lingual representation learning at scale. In: Proceedings of the 58th Annual Meeting of the Association for Computational Linguistics, pp. 8440–8451 (2020)
10. Daille, B.: Building bilingual terminologies from comparable corpora: the TTC TermSuite. In: 5th Workshop on Building and Using Comparable Corpora (2012)
11. Daniel, F., Kucherbaev, P., Cappiello, C., Benatallah, B., Allahbakhsh, M.: Quality control in crowdsourcing: a survey of quality attributes, assessment techniques, and assurance actions. ACM Comput. Surv. 51(1), 1–40 (2018)
12. Déjean, H., Gaussier, É., Sadat, F.: Bilingual terminology extraction: an approach based on a multilingual thesaurus applicable to comparable corpora. In: Proceedings of the 19th International Conference on Computational Linguistics COLING, pp. 218–224 (2002)
13. Devlin, J., Chang, M.W., Lee, K., Toutanova, K.: BERT: pre-training of deep bidirectional transformers for language understanding. In: Proceedings of the 2019 Conference of the North American Chapter of the Association for Computational Linguistics: Human Language Technologies, Volume 1 (Long and Short Papers), pp. 4171–4186 (2019)
14. Feng, F., Yang, Y., Cer, D., Arivazhagan, N., Wang, W.: Language-agnostic BERT sentence embedding (2020)
15. Jalili Sabet, M., Dufter, P., Yvon, F., Schütze, H.: SimAlign: high quality word alignments without parallel training data using static and contextualized embeddings. In: Findings of the Association for Computational Linguistics: EMNLP 2020, pp. 1627–1643. Association for Computational Linguistics, Online, November 2020

16. Joulin, A., Grave, E., Bojanowski, P., Douze, M., Jégou, H., Mikolov, T.: Fast-text.zip: compressing text classification models. ArXiv:abs/1612.03651 (2016)
17. Joulin, A., Grave, E., Bojanowski, P., Mikolov, T.: Bag of tricks for efficient text classification. In: Proceedings of the 15th Conference of the European Chapter of the Association for Computational Linguistics: Volume 2, Short Papers, pp. 427–431. Association for Computational Linguistics, Valencia, Spain, April 2017
18. Kaffee, L.A., Piscopo, A., Vougiouklis, P., Simperl, E., Carr, L., Pintscher, L.: A glimpse into babel: an analysis of multilinguality in Wikidata. In: Proceedings of the 13th International Symposium on Open Collaboration. OpenSym 2017 (2017)
19. Lan, Z., Chen, M., Goodman, S., Gimpel, K., Sharma, P., Soricut, R.: ALBERT: a lite BERT for self-supervised learning of language representations. In: 8th International Conference on Learning Representations, ICLR 2020, Addis Ababa, Ethiopia, 26–30 April 2020 (2020)
20. Lefever, E., Macken, L., Hoste, V.: Language-independent bilingual terminology extraction from a multilingual parallel corpus. In: Proceedings of the 12th Conference of the European Chapter of the ACL (EACL 2009), pp. 496–504 (2009)
21. Levenshtein, V.I.: Binary codes capable of correcting deletions, insertions, and reversals. Soviet Physics Doklady $10(8)$, 707–710 (1966)
22. Lewoniewski, W., Węcel, K., Abramowicz, W.: Modeling popularity and reliability of sources in multilingual Wikipedia. Information $11(5)$, 263 (2020)
23. Merhav, Y., Ash, S.: Design challenges in named entity transliteration. In: Proceedings of the 27th International Conference on Computational Linguistics, pp. 630–640 (2018)
24. Mora-Cantallops, M., Sánchez-Alonso, S., García-Barriocanal, E.: A systematic literature review on Wikidata. Data Technologies and Applications (2019)
25. Moussallem, D., Ngonga Ngomo, A.C., Buitelaar, P., Arcan, M.: Utilizing knowledge graphs for neural machine translation augmentation. In: Proceedings of the 10th International Conference on Knowledge Capture, pp. 139–146 (2019)
26. Pinnis, M.: Context independent term mapper for European languages. In: Proceedings of Recent Advances in Natural Language Processing (RANLP 2013). pp. 562–570 (2013)
27. Piscopo, A., Kaffee, L.-A., Phethean, C., Simperl, E.: Provenance information in a collaborative knowledge graph: an evaluation of Wikidata external references. In: d'Amato, C., et al. (eds.) ISWC 2017. LNCS, vol. 10587, pp. 542–558. Springer, Cham (2017). https://doi.org/10.1007/978-3-319-68288-4_32
28. Piskorski, J., et al.: Slav-NER: the 3rd cross-lingual challenge on recognition, normalization, classification, and linking of named entities across Slavic languages. In: Proceedings of the 8th Workshop on Balto-Slavic Natural Language Processing, pp. 122–133 (2021)
29. Shenoy, K., Ilievski, F., Garijo, D., Schwabe, D., Szekely, P.A.: A study of the quality of Wikidata. CoRR abs/2107.00156 (2021)
30. Ştefănescu, D.: Mining for term translations in comparable corpora. In: The 5th Workshop on Building and Using Comparable Corpora, pp. 98–103 (2012)
31. Turki, H., Vrandecic, D., Hamdi, H., Adel, I.: Using Wikidata as a multi-lingual multi-dialectal dictionary for Arabic dialects. In: 2017 IEEE/ACS 14th International Conference on Computer Systems and Applications (AICCSA), pp. 437–442 (2017)
32. Vīksna, R., Skadina, I.: Multilingual slavic named entity recognition. In: Proceedings of the 8th Workshop on Balto-Slavic Natural Language Processing, pp. 93–97 (2021)

33. Vrandečić, D., Krötzsch, M.: Wikidata: a free collaborative knowledgebase. Commun. ACM **57**(10), 78–85 (2014)
34. Yang, H., Zou, Y., Shi, P., Lu, W., Lin, J., Sun, X.: Aligning cross-lingual entities with multi-aspect information. In: Inui, K., Jiang, J., Ng, V., Wan, X. (eds.) Proceedings of the 2019 Conference on Empirical Methods in Natural Language Processing and the 9th International Joint Conference on Natural Language Processing, EMNLP-IJCNLP 2019, pp. 4430–4440 (2019)

# Quality Assessment of Subtitles – Challenges and Strategies

Julia Brendel[(✉)] and Mihaela Vela

Saarland University, Campus, 66123 Saarbrücken, Germany
s9jubren@stud.uni-saarland.de, m.vela@mx.uni-saarland.de

**Abstract.** This paper describes a novel approach for assessing the quality of machine-translated subtitles. Although machine translation (MT) is widely used for subtitling, in comparison to text translation, there is little research in this area. For our investigation, we are using the English to German machine translated subtitles from the SubCo corpus [11], a corpus consisting of human and machine-translated subtitles from English. In order to provide information about the quality of the machine-produced subtitles error annotation and evaluation is performed manually. Both the applied error annotation and evaluation schemes are covering the four dimensions *content, language, format* and *semiotics* allowing for a fine-grained detection of errors and weaknesses of the MT engine. Besides the human assessment of the subtitles, our approach comprises also the measurement of the inter-annotator agreement (IAA) of the human error annotation and evaluation, as well as the estimation of post-editing effort. The combination of these three steps represents a novel evaluation method that finds its use in both improving the subtiling quality assessment process and the machine translation systems.

**Keywords:** subtitles · quality assessment · machine translation

## 1 Introduction

In this paper, we present a method for evaluating the subtitling quality of machine translated (MT) subtitles. The demand for the production of subtitles and the translation into a variety of languages has increased tremendously. Caused by the development and accessibility of technology, audiovisual content is nowadays consumed worldwide on a daily basis. [15] describe how the subtitling workflow, at first consisting exclusively of human translation, has been adapted by integrating machine translation technologies in the subtitling workflow. Approaches to neural machine translation (NMT) were embedded into the workflow, in order to deliver high quality content in the shortest amount of time. Still, these scenarios are limited. A possible explanation therefore is given by [8], stating that the large amounts of high-quality data required for training the systems, as well as the necessary pre-processing phase for the data, makes the process a time-consuming task. Until now, the most profitable workflow is the

© Springer Nature Switzerland AG 2022
P. Sojka et al. (Eds.): TSD 2022, LNAI 13502, pp. 52–63, 2022.
https://doi.org/10.1007/978-3-031-16270-1_5

machine translation of subtitles followed by human post-editing. As machine translation engines have several limitations and weaknesses [6,8,10], multiple evaluation methods exist to assess the quality of the MT output, although there is no consensus on a universal definition for subtitling quality. [8] and [2] give an overview of applicable quality factors for subtitling, factors also considered by us in our approach. According to them, adequacy and fluency together with technical and linguistic parameters are the most important factors for subtitling quality. Built on the most recent findings, the error annotation scheme, as well as the evaluation taxonomy used to assess the machine translated subtitles in the SubCo corpus[1], correspond to the most recent findings in this research area [8]. We focused on the error sources and evaluated the results, to further investigate limitations of the MT output and possible weaknesses in the quality assessment process. Although the machine translated subtitles were produced by SUMAT, a statistical MT online service, specifically developed for subtitling [4,12,17], we can assert that the limitations concerning the MT adaptability similarly occur in NMT quality assessment and training. It can therefore be applied to the most recent NMT subtitle training studies. With a mixed approach of combining error annotation, evaluation measures, as well as the calculation of the inter-annotator agreement, we aim to determine the most important subtitle quality factors. With our method, both whole documents and single subtitle lines can be evaluated quickly and reliably, allowing statements regarding the subtitling quality. This way, we can identify subtitling quality ranging from perfect to unacceptable. For cases where the subtitle quality could not be identified, we assume that the translation of the subtitle was rather difficult for the MT engine to process. Particularly for the above mentioned issues, but also in general, we propose estimating the post-editing effort. We can thus evaluate the amount of time and work that is required to post-edit and improve the quality of each subtitle. Such measures can be useful to detect general MT quality, issues and weaknesses in the translation process and enhance the subtitling workflow.

## 1.1 Quality Assessment of Machine Translated Subtitles

Assessing the quality of a machine translated subtitle is a complex task. The literature lists two main ways of proceeding, namely approaches:

(i) addressing the translation process (use of templates or subtitle product chains), and approaches

(ii) addressing the translation product (error annotation or evaluation).

[13] and [1] concentrate on (i), investigating how the quality of a subtitle is dependant on the translation product. We will be focusing on the second approach (ii), the translation product and the use of error annotation and evaluation measures to assess the subtitle quality. In both approaches, the definition of quality is dependant on various factors such as the workflow efficiency, the target audience, the translator's experience and professional environment, and

---

[1] http://fedora.clarin-d.uni-saarland.de/subco/index.html.

more [9]. With reference to the subtitle translation industry, [14] conducted a survey where they addressed professional subtitlers and their clients. In analogy to [7], they identified subtitle quality factors, divided into specifications regarding (a) translation quality (content and transfer, grammar, spelling and punctuation, readability and appropriateness), as well as (b) technical issues (style guide, speed, spotting and formatting). In the process of assessing the quality for our data, we will identify the importance and nuances of these factors and how they contribute increasing and decreasing the quality of the final product.

## 2   Data and Methodology

In this section, we describe the data used for our investigation, but also the scales and methods used.

### 2.1   The Corpus

The data used for our investigation is the documentary film *Joining the Dots* by Pablo Romero Fresco [16]. The film consists of 132 English subtitles and a total of 1557 words. These English subtitles were automatically translated into German and are part of the SubCo [11] corpus. To date, there is no fully automated MT engine that can transfer the input of a source subtitle into a target translated product. Contrary to plain text translation, the translation of subtitles requires further individual production steps such as segmentation of the input, as well as compliance with spatial and timing constraints. Furthermore, post-editing the MT output by humans is indispensable. The SUMAT[2] project aimed to improve the subtitling workflow with the application of statistical machine translation (SMT) technologies. As part of the project [15] developed an online translation service for subtitles including 9 European language pairs that can be combined into 14 language pairs. The German machine translated subtitles in the SubCo corpus were produced with SUMAT's online demo [3].

### 2.2   Error Annotation and Evaluation

The manual error annotation and evaluation[3] of machine translated subtitles used for our analysis comes also from the SubCo corpus [11]. In order to test the reliability of the manual error annotation and evaluation in SubCo, we propose our own inter-annotator agreement measuring the data by generating boxplots. Subsequently, we derive our own measures for the estimation of subtitling quality and post-editing effort. Lastly, we re-evaluate the MT output in terms of errors and evaluation to compare our results to those in the SubCo corpus. The used error annotation scheme consists of the dimensions *content, language, format* and *semiotics*, each category covering different types of errors:

---

[2] http://www.fp7-sumat-project.eu.

[3] The subtitles were error annotated, evaluated and post-edited by novice translators, who were trained for several weeks to perform these tasks.

(a) content: addition, omission, content shift, terminology and untranslated,

(b) language: function words, morphology, orthography and syntax,

(c) format: capitalisation, punctuation, number of characters per line (cpl), number of characters per second (cps) and spacing errors,

(d) semiotics: inter-semiotic coherence (audiovisual phenomenon, where different channels contradict each other, contributing to the meaning of text and translation).

The first two error categories can be applied on any translation, whereas the last two categories describe issues concerning specific features of subtitling.

The evaluation was measured for all categories, on four levels depending on their acceptability:

- perfect: no error and no modification needed,
- acceptable: some minor errors, can be used without modification,
- revisable: one major error and/ or minor errors, revision is needed,
- unacceptable: revision is not worth the effort, re-translation is required.

In addition, we developed an additional MT error model based on the findings of [6], who collected errors exclusively produced by MT engines. The following error categories were considered:

(a) compounds: errors in compounding,

(b) paraphrased translation: MT fails to paraphrase translation to adhere to cpl and cps guidelines and produces a literal translation instead,

(c) literal vs. contextual translation: MT produces literal translation and fails to convey the correct meaning in the context,

(d) text not to translate: MT tends not to identify text to be excluded from the translation,

(e) language nuances: incorrect choice of pronouns,

(f) abbreviations: errors in the translation of abbreviations,

(g) word structure errors: MT translation output is grammatically correct but uses the wrong morphological form.

This special error model[4] was applied on top of the already existing error annotation, allowing us to detect more easily specific strengths and weaknesses of the MT, and thus to better predict the quality and post-editing effort of the MT output.

## 3   Estimating Subtitling Quality and Post-Editing Effort

The most common calculus for inter-annotator agreement is Fleiss' kappa correlation coefficient [5]. As it only accounts for numeral data, it could not be applied to our set of ordinal data. Furthermore, the kappa value only describes the agreement of the data set as a whole, not individual data points. As we were

---

[4] This error annotation was performed by one professional translator.

keen to identify not just the overall agreement, but the agreement for single lines to further determine error sources and special translation phenomena, we derived our own method to measure the inter-annotator agreement (IAA). For all of our deductions, we suggest the generation of boxplots and the use of the statistics resulting from that, to explain and depict the statistical dispersion of the measures. For measuring the inter-annotator agreement, we deduced that the interquartile range (IQR) (50% of the data) and the median (midpoint value) are indicators, which enable measuring the IAA per line for each subtitle. Figure 1 shows how we can automatically filter the quality of a subtitle by interpreting the elements of a boxplot.

We derived the measure for reliable subtitling quality as a combined observation of a IQR, which must be <1, and the position of the median (midpoint value) ranging from 1 (perfect quality) to 4 (unacceptable quality). We can thus make a statement about the reliable quality of a single subtitle. If we determine the subtitle quality of each subtitle, we get an impression of reliable perfect to unacceptable quality subtitles. Subtitles where an assertion about their quality

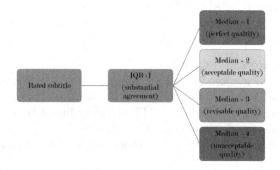

**Fig. 1.** Decision tree for estimating the quality of the MT generated subtitles. (Color figure online)

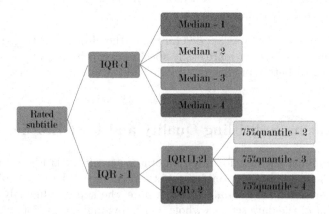

**Fig. 2.** Decision tree for estimating the post-editing effort. (Color figure online)

cannot be stated are treated as *indefinable* and will be considered when estimating the post-editing effort as depicted in Fig. 2.

The colours of the decision tree incorporate the degree of post-editing effort: green stands for no post-editing effort, yellow is low post-editing effort, orange indicates a medium post-editing effort and red implies the highest post-editing effort, a complete re-translation of the segment. The upper part of the scheme corresponds to the decision tree for subtitles with high agreement (IQR < 1), and the position of the median indicates the reliable quality of a subtitle. Whereas a (green) safe perfect quality subtitle does not require post-editing, the rise of the value of the median increases the post-editing effort. A safe unacceptable quality subtitle thus requires the highest post-editing effort possible. The lower part of the tree concerns all ratings where the IQR > 1. This means that the IAA is less reliable than in the upper case. A low IAA can be an indicator for problematic subtitles: a non-professional annotator might not detect errors that a professional would mark. Therefore his rating could be acceptable, simply because he missed the error. Or the subtitle could not be rated correctly, because the annotator could not decide between categories or classify the error correctly.

# 4    Analysis Results

In this section we present the analysis results based on the available error annotation, the evaluations and the performed post-editing on the machine translated subtitles. We will describe how the inter-annotator agreement is measured and what this means for subtitling quality. We will also show what post-editing effort and the additional error categories reveal about the quality of the analysed subtitles.

## 4.1    Inter-annotator Agreement

The mean interquartile range (IQR) as a measure for inter-annotator agreement (IAA) depicted in Fig. 3, indicates the overall agreement for each error category. With these values we can estimate tendencies for each category and compare them. The best mean IAA value was achieved in the *format* category with the lowest IQR value, followed by *content* and *language* with the poorest agreement values and an increasing IQR.

Figure 4 shows the IAA per line for the first 15 subtitles[5] of the *format* error category. We can directly filter all subtitles with a perfect agreement and assume that their quality is rather perfect. Subtitles with lower agreement need further observation that consists of two steps: (1) check if IQR is < 1 or > 1, and (2) according to the result, we can either estimate the subtitling quality or post-editing effort.

---

[5] In order to increase the visualisation effect, we depicted only the first 15 subtitles. Depicting all subtitles would have made the visualisation impossible.

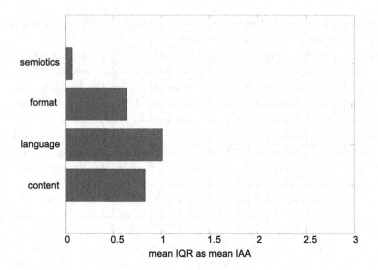

**Fig. 3.** Overall inter-annotator agreement.

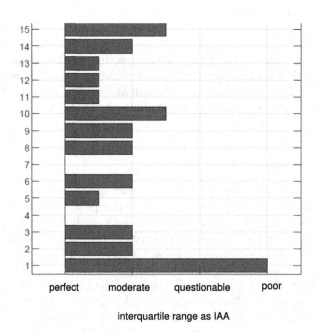

**Fig. 4.** Inter-annotator agreement per line for the *format* category.

## 4.2   Subtitling Quality

Comparably to the results from the overall inter-annotator agreement, we present in Fig. 5 the mean values of the subtitling quality for all subtitles with substantial agreement (IQR< 1)[6] for all four error categories: *content, language, format, semiotics.*

The category with the most *perfect* reliable quality subtitles is the *format* category. However, almost the same amount of subtitles was annotated with *revisable.* This example shows, that the overall quality of this error category is mixed. We are therefore interested in investigating how this trend evolved and where the error sources can be located. That is why we consider the reliable subtitle quality per line in Fig. 6, which shows the reliable quality of the first 15 subtitles[7] for the *language* category.

An empty line in Fig. 6 means that the subtitle quality per line could not be evaluated. This phenomenon occurs, when the IAA for a line is too poor. Then, no reliable statements can be made about the quality. Lines of that kind need to be evaluated further regarding the post-editing effort, thereby we can make statements regarding their quality.

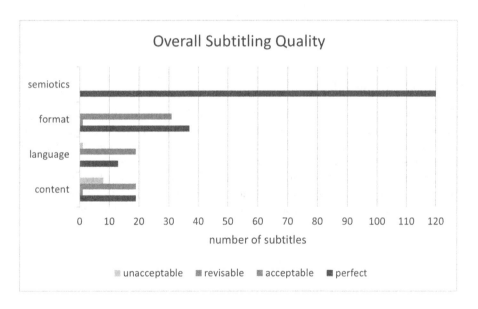

**Fig. 5.** Overall subtitling quality.

---

[6] IQR < 1 means that not all subtitles are depicted in Fig. 5, but only the ones with IQR < 1, leading to a different number of subtitles per error category.

[7] As in Fig. 4, we decided to show only the first 15 subtitles, increasing this way the visualisation effect. Depicting all subtitles would have made the visualisation impossible.

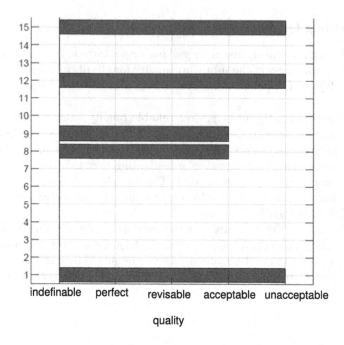

**Fig. 6.** Subtitling quality per line for the *language* category.

## 4.3 Post-editing Effort

We measure the post-editing effort for all subtitles with an IQR <1 and IQR ≥1, according to Fig. 2. The mean value of those results across all categories are collected in Fig. 7. We observed that the error category *language* requires the highest post-editing effort. In the *format* and *content* error category, subtitles with medium to high post-editing effort predominate as well. We can now confirm that, at least for our data, the performance of the MT has limitations on all levels and decreases the quality of the output. Taking into consideration the post-editing effort per line, allows us to identify the time and effort and determine MT adaptability problems for each subtitle.

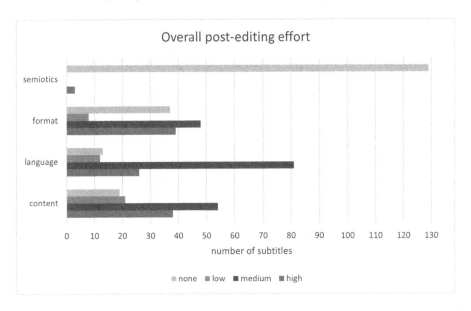

**Fig. 7.** Overall post-editing effort.

## 4.4  Error Analysis

The additional error annotation of the MT produced subtitles exhibit limitations in the *content* and *language* category. Based on the error categories in Sect. 2.2, the analysis is showing that MT failed to identify context and produced multiple content shift errors. With a total of 80 errors the *syntax* error category was the leading category for MT errors. Surprisingly in the *format* category, the MT system did not produce any spacing errors, but failed to comply with the characters per line (cpl) guidelines in more than two-thirds of the subtitles. Several intersemiotic coherence errors occurred as well. To conclude, the MT performed a poor translation quality on almost all levels. The post-editing effort of the MT is thus rather high and leads to a poor quality. An overview of the special MT error evaluation can be seen in Fig. 8 below. The results of the special MT error analysis shows that, for this investigation, the MT has limitations especially for the *paraphrased translation* category and thus observing the characters per line (cpl) and characters per second (cps) restrictions. Where a human translator shortens the translation to avoid violating the timing guidelines, the MT produces more literal translations. According to that, in the *content* category the most errors were produced and in the *literal vs. contextual* category also several errors were found. This is also reflected in the *word structure errors*; although the translation seems correct on the surface, contextually the translation is poor in quality. It was found that not just for single subtitles but across multiple subtitles, where sections shared the same context, the MT failed to convey the correct meaning and produced errors. The MT output thus requires high post-editing effort in those cases or even a complete re-translation of single segments.

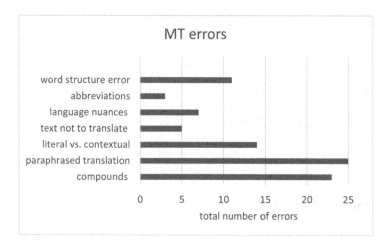

**Fig. 8.** Additional MT errors.

## 5   Conclusion

We presented here three subtitling quality evaluation methods. These can be applied to other MT and/or NMT engines to improve the quality assessment workflow, as well as MT and NMT training. The calculation of the inter-annotator agreement per line can provide information about specific translation issues: a potentially poor agreement indicates that the annotators struggled with assigning the categories correctly or the quality of a subtitle could not be determined at all. In order to test such cases, we developed a measure for the reliable subtitle quality and post-editing effort per line. For all lines we can make statements if (1) the quality can be determined and if not, we can (2) estimate the post-editing effort. A subtitle with a reliable perfect quality is thus not required to be reworked at all. Subsequently poorer quality subtitles require higher post-editing effort. With our approach, we aimed to improve the MT subtitle workflow. We found that there are three ways for improvement. Firstly, pre-processing the MT output, since in the error analysis we found that the strongest limitations of MT were context in the content category. A possible pre-processing of contextual sequences of the source text for better MT implementation could be helpful. Secondly, enhancing the guidelines, especially for the format layer. As we added more up-to-date categories, MT issues concerning subtitling constraints can be accessed more quickly. Thirdly, improving the quality assessment itself. Measuring IAA, reliable subtitling quality and post-editing effort per line is more profitable than observing the results for the whole document. We can thus identify the most difficult subtitles and find specific MT limitations. Furthermore, the amount of effort of those subtitles can be estimated immediately. Our additions to the error annotation scheme as well as the measure for all calculations per line can be applied to future work to help improve the quality assessment workflow and MT/NMT quality on multiple levels. With our approach we accomplished calculating all three dimensions not just for the whole document, but for all subtitles per line.

# References

1. Abdallah, K.: Audiovisual translation in close-up: practical and theoretical approaches. In: Quality Problems in AVT Production Networks: Reconstructing An Actor-network In The Subtitling Industry, pp. 173–186. Peter Lang, Bern (2011)
2. Díaz-Cintas, J., Remael, A.: Subtitling: Concepts and Practices. Translation practices explained. Routledge, London (2020)
3. Del Pozo, A.: SUMAT Final Report. VICOMTECH (2014)
4. Etchegoyhen, T., et al.: Machine translation for subtitling: a large-scale evaluation. Proceedings of the Ninth International Conference On Language Resources and Evaluation (LREC), pp. 46–53 (2014,5)
5. Fleiss, B., Cho Paik, M.: Statistical Methods for Rates and Proportions. Wiley (1973)
6. Gupta, P., Sharma, M., Pitale, K., Kumar, K.: Problems with automating translation of movie/TV show subtitles. CoRR
7. Ivarsson, J., Carroll, M.: Subtitling.: TransEdit (1998)
8. Karakanta, A., Negri, M., Turchi, M.: Are Subtitling Corpora really Subtitle-like?. Conference: Sixth Italian Conference on Computational Linguistics (CLiC-It), At Bari, Italy (2019)
9. Kuo, A.: Professional realities of the subtitling industry: The subtitlers perspective. Audiovisual Translation in a Global Context: Mapping An Ever-Changing Landscape, pp. 163–191 (2015)
10. Lommel, A., Burchardt, A. & Uszkoreit, H.: Multidimensional quality metrics: a flexible system for assessing translation quality. In: Proceedings of Translating and the Computer 35 (ASLIB), November 2013
11. Martínez, J., Vela, M.: SubCo: a learner translation corpus of human and machine subtitles. In: Proceedings of the 10th International Conference On Language Resources and Evaluation, pp. 2246–2254 (2016)
12. Müller, M., Volk, M.: Statistical Machine Translation of Subtitles: From OpenSubtitles to TED. Language Processing And Knowledge In The Web SE - **14**(8105), 132–138 (2013)
13. Nikolić, K. The Pros and Cons of Using Templates in Subtitling. Audiovisual Translation In A Global Context: Mapping An Ever-changing Landscape, pp. 192–202 (2015)
14. Robert, I., Remael, A.: Quality control in the subtitling industry: an exploratory survey study. Meta **61**, 578–605 (2016)
15. Petukhova, V., et al.: Data Collection and Parallel Corpus Compilation for Machine Translation of Subtitles. LREC (2012)
16. Romero-Fresco, P.: Accessible filmmaking: Joining the dots between audiovisual translation, accessibility and filmmaking. J. Specialised Trans., 201–223 (2013,1)
17. Volk, M.: The Automatic Translation of Film Subtitles. A Machine Translation Success Story. In: Resourceful Language Technology: Festschrift In Honor Of Anna Saagvall Hein, pp. 202–214 (2008)

# Computational Approaches for Understanding Semantic Constraints on Two-termed Coordination Structures

Julie Kallini$^{(\boxtimes)}$ ⬥ and Christiane Fellbaum

Computer Science Department, Princeton University, Princeton, NJ 08544, USA
jkallini@alumni.princeton.edu, fellbaum@princeton.edu

**Abstract.** Coordination is a linguistic phenomenon where two or more terms or phrases, called *conjuncts*, are conjoined by a coordinating conjunction, such as *and*, *or*, or *but*. Well-formed coordination structures seem to require that the conjuncts are semantically similar or related. In this paper, we utilize English corpus data to examine the semantic constraints on syntactically *like* coordinations, which link constituents with the same lexical or syntactic categories. We examine the extent to which these semantic constraints depend on the type of conjunction or on the lexical or syntactic category of the conjuncts. We employ two distinct, independent metrics to measure the semantic similarity of conjuncts: WordNet relations and semantic word embeddings. Our results indicate that both measures of similarity have varying distributions depending on the particular conjunction and the conjuncts' lexical or syntactic categories.

**Keywords:** Coordination · Corpus linguistics · Semantics

## 1 Introduction

Coordination is the syntactic phenomenon whereby two or more terms or phrases are linked into one larger phrasal structure. We examine two-termed coordination phrases, where two elements (the *conjuncts*) are linked by the coordinating conjunctions *and*, *or*, or *but*, as in example (1).

(1)  a.  The president will [VP understand the criticism] and [VP take action].
     b.  Would you like [NP soup] or [NP salad] with your meal?
     c.  The new student was [AP intelligent] but [AP lazy].

The widely accepted Law of the Coordination of Likes (LCL) [17], which was proposed to account for the syntactic constraints on coordination, requires that the conjuncts belong to the same lexical or syntactic category.[1] While the LCL

---

[1] We focus on the coordination of lexical categories like nouns, verbs, and adjectives, as well as syntactic (phrasal) categories such as noun phrases, verb phrases and adjective phrases. For simplicity, we refer to both as *categories* in this paper.

© Springer Nature Switzerland AG 2022
P. Sojka et al. (Eds.): TSD 2022, LNAI 13502, pp. 64–76, 2022.
https://doi.org/10.1007/978-3-031-16270-1_6

accounts for the acceptability of the examples in (1), there are cases where it is not restrictive enough, as it would allow structures such as those in (2) [12]:

(2)   a.   * John ate with [NP his mother] and [NP good appetite].

      b.   * John [AdvP probably] and [AdvP unwillingly] went to bed.

The ungrammaticality here results from the semantic nature of these coordinations rather than their syntax. A stronger version of the LCL would require that conjuncts must also be semantically compatible. In this case, the prepositional phrase "with his mother" expresses accompaniment, whereas "with good appetite" expresses manner, so coordinating "his mother" and "good appetite" in (2a) produces a zeugma [12]. In (2b), the semantic difference between two adverbs (manner vs. epistemic) seems to account for the unacceptability.

Previous work explored the syntactic properties of coordination through a corpus-based approach [7], but a similar examination of the semantic constraints on coordination remains an open challenge. This paper explores the semantic properties of coordination structures through a large-scale quantitative corpus analysis. We study syntactically *like* coordinations, where the conjuncts have the same categories, and measure semantic constraints in terms of WordNet relations and word embeddings, which provide two independent measures of semantic similarity. We investigate whether the constraints depend on the type of conjunction (*and, or, but*) or on the categories of the conjuncts (noun, verb, adjective, adverb). A broader goal is to share data that may inform linguistic hypotheses about coordination.

## 2   Background and Related Work

Traditional linguistic analyses have given a thorough treatment of various semantic use cases of coordination; the three main types are often referred to as *conjunctive, disjunctive*, and *adversative* coordinations [4,5]. Conjunctive coordination links equal elements and is signalled by English *and*; disjunctive coordination usually indicates mutually exclusive options and is signalled by English *or*; and adversative coordination displays semantic contrast and is signalled by English *but*. However, the three conjunctions are not limited to these functions.

Quirk et al. [13] note that *and* is the conjunction with the most general meaning and usage and that it can take on several different connotations in context. For instance, *and* can link semantically contrastive elements and be replaced by *but* to produce a phrase with equivalent meaning, as in "she tried hard *and* failed." Quirk et al. also point out that *or* can be logically equivalent to *and* when following a negative, as demonstrated by the semantic equivalence of (3a) and (3b) [13].

(3)   a.   He doesn't have long hair *or* wear jeans.

      b.   He doesn't have long hair, *and* he doesn't wear jeans.

A similar replacement can take place with permissive modals, as in "the play can be performed in public *or* private theaters." Furthermore, *or* is not constrained to disjunctive scenarios. In (4), the conjuncts linked by *or* do not necessarily represent mutually exclusive options.

(4)    a.  He is good at painting with watercolors *or* with oils.

       b.  You can boil an egg *or* make a sandwich.

With regard to computational approaches to understanding coordination, previous work has focused on syntax rather than semantics. While the LCL mentioned in the introduction overgenerates with regard to semantics, it is too restrictive with regard to syntax, as it rules out perfectly acceptable coordinations with syntactically unlike conjuncts [12,14]:

(5)    a.  Pat is [NP a Republican] and [AP proud of it].

       b.  John is [AP healthy] and [PP in good shape].

In a previous paper, we examined *unlike* category coordinations using constituency-parsed corpora to identify coordination structures and determine the distributions of unlike phrasal category combinations [7]. The findings show, broadly, that noun phrases tend to coordinate with subordinate clauses and that the first conjunct tends to be shorter in length than the second conjunct, supporting an anti-symmetric account for the syntactic structure of coordination.

## 3    Approach

This paper focuses on the *semantic* properties of coordination, which to our knowledge have not yet been explored through a computational approach. We extract coordinate structures from hand-annotated Universal Dependencies corpora, and employ two methods to measure the similarity of conjuncts: WordNet's paradigmatic relations [3,10], and Google's Word2Vec semantic vectors [8,9], which reflect syntagmatic similarity. With these metrics, we investigate whether semantic relatedness correlates with particular conjunctions or categories.

### 3.1    Universal Dependencies Corpora

We examine corpora annotated within the Universal Dependencies (UD) project, which aims to provide a consistent dependency treebank annotation across many languages [11]. The CONJ relation links the first conjunct to all subsequent conjuncts, and all coordinating conjunctions are attached to the immediately following conjunct by the CC relation. We utilize the enhanced dependencies of UD v2, which augment the CONJ dependency labels between conjuncts by explicitly including their coordinating conjunction in the label. This feature is useful for disambiguating conjuncts in nested coordination phrases where more than one conjunction is involved, as in (6).

(6)    UD v2 enhanced coordination annotation.

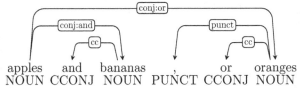

apples    and    bananas    ,    or    oranges
NOUN  CCONJ  NOUN  PUNCT  CCONJ  NOUN

The UD v2 dependencies also elegantly annotate ellipsis constructions by using null nodes to represent elided material, such as in example (7). This representation aids the disambiguation of ellipsis constructions from simple coordinations of constituents.[2]

(7)    UD v2 enhanced ellipsis annotation, where *(drank)* represents a null node.

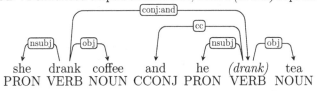

she    drank    coffee    and    he    *(drank)*    tea
PRON  VERB  NOUN  CCONJ  PRON  VERB  NOUN

We extract coordinations from three UD v2 corpora with enhanced dependencies: the English Web Treebank (EWT) [15], the Georgetown University Multilayer corpus (GUM) [1,18], and the English portion of the Parallel Universal Dependencies (PWT) treebanks [19]. Table 1 provides details about each corpus.

**Table 1.** Word counts, sentence counts, and example sources for each corpus we use.

| Corpus | Words | Sentences | Example media/sources |
|---|---|---|---|
| EWT | 254,825 | 16,621 | weblogs, newsgroups, emails, reviews, etc. |
| GUM | 135,886 | 7,397 | interviews, news stories, academic writings, etc. |
| GUMReddit | 16,356 | 895 | Reddit posts |
| PUD | 21,176 | 1,000 | news, wikipedia |

## 3.2    Coordination Extraction

Our coordination extraction script requires input files in the CoNLL-U format, the format in which UD annotations are provided. Sentences are represented using one or more lines, where each line corresponds to a single token or word. Ten fields fully describe each token or word, but for coordination extraction, we are only concerned with a subset of fields: the word `ID`, `FORM`, `LEMMA`, `UPOS`, `HEAD`,

---

[2] UD v2 also handles shared modifiers, such as the adjective *old* in "old men and women," using a distinct type of annotation.

DEPREL (basic universal dependency relation to the HEAD), and DEPS (enhanced dependency graph). We use a CoNLL-U parser to process corpus files into nested Python dictionaries [16].

**Table 2.** The usage and applicable lexical categories for each WordNet relation in our semantic analysis.

| Relation | Usage | Categories |
|---|---|---|
| Synonymy | Are the conjuncts within the same synset? | N, V, Adj, Adv |
| Co-hyponymy | Are the conjuncts co-hyponyms? | N, V |
| Antonymy | Are the conjuncts antonyms? | Adj, Adv |
| Hypernymy | Is the first conjunct a hypernym of the second, or is the second conjunct a hypernym of the first? | N, V |

Due to the nature of coordination annotation in UD, in which subsequent conjuncts are dependents of the first conjunct, we maintain coordination phrases as a dictionary mapping first conjunct IDs to sets of subsequent conjunct IDs. For each token in a sentence, the script searches the token's DEPS field for any dependencies of the form CONJ:CC, where CC is the lemma of a coordinating conjunction. If such a dependency is present, the current token is a conjunct of a coordination phrase, and the corresponding head is the first conjunct of that phrase. There can be only one such CONJ:CC dependency; we have checked this in the corpora programmatically, and one can also reason that it is impossible for a word to be a secondary conjunct of more than one coordination phrase. Importantly, the enhanced dependencies also indicate when a conjunct has been elided and thus should be excluded from the semantic analysis.[3]

### 3.3   Semantic Analysis

On the pragmatic assumption that conjuncts must be related in meanings, we examine and measure their semantic relatedness using two different, independent resources that capture paradigmatic and syntagmatic relatedness, respectively, WordNet [3,10] and Google's Word2Vec word embeddings [8,9]. We include coordination phrases with like conjuncts from the following open-class lexical categories: nouns, verbs, adjectives, and adverbs.

**WordNet-based Similarity.** WordNet's structure allows us to compare conjuncts in terms of "classical" semantic relations: synonymy, antonymy, and hypernymy/hyponymy. We expect many conjuncts to be co-hyponyms (as in *beer and wine*) or antonyms (as in *right and left*), since *and*, *or*, and *but* generally serve to conjoin elements with similar or contrasting meanings. We expect to find few synonyms (as in *cars and automobiles*), since conjoining words with

---

[3] Our code is available at https://github.com/jkallini/SemanticCoordinationAnalysis.

near-identical meanings seems redundant and uninformative.[4] We also expect to find relatively few conjoined words that are in a hypernymy/hyponymy relation (as in *roses and flowers*) except in cases where the hypernym in the second conjunct is modified and thus denotes co-hyponyms, as in *roses and other flowers*. We gather frequency data by counting coordination phrases that contain the basic presence or absence of these relations, and so the conjuncts' relative placement in the WordNet hierarchy does not affect our analysis. Table 2 summarizes the WordNet relations that we use for coordination semantic analysis in this project.

A challenge that accompanies the use of WordNet to analyze semantic relationships between conjuncts is *word sense disambiguation* (WSD), or the problem of selecting the correct sense/synset for strings that have multiple meanings. To handle ambiguous strings, we test the WordNet relations on all possible pairs of synsets corresponding to the two conjuncts of a coordination phrase.

**Table 3.** Summary of frequencies and chi-square tests comparing the presence of synonymy, antonymy, and co-hyponymy across the conjunctions *and*, *or*, and *but*. Statistically significant results are in bold.

| Conjunction | Synonymy | | Antonymy | | Co-hyponymy | |
|---|---|---|---|---|---|---|
| | yes | no | yes | no | yes | no |
| 'and' $n$ (%) | 160 (3.0) | 5209 (97.0) | 38 (6.2) | 576 (93.8) | 836 (17.6) | 3919 (82.4) |
| 'or' $n$ (%) | 23 (3.4) | 651 (96.6) | **16 (23.2)** | 53 (76.8) | 104 (17.2) | 501 (82.8) |
| 'but' $n$ (%) | 19 (3.4) | 542 (96.6) | 1 (1.9) | 53 (98.1) | 94 (18.5) | 413 (81.5) |
| Chi-square Test | $\chi^2(2, N = 5867) = 0.600$ $p = .741$ | | $\chi^2(2, N = 737) = 28.613$ $p < .001$ | | $\chi^2(2, N = 5867) = 0.378$ $p = .828$ | |

**Embedding-Based Similarity.** We measure semantic relations among conjuncts with Google's pre-trained Word2Vec word embeddings [8,9]. Speakers commonly conjoin words referring to concepts from a given semantic domain (as in *students and teachers*) that are not reflected by a WordNet-style relation. We ask whether the distributional similarity captured by semantic vectors is reflected in coordinate structures.

## 4    Results

We first present general statistics about coordination from our corpus data. Our corpora include 6,892 like-category, two-termed coordination phrases, and in 6,641 (96.4%) of these coordinations, both conjuncts are present in WordNet. 27 coordinations (0.4%) include one elided conjunct; we exclude these from the semantic analysis. 5,579 coordinations (80.9%) use *and* as the coordinating conjunction; 723 (10.5%) use *or*, and 572 (8.3%) use *but*. The coordinating conjunction *nor* is only present in 18 coordinations (0.3%), so we exclude it from our analysis. For the results of our semantic analysis detailed in the next sections, we consider *p*-values less than .05 to be statistically significant.

---

[4] To avoid potential false positives for synonymy, we filter out coordinations in which both conjuncts have the same lemma, as in "he ran *faster and faster*."

## 4.1   WordNet Analysis

We begin with the bidirectional WordNet relations: synonymy, antonymy, and co-hyponymy. We observe how the presence of these relations is affected by the coordination phrase's conjunction or the conjuncts' lexical categories.

Table 3 summarizes the results of several chi-square tests of independence to examine the association between the different WordNet relations and the three coordinating conjunctions (*and, or, but*). The relation between conjunctions and the presence of antonymy was found to be significant, with the coordinating conjunction *or* having the largest proportion of coordinations in which the two conjuncts are antonyms.[5]

Similarly, Table 4 summarizes the results of several chi-square tests of independence examining the association between WordNet relations and the closed-class categories (noun, verb, adjective, adverb). For each WordNet relation, the association between the presence of the relation and the category of the conjuncts was found to be significant. Verbal categories had the largest proportion of synonymy and co-hyponymy, and adverbs had the largest proportion of antonymy.

We also performed an analysis of hypernymy. The first conjunct of the phrase was a hypernym of the second conjunct in 334 coordinations, and the second conjunct was a hypernym of the first in 372 coordinations. Using a chi-square test for goodness-of-fit, we did not find a significant difference in the distribution of the two types of hypernymy relations, $\chi^2(1, N = 706) = 2.045$, $p = 0.153$.

## 4.2   Word Embedding Analysis

We next present the results of our embedding-based analysis. Table 5 presents summary statistics of cosine similarity between conjuncts for each coordinating conjunction. A one-way ANOVA was performed to compare the effect of the coordinating conjunction on cosine similarity of the conjuncts. The one-way ANOVA revealed that there was a statistically significant difference in cosine similarity between groups ($F(2, 6531) = 13.613$, $p < .001$). Tukey's HSD Test for multiple comparisons found that the mean value of cosine similarity was significantly different between *and* coordinations and *or* coordinations ($p < .001$, 95% C.I. $= [.016, .046]$), and between *or* coordinations and *but* coordinations ($p = .004$, 95% C.I. $= [-.064, -.021]$). There was no statistically significant difference between *and* coordinations and *but* coordinations ($p = .223$).

---

[5] Previous corpus analyses have shown that antonymous word pairs co-occur within the same sentence with frequencies far higher than chance [2,6].

**Table 4.** Summary of frequencies and chi-square tests comparing the presence of synonymy, antonymy, and co-hyponymy across the four main lexical categories. Statistically significant results are in bold.

| Conjunction | Synonymy | | Antonymy | | Co-hyponymy | |
|---|---|---|---|---|---|---|
| | yes | no | yes | no | yes | no |
| NOUN $n$ (%) | 40 (1.6) | 2407 (98.4) | - | - | 285 (11.6) | 2162 (88.4) |
| VERB $n$ (%) | **147 (4.3)** | 3289 (95.7) | - | - | **750 (21.8)** | 2686 (78.2) |
| ADJ $n$ (%) | 14 (2.2) | 618 (97.8) | 38 (6.0) | 594 (94.0) | - | - |
| ADV $n$ (%) | 2 (1.9) | 104 (98.1) | **17 (16.0)** | 89 (84.0) | - | - |
| Chi-square Test | $\chi^2(2, N = 6621) = 35.893$ $p < .001$ | | $\chi^2(1, N = 738) = 11.814$ $p = .001$ | | $\chi^2(1, N = 5883) = 101.474$ $p < .001$ | |

**Table 5.** Summary statistics of cosine similarity between conjuncts for different coordinating conjunctions.

| | $N$ | Mean | Std. Dev. | Std. Err. | Min | Max |
|---|---|---|---|---|---|---|
| *and* | 5334 | .258 | .157 | .002 | -.156 | .967 |
| *or* | 670 | .289 | .180 | .007 | -.069 | .964 |
| *but* | 530 | .246 | .142 | .006 | -.073 | .734 |

We also compared cosine similarity between conjuncts of different lexical categories. Table 6 presents summary statistics of cosine similarity between conjuncts for each lexical category. A one-way ANOVA was performed to compare the effect of the conjuncts' category on their cosine similarity. The one-way ANOVA revealed that there was a statistically significant difference in cosine similarity between groups $(F(3, 6547) = 83.590, p < .001)$. Tukey's HSD Test for multiple comparisons found that the mean value of cosine similarity was significantly different between all pairs of groups, shown in Table 7. Adverbial conjuncts had the highest cosine similarity on average, while verbal categories had the lowest on average.

**Table 6.** Summary statistics of cosine similarity between conjuncts for different categories.

| | $N$ | Mean | Std. Dev. | Std. Err. | Min | Max |
|---|---|---|---|---|---|---|
| NOUN | 2474 | .266 | .178 | .003 | -.156 | .965 |
| VERB | 3331 | .242 | .132 | .002 | -.104 | .764 |
| ADJ | 646 | .309 | .166 | .007 | -.075 | .893 |
| ADV | 100 | .443 | .224 | .022 | -.035 | .967 |

**Table 7.** Results of Tukey's HSD test for cosine similarity between conjuncts of different lexical categories. The table displays the difference between group means, confidence intervals, and $p$-values for each comparison.

|  | Difference | 95% C.I | $p$ |
|---|---|---|---|
| NOUN vs. VERB | −.024 | [−.035, −.016] | < .001 |
| NOUN vs. ADJ | .043 | [.025, .061] | < .001 |
| NOUN vs. ADV | .177 | [.137, .218] | < .001 |
| VERB vs. ADJ | .067 | [.050, .084] | < .001 |
| VERB vs. ADV | .202 | [.161, .242] | < .001 |
| ADJ vs ADV | .135 | [.092, .178] | < .001 |

# 5   Discussion

This section provides an in-depth discussion of the results presented in Sect. 4. We begin with the analysis of WordNet relations, followed by a discussion of embedding-based similarity.

## 5.1   WordNet Analysis

Table 8 contains several examples of synonymy, antonymy, and co-hyponymy pulled from the corpora. The relation between the presence of synonymy and the type of conjunction within a coordination phrase was not found to be statistically significant; the same was true for co-hyponymy. Overall, few examples of synonymy were found, which supports our hypothesis that conjoining words with very similar meanings is unnecessary and uninformative. With regard to co-hyponymy, while one might expect *and*-coordinations to have the highest percentage of co-hyponymy since *and* usually conjoins equal elements, *and*-coordinations had a lower percentage than *or*- and *but*-coordinations. This result supports the claims by Quirk et al. discussed in Sect. 2; if *and* is often used as a general-purpose conjunction independent of the meaning of the conjuncts, there would be weaker semantic constraints on *and*-coordinations and thus no strong correlation between *and* and the presence of a particular WordNet relation.

This result also suggests that the conjunction *or* is not restricted to its role as a disjunctive coordinator. As mentioned in Sect. 2, *or* may be used to conjoin options that are not mutually exclusive, as in "do you have any *brothers or sisters*." The data highlights other special use-cases for *or*; for instance, *or* is commonly used in appositive phrases, where one noun is used to define or modify another noun. One example from the corpora is shown in (8), where the two conjuncts are synonyms, and the second conjunct defines the first.

(8)   Corn, *or* maize, [...] formed the basis of their diet.

While such cases show the versatility of *or*, most of its usages in our corpora overwhelmingly reflect its role as a disjunctive coordinator; the relation between

**Table 8.** Example coordinations for each bidirectional WordNet relation, conjunct category, and conjunction. Cells for which the given WordNet relation does not apply are filled with 'N/A'. Empty cells indicate that no samples were found.

| Coordination Type | | Synonymy | Antonymy | Co-hyponymy |
|---|---|---|---|---|
| NOUN | and | It [...] is still valuable for its many [N examples] and [N exercises]. | N/A | Many [N books] and [N articles] in moral philosophy start with the observation [...] |
| | or | [N Corn], or [N maize], domesticated by 5000 BCE, formed the basis of their diet. | N/A | If you study [N physics] or [N chemistry] then you should describe the real world. |
| | but | - | N/A | Winter is definitely low [N season], [...], but also an ideal [N time] to save money [...] |
| VERB | and | Steven jiggled the handle [...], [V turning] and [V twisting] it most professionally and murmuring encouragements. | N/A | [...] he stayed up all night [V writing] letters to his Republican friends and [V composing] what would become his mathematical testament [...] |
| | or | These can be [V bought] at garden centers or [V purchased] online. | N/A | A healthy ecosystem [...] will [V reduce] the chance of these events happening, or will at least [V mitigate] adverse impacts. |
| | but | I also [V think] the National Endowment for the Arts is a waste, but [V guess] I would rather see my money go to the NEA [...] | N/A | [...] she [V began] appearing in films [...] but [V continued] to be primarily active in the theatre [...] |
| ADJ | and | I know that a transaction of this magnitude would make anyone [Adj apprehensive] and [Adj worried]. | Hundreds of vendors offered products [Adj new] and [Adj old], joined by celebrity guests [...] | N/A |
| | or | - | Just as concepts can be [Adj abstract] or [Adj concrete], we can make a distinction [...] | N/A |
| | but | - | Skin will be [Adj darker] but [Adj lighter] than the Silkies. | N/A |
| ADV | and | [Adv First] and [Adv foremost] was the provision of open space for the benefit of townspeople [...] | It's an entirely [Adv up] and [Adv down] experience, however. | N/A |
| | or | - | Wilson did not work "[Adv directly] or [Adv indirectly]" for the CIA since retiring. | N/A |
| | but | - | - | N/A |

conjunctions and antonymy was found to be significant, with *or* having the largest proportion of coordinations in which the two conjuncts are antonyms.

Coordinations containing *but* did not have a large percentage of any Word-Net relation. This might have to do with its tendency to demonstrate contrast between entire clauses rather than individual words, a semantic phenomenon that is not captured using word-level measures of similarity.

Now we discuss the associations between the bidirectional WordNet relations and the lexical categories of the conjuncts within a coordination phrase. For each WordNet relation, the association between the presence of the relation and the category of the conjuncts was found to be significant, with verbal categories having the largest proportion of synonymy and co-hyponymy, and adverbs having the largest proportion of antonymy. Although it is not entirely clear why verbal conjuncts tend to be more semantically similar, it is expected that the analyses of synonymy and co-hyponymy should be complementary. One hypothesis is that repeating similar verbs in conjoined predicates can express emphasis, as in example (9) taken from the corpora.

(9)  Trust me, and most especially, [$_V$ trust] and [$_V$ believe] yourself.

The high frequency of antonymous conjuncts in coordinations of adverbs seems to stem from common phrases involving contrasting adverbs, such as "back and forth," "up and down," "here or there," and "more or less."

Finally, we discuss the hypernymy relation. We hypothesized that hypernymy would be attested in certain contexts, and that the second conjunct would more often be a hypernym of the first, as in "I bought *strawberries and other fruit.*" The determiner *other* contextualizes that, in addition to strawberries, the rest of the items purchased are also kinds of fruit and therefore hyponyms of fruit, i.e., lexically unspecified co-hyponyms of the first conjunct. While the second conjunct was more often a hypernym of the first in our data, the difference in the distribution of the direction of the hypernymy relation was not statistically significant, suggesting that semantic asymmetry between the two conjunct positions is not very prominent.

## 5.2   Word Embedding Analysis

Our analysis of conjunct similarity using Word2Vec word embeddings revealed that *or*-coordinations had a significantly higher average cosine similarity between the conjuncts compared to *and*- and *but*-coordinations. This result complements the previous result regarding the large proportion of antonymous coordinations that use *or* as the conjunction. Word embeddings are created such that words that appear in similar contexts will have similar word vectors [8]. Direct antonyms often appear in similar contexts; for instance, *large* and *small* can interchangeably describe the size of an object, and as a result, they have similar word vectors. The vectors for *large* and *small* have a cosine similarity of .733, which is higher than the cosine similarity of near-synonyms like *large* and *big* (.556). Since *or* typically conjoins antonymous conjuncts, *or*-coordinations will have a high average cosine similarity between the conjuncts.

The nature of how word embeddings capture word similarity also accounts for the high average cosine similarity for adverbial conjuncts. Since a large percentage of adverbial coordination phrases contained antonymy, it follows that these coordination phrases would have a high cosine similarity between the conjuncts. Verbal coordinations had a significantly lower cosine similarity between conjuncts, despite having the largest proportion of synonymous coordinations; this can again be accounted for by the semantic tools we use. Near-synonymous verbs in WordNet like *grow* and *develop* or *print* and *publish* have similar word vectors, but the similarity is not quite as large as antonymous word vectors.

# 6   Conclusion

This paper analyzed the semantics of two-termed coordination phrases through a computational corpus analysis. We explore the differences in meaning between the two conjunct positions and the possible relationships they share by utilizing two representations of words: WordNet and word embeddings. The results show that *and* is a general-purpose coordinator that can conjoin conjuncts in various semantic relationships. The conjunction *or* is primarily used as a disjunctive coordinator, although it is not limited to this function. The relationships and similarities of the conjuncts also depend on their lexical categories. We see this analysis as a step towards a fuller understanding of speakers' real-world usage of coordination phrases.

# References

1. Behzad, S., Zeldes, A.: A cross-genre ensemble approach to robust Reddit part of speech tagging. In: Proceedings of the 12th Web as Corpus Workshop (WAC-XII), pp. 50–56 (2020)
2. Fellbaum, C.: Co-occurrence and antonymy. Int. J. Lexicogr. **8**(4), 281–303 (1995)
3. Fellbaum, C.: WordNet: An Electronic Lexical Database. MIT Press, Cambridge (1998)
4. Haspelmath, M.: Coordinating constructions: an overview. In: Coordinating Constructions. Typological Studies in Language, vol. 58, pp. 3–39. John Benjamins Publishing Company (2004). https://doi.org/10.1075/tsl.58.03has
5. Haspelmath, M.: Coordination. In: Shopen, T. (ed.) Language Typology and Syntactic Description, vol. 2, 2 edn., chap. 1. Cambridge University Press (2007). https://doi.org/10.1017/CBO9780511619434
6. Justeson, J.S., Katz, S.M.: Co-occurrences of antonymous adjectives and their contexts. Comput. Linguist. **17**(1), 1–19 (1991)
7. Kallini, J., Fellbaum, C.: A corpus-based syntactic analysis of two-termed unlike coordination. In: Findings of the Association for Computational Linguistics: EMNLP 2021, pp. 3998–4008. Association for Computational Linguistics, Punta Cana, Dominican Republic, November 2021. https://doi.org/10.18653/v1/2021.findings-emnlp.335, https://aclanthology.org/2021.findings-emnlp.335
8. Mikolov, T., Chen, K., Corrado, G.S., Dean, J.: Efficient estimation of word representations in vector space (2013). https://arxiv.org/abs/1301.3781
9. Mikolov, T., Sutskever, I., Chen, K., Corrado, G., Dean, J.: Distributed representations of words and phrases and their compositionality. In: Neural Information Processing Systems (NeurIPS) (2013). https://papers.nips.cc/paper/5021-distributed-representations-of-words-and-phrases-and-their-compositionality.pdf
10. Miller, G.A.: Wordnet: a lexical database for English. Commun. ACM **38**(11), 39–41 (1995)
11. Nivre, J., et al.: Universal dependencies v2: an evergrowing multilingual treebank collection. In: Proceedings of the 12th Language Resources and Evaluation Conference, pp. 4034–4043. European Language Resources Association, Marseille, France, May 2020. https://aclanthology.org/2020.lrec-1.497
12. Prażmowska, A.: Is unlike coordination against the law (of the coordination of likes)? (2015)

13. Quirk, R., Greenbaum, S., Leech, G., Svartvik, J.: A Comprehensive Grammar of the English Language. Longman, London (1985)
14. Sag, I.A., Gazdar, G., Wasow, T., Weisler, S.: Coordination and how to distinguish categories. Nat. Lang. Linguistic Theory **3**(2), 117–171 (1985). https://www.jstor.org/stable/4047644
15. Silveira, N., et al.: A gold standard dependency corpus for English. In: Proceedings of the Ninth International Conference on Language Resources and Evaluation (LREC 2014), pp. 2897–2904. European Language Resources Association (ELRA), Reykjavik, Iceland, May 2014. https://www.lrec-conf.org/proceedings/lrec2014/pdf/1089_Paper.pdf
16. Stenström, E.: CoNLL-U parser. https://github.com/EmilStenstrom/conllu/ (2021)
17. Williams, E.S.: Transformationless grammar. In: Linguistic Inquiry, vol. 12, pp. 645–653 (1981)
18. Zeldes, A.: The GUM corpus: creating multilayer resources in the classroom. Lang. Resour. Eval. **51**(3), 581–612 (2016). https://doi.org/10.1007/s10579-016-9343-x
19. Zeman, D., et al.: CoNLL 2017 shared task: multilingual parsing from raw text to universal dependencies. In: Proceedings of the CoNLL 2017 Shared Task: Multilingual Parsing from Raw Text to Universal Dependencies, pp. 1–19. Association for Computational Linguistics, Vancouver, Canada, August 2017. https://doi.org/10.18653/v1/K17-3001, https://aclanthology.org/K17-3001

# Review of Practices of Collecting and Annotating Texts in the Learner Corpus REALEC

Olga Vinogradova[1] and Olga Lyashevskaya[1,2]([✉])

[1] The National Research University Higher School of Economics,
Myasnitskaya ulitsa 20, Moscow 101000, Russia
`olgavinogr@gmail.com, olesar@yandex.ru`
[2] Vinogradov Russian Language Institute RAS,
Volkhonka Street 18/2, Moscow 119019, Russia

**Abstract.** REALEC, learner corpus released in the open access, had received 6,054 essays written in English by HSE undergraduate students in their English university-level examination by the year 2020. This paper reports on the data collection and manual annotation approaches for the texts of 2014–2019 and discusses the computer tools available for working with the corpus. This provides the basis for the ongoing development of automated annotation for the new portions of learner texts in the corpus. The observations in the first part were made on the reliability of the total of 134,608 error tags manually annotated across the texts in the corpus. Some examples are given in the paper to emphasize the role of the interference with learners' L1 (Russian), one more direction of the future corpus research. A number of studies carried out by the research team working on the basis of the REALEC data are listed as examples of the research potential that the corpus has been providing.

**Keywords:** learner academic writing in english · learner corpus · L1 Russian · corpus annotation · error taxonomy

## 1    Introduction

Researchers over the last four decades have claimed that learner corpora provide evidence necessary for second language acquisition theory and practices, as well as for many areas of linguistic studies (see [9–11,14]; and the important reviews by G. Gilquin [7] and by T. McEnery with co-authors [18], among many others). Learner texts themselves make up a valuable resource, and their value grows manyfold if the texts get annotation of features specific for a particular corpus. Russian Error-Annotated Learner English Corpus (REALEC), set up at HSE

The research was carried out within the project of the HSE University Research Foundation 2021 - Automated analysis of text written in English by learners with Russian L1 (ADWISER).

P. Sojka et al. (Eds.): TSD 2022, LNAI 13502, pp. 77–88, 2022.
https://doi.org/10.1007/978-3-031-16270-1_7

University, is a collection of essays written by 2nd- or 3rd-year university learners of English with Russian as their native language. REALEC is in the open access at the university portal. The errors in the texts have been manually annotated in the years 2014–2020, and Sect. 2 gives the details about the collection and annotation approaches adopted in REALEC.

## 2   Learner Corpora Available for Research Purposes

A number of large learner corpora have been presented to the research communities, and the results of using their data have been reported in numerous publications. The collection of smaller and larger learner corpora with different L1 of the contributors can be found on the site of the Learner Corpus Association [29]. The most frequently referenced corpora in corpus research community seem to be EFCAMDAT ([4, 6] - 1st version and [13] - 2nd version) - accessible to the public big collection of short learner texts from learners with different levels of proficiency; ICLE [12] with 5.5 million words of essays written by learners with 25 different native languages; Cambridge Learner Corpus, CLC [21], a 45-million word corpus of student responses to ESOL exams, which can be accessed in Sketch Engine in two main parts - the error-coded learner corpus (CLC coded) and the uncoded learner corpus (CLC uncoded); and also two corpora of spoken learner production: the Louvain International Database of Spoken English Interlanguage, LINDSEI [8], and the Trinity Lancaster Corpus, TLC [5], with 4.2 million words of transcribed L2 spoken interaction. All these corpora differ in size, in the number of native languages of the learner authors, in platforms they were released on, and most importantly for this paper, in availability of different types of annotation assigned to the learner texts. These corpora have already been successfully used for studying a broad range of lexical, grammatical and pragmatic features. As all of them have been well documented, we tried to adhere to the same level of detail and pointed out the same important features in our presentation of the Russian Error-Annotated Learner English Corpus.

## 3   Data Collection and Annotation Practices in REALEC

All Bachelor students at the HSE University take the Independent English Language Test (IELT) designed to evaluate English proficiency in academic register of English [28]. The exam format is the same as that of the leading international English certification tests, with IELTS being the closest. The examination is called Independent because EFL instructors from HSE do not participate in organizing this test or evaluating students' work in it. This task is done by independent certified examiners, who develop the materials every year and assess students' written and oral performance (essays and interviews, respectively) in accordance with international language standards. The test includes Reading, Listening, Writing and Speaking, and it is essays written in answer to the two tasks in Writing - a description of the graphical materials in 20 min and an opinion essay in 40 min, which have been submitted to REALEC since the year

2014. All students taking the IELT are at a similar academic level, as they are all undergraduate students (2nd or 3rd year at HSE), but because of differences in prior exposure to English language, examination essays show a wide range of levels, and our pilot experiments on automated predictions of CEFR levels attested CEFR levels from B1 to C1 for the majority of essays [1].

The collection in REALEC of these essays from the years 2014–2020 includes about 18,700 texts, with the total of approximately 4,336,000 words. When the administration of the examination involved only students of three departments typing essays on computer (in 2014–2019), we were able to annotate errors in those essays manually. This work was done by specially trained student annotators as their practical experience in corpus maintenance, and unfortunately we never had enough of those annotators to follow the conventional practice of double annotation of all texts. However, we did have an editing team responsible for editing student annotation to ensure some consistency in annotating approach. The new technological breakthrough came in 2020, when the test was administered online for students of all departments of the HSE university, and as a result REALEC received twice the number of texts as that in all the previous 5 years.

REALEC is made up of (1) the texts with the sentence borders established by using NLTK Punkt sentence tokenizer [2], (2) automated POS annotation tags received with the help of TreeTagger [22], and (3) of the files with manually annotated errors in the form of error spans, error tags assigned to them, and the correction of the error span suggested by the annotator. The learner corpus was released on BRAT platform [23] chosen for its convenience for annotating processes and for the highly satisfactory visualization opportunities. A team of specially trained Linguistics undergraduate students proficient in English annotated about 6,000 essays between 2014 and 2019. The annotators chose an appropriate label for each error they identified, and they could apply more than one error tag to the same error span if needed (see Figs. 1 and 2 for examples). The results of inter-annotator agreement experiment carried out across 2,128 errors annotated by 5 independent annotators were presented in (Vinogradova, 2016:743-748). Figures 1 and 2 illustrate REALEC annotations with two and four error tags assigned to one error span, and a pop-up window on the screenshots presents the corrected version suggested by the annotator.

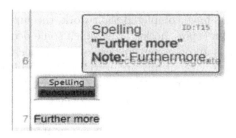

**Fig. 1.** Multiple categorisation of errors in REALEC - error span with 2 error tags.

There are 5,604 error spans with more than one error tag, which makes up 4% of the total number of error spans.

While choosing the appropriate tag for an error identified, annotators had to tick `delete` if an error span was to be deleted instead of being corrected. There was also an option to choose the tag `L1 Interference` as a possible cause of error, but so far it has not been marked consistently enough. An example of such error is the confusion in Russian learners' use of English verbs solve and decide Fig. 2: both English verbs have the same equivalent in Russian, so this wrong vocabulary choice (`Choice of lexical item` tag) was supposedly made under the influence of L1 interference.

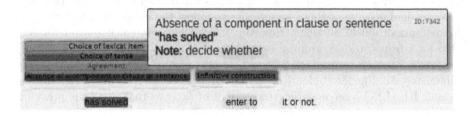

**Fig. 2.** Multiple categorisation of errors in REALEC - error span with 4 error tags.

One more function in annotation was to show that some changes had to be applied as a result of some other changes already made in the sentence, and for such cases there is a way to show with an arrow the relation between two tags called `Dependent change` coming from the initial suggestion of a change to the other tag depending on the former - see the example in Fig. 3.

**Fig. 3.** Dependent change relation in REALEC.

After the annotators have completed their work, the supervisor of the annotation practice does some spot-checks, after which some decisions get reviewed. Annotation reviewing is an on-going process, and the specific numbers (in particular, numbers of texts without any annotations - see Table 1) and some of the choices made by annotators are still subject to changes. Currently, the total is 134,608 error tags for 4,918 out of 6,054 texts collected in the corpus from 2014 to 2019.

There have been observed cases when POS automated annotation from Tree-tagger produced some misleading indices - like in the following cases:

(1) *All of us have their leisure time and there is no secret that a lot of us **like** some kind of sport activity.*

(2) *For example, my friend Andrew really **like** basketball.* Both verbs *like*, the correct form in (1) and the incorrect form in sentence (2), are marked with the tag PRP (preposition) instead of the necessary verbal tag.

(3) *It can be one of the main reasons why the mobiles phone's part **increase** for 2 times.* Word *increase* is marked with the tag NN1 (singular noun) instead of the necessary verbal tag.

While the first confusion does not stem from any error in the learner text, the second and the third ones can be accounted for by agreement errors made by student authors.

# 4 Corpus Statistics

Table 1 gives the basic statistics of the REALEC corpus collected in 2014–2019. The table gives numbers of texts, the total numbers of sentences, words and tokens, the average numbers of sentences, words, and tokens per text, the maximum number of words in a text, the total number of error tags assigned, the average number of errors per text, the average numbers of tokens and error tags per sentence, and the total number of annotated and unannotated texts for Task 1 and Task 2 essays separately, as well as separately for the years 2014-2017 and 2019. For the much greater number of texts collected in 2020, manual annotation was out of the question, so we applied a BERT-transformer-type neural network for both identification and correction of errors, and the analysis of the results is still in progress and will not be included in the current report.

**Table 1.** Corpus statistics for the texts collected in REALEC before 2020.

| Year – Task | Texts | Sent | Words | Tokens | Av. Snt /Txt | Av. Wrd /Txt | Av. Tok /Txt | Total Error Tags | Av. Err/ Txt | Av. Tok/ Snt | Av. Err/ Snt | Texts with annot |
|---|---|---|---|---|---|---|---|---|---|---|---|---|
| 14 – 1 | 829 | 7,757 | 147,953 | 166,906 | 9 | 178 | 201 | 17,284 | 26 | 22 | 3 | 668 |
| – 2 | 823 | 12,223 | 219,740 | 246,325 | 15 | 267 | 299 | 22,119 | 33 | 20 | 3 | 678 |
| 15 – 1 | 31 | 5,045 | 5,680 | 8 | 163 | 183 | 224 | 621 | 22 | 23 | 3 | 28 |
| – 2 | 30 | 401 | 7,709 | 8,612 | 13 | 257 | 287 | 981 | 36 | 21 | 3 | 27 |
| 16 – 1 | 670 | 5,902 | 123,522 | 136,130 | 9 | 184 | 203 | 9,498 | 18 | 23 | 3 | 522 |
| – 2 | 664 | 9,603 | 181,135 | 201,406 | 14 | 273 | 303 | 11,960 | 23 | 21 | 2 | 512 |
| 17 – 1 | 1,126 | 10,467 | 196,103 | 222,619 | 9 | 174 | 198 | 23,155 | 25 | 21 | 3 | 929 |
| – 2 | 1,124 | 16,816 | 315,001 | 351,628 | 15 | 280 | 313 | 29,227 | 35 | 21 | 3 | 839 |
| 19 – 1 | 377 | 3,293 | 70,665 | 79,449 | 9 | 187 | 211 | 8,242 | 23 | 24 | 3 | 354 |
| – 2 | 380 | 5,708 | 118,605 | 131,898 | 15 | 312 | 347 | 11,521 | 32 | 23 | 3 | 361 |
| Task1 | 3,033 | 27,663 | 543,288 | 610,784 | 9 | 179 | 201 | 58,800 | 24 | 22 | 3 | 2,501 |
| Task2 | 3,021 | 44,751 | 842,190 | 939,869 | 15 | 279 | 311 | 75,808 | 31 | 21 | 3 | 2,417 |
| Total | 6,054 | 72,414 | 1,385,478 | 1,550,653 | 12 | 229 | 256 | 134,608 | 27 | 21 | 3 | 4,918 |

It can be seen that in roughly the same numbers of Task 1 and Task 2 essays, the numbers of sentences, words and tokens, both total and average/maximum, correspond to the proportion of the required length: Task 1 essay is supposed to be not less than 150 words, while Task 2 essays are required to be not less than 250 words. The only parameter with much smaller, almost no, difference between Task1 and Task 2 texts is the average number of tokens per sentence, which makes sense because each student wrote both Task 1 and Task 2 essays. The statistics related to error counts is discussed in the next section.

## 5    Error Taxonomy in REALEC

Hierarchical error categorization for the corpus was initially developed on the basis of the pedagogical tradition in Russian EFL error-marking practices and included over 150 error tags [25]. After about two years of manual expert annotation with this categorization scheme and as a result of annotator-agreement experiment, the number of tags was reduced to about 100 on the grounds of infrequent use of about a third of them. Further application of this reduced scheme revealed the inconsistency and/or the need for high-level linguistic knowledge for the appropriate use of some more of the error tags, so another portion of about 50 tags was eliminated.

The new version of the error tags has 54 errors tags (see Table 2), of which 7 are upper-level tags (Grammar, Vocabulary, Verbs, Nouns, etc.) used only for grouping tags of similar nature. At each stage of applying changes to the error tags, most error spans that had been annotated with the eliminated tags were automatically reassigned the remaining error tags, but there were six that required manual updating. One example of these six is the tag `Conditionals`: annotators used this tag either for wrong tense forms, which in all other types of clauses were labelled with the tag `Choice of tense`, or for the wrong uses of the negative form (for example, with the conjunction unless), which in turn can be marked with `Negation` tag. The reassigning of tags had to be implemented manually.

## 6    Distribution of Learner Errors in REALEC

From the general statistics, we can see that errors are quite frequent in student essays collected in REALEC - error density parameter is 9.72 errors per 100 words. Roughly, every tenth word in the corpus is grammatically incorrect. This shows that not many student authors of the essays in the corpus have achieved a very high level of English proficiency, which in terms of CEFR, which in terms of CEFR level implies somewhere between levels B1 and B2 for the majority of student authors.

When we look at the distribution of errors across documents, we can make some interesting observation. Figure 4 shows the histograms of the number of error annotations per document for Task 1 essays and for Task 2 essays in different colour (blue and orange, correspondingly). The distribution for both classes

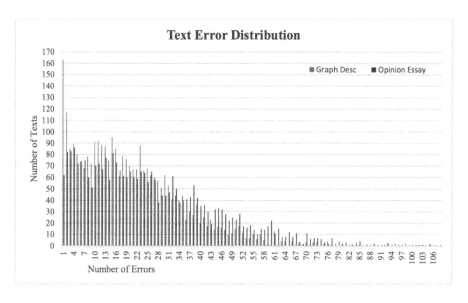

**Fig. 4.** Distribution of error annotations across documents in REALEC.

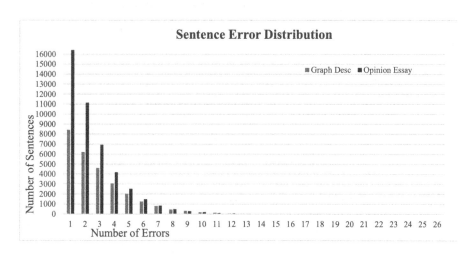

**Fig. 5.** Distribution of error annotations across sentences in REALEC.

**Table 2.** Error categorisation in REALEC.

| Upper-level tag | Error tag | Error spans and ≫ their corrections for some tags |
|---|---|---|
| | Punctuation | |
| | Spelling | |
| | Capitalisation | |
| Grammar | Determiners | The other ≫ Another example |
| | Articles | a lowest figure ≫ the lowest figure of 35% |
| | Quantifiers | much ≫ many efforts |
| Verbs | Tense | |
| | Choice of tense | There is ≫ was a rise in 2012 |
| | Tense form | It has taken many years |
| | Voice | was fluctuated ≫ fluctuated; |
| | | interested ≫ interesting fact |
| | Modals | must ≫ had to do |
| | Verb pattern | let them to create ≫ let them create; |
| | | Please introduce ≫ introduce yourself |
| | Gerund or participle construction | Create ≫ Creating modern house is |
| | Infinitive construction | Doing ≫ To do it means to develop |
| Nouns | Countable/uncountable nouns | advices ≫ advice |
| | Prepositional noun | ... a reason of ≫ reason for |
| | Possessive form of noun | This student ≫ student's reaction |
| | Noun+infinitive | the way of solving ≫ to solve |
| | Noun number | I know case ≫ cases of injustice |
| | Prepositions | in ≫ at night |
| | Conjunctions | new opportunities appear, ≫ and the whole world becomes |
| Adjectives | Prepositional adjective | independent on ≫ independent of |
| | Adjective as collective noun | poors ≫ the poor |
| Adverbs | Prepositional adverb | independently out of ≫ independently of |
| | Degree of comparison | the best ≫ better of the two |
| | Numerals | three millions of ≫ three million people |
| | Pronouns | |
| | Agreement | |
| | Word order | |
| | Relative clauses | offices which ≫ whose role is |
| | Parallel construction | They want to study ... and doing ≫ do sports. |
| | Negation | They have not ≫ do not have time to do it |
| | Comparative construction | twice more ≫ as many |
| | Confusion of structures | There is ≫ It is very important to |
| Vocabulary | Word choice | places in work industry ≫ work places |
| | Choice of lexical item | make ≫ fulfil its function |
| | Change, deletion, or addition | the jury is still on ≫ the jury is still out on |
| | of part of lexical item | |
| | Derivation | |
| | Formational affixes | controversional ≫ controversial issue |
| | Confusion of category | I am agree ≫ agree |
| | Compound word | crowd sourcing ≫ crowdsourcing |
| Discourse | Referential device | higher than of ≫ than that of male graduates |
| | Coherence | |
| | Linking device | To sum, ≫ To sum up, |
| | Inappropriate register | tiny ≫ insignificant increase |
| | Absence of a necessary | while appeared ≫ there appeared more people |
| | component in clause or sentence | |
| | Redundant component in clause | from both opposite ≫ both sides |
| | or sentence | |
| | Absence of necessary explanation | The percentage of people ≫ people |
| | or detail | in this group is about 70%. |

of essays is heavily skewed to the left with most documents (4617 out of 6054) having less than 32 errors, while some documents have significantly more errors than the average document: 16 graph descriptions and 34 opinion essays have more than 80 error annotations, and the highest number of error annotations in a document overall is 133. The mode (the most frequent value in the histogram) is 1 error/text for graph descriptions and 5 errors/text for opinion essays, and the median is 16 errors for Task1 and 21 errors for Task2.

A similar pattern can be observed when we look at the distribution of errors per sentence. Figure 5 shows a histogram of the number of error annotations per sentence in the REALEC corpus. The histogram shows that the largest number of sentences have no errors or one error, both in Task 1 and Task 2 essays. The frequency decreases quickly for higher error counts, and the highest observed number of error annotations in a sentence is 34 in Task 1 and 25 in Task 2 essays.

The skewed distribution of errors in the corpus was observed in (Dahlmeier et al. 2013), in which the authors explicated the long tail of the distribution by stating that if a learner has made a lot of mistakes in the beginning of the essay, the chance of making more errors in the remainder of the essay increases at least because of systematic errors, which are likely to be repeated.

As for the types of errors that language learners make, Fig. 6 shows a histogram of most frequent error categories (having 1,000 occurrences and more). The top three categories are misspelled words (about 27 thousand, 23%), wrong uses of articles (about 15 thousand, 13%), and wrong vocabulary choices (about 17 thousand, 15%). These top three error categories account for 51% of all error annotations. The next 5 categories are errors in punctuation, wrong choice of verb tense, inappropriate prepositions, agreement errors, and uses of redundant components, ranging from 9 to 4%.

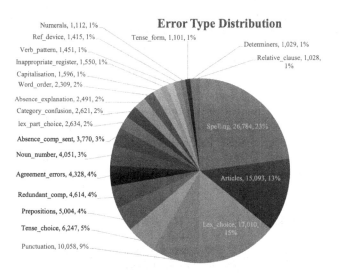

**Fig. 6.** Distribution of 22 most frequent REALEC error tags.

## 7　Corpus at Work

Drawing from the observations over the most frequent errors made by student authors with Russian L1, the research team working with REALEC set up the task to create, and reported the initial description of, a writing assistant for learners with Russian as L1 [26]. Annotated errors also formed the basis for a test-making program which worked at the HSE University as a placement program for a few years [26]. The third computer tool developed by the research team was a system for evaluating text complexity parameters [15].

Currently, two more directions for the researchers working with REALEC is to explore the relations between text complexity values and error counts in learner texts, on the one hand, and comparisons of English learner production by learners with different L1 [17,27]. The work on the writing assistant is still in progress, and an interesting question is how adding syntactic parsing with SpaCy [31] allowed us to increase the efficiency of the writing assistant in identifying four of the eight most frequent errors attested in REALEC, namely:

- errors in the subject-predicate agreement
- errors in the determiner-noun agreement
- errors in the use of commas
- errors in the use of verb tenses
- errors in the use of some prepositional constructions.

Some limitations in the ability of the parser to cope with the erroneous learner production, especially when errors were made by Russian learners of English under the influence of L1, have been observed by the REALEC research team. The possible ways to tackle the problems with wrong parsing was discussed in [17], but this specific line of research is beyond the scope of the present paper.

The difficulties of carrying out research across different learner corpora were noted by many authors (see, for example, [24, :44–45], and one of those were specific errors made under the influence of the interference with learners' L1. That is why annotation in REALEC has an additional focus on marking all errorenous occurrences that in some way resemble the features that exist in Russian. The examples can be brought in from such different areas as spelling (*democraty* instead of democracy - cf. Russian *demokratia*; *standarts* instead of *standards* - cf. Russian *standart*), word formation (*tendention* - cf. Russian *tendentsia*; *expluatated* instead of *exploited* - cf. Russian *ekspluatiroval*, lexical choice (see example in Fig. 3; *close their eyes to* instead of *turn a blind eye to* - cf. Russian *zakryvat' glaza na*). Errors in word order often have to be given as the complete sentences, and the corresponding Russian sentences have exactly the same word order as in the erroneous English sentence, as in the following example: *What it leads to?* instead of *What does it lead to?*

## 8　Conclusions and Future Research

The paper has reviewed our recent work towards development the REALEC corpus. Texts from our corpus can be downloaded, and the fact that the time-consuming and costly error annotation has been done and is being improved will hopefully make REALEC a valuable resource for EFL professionals, for SLA researchers, for linguists working in different walks in Linguistics, for NLP specialists and, finally, for students learning to become EFL instructors to practice error detection and correction in English classes. At HSE University, REALEC data are being used by both undergraduate and graduate students in Computer Linguistics program for their research activities.

Now that the first results of automated identification and correction in a large portion of learner texts have been received, it becomes even more important to increase the consistency of manual error annotation in the smaller part of the corpus in order to be able to create a procedure of the automated error classification as a follow-up to deep learning model.

# References

1. Bailler, N., Buzanov, A., Gaillat, T., Vinogradova, O.: A Cross-platform Investigation of Complexity for Russian Learners of English. EUROCALL 2021, presentation at the conference (2021)
2. Bird, S., Klein, E., Loper, E.: Natural language processing with Python: analyzing text with the natural language toolkit. O'Reilly Media, Inc. (2009)
3. Díaz-Negrillo, A., Valera, S., Meurers, D., Wunsch, H.: Towards interlanguage POS annotation for effective learner corpora in SLA and FLT. Language Forum **36**, 139–154 (2010)
4. Education First. http://www.englishtown.com. Englishtown (2012)
5. Gablasova, D., Brezina, V., McEnery, T.: The trinity lancaster corpus: development, description and application. Int. J. Learner Corpus Res. **5**(2), 126–158 (2019)
6. Geertzen, J., Alexopoulou, T., Korhonen, A.: Automatic linguistic annotation of large scale L2 databases: The EF-Cambridge Open Language Database (EFCAMDAT). In: Selected Proceedings of the 2012 Second Language Research Forum, Somerville, MA, USA (2013)
7. Gilquin, G.: Learner corpora. In: Paquot, M., Gries, S.T. (eds.) A Practical Handbook of Corpus Linguistics, pp. 283–303. Springer, Cham (2020). https://doi.org/10.1007/978-3-030-46216-1_13
8. Gilquin, G., de Cock, S., Granger, S.: The Louvain International Database of Spoken English Interlanguage. Handbook and CD-ROM. Press. univ. de Louvain, Louvain-la-Neuve (2010)
9. Granger, S.: Learner corpora. In: Lüdeling, A., Kytö, M. (eds.) Corpus Linguistics. An International Handbook, vol. 1, pp. 259–275. Walter de Gruyter, Berlin, New York (2008)
10. Granger S.: How to use foreign and second language learner corpora. In: Research Methods in Second Language Acquisition: A Practical Guide, ch. 2, pp. 5–29. Blackwell, Oxford (2012)
11. Granger S.: The contribution of learner corpora to reference and instructional materials design. In: The Cambridge Handbook of Learner Corpus Research, pp. 485–510. Cambridge University Press, Cambridge (2015)
12. Granger, S., Dupont, M., Meunier, F., Naets, H., Paquot, M.: The International Corpus of Learner English. Version 3. Press. univ. de Louvain, Louvain-la-Neuve (2020)

13. Huang Y., Geertzen, J., Baker, R., Korhonen, A., Alexopoulou, Th.: The EF Cambridge Open Language Database (EFCAMDAT): Information for Users, pp. 1–18. https://corpus.mml.cam.ac.uk (2017)
14. Lindquist, H.: Corpus Linguistics and the Description of English. Edinburgh University Press, Edinburgh (2009)
15. Lyashevskaya, O., Vinogradova, O., Panteleeva, I.: Automated assessment of learner text complexity. Assessing writing **49**, 100529 (2021)
16. Lyashevskaya, O., Panteleeva, I.: REALEC learner treebank: annotation principles and evaluation of automatic parsing. In: TLT 16, pp. 80–87 (2017)
17. Lyashevskaya, O., Vinogradova, O., Scherbakova, A. Accuracy, syntactic complexity, and task type at play in examination writing: A corpus-based study (forthc.)
18. McEnery, T., Brezina, V., Gablasova, D., Banerjee, J.: Corpus linguistics, learner corpora, and SLA: employing technology to analyze language use. Ann. Rev. Appl. Linguistics **39**, 74–92 (2019)
19. Meurers, D., Dickinson, M.: Evidence and interpretation in language learning research: opportunities for collaboration with computational linguistics. Lang. Learn. **67**(1), 66–95 (2017)
20. Nesi, H.: ESP and corpus studies. In: Paltridge, B., Starfield, S. (eds.) The Handbook of English for Specific Purposes. Handbooks in Linguistics Series, pp. 407–426. Wiley-Blackwell, Oxford (2013)
21. Nicholls, D.: The Cambridge Learner Corpus: Error coding and analysis for lexicography and ELT. In: Proceedings of the Corpus Linguistics Conference, pp. 572–581. Lancaster University: University Centre for Computer Corpus Research on Language (2003)
22. Schmid, H.: Probabilistic part-of-speech tagging using decision trees. In: Proceedings of International Conference on New Methods in Language Processing, Manchester, UK (1994)
23. Stenetorp, P., Pontus, P., Sampo, T., Goran, O., Tomoko, A. Tsujii, J.-I.: BRAT: A Web-based Tool for NLP-Assisted Text Annotation. In: EACL 13, Demonstrations, pp. 102–107. Stroudshourg, PA (2012)
24. Tetreault, J.R., Filatova, E., Chodorow, M.: Rethinking grammatical error annotation and evaluation with the amazon mechanical Turk. In: Proceedings of the Fifth Workshop on Innovative Use of NLP for Building Educational Applications, pp. 45–49. Los Angeles, USA (2010)
25. Vinogradova, O.: The Role and Applications of Expert Error Annotation in a Corpus of English Learner Texts. In: Computational Linguistics and Intellectual Technologies: Proceedings of Dialog 2016, pp. 740–751. Moscow, Russia (2016)
26. Vinogradova, O., Ershova, E., Sergienko, A., Overnikova, D., Buzanov, A.: Chaos is merely order waiting to be deciphered: corpus-based study of word order errors of Russian learners of English. In: Learner Corpus Research Conference, p. 115. Warsaw (2019)
27. Vinogradova, O., Smirnova, E. The L1 influence on the use of the English present perfect: a corpus analysis of Russian and Spanish learner essays (forthc.)
28. HSE Independent English Language Test regulations page. https://www.hse.ru/en/studyspravka/indexam. Accessed 20 Apr 2022
29. Learner Corpus Association page. https://uclouvain.be/en/research-institutes/ilc/cecl/learner-corpora-around-the-world.html. Accessed 5 May 2022
30. REALEC homepage. https://realec.org/index.xhtml#/exam. Accessed 5 May 2022
31. SpaCy homepage. https://spacy.io. Accessed 5 May 2022

# New Language Identification
# and Sentiment Analysis Modules
# for Social Media Communication

Radoslav Sabol and Aleš Horák[(✉)] [iD]

Natural Language Processing Centre, Faculty of Informatics, Masaryk University
Botanická 68a, 602 00 Brno, Czech Republic
{xsabol,hales}@fi.muni.cz

**Abstract.** The style and vocabulary of social media communication, such as chats, discussions or comments, differ vastly from standard languages. Specifically in internal business communication, the texts contain large amounts of language mixins, professional jargon and occupational slang, or colloquial expressions. Standard natural language processing tools thus mostly fail to detect basic text processing attributes such as the prevalent language of a message or communication or their sentiment.

In the presented paper, we describe the development and evaluation of new modules specifically designed for language identification and sentiment analysis of informal business communication inside a large international company. Besides the details of the module architectures, we offer a detailed comparison with other state-of-the-art tools for the same purpose and achieve an improvement of 10–13 % in accuracy with selected problematic datasets.

**Keywords:** social media communication · language identification · sentiment analysis

## 1 Introduction

Detailed content analysis of unstructured texts can bring valuable insights into otherwise hidden data ranging from emotion and sentiment information [4,9] through market analysis [2] to electronic health records investigations [20]. Most of the tasks rely on basic text attributes such as the prevalent language of the text. In standard text types, the *language identification* task is relatively well-managed with available *n*-gram modules like LangID [14] or pretrained neural models such as FastText [11] or Apple Bi-LSTM [19]. However, when these mainstream models process non-standard input texts like spoken language (in the form of movie subtitles) or internal business communication in the form of chats and discussions, they usually face severe accuracy drops. Reasons for such imprecision are relatively clear – conversational texts tend to use colloquial and

P. Sojka et al. (Eds.): TSD 2022, LNAI 13502, pp. 89–101, 2022.
https://doi.org/10.1007/978-3-031-16270-1_8

professional vocabulary, mix phrases and terms from different languages, refrain from using diacritics etc.

In the following text, we present the details of development of two new modules of *OfficeBot*, a system designed to understand the content of internal business communication, e.g. in the form of Slack [17] conversations. The first module's task is the above mentioned language identification, where we build a dictionary based ensemble model for eighteen languages to solve the problematic constructions in chat texts. The second module concentrates on the task of sentiment analysis of Czech messages as these were failing badly with standard multilingual tool Polyglot [5]. Both modules underwent a detailed evaluation and comparison with selected current tools improving the results on language identification with spoken texts of 3–13 % in accuracy (ratio of correct results to all cases) and the sentiment analysis detection of 10 % again in accuracy.

## 2 Language Identification

Most of the primary text analysis tasks the *OfficeBot* system needs to perform require the prerequisite of *language identification* – a classification task to determine the prevailing language of the message or conversation. An incorrect classification in this step implies almost inevitable failure in the subsequent tasks. For this reason, having a module that can adequately cope with messages in a social network setting is crucial.

The following section will briefly review existing language identification tools, offer a detailed description of new tools created for this task, and their evaluation and comparison.

### 2.1 Related Works

LangID [14] is an off-the-shelf Python library used for language identification. It comes pre-trained with support for 97 languages as a supervised Naive-Bayes classifier over byte $n$-grams (1–4). With reasonable success, the module was evaluated on both long document and micro-blog corpora.

FastText [11] is a C++ application for learning of word representations and text sequence classification. It includes bindings for use in Python, making it one of the fastest libraries currently available. FastText uses a bag of $n$-grams representation of the input text to train a linear classifier with hierarchical softmax. Within the distribution, a compact text classification model for language identification called *lid176.bin* that is trained to recognize 176 languages with texts from Wikipedia, SETimes, and Tatoeba is included.

Apple Bi-LSTM [19] is a relatively recent reproduction of Apple's approach using a neural network architecture for language identification. The module is designed for applications like automatic spell checkers during typing, where the input messages are typically shorter than usual benchmarking documents. The reproduction uses a Bidirectional LSTM [18] on character encodings, where the approach outperforms most of the current open-source language identification modules.

## 2.2    On the Difficulty of Identifying Internet Language

Based on the observations of data, we can make assumptions about some features of the "internet language[1]" and consider the complexity of their analysis.

**Short Messages.** Out-of-the-shelf language identification modules were designed to work with entire paragraphs or full-fledged sentences of text. In the internet language, messages shorter than three words are the most common (Fig. 1).

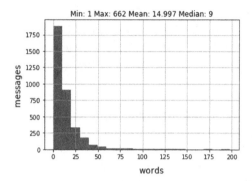

**Fig. 1.** Message length distribution in the internal business communication

**Frequent misspellings** can be problematic for methods dependent on the exact match of words or word $n$-grams; however, the most commonly used character $n$-gram models can deal with misspelling to some extent.

**Missing diacritics**, either partially or entirely. In both cases, languages that make heavy use of diacritics (Czech, Slovak, etc.) are more difficult to classify correctly, as diacritics is a prominent feature of the aforementioned languages. Also, as shown in Table 1, missing diacritics can create ambiguities that would not be present if the diacritics were present.

**Table 1.** The meaning and language of a word dependent on the correct use of diacritics

| Word | Language | Meaning |
|------|----------|---------|
| pit | English | a large hole in the ground |
| pič | Slovak | to drink |
| pít | Czech | to drink |

**Usage of Internet Slang Terms.** Most of the internet slang and acronyms (*thanx*, *imho*, *btw*) are derived from English, however, they are used independently of the true language of the text. Some language-specific slang terms also

---

[1] The language used in social media communications.

exist (e.g. "*jj*" as a positive answer in both Czech and Slovak, meaning "*jo jo*", *yeah yeah*). The ability to distinguish between slang terms that provide valuable information about the language and those that are just added "language noise" can be an important feature of a classifier.

## 2.3   Custom FastText Model

The initial attempt at language identification consisted in training a new Fast-Text classification module, where the training dataset was adapted to the specifics of internet language. Among the 20 supported languages,[2] two special "languages" were included, *Czech Without Diacritics* (csd) and *Slovak Without Diacritics* (skd). Their role is to distinguish the Czech and Slovak languages even when the messages partially or entirely miss diacritics (a prominent feature of these languages).

**Dataset and Preprocessing.** Multilingual Wikipedia[3] and Tatoeba corpora[4] were used as sources for the datasets to train the FastText model. The preprocessing part was different for two kinds of languages – the ones that use the Latin alphabet and the others. The standard preprocessing procedures include removal of punctuation, URLs and numerical data. For the Latin script languages, all sentences were transformed to lowercase. Especially for *Czech* and *Slovak* Without Diacritics, the datasets were created through transliteration of original Czech and Slovak texts. For Non-Latin script languages, all occurrences of Latin characters were removed to avoid confusion.

Once preprocessed, the resulting dataset contained around 15 million annotated sentences.

**Usage of the Model.** The module consists of two parts: the FastText model itself and a Python wrapper that handles preprocessing, postprocessing, and the usage of the FastText model itself.

In practical applications, the message is sometimes too short or filled with language-agnostic content that makes it impossible to classify into a single language. For this reason, a special class called "*unknown*" is introduced.

The input sentences require similar preprocessing as the training data, i.e. removal of URLs, emojis, and numerical data, as they are irrelevant to the classification itself. If the message becomes too short after these steps ($\leq 5$ characters), the message is automatically classified as "*unknown*". If the model is too uncertain about the outcome of the classification (confidence level less than 50 %), the message is classified as "*unknown*" as well.

---

[2] cs, csd, da, de, en, es, fi, fr, hu, it, jp, nl, no, pl, ru, se, sk, skd, sw, and zh.
[3] https://www.wikipedia.org/.
[4] https://tatoeba.org.

## 2.4   Dictionary-Based Language Identification

As may follow from the description above, the custom FastText module can handle the problematic languages without diacritics, but short messages still pose a problem. For instance, a two-word English message saying *"NO WAY"* is wrongly identified as Japanese by the original FastText model (with relatively low confidence) and as Spanish by the custom FastText model presented in the previous section. Since such messages are the most frequent in the chat and conversation texts, we propose a new method based on a combined score computation with word frequency dictionaries.

First, frequency wordlists were extracted using both very large text corpora [10] and the OpenSubtitles corpus [13] for each language separately. Each of the wordlists consists of two dictionaries – one contains 10,000 of the most common words in the language, while the other one includes 50,000 most common word bigrams. Every dictionary is ordered by the word/bigram frequency in the corpus. From now on, the term *token* is used to capture the shared properties of both words and word bigrams in the algorithm. To describe the method, we employ the following notation:

- $W$ denotes the input text, $L$ is a set of all supported languages.
- $rank(w, l)$ corresponds to the position of the token $w$ in the wordlist of language $l$.
  if $w$ does not occur in the wordlist of $l$, then $rank(w, l)$ is equal to 0.
- $c$ is a suitable constant to compensate for the dictionary size (10,000 for words, 50,000 for bigrams).
- $length\_mod(w)$ is a multiplicative modifier that takes the token length into account. Longer tokens tend to be more unique in the given language, and that has be reflected in the final score.
- $occ\_penalty(w, l)$, or the *occurrence penalty* of token $w$ in language $l$, is a measure of the token ambiguity w.r.t. the other languages. If a token occurs in multiple languages, then there is an increased uncertainty about the word being important for classification – so the overall score must be penalized.
  $p$ is a suitable normalization constant (1,000 for words, 5,000 for bigrams)

The combined language score of a message $W$ for a language $l$ is then computed as follows

$$language\_score(W, l) = \sum_{w \in W} score(w, l) \tag{1}$$

$$score(w, l) = log\left(\frac{\frac{c}{rank(w,l)}\, length\_mod(w)}{occ\_penalty(w, l)}\right) \tag{2}$$

$$occ\_penalty(w, l) = \sum_{k \in L, k \neq l} \frac{log(c - rank(w, k))}{p} \tag{3}$$

$$length\_mod(w) = 1 + log(length(w)) \tag{4}$$

Languages with the highest score are considered the most probable candidates for the actual language.

## 2.5    The Ensemble Method

The pretrained FastText model *lid176.bin* performs reasonably well for most instances of longer texts in one of the standard languages. The dictionary-based method (Sect. 2.4) is best suited to short messages of common words without unexpected misspellings. The custom FastText model (Sect. 2.3) works well with languages without diacritics and instances with English terms mixed up in a foreign language; however, the overall average performance is worse than with *lid176.bin*.

To improve upon the existing modules, we present an ensemble of these three classifiers, where the voting takes each module's strengths and weaknesses into account. Each of the classifiers predicts one language along with its confidence, and the voting commences in this exact order:

- if the majority agrees on the language $x$, then return $x$.
- if the custom FastText model predicts language $x$ with confidence large enough ($\geq 0.9$), then return $x$.
- if *lid176.bin* model predicts language $x$ with confidence large enough ($\geq 0.6$), then return $x$.
- if the dictionary-based module reaches a confidence for language $x$ higher than $0.10 \cdot log(length(W))$, then return $x$.
- otherwise return *"unknown"*.

## 2.6    Evaluation

In the following text, the performance of all the above presented techniques is evaluated and a comparison with current mainstream, publicly available solutions is provided.

First, Table 2 compares the performance of the original and the custom Fast-Text module on a small disjoint subset of Wikipedia articles (100 per language), where the results support the primary decision for preparing the custom model which shows significantly increased performance on languages without diacritics. Compared to the following evaluation with all languages, the accuracy of the custom FastText model diminishes due to lower precision on other languages where the diacritics do not play such important role and where the original FastText model performs more robustly.

For the full evaluation purposes, we use two specific datasets. The first dataset, called OfficeBot set, is a preselected collection of messages from the OfficeBot Slack workspace that were problematic to classify using the custom FastText module. The set was also used to fine-tune the parameters of the Ensemble module, so it may be considered as a sort of development set of 177 messages.

The second set is created from OpenSubtitles – a multilingual parallel corpus of movie subtitles [13]. This particular corpus was chosen due to its volume and because it offers conversational expressions from everyday speech that closely resembles internet conversations (compared to other commonly used multilingual corpora like Wikipedia or EuroParl). 10,000 sentences of each language were used as a test set to perform the evaluation.

The Table 3 shows the prediction accuracies with both datasets. For the OfficeBot Set, the custom FastText model reaches the least reasonable accuracy as the set is negatively biased against the module. The original FastText module achieves decent performance, with the best result of the foreign solutions being offered by the more recent pretrained Apple BiLSTM model. The ensemble can properly combine the strengths of various modules, and thanks to that, it achieves the best performance on the dataset.

**Table 2.** Comparison of both FastText modules on the development subset of Wikipedia articles

|  | Original FastText acc. (%) | Our FastText acc. (%) |
|---|---|---|
| English | **100.0** | 98.5 |
| Czech | **99.0** | 98.5 |
| Czech Without Diacritics | 89.5 | **98.5** |
| Slovak | 97.5 | **100.0** |
| Slovak Without Diacritics | 83.0 | **99.5** |

**Table 3.** Comparison of the prediction accuracy of the presented solutions with the OfficeBot and OpenSubtitles datasets

| Module | OfficeBot Set (%) | OpenSubtitles Set (%) |
|---|---|---|
| FastText | 84.74 | 73.96 |
| custom FastText | 65.56 | 58.91 |
| dictionary-based module (our) | 94.35 | **87.03** |
| Ensemble (our) | **94.91** | 76.30 |
| Apple BiLSTM | 91.52 | 65.10 |

The best-performing module on the OpenSubtitles dataset is the dictionary module. One of the reasons for success is that the dataset does not typically contain misspelling as internet conversations do, so the module does not struggle with lower recall on such sentences. The second best performance of the ensemble shows that the rule parameters are designed to the OfficeBot Set. Future work on the module should replace the handwritten rules with a learnable classifier that aggregates the predicted languages in a fashion that is less likely to overfit on larger datasets.

# 3   Sentiment Analysis

The OfficeBot system employs sentiment analysis to understand users' attitudes in existing workspace conversations. As the workspace functions in a multilingual setting, it is crucial to be capable of both working with the internet language and working with multiple languages simultaneously.

## 3.1   Related Works

The vast majority of sentiment analysis systems focus on a single language (most commonly English [6]). One of the main problems that are holding back the development of multilingual sentiment analysis systems is the lack of resources across languages [1].

An essential part of a successful multilingual sentiment analysis consists in dealing with the sparsity of sentiment lexicons that are difficult to create and maintain. One of the common approaches lies in using machine translation to translate the original content into English, where the resources are well developed. However, this method comes with its own set of problems, including additional noise generated by the translation and cases where the system does not translate essential parts of the content [1].

Polyglot [5] is an extensive multilingual NLP framework that supports tokenization, NER, POS tagging, language detection, but also sentiment analysis. The sentiment analysis module is a lexicon-based method that supports 136 languages. The seed sentiment lexicons were bootstrapped using WordNet [8], and the links to other languages were established using knowledge graphs.

## 3.2   Sentiment Analysis for Czech

The baseline solution for OfficeBot was to use the Polyglot sentiment analysis module for the task. However, the usage proved insufficient due to poor performance with the Czech language which is the most used language in the workspace where OfficeBot is deployed. Table 4 lists a few examples of words present in the lexicon. It is important to note that most examples are frequently used words (most of them can be found in stoplists), so they introduce a large amount of noisy parameters to the analysis.

**Table 4.** Examples of erroneous items in Polyglot Czech sentiment lexicon

| Word (Czech) | Word (English) | Claimed polarity | True polarity |
|:---:|:---|:---:|:---:|
| o | about (preposition) | negative | neutral |
| jako | like (preposition) | positive | neutral |
| malý | small (adjective) | negative | neutral |
| no | well (interjection) | positive | neutral |

In this solution, we are using the ensemble technique from Sect. 2.5 to identify the language. If the language is either Czech or CzechWithoutDiacritics, we will use a different module adapted to this single language instead of Polyglot. The sentiment analysis tool for Czech is an adaptation of a previously developed sentiment lexicon-based module [3] that was created for use in political discussion content.

If the current language is classified as *CzechWithoutDiacritics*, then all diacritics are removed (if any are left), and a specifically prepared Czech lexicon without diacritics is used. If the language is Czech, then the *czaccent* [16] tool is used to restore potentially missing diacritics of the content. The sentiment scoring procedure remains identical to the original work [3], with notable exceptions mentioned in the following subsections.

**Lexicon Expansion.** The original sentiment analysis module contained 3,550 affective words and a specific dictionary focused on political discussions.

The first expansion was the addition of *afinn.cz* [15] sentiment lexicon with approximately 20,000 words with polarities of −1 and 1. With such an extensive lexicon, inevitably, some of the words are not as affective, and to compensate for that, the following rule applies: if the word is present in *afinn.cz* lexicon and is not present in any other of the lexicons, the polarity value of the word is reduced to 50 %.

The second expansion employed *eval_words.txt* [12], a Czech sentiment lexicon of approximately 6,200 words originated as a Czech translation of the English SentiWordNet lexicon [7], where positive and negative sentiment intensity is listed separately. There is a number of instances where the sentiment intensity is low for both polarities, that it might as well be omitted, so the word should actually be treated as neutral. The confidence score of the word being neutral is thus computed as $1.0 - p - n$, where $p$ stands for the positive confidence and $n$ stands for the negative. If the neutral confidence is the highest, the word is omitted. Otherwise, the final polarity is the one with the higher confidence, where the confidence level is preserved in the preprocessed lexicon. After this pruning, 1,500 new affective words with polarity scores have been added to the new lexicon.

**Emojis.** The standard Slack workspace offers 875 emojis, each following a specific text format of `:lower_snake_case_name:` encoded as parts of the conversation messages. The emoji names have been converted to English words and the emoji sentiment was then determined by using Polyglot [5]. With this method, 105 emojis were classified as positive and 59 as negative, and those were added as a separate wordlist to the sentiment module.

**Module Tweaks.** The original module included several domain-dependent features that either do not apply in the internet conversations settings or they have to be adjusted.

Upper-cased words were detected as "yelling", which is usually interpreted as strongly negative content. However, upper-case acronyms are frequently used in internet discussions, which would bring them misinterpreted as negative yelling. For this reason, the feature was completely removed.

With massively increased lexicon size, the module is able to interpret the sentiment of many new words in the input messages which had to be reflected in recalculating numeric weights and parameters of the original module. Since the module's decision process uses separate values for positivity confidence $p$ and negativity confidence $n$, for a comparison with Polyglot the individual predictions for each polarity have to be reduced to a single number, which is done by the following formula:

$$sentiment(p, n) = \begin{cases} 0 & \text{for } |p - n| < 0.5 \\ 1, & \text{for } p > n \\ -1, & \text{for } p < n \end{cases}$$

### 3.3 Evaluation

Unfortunately, there are no publicly available Czech sentiment analysis datasets that would match the internet conversation domain. We have thus manually annotated 328 messages from the OfficeBot Slack workspace to compare our approach with selected baselines.

The messages were labeled by a single annotator using the following criteria. Messages that contain an abundance of positive emojis or express appraisal, positive news, and humorous content are labeled as positive messages. Negative sentiment was assigned to messages that express frustration, disapproval, overall tension or contain negative emojis. The content of the message has higher importance than the presence of emojis themselves (as they can be used sarcastically). If the message does not fit any criteria, the sentiment is kept as neutral.

The modules are evaluated in two ways. The first one computes accuracy on a complete match between labeled and predicted sentiments. The second one takes into account only those examples that have non-neutral emotion. This is because predicting the opposite polarity of the sentiment is a more severe mistake in practice than detecting neutral sentiment instead. All message languages are pre-set correctly in advance by an oracle.

**Table 5.** Confusion matrices of the sentiment prediction for all three modules

|          | Polyglot | | | Politics | | | OfficeBot | | |
|----------|-----|-----|-----|-----|-----|-----|-----|-----|-----|
|          | neu | pos | neg | neu | pos | neg | neu | pos | neg |
| Neutral  | 75  | 17  | 12  | 50  | 7   | 47  | 35  | 44  | 25  |
| Positive | 74  | 47  | 7   | 22  | 79  | 27  | 7   | 111 | 10  |
| Negative | 68  | 18  | 10  | 37  | 22  | 37  | 13  | 30  | 53  |

Table 5 shows the confusion matrices between predicted and actual labels for all three modules. For the Polyglot module, recall problems can be observed as most of the sentences are predicted as neutral. Overall, the Politics module performs better; however, it is more biased toward negative sentiment due to the misinterpretation of yelling. The OfficeBot module improves upon this and particularly excels at predicting positive sentiment.

**Table 6.** Overall test set accuracy results with separate measurements excluding the neutral class

|  | Accuracy | Accuracy without neutral |
|---|---|---|
| **Polyglot** | 40.42 | 69.51 |
| **Politics** | 50.61 | 70.30 |
| **OfficeBot** | 60.67 | 80.39 |

Table 6 concludes the overall performance for all three modules using both methods. In both cases, the proposed module outperforms the remaining modules considerably by at least 10%.

## 4   Conclusion

The presented paper details the development and evaluation of newly developed modules aiming at processing social media communication texts, i.e. internet chats, discussions and comments. The specifics of these non-standard texts were briefly discussed and the evaluation proved inadequacies of standard natural language processing tools when analysis informal multilingual conversations, specifically in the internal business communication environment.

The new modules concentrated on the language identification task for eighteen most common languages with respect to the European area and specifically for the Czech language sentiment analysis where the chosen multilingual Polyglot tool delivered distorted results. The modules evaluation compared the new tools with selected baselines and showed a stable and remarkable improvement ranging from 10 to 13 % in accuracy.

Both the modules are published with a free license available to other projects processing the non-conforming language variety of internet discussions.[5]

**Acknowledgments.** This work has been partly supported by the Ministry of Education of CR within the LINDAT-CLARIAH-CZ project LM2018101. Access to computing and storage facilities owned by parties and projects contributing to the National Grid Infrastructure MetaCentrum provided under the programme "Projects of Large Research, Development, and Innovations Infrastructures" (CESNET LM2015042), is greatly appreciated.

---

[5] https://gitlab.fi.muni.cz/nlp/internetlangident and
   https://gitlab.fi.muni.cz/nlp/internet-sentiment-analysis.

# References

1. Agarwal, B., Poria, S., Mittal, N., Gelbukh, A., Hussain, A.: Concept-level sentiment analysis with dependency-based semantic parsing: a novel approach. Cogn. Comput. **7**(4), 487–499 (2015)
2. Balducci, B., Marinova, D.: Unstructured data in marketing. J. Acad. Mark. Sci. **46**(4), 557–590 (2018)
3. Bilík, J.: Emotion detection in plain text (in Czech) (2014). https://is.muni.cz/th/ko3aa/
4. Chan, S.W., Chong, M.W.: Sentiment analysis in financial texts. Decis. Support Syst. **94**, 53–64 (2017)
5. Chen, Y., Skiena, S.: Building sentiment lexicons for all major languages. In: Proceedings of the 52nd Annual Meeting of the Association for Computational Linguistics (Short Papers), pp. 383–389 (2014)
6. Dashtipour, K., Poria, S., Hussain, A., Cambria, E., Hawalah, A.Y., Gelbukh, A., Zhou, Q.: Multilingual sentiment analysis: state of the art and independent comparison of techniques. Cogn. Comput. **8**(4), 757–771 (2016)
7. Esuli, A., Sebastiani, F.: SentiWordNet: a publicly available lexical resource for opinion mining. In: Proceedings of the Fifth International Con Language Resources and Evaluation (LREC'06) (2006)
8. Fellbaum, C. (ed.): WordNet: An electronic lexical database. MIT Press (1998)
9. Greco, F., Polli, A.: Emotional text mining: customer profiling in brand management. Int. J. Inf. Manage. **51**, 101934 (2020)
10. Jakubíček, M., Kilgarriff, A., Kovář, V., Rychlý, P., Suchomel, V.: The tenten corpus family. In: 7th International Corpus Linguistics Conference CL, pp. 125–127. Lancaster University (2013)
11. Joulin, A., Grave, E., Bojanowski, P., Mikolov, T.: Bag of tricks for efficient text classification. arXiv preprint arXiv:1607.01759 (2016)
12. Koublová, A.: Monitoring the use of subjective adjectives in connection with named entities in Czech internet news (in Czech) (2014). https://is.muni.cz/th/jlfc4/
13. Lison, P., Tiedemann, J., Kouylekov, M.: Opensubtitles 2018: statistical rescoring of sentence alignments in large, noisy parallel corpora. In: Proceedings of the Eleventh International Conference on Language Resources and Evaluation (LREC 2018) (2018)
14. Lui, M., Baldwin, T.: langid.py: An off-the-shelf language identification tool. In: Proceedings of the ACL 2012 System Demonstrations, pp. 25–30. Association for Computational Linguistics, Jeju Island, Korea, July 2012. https://aclanthology.org/P12-3005
15. Nielsen, F.Å.: Afinn, March 2011. http://www2.compute.dtu.dk/pubdb/pubs/6010-full.html
16. Rychlý, P.: CzAccent - simple tool for restoring accents in czech texts. In: Aleš Horák, P.R. (ed.) 6th Workshop on Recent Advances in Slavonic Natural Language Processing, pp. 15–22. Tribun EU, Brno (2012), https://nlp.fi.muni.cz/raslan/2012/paper14.pdf
17. Stray, V., Moe, N.B., Noroozi, M.: Slack me if you can! using enterprise social networking tools in virtual agile teams. In: 2019 ACM/IEEE 14th International Conference on Global Software Engineering (ICGSE), pp. 111–121. IEEE (2019)
18. Sundermeyer, M., Schlüter, R., Ney, H.: LSTM neural networks for language modeling. In: Thirteenth Annual Conference of the International Speech Communication Association (2012)

19. Toftrup, M., Asger Sørensen, S., Ciosici, M.R., Assent, I.: A reproduction of Apple's bi-directional LSTM models for language identification in short strings. In: Proceedings of the 16th Conference of the European Chapter of the Association for Computational Linguistics: Student Research Workshop, pp. 36–42. Association for Computational Linguistics, April 2021. 10.18653/v1/2021.eacl-srw.6, https://aclanthology.org/2021.eacl-srw.6

20. Wang, Y., Kung, L., Byrd, T.A.: Big data analytics: understanding its capabilities and potential benefits for healthcare organizations. Technol. Forecast. Soc. Chang. **126**, 3–13 (2018)

# Identification of Metaphorical Collocations in Different Languages – Similarities and Differences

Lucia Nacinovic Prskalo$^{(\boxtimes)}$ [ID] and Marija Brkic Bakaric [ID]

Faculty of Informatics and Digital Technologies, University of Rijeka, Radmile Matejcic 2, 51000 Rijeka, Croatia
{lnacinovic,mbrkic}@uniri.hr

**Abstract.** Metaphorical collocations are a subset of collocations in which a semantic shift has occurred in one of the components. The main goal of this paper is to describe the process of identifying metaphorical collocations in different languages – English, German and Croatian. Approaches to annotating metaphorical collocations from a list of word sketches for the three languages are presented using one of the most common nouns for all three languages – "year" for English, "Jahr" (Engl. year) for German, and "godina" (Engl. year) for Croatian. The compilation of a list of relevant grammatical relations in the identification of metaphorical collocations for each language is also described. Finally, the procedures for automatic classification of metaphorical collocations for Croatian, German and English are performed and compared.

**Keywords:** Metaphorical collocations · Collocations · Classification · Automatic collocation identification · Grammatical relations

## 1 Introduction

Metaphorical collocations are a subset of collocations in which there is a shift in the meaning of a component, usually the collocate. In this paper, procedures for identifying metaphorical collocations are described and compared for three different languages - English, German and Croatian. Procedures for (automatic) identification of metaphorical collocations require a number of sub-procedures, such as corpus selection, creation of an inventory of collocations and metaphorical collocations, selection of relevant grammatical relations, machine learning modelling, etc. They are described in details in the following sections.

According to research by [1], it was found that the noun mostly appears in the role of the base, while verbs and adjectives, which have the potential to acquire secondary meaning leading to polysemy, mostly appear in the role of the

Supported by Croatian Science Foundation under the project *Metaphorical collocations – Syntagmatic word combinations between semantics and pragmatics* (IP-2020-02-6319).

P. Sojka et al. (Eds.): TSD 2022, LNAI 13502, pp. 102–112, 2022.
https://doi.org/10.1007/978-3-031-16270-1_9

collocate. In the same article, the authors give an example of the metaphorical collocation in Croatian "zabiti gol" (Engl. to kick a goal), where the noun "gol" is the base and the verb "zabiti" has the function of a collocate. In the same example, the idiosyncratic character of collocational compounds, in which two lexemes are arbitrarily connected in a collocation, is evident. Therefore, it is very difficult for a non-native speaker to know which word combinations are common in another language and which are not acceptable. For example, the metaphorical collocation "zabiti gol" - (Engl. to hit a goal) mentioned above uses different collocates in other languages - in German the equivalent translation is "ein Tor schießen" - (Engl. to shoot a goal), and in English "kick a goal". The authors note that the collocate is expressed in different images in these languages and that the meaning is determined by different extralinguistic comparisons. However, they also note that the comparisons are based on the same concept, namely the physical encounter of the ball and the goal. They conclude, therefore, that the examples of collocation compounds in different languages indicate that the same extra-linguistic reality is lexicalized in different ways, which superficially gives the appearance of arbitrariness, but that the process of forming collocation compounds seems to follow the same pattern. Testing this assumption is one of the main long-term goals of our project, and the research presented in this paper represents the first steps in this direction.

Throughout our project, we intend to use a combination of computational-linguistic and theoretical-semantic approaches to obtain the most relevant results as quickly as possible. Manual annotation of metaphorical collocations in the corpus is an extremely time-consuming and tedious task. Therefore, by combining the two approaches, we aim to facilitate the task of finding different types of metaphorical collocations in different languages and identifying similarities and differences in the formation of metaphorical collocations in different languages.

In the second section we have singled out some of the important related work. The third section describes the research methodology - corpus selection, selection of the most relevant grammatical relations, annotation procedures, and model development using machine learning techniques. Finally, a description of the results and a conclusion follow.

## 2    Related Work

There is research that has addressed the automatic identification of metaphors in a text, such as in [2–5], but to our knowledge there is no research that has addressed the extraction of metaphorical collocations as a subset of collocations in general. The work in the remainder of this section relates to the extraction of collocations in general.

Most of the papers on the topic of automatic collocation extraction have dealt with the application of various association measures. For example, Church and Hanks [6] proposed an association ratio measure in 1990, Dunning [7] proposed a likelihood ratio measure in 1993, and Kita [8] and co-workers proposed a cost criteria measure in 1994. Smadja et al. [9] use the Dice coefficient to find translations of a source language collocation using a parallel corpus, and Thanopoulos et al. [10] propose a PMI (Pointwise mutual information) measure. All these works focus on statistical methods in the form of association measures.

Some papers have experimented with parsing in addition to statistical measures. For example, Seretan and Wehrli [11] use different types of parsing for flexible pair extraction, and Lin [12] proposes an approach using a parser to extract dependency triples from a corpus.

There have also been attempts to include other linguistic features in the models, such as POS tags. For example, Krenn [13] uses statistical POS taggers and a partial parser to extract collocation-specific syntactic constraints. Pearce [14] uses WordNet to present an approach based on constraints on the possible substitutions of synonyms within candidate phrases.

Karan et al. [15] evaluate classification algorithms and features for the purpose of collocation extraction in Croatian. They use several classification algorithms and conclude that the SVM classifier performs best on bigrams and the decision trees on trigrams.

Ljubešić et al. [16] compare two approaches to the ranking of collocates - the logDice method and the word embedding method - on two Slovenian data sets. The quantitative evaluation shows that the machine-learning approach gives better results, but the lexicographers consider the obtained listings of collocates to be very similar.

A detailed systematic literature review on collocation extraction can be found in [17].

## 3    Methodology

One of the main goals of our research is to extract metaphorical collocations in Croatian, English, German and Italian. We also want to find out if there are similarities and peculiarities in the creation and extraction of metaphorical collocations in different languages.

We are currently in the first phase of research, in which we are detecting the basic metaphorical collocations and investigating their composition. The second phase will involve the detection of translation equivalents and their extraction.

There are no evaluation resources for extracting metaphorical collocations. In order to evaluate our own experiments, we are forced to develop suitable gold standard reference data sets ourselves.

The following subsections describe the main steps we have taken so far. First, we describe the selected corpora. Then we give an overview of the grammatical relations of Croatian, German and English as used in the Sketch Engine [18] tool for creating the lists of word sketches.

The study begins with the noun as a part of speech, since it was determined to be the most productive part of speech in terms of creating metaphorical collocations. Therefore, the most frequent nouns in the Croatian language were identified. We used the Croatian Web Corpus [19] for that purpose. Since nouns that are not productive in collocation matching (e.g. proper nouns) also appeared among the identified nouns, such nouns were additionally excluded manually.

The same procedure was performed for the comparable corpora enTenTen20 for English [20], deTenTen18 [20] for German, and itTenTen20 [20] for Italian. The nouns overlapping in four identical corpora were selected to ensure empirically relevant data. Then, the collocation profiles of the most frequently occurring noun "year" are analyzed in Croatian ("godina"), English and German ("Jahr"), and the collocation compounds expressing a metaphorical meaning are manually annotated.

## 3.1   Corpora

As mentioned earlier, for the Croatian language, we used the Croatian Web Corpus [19], which consists of texts collected on the Internet and contains over 1.2 billion words. The hrWaC corpus was PoS-tagged using the MULTEXT-East Croatian POS tag-set version 5 [21].

The English Web Corpus (enTenTen20) [20] is an English language corpus consisting of texts collected from the Internet. The latest version of the enTenTen corpus contains more than 38 billion words. The authors state that sample texts from the largest web domains, which account for 40% of all texts in the corpus, were manually reviewed and content with poor text quality and spam was removed. The corpus was tagged with the TreeTagger tool using the English Web 2020 part-of-speech tag set.

The German Web Corpus (deTenTen18) [20] is a German corpus that also consists of texts collected from the Internet. The latest version includes 5.3 billion words. The corpus contains lemmatization including gender lemmas and part-of-speech tagging. It was annotated with the RFTagger tool using the German RFTagger part-of-speech tag-set.

## 3.2   Grammatical Relations and Annotation

When we use the Word Sketch function in the Sketch Engine, we get a list of word's collocates and other words in their environment, organized into categories called grammatical relations. These are, for example, words that serve as the subject of the verb, words that modify the word, etc. Each language/corpus has differently defined grammatical relations, which are specified by rules in the Sketch grammar. Sketch Engine uses the logDice measure [22] to identify collocations.

By default, the word sketches are sorted so that the sketches with the highest logDice score come first. logDice can be thought of as "typicality". A high score means that the collocate is frequently found with the base and there are not many other bases with which the collocate is combined. In this case, it is a strong collocation. A low score means that the collocate tends to combine not only with that particular base, but with many other words. In this case, it is a weak collocation.

The linguists analyzed the lists thus obtained for the most frequent word in all three languages (Croatian, German and English) - "godina", "Jahr" and "year" - and performed the annotation of collocations and metaphorical collocations.

Before compiling the final list of metaphorical collocations for each language, the experts held several discussion sessions until they felt confident enough to distinguish between the different types of collocations and thus extract metaphorical collocations. Two linguists per language participated in the task. The annotation varies in detail among the languages, so we provide the details for each language below.

The preliminary results of the analysis show that in all three languages, the most productive grammatical relations and combinations of parts of speech with respect to metaphorical collocations are combinations of an adjective in the function of a collocate + a noun in the function of the base and a verb in the function of the collocate + a noun in the function of the base. It is also noticed that phrasal verbs in English make a productive relation in terms of forming metaphorical collocations.

**Croatian.** For the word "godina", the Sketch Engine generates a total of 21 grammatical relations: *kakav?, oba-u-genitivu, u-genitivu-n, a-koga-čega, n-koga-čega, koga-što, particip, prijedlog, infinitive, koga-čega, s-prilogom, a-koga-što, a-komu-čemu, komu-čemu, glagol-ispred-prijedloga, prijedlog-iza, veznik, koordinacija, imenica-iza-prijedloga, biti-kakav?* and *subjek-od.* There are 1,747 unique collocates dispersed over different grammatical relations out of a total of 5,019 collocation candidates. After extensive analysis by linguists, it was decided that the following grammatical relations are most productive and relevant for the formation and identification of metaphorical collocations in Croatian: **kakav?** (like what), **n-koga-čega** (two nouns - one in genitive), **koga-što** (accusative), **subjekt-od** (subject of), **particip** (participle), **biti-kakav?** (be like what). Detailed explanations on why those relations were chosen can be found in [1] and [23]. The annotated data set for Croatian also includes labels for the type of metaphorical collocation, such as for example "lexicalized metaphor", "metaphor", "term-metonymy", etc.

The statistics of the annotated data set for Croatian is shown in Table 1.

**Table 1.** Statistics of the annotated data set for Croatian.

| Relation | # of cands | # of colls | # of m-colls | Ratio of m-colls |
|----------|-----------|-----------|-------------|------------------|
| kakav? | 99 | 54 | 54 | 55% |
| n-koga-čega | 100 | 41 | 38 | 41% |
| koga-što | 100 | 41 | 41 | 41% |
| particip | 100 | 16 | 11 | 11% |
| subjekt-od | 100 | 30 | 30 | 30% |
| biti-kakav? | 74 | 20 | 20 | 55% |
| **Total** | **673** | **202** | **193** | **29%** |

**German.** For the word "Jahr", the Sketch Engine generates a total of 18 grammatical relations: *Constructions, modifiers of Jahr, verbs with Jahr as subject, genitive objects of Jahr, nouns with Jahr as genitive object, dative objects of Jahr, nouns with Jahr as dative object, accusative objects of Jahr, nouns with Jahr as accusative object, verbs with Jahr as genitive object, verbs with Jahr as dative object, verbs with Jahr as accusative object, Jahr and/or ..., prepositions with Jahr as object, prepositional phrases, prepositional objects in dative, prepositional objects in accusative, prepositional objects in genitive.* After extensive analysis by linguists, it was decided that the following grammatical relations are most productive and relevant for the formation and identification of metaphorical col-locations in German: **modifiers of x** (e.g. kommende Jahr), **verbs with x as subject** (e.g. das Jahr beginnt), **verbs with x as accusative object** (e.g. Jahr verbringen) and **nouns with x as genitive object** (e.g. Anfang des Jahres). Similar to the Croatian dataset, the annotated data set for German also includes labels for the type of metaphorical collocation, such as "lexicalized metaphor", "metaphor", "term-metonymy", etc.

The statistics of the annotated data set for German is shown in Table 2.

**Table 2.** Statistics of the annotated dataset for German.

| Relatiom | # of cands | # of colls | # of m-colls | Ratio of m-colls |
|---|---|---|---|---|
| Modifier of x | 105 | 57 | 41 | 39% |
| Verbs with x as subject | 100 | 86 | 13 | 13% |
| Verbs with x as accusative object | 101 | 66 | 33 | 33% |
| Nouns with x as genitive object | 403 | 349 | 51 | 13% |
| **Total** | **709** | **558** | **138** | **19%** |

**English.** For the word "year", the Sketch Engine generates a total of 27 grammatical relations out of which 14 are of the type verbs with particle "x" and "year" as object: *modifiers of "year", nouns modified by "year", verbs with "year" as object, verbs with "year" as subject, "year" and/or ..., prepositional phrases, adjective predicates of "year", "year" is a ..., year's ..., possessors of "year", pronominal possessors of "year", ... is a "year", verbs with particle "x" and "year" as object, usage patterns.* After extensive analysis by linguists, it was decided that the following grammatical relations are most productive and relevant for the formation and identification of metaphorical collocations in English: **modifiers of "year", verbs with "year" as object, verbs with "year" as subject,** and **verbs with particle "x" and "year" as object.** For English, there are no annotations yet for the type of metaphorical collocation. There are also no annotated collocations for a part of the list, but only metaphorical collocations are annotated.

The statistics of the annotated data set for Croatian can be found in Table 3.

**Table 3.** Statistics of the annotated data set for English.

| Relation | # of cands | # of m-colls | Ratio of m-colls |
|---|---|---|---|
| modifiers of "year" | 94 | 28 | 30% |
| verbs with "year" as object | 98 | 13 | 13% |
| verbs with "year" as subject | 100 | 7 | 7% |
| verbs with particle "x" and "year" as object | 541 | 109 | 20% |
| **Total** | **833** | **157** | **19%** |

### 3.3 Experiment

We experimented with models for automatic identification of metaphorical collocations from the lists created by the linguists described in the previous section. We trained the models for Croatian German and English, as they are fully completed at the time of writing.

**Preprocessing.** Before the model could be trained, all non-standard language variants, misspelled words, incorrectly lemmatized forms, duplicated lemmas, etc. had to be removed or corrected from the list of collocations and metaphorical collocations.

**Models.** We experimented with several models, including Support Vector Machines (SVM), Multilayer Perceptron, C4.5, and Random Forest. When training the models, we performed 10-fold cross-validation.

**Features.** As features for model training, we used collocation frequency, logDice, grammatical relation, and pretrained word embeddings (containing 300 vectors for each word) as implemented in fastText [24]. While frequency and logDice are statistical measures, grammatical relation represents syntactic information and word embeddings represent semantic information as they are vector representations of the context in which a word occurs.

## 4    Results

We evaluated the classification models based on Accuracy (percentage of correctly classified instances), Precision (proportion of correctly classified positive instances out of all positive instances in the system output), Recall (proportion of correctly identified positive instances out of all instances that should have been identified as positive) and F-measure (a measure that combines the results of Precision and Recall).

Table 4 shows the results for the Croatian data set, Table 5 the results for the German data set, and Table 6 for the English data set.

**Table 4.** Results for Croatian data set.

| Model | Accuracy | Precision | Recall | F-measure |
|---|---|---|---|---|
| SVM | 71.4706 % | 0.715 | 0.715 | 0.714 |
| Multilayer Perceptron | **75.2941 %** | **0.754** | **0.753** | **0.752** |
| C4.5 | 69.7059 % | 0.697 | 0.697 | 0.697 |
| Random Forest | 68.8235 % | 0.688 | 0.688 | 0.688 |

**Table 5.** Results for German data set.

| Model | Accuracy | Precision | Recall | F-measure |
|---|---|---|---|---|
| SVM | **82.9023 %** | **0.865** | 0.932 | **0.897** |
| Multilayer Perceptron | 79.454 % | 0.853 | 0.898 | 0.875 |
| C4.5 | 76.5805 % | 0.855 | 0.853 | 0.854 |
| Random Forest | 81.3218 % | 0.826 | **0.971** | 0.893 |

From the results in the tables, we can see that all the models used perform similarly within each language, with the best results obtained with the Multilayer Perceptron model for the Croatian data set (Acc 75.2941%, P 0.754, R 0.753, F 0.752), with the SVM model for the German data set (Acc 82.9023%, P 0.865, F0.897) and with the Random Forest model for the English data set (Acc 72.242%, R 0.911, F0.826). We obtained the best Recall (0.865) for the German data set with Random forest model and the best Precision (0.788) for the English data set with the C4.5 model. Comparing the results between the languages, the best results are obtained for German.

We also found that the inclusion of word embeddings in the features improved Accuracy by almost 10%.

**Table 6.** Results for English data set.

| Model | Accuracy | Precision | Recall | F-measure |
|---|---|---|---|---|
| SVM | 67.6157 % | 0.743 | 0.842 | 0.789 |
| Multilayer Perceptron | 67.9715 % | 0.752 | 0.830 | 0.789 |
| C4.5 | 69.9288 % | **0.788** | 0.798 | 0.793 |
| Random Forest | **72.242 %** | 0.755 | **0.911** | **0.826** |

## 5    Conclusion

In this paper, we have described the steps that we and our colleagues on the project team have taken to identify metaphorical collocations as a subset of the general category of collocations in different languages. So far, we have set the theoretical and methodological framework and taken the first steps to create the golden standard for Croatian, English and German. We have also determined the set of nouns we will use in our study and analyzed the word sketches for the most frequent noun in all three corpora - Croatian ("godina"), German ("Jahr") and English ("year").

The project team linguists also selected the most productive grammatical relations for the formation of metaphorical collocations. For Croatian, these are: kakav? (like what), n-koga-čega (two nouns - one in the genitive), koga-što (accusative), subject-od (subject of), particip (participle), biti-kakav? (to be like what). For German these are: modifiers of x, verbs with x as subject, verbs with x as accusative object, and nouns with x as genitive object. For English these are: modifiers of "year", verbs with "year" as object, verbs with "year" as subject, and verbs with particles "x" and "year" as object.

The preliminary results of the analysis show that in all three languages the most productive grammatical relations and combinations of parts of speech in terms of metaphorical collocations are combinations of an adjective in the function of a collocate + a noun in the function of the base and a verb in the function of the collocate + a noun in the function of the base. Moreover, it is noted that phrasal verbs in English are a productive relation for the formation of metaphorical collocations.

The percentage of metaphorical collocations in the annotated data sets is slightly different for different languages - for Croatian it is 29%, for German 19% and for English 19%. It remains to be clarified whether these differences are due to different characteristics of the individual languages or to the different approaches of the annotators. It has already been noted in our project meetings that determining whether a collocation is also a metaphorical collocation might be subject to different approaches, since there are different types of metaphorical collocations (e.g. lexicalized metaphorical collocations, term, metonymy, etc.). It was also noted that further new guidelines need to be found to specify the annotation process for all languages as new insights are gained through the research process.

We also trained models for automatic recognition of metaphorical collocations from the candidate lists for Croatian, German and English created by the linguists. We experimented with four different models - Support Vector Machines (SVM), Multilayer Perceptron, C4.5, and Random Forest. We used collocation frequency, logDice, grammatical relation and pretrained word embeddings as features in model training. We obtained the best results with the Multilayer Perceptron model for the Croatian dataset (Acc 75.2941%, P 0.754, R 0.753, F 0.752), with the SVM model for the German data set (Acc 82.9023%, P 0.865, F0.897) and with the Random Forest model for the English data set (Acc 72.242%, R 0.911, F0.826). We obtained the best Recall (0.865) for the German data set with Random forest model and the best Precision (0.788) for the English data set with the C4.5 model. We also found that the inclusion of word embeddings significantly improved the results. The results we obtained seem to be promising, but they can only be considered as preliminary results since they are based on only one most common noun. It remains to be seen how the data sets will behave for other nouns.

Our future work includes compiling similar lists and conducting experiments for other nouns. We also plan to test other measures and linguistic features to find methods that give the best results in extracting metaphorical collocations.

**Acknowledgement.** This work has been fully supported by Croatian Science Foundation under the project *Metaphorical collocations - Syntagmatic word combinations between semantics and pragmatics* (IP-2020-02-6319).

# References

1. Stojić, A., Košuta, N.: Izrada inventara metaforičkih kolokacija u hrvatskome jeziku - na primjeru imenice godina. Fluminensia **34**(1), 9–29 (2022)
2. Shutova, E.: Models of Metaphor in NLP. In: Proceedings of the 48th Annual Meeting of the Association for Computational Linguistics, pp. 688–697. Association for Computational Linguistics, Uppsala, Sweden (2010)
3. Tsvetkov, Y., Boytsov, L., Gershman, A., Nyberg, E., Dyer, C.: Metaphor detection with cross-lingual model transfer. In: Proceedings of the 52nd Annual Meeting of the Association for Computational Linguistics, pp. 248–258. Association for Computational Linguistics, Baltimore (2014)
4. Choi, M., Lee, S., Choi, E., Park, H., Lee, J., Lee, D., Lee, J.: MelBERT: metaphor detection via contextualized late interaction using metaphorical identification theories. In: Proceedings of the 2021 Conference of the North American Chapter of the Association for Computational Linguistics: Human Language Technologies, pp. 1763–1773. Association for Computational Linguistics (2021)
5. Wan, H., Lin, J., Du, J., Shen, D., Zhang, M.: Enhancing metaphor detection by gloss-based interpretations. In: Findings of the Association for Computational Linguistics: ACL-IJCNLP 2021, pp. 1971–1981. Association for Computational Linguistics (2021)
6. Church, K.W., Patrick, H.: Word association norms, mutual information, and lexicography. Comput. Linguist. **16**(1), 22–29 (1990)
7. Dunning, T.: Accurate methods for the statistics of surprise and coincidence. Comput. Linguist. **19**(1), 61–74 (1993)
8. Kita, K., et al.: A comparative study of automatic extraction of collocations from corpora: mutual information vs. cost criteria. J. Natural Lang. Process., 21–33 (1994)
9. Smadja, F.: Retrieving collocations from text: Xtract. Comput. Linguist. **19**(1), 143–78 (1993)
10. Thanopoulos, A., Fakotakis, N., Kokkinakis, G: Comparative evaluation of collocation extraction metrics. In: Proceedings of the Third International Conference on Language Resources and Evaluation, pp. 620–25 (2002)
11. Seretan, V., Wehrli, E.: Multilingual collocation extraction with a syntactic parse. Lang. Resour. Eval. **43**(1), 71–85 (2009)

12. Lin, D.: Extracting collocations from text corpora. In: Proceedings of the First Workshop on Computational Terminology, pp. 57–63 (1998)
13. Krenn, B.: Collocation Mining: Exploiting Corpora for Collocation Identification and Representation. Entropy, 1–6 (2000)
14. Pearce, D.: Synonymy in Collocation Extraction. In: Proceedings of the Workshop on WordNet and Other Lexical Resources, Second Meeting of the North American Chapter of the Association for Computational Linguistics, pp. 41–46. Association for Computational Linguistics, (2021)
15. Karan, M., Šnajder, J., Dalbelo Bašić, B.: Evaluation of Classification Algorithms and Features for Collocation Extraction in Croatian. In: Proceedings of the Eighth International Conference on Language Resources and Evaluation (LREC'12), pp. 657–62. European Language Resources Association (ELRA), Istanbul, Turkey (2012)
16. Ljubešić, N., Logar, N., Kosem, I.: Collocation ranking: frequency vs semantics. Slovenscina 2.0, **9**(2), 41–70 (2021)
17. Brkic Bakaric, M., Nacinovic Prskao, L., Matetic, M.: Insights into automatic extraction of metaphorical collocations. Rasprave (Manuscript submitted for publication)
18. Kilgarriff, A. et al.: The Sketch Engine: Ten Years On. Lexicography, pp. 7–36 (2014)
19. Ljubešić, N., Erjavec, T.: hrWaC and slWac: compiling web corpora for croatian and slovene. In: Habernal, I., Matoušek, V. (eds.) TSD 2011. LNCS (LNAI), vol. 6836, pp. 395–402. Springer, Heidelberg (2011). https://doi.org/10.1007/978-3-642-23538-2_50
20. Jakubíček, M. et al.: The TenTen Corpus Family. In: Proceedings of the 7th International Corpus Linguistics Conference CL, pp. 125–127 (2013)
21. Ljubešić, N. et al.: New inflectional lexicons and training corpora for improved morphosyntactic annotation of Croatian and Serbian. In: Proceedings of the Tenth International Conference on Language Resources and Evaluation (LREC 2016). European Language Resources Association (ELRA), Parise, France (2016)
22. Rychlý, P.: A Lexicographer-Friendly Association Score. In: Proceedings of the Recent Advances in Slavonic Natural Language Processing, pp. 6–9 (2008)
23. Stojić, A., Košuta, N.: METAPHORISCHE KOLLOKATIONEN - EINBLICKE IN EINE KORPUSBASIERTE STUDIE. Linguistica **61**(1), 81–91 (2022)
24. Grave, E., Bojanowski, P., Gupta, P., Joulin, A., Mikolov, T.: Learning Word Vectors for 157 Languages. In: Proceedings of the International Conference on Language Resources and Evaluation (LREC 2018), pp. 3483–3487 (2018). https://fasttext.cc/

# Automatic Grammar Correction of Commas in Czech Written Texts: Comparative Study

Jakub Machura[1] , Adam Frémund[2] , and Jan Švec[2(✉)]

[1] Department of Czech Language, Masaryk University, Brno, Czech Republic
machura@phil.muni.cz
[2] Department of Cybernetics, University of West Bohemia, Pilsen, Czech Republic
{afremund,honzas}@kky.zcu.cz

**Abstract.** The task of grammatical error correction is a widely studied field of natural language processing where the traditional rule-based approaches compete with the machine learning methods. The rule-based approach benefits mainly from a wide knowledge base available for a given language. On the contrary, the transfer learning methods and especially the use of pre-trained Transformers have the ability to be trained from a huge number of texts in a given language. In this paper, we focus on the task of automatic correction of missing commas in Czech written texts and we compare the rule-based approach with the Transformer-based model trained for this task.

**Keywords:** Grammatical error correction · Linguistic rules · Transfer learning

## 1 Introduction

Sentence punctuation is a very important linguistic feature that helps the reader better understand the complex text flow. While the sentence separating punctuation (such as full stops and question marks) is crucial for marking the basic sentence units in the text, the intra-sentence punctuation (mostly commas) helps to structure the sentence on syntactic and semantic levels [2,18].

If we focus on tasks where the missing or wrongly-inserted punctuation is restored, two main tasks arise (1) punctuation restoration in speech transcripts from automatic speech recognition and (2) grammatical error correction in written texts. The first task is widely studied because the restored punctuation dramatically improves the readability of the recognized transcript. The current methods use sequence-to-sequence mapping or token classification. The neural

This work was supported by the project of specific research *Lexikon a gramatika češtiny II - 2022* (Lexicon and Grammar of Czech II - 2022; project No. MUNI/A/1137/2021) and by the Czech Science Foundation (GA CR), project No. GA22-27800S.

P. Sojka et al. (Eds.): TSD 2022, LNAI 13502, pp. 113–124, 2022.
https://doi.org/10.1007/978-3-031-16270-1_10

networks with recurrent units (such as LSTM or GRU) or self-attention mechanism (mostly Transformer) are used. The models can use only the lexical information [4,23] or also the acoustic features extracted from speech [9,12].

In his paper, we focus on the grammatical error correction in written text. Also, this task is widely studied in many languages (for example [3,7]). We present a comparison of two approaches for a specific task of automatic correction of commas in Czech written texts. We first introduce the typology of rules for writing commas in Czech language (Sect. 2). Then we describe the rule-based (Sect. 3.1) and the Transformer-based (Sect. 3.2) approaches which are evaluated on the same datasets described in Sect. 4. Section 5 presents the results of experimental evaluation and Sect. 6 concludes the paper.

## 2    Writing Commas in Czech Language

Regarding punctuation, the main attention is given to writing commas. The comma is the most frequent punctuation mark not only for Czech but also for Slovak, English or German (see [5,23]). Traditionally, writing commas in Czech is part of the orthography. However, rather than orthographic rules at the level of words, these are rules of higher syntactic units. The rules for writing commas are codified in *Pravidla českého pravopisu* (Rules of Czech Orthography) [1] and in *Akademická příručka českého jazyka* (Academic Handbook of the Czech Language) [19]. Thus, we would say that knowing how to use commas is a part of "knowing how to write".

Nunberg [17] recognizes two main classes of commas. He sees a difference between a comma which separates structures at the same level (the *separator comma*), and a comma which delimits the boundaries between syntactic structures at different levels (the *delimiter comma*). The *separator comma* is inserted between members of coordinated sentence elements of the same type (e.g., multiple subject, object, predicate etc.) or of coordinated clauses within the sentence (asyndeton, or parataxis). The *delimiter comma* marks the boundaries between the main clause and the subordinate clause (hypotaxis), vocatives, or parenthetical expressions. In view of this classification, we can probably think of the existence of a third type of comma which cannot be obviously assimilated to either of these others. Its presence affects the meaning of the utterance (see Sect. 2, D.ii).

### 2.1    Typology of the Comma Insertion Place

To formalize the linguistic rules, it was necessary not only to consider the classification of commas according to which textual categories they separate but also to specify the place (boundary) in the sentence structure where the comma is inserted. Such a typology was first outlined in [7] and it is extended and described in detail below. In addition, we created a small random sample of 183 sentences and classified the commas in the text according to the established typology (see Table 1).

## A. The Comma Precedes a Connective

A connective (conjunction, relative pronoun, or relative adverb) or group of connectives indicates:

(i) the boundary between main clauses or multiple elements of a sentence which are not in simple coordination relation (see "Koordinace" in [10]):
*Pozvali jsme Karla, **ale** přišel Petr. (We invited Charles, **but** Peter came.)*
***Buď** přijedou dnes večer, **nebo** zítra ráno. (They will come **either** tonight* ***or** tomorrow morning.)*

(ii) the boundary between the main clause and subordinate clause (see "Souvětí" in [10]):
*Otec neví, **na jaký** úřad má jít. (Father does not know **what** bureau to go in.)*

(iii) apposition with an additional modification:
*Společnost dosáhla nového vrcholu v zisku, **a to** 220 milionů korun. (The company has reached a new peak in profit, **namely** CZK 220 million)*

## B. The Comma Is Located Between Two Clauses Without the (close) Presence of a Connective

(i) Connections of clauses in asyndetic structures (see "Asyndeton" in [10]):
*Petr má rád červené víno, jeho žena miluje bílé. (Peter likes the red wine, his wife loves the white one.)*

(ii) A connective usually stands on the left side of the subordinate clause, and the subordinate clause is separated asyndetically from the right side:
*Auto, které stálo celou noc před dome, se rozjelo. (A car, which was standing in front of the house the whole night, moved off.)*

(iii) And finally, sentences containing direct speech or quotation:
*"Musíte jít na operaci, " řekl lékař. ("You must have surgery!" said the doctor.)*

## C. The Comma Separates Individual Components of Multiplied Syntactic Structure

(i) Multiple sentence elements or enumeration. We assume that multiple sentence elements group together words that agree in some grammatical category - e.g. part of speech or case. If it has more than two members, most often only the last two members are separated by a conjunction. Other members are separated asyndetically, only by the comma (see "Koordinace" in [10]):
*Mezi oblíbené turistické destinace letos patří Španělsko, Francie, Itálie a Chorvatsko. (This year Spain, France, Italy, and Croatia belong to popular tourist destinations.)*

(ii) The apposition – construction of two elements, usually noun phrases, which are placed side by side and the second element somehow describes the first element - is another type of structure where is obligatory to put the comma:
*Sněžka, nejvyšší hora české republiky (Sněžka, the highest mountain of the Czech Republic)*

The main difference between (i) and (ii) is characterized by the fact that components of (i) refer to different entities. However, components of (ii) relate fully or partially to a single entity (see "Apozice" in [10]).

### D. The Comma Might but Might Not Be Inserted or Affects the Meaning of the Utterance

(i) The writer sometimes has the option of whether or not to write a comma. These include parentheses or phrasal idioms:
   *Zítra(,) bohužel(,) přijít nemohu. (Unfortunately, I can't come tomorrow.)*
(ii) In some cases, the insertion of the comma changes the meaning of the utterance. The typical examples in Czech are a restrictive attribute and nonrestrictive attribute (see "Přívlastek" in [10]):
   *Jídlo, koupené v obchodních domě, jsem uložil do ledničky. (I put the food, which was bought in the mall, into the fridge* - all food was bought in the mall and I put all this food in the fridge.*)*
   *Jídlo koupené v obchodním domě jsem uložil do ledničky. (I put food bought in the mall into the fridge* - only food which was bought in the mall was put in the fridge.*)*

### E. Others
This includes the remaining cases, such as:

(i) vocatives:
   *Pojď sem, Petře! (Come here, Peter!)*
(i) particles and interjections that must be separated from the text by commas:
   *Haló, je tam někdo? (Hey, is anybody there?)*
   *Zase jsi ve škole zlobil, že? (You were naughty at school again, weren't you?)*

**Table 1.** *Estimated distribution of commas according to the presented typology. Total number of commas in the sample: 183*

| Typology | # cases | frequency |
|---|---|---|
| A. comma precede the connective | 94 | 51.4% |
| B. comma without the presence of the connective | 49 | 26.8% |
| C. components of multiplied syntactic structure | 31 | 16.9% |
| D. comma might but might not be inserted | 8 | 4.4% |
| E. others | 1 | 0.5% |

## 3    Automatic Grammar Correction of Commas

The work presented in this paper was motivated by our experiments, where we initially compared the rule-based SET parser (Sect. 3.1) for automatic grammar correction of commas in Czech texts with the BERT-based method proposed in [23]. The BERT-based model was trained for slightly different task – restoring punctuation in recognized speech transcriptions. It is capable of inserting commas, full-stops and question marks. Based on the promising results, we trained a new model targeted only to the comma correction task (Sect. 3.2).

## 3.1 Rule-based Approach

The SET system, firstly introduced in [14], was originally developed as a syntactic parser that matches patterns within text. Besides the main grammar for syntactic analysis, the system also contains specialised sets of patterns that deal with subtasks of the automatic language checking (e.g. commas detection and correction, subject-predicate agreement, capitalization, ungrammatical structures such as zeugma, incorrect pronoun forms, etc.). These sets of patterns ("grammars") are used as the foundation of modules for the new online proofreader tool for the Czech language [8]. Before matching patterns, the text has to be tokenized and tagged. For tokenization purposes, we use the *unitok* tokenizer [22]. After thorough testing and comparison of the result [16], we decided to use two systems for morphological analysis: (1) the *Majka* analyzer [26] and *Desamb* tagger [25], (2) the *MorphoDita* system [21].

Based on the comma insertion rules, the SET parser produces pseudo-syntactic trees that indicate where a comma should or should not be inserted in the sentence structure (by hanging a particular word under the <c> or <n> node), as illustrated in Fig. 1.

**Input:** Buď mi řekneš pravdu nebo je konec.

**Rule:**  TMPL: $CONJ1 $SPACE* $NEG $CONJ2   MARK 3 <c>

        $CONJ1(lemma): ať buď buďto
        $CONJ2(word): nebo či anebo
        $NEG(tag not): k8

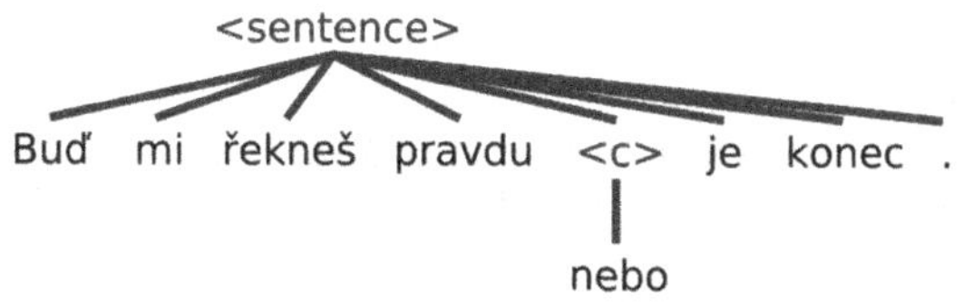

```
              <sentence>

Buď   mi   řekneš   pravdu   <c>   je   konec   .
                              |
                             nebo
```

**Output:** Buď mi řekneš pravdu, nebo je konec.

**Fig. 1.** One of the existing comma insertion rules, and its realization on a sample Czech sentence: *Buď mi řekneš pravdu nebo je konec* (missing comma before *nebo* - *Either you tell me the truth or it's over.*). In this case, the rule matches double-conjunction *buď - nebo* and if the conjunction *nebo* is not preceded by another conjunction (**$NEG(tag not): k8**), the analyzer inserts a comma before *nebo*.

The SET parser operates with a total of 1,400 rules. To formalize rules for type A (the comma precedes a connective) was the least complicated and had the highest recall. We can observe that Pareto's principle applies here - about 100 rules for subordinating conjunctions and relative pronouns cover 40% of all commas that should be inserted in a text. Next, we formalized rules for about ¼ of the commas of type B (the comma without the presence of the connective). These rules make use of the position of predicates or apply Wackernagel's law on the position of clitics in the sentence. The grammatical agreement of the case of components within a nominal phrase played a key role in formulating more than 600 rules for type C (components of multiplied syntactic structure). For this category, we also tried to make use of the semantics of words using the *Word Sketch* function in the *Sketch Engine* software that provides a summary of a word's grammatical and collocational behaviour [11]. Nevertheless, the parser finds just over 10% of the commas of type C (that is little less than 2% of searched commas). The remaining categories D, and E are dealt with marginally - partly because the identification of the vocative based on morphological analysis is quite unreliable partly because the comma affects the meaning of the utterance.

The advantage of rule-based systems is the ability to correct or extend existing rules. For example, creating rules for the conjunction *ale* (lit. but) is a more complex task because *ale* can also be a particle or an interjection. The rules comprehensively evaluated in [13] inserted a comma before the conjunction *ale* with the precision of 94%. Now, after modifying these rules, the precision increased to 96.2% while maintaining the same recall. [1]

### 3.2 Transformer-Based Approach

Recent advances in using transformer models for NLP have inspired us to use Czech pre-trained RoBERTa model for automatic grammar correction of commas. Then this approach has been compared to the rule-based approach.

We used our own pre-trained model from a collection of web data processed in our web mining tool [24], Common Crawl data[2] and texts collected from the Czech part of Wikipedia. We followed all the training steps, mentioned in [15], for pre-training the Czech RoBERTa model. As suggested we used dynamic masking of the tokens. This strategy generates the masking pattern every time a sequence is fed to the model. Also, the pre-training procedure does not use Next Sentence Prediction loss in contrast with the BERT model [6]. For tokenizing the input sequence we used Byte-Pair Encoding (BPE), introduced in [20], with a subword vocabulary containing 50K units. This implementation of BPE uses bytes instead of Unicode characters as the base subword units.

We used the ADAM optimization with linear warmup up to learning rate= $4 \cdot 10^{-4}$ for the first 24K steps followed by linear decay to 0. As the [15] suggested we pre-trained the model for 500K steps.

---

[1] You can try out the rule-based commas detection and correction at http://opravidlo. cz/.

[2] https://commoncrawl.org/.

For this experiment, we proposed RoBERTA model extended by a few extra classification layers. An input sequence is preprocessed using the tokenizer and special tokens are added (as shown in the Fig. 2). Next, we use the Czech pre-trained RoBERTa model with output dimension d=768. RoBERTa last hidden states are transformed by four regular densely-connected neural network layers. Three of these layers use the element-wise ReLU activation function and the last layer uses the softmax activation function. The last layer output defines whether the comma should be placed right after the current token. The overall scheme of the proposed neural network architecture is depicted in the Fig. 2.

As the training data set used for fine-tuning, we have used 10 GB of raw text extracted from the Czech CommonCrawl data set. Because the RoBERTa's output is related to input tokens (not words), we assigned the target label ("," for comma, "0" for no comma) to each token of the word, which is followed by a comma (as shown at the Fig. 2). In the prediction phase, it is necessary to combine the predictions for the partial tokens into a word-level predictions using a per-word pooling. We use a simple average pooling algorithm to obtain the word-level predictions. As the model defines this experiment as a two classes classification per each token, we use standard categorical cross-entropy loss. For optimization, we use the standard Adam optimization algorithm.

We use epoch size equal to 10K sequences, the batch size equal to 45 and epoch size equal to 25, 50 and 75. During the fine-tuning, we use linear learning rate with values starting at $1^{-4}$, ending at $1^{-5}$. The maximum sequence length is set to 128.

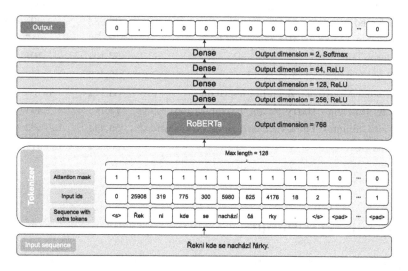

**Fig. 2.** Proposed model architecture. "0" and "," in the output layer indicates where the commas should be placed. It is necessary to post-process the model output and align the commas at the end of the words composed of multiple tokens.

## 4    Evaluation Data Sets

The same data presented in [13] were used to evaluate and compare the methods described above. These texts were prepared specifically for the automatic insertion of commas, and since the data are exactly the same, it is also possible to compare the current results with testing done in the past. In total, 7 texts of different nature and styles were used: 3 sources from the Internet (blog texts, horoscopes and selected chapters from the *Internet Language Reference Book*), and 4 fiction books (2 Czech authors: one classic – K. čapek, one contemporary – S. Monyová; 2 Czech translations of English authors: J. K. Rowling, N. Gaiman).

Blog texts and horoscopes were independently corrected by three proofreaders and the agreement rate among them was very high [13]. Selected chapters from the reference book were written by linguists from the Academy of Sciences, and for the remaining texts, we assumed that they were proofread before being published. The size of the individual texts and the number of commas in them can be found in Table 2. Some may question whether this data is large enough for objective testing. On the other hand, the testing was done on real texts with their actual size and the writers themselves usually need to review texts of this size or smaller. Thus, we conclude that chosen data are appropriate for testing and evaluation.

**Table 2.** *Statistics of the test data* [13].

| Testing set | # words | # commas |
|---|---|---|
| Selected blogs | 20,883 | 1,805 |
| Internet Language Reference Book | 3,039 | 417 |
| Horoscopes 2015 | 57,101 | 5,101 |
| Karel Čapek - selected novels | 46,489 | 5,498 |
| Simona Monyová - Ženu ani květinou | 33,112 | 3,156 |
| J.K. Rowling - Harry Potter 1 (translation) | 74,783 | 7,461 |
| Neil Gaiman - The Graveyard Book (translation) | 55,444 | 5,573 |
| Overall | 290,851 | 29,011 |

## 5    Experimental Results

As explained in [13], probably the fairest evaluation method is the one where all commas are removed from a text and a selected tool inserts commas back into the text. Then, we can measure how many commas the tool inserted correctly and incorrectly in comparison with the original (reference) text. We use standard precision, recall and F1 score on detected commas.

The texts with commas removed, but still containing all the remaining punctuation, were first processed using the rule-based SET parser and the BERT-based punctuation filling method. The BERT-based baseline was implemented the same way as in [23] and was able to insert three punctuation symbols: comma, full stop and question mark. The results are shown in Table 3 and Table 4.

The overall F1 performance of the BERT-based model was above the rule-based approach. The performance gain is significantly higher on the first three datasets (blogs, the language reference book and horoscopes). The success of the trainable model motivated the work presented in this paper. We used the RoBERTA model and we fine-tuned it only on the comma insertion task. The results are summarized in Table 5. In comparison with the BERT baseline, the F1 scores improved for all types of evaluation texts.

If we compare the Roberta-based method with the rule-based baseline, the Precision scores are approximately the same. The difference is in the Recall scores, where the Roberta-based method provides consistently higher scores. The consistent increase in Recall (from 58.8% to 89.5%) also implies the increase in F1 score (from 72.7% to 92.7%).

**Table 3.** *Results: rule-based approach.*

|                                                   | P [%] | R [%] | F1 [%] |
|---------------------------------------------------|-------|-------|--------|
| Selected blogs                                    | 95.7  | 61.4  | 74.8   |
| Internet Language Reference Book                  | 92.7  | 42.5  | 58.2   |
| Horoscopes 2015                                   | 96.9  | 71.3  | 82.2   |
| Karel Čapek - selected novels                     | 94.2  | 41.9  | 58.1   |
| Simona Monyová - Ženu ani květinou                | 92.2  | 66.2  | 77.1   |
| J.K. Rowling - Harry Potter 1 (translation)       | 94.7  | 61.7  | 74.7   |
| Neil Gaiman - The Graveyard Book (translation)    | 96.3  | 56.5  | 71.2   |
| Overall performance                               | 95.1  | 58.8  | 72.7   |

**Table 4.** *Results: Transformer-based approach (baseline BERT [23]).*

|                                                   | P [%] | R [%] | F1 [%] |
|---------------------------------------------------|-------|-------|--------|
| Selected blogs                                    | 94.5  | 81.6  | 87.6   |
| Internet Language Reference Book                  | 93.7  | 67.4  | 78.4   |
| Horoscopes 2015                                   | 94.6  | 88.4  | 91.4   |
| Karel Čapek - selected novels                     | 88.6  | 58.2  | 70.3   |
| Simona Monyová - Ženu ani květinou                | 87.9  | 67.3  | 76.2   |
| J.K. Rowling - Harry Potter 1 (translation)       | 89.3  | 68.1  | 77.2   |
| Neil Gaiman - The Graveyard Book (translation)    | 91.2  | 63.7  | 75.0   |
| Overall performance                               | 90.9  | 69.7  | 78.9   |

**Table 5.** *Results: Transformer-based approach (Roberta).*

|  | P [%] | R [%] | F1 [%] |
|---|---|---|---|
| Selected blogs | 95.5 | 88.3 | 91.8 |
| Internet Language Reference Book | 91.8 | 70.0 | 79.5 |
| Horoscopes 2015 | 96.4 | 93.9 | 95.2 |
| Karel Čapek - selected novels | 95.3 | 88.9 | 92.0 |
| Simona Monyová - Ženu ani květinou | 95.8 | 93.1 | 94.4 |
| J.K. Rowling - Harry Potter 1 (translation) | 96.6 | 88.4 | 92.3 |
| Neil Gaiman - The Graveyard Book (translation) | 96.8 | 87.2 | 91.8 |
| Overall performance | 96.1 | 89.5 | 92.7 |

# 6    Conclusion

In this paper, we compared the rule-based and the Transformer-based approaches to the task of automatic grammar correction of commas in the Czech language. The study was conducted using the production-ready representatives of each approach - the SET parser and Roberta-based model.

The experimental evaluation shows that training the Roberta-based model only for the comma insertion task provides better F1 performance, than using a generic BERT-based punctuation insertion model. A simple numerical comparison of the F1 scores shows consistently higher numbers for the Roberta-based model. On the other side, the Precision scores are comparable for the rule-based and Roberta-based approaches.

The great advantage of the rule-based SET parser is the explainability of the rules applied to the input sentence. The explainability of the Transformer models is unclear and almost impossible. The only way to interpret such models is to visualize the attention values. But this is complicated by the multi-layer and multi-head nature of the model.

RoBERTA model, for example, cannot insert a comma before the conjunction *a* (lit. and) followed by subordinating conjunction that starts a subordinate clause depending on the following main clause (*Pes čekal doma, a když pán přišel, radostně ho přivítal*). The model was unable to learn to deal with this type of syntactic construction because this type of comma does not usually appear in the training data from the Internet. We assume that the model could achieve even better results in the future if the training data will be without errors.

In future work, we would like to focus on the error analysis of the particular models. It would be helpful to know, what is the distribution of commas in our typology (A-E) among the erroneous predictions of the Roberta-based models. If there will be a common schema (for example lack of training data or consistent erroneous predictions), the rule-based approach can be used to extract the targeted training data and populate the rare cases to increase the overall performance. Another source of prediction errors in the Roberta-based model could be a mismatch between the training data (web text from CommonCrawl) and the evaluation data (especially the Internet Language Reference Book). Again, the rule-based model can be applied to pre-select the training data to better match the target dataset.

# References

1. Pravidla českého pravopisu, 2. rozšířené vydání. Academia, Praha (1993)
2. Boháč, M., Rott, M., Kovář, V.: Text punctuation: an inter-annotator agreement study. In: Ekštein, K., Matoušek, V. (eds.) TSD 2017. LNCS (LNAI), vol. 10415, pp. 120–128. Springer, Cham (2017). https://doi.org/10.1007/978-3-319-64206-2_14
3. Bryant, C., Felice, M., Andersen, Ø.E., Briscoe, T.: The BEA-2019 shared task on grammatical error correction. In: Proceedings of the Fourteenth Workshop on Innovative Use of NLP for Building Educational Applications, pp. 52–75. Association for Computational Linguistics, Florence, Italy (Aug 2019)
4. Cai, Y., Wang, D.: Question mark prediction by bert. In: 2019 Asia-Pacific Signal and Information Processing Association Annual Summit and Conference (APSIPA ASC), pp. 363–367 (2019). https://doi.org/10.1109/APSIPAASC47483.2019.9023090
5. Chordia, V.: PunKtuator: a multilingual punctuation restoration system for spoken and written text. In: Proceedings of the 16th Conference of the European Chapter of the Association for Computational Linguistics: System Demonstrations, pp. 312–320. Association for Computational Linguistics, Online (Apr 2021). https://doi.org/10.18653/v1/2021.eacl-demos.37, https://aclanthology.org/2021.eacl-demos.37
6. Devlin, J., Chang, M., Lee, K., Toutanova, K.: BERT: pre-training of deep bidirectional transformers for language understanding. CoRR abs/1810.04805 (2018). http://arxiv.org/abs/1810.04805
7. Hlaváčková, D., et al.: New online proofreader for Czech. Slavonic Natural Language Processing in the 21st Century, pp. 79–92 (2019)
8. Hlaváčková, D., Žižková, H., Dvořáková, K., Pravdová, M.: Developing online czech proofreader tool: Achievements, limitations and pitfalls. In: Bohemistyka, XXII, (1), pp. 122–134 (2022). https://doi.org/10.14746/bo.2022.1.7
9. Hlubík, P., Španěl, M., Boháč, M., Weingartová, L.: Inserting punctuation to ASR output in a real-time production environment. In: Sojka, P., Kopeček, I., Pala, K., Horák, A. (eds.) TSD 2020. LNCS (LNAI), vol. 12284, pp. 418–425. Springer, Cham (2020). https://doi.org/10.1007/978-3-030-58323-1_45
10. Karlík, P., Nekula, M., Pleskalová, J.e.: Nový encyklopedický slovník češtiny (2012–2020). https://www.czechency.org/
11. Kilgarriff, A., Baisa, V., Bušta, J., Jakubíček, M., Kovář, V., Michelfeit, J., Rychlý, P., Suchomel, V.: The Sketch Engine: ten years on. Lexicography 1(1), 7–36 (2014). https://doi.org/10.1007/s40607-014-0009-9
12. Klejch, O., Bell, P., Renals, S.: Sequence-to-sequence models for punctuated transcription combining lexical and acoustic features. In: 2017 IEEE International Conference on Acoustics, Speech and Signal Processing (ICASSP). pp. 5700–5704 (2017). https://doi.org/10.1109/ICASSP.2017.7953248

13. Kovář, V., Machura, J., Zemková, K., Rott, M.: Evaluation and improvements in punctuation detection for czech. In: Sojka, P., Horák, A., Kopeček, I., Pala, K. (eds.) TSD 2016. LNCS (LNAI), vol. 9924, pp. 287–294. Springer, Cham (2016). https://doi.org/10.1007/978-3-319-45510-5_33

14. Kovář, V., Horák, A., Jakubíček, M.: Syntactic analysis using finite patterns: a new parsing system for Czech. In: Vetulani, Z. (ed.) LTC 2009. LNCS (LNAI), vol. 6562, pp. 161–171. Springer, Heidelberg (2011). https://doi.org/10.1007/978-3-642-20095-3_15

15. Liu, Y., et al.: Roberta: A robustly optimized BERT pretraining approach. CoRR abs/1907.11692 (2019). http://arxiv.org/abs/1907.11692

16. Machura, J., Gerzová, H., Masopustová, M., Valíčková, M.: Comparing majka and morphodita for automatic grammar checking. In: Proceedings of Recent Advances in Slavonic Natural Language Processing, RASLAN, pp. 3–14. Brno (2019)

17. Nunberg, G.: The Linguistics of Punctuation. CSLI lecture notes, Cambridge University Press (1990). https://books.google.cz/books?id=Sh-sruuKjJwC

18. Păiş, V., Tufiş, D.: Capitalization and punctuation restoration: a survey. Artif. Intell. Rev. **55**(3), 1681–1722 (2021). https://doi.org/10.1007/s10462-021-10051-x

19. Pravdová, M., Svobodová, I.: Akademická příručka českého jazyka. Academia, Praha (2019)

20. Radford, A., Wu, J., Child, R., Luan, D., Amodei, D., Sutskever, I.: Language models are unsupervised multitask learners (2019)

21. Straková, J., Straka, M., Hajič, J.: Open-source tools for morphology, lemmatization, POS tagging and named entity recognition. In: Proceedings of 52nd Annual Meeting of the Association for Computational Linguistics: System Demonstrations. pp. 13–18. Association for Computational Linguistics, Baltimore, Maryland (Jun 2014). https://doi.org/10.3115/v1/P14-5003,https://aclanthology.org/P14-5003

22. Suchomel, V., Michelfeit, J., Pomikálek, J.: Text tokenisation using Unitok. In: Eight Workshop on Recent Advances in Slavonic Natural Language Processing, pp. 71–75. Tribun EU, Brno (2014). https://nlp.fi.muni.cz/raslan/2014/14.pdf

23. Švec, J., Lehečka, J., Šmídl, L., Ircing, P.: Transformer-based automatic punctuation prediction and word casing reconstruction of the ASR output. In: Ekštein, K., Pártl, F., Konopík, M. (eds.) TSD 2021. LNCS (LNAI), vol. 12848, pp. 86–94. Springer, Cham (2021). https://doi.org/10.1007/978-3-030-83527-9_7

24. Švec, J., et al.: General framework for mining, processing and storing large amounts of electronic texts for language modeling purposes. Lang. Resour. Eval. **48**(2), 227–248 (2014). https://doi.org/10.1007/s10579-013-9246-z

25. Šmerk, P.: Unsupervised learning of rules for morphological disambiguation. In: Sojka, P., Kopeček, I., Pala, K. (eds.) TSD 2004. LNCS (LNAI), vol. 3206, pp. 211–216. Springer, Heidelberg (2004). https://doi.org/10.1007/978-3-540-30120-2_27

26. Šmerk, P.: Fast morphological analysis of Czech. In: Proceedings of the RASLAN Workshop 2009. Masarykova univerzita, Brno (2009). https://nlp.fi.muni.cz/raslan/2009/papers/13.pdf

# Linear Transformations for Cross-lingual Sentiment Analysis

Pavel Přibáň[1,2(✉)] (ID), Jakub Šmíd[1] (ID), Adam Mištera[1,2], and Pavel Král[1] (ID)

[1] Department of Computer Science and Engineering, University of West Bohemia
Faculty of Applied Sciences, Pilsen, Czech Republic
{pribanp,amistera,pkral}@kiv.zcu.cz, biba10@students.zcu.cz
[2] NTIS – New Technologies for the Information Society, Univerzitni 8, 301 00 Pilsen,
Czech Republic
https://nlp.kiv.zcu.cz

**Abstract.** This paper deals with cross-lingual sentiment analysis in Czech, English and French languages. We perform zero-shot cross-lingual classification using five linear transformations combined with LSTM and CNN based classifiers. We compare the performance of the individual transformations, and in addition, we confront the transformation-based approach with existing state-of-the-art BERT-like models. We show that the pre-trained embeddings from the target domain are crucial to improving the cross-lingual classification results, unlike in the monolingual classification, where the effect is not so distinctive.

**Keywords:** sentiment analysis · cross-lingual · linear transformation · neural networks · semantic space transformation · classification

## 1 Introduction

Sentiment analysis (SA) is an essential task in the natural language processing (NLP) field and a lot of research interest has been devoted to this topic, especially in monolingual settings for English. However, cross-lingual sentiment analysis (CLSA) has been much less studied. Most of the approaches to SA require annotated data. CLSA aims to enable knowledge transfer between languages with enough data and languages with less or without annotated data (low-resource languages), thus allowing to run SA in these languages.

We can divide the existing approaches for CLSA into three groups. Machine translation can be used to translate annotated data into the target language and then the model is trained using the translated data. Secondly, the multilingual versions of pre-trained BERT-like models such as mBERT [14] or XLM-R [13] are applicable to CLSA. These models can be fine-tuned with annotated data from high-resource languages, usually English. Classification in the target language, such as Czech, is then performed without any training data [28]. The third approach uses linear transformations and other methods to transfer knowledge between languages. Usually, the linear transformations align semantic spaces

© Springer Nature Switzerland AG 2022
P. Sojka et al. (Eds.): TSD 2022, LNAI 13502, pp. 125–137, 2022.
https://doi.org/10.1007/978-3-031-16270-1_11

[30] in different languages into one common space. The common space (word embeddings) is then used during the training of a neural network, namely Long Short-Term Memory (LSTM) or Convolutional Neural Network (CNN).

As shown in [28], multilingual BERT-like models achieve SotA results. Their drawback is that they typically require much more resources and computational power in terms of memory and GPU performance than previous approaches. These greater requirements cause that they usually have to be fine-tuned on expensive and specialized GPUs with high electricity consumption. On the other hand, the approaches based on linear transformations and neural networks (e.g., CNN) can be easily trained on a standard computer using only a CPU. As we show in our paper, these cheaper cross-lingual approaches achieve competitive results in comparison to the multilingual BERT-like models.

In this paper, we focus on the *Sentiment Classification*[1] task (also known as *Polarity detection*) in cross-lingual settings for Czech, English and French. We perform zero-shot cross-lingual sentiment classification in the three languages. We compare the performance of five linear transformations for aligning semantic spaces in combination with two neural network models: CNN and LSTM. We show that the source of embeddings is a very important aspect when using linear transformations for the CLSA. Our experiments reveal that pre-trained in-domain embeddings can significantly improve (even more than 10%) cross-lingual classification results, unlike in monolingual classification, where the difference is only about 1%–2%. We compare our results with the available cross-lingual SotA results based on multilingual BERT-like models. In addition, to the best of our knowledge, none of the previous works applied linear transformations to the task of CLSA for the Czech language. We release all our resources and source codes[2].

Our main contributions are the following: 1) We compare the performance of five linear transformations on the task of CLSA and compare them with the available cross-lingual SotA results. 2) We show that the source of data for the embeddings used in the linear transformations is crucial for the CLSA task.

## 2    Related Work

Cross-lingual sentiment analysis has been moderately studied in recent years, but less attention has been paid to this research subtopic in comparison to the monolingual task. The approaches proposed in [5,11,40], the recent state-of-the-art BERT-like models applications [8,28,34,38], cross-lingual word embeddings and linear transformation can be applied to tackle this task. Most of the following cited works do not compare the linear transformations and their effect on CLSA performance in such detail as our work does.

Authors in [18] used a recursive autoencoder architecture and sentence aligned corpora of English and Hindi for CLSA and evaluated the system on the Hindi movie reviews dataset. A method specifically for sentiment cross-lingual word embeddings was proposed in [39]. The authors trained an SVM

---

[1] Here, we consider sentiment analysis and sentiment classification as the same task.

[2] https://github.com/pauli31/linear-transformation-4-cs-sa.

classifier based on embeddings for the polarity classification task. In [7], multiple techniques for cross-lingual aspect-based sentiment classification were compared, including the one from [27]. Also, in [1], the authors experimented with the linear transformation method from [27] on English, Spanish and Chinese. In [6], an approach for training bilingual sentiment word embeddings is presented. The embeddings are jointly optimized to represent (a) semantic information in the source and target languages using a small bilingual dictionary and (b) sentiment information obtained from the source language only. A cross-lingual algorithm using CNN is shown in [15] and evaluated on nine languages. Authors of [12] trained an adversarial neural network with bilingual embeddings for polarity classification in Chinese and Arabic using only English train data. In both [2,23], the authors used linear transformations for Persian and Turkish.

## 3 Experimental Setup

In this section, we describe the data, linear transformations and the models that we used for the experiments. We also cover the process of building bilingual dictionaries needed for the linear transformations along with the methodology of our zero-shot cross-lingual experiments.

### 3.1 Data

We use four publicly available datasets with binary polarity labels, i.e., *positive* and *negative* from the movie reviews domain. For Czech, we use the **CSFD** dataset of movie reviews introduced in [16]. It is built from 90k reviews from the Czech movie database[3] that were downloaded and annotated according to their star rating (0–1 stars as *negative*, 2–3 stars as *neutral*, 4–5 stars as *positive*). However, we use only the examples labeled as *positive* or *negative*. We use the data split from [28]. The French **Allocine** [36] dataset consists of 100k positive and 100k negative reviews. The dataset was scraped from the Allociné[4] website and annotated the same way as the CSFD dataset. English **IMDB** [26] dataset includes 50k movie reviews obtained from the Internet Movie Database[5] with *positive* and *negative* classes. We randomly selected 2.5k examples from the training part as development data. The second English **SST-2** [31] dataset contains almost 12k manually annotated movie reviews into two categories, see Table 1.

**Table 1.** Dataset statistics.

|        | CSFD (Czech) | | | IMDB (English) | | | SST-2 (English) | | | Allocine (French) | | |
|--------|-------|------|------|--------|-------|--------|-------|-----|------|---------|--------|--------|
|        | train | dev  | test | train  | dev   | test   | train | dev | test | train   | dev    | test   |
| Pos.   | 22,117 | 2,456 | 6,324 | 11,242 | 1,258 | 12,500 | 3,610 | 444 | 909  | 79,413  | 9,796  | 9,592  |
| Neg.   | 21,441 | 2,399 | 5,876 | 11,258 | 1,242 | 12,500 | 3,310 | 428 | 912  | 80,587  | 10,204 | 10,408 |
| Tot.   | 43,558 | 4,855 | 12,200 | 22,500 | 2,500 | 25,000 | 6,920 | 872 | 1,821 | 160,000 | 20,000 | 20,000 |

---

[3] https://www.csfd.cz.
[4] https://www.allocine.fr.
[5] https://www.imdb.com.

The linear transformations require bilingual dictionaries to align the semantic spaces, see Sect. 3.4. With Google Translate, we translated the 40k most common words from the CSFD dataset into English and French to obtain the required dictionaries. We repeat the process for IMDB and Allocine datasets. We also manually fixed some translation errors made by the translator.

## 3.2 Linear Transformations

We use linear transformations to create a bilingual semantic space. We align one semantic space (word embeddings) into the second semantic space in a different language. In such bilingual word embeddings, semantically similar words have similar vector representations across the two languages. Thanks to this property, we can use the bilingual space to train a neural network with a cross-lingual ability. The goal of the linear transformation is to find a transformation matrix $W^{s \rightarrow t} \in \mathbb{R}^{d \times d}$ that transforms vector space $X^s$ of the source language into the vector space $X^t$ of the target language by the following matrix multiplication:

$$\widehat{X}^s = W^{s \rightarrow t} X^s, \tag{1}$$

where $\widehat{X}^s$ is the transformed source vector space in the target space. Both matrices $X^t$ and $X^s$ contain $n$ vectors that correspond to translated pairs of words (called *seed words*) in dictionary $D$. Any word vector that is not present in the source matrix $X^s$ but comes from the same space can be transformed into the target space by multiplication of the transformation matrix $W^{s \rightarrow t}$.

We selected five transformation methods, the first was proposed in [27], where the transformation matrix is estimated by minimizing the mean squared error (**MSE**) between the pairs of vectors $(x_i^s, x_i^t)$ for the corresponding words from the dictionary $D$, as follows:

$$MSE = \sum_{i=1}^{n} \left\| W^{s \rightarrow t} x_i^s - x_i^t \right\|^2. \tag{2}$$

The second transformation is called Orthogonal (**Orto**) constraints the transformation matrix $W^{s \rightarrow t}$ to be *orthogonal*[6]. The orthogonal transformation has the same objective as MSE. The optimal transformation matrix $W^{s \rightarrow t}$ can be computed as follows:

$$W^{s \rightarrow t} = VU^{\mathsf{T}}, \tag{3}$$

where matrices $V$ and $U$ are computed by *Singular Value Decomposition* (SVD) of $X^{t^{\mathsf{T}}} X^s = U\Sigma V^{\mathsf{T}}$ as shown in [4]. The orthogonality constraint causes the transformation does not squeeze or re-scale the transformed space. It only rotates the space, thus it preserves most of the relationships of its elements (in our case, it is important that orthogonal transformation preserves angles between the words, so it preserves similarity between words in the transformed space).

---

[6] Matrix $W$ is orthogonal when it is a square matrix and the columns and rows are orthonormal vectors ($W^{\mathsf{T}}W = WW^{\mathsf{T}} = I$, where $I$ is the identity matrix).

The third method is based on *Canonical Correlation Analysis* (**CCA**). The method aligns both monolingual vector spaces $X^s$ and $X^t$ to a third shared space represented by matrix $Y^o$ [30]. CCA computes two transformation matrices $W^{s\to o}$ for the source language and $W^{t\to o}$ for the target language to map the spaces into one shared space $Y^o$. The transformation matrices can be computed analytically [17] using SVD. Using the approach from [3], the transformation matrix $W^{s\to t}$ can be computed as follows:

$$W^{s\to t} = W^{s\to o}(W^{t\to o})^{-1}. \tag{4}$$

The *Ranking Transformation* (**Rank**) [24] uses *max-margin hinge loss* (MML) instead of MSE to reduce the *hubness* problem [30]. The idea of this method is to rank correct translations of word $w_i$ (i.e., vectors $x_i^s$ and $x_i^t$) higher than random translation (negative example) of word $w_i$ (i.e., vectors $x_i^s$ and $x_j^t$).

The last *Orthogonal Ranking Transformation* (**Or-Ra**) [10] combines orthogonal and ranking transformations. The method tries to keep the transformation matrix $W^{s\to t}$ orthogonal and reduce hubness at once, see [10] for the objective function and details. Based on our experiments and our empirical experiences, we decided to set dictionary size to 20k word pairs in every experiment.

### 3.3 Neural Network Models

For our experiments, we implement a CNN inspired by [21] with one convolutional layer on top of pre-trained word embeddings. The first layer (embeddings layer) maps the input sentence of length $n$ to an $n \times d$ dimensional matrix, where $d = 300$ is the dimension of the word embeddings. We then use 1-dimensional convolution with filter sizes of 2, 3 and 4 (256 filters of each size) to extract features from the sentence. Next, we apply the ReLU activation and use max-over-time-pooling. After the pooling, we concatenate these scalars into a vector, which is then fed to a fully-connected layer to compute the prediction scores for the classes. The class with the highest score is selected as the prediction. As a regularization, we use a dropout [32] of 0.5 before the fully-connected layer.

We also train neural network based on the Bidirectional LSTM (BiLSTM). Our model consists of an embedding layer that again maps the input words to 300-dimensional input vectors. These vectors then pass to two BiLSTM layers, each with 512 units (hidden size). The output of the last BiLSTM layer is fed into the final fully-connected layer that computes prediction scores. We use a dropout of 0.5 before the fully-connected layer.

For our experiments, we use two types of pre-trained fastText [9] embeddings: (a) the existing[7] fastText embeddings. (b) In-domain embeddings trained by us on the text from the sentiment datasets. For English, we concatenate the texts from the SST-2 and IMDB datasets. We train embeddings for words with a minimum frequency of 5. During the training of the neural network models, we freeze the embeddings layer, meaning that we do not allow the embeddings to be

---

[7] Available from https://fasttext.cc/docs/en/crawl-vectors.html.

fine-tuned during training. For out-of-vocabulary words, we utilize the ability of fastText embeddings to generate a word vector. We train our model using Adam [22] with constant learning of 1e-3 or 1e-4. For some experiments, we use linear learning rate decay. We use a batch size of 32 and we train all our models for at most 10 epochs. We do not restrict the maximum input sequence length.

### 3.4 Cross-lingual Sentiment Classification

We perform zero-shot cross-lingual polarity detection for each pair of the three languages. The point of cross-lingual classification is to train a model on labeled data from one language (*source language*) and evaluate the model on data from another language (*target language*). The model must be able to transfer knowledge to the target language without any labeled data in the target language. For both languages in a pair, we train the model on data from one language and evaluate on data from the second language. The transformation of the semantic spaces is done in both directions, i.e., from the *source* space to the *target* space and vice versa. Since the French dataset is the largest one, for experiments where the source language is French, we use only French train data for training the model and as development data, we use French test data. For training models, where Czech is the source language, we use Czech train and test data parts of the CSFD dataset for training. We use the Czech dev part of the CSFD dataset as development data. In the case of the IMDB dataset, we randomly selected 2,500 examples as development data and the rest is used to train the model. For the SST-2 dataset, we use train and dev parts for training and test part as the development data.

In every experiment, we evaluate and report results for test data part in the target language. Only the test part of the data in the target language is used for evaluation, no other data from the target language are used to train the model.

## 4    Experiments and Results

We perform monolingual experiments, so we can compare the cross-lingual models with their monolingual equivalents. Secondly, we wanted to put our baselines and results into a context with the current SotA results. We use accuracy as the evaluation metric. We select the best models based on the results from the development data. We repeat each experiment at least six times and report the arithmetic mean value with the 95% confidence intervals. The label distribution is nearly perfectly balanced in all datasets and thus, the resulting $F_1$ Macro score was in a vast majority of experiments almost identical to our accuracy and is therefore not reported in the paper. Thanks to this, we are able to compare our results with the existing work in [28].

### 4.1    Monolingual Results

Table 2 compares our proposed monolingual models with the current monolingual state-of-the-art (SotA) models. We train both neural models with the existing fastText embeddings (rows CNN-F and LSTM-F) and with in-domain embeddings pre-trained by us (rows CNN and LSTM). As we can see, the modern BERT-like models outperform all our baselines. For English, the difference is the largest among all other languages, especially for the SST-2 dataset.

For Czech and French, the difference between best baselines and SotA models is only 1.7% and 1%, respectively. The difference between our baseline models trained on existing (rows CNN-F, LSTM-F) and our in-domain (rows CNN, LSTM) embeddings are at most 2.4% and 2.5% for CSFD and IMDB datasets, respectively. Based on the results, we can conclude that using custom pre-trained in-domain embeddings can slightly improve classification performance in monolingual settings, as one could expect. Our last observation is that our results are in general less competitive for English. This is most likely due to the fact that the current state-of-the-art approaches and models are generally more advanced in English, thus achieving better results.

**Table 2.** Comparison of the monolingual results as accuracy (upper section) with the current monolingual SotA (bottom section). The result with * was obtained on a custom data split. The results with ‡ are listed as $F_1$ score.

| **CSFD** (Czech) | | **IMDB** (English) | | **SST-2** (English) | | **Allocine** (French) | |
|---|---|---|---|---|---|---|---|
| CNN (ours) | $93.9^{\pm0.1}$ | | $91.8^{\pm0.1}$ | | $84.4^{\pm0.6}$ | | $95.0^{\pm0.1}$ |
| CNN-F (ours) | $91.5^{\pm0.2}$ | | $89.3^{\pm0.6}$ | | $83.7^{\pm0.2}$ | | $94.3^{\pm0.1}$ |
| LSTM (ours) | $94.3^{\pm0.1}$ | | $92.3^{\pm0.4}$ | | $84.5^{\pm0.5}$ | | $96.4^{\pm0.1}$ |
| LSTM-F (ours) | $92.1^{\pm0.2}$ | | $90.5^{\pm0.9}$ | | $84.3^{\pm0.5}$ | | $95.7^{\pm0.1}$ |
| **Current SotA** | | | | | | | |
| LSTM [28]‡ | $91.8^{\pm0.1}$ | BON-Cos [35] | 97.4 | RoB.$_{Smart}$ [19] | 97.5 | CamBERT [36] | 97.4 |
| mBERT [28]‡ | $93.1^{\pm0.3}$ | XLNet [37] | 96.2 | T5-11B [29] | 97.5 | CNN [36] | 93.7 |
| XLM-R$_{Large}$ [28]‡ | $96.0^{\pm0.0}$ | BERT$_{ITPT}$ [33] | 95.8 | XLNet [37] | 97.0 | | 93.0 |
| BERT$_{Distilled}$[25]* | 93.8 | oh-LSTM [20] | 94.1 | | | | |

## 4.2 Cross-lingual Results

We report our cross-lingual results for all three pairs of languages in Tables 3, 4 and 6. In each table, we present results trained with *in-domain* embeddings pre-trained by us and results for existing *fastText* embeddings, separated by the slash character. These pairs of results were always obtained by models trained with the same hyper-parameters (learning rate and the number of epochs). We report the results of experiments where the semantic spaces were transformed in both directions[8]. For easier comparison, we also include the monolingual results of our models from Table 2. The pairs where in-domain embeddings are better

---

[8] For example, the column labeled as **EN-s** ⇒ **CS-t** means that English space was transformed into Czech space. English is the source language (-s suffix) and Czech is the target language (-t suffix), in other words, the English dataset is used for training and Czech for the evaluation.

than the existing fastText embeddings have a gray background. The best results in absolute values are underlined and the results that overlap with the confidence interval of the best result are bold, we mark this separately in each column. As we mentioned, we trained the models for at most five epochs with constant learning rate or linear learning rate decay with learning rates of 1e-3 or 1e-4[9].

Our main observation is that in-domain embeddings significantly improve the results for the CLSA task (gray background in the Tables). The improvement is in some cases, even more than 10%. This statement is certainly true for the models trained on English and evaluated on Czech and French (with some minor exceptions). For the models evaluated on English, the improvement is not so noticeable, but in most cases, it is also valid. We can observe an analogical improvement in the monolingual results, but for these, the improvement is at most 2.5%.

**Table 3.** Cross-lingual accuracy results for English and Czech language pair.

| | | | Evaluated on **Czech** | | | Evaluated on **English** | |
| | | | EN-s ⇒ CS-t | CS-t ⇒ EN-s | | CS-s ⇒ EN-t | EN-t ⇒ CS-s |
| Dataset | Method | Monoling. | in-domain/fastText | in-domain/fastText | Monoling. | in-domain/fastText | in-domain/fastText |
|---|---|---|---|---|---|---|---|
| | | | | CNN | | | |
| | MSE | | $88.2^{\pm0.3}/75.7^{\pm1.5}$ | $72.3^{\pm2.2}/69.0^{\pm2.0}$ | | $77.5^{\pm1.5}/67.1^{\pm1.9}$ | $53.8^{\pm2.0}/67.1^{\pm1.4}$ |
| | Orto | 93.9/ | $88.5^{\pm0.1}/78.9^{\pm0.9}$ | $87.4^{\pm0.9}/72.5^{\pm1.4}$ | 91.8/ | $83.8^{\pm0.1}/76.8^{\pm0.3}$ | $81.3^{\pm0.3}/79.3^{\pm0.9}$ |
| | CCA | 91.5 | $88.4^{\pm0.1}/76.2^{\pm1.2}$ | $87.4^{\pm0.4}/79.5^{\pm0.6}$ | 89.2 | $83.9^{\pm0.1}/75.0^{\pm0.6}$ | $79.6^{\pm0.6}/67.2^{\pm4.4}$ |
| | Rank | | $85.7^{\pm0.3}/78.9^{\pm0.9}$ | $88.0^{\pm0.8}/76.7^{\pm0.8}$ | | $83.2^{\pm0.2}/76.1^{\pm0.7}$ | $82.0^{\pm1.0}/74.4^{\pm1.9}$ |
| IMDB | Or-Ra | | $83.3^{\pm0.7}/76.9^{\pm1.8}$ | $89.2^{\pm0.1}/79.2^{\pm1.0}$ | | $79.6^{\pm0.5}/78.4^{\pm0.6}$ | $82.3^{\pm0.4}/75.0^{\pm1.0}$ |
| CSFD | | | | LSTM | | | |
| | MSE | | $84.9^{\pm0.6}/80.6^{\pm1.3}$ | $83.4^{\pm2.0}/79.7^{\pm2.1}$ | | $84.8^{\pm0.6}/83.4^{\pm1.0}$ | $51.2^{\pm2.2}/62.9^{\pm3.7}$ |
| | Orto | 94.3/ | $87.1^{\pm0.3}/81.5^{\pm1.3}$ | $87.7^{\pm0.7}/82.2^{\pm0.8}$ | 92.3/ | $73.6^{\pm1.4}/79.8^{\pm1.7}$ | $68.2^{\pm1.5}/83.7^{\pm0.7}$ |
| | CCA | 92.1 | $85.9^{\pm1.7}/81.3^{\pm1.5}$ | $87.4^{\pm0.3}/82.6^{\pm0.4}$ | 90.5 | $82.7^{\pm2.9}/77.7^{\pm2.9}$ | $81.8^{\pm1.6}/82.6^{\pm0.7}$ |
| | Rank | | $82.5^{\pm2.4}/76.9^{\pm1.4}$ | $85.1^{\pm1.4}/80.9^{\pm2.9}$ | | $56.3^{\pm2.4}/82.9^{\pm1.9}$ | $83.8^{\pm0.9}/83.5^{\pm0.5}$ |
| | Or-Ra | | $86.2^{\pm0.5}/73.2^{\pm1.4}$ | $86.7^{\pm0.7}/82.9^{\pm2.1}$ | | $67.9^{\pm3.2}/82.8^{\pm2.0}$ | $83.6^{\pm1.2}/83.1^{\pm0.4}$ |
| | | | | CNN | | | |
| | MSE | | $84.1^{\pm2.1}/55.7^{\pm3.5}$ | $86.0^{\pm1.4}/78.1^{\pm1.0}$ | | $72.8^{\pm0.3}/73.1^{\pm0.3}$ | $50.5^{\pm1.5}/60.1^{\pm3.4}$ |
| | Orto | 93.9/ | $77.2^{\pm1.1}/50.9^{\pm2.2}$ | $81.8^{\pm1.7}/74.9^{\pm0.9}$ | 84.4/ | $77.8^{\pm0.2}/76.0^{\pm0.2}$ | $75.3^{\pm0.5}/74.3^{\pm0.9}$ |
| | CCA | 91.5 | $83.9^{\pm0.7}/51.2^{\pm1.1}$ | $83.1^{\pm0.7}/76.6^{\pm0.9}$ | 83.6 | $77.2^{\pm0.2}/75.0^{\pm0.3}$ | $72.4^{\pm0.2}/72.1^{\pm0.3}$ |
| | Rank | | $85.2^{\pm0.6}/55.8^{\pm2.7}$ | $83.2^{\pm1.6}/75.6^{\pm0.4}$ | | $77.0^{\pm0.5}/73.2^{\pm0.2}$ | $77.4^{\pm0.4}/75.2^{\pm0.4}$ |
| SST-2 | Or-Ra | | $80.1^{\pm1.5}/55.6^{\pm3.6}$ | $82.6^{\pm1.4}/76.9^{\pm0.3}$ | | $76.2^{\pm0.4}/75.5^{\pm0.4}$ | $77.4^{\pm0.3}/77.2^{\pm0.3}$ |
| CSFD | | | | LSTM | | | |
| | MSE | | $81.1^{\pm1.9}/76.4^{\pm2.9}$ | $82.0^{\pm2.3}/69.5^{\pm2.6}$ | | $76.1^{\pm0.4}/78.4^{\pm0.4}$ | $68.5^{\pm0.8}/73.0^{\pm2.2}$ |
| | Orto | 94.3/ | $80.4^{\pm2.1}/75.5^{\pm1.3}$ | $76.4^{\pm2.3}/74.8^{\pm1.3}$ | 84.5/ | $72.6^{\pm1.6}/78.4^{\pm0.5}$ | $72.9^{\pm0.5}/79.2^{\pm1.0}$ |
| | CCA | 92.1 | $83.0^{\pm1.4}/72.7^{\pm2.1}$ | $82.5^{\pm0.8}/72.9^{\pm2.2}$ | 84.3 | $76.5^{\pm2.0}/76.9^{\pm1.7}$ | $73.9^{\pm1.8}/75.9^{\pm1.0}$ |
| | Rank | | $83.1^{\pm1.3}/74.6^{\pm2.2}$ | $75.5^{\pm2.1}/77.8^{\pm2.0}$ | | $70.8^{\pm1.7}/77.1^{\pm0.8}$ | $77.5^{\pm1.5}/79.1^{\pm0.6}$ |
| | Or-Ra | | $83.0^{\pm0.7}/73.8^{\pm1.7}$ | $82.2^{\pm1.9}/78.3^{\pm2.4}$ | | $74.7^{\pm1.8}/76.1^{\pm2.1}$ | $75.9^{\pm2.5}/79.5^{\pm0.4}$ |

---

[9] We provide the details of the used hyper-parameters at our GitHub repository.

## 4.3 Comparison with Existing Works

Table 5 compares our best results with related work. This table shows that the proposed approach based on linear transformations is competitive with the current BERT-like models. There is an exception for English results obtained by the XLM-R$_{Large}$ model, which has a huge number of parameters (559M). We did not outperform the largest XLM-R$_{Large}$ model, but for example, for the

**Table 4.** Cross-lingual accuracy results for English and French language pair.

| | | | Evaluated on **French** | | | Evaluated on **English** | |
|---|---|---|---|---|---|---|---|
| | | | EN-s ⇒ FR-t | FR-t ⇒ EN-s | | FR-s ⇒ EN-t | EN-t ⇒ FR-s |
| Dataset | Method | Monoling. | in-domain/fastText | in-domain/fastText | Monoling. | in-domain/fastText | in-domain/fastText |
| | | | | **CNN** | | | |
| | MSE | | $86.5^{\pm0.2}/81.3^{\pm0.2}$ | $63.2^{\pm9.1}/79.9^{\pm0.7}$ | | $\mathbf{86.2^{\pm0.1}}/78.2^{\pm0.1}$ | $55.1^{\pm4.4}/72.8^{\pm1.2}$ |
| | Orto | 95.0/ | $90.4^{\pm0.0}/81.0^{\pm0.6}$ | $89.0^{\pm0.2}/81.3^{\pm0.3}$ | 91.8/ | $86.0^{\pm0.0}/81.3^{\pm0.4}$ | $\mathbf{87.0^{\pm0.0}}/81.0^{\pm0.6}$ |
| | CCA | 94.3 | $89.9^{\pm0.1}/81.0^{\pm0.5}$ | $89.0^{\pm0.1}/81.9^{\pm0.0}$ | 89.2 | $84.6^{\pm0.2}/80.2^{\pm0.4}$ | $85.3^{\pm0.2}/79.2^{\pm0.4}$ |
| | Rank | | $88.2^{\pm0.9}/77.1^{\pm2.6}$ | $88.7^{\pm0.0}/80.9^{\pm0.4}$ | | $83.6^{\pm0.1}/74.5^{\pm0.7}$ | $85.3^{\pm0.5}/74.9^{\pm0.9}$ |
| IMDB | Or-Ra | | $89.2^{\pm0.2}/75.9^{\pm0.8}$ | $\mathbf{89.4^{\pm0.0}}/80.8^{\pm0.6}$ | | $81.0^{\pm0.9}/78.3^{\pm1.5}$ | $86.3^{\pm0.1}/76.2^{\pm0.8}$ |
| Allocine | | | | **LSTM** | | | |
| | MSE | | $84.9^{\pm1.2}/80.2^{\pm9.0}$ | $68.7^{\pm9.7}/68.7^{\pm9.6}$ | | $81.7^{\pm1.0}/81.9^{\pm0.6}$ | $79.3^{\pm2.9}/78.4^{\pm1.1}$ |
| | Orto | 96.4/ | $\mathbf{91.2^{\pm0.3}}/81.2^{\pm8.2}$ | $86.9^{\pm4.8}/82.4^{\pm4.1}$ | 92.3/ | $81.6^{\pm1.2}/83.0^{\pm0.5}$ | $83.2^{\pm2.2}/80.3^{\pm2.1}$ |
| | CCA | 95.7 | $\mathbf{91.7^{\pm0.2}}/85.0^{\pm1.7}$ | $87.8^{\pm2.2}/85.9^{\pm1.1}$ | 90.5 | $\mathbf{85.2^{\pm0.9}}/82.2^{\pm0.1}$ | $\mathbf{86.8^{\pm0.3}}/71.5^{\pm2.4}$ |
| | Rank | | $88.3^{\pm1.6}/87.2^{\pm1.0}$ | $88.2^{\pm3.2}/82.9^{\pm3.6}$ | | $56.7^{\pm4.6}/81.1^{\pm0.9}$ | $85.2^{\pm0.6}/81.2^{\pm0.5}$ |
| | Or-Ra | | $86.3^{\pm3.4}/70.9^{\pm9.0}$ | $\mathbf{89.1^{\pm1.2}}/86.8^{\pm0.7}$ | | $56.4^{\pm3.1}/81.5^{\pm1.5}$ | $\mathbf{87.2^{\pm0.2}}/79.9^{\pm1.8}$ |
| | | | | **CNN** | | | |
| | MSE | | $86.7^{\pm0.8}/67.9^{\pm2.1}$ | $\mathbf{84.5^{\pm0.2}}/68.4^{\pm0.9}$ | | $\mathbf{79.6^{\pm0.1}}/79.2^{\pm0.3}$ | $50.8^{\pm1.3}/72.8^{\pm1.8}$ |
| | Orto | 95.0/ | $85.9^{\pm0.5}/65.7^{\pm2.9}$ | $81.0^{\pm0.7}/69.1^{\pm2.4}$ | 84.4/ | $78.9^{\pm0.3}/\mathbf{80.0^{\pm0.3}}$ | $80.1^{\pm0.3}/79.5^{\pm0.2}$ |
| | CCA | 94.3 | $\mathbf{87.8^{\pm0.1}}/61.7^{\pm2.4}$ | $84.2^{\pm0.6}/66.4^{\pm1.1}$ | 83.6 | $77.7^{\pm0.3}/78.9^{\pm0.2}$ | $79.2^{\pm0.3}/78.2^{\pm0.3}$ |
| | Rank | | $85.9^{\pm0.4}/68.1^{\pm1.8}$ | $81.9^{\pm1.2}/68.1^{\pm1.1}$ | | $75.4^{\pm1.0}/74.4^{\pm1.2}$ | $81.8^{\pm0.2}/78.8^{\pm0.2}$ |
| SST-2 | Or-Ra | | $83.8^{\pm0.3}/72.1^{\pm2.0}$ | $\mathbf{83.9^{\pm0.9}}/70.7^{\pm0.9}$ | | $73.4^{\pm1.3}/77.8^{\pm0.6}$ | $80.9^{\pm0.2}/79.1^{\pm0.3}$ |
| Allocine | | | | **LSTM** | | | |
| | MSE | | $78.6^{\pm3.7}/77.6^{\pm1.7}$ | $81.9^{\pm0.9}/71.6^{\pm9.2}$ | | $79.1^{\pm0.1}/78.8^{\pm0.7}$ | $76.2^{\pm0.8}/76.3^{\pm0.6}$ |
| | Orto | 96.4/ | $84.7^{\pm0.5}/76.2^{\pm4.6}$ | $81.1^{\pm2.8}/\mathbf{78.1^{\pm6.2}}$ | 84.5/ | $\mathbf{79.2^{\pm0.6}}/79.4^{\pm0.1}$ | $\mathbf{81.8^{\pm0.3}}/78.9^{\pm0.3}$ |
| | CCA | 95.7 | $85.3^{\pm0.8}/79.6^{\pm1.1}$ | $\mathbf{81.8^{\pm4.9}}/78.4^{\pm1.3}$ | 84.3 | $\mathbf{79.9^{\pm0.3}}/78.6^{\pm0.6}$ | $80.7^{\pm0.4}/78.1^{\pm0.4}$ |
| | Rank | | $85.3^{\pm1.7}/77.3^{\pm3.1}$ | $81.9^{\pm1.1}/79.5^{\pm1.1}$ | | $69.8^{\pm3.1}/77.4^{\pm0.2}$ | $\mathbf{82.5^{\pm0.4}}/79.0^{\pm0.4}$ |
| | Or-Ra | | $84.7^{\pm1.9}/75.7^{\pm2.7}$ | $\mathbf{82.3^{\pm5.0}}/76.6^{\pm3.4}$ | | $72.7^{\pm2.1}/78.5^{\pm0.6}$ | $81.7^{\pm0.4}/79.6^{\pm0.4}$ |

**Table 5.** Comparison of cross-lingual Macro $F_1$ results with other works. French result with * symbol is shown as accuracy.

| | IMDB | CSFD | Allocine |
|---|---|---|---|
| XLM-R$_{Base}$ [28] | $89.5^{\pm0.2}$ | $88.0^{\pm0.3}$ | |
| XLM-R$_{Large}$ [28] | $94.0^{\pm0.1}$ | $91.6^{\pm0.1}$ | |
| XLM [28] | $78.2^{\pm0.5}$ | $75.4^{\pm0.3}$ | |
| mBERT [28] | | $76.3^{\pm1.1}$ | |
| G/F-A [15]* | | | 93.0 |
| Our best | $87.2^{\pm0.2}$ (EN-t ⇒ FR-s) | $89.2^{\pm0.1}$ (CS-t ⇒ EN-s) | $91.7^{\pm0.2}$ (EN-s ⇒ FR-t) |

**Table 6.** Cross-lingual accuracy results for French and Czech language pair.

| | | | Evaluated on **Czech** | | | Evaluated on **French** | |
|---|---|---|---|---|---|---|---|
| | | | FR-s ⇒ CS-t | CS-t ⇒ FR-s | | CS-s ⇒ FR-t | FR-t ⇒ CS-s |
| Dataset | Method | Monoling. | in-domain/fastText | in-domain/fastText | Monoling. | in-domain/fastText | in-domain/fastText |
| | | | **CNN** | | | | |
| Allocine CSFD | MSE | 93.9/ 91.5 | $84.4^{\pm0.2}/75.2^{\pm1.2}$ | $56.0^{\pm3.1}/68.5^{\pm3.9}$ | 95.0/ 94.3 | $74.3^{\pm0.7}/65.6^{\pm1.0}$ | $52.7^{\pm0.4}/63.8^{\pm2.8}$ |
| | Orto | | $85.9^{\pm0.3}/77.5^{\pm0.5}$ | $86.0^{\pm0.3}/78.0^{\pm0.3}$ | | $\mathbf{84.6^{\pm0.2}}/80.8^{\pm0.2}$ | $84.0^{\pm0.3}/78.4^{\pm0.5}$ |
| | CCA | | $83.7^{\pm0.3}/75.9^{\pm0.4}$ | $82.7^{\pm0.6}/71.8^{\pm0.5}$ | | $\underline{84.7^{\pm0.3}}/79.8^{\pm0.3}$ | $76.9^{\pm0.5}/73.7^{\pm0.6}$ |
| | Rank | | $81.7^{\pm1.0}/75.1^{\pm1.3}$ | $86.2^{\pm0.3}/69.2^{\pm0.2}$ | | $82.4^{\pm0.8}/78.5^{\pm0.2}$ | $84.6^{\pm0.1}/68.9^{\pm1.3}$ |
| | Or-Ra | | $82.7^{\pm0.8}/72.6^{\pm1.6}$ | $87.0^{\pm0.1}/74.3^{\pm0.9}$ | | $75.9^{\pm1.4}/71.8^{\pm2.8}$ | $\mathbf{85.3^{\pm0.2}}/80.3^{\pm0.2}$ |
| | | | **LSTM** | | | | |
| Allocine CSFD | MSE | 94.3/ 92.1 | $85.3^{\pm0.6}/81.5^{\pm1.1}$ | $84.1^{\pm4.1}/76.5^{\pm2.8}$ | 96.4/ 95.7 | $81.7^{\pm2.1}/76.6^{\pm1.9}$ | $52.5^{\pm2.5}/62.2^{\pm5.7}$ |
| | Orto | | $\mathbf{87.6^{\pm0.6}}/80.2^{\pm0.6}$ | $\mathbf{88.0^{\pm0.7}}/81.5^{\pm0.7}$ | | $71.8^{\pm0.9}/70.7^{\pm4.5}$ | $68.9^{\pm1.1}/69.9^{\pm5.3}$ |
| | CCA | | $\mathbf{87.4^{\pm0.4}}/79.3^{\pm1.2}$ | $\mathbf{87.3^{\pm0.5}}/79.3^{\pm1.0}$ | | $76.5^{\pm2.9}/72.5^{\pm4.0}$ | $64.0^{\pm1.4}/72.5^{\pm3.3}$ |
| | Rank | | $76.6^{\pm5.9}/81.2^{\pm1.1}$ | $86.4^{\pm0.7}/76.1^{\pm1.3}$ | | $69.2^{\pm7.3}/77.1^{\pm2.9}$ | $\mathbf{85.4^{\pm0.8}}/78.5^{\pm1.0}$ |
| | Or-Ra | | $84.0^{\pm2.2}/78.7^{\pm3.4}$ | $87.6^{\pm0.6}/81.0^{\pm0.9}$ | | $78.4^{\pm5.8}/58.1^{\pm4.6}$ | $83.3^{\pm1.1}/82.7^{\pm0.7}$ |

CSFD dataset, we beat three BERT-like models that are much larger (in terms of a number of parameters) than our CNN and LSTM models. In the case of the mBERT and XLM models, the difference is very significant. The results in Table 5 are shown as Macro $F_1$, but we have to note that our Macro $F_1$ results are identical to the accuracy.

### 4.4  Discussion

From our perception, during the experiments and from the presented Tables, we consider the CCA and Orthogonal transformations to be the most stable in terms of performance. These two methods usually obtain very comparable (if not the best) results across all experiments, unlike the other methods. The other methods (MSE, Rank Or-Ra) tend to fail in some settings and their performance decreases significantly. For example, the performance of the MSE method often drops by a large margin for experiments where embeddings for the target language is mapped into the source language (the **FR-t ⇒ EN-s** columns).

We found no systematic differences in performance between the LSTM and CNN models. We recognized that the transformations sometimes fail and cause poor performance of the overall model. In future work, we want to focus on these particular incidents and we would like to improve the stability of the transformations, for example, by normalizing the semantic spaces before and after the transformation.

## 5  Conclusion

In this paper, we studied the task of cross-lingual sentiment analysis for Czech, English and French. We performed zero-shot cross-lingual classification on four datasets with linear transformations in combination with LSTM and CNN based classifiers. We demonstrate that pre-trained in-domain embeddings can significantly improve the cross-lingual classification, in some cases even by more than 10%. We show that the approaches based on linear transformations are, to some extent, competitive with the multilingual BERT-like models. We provide all the presented resources, including word embeddings, dictionaries and source codes, freely for research purposes on our GitHub (see footnote 2).

**Acknowledgments.** This work has been partly supported by ERDF "Research and Development of Intelligent Components of Advanced Technologies for the Pilsen Metropolitan Area (InteCom)" (no.: CZ.02.1.01/0.0/0.0/17 048/0007267); and by Grant No. SGS-2022-016 Advanced methods of data processing and analysis. Computational resources were supplied by the project "e-Infrastruktura CZ" (e-INFRA CZ LM2018140) supported by the Ministry of Education, Youth and Sports of the Czech Republic.

# References

1. Abdalla, M., Hirst, G.: Cross-lingual sentiment analysis without (good) translation. In: Proceedings of the Eighth International Joint Conference on NLP) (2017)
2. Aliramezani, M., Doostmohammadi, E., Bokaei, M.H., Sameti, H.: Persian sentiment analysis without training data using cross-lingual word embeddings. In: 2020 10th International Symposium onTelecommunications (IST) (2020)
3. Ammar, W., Mulcaire, G., Tsvetkov, Y., Lample, G., Dyer, C., Smith, N.A.: Massively multilingual word embeddings (2016)
4. Artetxe, M., Labaka, G., Agirre, E.: Learning principled bilingual mappings of word embeddings while preserving monolingual invariance. In: Proceedings of the 2016 Conference on Empirical Methods in NLP (2016)
5. Balahur, A., Turchi, M.: Multilingual sentiment analysis using machine translation? In: Proceedings of the 3rd Workshop in Computational Approaches to Subjectivity and Sentiment Analysis (2012)
6. Barnes, J., Klinger, R., Schulte im Walde, S.: Bilingual sentiment embeddings: Joint projection of sentiment across languages. In: Proceedings of the 56th Annual Meeting of the Association for Computational Linguistics (2018)
7. Barnes, J., Lambert, P., Badia, T.: Exploring distributional representations and machine translation for aspect-based cross-lingual sentiment classification. In: Proceedings of COLING 2016, the 26th International Conference on Computational Linguistics: Technical Papers (2016)
8. Barriere, V., Balahur, A.: Improving sentiment analysis over non-English tweets using multilingual transformers and automatic translation for data-augmentation. In: Proceedings of the 28th COLING (2020)
9. Bojanowski, P., Grave, E., Joulin, A., Mikolov, T.: Enriching word vectors with subword information. arXiv preprint arXiv:1607.04606 (2016)
10. Brychcín, T.: Linear transformations for cross-lingual semantic textual similarity. Knowledge-Based Systems 187 (2020)
11. Can, E.F., Ezen-Can, A., Can, F.: Multilingual sentiment analysis: An rnn-based framework for limited data. CoRR abs/1806.04511 (2018)
12. Chen, X., Sun, Y., Athiwaratkun, B., Cardie, C., Weinberger, K.: Adversarial deep averaging networks for cross-lingual sentiment classification. Transactions of the Association for Computational Linguistics 6 (2018)

13. Conneau, A., Khandelwal, K., Goyal, N., Chaudhary, V., Wenzek, G., Guzmán, F., Grave, E., Ott, M., Zettlemoyer, L., Stoyanov, V.: Unsupervised cross-lingual representation learning at scale. In: Proceedings of the 58th Annual Meeting of the Association for Computational Linguistics (2020)

14. Devlin, J., Chang, M.W., Lee, K., Toutanova, K.: BERT: Pre-training of deep bidirectional transformers for language understanding. In: Proceedings of the 2019 Conference of the North American Chapter of the Association for Computational Linguistics: Human Language Technologies (2019)

15. Dong, X., De Melo, G.: Cross-lingual propagation for deep sentiment analysis. In: Thirty-Second AAAI Conference on Artificial Intelligence (2018)

16. Habernal, I., Ptáček, T., Steinberger, J.: Sentiment analysis in Czech social media using supervised machine learning. In: Proceedings of the 4th Workshop on Computational Approaches to Subjectivity and Social Media Analysis (2013)

17. Hardoon, D.R., Szedmak, S., Shawe-Taylor, J.: Canonical correlation analysis: An overview with application to learning methods. Neural computation 16(12) (2004)

18. Jain, S., Batra, S.: Cross lingual sentiment analysis using modified BRAE. In: Proceedings of the 2015 Conference on Empirical Methods in NLP (2015)

19. Jiang, H., He, P., Chen, W., Liu, X., Gao, J., Zhao, T.: SMART: Robust and efficient fine-tuning for pre-trained natural language models through principled regularized optimization. In: Proceedings of the 58th Annual Meeting of the Association for Computational Linguistics (2020)

20. Johnson, R., Zhang, T.: Supervised and semi-supervised text categorization using lstm for region embeddings. In: Proceedings of the 33rd International Conference on International Conference on Machine Learning - Volume 48 (2016)

21. Kim, Y.: Convolutional neural networks for sentence classification. In: Proceedings of the 2014 Conference on Empirical Methods in NLP (2014)

22. Kingma, D.P., Ba, J.: Adam: A method for stochastic optimization. arXiv preprint arXiv:1412.6980 (2014)

23. Kuriyozov, E., Doval, Y., Gómez-Rodríguez, C.: Cross-lingual word embeddings for Turkic languages. In: Proceedings of the 12th LREC Conference (2020)

24. Lazaridou, A., Dinu, G., Baroni, M.: Hubness and pollution: Delving into cross-space mapping for zero-shot learning. In: Proceedings of the 53rd Annual Meeting of the Association for Computational Linguistics and the 7th International Joint Conference on Natural Language Processing. Beijing, China (2015)

25. Lehečka, J., Švec, J., Ircing, P., Šmídl, L.: Bert-based sentiment analysis using distillation. In: Espinosa-Anke, L., Martín-Vide, C., Spasić, I. (eds.) Statistical Language and Speech Processing (2020)

26. Maas, A.L., Daly, R.E., Pham, P.T., Huang, D., Ng, A.Y., Potts, C.: Learning word vectors for sentiment analysis. In: Proceedings of the 49th Annual Meeting of the Association for Computational Linguistics (2011)

27. Mikolov, T., Le, Q.V., Sutskever, I.: Exploiting similarities among languages for machine translation. CoRR abs/1309.4168 (2013)

28. Přibáň, P., Steinberger, J.: Are the multilingual models better? improving Czech sentiment with transformers. In: Proceedings of the International Conference on Recent Advances in Natural Language Processing (RANLP 2021) (2021)

29. Raffel, C., Shazeer, N., Roberts, A., Lee, K., Narang, S., Matena, M., Zhou, Y., Li, W., Liu, P.J.: Exploring the limits of transfer learning with a unified text-to-text transformer. Journal of Machine Learning Research 21(140) (2020)

30. Ruder, S., Vulić, I., Søgaard, A.: A survey of cross-lingual word embedding models. Journal of Artificial Intelligence Research 65 (2019)

31. Socher, R., Perelygin, A., Wu, J., Chuang, J., Manning, C.D., Ng, A., Potts, C.: Recursive deep models for semantic compositionality over a sentiment treebank. In: Proceedings of the 2013 Conference on Empirical Methods in NLP (2013)
32. Srivastava, N., Hinton, G., Krizhevsky, A., Sutskever, I., Salakhutdinov, R.: Dropout: a simple way to prevent neural networks from overfitting. The journal of machine learning research 15(1) (2014)
33. Sun, C., Qiu, X., Xu, Y., Huang, X.: How to fine-tune BERT for text classification? In: China National Conference on Chinese Computational Linguistics (2019)
34. Thakkar, G., Preradovic, N.M., Tadic, M.: Multi-task learning for cross-lingual sentiment analysis. In: CLEOPATRA@ WWW (2021)
35. Thongtan, T., Phienthrakul, T.: Sentiment classification using document embeddings trained with cosine similarity. In: Proceedings of the 57th Annual Meeting of the Association for Computational Linguistics: Student Research Workshop (2019)
36. Théophile, B.: French sentiment analysis with bert. https://github.com/TheophileBlard/french-sentiment-analysis-with-bert (2020)
37. Yang, Z., Dai, Z., Yang, Y., Carbonell, J., Le, Q.V.: Xlnet: Generalized autoregressive pretraining for language understanding. In: Wallach, H., Larochelle, H., Beygelzimer, A., d' Alché-Buc, F., Fox, E., Garnett, R. (eds.) Advances in Neural Information Processing Systems. vol. 32. Curran Associates, Inc. (2019)
38. Zhang, W., He, R., Peng, H., Bing, L., Lam, W.: Cross-lingual aspect-based sentiment analysis with aspect term code-switching. In: Proceedings of the 2021 Conference on Empirical Methods in NLP (2021)
39. Zhou, H., Chen, L., Shi, F., Huang, D.: Learning bilingual sentiment word embeddings for cross-language sentiment classification. In: Proceedings of the 53rd Annual Meeting of the Association for Computational Linguistics and the 7th International Joint Conference on Natural Language Processing (2015)
40. Zhou, X., Wan, X., Xiao, J.: Attention-based LSTM network for cross-lingual sentiment classification. In: Proceedings of the 2016 Conference on Empirical Methods in NLP (2016)

# TOKEN Is a MASK: Few-shot Named Entity Recognition with Pre-trained Language Models

Ali Davody[1,2], David Ifeoluwa Adelani[1(✉)], Thomas Kleinbauer[1], and Dietrich Klakow[1]

[1] Spoken Language Systems Group, Saarland Informatics Campus, Saarland University, Saarbrücken, Germany
{adavody,didelani,thomas.kleinbauer,dietrich.klakow}@lsv.uni-saarland.de
[2] Testifi.io, Munich, Germany

**Abstract.** Transferring knowledge from one domain to another is of practical importance for many tasks in natural language processing, especially when the amount of available data in the target domain is limited. In this work, we propose a novel few-shot approach to domain adaptation in the context of Named Entity Recognition (NER). We propose a two-step approach consisting of a variable base module and a template module that leverages the knowledge captured in pre-trained language models with the help of simple descriptive patterns. Our approach is simple yet versatile, and can be applied in few-shot and zero-shot settings. Evaluating our lightweight approach across a number of different datasets shows that it can boost the performance of state-of-the-art baselines by $2-5\%$ F1-score.

**Keywords:** Named entity recognition · Few-shot learning · Transfer learning · Prompt-tuning

## 1 Introduction

Transfer learning has received increased attention in recent years because it provides an approach to a common problem for many realistic Natural Language Processing (NLP) tasks: the shortage of high-quality, annotated training data. While different implementations exist, the basic tenet is to utilize available data in a source domain to help training a classifier for a low-resource target domain.

An interesting new direction of research leverages the world knowledge captured by pre-trained language models (PLMs) with cloze-style natural language prompts for few-shot classification (e.g. [1,18]) and regression [5]. These approaches are attractive because they require little to no training, making them especially suitable for low-resource settings.

In this paper, we contribute to this research area by introducing a novel cloze-style approach to Named Entity Recognition (NER), an important task which

© Springer Nature Switzerland AG 2022
P. Sojka et al. (Eds.): TSD 2022, LNAI 13502, pp. 138–150, 2022.
https://doi.org/10.1007/978-3-031-16270-1_12

has previously not been addressed via cloze-style prompts. In its classical setting, i.e. recognizing a small number of entity types in newspaper texts, NER achieves state-of-the-art F1 scores of $\sim 95\%$ [25]. This is not necessarily the case, however, for more specialized domains where data is more scarce and annotations cannot easily be provided because they may require expert knowledge, such as e.g. , for biomedical texts. With the approach presented here, the expertise of highly trained specialists can be utilized in a different way, by providing *representative words* for the named entity types, rather than having to annotate corpus data.

The main appeal of our method lies in its simplicity, as applying it to a new domain requires very little effort and technical expertise. Our contribution is three-fold: (1) we introduce a new method for Named Entity Recognition (NER) with a focus on simplicity; (2) our technique is scalable down to zero-shot in which case *no training* is required on top of the PLM; (3) we show how a hybrid combination of our method with a standard classifier based on a simple threshold outperforms both of the individual classifiers (Sect. 3).

The effectiveness of our method is demonstrated by a thorough evaluation comparing different variants of the approach across a number of different data sets (Sect. 5). For reproducibility, we release our code on Github[1]

## 2  Related Work

Named entity recognition is a well-studied task in NLP, and is usually approached as a sequence-labeling problem where pre-trained language models such as ELMO [12], BERT [2], RoBERTa [11] and LUKE [25] have brought significant improvements in recent years. All these methods are based on supervised learning but they do not generalize to new domains in zero and few-shot settings.

Meta-learning or *learning to learn* [3,17,20] is a popular approach to few-shot learning. In the context of few-shot NER, most applications of meta-learning make use of Prototypical Networks [4,7,8] or Model-Agnostic Meta-Learning (MAML) [9]. These approaches require training on diverse domains or datasets to generalize to new domains.

Pre-trained language models have shown impressive potential in learning many NLP tasks without training data [13,15]. [18] proposed using a cloze-style question to enable masked LMs in few-shot settings to perform text classification and natural inference tasks with better performance than GPT-3 [1]. As creating cloze-style questions is time consuming, there are some attempts to automate this process. [6] makes use of the T5 model [16] to generate appropriate template by filling a [MASK] phrase similar to how T5 was trained. Shin et al. (2020) [19] use a template that combines the original sentence to classify with some trigger tokens and a [MASK] token that is related to the label name. The trigger tokens are learned using gradient-based search strategy proposed in [23]. In this paper, we extend this PLM prompt technique to named entity recognition.

---

[1] https://github.com/uds-lsv/TOKEN-is-a-MASK.

## 3  Method

Our approach consists of two parts. We first describe the *base method* that can be used as a stand-alone, zero- or few-shot classifier (Sect. 3.1). In Sect. 3.2, we then lay out how a simple ensemble method can combine the base method with another classifier to potentially improve over the individual performance of both. We call this setup the *hybrid method*.

### 3.1  Zero-Shot Base Method

The base method for classifying NEs in a sentence consists of two steps, *detecting* candidate words and *querying* a PLM for the NE class of each candidate word. For example, let $s = I$ *will visit Munich next week* be the sentence to label. As is typical, most words in $s$ do not denote a named entity, only *Munich* does (LOC). We construct a cloze-style query to the PLM from the original sentence and a template, in which the candidate word has been inserted:

*I would like to visit Munich next week. Munich is a [MASK].*

The first part of the prompt serves as the context for the second part of the prompt, a template of a predefined form e.g. [TOKEN] is a [MASK]. The [TOKEN] is replaced with the term to label. For auto-regressive LMs like GPT-2, [MASK] is empty, the next word is predicted given a context that ends with "TOKEN is a".

The prediction of the PLM for the [MASK] is a probability distribution $P(w|s)$ over the tokens $w$ in the vocabulary $\mathcal{V}$. Intuitively, since NE labels themselves often are descriptive words (e.g. *location, person*, etc.) contained in $\mathcal{V}$, the answer to the query could be found by observing $P(label|s)$ for all labels and selecting the one with the highest probability. We found this approach not to perform well, possibly because NE labels tend to describe abstract higher-level concepts that are not commonly used in sentences realized by our template.

However, by associating with each entity type a list of words representative of that type, we reach competitive performance to state-of-the-art approaches (see Sect. 5). As an example, Table 1 shows representative words for the five named entity classes Location, Person, Organization, Ordinal and Date.

More formally, let $\mathcal{L}$ be the set of all labels for the NER classification task. We provide a list of representative words $\mathcal{W}_l$ for each label $l$. Denoting the output of the PLM by $P(\cdot|s + T(w))$ where $s$ is the original sentence, $T(w)$ is the prompt for token $w$, and $+$ stands for string concatenation, we assign label $l_w$ to the token $w$ by:

$$l_w = \arg\max_l P(v \in \mathcal{W}_l | s + T(w)). \tag{1}$$

For the example above ($s = I$ *will visit Munich next week*; $T(Munich) = Munich$ *is a [MASK]*), the top-5 predictions using the *BERT-large model* are: city, success, democracy, capital, dream. The largest probability (0.43) among all words is assigned to `city` which is among the representative words for label LOC. Thus, *Munich* is labeled as a location. A graphical depiction of the full method is shown in Fig. 1.

The outlined approach raises three design questions which we address in turn:

1. Given the input sentence, how to detect the candidate tokens to label?
2. What constitutes a good template for the second half of the prompt?
3. Which words to include in the list of representative words for each entity label?

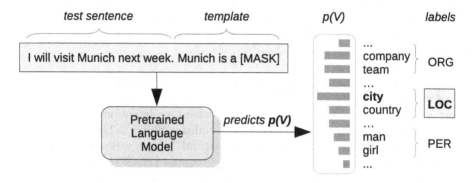

**Fig. 1.** Overview of the proposed template method: The PLM prompt consists of the sentence and the template instantiated with the word to label. The PLM predicts the probability of [MASK] for all representative words, and the label associated with the most probable word is returned.

**Table 1.** Examples of representative word lists for entity types `location` (LOC), `person` (PER), `organization` (ORG), `Ordinal` (ORDINAL), and `date` (DATE).

| Entity Type | Representative Words |
| --- | --- |
| LOC | location, city, country, region, area, province, state, town |
| PER | person, man, woman, boy, girl, human, someone, kid |
| ORG | organization, community, department, association, company, team |
| ORDINAL | number, digit, count, third, second |
| DATE | date, day, month, time, year |

A fourth decision to make is the choice of pre-trained language model. Our results comparing four state-of-the-art PLMs are listed in Sect. 5.1, but we shall first attend to the three questions listed above.

*Identifying Named Entities.* In sequence labeling tasks, it is common that the identification of token boundaries and the actual label of the token is performed jointly as both decisions are often informed by the same features. Here, we perform these steps separately. This is possible because named entities are usually realized as proper nouns (although some NE schemes also include entities such as numbers, date, and time expressions), licensing the use of a task-independent part-of-speech tagger to identify candidate tokens in the input sentence before labeling it with the template method. Part-of-speech (POS)[2] taggers can identify occurrences of proper nouns (or numerals, ordinals) with a high degree of accuracy. However, entity boundaries in case of multi-word expressions are usually not labeled explicitly. A phrase structure parser could be employed to determine the boundaries of multi-word named entities, but we found simply treating consecutive proper nouns as a single entity to be a reasonable heuristic in our experiments.

*Template Selection.* In order to gain insights into what constitutes a good template we have experimented with a number of variants. Overall, we found that most templates performed similarly, except where we intentionally tested the limits of the format. These experiments are detailed in Sect. 5.2. Generally speaking, a template should be grammatical and natural. Simple variants work better than overly complicated templates. The simple copula `[TOKEN] is a [MASK]` is a good recommendation as it performed well in all of our tested conditions.

*Representative Words.* If some examples of the target domain are available at training time, the representative word lists can be derived from predictions over this data. That is, the representative words for each entity type can be taken as the most probable mask fillers given the respective prompts. Alternatively, in a zero-shot setting or where otherwise appropriate, a set of words can be provided by a domain expert. For the experiments in the next section, this is the strategy we followed. Of course, it is possible to combine both methods, with an expert choosing a suitable subset from words with the highest probability in the automatic setting. Additionally, we can use static word embeddings like GloVe to extract a list of representative for each category based on word similarity.

## 3.2    Few-Shot Hybrid Method

The method described thus far can be used for zero-shot classification as it does not require any training. In a few-shot setting, however, we can improve the performance of the system by fine-tuning the PLM using the labeled data in the target domain.

A further performance gain can be made by combining our method with a standard supervised classifier in a simple two-fold ensemble. Based on a selection threshold $p_h$, we label the token according to the prediction of the base method

---

[2] We make use of Spacy POS tagger https://spacy.io/usage/linguistic-features.

if the probability of the predicted label is higher than the threshold $p_h$:

$$\max_l P(v \in \mathcal{W}_l | s + T(w)) > p_h, \tag{2}$$

otherwise we relay the output of the supervised classifier. The threshold $p_h$ is a hyper-parameter that can be tuned on the training examples from the target domain.

## 4  Data

We consider three popular NER datasets (CoNLL03, OntoNotes 5.0 and i2b2) from different domains and with different label sets.

The **CoNLL03** data [22] consists of documents from the English news domain that have been annotated with four named entity types: personal name (PER), organization (ORG), location (LOC), and miscellaneous entity (MISC).

The **OntoNotes 5.0** dataset [14] consist of NER in three languages (English, Chinese and Arabic). In this work we make use of the English dataset with six annotated domains: broadcast news (BN), broadcast conversation (BC), magazines (MZ), telephone conversation (TC), and web data (WB). The annotation scheme of OntoNotes 5.0 distinguishes between 18 entity types, making it a more challenging task than CoNLL03.

**Table 2.** F1-scores for four PLMs on the CoNLL03 dataset in the zero-shot setting.

|            | BERT | RoBERTa | GPT-2 | XLNet |
|------------|------|---------|-------|-------|
| LOC        | 69%  | 65%     | 42%   | 58%   |
| PER        | 80%  | 73%     | 45%   | 57%   |
| ORG        | 42%  | 43%     | 13%   | 34%   |
| Micro-Avg. | 60%  | 59%     | 36%   | 49%   |

The third dataset, **i2b2 2014** [21], is a BioNLP dataset commonly used for de-identification tasks. The dataset contains 25 entity types from seven Private Health Information (PHI) categories: Name, Profession, Location, Age, Date, Contact, and Ids.

In our few-shot experiments, 1, 5, or 100 data points are sampled per label from each training set, depending on the setting. In the zero-shot case, no training is used.

# 5    Experiments

## 5.1    Comparing Language Models

We study the role of the choice of PLM in our approach by comparing four state-of-the-art pre-trained language models: BERT [2], RoBERTa [11], GPT-2 [15] and XLNET [27]. BERT and RoBERTa are trained to predict masked tokens that are randomly corrupted in the training sentence. GPT-2 is based on autoregressive language modeling, but it is less efficient predicting masked tokens. XLNET attempts to address the limitations of BERT for next-word prediction (i.e. autoregressive LM) while retaining good performance on natural language understanding tasks.

Table 2 compares the four PLMs on the CoNLL03 dataset for the zero-shot setting as described above. In all of these experiments, the template [TOKEN] is a [MASK] and the representative word lists from Table 1 were used. We observe that BERT and RoBERTa outperform the other two LMs. Interestingly, GPT-2 does not perform well in this setting with an average F1 score of just 36%.

## 5.2    Choice of Template

A second variable in the setup is the choice of the template used in the prompt. We compare 15 different templates in the zero-shot setting, listed in Table 3. We examined these templates on the CoNLL03 and OntoNotes datasets using location, person and organization as entity classes. Tables 4 and 5 present the results of this experiment.

$T_1$ is a straight-forward default and copula template that directly identifies the token with the mask. $T_2$ template differs from $T_1$ only in the verb. We added it to study the influence of tense on the prediction quality. In our experiments, it lead to slightly worse results, but it might be useful e.g. for historical texts. $T_3$ is similar to the above but uses a modal auxiliary. We further experimented with stripping down a template to the minimum useful form in $T_4$. This template is ungrammatical, however, and does not perform well. $T_5$ is the smallest template possible modulo word order. It is the worst performing template in our experiments, especially failing to predict the PER class. The next four templates $T_6 - T_9$ are further variations of $T_1$ that replace the verb to be with longer constructions.

In all previous templates, the token to label appears as the first word. In $T_{10}$, we test whether a longer left-hand side context is beneficial to the PLM prediction. With $T_{11}$, we test the effect of extending the right-hand context. It does not produce the same performance gain as $T_{10}$, though. $T_{12}$ extends both the left-hand and the right-hand side context simultaneously, but also presents token and mask in a contrasting relation. It seems that the language model has more difficulties associating the mask and the token with each other in this template, as the performance drops considerably for CoNLL03. $T_{13}$ also reverses the order of mask and token but outperforms $T_{12}$ template in the case of CoNLL03.

Are the additional filler words responsible for the good performance of $T_{13}$, or is it the way the relation between mask and token are expressed using the word

**Table 3.** List of templates used in the comparative experiments. Aspects considered include tense, mood, expression length and complexity, verb choice, grammaticality, and TOKEN/MASK order, in different forms.

| ID | Template |
|---|---|
| $T_1$ | [TOKEN] is a [MASK]. |
| $T_2$ | [TOKEN] was a [MASK]. |
| $T_3$ | [TOKEN] would be a [MASK]. |
| $T_4$ | [TOKEN] a [MASK]. |
| $T_5$ | [TOKEN] [MASK]. |
| $T_6$ | [TOKEN] is an example of a [MASK]. |
| $T_7$ | [TOKEN] is an instance of a [MASK]. |
| $T_8$ | [TOKEN] denotes a [MASK]. |
| $T_9$ | [TOKEN] is well-known to be a [MASK]. |
| $T_{10}$ | Many people consider [TOKEN] to be a [MASK]. |
| $T_{11}$ | [TOKEN] is a common [MASK] known to many people. |
| $T_{12}$ | There are many [MASK]s but [TOKEN] stands out nevertheless. |
| $T_{13}$ | A [MASK] like [TOKEN] is often mentioned in conversations. |
| $T_{14}$ | A [MASK] like [TOKEN]. |
| $T_{15}$ | This [MASK], [TOKEN], is worth discussing. |

*like*? $T_{14}$ reduced template suggests the latter, as it performs even slightly better than $T_{13}$. Finally $T_{15}$ is similar in spirit to $T_5$ in that it tests whether proximity of mask and token are important, only with the order of the two reversed, and some context words added. It performs better than $T_5$ but not en par with most other templates.

The key message of these experiments is that our approach is robust against the details of the template format as long as it is not too artificial. Indeed, we do not observe a high variation in the performance of the model when using different natural sounding templates.

**Table 4.** Comparing different templates $T_1$–$T_{15}$ and their impact on the F1-score in the zero-shot setting on CoNLL03. The results suggest that the performance of a template depends mainly on its naturalness.

| | $T_1$ | $T_2$ | $T_3$ | $T_4$ | $T_5$ | $T_6$ | $T_7$ | $T_8$ | $T_9$ | $T_{10}$ | $T_{11}$ | $T_{12}$ | $T_{13}$ | $T_{14}$ | $T_{15}$ |
|---|---|---|---|---|---|---|---|---|---|---|---|---|---|---|---|
| LOC | 69% | 60% | 62% | 52% | 46% | 66% | 63% | 60% | 67% | 69% | 61% | 57% | 73% | 70% | 60% |
| PER | 80% | 72% | 73% | 65% | 7% | 81% | 82% | 71% | 76% | 82% | 83% | 15% | 76% | 81% | 57% |
| ORG | 42% | 48% | 51% | 35% | 35% | 44% | 39% | 41% | 47% | 44% | 41% | 36% | 48% | 54% | 34% |
| Micro-Avg. | 60% | 57% | 57% | 47% | 31% | 59% | 57% | 55% | 60% | 62% | 59% | 36% | 62% | 63% | 49% |

**Table 5.** Impact of template choice in the zero-shot setting for OntoNotes

|            | $T_1$ | $T_2$ | $T_3$ | $T_4$ | $T_5$ | $T_6$ | $T_7$ | $T_8$ | $T_9$ | $T_{10}$ | $T_{11}$ | $T_{12}$ | $T_{13}$ | $T_{14}$ | $T_{15}$ |
|------------|-----|-----|-----|-----|-----|-----|-----|-----|-----|------|------|------|------|------|------|
| LOC        | 71% | 72% | 71% | 64% | 50% | 69% | 67% | 72% | 67% | 67%  | 64%  | 68%  | 67%  | 68%  | 63%  |
| PER        | 49% | 45% | 43% | 47% | 24% | 51% | 51% | 44% | 48% | 49%  | 51%  | 43%  | 45%  | 43%  | 47%  |
| ORG        | 47% | 45% | 44% | 41% | 36% | 43% | 42% | 42% | 46% | 47%  | 47%  | 45%  | 44%  | 45%  | 42%  |
| Micro-Avg. | 57% | 55% | 54% | 52% | 38% | 56% | 54% | 54% | 55% | 56%  | 56%  | 54%  | 53%  | 54%  | 50%  |

## 5.3   Domain Adaptation

In this section, we assess the extent to which our prompt-based approach can improve the performance of available baseline methods for NER in a domain adaptation setting. Specifically, we are interested in a setting where knowledge of the source domain should be transferred to a target domain for which the number of available training samples is very limited. This is of particular importance as annotating a new large corpus is often prohibitive.

We consider three baselines: in the *AGG* baseline, we merge the training data of the source and target domain and train a NER classifier on the resulting aggregated dataset. In the *Fine-tuning* baseline, we first train the model on the source domain and then fine-tune it on the training set of the target domain. Both of these approaches have been shown to reach results competitive with other state-of-the-art methods [10]. In both cases, a BERT-large cased pre-trained LM followed by a linear layer is used as the NER classifier.

The third baseline is STRUCTSHOT, introduced by [26]. It is based on a feature extractor module obtained by training a supervised NER model on the source domain. The generated contextual representations are used at inference time by a nearest neighbor token classifier. Additionally, label dependencies are captured by employing a viterbi decoder of a conditional random field layer and estimating the tag transitions using source domain.

Following [24], we take one domain of the dataset as the target domain and the other domains as the source domain. We randomly select $K = 100$ sample sentences from the target domain as our target training set. For selecting

**Table 6.** Domain adaptation for NER: F1 score of using the OntoNotes and i2b2 datasets. Combining our prompt-based method $T$ with the Fine-Tuning approach achieves the best performance. For all few-shot methods, we use K=100 samples of target domain training set. In contrast, the In-domain method uses all available training samples and serves as a topline.

| Method          | BC       | BN       | MZ       | NW       | TC       | WB       | AVG      |
|-----------------|----------|----------|----------|----------|----------|----------|----------|
| AGG             | 46.3     | 47.9     | 46.9     | 52.7     | 51.7     | 43.8     | 48.2     |
| AGG+$T$         | 61.1     | 66.2     | 62.1     | 71.0     | 73.3     | 47.4     | 63.5     |
| Fine-Tuning     | 66.7     | 71.2     | 69.3     | 74.1     | 65.2     | 49.1     | 65.9     |
| Fine-Tuning+$T$ | **72.0** | 72.1     | 74.7     | **74.3** | 77.0     | 49.1     | 69.9     |
| STRUCTSHOT      | 63.2     | 70.6     | 71.6     | 71.8     | 67.3     | 51.2     | 65.9     |
| STRUCTSHOT +$T$ | 70.3     | **72.8** | **75.5** | 73.5     | **78.4** | **51.9** | **70.4** |
| In-domain       | 91.6     | 94.3     | 94.1     | 93.2     | 76.9     | 67.1     | 86.2     |

**Table 7.** Results of domain adaptation for NER using OntoNotes as the source domain and i2b2 as the target domain.

| In-domain | AGG | AGG+$T$ | Fine-Tuning | Fine-Tuning+$T$ | STRUCTSHOT | STRUCTSHOT +$T$ |
|-----------|-----|---------|-------------|-----------------|------------|-----------------|
| 94.8 | 53.5 | 57.2 | 62.3 | **65.1** | 60.2 | 64.2 |

source and target labels, heterogeneous setup is adopted in which we choose PERSON, ORG, PRODUCT as source labels and PERSON, ORG, PRODUCT, LOC, LANGUAGE, ORDINAL as target labels. This discrepancy between target and source labels makes transfer learning more challenging.

Table 6 depicts the results of our experiments on the various OntoNotes datasets averaged over five runs each. The table compares the performance of the baseline models with that of our hybrid approach. It also shows the results of an in-domain method, where we use all the training samples of target domain for training a fully supervised classifier. As is evident from this table, our prompt-based approach boosts the performance of all baseline models by a considerable margin. In our next experiment, we are interested in the impact of a greater discrepancy between source and target domain. We therefore take the OntoNotes 5.0 dataset as the source domain and the i2b2 2014 dataset as the target domain.

We use PERSON, ORG, DATE, LOC as source labels and PERSON, ORG, DATE, LOC, PROFESSION as target labels. Table 7 shows the results of our experiments. We observe the same pattern as before, i.e., combining our method with supervised baselines achieves the best performance. Lastly, we examine the role of tags on the performance of our method. To do so, we follow the same strategy as [26] and split the entity categories of the OntoNotes into three non-overlapping groups:

- Group A: ORG, NORP, ORDINAL, WORK OF ART, QUANTITY, LAW
- Group B: GPE, CARDINAL, PERCENT, TIME, EVENT, LANGUAGE
- Group C: PERSON, DATE, MONEY, LOC, FAC, PRODUCT

When we pick a group, e.g. A, as the target group, the corresponding tags are replaced with the O-tag in the training data. Thus, the model is trained only on source groups B and C. At inference time, we evaluate the model on the test set which contains only target labels (A). The results of this experiments

**Table 8.** Results of F1 scores on one-shot NER for different target labels.

| | one-shot | | | five-shot | | |
|---|---|---|---|---|---|---|
| | Group A | Group B | Group C | Group A | Group B | Group C |
| Fine-Tuning | $7.4 \pm 2.4$ | $8.9 \pm 4.3$ | $9.1 \pm 2.0$ | $13.1 \pm 1.8$ | $21.4 \pm 7.3$ | $20.8 \pm 4.2$ |
| Fine-Tuning+$T$ | $8.9 \pm 2.1$ | $11.8 \pm 3.9$ | $13.6 \pm 1.7$ | $14.9 \pm 1.6$ | $20.7 \pm 6.5$ | $22.5 \pm 2.6$ |
| STRUCTSHOT | $26.7 \pm 4.8$ | $33.2 \pm 15.6$ | $23.0 \pm 11.4$ | $\mathbf{47.8 \pm 3.5}$ | $56.5 \pm 9.3$ | $53.4 \pm 3.2$ |
| STRUCTSHOT +$T$ | $\mathbf{27.3 \pm 4.2}$ | $\mathbf{33.6 \pm 14.1}$ | $\mathbf{26.5 \pm 8.7}$ | $46.0 \pm 2.9$ | $\mathbf{57.7 \pm 7.8}$ | $\mathbf{55.1 \pm 2.1}$ |

are shown in Tables 8 for the one-shot and 5-shot setting. We again observe the improvement of baseline models by integrating them into template approach. The amount of performance gain depends on the target group, of course. In particular, we get a large amount of improvement for group C of tags around 3.5 in one-shot and 1.7 in the five-shot setting.

## 6   Conclusion and Future Work

We proposed a novel, lightweight approach to NER for zero- and few-shot settings, using pre-trained language models to fill in cloze-style prompts. It is based on extracting information available in PLMs and utilizes it to labels named entity instances identified by a domain-independent POS tagger. Results show that masked language models have a better performance in this setting compared with auto-regressive language models. We explored a wide range of possible prompts with different datasets. We observed that the proposed method is robust against contextual details of prompts. This is of practical significance in the low-resource setting where there is not enough data to tune the model. Our method is simple, general and can be used to boost the performance of available domain adaptation baselines. We also propose a hybrid approach that can easily combine the template method with any other supervised/unsupervised classifier, and demonstrated the effectiveness of this hybrid approach empirically.

Further work could investigate the possibility of fine-tuning templates while having access only to a few training samples. It would be also interesting to explore more sophisticated approaches for combining the predictions of the template model and other few-shot NER baselines. Two aspects of our approach currently require manual intervention, the template and the representative word lists. Finding ways to determine these fully automatically is another interesting direction to explore. As mentioned before, one way to extract representative words is by making use of word embeddings like GloVe. Indeed, we found that almost all subsets of our representative words perform fairly well in practice. We leave automatically extraction of representative words and its evaluation to future work.

**Acknowledgments.** This work was funded by the EU-funded Horizon 2020 projects: COMPRISE (http://www.compriseh2020.eu/) under grant agreement No. 3081705 and ROXANNE under grant number 833635.

## References

1. Brown, T., et al.: Language models are few-shot learners. In: Larochelle, H., Ranzato, M., Hadsell, R., Balcan, M., Lin, H. (eds.) In: NeurIPS, vol. 33, pp. 1877–1901 (2020)
2. Devlin, J., Chang, M.W., Lee, K., Toutanova, K.: BERT: pre-training of deep bidirectional transformers for language understanding. In: NAACL-HLT, pp. 4171–4186, June 2019

3. Finn, C., Abbeel, P., Levine, S.: Model-agnostic meta-learning for fast adaptation of deep networks. In: ICML (2017)
4. Fritzler, A., Logacheva, V., Kretov, M.: Few-shot classification in named entity recognition task. In: Proceedings of the 34th ACM/SIGAPP Symposium on Applied Computing, SAC 2019, pp. 993–1000 (2019)
5. Gao, T., Fisch, A., Chen, D.: Making pre-trained language models better few-shot learners. arXiv:2012.15723, 31 December 2020
6. Gao, T., Fisch, A., Chen, D.: Making pre-trained language models better few-shot learners (2020)
7. Hou, Y., et al.: Few-shot slot tagging with collapsed dependency transfer and label-enhanced task-adaptive projection network. In: ACL, pp. 1381–1393. Online, July 2020
8. Huang, J., et al.: Few-shot named entity recognition: a comprehensive study. ArXiv abs/2012.14978 (2020)
9. Krone, J., Zhang, Y., Diab, M.: Learning to classify intents and slot labels given a handful of examples. In: Proceedings of the 2nd Workshop on Natural Language Processing for Conversational AI, pp. 96–108. Association for Computational Linguistics, July 2020
10. Li, J., Shang, S., Shao, L.: Metaner: Named entity recognition with meta-learning. In: Proceedings of The Web Conference 2020, pp. 429–440. WWW 2020. Association for Computing Machinery, New York, (2020)
11. Liu, Y., et al.: Roberta: a robustly optimized bert pretraining approach. ArXiv abs/1907.11692 (2019)
12. Peters, M.E., et al.: Deep contextualized word representations. In: NAACL-HLT, pp. 2227–2237, June 2018
13. Petroni, F., et al.: Language models as knowledge bases? (2019)
14. Pradhan, S., et al.: Towards robust linguistic analysis using OntoNotes. In: Proceedings of the Seventeenth Conference on Computational Natural Language Learning, pp. 143–152. Association for Computational Linguistics, Sofia, Bulgaria, August 2013
15. Radford, A., Wu, J., Child, R., Luan, D., Amodei, D., Sutskever, I.: Language models are unsupervised multitask learners (2019). https://d4mucfpksywv. cloudfront.net/better-language-models/language_models_are_unsupervised_ multitask_learners.pdf
16. Raffel, C., et al.: Exploring the limits of transfer learning with a unified text-to-text transformer. J. Mach. Learn. Res. **21**, 140:1–140:67 (2020)
17. Ravi, S., Larochelle, H.: Optimization as a model for few-shot learning. In: ICLR (2017)
18. Schick, T., Schütze, H.: Exploiting cloze questions for few shot text classification and natural language inference. In: EACL, 19–23 April 2021
19. Shin, T., Razeghi, Y., Logan IV, R.L., Wallace, E., Singh, S.: AutoPrompt: Eliciting Knowledge from Language Models with Automatically Generated Prompts. In: EMNLP. pp. 4222–4235. Online (Nov 2020)
20. Snell, J., Swersky, K., Zemel, R.: Prototypical networks for few-shot learning. In: Guyon, I., Luxburg, U.V., Bengio, S., Wallach, H., Fergus, R., Vishwanathan, S., Garnett, R. (eds.) NeurIPS, vol. 30, pp. 4077–4087. Curran Associates, Inc. (2017)
21. Stubbs, A., Kotfila, C., Uzuner, O.: Automated systems for the de-identification of longitudinal clinical narratives. J. Biomed. Inf. **58**(S), S11–S19 (2015)
22. Tjong Kim Sang, E.F., De Meulder, F.: Introduction to the CoNLL-2003 shared task: Language-independent named entity recognition. In: Proceedings of the 7th CoNLL at HLT-NAACL 2003, pp. 142–147 (2003)

23. Wallace, E., Feng, S., Kandpal, N., Gardner, M., Singh, S.: Universal adversarial triggers for attacking and analyzing NLP. In: EMNLP/IJCNLP (2019)
24. Wang, J., Kulkarni, M., Preotiuc-Pietro, D.: Multi-domain named entity recognition with genre-aware and agnostic inference. In: ACL. pp. 8476–8488. Online (Jul 2020)
25. Yamada, I., Asai, A., Shindo, H., Takeda, H., Matsumoto, Y.: LUKE: deep contextualized entity representations with entity-aware self-attention. In: EMNLP, pp. 6442–6454, November 2020
26. Yang, Y., Katiyar, A.: Simple and effective few-shot named entity recognition with structured nearest neighbor learning. In: EMNLP, pp. 6365–6375, November 2020
27. Yang, Z., Dai, Z., Yang, Y., Carbonell, J., Salakhutdinov, R.R., Le, Q.V.: Xlnet: Generalized autoregressive pretraining for language understanding. In: NeurIPS. vol. 32, pp. 5753–5763 (2019)

# Use of Machine Learning Methods in the Assessment of Programming Assignments

Botond Tarcsay[(✉)] [iD], Jelena Vasić [iD], and Fernando Perez-Tellez [iD]

Technological University Dublin, Dublin, Ireland
botond@shoployal.ie

**Abstract.** Programming has become an important skill in today's world and is taught widely both in traditional and online settings. Educators need to grade increasing numbers of student submissions. Unit testing can contribute to the automation of the grading process; however, it cannot assess the structure, or partial correctness, which are needed for finely differentiated grading. This paper builds on previous research that investigated several machine learning models for determining the correctness of source code. It was found that some such models can be successful, provided that the code samples used for fitting and prediction fulfil the same sets of requirements (corresponding to coding assignments). The hypothesis investigated in this paper is that code samples can be grouped by similarity of the requirements that they fulfil and that models built with samples of code from such a group can be used for determining the quality of new samples that belong to the same group, even if they do not correspond to the same coding assignment, which would make for a much more useful predictive model in practice. The investigation involved ten different machine learning algorithms used on over four hundred thousand student code submissions and it confirmed the hypothesis.

**Keywords:** Applied Machine Learning for Code Assessment · Student Programming Code Grading · Automated Grading

## 1 Introduction

Manually grading student code submissions on a large scale is a tedious and time-consuming process for educators. With the rise of online programming courses, thousands of submissions must be graded in a brief time. Most automated solutions use question-specific unit testing to check if the code is runnable, and if it generates the desired output. However, there are multiple ways to write code that generate the same result. For example, printing numbers from 1 to 10 can be solved with a loop or hard coded to print the numbers individually. A unit test-based grade would be the same for these two solutions. The aim of this research work is to automate the discovery of these differences and assist in grading them accordingly. The research investigates Machine Learning (ML) algorithms for

© Springer Nature Switzerland AG 2022
P. Sojka et al. (Eds.): TSD 2022, LNAI 13502, pp. 151–159, 2022.
https://doi.org/10.1007/978-3-031-16270-1_13

automated grading based on content, rather than externally testable behavior. The paper investigates four different feature sets and suitably chosen ML methods.

The requirement for computing resources increases with the token count, therefore ByteCode was used and compared to Python code to explore how the lower-level language in this context would fare in terms of computational efficiency and model performance. ByteCode used significantly fewer tokens than Python code, saving significant amount of training time.

The hypothesis was that the student code submissions might contain common features at different levels of quality (corresponding to different grades), which can be picked up by ML methods. Pre-trained models can then assist educators in the grading process for basic programming exercises along with the current unit testing methods.

The main models were trained for binary prediction, with a pass/fail result of unit tests previously run on the coding exercises as the target feature. The process is displayed in Fig. 1 from compiling, preparing, and training the different models. The main contributions of this paper are:

1. It shows the potential of using multiple pre-trained ML models to assist educators to grade student submissions.
2. The use of a smaller lower-level language instruction set (ByteCode) can reduce the resource requirements for ML algorithms without significant loss of performance.

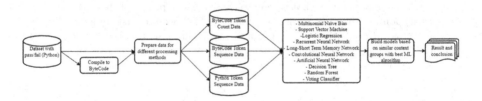

**Fig. 1.** Process Flow

## 2   Related Work

There were several previous works on describing source code in computationally solvable environment, SemCluster [2] which uses two different clustering algorithms to understand how the input is partitioned into classes, and how these classes address the problem, which is a different approach. A solution using ML is discussed in a method called InferCode [3], which examines the usage of self-supervised learning algorithms with NLP processing the Abstract Syntax Trees of the programming language in question. Different approaches were deployed to solve different but related problems, from finding security vulnerabilities directly in source code using Neural Network Language Model-guided Engine Fuzzer with Montage [4] to information retrieval techniques for plagiarism detection [6,11] and code review to predict if a code change will be approved [10] utilizing CNN in their proposed model: DeepReview. A more recent paper related to Python code proposes a Deep Similarity Learning approach Type4py [9] using word2vec and word embeddings. The authors were creating type hints based on natural information and code context.

Analyzing and understanding source code is a vital element in assisting educators in grading it. Solving the problem of grading student's coding submission at a scale has also been a widely researched subject, especially in the last couple of years, due to the increasing number of online programming courses. A paper proposing a method called ProgEdu [7] deals with an automated code quality assessment and student feedback using unit testing, while other papers discuss techniques to evaluate, run and grade a code using sophisticated scripts [5]. There are also question and language-independent solutions [8] using best practices and closeness to response given by logic and data dependencies and bag of words, while AutoGrader [12] is using formal-semantics-based approach to grade a submission based on a reference implementation and the semantic difference between the reference and the student code.

The research is different from the above-mentioned papers as it is focused on exploring whether student submissions can be assessed based on content only and whether partial correctness can be determined independent of question. The paper does not compare the code to a reference solution, or Abstract Syntax Tree, or investigate the question itself, but tries to understand if there is a possibility to determine content correctness and small differences from the code itself for assigning the final grade.

## 3   Dataset

The data was collected as part of previous research [1] aimed at profiling students based on their source code to identify learning development potential. The data contained half a million student source code submissions from more than 660 students (students were able to continually submit their code until the final deadline, resulting in multiple submissions per student for each question) across 3 years and 5 different courses, answering 657 different questions. All submissions were graded by an automatic unit testing system, removing any human bias from the results. An indicator of pass/fail status, for each submission, based on relevant unit tests was included. The submissions varied significantly in length. The average code length in ByteCode format was 4,000 characters, with a maximum of 21,000 and a minimum of 1, while the average length of Python code was 350 characters with a maximum of 35,000 and minimum of 1. The difference between the ByteCode and Python length is explained by the different way these languages are presented in the source code.

The data contain various programming assignments; however, all other languages were removed apart from Python code to prepare for processing. The data was anonymized by discarding all information except the source code, question name and the auto-grading results. Only code with a maximum length of 15,000 characters was used, to reduce the noise in the data created by outliers. The removed data accounted for 3.8% of the whole dataset. Transformed code, consisting of Python ByteCode was also used. ByteCode consists of a set of about 200 instructions, of which the students were using 85. The pieces of code that could not be transformed or had empty content were discarded, leaving us with a dataset of 202,000 submissions. Of these 58% were labelled 'fail' and 42% 'pass'.

Four sets of features were derived from the raw data i.e. the files containing code: 1. a set with a single attribute, the Python code length, 2. a set containing ByteCode token counts, 3. a set with NLP word tokenizer output for decompiled ByteCode instructions and 4. a set with NLP word tokenizer output for Python code. The ByteCode token count feature set was used to investigate the possible relationship between the pass/fail test result of the code and the number of times each ByteCode instruction appeared in the decompiled code. Instructions that did not appear throughout the whole dataset were discarded. Features in sets 3 and 4 represent token positions (with tokens as values) and were created using the word tokenizer from the *keras.preprocessing.text* library.

### 3.1   Preliminary Data Analysis

Feature set 2 (token counts) was investigated from an n-gram perspective, for how certain word sequences might influence the algorithms. The number of times the same token appears across the whole feature set was counted, and the same was done for bigrams, trigrams, and quadrigrams. The single token counts indicated that a limited number of features (top 30 most frequent tokens) would be sufficient for the models. The bigram counts are shown in Fig. 2. An interesting observation that can be made from these data is that passing (i.e. good) programs contain more functions (*load_const, make_function* ByteCode tokens and *def, self* Python tokens).

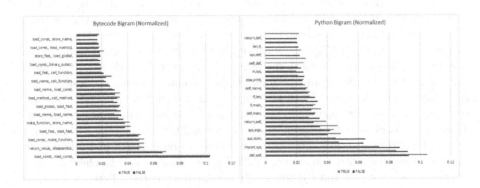

**Fig. 2.** ByteCode and Python Bigrams

The feature importance analysis for individual tokens in ByteCode showed similar results to feature importance reported by the decision tree model. There are 10 words which drive the decisions, with top 5 being *pop_top, load_name, load_fast, call_function, load_const.* This information assisted in the hyperparameter tuning of the ML algorithms used.

## 4   Model Exploration

Using pre-trained networks in NLP is common practice, however these solutions are not applicable to Python code and ByteCode as they are not natural languages.

Using standard 5-fold cross validation every algorithm was run 3 times with different random folds, which ensured that the models would not be biased. All algorithms had individual parameter optimization in place. Parameters were set to be close to each other while using different approaches, for result comparability, such as word count, maximum length, epoch, batch size etc. The algorithms used the relevant *tensorflow.keras* libraries.

A one-layer Artificial Neural Network predicting the result of the submissions (pass or fail) from the length of the relevant code was used to exclude the possibility that this one feature by itself (feature set 1) would be as effective as the more complicated approaches.

### 4.1   Token Count Based Models (Feature Set 2)

Multinomial Naïve Bayes was used to explore if the features are mutually independent in the dataset, Support Vector Machine to investigate if the algorithm can distinctly classify the pass/fail categories based on the token counts and Logistic Regression to examine if probability-based prediction is possible. Voting Classifier was also used with hard voting to see if the three previous algorithms can reach better results in an ensemble way. Additionally, Decision Tree and Random Forest was implemented to examine if a rule-based approach would be able to predict pass/fail outcomes from the token count-based dataset (feature set 2).

### 4.2   Language Based Approach - Token Sequences (Feature Sets 3 and 4)

For NLP based approaches, one layer Recurrent Neural Networks were used to explore if there are long-term dependencies within the data, two layer Long Short Term Memory Networks to account for more learning in context, and one dimensional Convolutional Neural Network to investigate if the word sequence can give an indication of the result. All deep learning methods used an embedding layer, to make sure that the tokenized data is further processed in a similar vector space. The preliminary data analysis using n-grams assisted in establishing the correct embedding features. The maximum number of words and embedding dimensions were set to 30 based on the results explained in Sect. 3.1. The Python token sequence (feature set 4) based investigation used the same algorithms however due to the high number of tokens, the training required more powerful machines and longer training times while the end results were very similar to the Bytecode token sequence (feature set 3) based algorithms.

## 5　Discussion of Results

All of the ByteCode based models could be fitted on basic computers, however, the Python code based ones required significantly stronger computing power as they use all relevant context (including keywords, numbers, variable names, comments). The memory requirement is also greatly increased when using the full Python token sequence based models, and the training time was considerably longer while the results were remarkably similar.

The results reported in Fig. 3 are the average of the 5-fold cross validation across 3 runs. The weighted F1 score rarely varied more than 1% between the folds. The rare occurrence of outliers was explainable by the small number of folds, where one of the classes was represented in a significantly higher number resulting in a one-sided prediction. These outlier results were removed from the final reported weighted F1 scores. One attribute model (feature set 1) using only the length of the code as a feature did not result in any satisfying accuracy, achieving a weighted F1 score of 0.24.

| Bytecode Token Count (feature set 2) | | | |
|---|---|---|---|
| **Multinomial Naïve Bias** | | **Random Forest** | |
| Precision | Recall | Precision | Recall |
| Fail | 0.61 | 0.69 | 0.82 | 0.88 |
| Pass | 0.45 | 0.40 | 0.81 | 0.72 |
| Weighted F1 Score | 0.54 | | 0.81 | |

| **Logistic Regression** | | **Voting Classifier** | |
|---|---|---|---|
| Precision | Recall | Precision | Recall |
| Fail | 0.60 | 0.93 | 0.60 | 0.96 |
| Pass | 0.56 | 0.12 | 0.64 | 0.10 |
| Weighted F1 Score | 0.51 | | 0.46 | |

| **Decision Tree** | | **Support Vector Machine** | |
|---|---|---|---|
| Precision | Recall | Precision | Recall |
| Fail | 0.92 | 0.84 | 0.60 | 0.95 |
| Pass | 0.80 | 0.89 | 0.54 | 0.09 |
| Weighted F1 Score | 0.86 | | 0.49 | |

| Bytecode and Python Token Sequence (feature set 3,4) | | | |
|---|---|---|---|
| **Artificial Neural Network** | | | |
| **ByteCode NLP** | | **Python NLP** | |
| Precision | Recall | Precision | Recall |
| Fail | 0.90 | 0.80 | 0.61 | 0.99 |
| Pass | 0.76 | 0.88 | 0.72 | 0.04 |
| Weighted F1 Score | 0.84 | | 0.48 | |
| **Long-Short Term Memory Network** | | | |
| **ByteCode NLP** | | **Python NLP** | |
| Precision | Recall | Precision | Recall |
| Fail | 0.67 | 0.83 | 0.72 | 0.82 |
| Pass | 0.63 | 0.65 | 0.66 | 0.53 |
| Weighted F1 Score | 0.64 | | 0.70 | |
| **Recurrent Neural Networks** | | | |
| **ByteCode NLP** | | **Python NLP** | |
| Precision | Recall | Precision | Recall |
| Fail | 0.69 | 0.68 | 0.70 | 0.81 |
| Pass | 0.65 | 0.63 | 0.63 | 0.48 |
| Weighted F1 Score | 0.67 | | 0.67 | |
| **Convolutional Neural Network** | | | |
| **ByteCode NLP** | | **Python NLP** | |
| Precision | Recall | Precision | Recall |
| Fail | 0.80 | 0.79 | 0.90 | 0.76 |
| Pass | 0.74 | 0.72 | 0.71 | 0.88 |
| Weighted F1 Score | 0.78 | | 0.81 | |

**Fig. 3.** Consolidated Results

The token count-based approach (feature set 2) with Decision Tree (F1 score: 0.86) and Random Forest (F1 score: 0.81) results indicate that these algorithms are able to predict whether the code itself answered the questions posed by the educator, based on the unit testing results. Multinominal Naive Bayes (F1 = 0.54), Logistic Regression (F1 = 0.51), SVM (F1 = 0.49) or Voting Classifier (F1 = 0.46) did not perform well enough to predict the class consistently. High differences in the results can be explained with how these algorithms approach the data from a different perspective and might lack a sequential processing view required to interpret student code.

The token sequence-based data approach (feature set 3 and 4) with LSTM, CNN and RNN had better than chance results as per Fig. 3, (which means that the prediction was better than a coin flip, or 50%) which is expected given the sequential nature of a coding submission.

Precision, recall, and weighted F1 score was measured for each of the algorithms. The results in Fig. 3 show that using Python token sequence as the training data, with Deep Learning produces very similar F1 score as using Byte-Code token sequence. This is an important finding, as using the full Python examples with comments consumes considerably more resources than using the smaller, instruction-only data, without any significant improvement in prediction. Comments can also be considered as noise in the data.

The results on Fig. 3 also show that CNNs are the most suitable algorithms to learn context from source code. However as the train-test split (using *sklearn.model_selection - train_test_split*) was random, code for all questions was seen during training and the successful learning could have been question-dependent. A train/test split was created to investigate question-dependence of the prediction. In this new split, code answering any one of the questions appeared in either the train or test portion, but not in both. This data split caused the F1 score on the best performing CNN model, to drop significantly from 0.81 to 0.51. This finding led to a refined approach, where the questions in the training dataset were grouped by similar tasks. As an example, question source codes such as: *count numbers, count items, count up, count even, count up to odd* were used as training set, and *count down, count even* question source codes were used as test set. This has resulted an increase in F1 score, from 0.51 to 0.70.

Based on these findings, the hypothesis that student submission source code content can be used to measure code correctness is possible if the training dataset contains similar questions.

## 6    Conclusion and Further Work

This research provides the results of the proposed assessment of code based on content. Dichotomous classification gave results that are better than the baseline. Prediction success is best if code pertaining to the same questions appears in the training and test sets but some success was achieved with a test set containing code for questions similar to those in the training set. Prediction of pass/fail status of code was not successful in cases where code for the same or similar questions was not previously seen by the fitted model.

The paper concludes that smaller files (using Bytecode or other instruction-based content without comments) give similarly accurate results reducing training time and computational requirements.

During the course of the research several different types of ML algorithms were investigated with token count based and token sequence based feature sets. The conclusion is that one dimensional CNNs with an embedding layer are the most suitable to process student coding submissions, where the student code is tokenized in a sequential format. For less resource intensive training ByteCode token sequences are preforming close to Python token sequences.

The possibility to assist lecturers with fine-graded results might be achievable, with further work using Transfer Learning and graded dataset, building on the existing pass/fail trained algorithm structure. This requires further work.

The final, fine-tuned model structure using Transfer Learning is planned to be released as a web service, where lecturers can submit their student's code, and receive grading suggestions from the most similar algorithm. In the future, this can further evolve to be a Reinforcement Learning model, where lecturers can signal if they agree with the grade, and the system will learn the lecturer's individual style, and refine the grade suggestions based on the feedback.

Another application of the research, and more immediately applicable, can be instant feedback to the students, where they can test their code before submission as a web service.

# References

1. Azcona, D., Arora, P., Hsiao, I.H., Smeaton, A.: user2code2vec: embeddings for profiling students based on distributional representations of source code. In: Proceedings of the 9th International Conference on Learning Analytics & Knowledge, pp. 86–95 (2019)
2. Perry, D.M., Kim, D., Samanta, R., Zhang, X.: SemCluster: clustering of imperative programming assignments based on quantitative semantic features. In: Proceedings of the 40th ACM SIGPLAN Conference on Programming Language Design and Implementation, pp. 860–873 (2019)
3. Bui, N.D., Yu, Y., Jiang, L.: InferCode: self-supervised learning of code representations by predicting subtrees. In: 2021 IEEE/ACM 43rd International Conference on Software Engineering (ICSE), pp. 1186–1197. IEEE (2021)
4. Lee, S., Han, H., Cha, S.K., Son, S., Montage: a neural network language model-GuidedJavaScript Engine Fuzzer. In: 29th USENIX Security Symposium (USENIX Security 20), pp. 2613–2630 (2020)
5. Hegarty-Kelly, E., Mooney, D.A.: Analysis of an automatic grading system within first year computer science programming modules. In: Computing Education Practice 2021, CEP 2021, pp. 17–20 Association for Computing Machinery, New York (2021)
6. Jayapati, V.S., Venkitaraman, A.: A Comparison of Information Retrieval Techniques for Detecting Source Code Plagiarism. arXiv preprint arXiv:1902.02407 (2019)

7. Chen, H.M., Chen, W.H., Lee, C.C.: An automated assessment system for analysis of coding convention violations in Java programming assignments. J. Inf. Sci. Eng. **34**(5), 1203–1221 (2018)
8. Rai, K.K., Gupta, B., Shokeen, P., Chakraborty, P.: Question independent automated code analysis and grading using bag of words and machine learning. In: 2019 International Conference on Computing, Power and Communication Technologies (GUCON), pp. 93–98. IEEE (2019)
9. Mir, A.M., Latoskinas, E., Proksch, S. and Gousios, G.: Type4py: Deep similarity learning-based type inference for python. arXiv preprint arXiv:2101.04470 (2021)
10. Li, H.Y., et al.: Deepreview: automatic code review using deep multi-instance learning. In: Pacific-Asia Conference on Knowledge Discovery and Data Mining, pp. 318–330. Springer, Cham (2019)
11. Setoodeh, Z., Moosavi, M.R., Fakhrahmad, M., Bidoki, M.: A proposed model for source code reuse detection in computer programs. Iranian J. Sci. Technol. Trans. Electr. Eng. **45**(3), 1001–1014 (2021). https://doi.org/10.1007/s40998-020-00403-8
12. Liu, X., Wang, S., Wang, P., Wu, D.: Automatic grading of programming assignments: an approach based on formal semantics. In: 2019 IEEE/ACM 41st International Conference on Software Engineering: Software Engineering Education and Training (ICSE-SEET), pp. 126–137. IEEE (2019)

# Ontology-Aware Biomedical Relation Extraction

Ahmad Aghaebrahimian[1,2]([✉]) [iD], Maria Anisimova[1,2] [iD], and Manuel Gil[1,2]

[1] Institute of Computational Life Sciences, Department of Life Sciences and Facility Management, Zurich University of Applied Sciences, 8820 Waedenswil, Switzerland
{agha,anis,giln}@zhaw.ch
[2] Swiss Institute of Bioinformatics, 1015 Lausanne, Switzerland

**Abstract.** Automatically extracting relationships from biomedical texts among multiple sorts of entities is an essential task in biomedical natural language processing with numerous applications, such as drug development or repurposing, precision medicine, and other biomedical tasks requiring knowledge discovery. Current Relation Extraction systems mostly use one set of features, either as text, or more recently, as graph structures. The state-of-the-art systems often use resource-intensive hence slow algorithms and largely work for a particular type of relationship. However, a simple yet agile system that learns from different sets of features has the advantage of adaptability over different relationship types without an extra burden required for system re-design.

We model RE as a classification task and propose a new multi-channel deep neural network designed to process textual and graph structures in separate input channels. We extend a Recurrent Neural Network with a Convolutional Neural Network to process three sets of features, namely, tokens, types, and graphs. We demonstrate that entity type and ontology graph structure provide better representations than simple token-based representations for Relation Extraction. We also experiment with various sources of knowledge, including data resources in the Unified Medical Language System to test our hypothesis. Extensive experiments on four well-studied biomedical benchmarks with different relationship types show that our system outperforms earlier ones. Thus, our system has state-of-the-art performance and allows processing millions of full-text scientific articles in a few days on one typical machine.

**Keywords:** Biomedical Relation Extraction · Graph Embedding · Deep Neural Network · Ontology · UMLS

## 1 Introduction

The job of a biomedical Relation Extraction (RE) system is to identify semantic relationships among biomedical named entities such as genes, drugs, proteins, or chemical substances. There can be a large number of such relationships among different entities. Associations between genes and diseases, interactions among

P. Sojka et al. (Eds.): TSD 2022, LNAI 13502, pp. 160–171, 2022.
https://doi.org/10.1007/978-3-031-16270-1_14

proteins and chemicals, or relationships among drugs and their side effects are a few examples. RE plays an essential role in many biomedical applications such as clinical decision-making or information retrieval. Furthermore, RE is an integral component of Literature-Based Discovery (LBD) systems, commonly used to generate hypotheses for drug repurposing or drug discovery.

The advent of modern Machine Learning (ML) paradigms led to a significant boost in the performance of different RE systems, including Chemical-Protein Interactions (CPI) [19] or Chemical-Induced Diseases (CID) [14] to name a few. [27] use Support Vector Machines (SVMs) [3] for modeling Protein-Protein Interaction (PPI) and [14] use SVM and decision trees to model CID.

Deep Learning (DL) is the most recent and common class of ML techniques that attempted to address RE. Many studies on PPI extraction use variants of DL-based algorithms such as Recurrent Neural Network (RNN) [5]. [9,20] employed DL to develop an end-to-end system for adverse drug event and drug-drug relationship detection. Using another DL-based algorithm named Convolutional Neural Network (CNN) [8], [12] proposed segment CNN for RE in clinical notes. [10] also made use of RNN to combine the feature vectors trained on MEDLINE with the semantic information obtained from external Knowledge Bases (KB) for relation and entity recognition.

Similar to our work, there are a few studies that attempted to integrate different neural architectures. The purpose is to benefit from the advantages and overcome the disadvantages of different shallow and deep algorithms. For instance, [28] combined RNN and CNN in a hybrid model or [15] combined RNN, CNN, and SVM as an ensemble system.

Contextualized language models help RE to obtain better results [11,24]. However, they are considered highly resource-intensive algorithms. Dependence on massive machinery infrastructure usually raises concerns about scalability when considering large-scale RE. Aiming at developing a large-scale system, we avoid using any resource-intensive, hybrid, or ensemble system. Instead, we design a unified model that minimizes the load and complexity of the system via integrating ontology graph and typing information such that it can process millions of full-text articles in a reasonable time and on a sensible infrastructure.

We apply our method to four benchmarks with different biomedical relationship types and linguistic characteristics individually to ensure that our model handles agnostic datasets without requiring any particular tuning per dataset. These datasets include ChemProt [6], DDI [18], i2b2 [23], and AGAC [25]. Our method shows a substantial improvement (based on the F1 score) compared to the current SotA RE systems.

## 2    Methods

Instead of moving towards a more complex DL approach which is less effective [7], we use a simple architecture with several channels that allows us to integrate various sources of data into the training stream without over-complicating the problem.

Meantime to ensure optimum system throughput, and to benefit from graph-level and sentence-level information, we train an embedding space on a graph and integrate it into a sentence-level deep neural model. This way, we can enhance the system's performance while letting it process more than a thousand sentences a second. The required time would be higher by at least one order of magnitude if we would implement it in a graph neural network.

Three sets of features are integrated into our model, namely tokens, entity types, and graph structures extracted from ontologies in the form of graph embeddings. Assume the sentence $S = t_1, t_2, ..., t_n$ to consist of tokens $t_i$ and to contain two named entities $e_1$ and $e_2$. We denote $r$ as the relationship point-ing to a pair of named entities $e_1$ and $e_2$.

In contrast to tokens which are merely occurrences of linguistic units (i.e., words, punctuation marks, symbols, etc.), named entities in life sciences are referred to well-recognized drugs, species, diseases, etc. They may consist of one or more consecutive tokens. Consider the following example:

> ... of the PDE inhibitors tested, dipyridamole was most effective, with IC50 values of 1.2 and 0.45 microM for inhibition of cAMP and cGMP hydrolysis, respectively.

The named entities are printed in red and blue. For the sake of brevity, we use entity to refer to a named entity from now on. In the ChemProt dataset, $CPR - 9$ is the relationship between the two red entities. Note that there may be other relationships among the blue entities as well.

The task is then to find $r$ such that

$$argmax_{r \in R} \quad p(r|S, e_i, e_j, T, G; \theta) \tag{1}$$

maximizes the probability of $r$ where $T$ is a set of associated entity types rep-resented in $t$ dimensional embedding space, and $G$ is a graph consisting of all entities and relations available in the training data. Tokens in $S$, as well as the entities, are represented in $d$ dimensional embedding space. $G$ also is represented as $g$ dimensional embeddings vectors. $R$ is a set of relationships, and $\theta$ are the network parameters. We describe $S$, $T$, and $G$ embeddings in more detail in sub-sections 2.1, 2.2, and 2.3 accordingly.

## 2.1   Token Embedding

The most efficient way for representing tokens in almost all NLP tasks is via low-dimensional word vectors, also known as word embeddings. From a broad perspective, word embeddings can be of two types, namely static or dynamic. A static word embeddings algorithm (e.g., Word2Vec [13], Glove [16]) maps each token to a unique low-dimensional vector irrespective of the context where the token occurs. In contrast, a dynamic (i.e., contextual) word embeddings algorithm (e.g., ELMo [17], BERT [4]) maps each token to several different low-dimensional word vectors depending on their surrounding words. Due to the high computational demand of the latter, we only use static embeddings to ensure a lean and scalable RE system. We use Word2Vec embeddings to represent $S$.

## 2.2  Type Embedding

Typing information provides a mechanism for disambiguation when the system is not confident about the relationship between two entities. We integrate type embeddings into the system to examine their impact on the system performance.

In contrast to tokens, there are usually very few types available in a dataset. Consequently, a shallow embeddings technique known as the one-hot encoding (OHE) is sufficient for representing $T$.

## 2.3  Ontology Graph Embeddings

The idea in ontology graph embeddings is to map the graph of an ontology to low-dimensional vectors such that similar components in the graph are close to each other in the low-dimensional space. Therefore, in addition to isolated tokens represented via token embeddings, the network benefits from the information about the interaction of graph components and their neighbors. As the results show in Sect. 3, the embeddings of the ontology graph is a beneficial feature for RE. Graph structures provide three levels of features, namely node, link, and graph as a whole. We only estimate and use node-level embeddings to prove the concept and postpone the two other levels to further studies. To set up the input graph for embeddings generation, we construct a graph where entities (i.e., genes, diseases, drugs, etc.) are the vertices, and their relationships are the edges. Transforming this graph into a set of linear random walks (i.e., linearization) is the first step for embeddings generation. After setting the number and the length of random walks, we use a simple sampling agent to linearize the graph. The graph is a directed graph, hence backward moves are not possible. Therefore, at each vertex, the agent decides which outgoing edge to take using a uniform distribution.

Two hyper-parameters, namely the number and the length of random walks, control the agent's walking behavior. The model uses a portion of training data called the development data to tune these hyper-parameters. After transforming the graph into a set of random walks, we assume each walk as a sequence and use Word2Vec's Skip-gram algorithm to estimate the embeddings.

## 2.4  UMLS Graph Embeddings

The ontology graph provides a beneficial means of structured data for learning algorithms. However, for some datasets, the ontology graph is not available. A more robust way for generating ontology graph embeddings is to use external resources such as the Unified Medical Language System (UMLS) or Open Biomedical and Biological Ontology (OBO).

We consider the UMLS as an ontology of biomedical concepts. It consists of three main components, namely Metathesaurus, Semantic network, and Specialist lexicon. The Metathesaurus contains over four million biomedical concepts and their associated terms from over 200 source vocabularies. The Semantic network defines 133 broad types (e.g., disease, drug, disorder, etc.) and 54 relationships. It includes semantic types and semantic relationships such as "clinical drug A treats disease B or syndrome C". Finally, the Specialist lexicon provides lexical information for language processing.

Extracting the clusters of concepts from different vocabularies similar to the UMLS's Metathesaurus or extracting semantic typing information like the UMLS's Semantic network requires extensive querying among all available ontologies in the OBO Foundry. Given this constraint and for the sake of accessibility and reproducibility, in this study, we use UMLS and postpone OBO integration to further studies.

We extract the words and strings and their associations with their concepts from the UMLS 2021 package. Extracting the concepts, semantic types, and relationships, we construct a semantic graph. After the graph is constructed, a similar mechanism as described in the last subsection projects the concepts and relationships into an embedding space.

### 2.5    Architecture

Recent advances in DL have significantly enhanced RE. Here, we propose a new DL architecture to improve RE over biomedical data (see Fig. 1 for the schema). This architecture complements an RNN with a CNN to extract two types of information that are deemed critical in RE.

On the one hand, Gated Recurrent Unit (GRU) [2] as an advanced variant of RNNs deals with strings with relatively long dependencies. GRUs in neural networks are often used in form of bidirectional units (i.e., BiGRU). Given a string, one GRU in a BiGRU unit extracts the textual features from right to left and the other from left to right and the resulting vectors are concatenated. CNN, on the other hand, is a great architecture for extracting keywords or key-phrases [8]. The combination of BiGRU and CNN assures that the model extracts the most informative sequential, local, and time-invariant features.

We hypothesize that combining GRU- and CNN-generated features provides RE with a more meaningful representation. Therefore, we propose a Bidirectional Gated Recurrent Unit-Convolutional Neural Network (BiGRU-CNN) multi-channel multi-input model for biomedical RE.

This architecture accepts a wide range of features. While tokens and their sequences are valuable features for RE, as we demonstrate via extensive experimentation (please refer to Sect. 6), entity types and ontology graph embeddings facilitate RE as well. Type information helps RE to disambiguate the detected relationships, while ontology embedding provides the model with implicit but beneficial information about entities and their connections in their ontology graph structure.

The first channel in Fig. 1 is fed with the isolated token embeddings. While individual tokens provide strong signals for some relationships, the sequence of tokens known as $n$-grams allows better recognition of some other relationships. The combination of BiGRU and CNN ensures that both of these feature types are extracted. The model concatenates the resulting vectors of BiGRU and CNN to get the overall feature vector. The number of hidden layers for the BiGRU network, sequence length, CNN activation function, the dropout rate, and the optimizer are some of the hyperparameters for this channel.

More recent studies on RE use contextualized word embeddings. Computationally, such algorithms are highly demanding with hundreds of millions of parameters. Therefore, to estimate the $S$ embeddings in the first channel, we use Word2Vec (Skip-gram) as a static word embeddings algorithm and train it on the PubMed abstracts released by BioASQ [22].

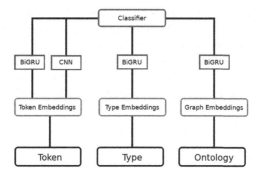

**Fig. 1.** Data-agnostic biomedical RE system architecture.

The second channel accepts the type embeddings, and the third channel receives the ontology graph embeddings. Sections 2.2, and 2.3 describe the procedure for estimating the embeddings representing $T$, and $G$ required for these channels. The number and length of random walks for the ontology graph embeddings and the embeddings vector size are two other hyperparameters specific to these channels. Finally, the classifier on the top is a softmax function.

The hyperparameters in Table 1 are reported to ensure reproducibility. All hyperparameters are optimized on the development set if available (the Chemprot dataset only), otherwise on randomly extracted 20% of the training set.

**Table 1.** System hyper-parameters

| Hyper-parameter | Value | Hyper-parameter | Value |
| --- | --- | --- | --- |
| Emb. size $d$ (tokens) | 200 | Optimizer | adam |
| Emb. $g$ (Ontology) | 128 | hidden layers | 64 |
| Num. random walks | 100 | CNN filters | 32 |
| Length of walks | 16 | CNN kernel size | 4 |
| Drop-out | 0.05 | CNN activation | relu |

# 3  Implementation and Results

A key motivation for our study is to enable to process millions of full-text articles while providing SotA accuracy. While many studies in RE focus on a particular dataset, we aim towards designing a dataset-agnostic system. To test the system, we selected four different benchmarks of relationship extraction tasks from various biomedical domains. They include the Active Gene Annotation Corpus (AGAC), the Informatics for Integrating Biology and the Bedside (i2b2), Drug-Drug Interaction (DDI), and CHEMical-PROTein interactions (ChemProt). This selection tries to reflect the thematic diversity, as well as the complexity of the task in terms of sequence length, number of classes, linguistic genre, and vocabulary. Training the models for different datasets takes from less than an hour to at most three hours on a standard machine with a Core-i7 CPU and 16 GB ram. Depending on the dataset and sequence length of the sentences, the models take a second to make inference over one thousand sentences with an average length of 70 to 120 tokens each. That makes relation extraction for the entire PubMed feasible in a few days and only using one typical machine. Tables 2, 3, 4, and 5 report the results of the system on AGAC, DDI, i2b2, and ChemProt datasets accordingly. The hyperparameters are tuned using the grid search strategy. The maximum length of all strings for each dataset is set as the

**Table 2.** AGAC test results. The results of the current system are reported in the Micro F1 score with two significant figures. Samples without relationships are extracted as described in [21]

| System | Without none relation | | | With none relation | | |
|---|---|---|---|---|---|---|
| Relation/Score | P. (%) | R. (%) | F1 (%) | P. (%) | R. (%) | F1 (%) |
| No-Rel | - | - | - | 95 | 93 | 94 |
| COM | 100 | 100 | 100 | 0 | 0 | 0 |
| GOF | 95 | 82 | 88 | 0.033 | 0.045 | 0.038 |
| LOF | 74 | 87 | 80 | 0.054 | 0.062 | 0.057 |
| REG | 100 | 25 | 40 | 0.031 | 0.042 | 0.035 |
| Current system | **84** | **72** | **78** | **87** | **87** | **87** |
| [21] | - | - | - | 86 | 86 | 86 |

**Table 3.** i2b2 test results. The results of the current system are reported with two significant figures due to the number of test samples. Similar to Table 10 in [26], a weighted F-Score is used to ensure a fair comparison. Since there are not enough training data in some classes in the i2b2 dataset, following [26], we did not use TrWP, TrIP, and TrNAP classes for training and development

| System | [26] | | | Current system | | |
|---|---|---|---|---|---|---|
| Relation/Score | P. (%) | R. (%) | F1 (%) | P. (%) | R. (%) | F1 (%) |
| TrCP | 68 | 65 | 66 | 73 | 34 | 47 |
| TrAP | 79 | 82 | 81 | 86 | 94 | 90 |
| TeRP | 87 | 87 | 87 | 83 | 94 | 88 |
| TeCP | 63 | 63 | 63 | 64 | 46 | 54 |
| PIP | 73 | 67 | 70 | 100 | 100 | 100 |
| Macro/Micro score | 74/- | 73/- | 73/- | **81/89** | **74/89** | **76/89** |

length of the sequences for that dataset. If required, Micro F1, Macro F1, or both are reported to make comparison with earlier works possible.

**Table 4.** DDI test results. The results of the current system are reported with three significant figures to account for the number of test instances. Similar to [1], the F1 score is Micro-averaged F1 score.

| Relation/Score | P. (%) | R. (%) | F1 (%) |
|---|---|---|---|
| Advise | 81.9 | 90.0 | 85.8 |
| Effect | 86.0 | 85.3 | 85.6 |
| Int | 94.4 | 35.4 | 51.5 |
| Mechanism | 89.9 | 91.7 | 90.8 |
| Current system | **86.5** | **83.5** | **85.0** |
| [1] | 85.36 | 82.83 | 84.08 |

**Table 5.** ChemProt results. The results of the current and SotA systems are reported in Macro/Micro F1 scores.

| System | [19] | Current system | | |
|---|---|---|---|---|
| Relation/Score | F1 (%) | P. (%) | R. (%) | F1 (%) |
| CPR:3 | 71.48 | 71.8 | 53.4 | 61.2 |
| CPR:4 | 81.28 | 78.8 | 87.9 | 83.1 |
| CPR:5 | 70.90 | 81.2 | 65.7 | 72.6 |
| CPR:6 | 79.86 | 78.0 | 88.4 | 82.9 |
| CPR:9 | 69.87 | 85.2 | 69.6 | 76.6 |
| Macro/Micro score | - | **79/78.8** | **73/76.6** | **75.2/77.7** |
| Macro/Micro score | 74.6/76.5 | - | - | - |

The results in this section are reported based on the ontology graphs generated via the data-driven approach. Although the UMLS-based ontology graphs have a positive impact on the system performance, they yield inferior results compared to the data-driven approach. The distinction between the UMLS-based system and the data-driven approach is reported in the ablation study in Sect. 6. The reason for this inferiority comes from the fact that the coverage rate (i.e., the ratio of entities and relationships in a test set available in the relevant graph embeddings) of the data-driven approach is higher than the UMLS-based approach. Including other biomedical knowledge graphs leads to increasing the term coverage hence improving the performance. We postpone this integration to further studies.

## 3.1 Ablation

This section reports the impact of each layer and several design decisions on the system performance. We limit the parameters of this study to the BiGRU and CNN base models and the result of adding the type and ontology graph embeddings into the network. The ablation study is performed over all datasets to eradicate possible bias as much as possible.

**Table 6.** Ablation results; the impact of adding each network layer on the system performance. Statistically, significant changes are reported in bold. All scores are reported as Micro F1 score for the sake of consistency.

| Config | Model-Dataset | AGAC(%) | DDI(%) | i2b2(%) | ChemProt(%) |
|--------|---------------|---------|--------|---------|-------------|
| 1 | Base CNN | 71 | 76.1 | 80 | 70.9 |
| 2 | Base GRU | 72 | 77.2 | 81 | 72.8 |
| 3 | 1 + 2 | 73 | 78.6 | 82 | 74.1 |
| 4 | 3 + Type layer | 75 | 81.4 | 85 | 75.4 |
| 5 | 4 + Ontology layer (UMLS) | 77 | 83.2 | 88 | 77.4 |
| 6 | 4 + Ontology layer (data-driven) | **78** | **85** | **89** | **77.7** |

The results in Table 6 show that the base BiGRU configuration consistently outperforms the CNN one, although the performance of the combined model is always higher than the sole BiGRU. It suggests that CNN captures some discriminative features which BiGRU encoders commonly lose. Our error analysis empirically shows that CNN does not work well for strictly directional relationships. For instance, CNN makes a lot of mistakes in recognizing CPR:5 and CPR:6 (Agonist and Antagonist relations) in the ChemProt dataset while it recognizes CPR:3 (Upregulator and activator) slightly better than BiGRU. The impact of type and ontology embeddings layers is also evident from the results.

## 4   Discussion

Biomedical relation extraction is a complex task. This complexity is partly due to the linguistic ambiguity and variability inherent in the biomedical entities. The difficulties involved in RE for different linguistic genres such as scientific papers (e.g., ChemProt) versus clinical texts (e.g., i2b2) add to this linguistic complexity. Another reason for such complexity is the wide range of ontologies in life sciences which lead to the definition of numerous relationships' types. Yet another source of complexity is added to RE because relationships are often directional connections between two entities. However, the text does not always preserve the order of the entities.

All studied datasets in this work are highly class-imbalanced that poses a significant issue in multi-class classification tasks. This includes an imbalance among classes as well as an imbalance between positive and negative instances of each class. Class imbalance usually works in favor of the majority class via disregarding the minority class at the training step. TeRP and TrAP in the i2b2 dataset are two evident examples of errors caused by class imbalance. TrCP and TeCP are the worst-performing classes in this dataset; TeCP is often misclassified with TeRP and TrCP is often misclassified with TrAP. In both cases, the class to which the true classes are wrongly assigned belongs to the majority classes.

Another reason for making errors in classification is that in both cases the misclassified classes are semantically similar to true classes; In the first case "Test Conducted to investigate Problem (TeCP)" and "Test Reveal Problem (TeRP)" and in the second case "Treatment Cause problems (TrCP)" and "Treatment Administered Problem (TrAP)" are considerably similar. Our experiments on various embeddings show that an embedding trained on biomedical data yields fewer misclassified instances of this type.

The worst-performing class in the DDI dataset is also the minority class *Int* which often is overshadowed by *Effect*. One reason for this is that *Int* is the super-class denoting any interaction which conveys the same semantics as *Effect* may do.

## 5  Conclusion

Relation Extraction is a fundamental task in biomedical text analytics. There is a wide range of domains within biomedical and health sciences. Therefore a universal model capable of extracting relationships across various biomedical subdomains is highly desirable since it reduces the time and effort required to design domain-specific architectures. Employing graph ontology and biomedical types represented as embeddings, we designed a deep neural network for relation extraction adaptable to various domains given the ontology and type information encoded as embeddings layers. The network takes this information directly from the datasets in a data-driven approach or indirectly from the UMLS as an external resource. Our system obtains state-of-the-art results on four datasets from different biomedical sub-domains, namely; Chemical Protein Interactions (CPI), Drug-Drug Interactions (DDI), Gene functions, and clinical problems and tests. Due to its uncomplicated yet quick encoders and classifier, it makes relation extraction feasible on a large volume of textual data and within a limited time.

**Funding Information.** This work was funded by the ZHAW Health@N initiative (grant 9710.3.01.5.0001.08 to M.G.).

## References

1. Asada, M., Miwa, M., Sasaki, Y.: Using drug descriptions and molecular structures for drug-drug interaction extraction from literature. Bioinformatics **37**(12) (2020)
2. Cho, K., et al.: Learning phrase representations using RNN encoder-decoder for statistical machine translation (2014)
3. Cortes, C., Vapnik, V.: Support-vector networks. Mach. Learn. **20**, 273–297 (1995). https://doi.org/10.1007/BF00994018
4. Devlin, J., Chang, M.W., Lee, K., Toutanova, K.: BERT: pre-training of deep bidirectional transformers for language understanding. In: NAACL-HLT (2019)

5. Elman, J.L.: Finding structure in time. Cogn. Sci. **14**(2), 179–211 (1990)
6. Hirschman, L., Yeh, A., Blaschke, C., Valencia, A.: Overview of BioCreAtIvE: critical assessment of information extraction for biology. BMC Bioinform. **6**(suppl 1) (2005). https://doi.org/10.1186/1471-2105-6-S1-S1
7. Huynh, T., He, Y., Willis, A., Rueger, S.: Adverse drug reaction classification with deep neural networks. In: Proceedings of COLING 2016, the 26th International Conference on Computational Linguistics: Technical Papers, pp. 877–887. The COLING 2016 Organizing Committee, Osaka, Japan (2016)
8. Lecun, Y., Bottou, L., Bengio, Y., Haffner, P.: Gradient-based learning applied to document recognition. Proc. IEEE **86**(11), 2278–2324 (1998). https://doi.org/10.1109/5.726791
9. Li, F., Liu, W., Yu, H.: Extraction of information related to adverse drug events from electronic health record notes: design of an end-to-end model based on deep learning. JMIR Med. Inform. **6**(4), e12159 (2018)
10. Li, Z., Lian, Y., Ma, X., Zhang, X., Li, C.: Bio-semantic relation extraction with attention-based external knowledge reinforcement. BMC Bioinform. **21**(1) (2020)
11. Lin, Y., Shen, S., Liu, Z., Luan, H., Sun, M.: Neural relation extraction with selective attention over instances. In: Proceedings of the 54th Annual Meeting of the Association for Computational Linguistics (vol. 1: Long Papers), pp. 2124–2133. Association for Computational Linguistics, Berlin, Germany (2016)
12. Luo, Y., Cheng, Y., Uzuner, O., Szolovits, P., Starren, J.: Segment convolutional neural networks (Seg-CNNs) for classifying relations in clinical notes. J. Am. Med. Inform. Assoc. **25**(1), 93–98 (2017). https://doi.org/10.1093/jamia/ocx090
13. Mikolov, T., Chen, K., Corrado, G., Dean, J.: Efficient estimation of word representations in vector space (2013)
14. Onye, S.C., Akkeleş, A., Dimililer, N.: relSCAN - a system for extracting chemical-induced disease relation from biomedical literature. J. Biomed. Inform. **87**, 79–87 (2018)
15. Peng, Y., Rios, A., Kavuluru, R., lu, Z.: Extracting chemical-protein relations with ensembles of SVM and deep learning models. Database **2018**(141), bay073 (2018)
16. Pennington, J., Socher, R., Manning, C.: GloVe: Global vectors for word representation. In: Proceedings of the 2014 Conference on Empirical Methods in Natural Language Processing (EMNLP), pp. 1532–1543. Association for Computational Linguistics, Doha, Qatar (2014)
17. Peters, M., et al.: Deep contextualized word representations. In: Proceedings of the 2018 Conference of the North American Chapter of the Association for Computational Linguistics: Human Language Technologies, vol. 1 (Long Papers), pp. 2227–2237. Association for Computational Linguistics, New Orleans, Louisiana (2018)
18. Segura-Bedmar, I., Martinez, P., Sanchez-Cisneros, D.: The 1st DDIExtraction-2011 challenge task: extraction of drug-drug interactions from biomedical texts. In: Challenge Task Drug-Drug Interaction Extraction, vol. 2011, pp. 1–9 (2011)
19. Sun, C., et al.: Chemical-protein interaction extraction via Gaussian probability distribution and external biomedical knowledge. Bioinform. **36**(15) (2020)
20. Sänger, M., Leser, U.: Large-scale entity representation learning for biomedical relationship extraction. Bioinform. **37**(2), 236–242 (2020)
21. Thillaisundaram, A., Togia, T.: Biomedical relation extraction with pre-trained language representations and minimal task-specific architecture. CoRR abs/1909.12411 (2019)
22. Tsatsaronis, G., et al.: An overview of the BIOASQ large-scale biomedical semantic indexing and question answering competition. BMC Bioinform. **16**(1), 138 (2015)

23. Uzuner, O., South, B., Shen, S., DuVall, S.: 2010 i2b2/VA challenge on concepts, assertions, and relations in clinical text. J. Am. Med. Inform. Assoc. **18**(5), 552–556 (2011)
24. Verga, P., Strubell, E., McCallum, A.: Simultaneously self-attending to all mentions for full-abstract biological relation extraction. In: Proceedings of the 2018 Conference of the North American Chapter of the Association for Computational Linguistics: Human Language Technologies, vol. 1 (Long Papers), pp. 872–884. Association for Computational Linguistics, New Orleans, Louisiana (2018)
25. Wang, Y., Zhou, K., Gachloo, M., Xia, J.: An overview of the active gene annotation corpus and the BioNLP OST 2019 AGAC track tasks. In: Proceedings of The 5th Workshop on BioNLP Open Shared Tasks, pp. 62–71. Association for Computational Linguistics, Hong Kong, China (2019)
26. Yadav, S., Ramesh, S., Saha, S., Ekbal, A.: Relation extraction from biomedical and clinical text: unified multitask learning framework. IEEE/ACM Trans. Comput. Biol. Bioinform. **PP**(99), 1–1 (2020)
27. Yan, C., Dobbs, D., Honavar, V.: Identification of surface residues involved in protein-protein interaction — a support vector machine approach. In: Abraham, A., Franke, K., Köppen, M. (eds.) Intelligent Systems Design and Applications. ASC, vol. 23, pp. 53–62. Springer, Heidelberg (2003). https://doi.org/10.1007/978-3-540-44999-7_6
28. Zhang, Y., et al.: A hybrid model based on neural networks for biomedical relation extraction. J. Biomed. Inform. **81**, 83–92 (2018)

# Balancing the Style-Content Trade-Off in Sentiment Transfer Using Polarity-Aware Denoising

Sourabrata Mukherjee[✉] [iD], Zdeněk Kasner[iD], and Ondřej Dušek[iD]

Faculty of Mathematics and Physics, Institute of Formal and Applied Linguistics,
Charles University, Prague, Czechia
{mukherjee,kasner,odusek}@ufal.mff.cuni.cz

**Abstract.** Text sentiment transfer aims to flip the sentiment polarity of a sentence (positive to negative or vice versa) while preserving its sentiment-independent content. Although current models show good results at changing the sentiment, content preservation in transferred sentences is insufficient. In this paper, we present a sentiment transfer model based on polarity-aware denoising, which accurately controls the sentiment attributes in generated text, preserving the content to a great extent and helping to balance the style-content trade-off. Our proposed model is structured around two key stages in the sentiment transfer process: better representation learning using a shared encoder and sentiment-controlled generation using separate sentiment-specific decoders. Empirical results show that our methods outperforms state-of-the-art baselines in terms of content preservation while staying competitive in terms of style transfer accuracy and fluency. Source code, data, and all other related details are available on Github (https://github.com/SOURO/polarity-denoising-sentiment-transfer).

**Keywords:** Sentiment Transfer · Text Style Transfer · Natural Language Generation

## 1 Introduction

Text sentiment transfer is the task of changing the sentiment polarity of a text while retaining sentiment-independent semantic content (e.g., "The food was tasteless" to "The food was delicious") [12,14,20,26]. It has been introduced in the context of textual style transfer, where positive and negative sentiment are considered distinct styles [14]. Style transfer is motivated by various writing assist tasks for copywriting or personalized chatbots, e.g. changing review sentiment, debiasing or simplifying a news text, or removing offensive language [9,14,25].

With the success of deep learning in the last decade, a variety of neural methods have been proposed for this task [9,27]. If parallel data are provided, standard sequence-to-sequence models can be directly applied [23]. However, due to lack of parallel corpora (paired sentences with opposite sentiment and

© Springer Nature Switzerland AG 2022
P. Sojka et al. (Eds.): TSD 2022, LNAI 13502, pp. 172–186, 2022.
https://doi.org/10.1007/978-3-031-16270-1_15

otherwise identical content), learning sentiment transfer – and text style transfer in general – from unpaired data represents a substantial research challenge.

A first approach to learning text style transfer from unpaired data disentangles text representation in a latent space into style-independent content and stylistic attributes (such as sentiment polarity) and applies generative modeling [7,20,26]. The latent representation needs to preserve the meaning of the text while abstracting away from its stylistic properties, which is not trivial [11]. In fact, disentanglement is impossible in theory without inductive biases or other forms of supervision [13]. A second line of research is prototype editing [3,12], which focuses specifically on style marker words (also called *pivot* words, e.g. sentiment polarity indicating words such as "good" or "bad"). The approach typically extracts a sentence "template" without the pivots and then fills in pivots marking the target style. However, since the pivot words are typically extracted using simple unsupervised probabilistic methods, they are difficult to distinguish from content words, which again leads to content preservation errors.

Our work combines both research branches and extends them, using additional supervision. The supervision comes from a sentiment dictionary, which is applied on pivot words within the context of generative models to learn better latent representations via the task of polarity-aware denoising. First, we randomly delete (or mask) pivot word(s) of input sentences. Then a shared encoder pre-trained on general domain helps in preparing a latent representation, followed by separate sentiment-specific decoders that are used to change the sentiment of the original sentence. We follow back-translation for style transfer approach proposed by Prabhumoye et al. [20] to represent the sentence meaning in the latent space.

Our contributions are summarized as follows:

- We design a sentiment transfer model using an extended transformer architecture and polarity-aware denoising. Our use of separate sentiment-specific decoders and polarity-aware denoising training allow more control over both the target sentiment and the sentiment-independent content.
- We derive a new non-parallel sentiment transfer dataset from the Amazon Review Dataset [17]. It is more topically diverse than earlier used datasets Yelp [12] and IMDb [2], which were majorly focused on movie and restaurant/business-related reviews. Our dataset and code is publicly available.[1]
- We introduce polarity-masked BLEU (MaskBLEU) and similarity score (MaskSim) for automatic evaluation of content preservation in this task. These metrics are derived from the traditional BLEU score [19] and Sentence BERT-based cosine similarity score [24]. In our approach, we mask polarity words beforehand for sentiment-independent content evaluation.
- Both automatic and human evaluations on our dataset show that our proposed approach generally outperforms state-of-the-art (SotA) baselines. Specifically, with respect to content preservation, our approach achieves substantially better performance than other methods.

---

[1] https://github.com/SOURO/polarity-denoising-sentiment-transfer.

## 2    Related Work

*Sentiment Transfer.* A common approach to the sentiment transfer task is to separate content and style in a latent space, and then adjust the separated style. Hu et al. [7] use a variational autoencoder and factor its latent representation into a style-independent and stylistic parts. Fu et al. [4] compare a multi-decoder model with a setup using a single decoder and style embeddings. Shen et al. [26] propose a cross-aligned auto-encoder with adversarial training. Prabhumoye et al. [20] propose to perform text style transfer through back-translation. In a recent work, He et al. [6] apply variational inference. Although these approaches successfully change the text style, they also change the text content, which is a major problem. Many previous methods [4,7,20,26] formulate the style transfer using the encoder-decoder framework. The encoder maps the text into a style-independent latent representation, and the decoder generates the target text using the latent representation and a style marker. Again, a major issue of these models is poor preservation of non-stylistic semantic content.

*Content Preservation.* To further deal with the above problem, Li et al. [12] first extract content words by deleting phrases, then retrieve new phrases associated with the target attribute, and finally use a neural model to combine these into a final output. Luo et al. [14] employ a dual reinforcement learning framework with two sequence-to-sequence models in two directions, using style classifier and back-transfer reconstruction probability as rewards. Though these works show some improvement, they are still not able to properly balance preserving the content with transferring the style. Our polarity-aware denoising technique aims to solve this problem by specifically targeting and changing polarity words while preserving the rest of the content (see Sect. 4.3).

*Evaluation.* Another challenge remains in the evaluation of textual style transfer. Previous work on style transfer [2,6,7,20] has re-purposed evaluation metrics from other fields, such as BLEU from machine translation [19] and PINC from paraphrasing [1]. However, these metric cannot evaluate style transfer specifically with respect to preservation of content [27] as they do not take into account the necessity of changing individual words when altering the style. Intended differences between the source sentence and the transferred sentence are thus penalized. In this regard, we have introduced polarity masked BLEU score (MaskBLEU) and polarity masked similarity measure (MaskSim), where we have masked the polarity words beforehand (see Sect. 5.3).

## 3    Approach

### 3.1    Task Definition

Given two datasets, $X_{pos} = \{x_1^{(pos)}, \ldots, x_m^{(pos)}\}$ and $X_{neg} = \{x_1^{(neg)}, \ldots, x_n^{(neg)}\}$ which represent two different sentiments *pos* and *neg*, respectively, our task is to generate sentences of the desired sentiment while preserving the meaning of the input sentence. Specifically, we alter samples of dataset $X_{pos}$ such that they belong to sentiment *neg* and samples of $X_{neg}$ such that they belong to sentiment *pos*, while sentiment-independent content is preserved. We denote the output of dataset $X_{pos}$ transferred to sentiment *neg* as $X_{pos \rightarrow neg} = \{\hat{x}_1^{(neg)}, \dots, \hat{x}_m^{(neg)}\}$ and the output of dataset $X_{neg}$ transferred to sentiment *pos* as $X_{neg \rightarrow pos} = \{\hat{x}_1^{(pos)}, \dots, \hat{x}_n^{(pos)}\}$.

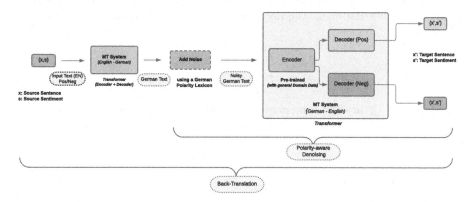

**Fig. 1.** Our sentiment transfer pipeline. In the pipeline, we (1) *translate* the source sentence from English to German using a transformer-based machine translation (MT) system; (2) *apply noise* on the German sentence using a German polarity lexicon; (3) *encode* the German sentence to latent representation using an encoder of German-to-English translation model; (4) *decode* the shared latent representation using the decoder for the opposite sentiment.

## 3.2 Model Overview

Figure 1 shows the overview of our proposed architecture. Following Prabhumoye et al. [20], we first translate the input text $x$ in the base language to a chosen intermediate language $\bar{x}$ using a translation model (see Sect. 4.1).[2] Next, we prepare a noisy text $x_{noise}$ from $\bar{x}$ using polarity-aware noising with word deletion or masking probabilities $\theta_N$ (see Sect. 4.3):

$$x_{noise} = Noise(\bar{x}; \theta_N). \qquad (1)$$

We provide $x_{noise}$ to the encoder of the $\bar{x} \rightarrow \hat{x}$ back-translation model (where $\hat{x}$ is a text in the base language with changed sentiment polarity). The encoder first converts the text to the latent representation $z$ as follows:

$$z = Encoder(x_{noise}; \theta_E), \qquad (2)$$

---

[2] We work with English as base language and German as intermediate language, see Sect. 5.1.

where $\theta_E$ represent the parameters of the encoder.

Two separate sentiment-specific decoders are trained to decode the original positive and negative inputs by passing in their latent representations $z$:

$$x_{pos} = Decoder_{pos}(z; \theta_{D_{pos}}) \qquad (3)$$
$$x_{neg} = Decoder_{neg}(z; \theta_{D_{neg}}). \qquad (4)$$

At inference time, sentiment transfer is achieved by decoding the shared latent representation using the decoder trained for the opposite sentiment, as follows:

$$\hat{x}_{neg} = Decoder_{pos}(z; \theta_{D_{pos}}) \qquad (5)$$
$$\hat{x}_{pos} = Decoder_{neg}(z; \theta_{D_{neg}}) \qquad (6)$$

where $\hat{x}_{neg}$, $\hat{x}_{pos}$ are the sentences with transferred sentiment conditioned on $z$ and $\theta_{D_{pos}}$ and $\theta_{D_{neg}}$ represent the parameters of the positive and negative decoders, respectively.

## 4   Model Variants

In all our experiments, we train sentiment transfer models using back-translation (Sect. 4.1) based on the transformer architecture [28]. First, we present baselines for sentiment transfer with simple style conditioning (Sect. 4.2). Next, we propose an approach based on an extended transformer architecture where we use separate modules (either the whole transformer model, or the transformer decoder only) for the respective target sentiment (Sect. 4.2). We further improve upon our approach using polarity-aware denoising (Sect. 4.3), which we propose as a new scheme for pre-training the sentiment transfer models.

### 4.1   Back-translation

Back-translation for style transfer was introduced in Prabhumoye et al. [20]. Following their approach, we use translation into German and subsequent encoding in a back-translation model to get a latent text representation for our sentiment transfer task. Prior work has also shown that the process of translating a sentence from a source language to a target language retains the meaning of the sentence but does not preserve the stylistic features related to the author's traits [21]. A pure back-translation approach (without any specific provisions for sentiment) is referred to as *Back-Translation* in our experiments.

We also experimented with an auto-encoder, but we have found that the back-translation model gives better results for sentiment transfer. We hypothesise that it is due to the fact that back-translation prevents the system from sticking to a particular wording, resulting in a more abstract latent representation.

## 4.2   Our Baseline Models

In addition to a pure back-translation model, we present several straightforward baselines:

- *Style Tok* is a back-translation model with added sentiment identifiers ($<$ *pos* $>$ or $<$ *neg* $>$) as output starting tokens. At the time of sentiment transfer, we decode the output with a changed sentiment identifier ($<$ *pos* $>$ $\rightarrow$ $<$ *neg* $>$, $<$ *neg* $>$ $\rightarrow$ $<$ *pos* $>$).
- *Two Sep. transformers:* To get more control over sentiment-specific generation, we train two separate transformer models for positive and negative sentiment, using only sentences of the respective target sentiment. During inference, the model is fed with inputs of the opposite sentiment, which it did not see during training.
- *Shrd Enc + Two Sep Decoders:* We extend the above approach by keeping decoders separate, but using a shared encoder. During training, all examples are passed through the shared encoder, but each decoder is trained to only generate samples of one sentiment. Sentiment transfer is achieved by using the decoder for the opposite sentiment.
- *Pre Training Enc:* Following Gururangan et al. [5], we introduce a variant where the shared encoder is pretrained for back-translation on general-domain data. The pre-trained encoder is then further fine-tuned during sentiment transfer training.

## 4.3   Polarity-Aware Denoising

We devise a task-specific pre-training [5] scheme for improving the sentiment transfer abilities of the model. The idea of our pre-training scheme—*polarity-aware denoising*—is to first introduce noise, i.e. delete or mask a certain proportion of words in the intermediate German input to the back-translation step, then train the model to remove this noise, i.e. produce the original English sentence with no words deleted or masked. To decide which words get deleted or masked, we use automatically obtained sentiment polarity labels (see Sect. 5.2 for implementation details). This effectively adds more supervision to the task on the word level. We apply three different approaches: deleting or masking (1) *general* words (i.e., all the words uniformly), (2) *polarity* words (i.e., only high-polarity words according to a lexicon), or (3) both *general* and *polarity* words (each with a different probability).

We use polarity-aware denoising during encoder pretraining, following the shared encoder and separate decoders setup from Sect. 4.2. The encoder is further fine-tuned during the sentiment transfer training.

## 5   Experiments

We evaluated and compared our approaches described in Sect. 4 with several state-of-the-art systems [6,12,14,20,26,29] on two datasets (see Sect. 5.1). We

first describe our training setup (Sect. 5.2), then detail our automatic evaluation metrics (Sect. 5.3) and human evaluation (Sect. 5.4), and finally discuss the
results (Sect. 5.5).

## 5.1  Datasets

For our back-translation process and model pretraining, we used the WMT14
English-German *(en-de)* dataset (1M sentences) from Neidert et al. [16].

For finetuning and experimental evaluation, we built a new English dataset
for sentiment transfer, based on the Amazon Review Dataset [17]. We have
selected Amazon Review because it is more diverse topic-wise (books, electronics,
movies, fashion, etc.) than existing sentiment transfer datasets, Yelp [12] and
IMDb [2], which are majorly focused on movie and restaurant/business-related
reviews. For comparison with previous work, we also evaluate our models on the
benchmark IMDb dataset [2].

While the Amazon Review data is originally intended for recommendation, it
lends itself easily to our task. We have split the reviews into sentences and then
used a pre-trained transformer-based sentiment classifier [30] to select sentences
with high polarity. Our intuition is that high-polarity sentences are more informative for the sentiment transfer task than neutral sentences. We filter out short
sentences (less than 5 words) since it is hard to evaluate content preservation
for these sentences. We also ignored sentences with repetitive words (e.g., *"no
no no no thanks thanks."*) because these sentences are noisy and do not serve
as good examples for the sentiment transfer model. We aim at comparable size
to existing datasets [12]: the resulting data has 102k positive and 102k negative examples in total, with 1+1k reserved for validation and testing for each
sentiment. The average sentence length in our data is 13.04 words.

## 5.2  Training Setup

In all our experiments, we use a 4-layer transformer [28] with 8 attention heads
per layer. Both embedding and hidden layer size are set to 512. The same model
shape is used for both the initial translation into German and the subsequent
model handling back-translation, denoising, and sentiment transfer.

We use a German polarity lexicon to automatically identify pivot words
for polarity-aware denoising. We prepared the German polarity lexicon by first
translating the words from German to English using an off-the-shelf translation
system [10], followed by labeling the words with *positive* and *negative* labels
using the English NLTK Vader lexicon [8]. We performed a manual check of the
results on a small sample.

We test various combinations of noise settings w.r.t. noise probability, noise
type (general or polarity-aware denoising), and noise mode (deleting or masking).
Parameter values are pre-selected based on our preliminary experiments with the
translation model (see Sect. 4.1). The parameters are encoded in the name of the
model as used in Table 1 (see the table caption for details).

## 5.3   Automatic Evaluation Metrics

To evaluate the performance of the models, we compare the generated samples along three different dimensions using automatic metrics, following previous work: (1) style control, (2) content preservation, and (3) fluency.

### Standard Metrics

- *Style Accuracy:* Following prior work, we measure sentiment accuracy automatically by evaluating the sentiment of transferred sentences. We use a pretrained transformer-based sentiment analysis pipeline[3] from Huggingface [30].
- *Fluency:* We use the negative log-likelihood from the GPT-2 [22] language model as an indirect metric for evaluating fluency. For context, we also calculate average sentence lengths of the sentiment-transferred sentences.
- *Content Preservation:* Following previous work, we compute BLEU score [19] between the transferred sentence and its source. Higher BLEU indicates higher n-gram overlap between the sentences, which is generally viewed as proxy for content preservation. We also compute Sentence BERT [24] based cosine similarity score to match the vector space semantic similarity between the source and the transferred sentence. None of the techniques is capable of evaluating style transfer methods specifically with respect to preservation of content in style transfer [27]. These metrics do not take into account the necessity of changing individual words while altering the sentence style. Intended differences between the source sentence and the transferred sentence are thus penalized.

**Newly Introduced Metrics for Content Preservation.** To avoid the problems of the commonly used metrics, it makes sense in sentiment transfer to evaluate the content and similarity while ignoring any polarity tokens. Thus, we introduce MaskBLEU and MaskSim scoring methods – these are identical to BLEU and cosine similarity, but they are computed on sentences where pivot words (based on NLTK Vader sentiment dictionary [8]) have been masked. This allows measuring content preservation while ignoring the parts of the sentences that need to be changed.

---

[3] https://huggingface.co/distilbert-base-uncased-finetuned-sst-2-english.

**Table 1. Automatic evaluation.** *Accuracy*: Sentiment transfer accuracy. *Sim* and *B*: Cosine similarity and BLEU score between input and sentiment-transferred sentence. *M/Sim* and *M/B*: MaskSim and MaskBLEU (similarity and BLEU with polarity words masked, see Sect. 5.3). *LM*: Average log probability assigned by vanilla GPT-2 language model. *Avg*: Average length of transferred sentences. *Avg*: Average of sentiment transfer accuracy, 100*MaskSim and MaskBLEU. Scores are based on a single run, with identical random seeds. First two sections show our own baselines, third section shows our models with denoising (with the best settings denoted $SCT_1$ and $SCT_2$, see Sect. 5.5). The bottom section shows a comparison with state-of-the-art models. Names of models with denoising reflect settings as follows: *W* denotes WMT pretraining data, *A* denotes Amazon finetuning data; the following tokens denote noise probability values are associated with the respective data. *G/P* represents general/polarity token noising, *D/M* represents noising mode deletion/masking. E.g. *WG03P08-AG03P08-D*: noise probabilities on WMT and Amazon data are identical, noising by deletion on both general and polarity token noising is applied (with probabilities 0.3 and 0.8, respectively).

| Models | Acc | Sim | M/Sim | B | M/B | LM | Len | Avg |
|---|---|---|---|---|---|---|---|---|
| **Back-Translation Only (Section 4.1)** | | | | | | | | |
| *Back-translation only* | 0.4 | 0.828 | 0.768 | 28.0 | 45.3 | -78.6 | 11.9 | 40.9 |
| **Our Baseline Models (Section 4.2)** | | | | | | | | |
| *Style Tok* | 13.2 | 0.536 | 0.560 | 4.8 | 8.6 | -52.1 | 7.6 | 25.9 |
| *Two Sep. transformers* | 89.3 | 0.394 | 0.611 | 6.8 | 19.6 | -79.0 | 13.7 | 56.7 |
| *Shrd Enc + Two Sep Decoders* | 88.1 | 0.397 | 0.600 | 7.3 | 20.1 | -78.0 | 12.5 | 56.0 |
| *Pre Training Enc* | 55.3 | 0.592 | 0.732 | 22.6 | 33.9 | -93.3 | 13.4 | 54.1 |
| **Our Models (with Denoising) (Section 4.3)** | | | | | | | | |
| *WG01-AG01-D* | 71.4 | 0.517 | 0.694 | 17.1 | 29.8 | -88.7 | 13.7 | 56.9 |
| *WG01-AG01-M* | 68.0 | 0.536 | 0.711 | 19.4 | 31.1 | -86.3 | 12.6 | 56.7 |
| *WG03-AG03-D* | 83.0 | 0.447 | 0.648 | 11.7 | 24.4 | -83.0 | 13.7 | 57.4 |
| *WG03-AG03-M* | 78.8 | 0.481 | 0.669 | 14.2 | 28.2 | -82.7 | 13.0 | 58.0 |
| *WP08-AP08-D* | 66.9 | 0.528 | 0.701 | 19.5 | 31.3 | -82.8 | 12.4 | 56.1 |
| *WP08-AP08-M* | 64.0 | 0.547 | 0.726 | 21.4 | 34.0 | -89.1 | 12.9 | 56.9 |
| *WP1-AP1-D* | 58.7 | 0.570 | 0.727 | 22.7 | 33.1 | -87.2 | 12.2 | 54.8 |
| *WP1-AP1-M* | 58.9 | 0.567 | 0.716 | 22.2 | 33.0 | -86.5 | 12.2 | 54.5 |
| *WG03-AG01-D* | 68.0 | 0.529 | 0.697 | 17.9 | 30.9 | -89.5 | 13.3 | 56.2 |
| *WG03-AG01-M* | 80.7 | 0.473 | 0.665 | 13.9 | 27.5 | -82.8 | 13.1 | 58.2 |
| *WG01-AG03-D* (=$SCT_2$) | 85.2 | 0.441 | 0.646 | 11.8 | 25.4 | -79.8 | 13.1 | 58.4 |
| *WG01-AG03-M* | 70.0 | 0.534 | 0.711 | 19.7 | 32.3 | -84.3 | 12.4 | 57.8 |
| *WP08-AP1-D* | 61.6 | 0.578 | 0.736 | 22.5 | 35.0 | -94.4 | 13.4 | 56.7 |
| *WP08-AP1-M* | 60.9 | 0.554 | 0.724 | 22.0 | 33.3 | -85.5 | 12.6 | 55.6 |
| *WP1-AP08-D* | 68.5 | 0.525 | 0.699 | 19.3 | 31.1 | -84.0 | 12.4 | 56.5 |
| *WP1-AP08-M* | 61.1 | 0.560 | 0.714 | 21.5 | 32.9 | -86.0 | 12.1 | 55.1 |
| *WG03-AP08-D* | 67.0 | 0.533 | 0.697 | 20.3 | 31.7 | -84.3 | 12.5 | 56.1 |
| *WG03-AP08-M* | 65.7 | 0.546 | 0.725 | 21.2 | 33.5 | -85.0 | 12.5 | 57.2 |
| *WP08-AG03-D* | 83.3 | 0.436 | 0.635 | 11.0 | 24.3 | -80.5 | 13.3 | 57.0 |
| *WP08-AG03-M* | 79.6 | 0.473 | 0.665 | 13.2 | 26.9 | -83.1 | 13.2 | 57.6 |
| *WG03P08-AG03P08-D* | 65.5 | 0.547 | 0.705 | 20.3 | 32.6 | -90.4 | 13.2 | 56.2 |
| *WG03P08-AG03P08-M* (=$SCT_1$) | 82.0 | 0.460 | 0.665 | 13.7 | 27.4 | -79.6 | 12.8 | **58.6** |
| **State-of-the-Art Models** | | | | | | | | |
| Shen et al. [26] | 88.6 | 0.346 | 0.513 | 3.2 | 18.3 | -74.0 | 10.9 | 52.7 |
| Li et al. [12] | 69.9 | 0.457 | 0.632 | 14.7 | 25.3 | -85.1 | 12.2 | 52.8 |
| Luo et al. [14] | 92.4 | 0.279 | 0.468 | 0.0 | 9.1 | -42.0 | 7.8 | 49.4 |
| Prabhumoye et al. [20] | 93.5 | 0.308 | 0.504 | 0.9 | 15.2 | -61.0 | 10.3 | 53.0 |
| Wang et al. [29] | 79.3 | 0.385 | 0.545 | 10.6 | 20.3 | -116.8 | 15.1 | 51.4 |
| He et al. [6] | 91.5 | 0.352 | 0.542 | 9.5 | 21.8 | -65.9 | 8.2 | 55.8 |

**Table 2.** Automatic evaluation on the IMDb Dataset (see Table 1 for metrics explanation).

| Models | Acc | Sim | M/Sim | B | M/B | LM | Len | Avg |
|---|---|---|---|---|---|---|---|---|
| Prabhumoye et al. [20] | 87.1 | 0.345 | 0.480 | 2.7 | 14.3 | -63.5 | 10.0 | 49.8 |
| Li et al. [12] | 21.0 | 0.587 | 0.668 | 18.3 | 25.9 | -83.6 | 15.3 | 37.9 |
| Wang et al. [29] | 84.0 | 0.357 | 0.456 | 9.2 | 13.2 | -63.9 | 10.8 | 47.6 |
| He et al. [6] | 81.7 | 0.458 | 0.576 | 29.0 | 41.8 | -83.6 | 15.3 | 60.4 |
| SCT$_1$ (WG03P08-AG03P08-M) | 85.3 | 0.435 | 0.612 | 28.6 | 42.3 | -86.4 | 15.9 | **62.9** |
| SCT$_2$ (WG01-AG03-D) | 88.2 | 0.379 | 0.588 | 25.8 | 39.2 | -79.6 | 15.1 | 62.1 |

**Table 3.** Human evaluation of sentiment transfer quality, content preservation, and fluency. Average of 1-5 Likert scale ratings on 100 examples from our Amazon Review data.

| Models | Sentiment | Content | Fluency |
|---|---|---|---|
| Prabhumoye et al. [20] | 3.95 | 1.19 | 3.56 |
| Li et al. [12] | 3.35 | 2.3 | 3.34 |
| Wang et al. [29] | 3.48 | 1.67 | 2.54 |
| He et al. [6] | 3.69 | 1.66 | 3.26 |
| SCT$_1$ (WG03P08-AG03P08-M) | 3.94 | **2.61** | 3.73 |
| SCT$_2$ (WG01-AG03-D) | **3.99** | 2.56 | **3.79** |

## 5.4  Human Evaluation

As automated metrics for language generation do not correlate well with human judgements [18], we conduct an in-house human evaluation with five expert annotators. We randomly select 100 sentences (50 for each sentiment) from the our Amazon Review test set. The annotators rate model outputs on using a 1-5 Likert scale for style control, content preservation and fluency.

## 5.5  Results

**Automatic Metrics** results on our Amazon Review data are shown in Table 1. Overall, there is clearly a tradeoff between preserving sentiment-independent content and achieving the desired target sentiment. Models which perform very well in sentiment transfer usually achieve worse results on content preservation. This tradeoff is documented by correlations between the automatic metrics (see Fig. 2). Sentiment accuracy is negatively correlated with BLEU score, similarity measures as well as our newly introduced MaskBLEU and MaskSim scores.

The translation-only and style token baselines do not perform well on changing the sentiment. Using two separate decoders leads to major sentiment transfer

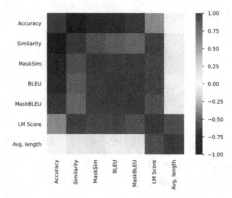

**Fig. 2.** Correlations between automatic evaluation metrics on our Amazon Review data: sentiment accuracy is negatively correlated with BLEU, semantic similarity, and their masked variants.

improvements, but content preservation is poor. Using the pre-trained encoder has helped to improve the content preservation, but sentiment transfer accuracy degrades significantly.

The main motivation for our work was to find a denoising strategy which offers the best balance between sentiment transfer and content preservation. Our results suggest putting an emphasis on denoising high-polarity words results in the best ratio between the sentiment transfer accuracy and content preservation metrics. Additionally, our models show the ability to produce fluent sentences, as shown by the language model score: our models' scores are similar to the back-translation baseline; other models only reach higher language model scores when producing very short outputs.

Overall, our denoising approaches are able to balance well between sentiment transfer and content preservation. On content preservation, they perform much better than state-of-the-art models, and they stay competitive on style accuracy. We selected two of our model variants – $SCT_1 = WG03P08\text{-}AG03P08\text{-}M$ and $SCT_2 = WG01\text{-}AG03\text{-}D$ – as the ones giving the best style-content trade-off (SCT) according to the average of sentiment accuracy, masked similarity and MaskBLEU (see Table 1).

Automatic metrics on the IMDb dataset [2] are shown in Table 2, comparing our selected $SCT_1$ and $SCT_2$ models with state-of-the-art. Our models outperform the state-of-the-art in terms of sentiment accuracy and reach competitive results in terms of similarity, BLEU, and fluency. Same as on our Amazon Review data, they provide the best style-content trade-off (according to the averaged metric defined in Table 1).

**Human Evaluation Results:** We compare our best $SCT_1$ and $SCT_2$ models (selected above) with four state-of-the-art models: two of the most recent models [6,29], and the models with best accuracy [20] and MaskBLEU score [12].

We have evaluated over 600 model outputs. Results are presented in Table 3. The human evaluation results mostly agree with our automatic evaluation results. The results also show that our models are better in content preservation than the competitor models.

**Table 4.** Example outputs comparison on samples from our Amazon Reviews dataset. Sentiment marker words (pivots) are colored. Note that our models preserve content better than most others.

|  | Negative → **Positive** | **Positive** → Negative |
|---|---|---|
| **Source** | movie was a waste of money : this movie totally sucks . | my daughter loves them : ) |
| Prabhumoye et al. [20] | stan is always a great place to get the food . | do n't be going here . |
| Li et al. [12] | our favorite thing was a movie story : the dream class roll ! | my daughter said i was still not acknowledged . |
| Wang et al. [29] | movie is a delicious atmosphere of : this movie totally sucks movie ! | i should not send dress after me more than she would said not ? |
| He et al. [6] | this theater was a great place , we movic totally amazing . | yup daughter has left ourselves . |
| SCT₁ (WG03P08-AG03P08-M) | movie : a great deal of money : this movie is absolutely perfect . | my daughter hates it : my daughter . |
| SCT₂ (WG01-AG03-D) | this movie is a great deal of money. | my daughter hated it . |
| **Source** | nothing **truly interesting happens in this book** . | **best fit for my baby : this product is wonderful ! !** |
| Prabhumoye et al. [20] | very good for the best . | bad customer service to say the food , and it is n't . |
| Li et al. [12] | nothing truly interesting happens in this book . | my mom was annoyed with my health service is no notice . |
| Wang et al. [29] | nothing truly interesting happens in this book make it casual and spot . | do not buy my phone : this bad crap was worst than it ? |
| He et al. [6] | haha truly interesting happens in this book . | uninspired . |
| SCT₁ (WG03P08-AG03P08-M) | in this book is truly a really great book . | not good for my baby : this product is great ! ! ! ! ! ! ! ! |
| SCT₂ (WG01-AG03-D) | in this book is truly awesome . | not happy for my baby : this product is not great ! ! |

We further examined a sample of the outputs in more detail to understand the behavior of different models. We found that state-of-the-art models tend to lose the content of the source sentence, as shown in the example outputs in Table 4. On the other hand, our models mostly preserve sentiment-independent content well while successfully transferring the sentiment. We conclude that with our models, there is a good balance between preserving the original sentiment-independent content and dropping the source sentiment, and existing state-of-the-art models tend to sacrifice one or the other.

## 6    Conclusions and Future Work

We proposed an approach for text sentiment transfer based on the transformer architecture and polarity-aware denoising. Experimental results on two datasets showed that our method achieves competitive or better performance compared to state-of-the-art. Our architecture provides a good style-content tradeoff mainly due to two elements: (1) separate sentiment-specific decoders providing explicit target sentiment control, and (2) polarity-aware enhanced denoising removing sentiment implicitly at the token level. As shown by human evaluation and our manual inspection, our models still sometimes fail to preserve the meaning of the original. While we improve upon previous works on content preservation, this remains a limitation.

In the future, we plan to adapt our method to the different kind of style transfer tasks such as formality transfer or persona-based text generation. Lexicons for the required attribute makers can be extracted by mining stylistic markers from generic dictionaries, or from personality-annotated data [15]. We also intend to focus on better controlling content preservation with the use of semantic parsing.

**Acknowledgments.** This research was supported by Charles University projects GAUK 392221, GAUK 140320, SVV 260575 and PRIMUS/19/SCI/10, and by the European Research Council (Grant agreement No. 101039303 NG-NLG). It used resources provided by the LINDAT/CLARIAH-CZ Research Infrastructure (Czech Ministry of Education, Youth and Sports project No. LM2018101).

## References

1. Chen, D., Dolan, W.B.: Collecting highly parallel data for paraphrase evaluation. In: Proceedings of the 49th Annual Meeting of the Association for Computational Linguistics: Human Language Technologies, ACL-HLT, pp. 190–200 (2011)
2. Dai, N., Liang, J., Qiu, X., Huang, X.: Style transformer: unpaired text style transfer without disentangled latent representation. In: Proceedings of the 57th Annual Meeting of the Association for Computational Linguistics, ACL, pp. 5997–6007 (2019)
3. Fu, Y., Zhou, H., Chen, J., Li, L.: Rethinking text attribute transfer: a lexical analysis. In: Proceedings of The 12th International Conference on Natural Language Generation, INLG, pp. 24–33 (2019)

4. Fu, Z., Tan, X., Peng, N., Zhao, D., Yan, R.: Style transfer in text: exploration and evaluation. In: Proceedings of the Thirty-Second AAAI Conference on Artificial Intelligence and Thirtieth Innovative Applications of Artificial Intelligence Conference and Eighth AAAI Symposium on Educational Advances in Artificial Intelligence, AAAI, pp. 663–670 (2018)
5. Gururangan, S., et al.: Don't stop pretraining: adapt language models to domains and tasks. In: Proceedings of the 58th Annual Meeting of the Association for Computational Linguistics, ACL, pp. 8342–8360 (2020)
6. He, J., Wang, X., Neubig, G., Berg-Kirkpatrick, T.: A probabilistic formulation of unsupervised text style transfer. In: Proceedings of the International Conference on Learning Representations (ICLR) (2020)
7. Hu, Z., Yang, Z., Liang, X., Salakhutdinov, R., Xing, E.P.: Toward controlled generation of text. In: Proceedings of the 34th International Conference on Machine Learning, (ICML), Sydney, Australia, vol. 70, pp. 1587–1596 (2017)
8. Hutto, C.J., Gilbert, E.: Vader: a parsimonious rule-based model for sentiment analysis of social media text. In: Proceedings of the Eighth International AAAI Conference on Weblogs and Social Media, ICWSM (2014)
9. Jin, D., Jin, Z., Hu, Z., Vechtomova, O., Mihalcea, R.: Deep learning for text style transfer: a survey. Comput. Linguist. **47**(4), 1–51 (2021)
10. Košarko, O., Variš, D., Popel, M.: LINDAT translation service (2019). http://hdl.handle.net/11234/1-2922
11. Lample, G., Subramanian, S., Smith, E.M., Denoyer, L., Ranzato, M., Boureau, Y.: Multiple-attribute text rewriting. In: Proceedings of the International Conference on Learning Representations, (ICLR) (2019)
12. Li, J., Jia, R., He, H., Liang, P.: Delete, retrieve, generate: a simple approach to sentiment and style transfer. In: Proceedings of the 2018 Conference of the North American Chapter of the Association for Computational Linguistics: Human Language Technologies, Volume 1 (Long Papers), NAACL-HLT, pp. 1865–1874 (2018)
13. Locatello, F., et al.: Challenging common assumptions in the unsupervised learning of disentangled representations. In: Proceedings of the 36th International Conference on Machine Learning, Long Beach, California, vol. 97, pp. 4114–4124 (2019)
14. Luo, F., et al.: Towards fine-grained text sentiment transfer. In: Proceedings of the 57th Annual Meeting of the Association for Computational Linguistics, ACL, pp. 2013–2022 (2019)
15. Mairesse, F., Walker, M.A.: Controlling user perceptions of linguistic style: trainable generation of personality traits. Comput. Linguist. **37**(3), 455–488 (2011)
16. Neidert, J., Schuster, S., Green, S., Heafield, K., Manning, C.D.: Stanford university's submissions to the WMT 2014 translation task. In: Proceedings of the Ninth Workshop on Statistical Machine Translation, WMT, pp. 150–156 (2014)
17. Ni, J., Li, J., McAuley, J.J.: Justifying recommendations using distantly-labeled reviews and fine-grained aspects. In: Proceedings of the 2019 Conference on Empirical Methods in Natural Language Processing and the 9th International Joint Conference on Natural Language Processing, (EMNLP-IJCNLP), pp. 188–197 (2019)
18. Novikova, J., Dusek, O., Curry, A.C., Rieser, V.: Why we need new evaluation metrics for NLG. In: Proceedings of the 2017 Conference on Empirical Methods in Natural Language Processing, EMNLP, pp. 2241–2252 (2017)
19. Papineni, K., Roukos, S., Ward, T., Zhu, W.: Bleu: a method for automatic evaluation of machine translation. In: Proceedings of the 40th Annual Meeting of the Association for Computational Linguistics, ACL, pp. 311–318 (2002)

20. Prabhumoye, S., Tsvetkov, Y., Salakhutdinov, R., Black, A.W.: Style transfer through back-translation. In: Proceedings of the 40th Annual Meeting of the Association for Computational Linguistics, ACL, pp. 866–876 (2018)
21. Rabinovich, E., Patel, R.N., Mirkin, S., Specia, L., Wintner, S.: Personalized machine translation: preserving original author traits. In: Proceedings of the 15th Conference of the European Chapter of the Association for Computational Linguistics: Volume 1, Long Papers, EACL, pp. 1074–1084 (2017)
22. Radford, A., Wu, J., Child, R., Luan, D., Amodei, D., Sutskever, I.: Language models are unsupervised multitask learners. Technical Report, Open AI (2019)
23. Rao, S., Tetreault, J.R.: Dear sir or madam, may i introduce the GYAFC dataset: corpus, benchmarks and metrics for formality style transfer. In: Proceedings of the 2018 Conference of the North American Chapter of the Association for Computational Linguistics: Human Language Technologies, Volume 1 (Long Papers), NAACL-HLT, pp. 129–140 (2018)
24. Reimers, N., Gurevych, I.: Sentence-BERT: sentence embeddings using Siamese BERT-Networks. In: Proceedings of the 2019 Conference on Empirical Methods in Natural Language Processing and the 9th International Joint Conference on Natural Language Processing, EMNLP-IJCNLP, pp. 3980–3990 (2019)
25. dos Santos, C.N., Melnyk, I., Padhi, I.: Fighting offensive language on social media with unsupervised text style transfer. arXiv preprint arXiv:1805.07685 (2018)
26. Shen, T., Lei, T., Barzilay, R., Jaakkola, T.S.: Style transfer from non-parallel text by cross-alignment. In: Proceedings of the 31st International Conference on Neural Information Processing Systems, NeurIPS, pp. 6830–6841 (2017)
27. Toshevska, M., Gievska, S.: A review of text style transfer using deep learning. In: IEEE Transactions on Artificial Intelligence (2021)
28. Vaswani, A., et al.: Attention is all you need. In: Proceedings of the 31st Conference on Neural Information Processing Systems (NIPS 2017), Long Beach, CA, USA, pp. 5998–6008 (2017)
29. Wang, K., Hua, H., Wan, X.: Controllable unsupervised text attribute transfer via editing entangled latent representation. In: Proceedings of the 33rd Conference on Neural Information Processing Systems (NeurIPS 2019), Vancouver, Canada, pp. 11034–11044 (2019)
30. Wolf, T., et al.: Transformers: state-of-the-art natural language processing. In: Proceedings of the 2020 Conference on Empirical Methods in Natural Language Processing: System Demonstrations, EMNLP, pp. 38–45 (2020)

# A Self-Evaluating Architecture
# for Describing Data

George A. Wright[1(✉)] and Matthew Purver[1,2]

[1] School of Electronic Engineering and Computer Science,
Queen Mary University of London, London, UK
{george.a.wright,m.purver}@qmul.ac.uk

[2] Department of Knowledge Technologies, Jožef Stefan Institute, Ljubljana, Slovenia

**Abstract.** This paper introduces LINGUOPLOTTER, a workspace-based architecture for generating short natural language descriptions. All processes within LINGUOPLOTTER are carried out by *codelets*, small pieces of code each responsible for making incremental changes to the program's state, the idea of which is borrowed from Hofstadter *et al.* [6]. Codelets in LINGUOPLOTTER gradually transform a representation of temperatures on a map into a description which can be output. Many processes emerge in the program out of the actions of many codelets, including language generation, self-evaluation, and higher-level decisions such as when to stop a given process, and when to end all processing and publish a final text. The program outputs a piece of text along with a *satisfaction* score indicating how good the program judges the text to be. The iteration of the program described in this paper is capable of linguistically more diverse outputs than a previous version; human judges rate the outputs of this version more highly than those of the last; and there is some correlation between rankings by human judges and the program's own satisfaction score. But, the program still publishes disappointingly short and simple texts (despite being capable of longer, more complete descriptions). This paper describes: the workings of the program; a recent evaluation of its performance; and possible improvements for a future iteration.

**Keywords:** Language generation · Self-evaluation · Workspace · Codelet

## 1 Introduction

Work on language generation and language understanding are often kept separate, but in humans the two processes are intertwined [9]: for example, simultaneous use of production and comprehension allow people to interweave contributions in dialogue [2]. This paper introduces LINGUOPLOTTER, an attempt

The authors were partially supported by the UK EPSRC under grants EP/R513106/1 (Wright) and EP/S033564/1 (Sodestream: Streamlining Social Decision Making for Improved Internet Standards).

P. Sojka et al. (Eds.): TSD 2022, LNAI 13502, pp. 187–198, 2022.
https://doi.org/10.1007/978-3-031-16270-1_16

at a cognitively plausible model of language generation in which constant self-evaluation and selection between competing ideas are integral to the generative process. The model is tested in a toy domain of temperatures on a fictional map.

Many of the core ideas of the program are borrowed from the Fluid Analogies Research Group, whose programs model high-level perceptual processes involved in analogy making [6]. Their programs such as COPYCAT [8] and TABLETOP [4] operate in different toy domains, but in essence do the same thing: search for a compact representation of their two inputs which allows for a satisfying mapping and an inference that solves a problem. Unlike other contemporary models of analogy-making such as the Structure Mapping Engine [3], the programs are not provided with a ready-made high-level representation of the input, but generate their own representation as part of the analogy making process.

LINGUOPLOTTER is not directly concerned with analogy making, but does create mappings from data into natural language descriptions and generates high-level representations of its input as part of the process. It avoids a pipeline architecture typical of many language generating programs which keep the analysis of data separate from the conversion to linguistic form (For example Reiter [11], Leppänen [7]). The program is thus more concordant with work such as by Turner [13] suggesting that language and narrative frames can influence the way we perceive the world.

This work is open to the charge of being old-fashioned and restricted to toy domains, but its aim is to produce an architecture which, like a neural network, displays high-level behaviour emergent from the interactions of small parts, while, like symbolic programs, is self-explanatory and easy to interpret.

## 2    How LINGUOPLOTTER Works

LINGUOPLOTTER[1] centers on a bubble chamber which contains a number of spaces representing the program's long- and short-term memory. Structures are built and connected to each other in these spaces and the best, most relevant structures bubble to the surface of the program's attention by receiving boosts in activation and spreading activation to related structures.

Long-term memory includes *concepts* (nodes located at prototypical points in conceptual spaces), *frames* (recursive structures which map between semantics and text), and *letter-chunks* (chunks of text ranging from morphemes to sentences) in a network of spreading activation.

Short-term structures built as the program runs include *chunks* which group together similar data points; *labels* which indicate that a node is an instance of a particular concept; *relations* which link items to create instances of relational concepts such as MORE or LESS); *correspondences* which map between items in different spaces (usually for the purpose of filling a slot in a frame); and *views* which collect together a consistent group of correspondences. Views have an output space where a piece of text made of *letter-chunks* is built (Fig. 1).

---

[1] Source code is available at https://github.com/georgeawright/linguoplotter.

All processing on structures is performed by *codelets*. Each codelet has a small, specific task and after running, spawns another codelet to carry out follow-up work. Codelets have an urgency representing the importance of their work which the *coderack* uses when stochastically selecting the next codelet to be run.

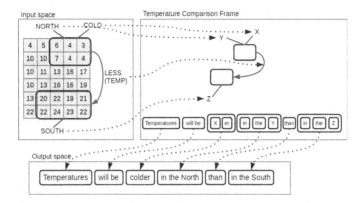

**Fig. 1.** Structures built by codelets inside a single view. Solid blue lines are labels and relations; dotted red lines are correspondences; green boxes are chunks. (Color figure online)

Most codelets belong to a cycle which begins with a *suggester* codelet. A suggester finds target structures and suggests a chunk or link that can be built with them. For example, a *label suggester* classifies the proximity of a chunk to a concept and spawns a *label builder* with an urgency reflecting its confidence that the chunk belongs to that concept. A *builder* codelet builds structures and spawns an *evaluator* codelet. An *evaluator* decides how good a structure is and assigns it a quality score. It then spawns a *selector* codelet that chooses between alternative structures, for example two different labels belonging to the same chunk, and probabilistically boosts the activation of the best one. The *selector* codelet spawns a *suggester* codelet to continue building related structures and an *evaluator* so as to maintain the process of selecting the best structure.

Left unchecked, this forking of codelet cycles would cause an explosion in the population of the coderack, hence *coderack cleaners* remove codelets that are no longer contributing to an increase in the program's satisfaction. In order to avoid the depletion of the coderack population and to make sure that active concepts and frames have structures suggested for them, *factory* codelets spawn suggesters to initiate new cycles of codelets (Fig. 2).

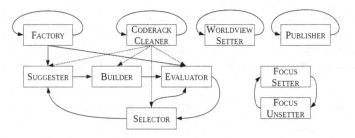

**Fig. 2.** Codelet types that run in the program. Solid arrows show each type's follow-up type. Dashed arrows show which types a *coderack cleaner* can remove.

The running of codelets and selection of structures all happens with some degree of randomness which is determined by *satisfaction*. This is a measure of the overall quality of structures in the bubble chamber. When the program lacks active high quality structures, it is more random and pursues more options in the search for a solution, but once good quality structures have been built and activated, it proceeds more deterministically towards a finished piece of text.

Earlier iterations of the program were prone to too much randomness and failed to narrow down on a single pathway towards a solution. This iteration of the program has a *focus setter* codelet which chooses a single view at a time as *focus*. Once a view is set as focus, codelets are targeted towards it and fill in the slots in its frame. Having a *focus* gives the program a short-term sub-goal and a narrower search space. A lack of progress or completion of the view causes a *focus unsetter* to remove the view from focus. The satisfaction of the program then falls; randomness increases; and the search space broadens (Fig. 3).

LINGUOPLOTTER also has a longer-term *Worldview* (an idea borrowed from TABLETOP [4]) which represents the best view completed so far. Its output space contains a candidate piece of text for publication. Every time a *worldview setter* codelet runs it searches for a better alternative to the current worldview. If it

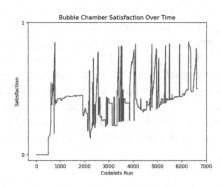

**Fig. 3.** Bubble chamber satisfaction over a run of the program. Satisfaction spikes when the focus is set and its slots filled in. Satisfaction dips when the focus is unset. Satisfaction increases over time as the worldview is set or improved upon.

fails, it sends activation to the PUBLISH concept. Eventually the program fails to improve on itself and if a *publisher* codelet runs when the PUBLISH concept is fully activated, the program halts and the text in the worldview is output.

## 2.1   Macro-level Processes in LINGUOPLOTTER

Macro-level processes emerge from LINGUOPLOTTER's interacting components such as: cycles that reinforce certain concepts and frames; alternation between more engaged and more reflective behaviour; and the gradual decision to publish.

**Self-Reinforcing Concepts.** When a selector codelet chooses from competing alternatives, it spawns a follow up suggester to suggest another related structure, for example another link with the same concept or another view with the same frame. This results in a snowballing of the use of certain conceptual structures. For example, having created a sentence with a certain frame, the program would be likely to start another sentence with the same frame.

**Cycles of Engagement and Reflection.** As the program runs, the changing satisfaction score affects the breadth of processing. When the focus is set and slots in its frame are filled in, satisfaction spikes and processing becomes more deterministic and dedicated to that set of structures. But when there is no focus, or when little progress is being made on the focus, processing is more random and lacks a clear aim. This is analogous to Sharples' cycle of engagement and reflection [12], the idea that humans alternate between bursts of purposeful behaviour and periods of greater reflection and exploration. Unlike MEXICA [10], a model of narrative generation based on Sharples' idea, this program's cycle of engagement and reflection is not explicitly coded, but results from a feedback loop between codelets altering the bubble chamber and bubble chamber satisfaction adjusting the randomness of codelet selection.

**Publishing.** The decision to publish is the responsibility of *worldview setter* and *publisher* codelets, but can be affected by the intervention of other codelets. Repeated failure of *worldview setters* results in the boosting of the PUBLISH concept. This increases the likelihood of publication. But, if other codelets run and maintain other processes, the PUBLISH concept will decay. The interactions of different processes thus result in a period of indecision. Only a sustained stream of failed worldview-setting can lead to publication.

## 2.2   Developing the Program

LINGUOPLOTTER's many interleaved processes give it great potential, but also make it difficult to optimize. Its behaviour can be altered by tweaking a number of parameters, such as the method for calculating each codelet's urgency; the method used to define the quality of each structure; and the formula for calculating satisfaction. There are also a number of hyper-parameters, such as the rate at which activation spreads between structures, the decay rate of activation, and the method for determining how random the program should be.

As shown by the outputs of the program in Table 1, the program in its current form is stuck in a local optimum where it is capable of producing outputs which are, for the most part, true descriptions of the input, but which lack detail and leave some of the input undescribed, even though it is capable of linking sentences with connectives such as *and* to produce a more full description.

**Calculating the Satisfaction Score.** Satisfaction has three components: general satisfaction $G$, focus satisfaction $F$, and worldview satisfaction $W$. The overall satisfaction of the program $S$ is given by:

$$S = \max(F, mean(G, W))$$

If there is a view in the focus, otherwise:

$$S = mean(G, W)$$

This limits satisfaction to 0.5 when there is no worldview and no focus and prevents satisfaction from dropping to 0 when an empty view is placed in the focus (this would result in highly random and unfocused behaviour).

*General Satisfaction.* $G$ is the mean quality of all the input and output spaces of the bubble chamber's views. A space's quality is determined by:

$$space\_quality = \frac{\sum_{a \in A} quality(a) \times activation(a)}{|A|}$$

where $A$ is the set of structures in the space with an activation greater than 0.5. A high quality space must contain active high quality structures.

*Worldview Satisfaction.* $W$ is calculated as:

$$W = AND(OR(Q, \frac{D}{10}), OR(P, \frac{1}{T}))$$

where

$$AND(X, Y) = X \times Y$$
$$OR(X, Y) = X + Y - X \times Y$$

$Q$ is the quality of the worldview as determined by evaluator codelets; $D$ is the depth of the view's parent frame (depth is a number between 1 and 10, with lower numbers given to frames for simple phrases and higher numbers given to sentences and conjunctions); $P$ is the proportion of the input involved in the view; $T$ is the total number of frame types used by the view (i.e. types of phrase constituting the sentence). This satisfaction metric encourages the program to output sentences which are correct (high $Q$), complete (high $P$), grammatically complete (high $D$), and succinct (low $T$).

*Focus Satisfaction.* $F$ is calculated as:

$$F = mean(mean\_correspondence\_quality, \frac{|FilledSlots|}{|Slots|})$$

where correspondence qualities are determined by codelets according to the quality of their arguments and how well they fill in frame slots.

**Optimizing the Satisfaction Score.** Changes to the satisfaction score affect the program's randomness and the texts that it prefers to publish. For example, calculating worldview satisfaction as the product of $Q$, $\frac{D}{10}$, $P$, and $\frac{1}{T}$ generally lowers overall satisfaction and makes the program unlikely to terminate, even after finding a more complete description than the current iteration. Alternatively, using the mean of the four components to calculate worldview satisfaction can result in very high satisfaction scores and causes the program to publish an output much earlier than the current iteration before any significant traversal of the search space. Further investigation is required in the search for a satisfaction formula which allows the program to distinguish between good and bad outputs and to estimate a good time to stop working and publish.

## 3    Performance of LINGUOPLOTTER

LINGUOPLOTTER was tested on the four inputs shown in Fig. 4. Three of these are variations of a similar input. The fourth is a more challenging map which has little or no pattern in the temperatures. The program was run 30 times for each map. Table 1 shows the mean and standard deviation for the number of codelets that were run before the program published a description of each input. It also shows the output that gave the highest mean satisfaction score, the output that was most frequently output (if there were two or more equally frequent outputs, the one one with highest mean satisfaction is shown), and the output with the lowest mean satisfaction score. Also shown for each input are two hand-selected human generated texts (one a detailed description and one written in note-form), and a text output by a previous version (judged by humans to be more correct than its other outputs.)

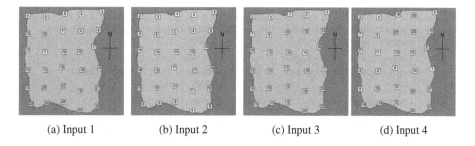

(a) Input 1          (b) Input 2          (c) Input 3          (d) Input 4

**Fig. 4.** The four maps described by the program.

## 3.1    Method for Evaluation by Human Judges

The program's outputs are evaluated through pairwise comparison. This avoids the difficulty of requesting a numeric score for a subjective judgement (describing a text as 100% interesting would be nonsensical) and results in less variance between respondents [1]. It also allows for direct comparison between different iterations of the program and humans. This iteration of the program was evaluated using the 24 texts in Table 1.

**Table 1.** Texts for inputs 1-4 (D: human (detailed); N: human (note-form); B: best satisfaction; F: most frequent; W: worst satisfaction; O: old version). Mean satisfaction scores are given in parentheses after machine-generated texts.

|  | Input 1 | Input 2 |
|---|---|---|
|  | Mean run length: 10425 ($\sigma$: 6197) | Mean run length: 12857 ($\sigma$: 6353) |
| D | The temperature is cold in the north but progressively warm moving south, reaching 24°C. | It is generally warmer in the south than the north but warmest in the central regions. |
| N | Cool in the north, warm in the south. | Cold in the north, milder in the centre. cooler in the south |
| B | Temperatures will be higher in the east than in the north. (0.675) | Temperatures will be colder in the east than in the west. (0.670) |
| F | Temperatures will be colder in the north than in the south. (0.644) | Temperatures will be warm in the east. (0.405) |
| W | Temperatures will be better in the southwest than in the northwest. (0.326) | Temperatures will be cool in the west. (0.290) |
| O | It is hot in the southeast. | It is mild in the south. |
|  | Input 3 | Input 4 |
|  | Mean run length: 10560 ($\sigma$: 7824) | Mean run length: 13583 ($\sigma$: 9660) |
| D | The temperature gets much warmer as you go from northwest to southeast. it's very chilly in the northwest and warm in the southeast. | The temperature is inconsistent across the region with isolated pockets of high and low temperatures in various places. |
| N | It is cold in the north, a little warmer elsewhere, but warm in the south east. | The temperatures are very erratic. |
| B | Temperatures will be higher in the southeast than in the northwest. (0.674) | Temperatures will be cooler in the west than in the northeast. (0.673) |
| F | Temperatures will be cool in the north. (0.604) | Temperatures will be hot in the north. (0.540) |
| W | Temperatures will be higher in the south than in the northwest. (0.350) | Temperatures will be lower in the southwest than in the southeast. (0.338) |
| O | The north is cold. | The southeast is hot. |

For each possible pair of texts, human judges were asked five questions in order to evaluate the texts along different dimensions:

1. Which text is easier to understand?
2. Which text is written more fluently?
3. Which text do you find more interesting?
4. Which text is more factually correct with regard to the temperatures on the map?
5. Which text provides a more complete description of the map?

Respondents could answer by either stating that one text was better than the other or that they were both the same. At no point were the respondents told that texts were machine-generated or human-generated.

Previous evaluation of the program only sought judgements on *easiness*, *fluency*, *correctness*, and *completeness*. These are typical characteristics considered in the evaluation of the quality and accuracy of machine generated language [5]. This time *interestingness* is also considered so as to measure the extent to which the computer program can match humans' creative flair when writing.

## 3.2   Results of Human Evaluation

Table 2 shows aggregate rankings of the different texts for each map calculated using the pairwise preferences given by human judges answering a survey on Amazon Mechanical Turk. Rankings were calculated by giving a text a score where it gained 1 point each time it was preferred over another text and lost 1 point each time another text was preferred over it. Overall, the outputs of the program are judged better than outputs of the previous version, but still lag behind the best texts generated by humans.

It should be noted that there was little agreement between human judges. Fleiss' Kappa was $-0.016$ for *easiness*, $-0.018$ for *fluency*, $-0.018$ for *interestingness*, $-0.014$ for *correctness*, and $-0.007$ for *completeness*. Low agreement is inevitable with subjective judgements, but this is also partly due to a large number of annotators – 36: only 2 annotators answered all questions in the survey. Agreement was greater between those two annotators, especially along the more objective dimensions of *correctness* (0.266) and *completeness* (0.589). It might be better in future for each annotator to provide rankings for all texts instead of just pairwise preferences so that a greater number of judgements per person can be obtained.

The latest iteration of the program consistently performs better than the previous evaluated version along the dimensions of *interestingness*, *correctness*, and *completeness*, but fails to match the best human performance.

As found when evaluating the previous version, humans tend to perform worse in terms of *easiness*, most likely because the computer-generated texts are simpler. Sometimes the previous iteration of the program (which produced shorter sentences) also outperformed the latest iteration along this dimension.

Interestingly, the latest iteration's best output ranked highest for all inputs in terms of fluency, usually followed by the detailed human text. The mean

Spearman's rank correlation coefficient for each input between the rankings of the program's satisfaction scores and the aggregated human judge rankings for fluency is 0.875. Correlation is lower for the other dimensions (0.625 for interestingness, 0.25 for completeness, 0 for correctness, and 0 for easiness). Since the number of texts being compared is so small, little weight should be given to these correlation scores. Nevertheless this does suggest that more work is needed to improve the program's satisfaction score, not only to optimize the running of the program, but also to improve its judgement.

**Table 2.** Average rankings according to pairwise preferences for inputs 1-4.

| Input 1 | Easy | Fluent | Interesting | Correct | Complete |
|---|---|---|---|---|---|
| 1 | F | B | D | D | D |
| 2 | N | D | B | F | F |
| 3 | B | F | F | N | N |
| 4 | O | O | N | B | B |
| 5 | D | W | W | O | W |
| 6 | W | N | O | W | O |
| Input 2 | Easy | Fluent | Interesting | Correct | Complete |
| 1 | F | B | D | D | D |
| 2 | W | D | N | N | N |
| 3 | B | W | B | F | F |
| 4 | O | F | W | W | W |
| 5 | D | O | F | O | O |
| 6 | N | N | O | B | B |
| Input 3 | Easy | Fluent | Interesting | Correct | Complete |
| 1 | O | B | D | D | D |
| 2 | F | D | N | W | N |
| 3 | B | F | B | B | W |
| 4 | W | W | W | N | B |
| 5 | D | N | F | F | F |
| 6 | N | O | O | O | O |
| Input 4 | Easy | Fluent | Interesting | Correct | Complete |
| 1 | O | B | D | O | D |
| 2 | F | F | B | W | B |
| 3 | B | W | W | D | W |
| 4 | W | D | N | N | N |
| 5 | N | O | F | B | O |
| 6 | D | N | O | F | F |

### 3.3    Discussion

Overall, the program produces better outputs than its earlier iteration, but still falls short of human performance. It has some wherewithal to recognize poor performance in the form of its satisfaction score, but this also needs improving. The current configuration of the program takes on the order of $10^4$ codelets to run and normally outputs a single sentence comparing two areas of the input map, though it sometimes produces a sentence describing a single area.

Its descriptions either make use of the TEMPERATURE space of the original input (*temperatures will be colder in the north than in the south*) or the HEIGHT or GOODNESS spaces (*temperatures will be higher in the east that in the north, temperatures will be better in the southwest than in the northwest*). There is little variation in the program's language but more than in the previous version which only used TEMPERATURE adjectives and simpler sentences. The program's outputs still fall far short of the richer human produced texts, but this is partly due to a lack of sentence frames available to the program.

The program's comparisons do not always seem sensible to the human ear, although they may be acceptable in terms of being truthful. For example, the program's "best" output for input 1 is a comparison between the *east* and the *north*. This description is odd, partly because it neglects a large part of the map, but also because it is ambiguous about the northeast. The program's more frequent output comparing the *north* and the *south* is ranked higher by human judges in terms of correctness, completeness, and easiness. It is strange that the "best" output is ranked higher in terms of fluency and interestingness, but there is especially low agreement for these dimensions.

On average the program took longest to describe input 4, but the difference is not significant and it shows a similar range of satisfaction scores for the outputs. Since input 4 ought to have been more difficult for the program to describe, a longer run time was to be expected, but the similar outputs and similar spread of satisfaction scores was not. Inspections of the structures built inside the program for each input indicate that relatively small chunks are being used to fill in frame slots and generate descriptions. The program therefore judges its descriptions to represent similar proportions of the map even though the descriptions for inputs 1-3 should be interpreted as describing larger areas. The program either builds large chunks and neglects to use them or fails to build larger chunks before generating text.

## 4    Future Improvements

It is clear from analysis of both the program's behaviour and its outputs, that further work is required to improve the program's satisfaction score and its ability to judge between good or bad outputs. This includes making sure that the program recognizes how correct and complete its descriptions are.

The program must remedy its description's lack of completeness by both building chunks which cover a wider area of the input when possible so as to gauge more accurately how much of the input a sentence can be interpreted as describing, but also to continue processing and generate more sentences when the text produced so far does not provide a full description.

Knowledge represented in the program and taken into account by self-evaluation ought also to include more aesthetic considerations. For example, the program ought to prefer comparison between opposite locations. Odd statements should not be forbidden in case a different context makes them relevant, but the program should generally avoid them.

Future work should also include a more thorough search for a set of hyperparameters that will encourage good quality and complete descriptions of the input. This will not necessarily require large-scale changes to the program, but remains a challenge considering the complexity of the search space.

Ultimately, the program must also be put to work in a more complex domain in order to test its general applicability to the task of generating descriptions.

## 5   Conclusion

This paper presents an advance towards an explainable model of language generation which can evaluate its own work and is directly affected by its own self-evaluation. The idea has great cognitive plausibility due to the intertwining of different processes, but the implementation thus far still lags behind humans in terms of both language generation and language evaluation. Future work must focus on improving the program's in-built aesthetic measures so that it can more reliably predict human judgements; produce better descriptions; and know when to publish them.

## References

1. Belz, A. and Kow, E.: Comparing rating scales and preference judgements in language evaluation. In: Proceedings of the 6th International Conference on Natural Language Generation, pp. 7–15 (2010)
2. Clark, H.H.: Using Language. Cambridge University Press (1996)
3. Falkenhainer, B., Forbus, K.D., Gentner, D.: The structure mapping engine: algorithm and examples. Artif. Intell. **41**, 1–63 (1989)
4. French, R.M: The Subtlety of Sameness: A Theory and Computer Model of Analogy-Making. MIT Press (1995)
5. Gatt, A., Krahmer, E.: Survey of the state of the art in natural language generation: core tasks, applications, and evaluation. J. Artif. Intell. Res. **61**, 65–170 (2018)
6. Hofstadter, D.: FARG: Fluid Concepts and Creative Analogies. Basic Books (1995)
7. Leppänen, L., Munezero, M., Granroth-Wilding, M., Toivonen, H.: Data-driven news generation for automated Journalism. In: Proceedings of the 10th International Natural Language Generation Conference, pp. 188–197 (2017)
8. Mitchell, M.: Analogy-Making as Perception: A Computer Model. MIT Press (1993)
9. Pickering, M.J., Garrod, S.: An integrated theory of language production and comprehension. Behav. Brain Sci. **36**, 329–392 (2013)
10. Pérez y Pérez, R., Sharples, M.: Mexica: a computer model of a cognitive account of creative writing. J. Exp. Theor. Artif. Intell. **13**(2), 119–139 (2001)
11. Reiter, E: An architecture for data-to-text systems. In: Proceedings of the Eleventh European Workshop on Natural Language Generation, pp. 97–104 (2007)
12. Sharples, M.: How We Write: Writing as Creative Design. Routledge (1998)
13. Turner, M.: The Literary Mind: The Origins of Thought and Language. Oxford University Press (1996)

# A Novel Hybrid Framework to Enhance Zero-shot Classification

Yanan Chen and Yang Liu[(✉)]

Faculty of Science, Wilfrid Laurier University, Waterloo, ON, Canada
`chen0040@mylaurier.ca`, `yangliu@wlu.ca`

**Abstract.** As manually labelling data can be error-prone and labour-intensive, some recent studies automatically classify documents without any training on labelled data and directly exploit pre-trained language models (PLMs) for many downstream tasks, also known as zero-shot text classification. In the same vein, we propose a novel framework aims at improving zero-short learning and enriching domain specific information required by PLMs with transformer models. To unleash the power of PLMs pre-trained on massive cross-section corpus, the framework unifies two transformers for different purposes: 1) expanding categorical *labels* required by PLMs by creating coherent representative samples with GPT2, which is a language model acclaimed for generating sensical text outputs, and 2) augmenting *documents* with T5, which has the virtue of synthesizing high quality new samples similar to the original text. The proposed framework can be easily integrated into different general testbeds. Extensive experiments on two popular topic classification datasets have proved its effectiveness.

**Keywords:** Natural language processing · Zero shot classification · Pre-trained language models

## 1 Introduction

Zero-shot text classifications 0SHOT-TC [32] refers to the tasks of making a prediction by gauging the matching score between documents and candidate labels without counting on any training data. One straightforward benefit of this method is to accommodate emerging labels and provide promising predictions not shown in the past. For example, to classify newly arrived Tweets into diverse topics, the prediction model will recognize previously unseen topics and assign them to incoming Tweets without relying on any training data. Another benefit is that the output layer (usually expressed with a Softmax function) of the neural networks does not need to be changed to cater for the dynamic label set, which eases the design and implementation of the system.

Compared to those well-studied supervised text classification tasks, 0SHOT-TC is far from satisfactory in many real-world scenarios. One of the major reasons behind this is that people tend to conduct classification through very

© Springer Nature Switzerland AG 2022
P. Sojka et al. (Eds.): TSD 2022, LNAI 13502, pp. 199–211, 2022.
https://doi.org/10.1007/978-3-031-16270-1_17

limited information of surface labels, but expect models to digest the underlying meanings and even make reasoning and associations for generalization purpose.

Previous studies in this direction mainly project documents and their label names into the same (latent) representation space, where their similarities can be captured by different metrics such as Cosine similarity functions [1,6,18, 25,28]. Further, additional information of the label, acquired through external resources such as Wikipedia and various knowledge graphs, can be included [25] to shed the light on the nature of classification topics. Nonetheless, these approaches are still in infancy due to high dependence on external resources and undesirable classification performance [32]. With the flourish of PLMs in recent years, people have explored their usages in various classification tasks to provide 1) better representations of text come out [20]; 2) deeper and well-rounded interactions between labels and documents, replacing classic cosine-based solutions [22,27,32]. Thanks to the in-depth knowledge gained through large and cross-section corpus, PLMs significantly reduce manual interventions and demonstrate an ubiquitous power in different learning tasks. Nonetheless, to the best of our knowledge, few work has been proposed to systematically improve the performance of 0SHOT-TC using PLMs.

To fill in this gap, we propose a novel framework to enhance 0SHOT-TC paradigm in an end-to-end manner. The proposal can be divided into three major modules. First, at the label level, we construct label-incorporated prompts to induce new label-conditioned texts with the help of GPT2, and calculate the similarity score between generated texts and the document using the NSP function of BERT. Second, at the document level, we utilize T5 to harvest augmented samples with the assist of text2text transformations. Finally, the knowledge derived from the above two modules are unified together with the matching score of the existing zero-short learning method to better capture the relatedness between documents and labels. Although both GPT2 and T5 models are transformer-based algorithms, they are explored in this work for different purposes based on their uniqueness. As one of the major contributions, our framework solely relies on the results of pre-training, saving the cost of generating handcrafted rules, the requirement of expert interventions, and the dependence on external resources. In experiments, we thoroughly evaluate the effectiveness of the unified framework and carefully compare each module with alternative methods. A detailed analysis of multiple factors that could affect the performance is provided.

## 2 Related Work

Previous studies on 0SHOT-TC can be roughly grouped into two categories. *Similarity model based approaches* attempt to construct a good representation for both labels and documents, and project them into the same embedding representation space where similarity functions, such as cosine similarity, can be applied to gauge the relatedness [1,6,18,25,28]. External resources such as Wikipedia are sometimes integrated in this process [8,33]. Given recent success of PLMs [5,15], a few studies, such as Sentence-BERT [20], create better representations using self-training and contrast learning over colossal corpus. *Language*

***model based approaches*** model the relatedness score between documents and labels internally within deep neural networks or PLMs. For example, [32] tackles the problem by using the entailment score of BERT trained on NLI dataset. This line of research often wraps the label into pre-defined templates and feeds them into PLMs. For example, prompt-tuning wraps the input sentence into a pre-defined template and lets PLM conduct cloze completion tasks, such as "A [MASK] article: **x**.", or "**x**, this is [MASK] News.", where **x** is the text to be classified. The prediction is usually made based on the probability a LM returns for the [MASK] [14].

## 3    Problem Formulation

Given a document collection $\mathcal{D} = \{d_1, \ldots, d_i, \ldots, d_n\}$, each document $d \in \mathcal{D}$ which contains multiple sentences and correspondingly a sequence of tokens of variable lengths, is assigned with a probability distribution over a list of candidate labels $\mathcal{L} = \{l_1, \ldots, l_i, \ldots, l_k\}^1$ by the zero-shot classification model $\mathcal{M}_{zsl}$. Somewhat different from traditional supervised training, in 0SHOT-TC $l_i$ is denoted as label surface names such as *politics, sports, business, finance, science* which are essential and fully exploited for classification. To categorize a document $d$, a 0SHOT-TC model $\mathcal{C}$ first takes $d$ and every label $l \in \mathcal{L}$ as inputs, and calculate the assignment score that $d$ belongs to $l$.

$$score_{zsl} = \mathcal{C}(d, l) \tag{1}$$

The label with the highest score then becomes the classification result of $\mathcal{C}$, i.e., picking up the label that has the highest semantic relatedness to the document. Our objective in this paper is to enhance the 0SHOT-TC process by simulating the decision making process of human being: to understand and construct associations both for $d$ and $l$.

## 4    An Unified Framework

In this section, we propose a cost effective 0SHOT-TC framework based on two pre-trained transformer models that do not require pre-processing, post-processing and saving any intermittent results. It contains three modules where the first two focus on label name expansion and document augmentation respectively, and the last integrates different components together. The architecture of the framework is shown in Fig. 1.

### 4.1    Label Name Expansion Using GPT2

Previous zero-shot classifiers perform text classifications only if suitable descriptions or indicative seed words of the labels are provided. This reliance causes

---

[1] $\mathcal{L}$ may not be pre-defined in practical scenarios, while in the experiments we fix it for convenient evaluations.

0SHOT-TC to be highly sensitive to the choice of label descriptions and human expert designs, and hinders its broader applications in different domains. Classic embedding approaches, including word2vec or even transformer-based embeddings, tend to exploit label names that consist of just one single word or phrase, where the latent representation of embedding can not carry sufficient meaning and therefore lose important contextual information. To mitigate this problem, we propose to leverage GPT2 to enrich the representation of labels.

Given a prompt, we use GPT2 to harvest synthetic samples $X$ at each time step auto-regressively as follows:

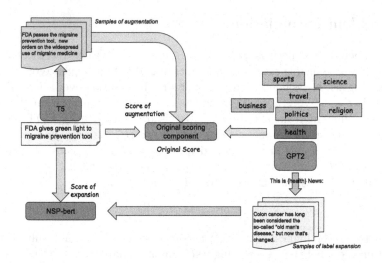

**Fig. 1.** The proposed framework

$$X_t = \mathcal{G}_{GPT2}\left(prompt; X_{<t}\right). \tag{2}$$

Here we formulate the prompt $\mathcal{P}(l)$ as a template ``This is {l} News:'', where $l$ is an incorporated label. For example, a template of politics can be expressed as ``This is politics News:''. This is to provide an indicative start alluring GPT2 to write continuations that are more likely to fall into the topic of the corresponding label $l$. In addition, to reduce the bias, we perform samplings at each time step of generation to increase the diversity of synthetic samples. This process can be formulated as

$$D_l^{GPT2} = \mathcal{F}_{expand}\left(GPT2, \mathcal{P}(l)\right), \tag{3}$$

where $D_l^{GPT2}$ is a collection of continuation texts from GPT2 based on $\mathcal{P}(l)$, and the maximum length of continuations is set to be the average length of the documents in $\mathcal{D}$. Accordingly $D_{l \in \mathcal{L}}^{GPT2}$ can be considered as representing label $l$ at the level of sentences/documents rather than words, which is significantly different from embedding-based solutions.

To ensure the prompt will produce closely related contents, we borrow the idea of Next Sentence Prediction (NSP) in BERT. NSP is one of the sentence-level pre-training objects of BERT (the other is MLM), and is frequently used in binary classification tasks to predict whether two sentences may appear consecutively. In other words, NSP can determine if a pair of samples fall into the same topic or express the same semantics, regardless of their order. In this work, such functionality is exploited in the label name expansion module to measure the alignment between $d$ and $t$ in terms of topic consistency.

Specifically, $\mathcal{M}_{bert}$ represents the model of BERT and takes a pair of texts $X$ and $\tilde{X}$ as inputs:

$$score_{nsp} = \mathcal{M}_{bert} \left( [CLS]X[SEP].\tilde{X}[EOS] \right), \tag{4}$$

where $score_{nsp}$ indicates the output of $\mathcal{M}_{bert}$'s NSP head, which is a probability value ranging from 0 to 1.[2] We next apply Eq. 4 to document $d$ and every synthetic text $t_l \in D_l^{GPT2}$ with respect to every label $l \in \mathcal{L}$, to calculate the overall compatibility between $d$ and $l$:

$$score_{expand}^{d,l} = \frac{1}{|D_l^{GPT2}|} \sum_{t_l \in D_l^{GPT2}} \left( \mathcal{M}_{bert} \left( d, t_l \right) + \mathcal{M}_{bert} \left( t_l, d \right) \right) \tag{5}$$

A higher score suggests document $d$ is more likely to belong to label $l$, where $D_l^{GPT2}$ can be considered as proxy of $l$.

### 4.2 Document Augmentation Using T5

Parallel to the attempt at expanding prompt labels, we explore data augmentation (DA) at document level to synthesize more samples in training set and to regularize the classifier. Witnessed the great success of T5 as another transformer-based PLM, we leverage T5 to generate new document samples for $d$. Unlike the auto-regressive model GPT2, T5 belongs to *directed generation* where the output can be regarded as a constrained transformation of the input [9]. In the generation process, each token is generated with

$$\tilde{X}_t = \mathcal{G}_{T5} \left( X \mid \tilde{X}_{<t} \right). \tag{6}$$

Besides, T5 model is of an encoder-decode architecture, attending to both source text $X$ and generated $\tilde{X}_{<t}$ simultaneously. It has widely been used in machine translation, text summarization and answer generation; nonetheless, less investigated in DA. In this work, we use T5 to synthesize augmentation samples without providing a specific task prefix,

$$D_d^{T5} = \mathcal{F}_{augment} \left( T5, d \right). \tag{7}$$

---

[2] In this study, we use the publicly available BERT of uncased version https://huggingface.co/bert-base-uncased. The output of BERT's NSP has two logits: the first is the probability of *IsNext* and the second is the probability of *NotNext*, both of which are outputs of the SoftMax function from the previous layer.

The augmentation score of this component can be calculated with

$$score_{aug}^{d,l} = \frac{1}{|D_d^{T5}|} \sum_{\tilde{d} \in D_d^{T5}} (\mathcal{C}\left(\tilde{d}, l\right)).$$ (8)

Note that $D_d^{T5}$ does not include the original sample $d$. Instead it is only used in the original 0SHOT-TC suggested in Eq. 1.

## 4.3 Integration of Modules

To generate an informed decision of 0SHOT-TC, we finally fuse all three scores obtained at estimations on vanilla zero-short learning, prompt label expansions and document augmentation. For each document-label pair, we calculate $score_{fuse}$ as the sum of the logarithm values of three individual factors. In this study, each compounding score is assigned with a same weight for simplicity; however, it is also possible to evaluate their impacts on different applications and suggest different importance for each of them.

$$score_{fuse} \propto \log score_{zsl} + \log score_{expand} + \log score_{aug}$$ (9)

# 5   Experiments

## 5.1   Datasets

We evaluate our proposed framework on two public topic classification datasets: **AG** and **Yahoo** [34] which have been widely adopted in related studies. Both datasets are balanced, and the numbers of candidate labels of each dataset are $|\mathcal{L}_{ag}| = 4$ and $|\mathcal{L}_{yahoo}| = 10$. Following previous studies, we use accuracy which will be a reliable indicator while the data are balanced, to evaluate 0SHOT-TC's performance.

## 5.2   Benchmark Solutions

To justify the proposal is model-agnostic and can be easily combined with other models irrespective of their local constraints, we include three benchmark models that address 0SHOT-TC from different views, and incorporate them with our proposed framework to evaluate the gain in performance.

1. **EMBEDDING** has been widely used in previous studies [2,7,12,13,21, 25,26,28] and adopts pre-trained word embedding for documents and label words. We use cmlm [31] as text encoder[3]. The label with the highest cosine similarity $\mathcal{M}_{cos}$ is selected for prediction. We do not add external information, such as class descriptions as those in [19,33] since they vary a lot and essentially do not change the architecture.

---

[3] https://tfhub.dev/google/universal-sentence-encoder-cmlm/en-base/1.

$$score\,(d,l) = \mathcal{C}\,(d,l)$$
$$= \mathcal{M}_{cos}\,(embed(d), embed(l)) \tag{10}$$

2. **NLI** [32] regards 0SHOT-TC as a textual entailment problem and learns from entailment datasets through pre-training over sentence pair classifications. This method simulates the decision process of raising and proving hypothesis by human being. By using textual entailment, classifiers understand the underlying meaning of documents labels, acquiring certain generalization ability. Following template $\mathcal{T}$ of `This text is about {label}` in [32], we take $d$ to be labeled as **premise** and turn each candidate label $l$ into **hypothesis**. Both the sentence (premise) and the label (hypothesis) are fed into the NLI model to return an entailment score $score_{nli}$ computed by $\mathcal{M}_{nli}$

$$score\,(d,l) = \mathcal{C}\,(d,l)$$
$$= \mathcal{M}_{nli}\,(hypothesis, premise) \tag{11}$$
$$= \mathcal{M}_{nli}\,(d, \mathcal{T}(l))$$

A higher score implies that the premise is more likely to entail the hypothesis. roberta-large fine-tuned over XNLI [3] and ANLI [17] datasets is adopted as $\mathcal{M}_{nli}$ in this study.

3. **CLOZE** [22] reformulates text classification as a cloze task. To perform 0SHOT-TC, a document is incorporated into templates with a `{MASK}` slot. The pre-trained MLM model predicts the words to be filled in `{MASK}` based on their possibilities to occur. Following method introduced in [22], three templates $\mathcal{T}$ are included. roberta-large [15] is adopted as $\mathcal{M}_{mlm}$ to derive the probability distribution over the vocabulary on the masked token.
`{Document} This text is about {MASK}.`
`{Document} News: {MASK}.`
`[Category: {MASK}] {Document}.`
In addition, the score of each label is set to be the sum of the three probabilities.

$$score\,(d,l) = \mathcal{C}\,(d,l)$$
$$= \sum_{\mathcal{T}}\sum_{w\in l} \mathcal{M}_{mlm}\,(\mathcal{T}(d); w) \tag{12}$$

## 5.3   Main Results and Analysis

**Evaluation on Benchmarks.** We perform experiments on three benchmarks introduced in Sect. 5.2 and demonstrate the results in Fig. 2. Specifically, we set $|D_d^{T5}| = 32$ and $|D_l^{GPT2}| = 256$ for each test sample represented as a document-label pair.

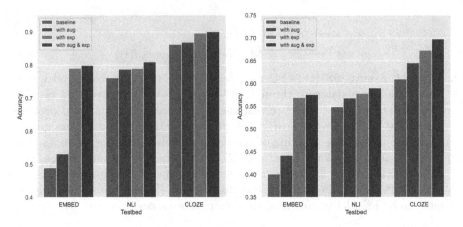

**Fig. 2.** Evaluation on three testbeds. **with aug** refers to the ablation approach of only including the DA module; **with exp** suggests only adding the label expansion module; **with aug & exp** indicates uniting both modules together. (left, for AG, and right, for YAHOO)

It is clear that the proposed framework significantly improves the baseline benchmarks. From the view of ablation, the expansion module at labels generally contributes more, especially for **EMBEDDING**. It proves our hypothesis that GPT2 helps generate more relevant texts to expand labels in prompts, and compensates information deficiency along label side. In addition, expansions can mitigate the ambiguity issue of certain labels such as *World* in AG dataset. Finally, the combination of the two components brings extra gains in accuracy, which justifies the power of ensemble.

**Tuning the Number of Samples in Expansion and Augmentation Component.** As including excessive samples could introduce noises while too few samples may under-represent documents and labels, we examine the impact of adopting different $|D_d^{T5}|$s and $|D_l^{GPT2}|$s. Beside, as enlarging the number of synthetic samples may incur extra computing costs, we wish to limit the expansion as much as possible.

As shown in Fig. 3, increasing the number of augmented documents $|D_d^{T5}|$ improves performance remarkably at the initial stage; while further enlarging the number does not help much and triggers a higher computation cost. Similar observations are made in label expansion, where 256 is identified the optimal number. Adding more continuation texts with GPT2 tends to undermine the performance in accuracy.

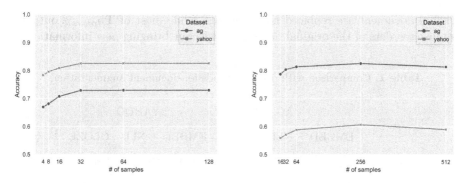

**Fig. 3.** Impact of number of synthetic samples, under setting of left: **with aug** and right:**with exp**

### 5.4   Comparison with Alternative Methods

In this section, we replace the two modules with some alternatives that may serve the same purpose. Instead of justifying the importance of each module as discussed in Sect. 5.3, this experiment sticks with the proposed framework and examine the virtues of the two LMs: GPT2 and T5.

**Alternative DAs.** To answer the call of performing effective document augmentation, we compare three DA approaches with $T5_{vanilla}$ which is adopted in our study.

- **EDA** [29] is the widely used word-replacement DA method, and it contains four basic randomization operations, i.e., *replacement, insertion, swap, and deletion.*[4]
- **Back-Translation (BT)** [23] is originated from language translation and extended to DA to bring linguistic diversities [11,16,24,30]. This experiment uses Chinese as the intermediate language and performs translation first from English to Chinese and then from Chinese back to English with models implemented in EN-ZH[5] and ZH-EN[6].
- **Fine-tuned T5** is a version of T5 fine-tuned[7] on Google PAWS paraphrasing dataset[8]. We add "`paraphrase:`" as a guide prefix to induce documents.

To make a fair comparison, the same experiment setting is applied to alternative methods as that in Sect. 5.3, where $|D_d^{EDA}| = |D_d^{BT}| = |D_d^{T5_{paws}}| = 32$. As shown in Table 1, $T5_{vanilla}$ consistently outperforms other approaches which suggests the effectiveness of T5. For **EDA** and **BT**, only a small fraction of words in the

---

[4] https://github.com/jasonwei20/eda_nlp.
[5] https://huggingface.co/Helsinki-NLP/opus-mt-en-zh.
[6] https://huggingface.co/Helsinki-NLP/opus-mt-zh-en.
[7] https://huggingface.co/Vamsi/T5_Paraphrase_Paws.
[8] https://github.com/google-research-datasets/paws.

original document are replaced by synonyms, while most of $\mathbf{T5_{paws}}$'s outputs are just reorders of the original documents without bringing new information.

**Table 1.** Comparison with other methods for document augmentation

|  | AG | | | YAHOO | | |
|---|---|---|---|---|---|---|
|  | EMBED | NLI | CLOZE | EMBED | NLI | CLOZE |
| EDA | 0.5199 | 0.7636 | 0.8603 | 0.3804 | 0.5612 | 0.6354 |
| BT | 0.5265 | 0.7769 | 0.8617 | 0.3971 | 0.5679 | 0.6419 |
| $T5_{paws}$ | 0.5301 | 0.7849 | 0.8644 | 0.4419 | 0.5669 | 0.6448 |
| $T5_{vanilla}$ | **0.5314** | **0.7876** | **0.8686** | **0.4422** | **0.5682** | **0.6452** |

**Alternative Label Expansions.** We expect the expanded text labels should be in good alignment with the originals, and choose two other state-of-the-art models that may provide such functionality. In this section, we examine their potentials in improving the label expansion module, and manually select a list of seed words $\{w_0^l, w_1^l, \ldots, w_k^l\} \in \mathcal{W}^l$ for each label to steer text generation, where $k$ is not a fixed number among labels. As an example, for *World* in AG dataset, some seeds could be {'Election', 'Terrorism', 'Politics', 'Tyranny', 'Military', 'Democracy', 'Totalitarian' ... }

- **CTRL** [10] We use the off-the-shelf CTRL[9] although most of our seed words are not covered by the original control codes given by the authors. We insert a fraction of seed words $\sim \mathcal{W}^l$ (randomly selected each time) into the template ``Links in {seed words}'' as prompt $\mathcal{P}(l)$ for CTRL's continuation towards $l$.
- **PPLM** [4] is another approach for controllable text generation which combines one or multiple simple attributes with a steerable layer. In 0SHOT-TC, there is no trained classifier; therefore we consider label seed words $\mathcal{W}^{l\in\mathcal{L}}$ as a predefined bag of words to suggest possible topic directions while making an update of $p(l|x)$ with $\log p(l|x) = \log\left(\sum_{i=1}^k p_{t+1}[w_i]\right)$. To be consistent with previous settings, we use GPT2 in Sect. 4.1 as the generative model.

In this experiment, we set $|D_{l\in\mathcal{L}}^{CTRL}| = |D_{l\in\mathcal{L}}^{GPT2_{PPLM}}| = |D_{l\in\mathcal{L}}^{GPT2_{vanilla}}| = 256$, and demonstrate the comparison results in Table 2. Clearly, alternative controllable label generations bring marginal improvements in accuracy. However, considering their computational costs - CTRL contains 1.63 billion parameters and PPLM requires additional parameter updates on every token generation, using the vanilla GPT2 is still a cost-effective and efficient practice.

---

[9] https://huggingface.co/docs/transformers/model_doc/ctrl.

**Table 2.** Comparison with other methods for label expansion

|  | AG | | | YAHOO | | |
|---|---|---|---|---|---|---|
|  | EMBED | NLI | CLOZE | EMBED | NLI | CLOZE |
| CTRL | 0.8048 | **0.8049** | 0.9064 | **0.5732** | **0.5825** | **0.6812** |
| GPT2$_{PPLM}$ | **0.8055** | 0.8015 | **0.9087** | 0.571 | 0.5808 | 0.6793 |
| GPT2$_{vanilla}$ | 0.7907 | 0.7901 | 0.8963 | 0.5695 | 0.5783 | 0.6731 |

# 6    Conclusion and Future Work

In this paper, we propose to improve 0SHOT-TC through document augmentations and label expansions. Extensive experiments on real datasets prove this framework is robust and easy to implement. In addition, it does not require much human intervention as those are usually seen in other methods. In future work, it is worth exploring the benefit on other natural language processing tasks such as classifying sentiments and question types in 0SHOT-TC.

**Acknowledgement.** This work was supported by the NSERC Discovery Grants.

# References

1. Chang, M.W., Ratinov, L.A., Roth, D., Srikumar, V.: Importance of semantic representation: dataless classification. In: AAAI2008 Proceedings of the 23rd National Conference on Artificial Intelligence, vol. 2, pp. 830–835 (2008)
2. Chen, X., Xia, Y., Jin, P., Carroll, J.: Dataless text classification with descriptive IDA. In: AAAI2015 Proceedings of the Twenty-Ninth AAAI Conference on Artificial Intelligence, vol. 29, pp. 2224–2231 (2015)
3. Conneau, A., et al.: XNLI: Evaluating cross-lingual sentence representations. In: Proceedings of the 2018 Conference on Empirical Methods in Natural Language Processing, EMNLP (2018)
4. Dathathri, S., et al.: Plug and play language models: a simple approach to controlled text generation. CoRR abs/1912.02164 (2019)
5. Devlin, J., Chang, M.W., Lee, K., Toutanova, K.: BERT: pre-training of deep bidirectional transformers for language understanding. In: Proceedings of the 2019 Conference of the North American Chapter of the Association for Computational Linguistics: Human Language Technologies, NAACL-HLT 2019, Minneapolis, MN, USA, pp. 4171–4186 (2019)
6. Elhoseiny, M., Saleh, B., Elgammal, A.: Write a classifier: zero-shot learning using purely textual descriptions. In: 2013 IEEE International Conference on Computer Vision, ICCV, pp. 2584–2591 (2013)
7. Gabrilovich, E., et al.: Computing semantic relatedness using Wikipedia-based explicit semantic analysis. In: IJCAI2007 Proceedings of the 20th International Joint Conference on Artifical Intelligence, IJCAI, vol. 7, pp. 1606–1611 (2007)

8. Harrando, I., Troncy, R.: Explainable zero-shot topic extraction using a common-sense knowledge graph. In: Third Biennial Conference on Language, Data and Knowledge, LDK (2021)

9. Holtzman, A., Buys, J., Du, L., Forbes, M., Choi, Y.: The curious case of neural text degeneration. CoRR abs/1904.09751 (2019)

10. Keskar, N.S., McCann, B., Varshney, L., Xiong, C., Socher, R.: CTRL - a conditional transformer language model for controllable generation. CoRR abs/1909.05858 (2019)

11. Kumar, V., Choudhary, A., Cho, E.: Data augmentation using pre-trained transformer models. CoRR abs/2003.02245 (2020)

12. Li, C., Xing, J., Sun, A., Ma, Z.: Effective document labeling with very few seed words: a topic model approach. In: CIKM 2016 Proceedings of the 25th ACM International on Conference on Information and Knowledge Management, CIKM, pp. 85–94 (2016)

13. Li, Y., Zheng, R., Tian, T., Hu, Z., Iyer, R., Sycara, K.: Joint embedding of hierarchical categories and entities for concept categorization and dataless classification. CoRR abs/1607.07956 (2016)

14. Liu, P., Yuan, W., Fu, J., Jiang, Z., Hayashi, H., Neubig, G.: Pre-train, prompt, and predict: a systematic survey of prompting methods in natural language processing. CoRR abs/2107.13586 (2021)

15. Liu, Y., et al.: RoBERTa: a robustly optimized BERT pretraining approach. CoRR abs/1907.11692 (2019)

16. Longpre, S., Wang, Y., DuBois, C.: How effective is task-agnostic data augmentation for pretrained transformers? In: the 2020 Conference on Empirical Methods in Natural Language Processing, EMNLP, pp. 4401–4411 (2020)

17. Nie, Y., Williams, A., Dinan, E., Bansal, M., Weston, J., Kiela, D.: Adversarial NLI: a new benchmark for natural language understanding. In: Proceedings of the 58th Annual Meeting of the Association for Computational Linguistics, ACL (2020)

18. Palatucci, M.M., Pomerleau, D.A., Hinton, G.E., Mitchell, T.: Zero-shot learning with semantic output codes. In: NIPS2009 Proceedings of the 22nd International Conference on Neural Information Processing Systems, NIPS, vol. 22 (2009)

19. Rei, M., Søgaard, A.: Zero-shot sequence labeling: transferring knowledge from sentences to tokens. In: Proceedings of the 2018 Conference of the North American Chapter of the Association for Computational Linguistics: Human Language Technologies, Volume 1 (Long Papers), NAACL-HLT, pp. 293–302 (2018)

20. Reimers, N., Gurevych, I.: Sentence-BERT: Sentence embeddings using Siamese BERT-networks. In: Proceedings of the 2019 Conference on Empirical Methods in Natural Language Processing and the 9th International Joint Conference on Natural Language Processing, EMNLP-IJCNLP, pp. 3982–3992 (2019)

21. Rios, A., Kavuluru, R.: Few-shot and zero-shot multi-label learning for structured label spaces. In: Proceedings of the 2018 Conference on Empirical Methods in Natural Language Processing, EMNLP, pp. 3132–3142 (2018)

22. Schick, T., Schütze, H.: Exploiting cloze questions for few-shot text classification and natural language inference. Computing Research Repository arXiv:2001.07676 (2020)

23. Sennrich, R., Haddow, B., Birch, A.: Improving neural machine translation models with monolingual data. In: Proceedings of the 54th Annual Meeting of the Association for Computational Linguistics (Volume 1: Long Papers), ACL, pp. 86–96 (2016)

24. Shleifer, S.: Low resource text classification with ulmfit and backtranslation. CoRR abs/1903.09244 (2019)
25. Song, Y., Roth, D.: On dataless hierarchical text classification. In: AAAI2014 Proceedings of the Twenty-Eighth AAAI Conference on Artificial Intelligence, AAAI, pp. 1579–1585 (2014)
26. Song, Y., Upadhyay, S., Peng, H., Roth, D.: Cross-lingual dataless classification for many languages. In: Proceedings of the Twenty-Fifth International Joint Conference on Artificial Intelligence, IJCAI, pp. 2901–2907 (2016)
27. Sun, Y., Zheng, Y., Hao, C., Qiu, H.: NSP-BERT: a prompt-based zero-shot learner through an original pre-training task-next sentence prediction. arXiv:2109.03564 (2021)
28. Veeranna, S.P., Nam, J., Mencía, E., Furnkranz, J.: Using semantic similarity for multi-label zero-shot classification of text documents. In: European Symposium on Artificial Neural Networks, ESANN, pp. 423–428 (2016)
29. Wei, J., Zou, K.: Eda: Easy data augmentation techniques for boosting performance on text classification tasks. In: Proceedings of the 2019 Conference on Empirical Methods in Natural Language Processing and the 9th International Joint Conference on Natural Language Processing, EMNLP-IJCNLP, pp. 6383–6389 (2019)
30. Xie, Q., Dai, Z., Hovy, E., Luong, T., Le, Q.: Unsupervised data augmentation for consistency training. In: Advances in Neural Information Processing Systems 33 (2020)
31. Yang, Z., Yang, Y., Cer, D., Law, J., Darve, E.: Universal sentence representation learning with conditional masked language model. In: Proceedings of the 2021 Conference on Empirical Methods in Natural Language Processing, EMNLP, pp. 6216–6228 (2021)
32. Yin, W., Hay, J., Roth, D.: Benchmarking zero-shot text classification: datasets, evaluation and entailment approach. In: Proceedings of the 2019 Conference on Empirical Methods in Natural Language Processing and the 9th International Joint Conference on Natural Language Processing, EMNLP-IJCNLP, pp. 3905–3914 (2019)
33. Zhang, J., Lertvittayakumjorn, P., Guo, Y.: Integrating semantic knowledge to tackle zero-shot text classification. In: Proceedings of the 2019 Conference of the North American Chapter of the Association for Computational Linguistics: Human Language Technologies, NAACL-HLT, pp. 1031–1040 (2019)
34. Zhang, X., Zhao, J., LeCun, Y.: Character-level convolutional networks for text classification. In: NIPS2015 Proceedings of the 28th International Conference on Neural Information Processing Systems, NIPS, vol. 1, pp. 649–657 (2015)

# Attention-Based Model for Accurate Stance Detection

Omama Hamad[1](✉) ⓘ, Ali Hamdi[2], and Khaled Shaban[1]

[1] Computer Science and Engineering Department, Qatar University, Doha, Qatar
{omama.hamad,khaled.shaban}@qu.edu.qa
[2] Computer Science School, University of Adelaide, Adelaide, Australia
alihamdi.ali@adelaide.edu.au

**Abstract.** Effective representation learning is an essential building block for achieving many natural language processing tasks such as stance detection as performed implicitly by humans. Stance detection can assist in understanding how individuals react to certain information by revealing the user's stance on a particular topic. In this work, we propose a new attention-based model for learning feature representations and show its effectiveness in the task of stance detection. The proposed model is based on transfer learning and multi-head attention mechanisms. Specifically, we use BERT and word2vec models to learn text representation vectors from the data and pass both of them simultaneously to the multi-head attention layer to help focus on the best learning features. We present five variations of the model, each with a different combination of BERT and word2vec embeddings for the query and value parameters of the attention layer. The performance of the proposed model is evaluated against multiple baseline and state-of-the-art models. The best of the five proposed variations of the model improved the accuracy on average by 0.4% and achieved 68.4% accuracy for multi-classification, while the best accuracy for binary classification is 86.1% with a 1.3% improvement.

**Keywords:** Transfer learning · Multi-head attention · Text classification · Stance detection · Deep learning · COVID-19 pandemic

## 1 Introduction

Social networks, notably the Twitter platform, have become a hot spot for individuals to share their opinions on a variety of topics during the COVID-19 pandemic, one of which is online schooling. The task of identifying a person's position on a specific topic is called stance detection, where the stances might be agree, disagree or neutral. Considerable efforts have been given to classifying stances on social media [1,14]. However, the problem lies in that existing proposed methods fail to capture the semantics of text features, resulting in poor performance. For instance, the ambiguous stance of a user's slang-expressed tweet on a particular problem confuses the model, resulting in inaccurate predictions. One of

© Springer Nature Switzerland AG 2022
P. Sojka et al. (Eds.): TSD 2022, LNAI 13502, pp. 212–224, 2022.
https://doi.org/10.1007/978-3-031-16270-1_18

the effective approaches to improving the performance of models consisting of millions of parameters is to train the model on a large amount of training data to understand the underlying meaning of the language. However, the datasets for stance detection are generally limited due to the high annotation costs.

Multiple studies have proposed multiple models for stance detection, indicating that this type of text classification is extremely challenging. The majority of recent methods employed attentional networks [22,28] and transfer learning [23]. However, several models were capable of detecting one or two stances at the cost of performance in the remaining classes [2]. For example, when multi-classification models used stances such as "favor", "against", and "neither", the "against" class almost overwhelmed the classification results, with a high percentage of true positives compared to the "neither" classes, which were almost detected as true negatives due to the unclear position of the text toward a specific issue. As a result, there is a need for models that produce accurate text representation vectors with respect to the stance, which we address in this work. We propose a novel method for detecting stances in text using a multi-head attention layer. The proposed method learns context-dependent and context-independent features from baseline and deep learning models, which are then passed in parallel to an attention-based model as shown in Fig. 1. Therefore, the multi-head attention layer learns new feature representations from multiple inputs by leveraging the query, key, and value parameters.

The reset of the article is organised as follows: Sect. 2 reviews related works. Section 3 explains the proposed model. Section 4 describes the dataset, machine and deep learning models used as baseline models, as well as the experimental setup. Section 5 presents the results and analysis. Section 6 concludes the paper.

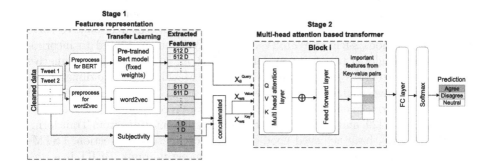

**Fig. 1.** Proposed model.

## 2   Related Work

Various studies have used debate-side classification [4] and stance classification [24] to describe stance detection. Essentially, stance detection assists in understanding how individuals react to target information, revealing the user's stance on a particular topic [6]. The rise of social media has brought this classification task into focus. Formally, we denote the dataset as $D = \{x_i = (t_i, s_i)\}_{i=1}^{N}$, where $N$ is the number of samples in the dataset $D$ and each sample $x$ contains a tweet $t_i$ and each tweet belongs to a class of specific stance $s_i$. The aim is to predict the probability $p \in \mathbb{R}^S$ that this piece of text belongs to a particular stance:

$$p = \text{softmax}\,(W_{\text{clf}}s + b_{\text{clf}}) \tag{1}$$

where $W$ and $b$ indicate the parameters of the classification layer, and $S$ is the learnt feature representation [12].

Modeling stance detection has been proposed using different learning methods, such as Convolutional Neural Networks (CNN) and Long Short-Term Memory (LSTM) [5] and transfer learning [23]. Several studies employed zero-shot stance detection to overcome the lack of annotated datasets for all topics. Allaway et al. [3] used adversarial learning to generalise across topics. They concluded that stance classification is a topic-dependent, and they focused on identifying topic-invariant stance representations to increase generalization. However, generalisation across social media topics is still a challenge. An attentional CNN model was developed in [30] to detect tweet stances. Specifically, a self-attention mechanism was implemented over CNN for adaptive enhancement of word embeddings with global textual data. Their approach was useful for identifying stance-indicative words where stance clues usually exist within non-informative words. The authors of [12] developed an attention-based BiLSTM model that identified features relevant to the particular target by explicitly adding the target information into the BiLSTM model.

Text representation learning is an essential component in stance detection. CNN for instance, combine different local textual characteristics for classifying stances. However, global textual information is generally ignored by CNN, leading to the missing of important discriminative textual features [30]. To solve this issue, methods such as Word2Vec and GloVe were presented to incorporate important global text features. Ghafarian et al. [13] identified informative tweets related to crises using a Support Measure Machine over one-dimensional vector-embeddings using Word2Vec. Bao et al. [5] used GloVe, a pre-trained word embedding matrix, to encode the input words. More recent models, such as bidirectional LSTM [29] and Bidirectional Encoder Representations from Transformers (BERT) [11], have achieved good performance in stance detection. LSTM-based models capture long-term dependencies among n-grams. BERT is a pre-trained model that learns contextual relations between words and predicts the masked words. However, using only pre-trained models proved to be unreliable when used with domain-specific text data [15].

## 3   Proposed Model

We propose a novel attention-based model for better representation learning for stance detection. The proposed model is designed to address the problem of classifying tweets correctly by improving the performance of the three stance classes. The proposed approach is divided into two stages as depicted in Fig. 1 to help in generating effective vectors that remove ambiguities and resolve vocabulary overlap across classes. The class overlap problem occurs when the features used to represent each class are insufficient or ineffective of capturing the necessary properties for drawing a clear boundary between them and distinguishing samples from each class [10]. (Table 1)

**Table 1.** Examples of classified tweets.

| Class | Tweet |
|---|---|
| **Agree** | So this mean ALL students are required to return back to in-person school?? What if we choose online learning due to level of risk?? I will no expose my children or elders in our home!! |
| **Disagree** | #onlinelearning Put kids at risk for suicide & depression. Punishment & lack of concern is not the solution & mental illness is not the goal. Intervene or they'll shut down. |
| **Neutral** | remote learning has never been and will never be a 100% effective replacement for anything, but it's complimentary and can be effective when it is designed to be effective, which is very much not what we're doing here |

### 3.1  Stage 1: Features Representation

In the first stage we employ two pre-trained language models, BERT [11], and the word2vec [18] to extract features. Embeddings extracted by these two models are context-dependent and context-independent, which are injected simultaneously as an input into the next attention-based model. BERT learns bidirectional representations by conditioning both left and right contexts in all layers concurrently, while the word2vec model generates word vectors from a massive amount of text input by detecting the contextual data in which the input words appear. Thus, words in a similar context tend to have collinear vectors. For example, words like "learning" and "education" should have a smaller semantic distance, hence word embedding develops semantics.

### 3.2  Stage 2: Multi-Head Attention

Here, we employ the transformer encoder architecture consisting of six encoder layers stacked on top of each other. Each encoder layer includes a multi-head attention layer and a feed-forward network. The multi-head attention layer takes three inputs for each head: Query $q$, Key $k$, and Value $v$. Unlike the original transformer architecture, the proposed model accepts two independent inputs from different sources to capture the complex relationships between these inputs. For example, the query $q_b^i$ is derived from the BERT hidden layer, while value $v_w^i$ and key $k_w^i$ are derived from the word2vec output. First, we compute the similarity between the query, which is BERT embeddings and the key, which is word2vec embeddings, and then perform the dot product operations with the value, which is the word2vec embeddings. In addition, the subjectivity feature is computed using the TextBlob library and ranges from 0.0 to 1.0, denoting very objective and very subjective, respectively. There are five versions of the dot product operations score, as follows:

- Version-1: To capture the best representation of BERT features given BERT features as query, $scores = q_b^i * v_b^i$.
- Version-2: To capture the best representation of BERT features given word2vec features concatenated with subjectivity feature as query, $scores = (q_w^i + q_s^i) * v_b^i$.
- Version-3: To capture the best representation of word2vec features concatenated with subjectivity feature given the query BERT features, $scores = q_b^i * (v_w^i + v_s^i)$
- Version-4: To capture the best representation of word2vec features given the word2vec features, $scores = q_w^i * v_w^i$
- Version-5: To capture the best representation features of the concatenated word2vec and BERT features, $scores = q_{bw}^i * v_{bw}^i$

The attention scores for all heads are concatenated as follows:

$$\text{MultiHead}\,(Q, K, V) = \text{Concat}\,(\text{head}_1, \ldots, \text{head}_h)\,W$$
$$head_i = \text{Attention}\left(QW_i^Q, KW_i^K, VW_i^V\right) \qquad (2)$$

## 4  Experiment

### 4.1  Dataset

We use StEduCov dataset[1] for detecting stances in tweets towards online education during the COVID-19 Pandemic. The dataset includes 16,572 tweets classified as "agree", "disagree", or "neutral". The distribution of tweets is as follows: 6,511 agree, 5,115 disagree, and 4,946 are neutral. Standard preprocessing operations are performed, such as lower-casing words and removing non-English and duplicate tweets. Cleaning the text from noise such as mentions and hashtags is an important step, since all extracted tweets have the same mentions and hashtags, such as "online learning, coronavirus". Therefore, removing such noise enables more accurate stance learning. In addition, we remove punctuation, stop words and URLs. Additionally, as Twitter users tend to utilise abbreviated forms of words, we break up contractions and give up the relevant lemmas.

---

[1] http://ieee-dataport.org/9221.

## 4.2   Baseline and State-of-the-Art Models

Various models are implemented and trained using the StdEduCov dataset. We introduce them in the following while categorising them into machine and deep learning (DL) models. Traditional machine learning models are: Logistic Regression (LR) [20], Random Forest (RF) [8], K-Nearest Neighbour (KNN) [17], Support Vector Machines (SVM) [9], Naive Bayes (NB) [21] and Decision Trees (DT) [19]. We train DL models as follows:

- **Bi-LSTM**: Bi-Directional Long Short Term Memory Networks is based on LSTM and initialized with GloVe embeddings, which can capture contextual information and long-term dependencies [16].
- **Att biLSTM**: Multi-head attention based biLSTM model, where using multiple heads of attention, the model may simultaneously pay attention to data coming from several representation subspaces located at various points in space [26].
- **BERT base**: A transformer-based architecture and a bidirectional model. As opposed to static embeddings produced by fastText and word2vec, BERT produces contextualised word embeddings where the vector for the word is computed based on the context in which it appears [11].
- **CNN**: A neural network made up of three types of layers: convolutional, pooling, and fully connected layers. The first two layers, convolution and pooling, extract features, and the third, a completely connected layer, maps the extracted features into final classification [27].
- **NBSVM**: proposed by [25] and is implemented as a neural network, which demonstrated that it could compete with more advanced neural network architectures. The implementation of this model employs two embedding layers for storing Navie Bayes log-count ratios and the set of weights that have been learnt. The dot product of these two vectors is then computed, which becomes the prediction.

## 4.3   Training and Hyper-parameters

**Experimental Setup.** A HuggingFace transformers is used to fine-tune the BERT model utilising the Pytorch framework, which supports GPU processing. Also, the Keras framework is used to implement and customise the LSTM, CNN and NBSVM models. The Ktrain library is used to train the NBSVM model which is implemented as a neural network. Two PCs are utilised to train the classification algorithms simultaneously: (a) an AsusTek PC computer with 125 GiB of RAM and four Quadro RTX 6000 GPUs; and (b) a Google Cloud Platform virtual instance with 8 vCPUs, 52 GB of RAM and one Nvidia Tesla K80.

**Hyper-Parameters.** Several experiments are performed to fine-tune the proposed model's hyper-parameters. The number of epochs and batch size are 50 and 8, respectively. The learning rate is estimated for BERT using the ktrain library, which is 1e-04 and the dropout ratio on all layers is 0.1. The hidden dimension is 256 and the optimizer is AdamW. The hyper-parameters for other DL models are: learning rate is 1e-4, hidden dimension is 300, dropout ratio is 0.3 and batch size is 16 for CNN and 64 for biLSTM.

## 5   Results and Analysis

The performance is evaluated using ten-fold cross validation on a shuffled dataset. To conduct the evaluation, a weighted average of the precision, and F1 scores is used, as well as accuracy. Table 2 shows the performance of six traditional machine learning models, five state-of-the-art machine learning models, and model v1, which is the best performing variant of our proposed model in terms of average results. Even though model v1 and the BERT model have comparable F1 scores, model v1 outperforms all state-of-the-art and baseline models on the average accuracy and precision, as shown in Table 2. In terms of the performance of the models in each class, an ablation study was conducted to show the performance of each version of the model, as shown in Table 4. Model v2 has the highest accuracy for the agree class, with an improvement of 7.2%, while the NBSVM model gives better results for the disagree class and BiLSTM gives better results for the neutral class. Notably, while all models' precision for the neutral class is quite low, model v2 followed by RF gives results of 64% and 63%, respectively. The confusion matrices for BERT and model v1 show that the neutral class has a significant impact on performance, with more than half of neutral tweets being false negatives and the majority of tweets predicted as agree class in both models, as shown in Fig. 2. To investigate the behaviour of our proposed model, we performed binary classification experiment by excluding the neutral class. The average results for the binary classification are in Table 3, showing that our model v2, which queries the word2vec features to pay attention

**Table 2.** Performance of models on every class using StEduCov Dataset. Acc: Accuracy, Pr: Precision and weighted F1 score.

| | LR | RF | KNN | SVM | NB | DT | nbsvm | biLSTM | CNN | BERT | Att biLSTM | Proposed model v1 |
|---|---|---|---|---|---|---|---|---|---|---|---|---|
| | | | | | Target: Agree with online education (Agree) | | | | | | | |
| Acc | 70.90% | 73.60% | **80.00%** | 67.00% | 70.70% | 56.70% | 59.10% | 59.30% | 73.80% | 74.60% | 79.90% | **78.80%** |
| Pr | **67.00%** | 58.00% | 45.00% | 60.00% | 63.00% | 52.00% | **67.00%** | 63.00% | 60.00% | 65.00% | 60.00% | 64.00% |
| F1 | **69.00%** | 65.00% | 57.00% | 63.00% | 66.00% | 54.00% | 63.00% | 61.00% | 66.00% | **69.00%** | **69.00%** | 71.00% |
| | | | | | Target: Disagree with online education (Disagree) | | | | | | | |
| Acc | 83.40% | 80.20% | 59.30% | 76.90% | 91.10% | 65.10% | **91.80%** | 72.50% | 75.60% | 84.90% | 69.20% | **86.90%** |
| Pr | 68.00% | 63.00% | 66.00% | 68.00% | 64.00% | 64.00% | 63.00% | 70.00% | 73.00% | **75.00%** | 74.00% | **75.00%** |
| F1 | 75.00% | 71.00% | 62.00% | 72.00% | 75.00% | 64.00% | 75.00% | 71.00% | 74.00% | **80.00%** | 72.00% | **80.00%** |
| | | | | | Target: Neutral | | | | | | | |
| Acc | 33.00% | 26.00% | 14.60% | 40.30% | 18.20% | 32.00% | 32.40% | **44.90%** | 34.60% | 33.70% | 31.80% | 28.10% |
| Pr | 50.00% | **63.00%** | 52.00% | 55.00% | 62.00% | 37.00% | 60.00% | 44.00% | 50.00% | 54.00% | 51.00% | 60.00% |
| F1 | 40.00% | 37.00% | 23.00% | **47.00%** | 28.00% | 34.00% | 42.00% | 45.00% | 41.00% | 41.00% | 39.00% | 38.00% |
| | | | | | Average results | | | | | | | |
| Acc | 63.10% | 62.80% | 52.60% | 62.00% | 62.70% | 52.90% | 63.10% | 60.20% | 63.00% | **68.00%** | 62.70% | **68.40%** |
| Pr | 63.20% | 62.30% | 54.40% | 61.10% | 62.80% | 52.50% | 63.00% | 60.20% | 62.00% | **66.00%** | 62.00% | **67.50%** |
| F1 | 62.80% | 59.90% | 49.80% | 61.30% | 58.50% | 52.60% | 60.60% | 60.20% | 62.00% | **66.00%** | 61.10% | 66.00% |

to the important features from BERT embeddings, outperforms all other models on all metrics.

The results show that the model is confused between "agree" and "neutral" classes due to the use of subjectivity and objectivity in tweets. As an example, "Because schools refuse to host any classes online, students are generally not compelled to complete any work or maintain regular contact with teachers". This tweet provides a fact while also indicating a certain point of view. However, in certain ambiguous tweets, the suggested model can predict the correct class, which proves that it improves the feature representations, as shown in Table 5. The importance of combining context-independent and context-dependent features is that the features based on non-contextualised models will, in some cases, improve the performance of the model on unseen data when different ways of expressing the opinion and different vocabularies are used than in the training set. So the hybrid method can have a positive effect, as shown in this study. However, such neural networks with millions of parameters require a large corpus to be fine-tuned for a particular domain, such as education. On the other hand, other research revealed that segmenting data into more specific categories improved the performance of models on text classification [7]. As a result, additional research efforts are required to develop novel techniques for improving the classification accuracy of such complex and overlapping data.

**Table 3.** Performance of models on binary classification (Agree and Disagree Classes).

|  | LR | RF | KNN | SVM | NB | DT | nbsvm | biLSTM | CNN | BERT | Att biLSTM | Proposed model v2 |
|---|---|---|---|---|---|---|---|---|---|---|---|---|
| **Acc** | **84.8%** | 83.6% | 76.0% | 84.0% | 83.8% | 75.0% | 83.1% | 83.0% | 84.6% | 84.3% | 81.7% | **86.1%** |
| **Pr** | 84.8% | 83.7% | 76.7% | 84.0% | 84.8% | 75.0% | 84.7% | 83.0% | **85.0%** | 83.6% | 81.8% | **86.0%** |
| **F1** | 84.8% | 83.6% | 76.0% | 83.9% | 83.7% | 75.0% | 82.8% | 83.0% | **85.3%** | 84.9% | 81.6% | **86.2%** |

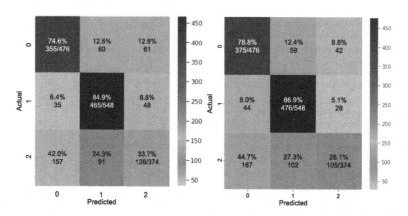

**Fig. 2.** Confusion matrix for BERT (left) and model v1 (right) for multi-classification (0: agree, 1: disagree and 2: neutral).

## 5.1   Error Analysis

As shown in Table 5, BERT and the proposed model perform well on examples where the stance is stated explicitly, such as tweets 1, 3, and 5. However, only model v1 successfully predicts the stance in tweet 2, where the meaning is represented through negation. When the true meaning is obscured, as in tweet 4, model v1 predicts it accurately while others fail. Even in tweet 6, where humans struggle to understand the meaning, model v2 accurately predicts. As shown in Fig. 3, the neutral class shares the top bigram words with either the agree or disagree classes, as it is usually expressed using the two classes. Thus, the most uncertainty occurred when predicting the neutral class. When considering these top words as stop words, the accuracy is decreased since these words are important for the context. However, keeping these common words when training model v1 reduces errors by 0.4% compared to BERT and 5.4% compared to the

**Table 4.** Ablation study results of five variants of the proposed model.

|    | Agree | | | Disagree | | | Neutral | | | Average | | |
|----|--------|--------|--------|--------|--------|--------|--------|--------|--------|--------|--------|--------|
|    | Acc | Pr | F1 | Acc | Pr | F1 | Acc | Pr | F1 | Acc | Pr | F1 |
| v1 | 78.80% | 64.00% | **71.00%** | 86.90% | 75.00% | **80.00%** | 28.10% | 60.00% | 38.00% | **68.40%** | **67.50%** | **66.00%** |
| v2 | **87.20%** | 59.00% | 70.00% | 80.50% | **78.00%** | 79.00% | 21.70% | **64.00%** | 32.00% | 67.00% | 61.30% | 64.00% |
| v3 | 76.10% | 60.00% | 67.00% | 76.10% | 71.00% | 74.00% | 28.60% | 51.00% | 37.00 | 64.00% | 62.10% | 62.00% |
| v4 | 53.40% | 57.00% | 55.00% | 77.40% | 68.00% | 72.00% | **36.60%** | 42.00% | 39.00% | 58.20% | 57.20% | 58.50% |
| v5 | 72.70% | **65.00%** | 69.00% | **87.20%** | 72.00% | 79.00% | 30.70% | 57.00% | **40.00%** | 67.20% | 66.00% | 65.00% |

**Table 5.** A comparison of the models predictions.

|   | Tweet | Actual label | BERT | Model v1 | Model v2 |
|---|-------|--------------|------|----------|----------|
| 1 | Thank you quarantine for allowing me to log in to my online lecture and then go back to bed because i dont have the brain cells to endure learning today | Agree | Agree | Agree | Agree |
| 2 | When schools close, students don't have to stop learning. In recent years, eLearning has made huge advancements. However, before choosing or implementing a new eLearning program, first, follow these three key steps | Agree | Disagree | Agree | Disagree |
| 3 | Distance learning is awful for my kindergartener's mental health. You know what would be worse? Her being saddled with guilt at age 5 that she may have contributed to her (very high risk) live-in grandmother's death | Disagree | Disagree | Disagree | Disagree |
| 4 | Year 7 and Year 10, you absolutely smashed it today with the remote learning. Amazed at how many of you were able to log on and even see all of your lovely faces at home. Already missing you all, can't wait to get you back in my classroom! Super work guys! | Disagree | Agree | Disagree | Agree |
| 5 | Boston University, Harvard University and others are discussing potential scenarios for a different start to the upcoming school year due to the coronavirus pandemic | Neutral | Neutral | Neutral | Neutral |
| 6 | Student learning is largely falling to families as Michigan schools opt not to attempt to hold any classes online. The result? Students mostly aren't being required to complete any work or to have regular contact with teachers. | Neutral | Disagree | Disagree | Neutral |

SVM model. Models v2 and v3 rely heavily on preprocessing because they use embeddings from BERT and word2vec models, requiring different preprocessing for each one. Word2vec establishes a word's association with other words, such as "learning with education", hence they will have vectors that are quite similar. On the other hand, BERT captures the semantics of the context. Thus, while training models v2 and v3, we consider removing the most common terms when training word2vec while keeping them in BERT, which improves models v2 and v3 performance.

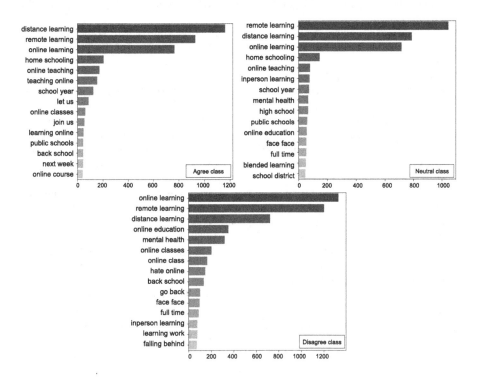

**Fig. 3.** Error analysis: comparison of the top 15 bi-gram words in every class.

# 6   Conclusion

In this study, we propose an attentional neural network architecture for learning better feature representation. The proposed model is composed of two stages, the first of which involves transfer learning in order to generate embeddings from pretrained BERT and word2vec models. The second stage employs the attention mechanism, which takes inputs from two sources (BERT and word2vec embeddings) to focus on the critical input sequences. This technique outperforms state-of-the-art models in detecting stances in tweets by combining context-based and non-context-based models to overcome vocabulary overlap across classes. As for future work, there is a need to develop an ensemble using the best performing models in each class, which may result in improved performance. Moreover, other transfer learning approaches that can improve model performance will also be investigated.

# References

1. Miao, L., Last, M., Litwak, M.: Tracking social media during the COVID-19 pandemic: the case study of lockdown in New York state. Expert Syst. Appl. **187**, 115797 (2022)
2. Al-Ghadir, A.I., Azmi, A.M., Hussain, A.: A novel approach to stance detection in social media tweets by fusing ranked lists and sentiments. Inf. Fusion **67**, 29–40 (2021)
3. Allaway, E., Srikanth, M., McKeown, K.: Adversarial learning for zero-shot stance detection on social media. In: Proceedings of the 2021 Conference of the North American Chapter of the Association for Computational Linguistics: Human Language Technologies. Association for Computational Linguistics, Online (2021)
4. Anand, P., Walker, M., Abbott, R., Tree, J.E.F., Bowmani, R., Minor, M.: Cats rule and dogs drool!: classifying stance in online debate. In: Proceedings of the 2nd Workshop on Computational Approaches to Subjectivity and Sentiment Analysis (WASSA 2.011), pp. 1–9 (2011)
5. Bao, J., Zhang, L., Han, B.: Collaborative attention network with word and n-gram sequences modeling for sentiment classification. In: Tetko, I.V., Kůrková, V., Karpov, P., Theis, F. (eds.) ICANN 2019. LNCS, vol. 11730, pp. 79–92. Springer, Cham (2019). https://doi.org/10.1007/978-3-030-30490-4_8
6. Barbieri, F., Camacho-Collados, J., Neves, L., Espinosa-Anke, L.: TweetEval: unified benchmark and comparative evaluation for tweet classification. arXiv preprint arXiv:2010.12421 (2020)
7. Bello-Orgaz, G., Hernandez-Castro, J., Camacho, D.: Detecting discussion communities on vaccination in twitter. Futur. Gener. Comput. Syst. **66**, 125–136 (2017)
8. Breiman, L.: Bagging predictors. Mach. Learn. **24**(2), 123–140 (1996)
9. Crammer, K., Singer, Y.: On the algorithmic implementation of multiclass Kernel-based vector machines. J. Mach. Learn. Res. **2**, 265–292 (2001)
10. Das, B., Krishnan, N.C., Cook, D.J.: Handling imbalanced and overlapping classes in smart environments prompting dataset. In: Yada, K. (ed.) Data Mining for Service. SBD, vol. 3, pp. 199–219. Springer, Heidelberg (2014). https://doi.org/10.1007/978-3-642-45252-9_12
11. Devlin, J., Chang, M.W., Lee, K., Toutanova, K.: BERT: pre-training of deep bidirectional transformers for language understanding. In: Proceedings of the 2019 Conference of the North American Chapter of the Association for Computational Linguistics: Human Language Technologies, Volume 1 (Long and Short Papers). Association for Computational Linguistics, Minneapolis, Minnesota (2019)
12. Du, J., Xu, R., He, Y., Gui, L.: Stance classification with target-specific neural attention networks.In: Proceedings of the Twenty-Sixth International Joint Conference on Artificial Intelligence (2017)
13. Ghafarian, S.H., Yazdi, H.S.: Identifying crisis-related informative tweets using learning on distributions. Inf. Process. Manage. **57**(2), 102145 (2020)

14. Glandt, K., Khanal, S., Li, Y., Caragea, D., Caragea, C.: Stance detection in COVID-19 tweets. In: Proceedings of the 59th Annual Meeting of the Association for Computational Linguistics and the 11th International Joint Conference on Natural Language Processing (Volume 1: Long Papers). Association for Computational Linguistics, Online (2021)

15. Khadhraoui, M., Bellaaj, H., Ammar, M.B., Hamam, H., Jmaiel, M.: Survey of BERT-base models for scientific text classification: COVID-19 case study. Appl. Sci. **12**(6), 2891 (2022)

16. Lai, S., Xu, L., Liu, K., Zhao, J.: Recurrent convolutional neural networks for text classification. In: AAAI2015: Proceedings of the Twenty-Ninth AAAI Conference on Artificial Intelligence, pp. 2267–2273 (2015)

17. Lanjewar, R., Mathurkar, S., Patel, N.: Implementation and comparison of speech emotion recognition system using Gaussian mixture model (GMM) and k-nearest neighbor (k-NN) techniques. Procedia Comput. Sci. **49**, 50–57 (2015)

18. Mikolov, T., Sutskever, I., Chen, K., Corrado, G.S., Dean, J.: Distributed representations of words and phrases and their compositionality. In: Advances in Neural Information Processing Systems, pp. 3111–3119 (2013)

19. Mingers, J.: An empirical comparison of pruning methods for decision tree induction. Mach. Learn. **4**(2), 227–243 (1989)

20. Ramadhan, W., Novianty, S.A., Setianingsih, S.C.: Sentiment analysis using multinomial logistic regression. In: 2017 International Conference on Control, Electronics, Renewable Energy and Communications (ICCREC), pp. 46–49. IEEE (2017)

21. Ren, J., Lee, S.D., Chen, X., Kao, B., Cheng, R., Cheung, D.: Naive Bayes classification of uncertain data. In: 2009 Ninth IEEE International Conference on Data Mining, pp. 944–949. IEEE (2009)

22. Song, Y., Wang, J., Jiang, T., Liu, Z., Rao, Y.: Targeted sentiment classification with attentional encoder network. In: Tetko, I.V., Kůrková, V., Karpov, P., Theis, F. (eds.) ICANN 2019. LNCS, vol. 11730, pp. 93–103. Springer, Cham (2019). https://doi.org/10.1007/978-3-030-30490-4_9

23. Vizcarra, G., Mauricio, A., Mauricio, L.: A deep learning approach for sentiment analysis in spanish tweets. In: Kůrková, V., Manolopoulos, Y., Hammer, B., Iliadis, L., Maglogiannis, I. (eds.) ICANN 2018. LNCS, vol. 11141, pp. 622–629. Springer, Cham (2018). https://doi.org/10.1007/978-3-030-01424-7_61

24. Walker, M.A., Anand, P., Abbott, R., Tree, J.E.F., Martell, C., King, J.: That is your evidence?: classifying stance in online political debate. Decis. Support Syst. **53**(4), 719–729 (2012)

25. Wang, S.I., Manning, C.D.: Baselines and bigrams: simple, good sentiment and topic classification. In: Proceedings of the 50th Annual Meeting of the Association for Computational Linguistics (Volume 2: Short Papers), pp. 90–94 (2012)

26. Wei, J., Liao, J., Yang, Z., Wang, S., Zhao, Q.: BiLSTM with multi-polarity orthogonal attention for implicit sentiment analysis. Neurocomputing **383**, 165–173 (2020)

27. Wei, W., Zhang, X., Liu, X., Chen, W., Wang, T.: Pkudblab at SemEval-2016 task 6: a specific convolutional neural network system for effective stance detection. In: Proceedings of the 10th International Workshop on Semantic Evaluation (SemEval-2016), pp. 384–388 (2016)

28. Wu, H., Qin, S., Nie, R., Cao, J., Gorbachev, S.: Effective collaborative representation learning for multilabel text categorization. In: IEEE Transactions on Neural Networks and Learning Systems (2021)

29. Zhou, J., Xu, W.: End-to-end learning of semantic role labeling using recurrent neural networks. In: Proceedings of the 53rd Annual Meeting of the Association for Computational Linguistics and the 7th International Joint Conference on Natural Language Processing (Volume 1: Long Papers), pp. 1127–1137 (2015)
30. Zhou, S., Lin, J., Tan, L., Liu, X.: Condensed convolution neural network by attention over self-attention for stance detection in twitter. In: 2019 International Joint Conference on Neural Networks (IJCNN), pp. 1–8. IEEE (2019)

# OPTICS: Automatic MT Evaluation Based on Optimal Transport by Integration of Contextual Representations and Static Word Embeddings

Hiroshi Echizen'ya[1](✉) , Kenji Araki[2] , and Eduard Hovy[3]

[1] Hokkai-Gakuen University, 1-1, South-26, West-11, Chuo-ku,
Sapporo 064-0926, Japan
echi@lst.hokkai-s-u.ac.jp
[2] Hokkaido University, North-14, West-9, Kita-ku, Sapporo 060-0814, Japan
araki@ist.hokudai.ac.jp
[3] University of Melbourne and Carnegie Mellon University, Melbourne Connect,
cor. Swanston and Grattan Streets, Parkville, VIC 3052, Australia
eduard.hovy@unimelb.edu.au, hovy@cmu.edu
http://www.lst.hokkai-s-u.ac.jp/~echi/eng-index.html
http://arakilab.media.eng.hokudai.ac.jp/~araki/araki_english.html
http://www.cs.cmu.edu/~hovy

**Abstract.** Automatic MT metrics using word embeddings are extremely effective. Semantic word similarities are obtained using word embeddings. However, similarities using only static word embeddings are insufficient for lack of contextual information. Automatic metrics using fine-tuned models can adapt to a specific domain using contextual representations obtained by learning, but that adaptation requires large amounts of data to learn suitable models. As described herein, we propose an automatic MT metric based on optimal transport using both contextual representations and static word embeddings. The contextual representations are obtained by learning the neural models. In that case, our proposed metric requires no other data except source sentences and references, which correspond to the evaluation target hypotheses, to learn the models that are used to extract the contextual representations. Therefore, our proposed metric can adapt to the domain appropriately without requiring large amounts of learning data. Experiment results obtained using the WMT 20 metric shared task data indicated that correlations with human judgment using our proposed metric are higher than those using a metric based only on static word embeddings. Moreover, our proposed metric achieved state-of-the-art performance with system-level correlation and to-English segment-level correlation.

**Keywords:** Automatic metric · Contextual representations · Optimal transport · Static word embeddings

© Springer Nature Switzerland AG 2022
P. Sojka et al. (Eds.): TSD 2022, LNAI 13502, pp. 225–237, 2022.
https://doi.org/10.1007/978-3-031-16270-1_19

# 1    Introduction

Automatic metrics are necessary for machine translation research. Quantitative evaluation of machine translation systems without an automatic metric is difficult because human evaluation needs expensive and time-consuming. Therefore, the metrics which can achieve high correlation with human judgment are necessary, and the investigation for the metrics, that have the highest accuracy, is also performed [1]. Actually, BLEU [2] has been used widely as an industry standard metric to evaluate various machine translation systems. Nevertheless, metrics based on surface matching (*e.g.* BLEU, TER [3], chrF [4], chrF++ [5]) are unsuitable to measure semantic similarity between a reference and hypothesis because they use only surface information.

In recent years, various metrics based on semantic similarity have been proposed as neural network technology has developed. In metrics using pre-trained models (*e.g.* YiSi-1 [6], WE_WPI [7]), various static embedding models (*e.g.* word2vec [8], fastText [9], GloVe [10], BERT [11]) are used to obtain semantic similarities between pairwise word embeddings in references and hypotheses. However, these metrics show difficulty in application to suitable specific domains because they depend on static word embedding models. In metrics using fine-tuned models such as BLEURT [12], COMET [13], and OpenKiwi [14], the estimator models are built by fine-tuned language models using earlier WMT data. Moreover, in metrics using neural models (*e.g.* esim [15], prism [16]), contextual representations that adapt to a specific domain are extracted from the learned model using earlier WMT data. These metrics can accommodate various sentences by fine-tuning of the models. However, they require large amounts of learning data to fine-tune the language models.

As described herein, we propose a new metric based on optimal transport by integration of contextual representations and static word embeddings. The contextual representations are extracted from the neural model (*e.g.* an attention-based LSTM [17]) learned only using source sentences and references, which correspond to the evaluation target hypotheses. Therefore, our proposed metric can adapt to a specific domain without requiring large amounts of learning data such as earlier WMT data. Moreover, in our proposed metrics, the contextual representations are used as the weights for the static word embeddings. This means that the static word embeddings are corrected to adapt the domain in the vector space. Furthermore, the evaluation scores are calculated based on the Earth Mover's Distance (EMD) [18] algorithm, which solves the optimal transport problem, in our proposed metric. As described herein, we call this proposed metric **OPTICS** (automatic metric based on **OP**timal **T**ransport by **I**ntegration of **C**ontextual representations and **S**tatic word embeddings). Through the experiments using WMT 20 metric shared task data, OPTICS outperformed the metric using only the static word embeddings (*i.e.* WE_WPI [7]). Moreover, we confirmed that OPTICS achieves state-of-the-art performance in correlations with human judgments except out-of-English segment-level correlation.

## 2  Related Work

### 2.1  Metrics Using Pre-trained Models

YiSi-1 [6] obtains evaluation scores using idf-weighted lexical semantic similarity by the pre-trained embedding models. The idf-weighted lexical semantic similarity is based on cosine similarity between lexical embeddings. In WMT 20 metric shared task, YiSi-1 uses lexical embeddings extracted from pre-trained language models (*e.g.* BERT [11], CamemBERT [19], RoBERTa [20], XLM [21], XLM-RoBERTa [22]). Moreover, it optionally requires a semantic role labeler in the hypotheses for evaluating structural semantic similarity. Also, WE_WPI [7] is a metric based on EMD [18] which solves the problem of the optimal transport. In that case, fastText [9] as static word embedding model is used to calculate similarities between word embeddings in reference and hypothesis. Moreover, it uses the relative difference of word order between a reference and hypothesis as the weight in the calculation of similarity. As a result, it can perform evaluation that specifically examines differences of word order.

### 2.2  Metrics Using Fine-Tuned Models

BLEURT [12] is a BERT-based regression model. This model is fine-tuned on human ratings from WMT 2015 Metrics to WMT 2019 Metrics. Moreover, it learns to predict widely diverse similarity that includes existing metrics (BERTScore [23] etc.) as mid-training. COMET [13] metrics are built using the Estimator model or the Translation Ranking model. The Estimator model regresses on human judgment such as direct assessment (DA) from WMT 2017 Metrics to WMT 2019 Metrics. The Translation Ranking model is trained to minimize the distance between a better hypothesis and both its corresponding reference and its source sentence. Both models constitute a cross-lingual encoder and a pooling layer. OpenKiwi [14] metrics are Quality Estimation models; they are trained with WMT Metrics data from 2017–2019. OpenKiwi-BERT and OpenKiwi-XLMR respectively use fine-tuning BERT and XLM models in a predictor–estimator architecture.

### 2.3  Metrics Using Neural Models

Esim [15], a neural model proposed for Natural Language Inference as described in an earlier report [24], has been adapted for MT evaluation. This model encodes a reference and hypothesis with a BiLSTM, and computes attention-weighted representations of each word embedding in the hypothesis with respect to each word embedding in the reference. Moreover, a feedforward regressor over the concatenation of the reference and hypothesis is applied to compute the final predicted score. Esim requires human evaluation data from WMT Metrics as training data. Prism [16] is a multilingual NMT system trained on data for 39 language pairs, with data derived largely from WMT and Wikimatrix, although it requires no human judgment for training. At evaluation time, the model is used in zero-shot mode to score hypotheses conditioned on their corresponding references.

# 3   New Automatic Metric: OPTICS

Our proposed metric is constructed from two stages: learning of the encoder for extraction of contextual representations, and calculation of scores based on optimal transport using contextual representations by the trained encoder and the static word embeddings.

## 3.1   Learning of Encoder for Extracting Contextual Representations

Our proposed metric obtains the encoder for extraction of contextual representations. As described herein, attention-based LSTM, which is a basic encoder–decoder model, is used to obtain the encoder. It remains unclear whether the attention-based LSTM is the best model among various encoder–decoder models, or not. Therefore, this point is an issue that remains for future study. Figure 1 depicts the outline for learning of attention-based LSTM.

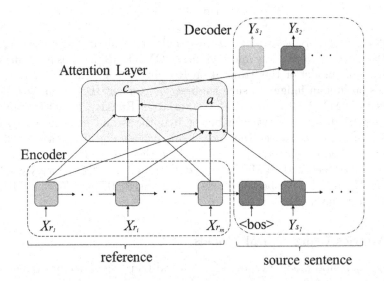

**Fig. 1.** Outline of learning of attention-based LSTM model.

In Fig. 1, the reference and source sentence corresponding to the evaluation target hypothesis, are used, respectively, as encoder and decoder inputs. As a result, our proposed metric can convert the reference and hypothesis respectively into contextual representations by the encoder of the learned attention-based LSTM model.

## 3.2   Score Calculation Based on Optimal Transport Using Contextual Representations and Static Word Embeddings

The encoder of the learned neural model is used to obtain the contextual representations of words in the reference and hypothesis. Moreover, those contextual representations are used as features of distributions in EMD, which is an algorithm to solve the optimal transport problem. Figure 2 presents an outline of score calculation.

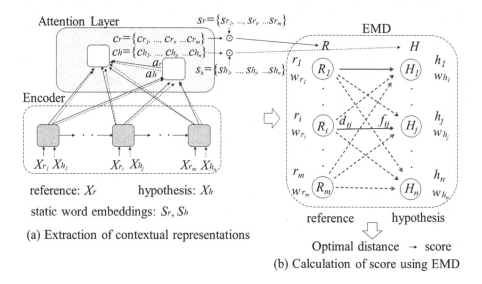

reference: $X_r$          hypothesis: $X_h$

static word embeddings: $S_r$, $S_h$

(a) Extraction of contextual representations

reference          hypothesis

Optimal distance → score

(b) Calculation of score using EMD

**Fig. 2.** Outline of score calculation.

In Fig. 2 (a), the contextual representations $c_{r_{1 \sim m}}$ of the words in reference $X_{r_{1 \sim m}}$ and the contextual representations $c_{h_{1 \sim n}}$ of the words in hypothesis $X_{h_{1 \sim n}}$ are respectively extracted from the trained encoder; also, $m$ and $n$ indicates the word numbers of reference and hypothesis, respectively. The $c_{r_i}$ and $c_{h_j}$ are respectively integrated into the static word embeddings $s_{r_i}$ and $s_{h_j}$. The $r_i$ and $h_j$, which are used as the features in EMD, are obtained as Eqs. (1) and (2).

$$r_{i_k} = exp(\alpha \times c_{r_{i_k}}) \times s_{r_{i_k}} \tag{1}$$

$$h_{j_k} = exp(\alpha \times c_{h_{j_k}}) \times s_{h_{j_k}} \tag{2}$$

In Eqs. (1) and (2), $\alpha$ is a high parameter, and $k$ means each element position of the vector. In Eq. (1), $r_{i_k}$ is calculated using the contextual representation $c_{r_i}$, which is extracted from the encoder of the attention-based LSTM model, and the static word embedding $s_{r_i}$. The calculation in Eq. (1) is performed using all elements $\{c_{r_{i_1}}, ..., c_{r_{i_k}}, ..., c_{r_{i_l}}\}$ and $\{s_{r_{i_1}}, ..., s_{r_{i_k}}, ..., s_{r_{i_l}}\}$. In Eq. (2), $h_{j_k}$ is calculated using the contextual representation of $c_{h_j}$, which is extracted from the encoder of the attention-based LSTM model, and the static word embedding $s_{h_j}$. This indicates that the calculation in Eq. (2) is performed using all elements $\{c_{h_{j_1}}, ..., c_{h_{j_k}}, ..., c_{h_{j_l}}\}$ and $\{s_{h_{j_1}}, ..., s_{h_{j_k}}, ..., s_{h_{j_l}}\}$. In Eqs. (1) and (2), the contextual representations $c_{r_i}$ and $c_{h_j}$ are used as the weight for the static word embeddings $s_{r_i}$ and $s_{h_j}$. Therefore, the static word embeddings are corrected to adapt the domain by using the contextual representations in the vector space.

Word vector $r_i$ in the reference and word vector $h_j$ in the hypothesis are used as EMD features. In Fig. 2 (b), the distributions $R$ and $H$ respectively correspond to the reference and hypothesis. Each signature $\{R_1, ..., R_i, ..., R_m\}$ of distribution $R$ has word vector $\{r_1, ..., r_i, ..., r_m\}$ and weight $\{w_{r_1}, ..., w_{r_i}, ..., w_{r_m}\}$. Each signature $\{H_1, ..., H_j, ..., H_n\}$ of distribution $H$ also has word vector $\{h_1, ..., h_j, ..., h_n\}$ and weight $\{w_{h_1}, ..., w_{h_j}, ..., w_{h_n}\}$. Moreover, $m$ and $n$ respectively means the word numbers of reference and hypothesis. Weights $w_{r_i}$ and $w_{h_j}$ are obtained using sentence-level $tf \cdot idf$. Each weight based on sentence-level $tf \cdot idf$ is defined as Eq. (3).

$$w = tf \times \left( \log \frac{N}{df} + 1.0 \right) \tag{3}$$

In Eq. (3), $tf$ represents the number of times that the word appears in a reference or hypothesis. Also, $N$ denotes the number of all references or all hypotheses, and $df$ stands for the sentence number that the word appears for all references or all hypotheses. Moreover, each weight $w_{r_i}$ and $w_{h_j}$ is respectively defined as Eqs. (4) and (5).

$$\tilde{w}_{r_i} = \frac{w_{r_i}}{\sum_{k=1}^{m} w_{r_k}} \tag{4}$$

$$\tilde{w}_{h_j} = \frac{w_{h_j}}{\sum_{k=1}^{n} w_{h_k}} \tag{5}$$

By Eqs. (4) and (5), the weights are normalized between 0.0 and 1.0. The cosine similarity between two word vectors $r_i$ and $h_j$ is used to calculate the distance $d_{ij}$. In that case, the penalty based on the difference of word order is applied to cosine similarity. Also, $d_{ij}$ is obtained using the following Eq. (6) as shown below.

$$d_{ij} = \begin{cases} 1.0 - cos\_sim(r_i, h_j) \times exp(-pos\_inf(X_{r_i}, X_{h_j})) \\ \quad \text{if } cos\_sim(r_i, h_j) \text{ is the highest among } cos\_sim \text{ between } r_i \text{ and } h_{1 \sim n} \\ 1.0 \quad \text{otherwise} \end{cases} \tag{6}$$

$$pos\_inf(X_{r_i}, X_{h_j}) = \left| \frac{pos(X_{r_i})}{m} - \frac{pos(X_{h_j})}{n} \right| \tag{7}$$

In Eq. (6), $cos\_sim(r_i, h_j)$ represents cosine similarity between $r_i$ by Eq. (1) and $h_j$ by Eq. (2), and $exp(-pos\_inf(X_{r_i}, X_{h_j}))$ represents the penalty to

$cos\_sim(r_i, h_j)$ because it is smaller (*i.e.* less than 1.0) as the difference of word order $pos\_inf(X_{r_i}, X_{h_j})$ becomes larger. The $pos\_inf(X_{r_i}, X_{h_j})$ is obtained by Eq. (7). Here, $pos(X_{r_i})$ and $pos(X_{h_j})$ respectively correspond to word positions in the reference and hypothesis. Our proposed metric can obtain the correct score which specifically emphasizes the difference of word order between the reference and hypothesis. Moreover, in EMD, the overall cost is defined as in Eq. (8).

$$WORK(R, H, F) = \sum_{i=1}^{m} \sum_{j=1}^{n} d_{ij} f_{ij} \tag{8}$$

In Eq. (8), $F = [f_{ij}]$ denotes the total flow; also, EMD obtains $F$ which minimizes the overall cost. Moreover, four constraints are defined for $f_{ij}$ to find minimum $F$ as in the following Eqs. (9)–(12).

$$f_{ij} \geq 0 \qquad 1 \leq i \leq m, \qquad 1 \leq j \leq n \tag{9}$$

$$\sum_{j=1}^{n} f_{ij} \leq w_{r_i} \qquad 1 \leq i \leq m \tag{10}$$

$$\sum_{i=1}^{m} f_{ij} \leq w_{h_j} \qquad 1 \leq j \leq n \tag{11}$$

$$\sum_{i=1}^{m} \sum_{j=1}^{n} f_{ij} = min \left( \sum_{i=1}^{m} w_{r_i}, \sum_{j=1}^{n} w_{h_j} \right) \tag{12}$$

In fact, Eq. (9) shows that "supplies" must be transferred from $R$ to $H$, not from $H$ to $R$. Also, Eq. (10) shows that supplies exceeding the weights of $R$ cannot be transferred to $H$; Eq. (11) shows that supplies exceeding the weights of $H$ cannot be received from $R$. Moreover, Eq. (12) means that the upper limit of the total supply corresponds to the smaller of the total weight of $R$ and the total weight of $H$. Also, EMD is defined as shown below.

$$EMD(R, H) = \frac{min(WORK(R, H, F))}{\sum_{i=1}^{m} \sum_{j=1}^{n} f_{ij}} \tag{13}$$

The EMD in Eq. (13) is normalized from 0.0 to 1.0. The value approaches 0.0 as the distance between the two distributions becomes smaller. In our proposed metric, the final score is defined as Eq. (14).

$$score = 1.0 - EMD(R, H) \tag{14}$$

Therefore, the score value in Eq. (14) is closer to 1.0 as the evaluation is higher.

## 4 Experiments

### 4.1 Experiment Data and Procedure

We used WMT20 metrics shared task [25] data for experiments. For learning the attention-based LSTM in our proposed metric, we copied the sentence pair, which is the source sentence and its reference, ten times to increase the learning data for each language pair. In that case, we used only source sentences and their references, which correspond to the evaluation target hypotheses in WMT20 metrics shared task data. The maximum number of pairs of source sentences and its references among all language pairs is 29,710, which is the number of pairs of both Inuktitut–English and English–Inuktitut. On the other hand, the minimum number of pairs is 7,850 which is the number of pairs of German–English. Using those learning data, we produced the attention-based LSTM model in Fig. 1 to extract the contextual representations in each language pair.

In Fig. 2, the numbers of dimensions $r_i$, $h_j$, $c_{r_i}$, $c_{h_j}$, $s_{r_i}$, and $s_{h_j}$ respectively denote 300. The number of epochs is 80 in each language pair. The contextual representations of the reference $c_{r_i}$ and those of the hypothesis $c_{h_j}$ are extracted, respectively, from the encoder of the learned attention-based LSTM models. Moreover, 0.1 was used as the high parameter $\alpha$ in Eqs. (1) and (2) by preliminary experimentation. Our proposed metric (*i.e.* OPTICS) and WE_WPI [7] used fastText [9] as the static word embedding models for reference and hypothesis. In OPTICS and WE_WPI, the averages of the segment-level scores are used as system-level scores.

Next, we obtained the correlation coefficients with human judgments to evaluate OPTICS and the state-of-the-art metrics using the script provided by WMT20. The script is provided at http://www.statmt.org/wmt20/results.html.

In WE_WPI and OPTICS, fastText model of Inuktitut is not provided at https://fasttext.cc/docs/en/crawl-vectors.html. Therefore, correlations of English–Inuktitut in WE_WPI were not obtained. In OPTICS, only contextual representations, which are extracted from the encoder of the neural model learned using the pairs of English source sentence and Inuktitut reference, were used. In that case, the vectors, of which all elements are 1.0, were used as the static word embeddings (*i.e.* $s_{r_{i_k}}$, $s_{h_{j_k}}$) of Inuktitut.

## 4.2  Experiment Results and Discussion

**Table 1.** Pearson correlations of to-English at the system-level.

| | cs-en | de-en | ja-en | pl-en | ru-en | ta-en | zh-en | iu-en | km-en | ps-en | Avg. |
|---|---|---|---|---|---|---|---|---|---|---|---|
| BLEURT | | | | | | | | | | | |
| -extend | **0.771** | 0.985 | **0.961** | **0.551** | 0.900 | **0.897** | 0.945 | 0.789 | 0.985 | **0.942** | 0.873 |
| COMET | **0.783** | **0.998** | 0.964 | **0.591** | **0.923** | 0.880 | **0.952** | 0.852 | 0.971 | **0.941** | 0.886 |
| esim | **0.790** | **0.998** | **0.983** | **0.591** | **0.928** | 0.885 | **0.963** | 0.807 | 0.929 | **0.929** | 0.8803 |
| OpenKiwi | | | | | | | | | | | |
| -Bert | 0.726 | 0.989 | 0.735 | 0.355 | **0.862** | 0.645 | 0.625 | −0.126 | 0.751 | 0.753 | 0.632 |
| OpenKiwi | | | | | | | | | | | |
| -XLMR | **0.760** | 0.995 | 0.931 | 0.442 | 0.859 | 0.792 | 0.905 | 0.271 | 0.880 | 0.865 | 0.770 |
| prism | **0.818** | **0.998** | **0.974** | **0.502** | **0.908** | 0.898 | **0.957** | 0.833 | 0.950 | **0.966** | 0.8804 |
| YiSi-1 | **0.832** | **0.998** | **0.982** | **0.543** | **0.915** | **0.925** | **0.961** | 0.834 | 0.977 | **0.953** | 0.892 |
| WE_WPI | | | | | | | | | | | |
| (Baseline) | **0.838** | **0.998** | **0.973** | **0.573** | **0.939** | **0.933** | **0.965** | 0.776 | **0.993** | 0.922 | 0.891 |
| OPTICS | | | | | | | | | | | |
| (This work) | **0.849** | **0.998** | **0.972** | **0.541** | **0.934** | **0.933** | 0.964 | 0.824 | **0.993** | 0.929 | 0.894 |

**Table 2.** Pearson correlations of out-of-English at the system-level.

| | en-cs | en-de | en-ja | en-pl | en-ru | en-ta | en-zh | en-iu _fill | en-iu _news | Avg. |
|---|---|---|---|---|---|---|---|---|---|---|
| BLEURT-extend | 0.989 | **0.969** | 0.944 | **0.982** | **0.980** | 0.940 | 0.928 | 0.823 | 0.762 | 0.924 |
| COMET | 0.978 | **0.972** | 0.974 | **0.981** | 0.925 | 0.944 | 0.007 | 0.860 | **0.858** | 0.833 |
| esim | 0.908 | **0.979** | 0.993 | **0.969** | **0.967** | 0.937 | **0.972** | 0.814 | 0.760 | 0.922 |
| OpenKiwi-Bert | 0.920 | 0.852 | 0.363 | 0.903 | 0.834 | 0.846 | 0.551 | 0.573 | 0.808 | 0.739 |
| OpenKiwi-XLMR | 0.972 | **0.968** | 0.992 | 0.957 | 0.875 | 0.910 | −0.010 | 0.513 | 0.680 | 0.762 |
| prism | 0.949 | 0.958 | 0.932 | 0.958 | 0.724 | 0.863 | 0.221 | **0.957** | **0.945** | 0.834 |
| YiSi-1 | 0.922 | **0.971** | 0.969 | **0.964** | **0.926** | 0.973 | 0.959 | 0.554 | 0.523 | 0.862 |
| WE_WPI (Baseline) | 0.879 | 0.941 | 0.964 | 0.894 | **0.945** | 0.936 | 0.911 | – | – | – |
| OPTICS (This work) | 0.868 | 0.944 | 0.964 | 0.913 | **0.952** | 0.935 | 0.910 | 0.586 | 0.695 | 0.863 |

**Table 3.** Kendall correlations of to-English at the segment-level.

| | cs-en | de-en | iu-en | ja-en | km-en | pl-en | ps-en | ru-en | ta-en | zh-en | Avg. |
|---|---|---|---|---|---|---|---|---|---|---|---|
| BLEURT | | | | | | | | | | | |
| -extend | 0.127 | 0.448 | 0.259 | 0.271 | 0.330 | 0.044 | 0.161 | 0.101 | 0.246 | 0.137 | 0.212 |
| COMET | 0.129 | 0.485 | 0.281 | 0.274 | 0.298 | 0.099 | 0.158 | 0.156 | 0.241 | 0.171 | 0.229 |
| esim | 0.110 | 0.454 | 0.241 | 0.239 | 0.300 | 0.058 | 0.147 | 0.084 | 0.208 | 0.138 | 0.198 |
| OpenKiwi | | | | | | | | | | | |
| -Bert | 0.036 | 0.379 | −0.005 | 0.110 | 0.168 | −0.033 | 0.076 | −0.033 | 0.118 | 0.029 | 0.085 |
| OpenKiwi | | | | | | | | | | | |
| -XLMR | 0.093 | 0.463 | 0.056 | 0.220 | 0.244 | 0.059 | 0.106 | 0.092 | 0.188 | 0.115 | 0.164 |
| prism | 0.143 | 0.475 | 0.255 | 0.272 | 0.304 | 0.109 | 0.165 | 0.145 | 0.237 | 0.167 | 0.227 |
| YiSi-1 | 0.117 | 0.468 | 0.253 | 0.277 | 0.316 | 0.042 | 0.147 | 0.091 | 0.248 | 0.146 | 0.211 |
| WE_WPI | | | | | | | | | | | |
| (Baseline) | 0.102 | 0.474 | 0.218 | 0.238 | 0.239 | 0.080 | 0.134 | 0.133 | 0.222 | 0.151 | 0.199 |
| OPTICS | | | | | | | | | | | |
| (This work) | 0.103 | 0.475 | 0.231 | 0.233 | 0.235 | 0.089 | 0.149 | 0.134 | 0.222 | 0.154 | 0.203 |

Tables 1 and 2 respectively present Pearson correlations of to-English and out-of-English system-level metrics with direct assessment (DA) human assessment over MT systems using the *newstest2020* references. Tables 3 and 4 respectively present segment-level metric results for to-English and out-of-English language pairs. These coefficients are Kendall's Tau formulations of the segment-level metric. The highlighted values shown in bold typeface in Tables 1–2 denote that the correlations of metrics are not significantly outperformed by any other for that language pair. "Avg." stands for the average of correlations of all language pairs.

**Table 4.** Kendall correlations of out-of-English in the segment-level.

|  | en-cs | en-de | en-iu | en-ja | en-pl | en-ru | en-ta | en-zh | Avg. |
|---|---|---|---|---|---|---|---|---|---|
| BLEURT-extend | 0.689 | 0.447 | 0.359 | 0.533 | 0.430 | 0.305 | 0.643 | 0.460 | 0.483 |
| COMET | 0.668 | 0.468 | 0.322 | 0.624 | 0.462 | 0.344 | 0.671 | 0.432 | 0.499 |
| esim | 0.469 | 0.347 | 0.122 | 0.522 | 0.312 | 0.224 | 0.599 | 0.391 | 0.373 |
| OpenKiwi-Bert | 0.262 | 0.168 | −0.115 | −0.529 | 0.153 | 0.164 | 0.169 | 0.077 | 0.044 |
| OpenKiwi-XLMR | 0.607 | 0.369 | 0.060 | 0.553 | 0.347 | 0.279 | 0.604 | 0.377 | 0.400 |
| prism | 0.619 | 0.447 | 0.452 | 0.579 | 0.414 | 0.283 | 0.448 | 0.397 | 0.455 |
| YiSi-1 | 0.550 | 0.427 | 0.251 | 0.568 | 0.349 | 0.256 | 0.669 | 0.463 | 0.442 |
| WE_WPI (Baseline) | 0.477 | 0.331 | − | 0.502 | 0.276 | 0.192 | 0.376 | 0.379 | − |
| OPTICS (This work) | 0.471 | 0.339 | 0.250 | 0.500 | 0.280 | 0.184 | 0.367 | 0.381 | 0.347 |

The "Avg." of correlations with human judgment in Tables 1 and 3 expresses that OPTICS outperforms WE_WPI, which is the metric based on optimal transport using static word embeddings only. Moreover, OPTICS achieves state-of-the-art performance except out-of-English segment-level correlations of Table 4. The difference between "Avg." of top rank (*i.e.* COMET) and that of OPTICS is not small in out-of-English segment-level correlations of Table 4 because the correlation of "en-ta" in OPTICS is low. To ascertain the cause, it is necessary to investigate the related details. On the other hand, the correlation of "en-iu" of OPTICS in Table 4 is not a severe difficulty compared with that of "en-ta" of OPTICS, although OPTICS calculated the scores only using the contextual representations in **"en-iu"**. Therefore, this result represents the effectiveness of the contextual representations in OPTICS.

## 5   Conclusion

As described in this paper, we proposed OPTICS as a new automatic metric based on optimal transport by integration of contextual representations and static word embeddings. In OPTICS, after the contextual representations are extracted from the encoder of the learned neural models, they are used as weights for static word embeddings. Through the experimentally obtained results, we confirmed that OPTICS can obtain high correlations with human judgment to WE_WPI, which uses only static word embeddings. Moreover, OPTICS achieved state-of-the-art performance, although the correlations of out-of-English segment-level are insufficient.

Future work will be undertaken to investigate the effects of other neural models (*e.g.* Transformer [26]), which extract contextual representations. In that case, the investigation about the epoch number and the suitable learning data is also required. Moreover, we expect to perform a meta-evaluation using various data (*e.g.* WMT 21 data using MQM-based human evaluation [27]).

**Acknowledgement.** This work was partially supported by grants from Hokkai-Gakuen University.

# References

1. Kocmi, T., Federmann, C., Grundkiewicz, R., Junczys-Dowmunt, M., Matsushita, H., Menezes, A.: To ship or not to ship: an extensive evaluation of automatic metrics for machine translation. In: Proceedings of the Sixth Conference on Machine Translation, pp. 478–494 (2021)
2. Papineni, K., Roukos, S., Ward, T., Zhu, W.-J.: BLEU: a method for automatic evaluation of machine translation. In: Proceedings of the 40th Annual Meeting of the Association for Computational Linguistics, pp. 311–318 (2002)
3. Snover, M., Dorr, B., Schwartz, R., Micciulla, L., Makhoul, J.: A study of translation edit rate with targeted human annotation. In: Proceedings of the 7th Conference of the Association for Machine Translation in the Americas, pp. 223–231 (2006)
4. Popović, M.: chrF: character n-gram F-score for automatic MT evaluation. In: Proceedings of the Tenth Workshop on Statistical Machine Translation, pp. 392–395 (2015)
5. Popović, M.: chrF++: words helping character n-grams. In: Proceedings of the Conference on Machine Translation, Volume 2: Shared Task Papers, pp. 612–618 (2017)
6. Lo, C.: YiSi - a unified semantic MT quality evaluation and estimation metric for languages with different levels of available resources. In: Proceeding of the Fourth Conference on Machine Translation, Volume 2: Shared Task Papers, pp. 507–513 (2019)
7. Echizen-ya, H., Araki, K., Hovy, E.: Word embedding-based automatic MT evaluation metric using word position information. In: Proceedings of the 17th Annual Conference of the North American Chapter of the Association for Computational Linguistics: Human Language Technologies, pp. 1874–1883 (2019)
8. Mikolov, T., Sutskever, I., Chen, K., Corrado, G., Dean, J.: Distributed representations of words and phrases and their compositionality. Adv. Neural. Inf. Process. Syst. **26**, 3111–3119 (2013)
9. Bojanowski, P., Grave, E., Joulin, A., Mikolov, T.: Enriching word vectors with subword information. Trans. Assoc. Comput. Linguist. **5**, 135–146 (2017)

10. Pennington, J., Socher, R., Manning, C.D.: Glove: global vectors for word representation. In: Proceedings of the 2014 Conference on Empirical Methods in Natural Language Processing, pp. 1532–1543 (2014)

11. Devlin, J., Chang, M.-W., Lee, K., Toutanova, K.: BERT: pre-training of deep bidirectional transformers for language understanding. In: Proceedings of the 17th Annual Conference of the North American Chapter of the Association for Computational Linguistics: Human Language Technologies, pp. 4171–4186 (2019)

12. Sellam, T., et al.: Learning to evaluate translation beyond English: BLEURT submissions to the WMT metrics 2020 shared task. In: Proceedings of the 5th Conference on Machine Translation, pp. 921–927 (2020)

13. Rei, R., Stewart, C., Farinha, A.C., Lavie, A.: COMET: a neural framework for MT evaluation. In: Proceedings of the 2020 Conference on Empirical Methods in Natural Language Processing, pp. 2685–2702 (2020)

14. Kepler, F., Trénous, J., Treviso, M., Vera, M., Martins, A.F.T.: OpenKiwi: an open source framework for quality estimation. In: Proceedings of the 57th Annual Meeting of the Association for Computational Linguistics: System Demonstrations, pp. 117–122 (2019)

15. Mathur, N., Baldwin, T., Cohn, T.: Putting evaluation in context: contextual embeddings improve machine translation evaluation. In: Proceedings of the 57th Annual Meeting of the Association for Computational Linguistics, pp. 2799–2808 (2019)

16. Thompson, B., Post, M.: Automatic machine translation evaluation in many languages via zero-shot paraphrasing. In: Proceedings of the 2020 Conference on Empirical Methods in Natural Language Processing, pp. 90–121 (2020)

17. Bahdanau, D., Cho, K., Bengio, Y.: Neural machine translation by jointly learning to align and translate. In: Proceedings of the Third International Conference on Learning Representations (2015)

18. Rubner, Y., Tomasi, C., Guibas, L.J.: A metric for distributions with applications to image databases. In: Proceedings of the 1998 IEEE International Conference on Computer Vision, pp. 59–66 (1998)

19. Martin, L., et al.: CamemBERT: a Tasty French Language Model. In: Proceedings of the 58th Annual Meeting of the Association for Computational Linguistics, pp. 7203–7219 (2020)

20. Liu, Y., et al.: RoBERTa: a robustly optimized BERT Pretraining Approach. In: Proceedings of the Eighth International Conference on Learning Representations (2020)

21. Conneau, A., Lample, G.: Cross-lingual language model pretraining. In: Proceedings of the 33rd Conference on Neural Information Processing Systems, pp. 7059–7069 (2019)

22. Conneau, A., et al.: Unsupervised cross-lingual representation learning at scale. In: Proceedings of the 58th Annual Meeting of the Association for Computational Linguistics, pp. 8440–8451 (2020)

23. Zhang, T., Kishore, V., Wu, F., Weinberger, K.Q., Artzi, Y.: BERTScore: evaluating text generation with BERT. In: Proceedings of the International Conference on Learning Representations (2020)

24. Chen, Q., Zhu, X., Ling, Z., Wei, S., Jiang, H., Inkpen, D.: Enhanced LSTM for natural language inference. In: Proceedings of the 55th Annual Meeting of the Association for Computational Linguistics, pp. 1657–1668 (2017)

25. Mathur, N., Wei, J.T.-Z., Freitag, M., Ma, Q., Bojar, O.: Results of the WMT20 metrics shared task. In: Proceedings of the 5th Conference on Machine Translation, pp. 688–725 (2020)
26. Vaswani, A., et al.: Attention is all you need. In: Proceedings of the 31st Conference on Neural Information Processing Systems, pp. 6000–6010 (2017)
27. Freitag, M., et al.: Results of the WMT21 metrics shared task: evaluating metrics with expert-based human evaluations on TED and news domain. In: Proceedings of the Sixth Conference on Machine Translation, pp. 733–774 (2021)

# Exploration of Multi-corpus Learning for Hate Speech Classification in Low Resource Scenarios

Ashwin Geet D'Sa[✉], Irina Illina[✉], Dominique Fohr, and Awais Akbar

Université de Lorraine, CNRS, Inria, LORIA, 54000 Nancy, France
{ashwin-geet.dsa,irina.illina,dominique.fohr}@loria.fr

**Abstract.** The dramatic increase in social media has given rise to the problem of online hate speech. Deep neural network-based classifiers have become the state-of-the-art for automatic hate speech classification. The performance of these classifiers depends on the amount of available labelled training data. However, most hate speech corpora have a small number of hate speech samples. In this article, we aim to jointly use multiple hate speech corpora to improve hate speech classification performance in low-resource scenarios. We harness different hate speech corpora in a multi-task learning setup by associating one task to one corpus. This multi-corpus learning scheme is expected to improve the generalization, the latent representations, and domain adaptation of the model. Our work evaluates multi-corpus learning for hate speech classification and domain adaptation. We show significant improvements in classification and domain adaptation in low-resource scenarios.

**Keywords:** hate speech detection · multi-task learning · low-resource text classification

## 1 Introduction

An increase in online social media usage has led to a rise in hate speech. Hate speech is an anti-social behavior that targets a small part of the society, based on race, gender, etc. [10]. In many countries, hate speech is prohibited by the law and has to be filtered from social media platforms. However, manually analyzing the user contents is time-consuming and expensive. Natural language processing techniques can be used to automatically detect and filter hate speech content. Hence, there is an increased interest in automatic hate speech classification. Deep learning-based approaches have become the state-of-the-art for this task [3,9,15, 18,20]. However, the performance of these classifiers depends on the amount of available labelled training data [2].

Typically, hate speech datasets are collected from sources such as Twitter [4,8,14], Wikipedia [26], etc. Characteristics of the dataset, such as the sampling strategy, the time frame [12] of the comments, and the definition of class labels [13], often bias the models trained on each dataset. Particularly, a model

P. Sojka et al. (Eds.): TSD 2022, LNAI 13502, pp. 238–250, 2022.
https://doi.org/10.1007/978-3-031-16270-1_20

trained on one dataset can be inefficient on another dataset [25], resulting in the restricted generalizability of the model. Furthermore, these datasets have a small number of labelled samples. In order to bring diversity in the training data, and increase the number of samples to train the model, multiple hate speech corpora can be harnessed to consider the corpus diversity and reduce the data sparsity issue. In this paper, we investigate a multi-task learning (MTL) approach, instead of a simple combination of different corpora.

MTL aims to jointly learn from multiple related tasks. MTL combines the domain-specific information and shares representations between related tasks, hence, can improve the generalization capabilities of the model on the target task [7]. MTL has applications in various domains, such as computer vision, bioinformatics, speech, natural language processing (NLP), etc. [23,27].

MTL has been explored for hate speech classification. An MTL architecture having shared and private task-specific layers to capture shared and task-specific features, respectively, from different hate speech classification tasks is proposed in [16]. A joint model of emotion and abusive language detection, that allows one task to receive relevant information from the other tasks is introduced in [22]. They combine the features of single task-learning and MTL using an attention mechanism. Although these prior works have shown the effectiveness of MTL architectures, they haven't exploited the pre-trained models.

In this article, we design an MTL approach based on the work in [19], wherein the authors combined a range of NLP tasks using shared layers represented by the pre-trained BERT model and several groups of task-specific layers; each group corresponding to a single task. Compared to this work, we adapt the paradigm of multi-task learning to multi-corpus learning. In our approach, *a task* corresponds to *a corpus*. Compared to the works in [16,22], we use the pre-trained Bidirectional Encoder Representations from Transformers (BERT [11]) model for our MTL to benefit from extensive knowledge learned by BERT pre-training. A Spanish BERT model in an MTL setup has showed improvements for hate speech classification tasks in [21]. However, they incorporate sentiment analysis and emotion analysis tasks in their MTL. Instead, we exploit the relatedness of hate speech classification tasks by using five well-known hate speech datasets extracted from Twitter and Wikipedia. Furthermore, these prior works do not study the performance of the MTL approach in low-resource scenarios. Thus, we explore a low-resource domain adaptation scenario in the framework of multi-corpus learning.

Our contributions are summarized as follows:

1. We adapt MTL approach to *multi-corpus learning* (MCL) for hate speech classification and validate it on widely used hate speech corpora.
2. We study the robustness of the proposed MCL in low-resource scenarios.
3. We study low-resource domain adaptation.

## 2   Proposed Methodology

In this section, we first describe MTL. This is followed by our approaches for MCL and domain adaptation in low-resource scenario.

## 2.1  Objective of Multi-Task Learning

Given $T$ related tasks $\{t_i\}_{i=1}^T$, MTL aims to jointly learn these tasks to improve the model performance on each task $t_i$. Let us consider supervised learning task $t_i$, with $n_i$ samples $(x_1^i, x_2^i \ldots x_{n_i}^i) \in X^i$ and labels $(y_1^i, y_2^i \ldots y_{n_i}^i) \in Y^i$. For the task $t_i$, a MTL model learns the parameter set $\{\theta^s, \theta^i\}$ using a function $f^i$ as follow:

$$f^i(X^i; \theta^s, \theta^i) : X^i \to Y^i \tag{1}$$

where $\theta^s$ are the model parameters shared between all the tasks in $\{t_i\}_{i=1}^T$, and $\theta^i$ represents the task-specific model parameters. The objective is to minimize the overall loss $L$:

$$L(\theta^s, \theta^1, \theta^2, \ldots \theta^T) = \sum_{i=1}^T L^i(\theta^s, \theta^i) \tag{2}$$

where $L^i(\theta^s, \theta^i)$ is the loss for task $t_i$, and, in the supervised case, can be evaluated as follow:

$$L^i(\theta^s, \theta^i) = \frac{1}{n_i} \sum_{j=1}^{n_i} \mathcal{L}(f^i(x_j^i; \theta^s, \theta^i), y_j^i) \tag{3}$$

where, $\mathcal{L}$ is a loss function measuring how well the function $f^i$ fits the training data $(X^i, Y^i)$. The objective of MTL is to reduce the overall loss $L$, by optimizing the task-specific parameters $\{\theta^i\}_{i=1}^{Ts}$, and the parameters shared across all the tasks $\theta^s$. In a single task learning approach, $T = 1$ and the dataset of task $t_1$ is processed by a model with parameters $\theta^1$.

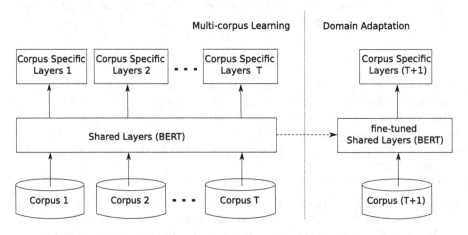

**Fig. 1.** Architecture of the multi-corpus model (left part) and the procedure of domain adaptation (right part).

## 2.2  Our Approach for Multi-Corpus Learning

MTL can be done with either *hard* or *soft* parameter sharing of hidden layers [23]. In our work, we use the most common approach of MTL: the hard parameter sharing. In this case, all the datasets are first processed by the shared layers having learnable parameters $\theta^s$. These layers learn a shared representation for all the tasks from all the available input data. The outputs of the shared layers are passed into the task-specific layers with parameters $\theta^i$ when the model input corresponds to the data of task $t_i$.

Our methodology is based on MTL proposed in [19], where a pre-trained BERT model is incorporated. We adapt this model for our task of low-resource hate speech classification and apply it in a multi-corpus scenario. Usually, supervised classification approaches require a large amount of annotated data. By combining several corpora, MCL mitigates the problems of less amount of training data to efficiently train a model and reduces the overfitting problem.

Figure 1 (left part) shows the architecture of our approach. We consider *a corpus as a task*. The number of tasks corresponds to the number of available annotated corpora used to train the model. The MCL model consists of two parts: (a) the shared layers; (b) a set of corpus-specific layers.

**Shared Layers:** The shared layers are shared by all the tasks. We chose the pre-trained BERT model [11] as shared layers. The training samples from all the tasks are passed as input to the shared layers. These layers benefit from an implicit data augmentation as they process the data from all the tasks. This enriches the representations learned by the shared layers.

**Corpus-specific Layers:** The outputs of the shared layers are used as input to the corpus-specific layers. The objective of the corpus-specific layers is to optimize the model for a given corpus.

## 2.3  Domain Adaptation Using Multi-Corpus Learning

The goal of an efficient model is to generalize to unseen data. When the distribution of train and test sets differ (domain shift) [6], the ability of a model trained on one domain to perform on another domain reduces. Supervised domain adaptation techniques allow a model trained on the source domain to adapt to a target domain with a limited amount of labelled data.

The procedure for domain adaptation using the MCL is presented in Fig. 1 (right). We first train an MCL model with all the available corpora except one, which is our target corpus for adaptation. Then we adapt the trained MCL model to our target corpus. After adding new corpus-specific layers for the new target corpus, during adaptation, we update the shared layers along with the newly added corpus-specific layers using the target corpus.

## 3  Experimental Setup

In this section, we briefly describe the considered datasets, the text pre-processing, and the choice of model parameters for our MCL approach.

## 3.1  Corpora

We consider five widely used hate speech corpora to train our MCL model. Four of these corpora are tweets sampled from Twitter, namely *Davidson* [8], *Founta* [14], *Hateval* [4], and *Waseem* [24]. The fifth corpus is sampled from *Wikipedia* talk pages [26]. We perform binary classification for the Hateval, Waseem and Wikipedia datasets. The Davidson and Founta corpora are used for the multi-class classification of hate speech. The statistics of these corpora are provided in Table 1.

**Table 1.** Corpus statistics: number of tweets or comments.

| Corpus | Total | Class labels | | |
|---|---|---|---|---|
| | | Normal | Abusive | Hateful |
| **Davidson** | 24.8k | 4.2k | 19.2k | 1.4k |
| **Founta** | 86.0k | 53.8k | 27.2k | 5.0k |
| | | Non-hateful | | Hateful |
| **Hateval** | 13.0k | 7.5k | | 5.5k |
| **Waseem** | 10.9k | 8.0k | | 2.9k |
| | | Non-Toxic | | Toxic |
| **Wikipedia** | 159.7k | 131.7k | | 28.0k |

**Davidson:** This dataset is collected by sampling tweets using some keywords from the hatebase lexicon.[1] The corpus is annotated into three classes *neither*, *offensive language*, and *hate speech*. We refer to these classes as *normal*, *abusive*, *hateful*, respectively.

**Founta:** The Founta corpus has four classes, namely, *normal*, *abusive*, *hateful*, and *spam*. We removed samples labelled as *spam* class, which reduced the size of this dataset from 100k tweets to 86.9k tweets.

**Hateval:** This corpus was designed for the 'SemEval-2019' shared task. For our study, we have used the English part of the dataset. The corpus is annotated into two classes, namely, *hateful* and *non-hateful*. The corpus provides 9k, 3k, and 1k samples for training, development, and test sets, respectively.

**Waseem:** This dataset is sampled using keywords containing racial and sexual slurs. This dataset has three classes, *racism*, *sexism*, and *none* with 2.0k, 3.4k, and 11.6k samples, respectively. Due to the filtering strategy of Twitter to remove hateful content, we retrieved only 20, 2.9k, and 8.0k samples for *racism*, *sexism*, and *none* classes, respectively, using the tweet-ids provided by the authors, as in [5]. We refer to the *sexism* class as *hateful*, and the *none* class as *non-hateful*. We discard samples from the *racism* class due to very few samples.

---

[1] https://www.hatebase.org.

**Wikipedia:** This corpus contains comments from the user talk pages. We use the 'toxicity' part of the dataset, annotated with five labels - *very toxic, toxic, neither, healthy,* and *very healthy.* Each comment is annotated by approximately ten annotators. We chose to split the corpus into two classes: *toxic* versus *non-toxic* for each comment. We consider the comment as toxic if at least two annotators have labelled the comment as *toxic* or *very toxic,* and if the number of annotations as *toxic* or *very-toxic* is higher than the number of annotations as *healthy* and *very-healthy.* The dataset provides 95.7 k, 32.1 k, and 31.9 k samples for training, development, and test sets, respectively.

### 3.2   Dataset Split

For Davidson, Founta, and Waseem, we randomly split the datasets into three parts, training, validation, and test sets, each containing 70%, 10%, and 20%, respectively. For Hateval and Wikipedia corpora, we utilize the splits provided by the datasets. The training set is used to train the model, the validation set to adjust the model parameters, and the test set to evaluate the model performance.

### 3.3   Input Pre-processing

For Twitter corpora, the user handles are changed to '@USER'. The '#' symbol in the hashtag is removed, and the multi-word hashtags are split based on the presence of the uppercase characters. For example, '#leaveThisPlace' is changed to 'leave This Place'. The tweets containing the term 'RT' indicating re-tweet are also removed. For all the datasets, we remove all numbers, newlines, and special characters except '.', ',', '!', '?', and *apostrophes.* The repeated occurrences of the same special character are reduced to a single one. All the URLs and emoticons are also removed. Finally, all the data is lower-cased.

### 3.4   Multi-corpus Model and Training Description

The shared layers consist of the pre-trained English 'bert-base-uncased' model. We use five sets of corpus-specific layers as we have five corpora. The output of the [CLS] token of the BERT model is used as input to the corpus-specific layers. We define a single dense layer as our corpus-specific layer. The outputs of this hidden layer are passed through a softmax classifier with the number of units equal to the number of classes of the respective corpus. We use ReLU [1] activation for the dense layers, a learning rate of $1e-5$, Adam optimizer [17], a maximum of 30 epochs, mini-batch size of 32, and early stopping.

Compared to the standard way of a random selection of training samples for a mini-batch, we perform a task-specific selection of mini-batches. All the samples of a given mini-batch are extracted from a single corpus. For example, given two datasets, for one mini-batch, we select a fixed number of random training samples from one dataset, and for the other mini-batch we select the same number of samples from the other dataset. This procedure is repeated for the remaining mini-batches. When one corpus has fewer samples compared to another corpus, the samples from the smaller dataset are repetitively selected. This kind of mini-batch selection ensures that the multi-task learning model is trained with an equal number of samples from all the corpora. Our source code for MCL is made available[2].

## 4   Results and Discussion

In this section, we report the classification performance. We compute average macro-F1 and standard deviation over five runs of the model with different random initialization.

### 4.1   Multi-Corpus Learning

We evaluate the following configurations:

**Single-Corpus Learning (SCL):** We create five models, one for each corpus. Each model is obtained by fine-tuning the pre-trained BERT on the training part of the corresponding corpus. The test set is used to evaluate the model.

**Multi-Corpus Learning (MCL):** We create a single model using all the training corpora (see Sect. 2.2). The test set of each corpus is used separately to evaluate the model.

**Multi-Corpus Learning with corpus-specific fine-tuning (MCL$_{finetuned}$):** The model learned using the MCL setup, is further fine-tuned using five target corpora. We create five models, one for each corpus. In the beginning, one MCL model is learned. Then, this model is fine-tuned using five training corpora separately. This results in five models. The test part of each corpus is used to evaluate the corresponding fine-tuned MCL model.

The results obtained on the five corpora are presented in Table 2.

**Table 2.** Macro-F1 and standard deviation of five runs. Results on test sets for the different approaches. Average column presents the mean on five test corpora.

|  | Davidson | Founta | Hateval | Waseem | Wikipedia | Average |
|---|---|---|---|---|---|---|
| SCL | 76.0 ± 0.6 | 75.8 ± 0.4 | 49.3 ± 1.8 | 84.0 ± 0.5 | 86.9 ± 0.1 | 74.4 |
| MCL | 76.3 ± 1.1 | 75.5 ± 0.2 | 50.4 ± 3.0 | 84.1 ± 0.4 | 86.4 ± 0.2 | 74.5 |
| MCL$_{finetuned}$ | 75.7 ± 1.0 | 75.8 ± 0.7 | 52.1 ± 2.6 | 84.6 ± 0.6 | 86.7 ± 0.2 | **75.0** |

We observe that the average macro-F1 obtained for the SCL approach is 74.4%. The average macro-F1 of the MCL approach 74.5% is close to the SCL approach. We note that for the two smaller training corpora (Davidson and Hateval) the performance slightly increased, but for the two larger training corpora (Founta and Wikipedia) the performance marginally reduced, thus showing

---

[2] https://gitlab.inria.fr/adsa/multitasklearning_lrec.

higher improvements in low-resource corpora. For the MCL$_{finetuned}$ setup, we obtain an average macro-F1 of 75.0%. This shows an improvement compared to SCL and MCL approaches. We observe that all the corpora, except Davidson, benefit from the fine-tuning of the MCL model. This improvement observed for the MCL$_{finetuned}$ approach can be due to the fact that the MCL model is not fully optimized for every considered corpus. Hence, fine-tuning the MCL model on a specific corpus can help.

We would like to highlight that, although we obtain poor classification results on the Hateval dataset, our results are higher than the average macro-F1 of 44.84% obtained by the participants of the SemEval-2019 Task 5 challenge [4].

In the MCL approach, only the shared layers benefit from jointly training with several corpora. Whereas, each corpus-specific layer is trained only with the corpus-specific data. To increase the amount of data used to train corpus-specific layers, we *combine the training sets* of related corpora. To achieve this, we merge the training sets of the three-class datasets together, and similarly, the training sets of the two-class datasets. We represent the combined training sets as {Davidson & Founta} and {Hateval & Waseem & Wikipedia} in Table 3. This setup reduces the number of corpus-specific layers used for the MCL architecture, and the the number of parameters to train. Compared to the standard MCL approach, which consists of five sets of corpus-specific layers, by combining the training sets, we have only two sets of corpus-specific layers. In this setup, for all the configurations, we fine-tune the MCL model using the combined training sets. However, the model is evaluated on a specific test set and the results are reported separately to allow their comparison with the previous results.

**Table 3.** Macro-F1 and standard deviation of five runs. Results on test sets for the different approaches by combining tasks. Average column presents the mean on five test corpora.

| Train set | {Davidson & Founta} | | {Hateval & Waseem & Wikipedia} | | | Average |
|---|---|---|---|---|---|---|
| Test set | Davidson | Founta | Hateval | Waseem | Wikipedia | |
| SCL | 82.1 ± 4.7 | 77.2 ± 0.7 | 39.8 ± 2.3 | 80.4 ± 1.7 | 86.7 ± 0.2 | 73.2 |
| MCL | 82.2 ± 3.3 | 77.7 ± 1.1 | 42.5 ± 3.6 | 80.0 ± 1.2 | 86.4 ± 0.3 | 73.7 |
| MCL$_{finetuned}$ | 88.1 ± 1.7 | 78.4 ± 0.2 | 42.3 ± 2.5 | 81.9 ± 0.7 | 86.0 ± 0.3 | **75.3** |

Table 3 presents the results obtained using the MCL by combining corpora. For SCL, we obtain better results for Davidson and Founta test sets compared to the SCL approach without combining the training sets (results in Table 2). Perhaps this is because Davidson and Founta datasets have a similar label definition. However, we observe a reduced performance for Hateval and Waseem test sets. This can be due to the fact that abusive speech and toxic speech are close but represent different concepts and bias the system. The MCL approach by combining the tasks provides a small improvement compared to the SCL approach (73.7% versus 73.2%). Furthermore, for MCL$_{finetuned}$ approach, we obtain the best results (75.3%). In conclusion, we note that corpus-specific fine-tuning of the trained MCL model shows improvements compared to the MCL approach.

## 4.2   Multi-Corpus Learning in Low-Resource Scenarios

We explore the MCL approach in low-resource training scenarios. We down-sample the available training sets of all the corpora to 100, 200, 500, and 1000 samples. We then perform the training using SCL, MCL, and MCL$_{finetuned}$ approaches on the reduced training data.

Table 4 presents the average macro-F1 on the five datasets in low-resource scenarios. Figure 2 shows the macro-average F1 for SCL, MCL, and MCL$_{finetuned}$ setup for the Founta and Wikipedia test sets. For illustration, we plot the results only for the Wikipedia and Founta datasets, as examples of two-class and three-class classification performance. We obtained similar results for other datasets.

From Table 4 and Fig. 2, we can note that MCL and MCL$_{finetuned}$ setups show similar or better results than SCL. However, MCL and MCL$_{finetuned}$ give higher performance gains in very low-resource scenarios. When we use 100 samples for the training sets, we obtain a relative improvement of 16.8% and 23.9% for MCL and MCL$_{finetuned}$, respectively, compared to SCL (61.2%, 57.7% versus 49.4%). For 200 samples, we obtain a relative improvement of 18.5% and 22.3% for MCL and MCL$_{finetuned}$, respectively (65.3% and 63.3% versus 53.4%). These improvements are statistically significant.

**Table 4.** Average macro-F1 results on test sets for five corpora in low-resource scenarios.

| Approaches | Number of training samples | | | |
|:---:|:---:|:---:|:---:|:---:|
| | 100 | 200 | 500 | 1000 |
| SCL | 49.4 | 53.4 | 67.7 | 70.2 |
| MCL | 57.7 | 63.3 | 67.0 | 69.6 |
| MCL$_{finetuned}$ | **61.2** | **65.3** | **68.7** | **70.6** |

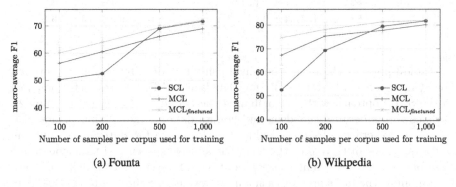

(a) Founta                    (b) Wikipedia

**Fig. 2.** Macro-average F1 results on test sets for low-resource scenarios.

This shows that when the number of available samples is low, the MCL gains from jointly training the model using several datasets. Furthermore, the results also indicate that corpus-specific fine-tuning of the MCL model gives significant performance improvements in low-resource scenarios.

## 4.3  Domain Adaptation Using Multi-Corpus Learning Approach

We perform supervised domain adaptation for hate speech classification as described in Sect. 2.3. We simulate low-resource scenarios for domain adaptation. We train the MCL model with entire training sets of four tasks. Whereas, for the target corpus, we use only 100, 200, 500, and 1000 training samples. The average macro-F1 results obtained on five target corpora in low-resource scenarios are presented in Table 5. The results of domain adaptation are compared against low-resource single-corpus learning, where the SCL model is fine-tuned with the varying amount of training data of the target set (same model as in Sect. 4.2). Figure 3 presents the results obtained for domain adaptation for Founta and Wikipedia as target datasets.

Compared to the SCL, for domain adaptation, we obtain a significant relative improvement of 37% and 31.5%, using 100 and 200 training samples for the target datasets, respectively (67.7% versus 49.4% and 70.2% versus 53.4%). The improvement is higher when the amount of available data is lower. This can be because the shared layer of MCL captures information from multiple related corpora, that can be transferred to a new corpus. Figure 3b shows a considerable amount of improvements in the low-resource domain adaptation for the Wikipedia dataset, although the MCL model was trained with four Twitter datasets. This indicates that the MCL approach can still be helpful when the task is related but the corpora come from different domains. Using the entire training set as a target corpus for domain adaptation, an average macro-F1 of 74.7% is obtained. This result is better than macro-F1 of 73.2% obtained using SCL. Thus, from Table 5, we conclude that domain adaptation in low-resource scenarios gives better performance than the SCL approach.

**Table 5.** Average of macro-F1 results for five test datasets as target datasets for domain adaptation: low-resource scenario and all training samples.

| Approaches | Low-resource scenario | | | | All training samples |
|---|---|---|---|---|---|
| | Number of adaptation samples | | | | |
| | 100 | 200 | 500 | 1000 | |
| SCL (without adaptation) | 49.4 | 53.4 | 67.7 | 70.2 | 73.2 |
| MCL domain adaptation | **67.7** | **70.2** | **71.2** | **72.1** | **74.7** |

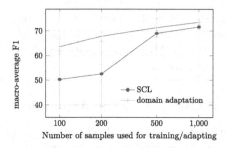
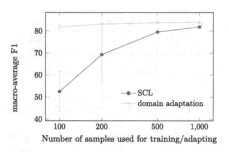

(a) Macro-F1 on **Founta** test set. The MCL model is trained using Davidson, Hateval, Waseem, and Wikipedia training sets. Model adapted using varying amount of Founta training set.

(b) Macro-F1 on **Wikipedia** test set. The MCL model is trained using Davidson, Founta, Hateval, and Waseem training sets. Model adapted using varying amount of Wikipedia training sets.

**Fig. 3.** Macro-average F1 results for domain adaptation.

## 5   Conclusion

In this article, we explored multi-corpus learning (MCL) for low-resource hate speech classification. Our approach for MCL is based on the paradigm of multi-task learning. Our idea is to utilize the shared layers of MCL to learn a common representation for several corpora, and corpus-specific layers to take into account the corpus-specific characteristics. We showed that the fine-tuning of the MCL model improves the performance compared to the SCL model.

In very low-resource scenarios, the MCL showed significant performance improvement when compared to SCL. We also used the MCL approach to perform domain adaptation. Compared to fine-tuning a pre-trained BERT, our adaptation approach showed significant improvements, especially when the amount of available adaptation data is very low. Overall, we experimentally demonstrated the efficiency of MCL for low-resource hate speech classification and domain adaptation.

**Acknowledgment.** This work was funded by the M-PHASIS project supported by the French National Research Agency (ANR) and German National Research Agency (DFG) under contract ANR-18-FRAL-0005. Experiments presented in this article were carried out using the Grid'5000 testbed, supported by group hosted by Inria, CNRS, RENATER and several Universities and organizations.

## References

1. Agarap, A.F.: Deep learning using rectified linear units (ReLU). arXiv preprint arXiv:1803.08375 (2018)
2. Alwosheel, A., van Cranenburgh, S., Chorus, C.G.: Is your dataset big enough? Sample size requirements when using artificial neural networks for discrete choice analysis. J. Choice Modell. **28**, 167–182 (2018)

3. Badjatiya, P., Gupta, S., Gupta, M., Varma, V.: Deep learning for hate speech detection in tweets. In: Proceedings of the 26th International Conference on World Wide Web Companion, pp. 759–760 (2017)
4. Basile, V., et al.: SemEval-2019 task 5: multilingual detection of hate speech against immigrants and women in Twitter. In: Proceedings of the 13th International Workshop on Semantic Evaluation, pp. 54–63. Association for Computational Linguistics, June 2019
5. Bodapati, S., Gella, S., Bhattacharjee, K., Al-Onaizan, Y.: Neural word decomposition models for abusive language detection. In: Proceedings of the Third Workshop on Abusive Language Online, pp. 135–145 (2019)
6. Bose, T., Aletras, N., Illina, I., Fohr, D.: Dynamically refined regularization for improving cross-corpora hate speech detection. In: ACL 2022 60th Meeting Association for Computational Linguistics Findings (2022)
7. Caruana, R.: Multitask learning. Mach. Learn. **28**(1), 41–75 (1997)
8. Davidson, T., Warmsley, D., Macy, M., Weber, I.: Automated hate speech detection and the problem of offensive language. In: Proceedings of the International Association for the AAAI Conference on Web and Social Media, vol. 11, pp. 512–515 (2017)
9. Del Vigna, F., Cimino, A., Dell'Orletta, F., Petrocchi, M., Tesconi, M.: Hate me, hate me not: Hate speech detection on Facebook. In: Proceedings of the First Italian Conference on Cybersecurity, pp. 86–95 (2017)
10. Delgado, R., Stefancic, J.: Hate speech in cyberspace. Wake Forest L. Rev. **49**, 319 (2014)
11. Devlin, J., Chang, M.W., Lee, K., Toutanova, K.: BERT: pre-training of deep bidirectional transformers for language understanding. In: Proceedings of the 2019 Conference of the North American Chapter of the Association for Computational Linguistics: Human Language Technologies, vol. 1 (Long and Short Papers), pp. 4171–4186 (2019)
12. Florio, K., Basile, V., Polignano, M., Basile, P., Patti, V.: Time of your hate: the challenge of time in hate speech detection on social media. Appl. Sci. **10**(12), 4180 (2020)
13. Fortuna, P., Soler, J., Wanner, L.: Toxic, hateful, offensive or abusive? What are we really classifying? An empirical analysis of hate speech datasets. In: Proceedings of the 12th Language Resources and Evaluation Conference (LREC), pp. 6786–6794 (2020)
14. Founta, A.M., et al.: Large scale crowdsourcing and characterization of twitter abusive behavior. In: Twelfth International AAAI Conference on Web and Social Media, pp. 491–500 (2018)
15. Gambäck, B., Sikdar, U.K.: Using convolutional neural networks to classify hate-speech. In: Proceedings of the First Workshop on Abusive Language Online, pp. 85–90 (2017)
16. Kapil, P., Ekbal, A.: A deep neural network based multi-task learning approach to hate speech detection. Knowl.-Based Syst. **210**, 106458 (2020)
17. Kingma, D.P., Ba, J.: Adam: a method for stochastic optimization. In: 3rd International Conference on Learning Representations, ICLR 2015 (2015)
18. Lee, Y., Yoon, S., Jung, K.: Comparative studies of detecting abusive language on twitter. In: Proceedings of the 2nd Workshop on Abusive Language Online (ALW2), pp. 101–106 (2018)
19. Liu, X., He, P., Chen, W., Gao, J.: Multi-task deep neural networks for natural language understanding. In: Proceedings of the 57th Annual Meeting of the Association for Computational Linguistics, pp. 4487–4496 (2019)

20. Park, J.H., Fung, P.: One-step and two-step classification for abusive language detection on twitter. In: Proceedings of the First Workshop on Abusive Language Online, pp. 41–45 (2017)
21. Plaza-Del-Arco, F.M., Molina-González, M.D., Ureña-López, L.A., Martín-Valdivia, M.T.: A multi-task learning approach to hate speech detection leveraging sentiment analysis. IEEE Access **9**, 112478–112489 (2021)
22. Rajamanickam, S., Mishra, P., Yannakoudakis, H., Shutova, E.: Joint modelling of emotion and abusive language detection. In: Proceedings of the 58th Annual Meeting of the Association for Computational Linguistics, pp. 4270–4279 (2020)
23. Ruder, S.: An overview of multi-task learning in deep neural networks. arXiv preprint arXiv:1706.05098 (2017)
24. Waseem, Z., Hovy, D.: Hateful symbols or hateful people? Predictive features for hate speech detection on twitter. In: Proceedings of the NAACL Student Research Workshop, pp. 88–93 (2016)
25. Wiegand, M., Ruppenhofer, J., Kleinbauer, T.: Detection of abusive language: the problem of biased datasets. In: Proceedings of the 2019 conference of the North American Chapter of the Association for Computational Linguistics: Human Language Technologies, vol. 1 (long and short papers), pp. 602–608 (2019)
26. Wulczyn, E., Thain, N., Dixon, L.: Ex Machina: personal attacks seen at scale. In: Proceedings of the 26th International Conference on World Wide Web, pp. 1391–1399 (2017)
27. Zhang, Y., Yang, Q.: A survey on multi-task learning. IEEE Trans. Knowl. Data Eng. **1** (2021)

# On the Importance of Word Embedding in Automated Harmful Information Detection

Salar Mohtaj[1,2]([⊠]) [iD] and Sebastian Möller[1,2]

[1] Technische Universität Berlin, Berlin, Germany
{salar.mohtaj,sebastian.moeller}@tu-berlin.de
[2] German Research Centre for Artificial Intelligence (DFKI),
Labor Berlin, Germany

**Abstract.** Social media have been growing rapidly during past years. They changed different aspects of human life, especially how people communicate and also how people access information. However, along with the important benefits, social media causes a number of significant challenges since they were introduced. Spreading of fake news and hate speech are among the most challenging issues which have attracted a lot of attention by researchers in past years. Different models based on natural language processing are developed to combat these phenomena and stop them in the early stages before mass spreading. Considering the difficulty of the task of automated harmful information detection (i.e., fake news and hate speech detection), every single step of the detection process could have a sensible impact on the performance of models. In this paper, we study the importance of word embedding on the overall performance of deep neural network architecture on the detection of fake news and hate speech on social media. We test various approaches for converting raw input text into vectors, from random weighting to state-of-the-art contextual word embedding models. In addition, to compare different word embedding approaches, we also analyze different strategies to get the vectors from contextual word embedding models (i.e., get the weights from the last layer, against averaging weights of the last layers). Our results show that XLNet embedding outperforms the other embedding approaches on both tasks related to harmful information identification.

**Keywords:** Fake news detection · Hate speech detection · Word embedding · Contextual word embedding

## 1 Introduction

Social media play an important role in people's life nowadays and affected different aspects of communication and accessing to information. Although they have given the opportunity to people to publish content online in a fast and

© Springer Nature Switzerland AG 2022
P. Sojka et al. (Eds.): TSD 2022, LNAI 13502, pp. 251–262, 2022.
https://doi.org/10.1007/978-3-031-16270-1_21

easy way, they also lead to ease of publishing harmful content by ease of generating content online and the anonymity that they provide [9]. South West Grid for Learning Organization[1] defined harmful content in simple terms as "anything online which causes a person distress or harm." In this paper, by harmful information we refer to fake news and hate speech content in social media.

Huge amount of online content in social media and the other online resources make it almost impossible to manually detect and remove harmful content from these communication mediums [25]. As a result, Machine Learning (ML) based approaches are being developed to increase the potential to combat these types of information. Due to complexity of the task of automated harmful content detection, hybrid approaches where Artificial Intelligence (AI) and human could empower each other in order to fight harmful content have attracted considerable attention from researchers, recently [4,14].

Automated fake news and hate speech detection in social media are considered as challenging prediction tasks because of various factors includes noisy content and the dynamic nature of social networks [24,29]. The difficulty of these tasks increases the importance of all the components in the whole Natural Language Processing (NLP) pipeline. In other words, the pre-processing approach, how to convert raw texts into vectors, the hyper-parameters and so forth could play a significant role on the overall performance of a harmful content identification system. For instance, it has been shown that how to deal with URLs to develop a machine learning based model to detect fake news in social media could considerably impact the performance of different models.

In this paper, we focus on measuring the importance of word embedding on the performance of ML models on two tasks related to harmful content identification, namely *fake news* and *hate speech* detection. For this purpose, we compared the performance of a deep neural network on two standard datasets for these two tasks, by using different word embedding approaches. We tested a broad range of word vectorization approaches from random embedding to the state-of-the-art contextual word embedding from pre-trained models like BERT [5], XLNet [28], and RoBERTa [15]. In addition to compare different embedding models, in the case of contextual embedding models we extracted the activations from different layers (i.e., one or more last layers) to find the best setting for the tasks of harmful content detection.

The impact of word embedding on NLP tasks are studied in different papers. For instance, the distance of human judgment and ELMO [22] and BERT embeddings have been compared in [11], and the performance of word embedding models for the tasks of multi-lingual plagiarism detection has been measures in [1]. Also, the contextualized representation of different contextual word embedding models (e.g., BERT [5], ELMO and GPT-2 [23]) are studied in [6]. Although the impact of word embedding on the task of hate speech detection has been studied in [13], in this paper we attempt to compare and measure different embedding approaches not only for hate speech detection, but also for the task of fake news detection.

---

[1] https://swgfl.org.uk/.

The rest of the paper is organized as follow; in Sect. 2 we discuss some of the recent models for fake news and hate speech identification in social media. Section 3 contains a brief introduction about the datasets that are used for the experiments. Sections 4 and 5 present a proposed experiments to compare different word embedding models and the obtained results by the models, respectively. Finally in Sect. 6 we briefly conclude the paper and discuss some directions in which the experiments could be extended.

## 2    Related Work

In this section, we review a number of research on identification of harmful information. We discuss some of the recently developed models for automatically detect fake news in social media. Moreover, some of the state-of-the-art models for the task of hate speech detection in user generated contents are discussed in this section.

### 2.1    Fake News Detection

There are different approaches and task definitions for fake news detection in online content. However, most of the recently developed approached could be categorized into the knowledge-based and style-based approaches [19]. While ground truth knowledge bases are used in the knowledge-based approaches to check the veracity of claims in textual data (i.e., fact-checking), style-based approaches rely on capturing the writing style of textual content (e.g., news content).

Ghanem et al., modeled the flow of effective information in fake news articles using a neural architecture [8] named as *FakeFlow* model. As a style-based approach, the FakeFlow model divides an input document into N segments and uses word embeddings and other features to catch the flow of emotions in the document. They used Convolutional Neural Network (CNN) to extract topic-based information from articles and Bidirectional Gated Recurrent Units (Bi-GRUs) to extract flow of the affective information.

As another experiment on word embedding for fake news detection, Verma et al., proposed *WELFake* [26] as another style-based method. *WELFake* is based on word embedding over linguistic features for fake news detection using ML classification. They applied TF-IDF and count vectorizer as embedding methods on a set of classification models like Support Vector Machine (SVM) and K-Nearest Neighbors (KNN) on 20 extracted linguistic features from news articles. The achieved results show that the combination of count vectorizer and SVM can outperform the other methods.

As a knowledge-based approach, Hu et al., proposed an end-to-end graph neural model, named as *CompareNet* [12]. *CompareNet* compares news to the knowledge base for fake news detection. Based on the proposed model they first construct a directed heterogeneous document graph from news articles, considering topics and entities for enriching news representation [12]. The topic-enriched news representation to encode the semantics of the news has been learned based on a heterogeneous graph attention network. As the last step, they compare the contextual entity representations with the corresponding KB-based entity representations. The achieved results show that the proposed model could outperform the other deep learning based models consisting of different architectures from LSTMs to CNNs and BERT pre-trained model [12].

## 2.2   Hate Speech Detection

The approaches for hate speech detection can be categorized into lexicon-based and machine learning-based models. While lexicon-based models try to identify hate speech expressions based on a set of pre-defined lexicons and rules, machine learning-based models turn hate speech detection into a text classification problem. We will review a few research from each of the approaches in the following.

Mohtaj et al., proposed two different models for the task of hate speech detection in [17,18]. The first model is a character-based LSTMs model that predicts harmful content in tweets, after replacing Twitter handles, URLs and emojis in the text with representing phrases. The second model relies on BERT [5] pre-trained language model. Their achieved results show that the BERT model could outperform the LSTMs model, using the same pre-processing steps [17].

In another classification based approach, Frenda et al., studied hate speech detection where women are the target [7]. The proposed model consists of a SVM classifier that was fed with different textual features, includes "bag and sequences of words", "characters n-grams", and "lexicons" related to the target group. Their experiments show that characters n-grams work slightly better than the other approaches in different testing corpora [7].

In a lexicon-based approach, Gitari et al., proposed a rule-based model to detect hateful content in social media [10]. The proposed model includes a lexicon building stage, in which the list of terms related to hateful content has been extracted. As the next step, they developed a set of rules to check the presence of pre-defined terms in the targeted sentences.

To the best of our knowledge, the experiments in this research is the first attempt to measure the importance of word embedding step on the overall performance of harmful content identification. The proposed method for measuring the performances is described thoroughly in the following sections.

## 3   Data

In this section we briefly discuss the chosen datasets for running experiments for fake news detection and hate speech detection. We also present a few statistics from each of the datasets.

### 3.1   Fake News Data

For the fake news detection experiments we used a *COVID-19* related fake news detection dataset containing English *fake* and *real* tweets and news [20]. The data have been collected from different social media and fact checking web-sites and contain *10,700* records in train, validation and test sections[2]. For the experiments in this paper, we merged these three parts and then split the whole data into 5 folds to measure results in a 5-fold cross validation setting. Some statistics of the dataset are presented in Table 1.

## 3.2   Hate Speech Data

For the hate speech detection experiments, we chose the English training dataset of the shared task on "Hate Speech and Offensive Content Identification in English and Indo-Aryan Languages" HASOC 2021[3].

**Table 1.** *COVID-19* Fake News Detection Dataset Statistics

| Attribute | # |
|---|---|
| Total number of documents | 10700 |
| Number of *real* documents | 5600 (52%) |
| Number of *fake* documents | 5100 (48%) |
| Average length of documents (in character) | 181.8 |
| The length of shortest document (in character) | 18 |
| The length of longest document (in character) | 10170 |

HASOC 2021 offered 2 subtasks for hateful content identification in different languages, including English [16]. Task 1 is a binary classification task in which tweet are classified into two classes, namely: Hate or Offensive *(HOF)* and Non-Hate and Non-Offensive *(NOT)*. The second task is a multi-class classification problem in which Hate or Offensive *(HOF)* are categorized into more detailed classes [16].

Based on the dataset publishers, the *Hate and Offensive* label in the dataset presents posts that contain hate, offensive or profane content, while posts with *Non Hate-Offensive* label do not contain any Hate Speech, profanity or offensive content. The *(NOT)* posts contain normal content, statements or anything else [16].

In this paper we focus on the binary label of the tweets and developed models to assign text into one of the *(HOF)* or *(NOT)* label. Table 2 presents some statistics of the HASOC 2021 dataset. For this purpose, we split the training set of the provided dataset into 5 folds as what we did for the fake news detection dataset.

---

[2] https://competitions.codalab.org/competitions/26655.
[3] https://hasocfire.github.io/hasoc/2021/index.html.

**Table 2.** *HASOC 2021* English Hate Speech Detection Dataset Statistics

| Attribute | # |
|---|---|
| Total number of documents | 3843 |
| Number of *(HOF)* documents | 2501 (65%) |
| Number of *(NOT)* documents | 1342 (35%) |
| Average length of documents (in character) | 167.3 |
| The length of shortest document (in character) | 4 |
| The length of longest document (in character) | 812 |

## 4   Experiments

To measure the importance of word embedding on two above mentioned tasks for harmful information identification in social media, we tested the impact of word embedding on a deep neural network architecture by fixing all the other parameters in the experiment. A set of pre-processing steps were applied on the input text to help models better generalize. The pre-processing steps and the developed classification models are entirely described in this section.

### 4.1   Pre-processing

Having fed raw text into the developed models, we applied a set of processes as the pre-processing phase. Since the data for both tasks mainly come from social media content, we focused on normalizing input data–considering the nature of social network text.

As one of the pre-processing steps, we replaced social network handles (e.g., Twitter usernames) with a constant text ("**username**"). Also, we replaced URLs with "**weblink**" constant text. The reason for the replacement is to keep a part of information instead of removing it. These constant texts show that there is an URL in a tweet or/and someone is mentioned in a tweet. Although an username or URL does not matter by itself, keeping this information could be helpful on assigning the tweet to a correct category (i.e., fake/real or hate full/not hate full).

Moreover, we replaced Emojis in the texts with a descriptive text that express them (e.g., replacing the emoji of Germany's flag with the text "flag of Germany"). As the previous pre-processing steps, adding more textual content to the input data could help models to better distinguish text based on classes. These pre-processing steps have been used in [17,18] and could improve the overall performance of prediction models.

### 4.2   Classification Models

For developing a model to classify text into the corresponding classes for the fake news and hate speech detection tasks, we used Recurrent Neural Network

(RNN) architectures due to the fact that they have shown good performances for the task of text classification [30]. We used Gated Recurrent Units (GRUs) [3] to develop the model.

The developed deep neural network model includes an embedding layer, where different embedding models have been tested. The embedding layer feeds its output into a Bidirectional GRU unit in order to process the sequence of input tokens. Then, the GRU's output passed into a dropout layer to improve the model's generalization. Finally, a linear layer pass inputs to the output layer.

We set *64* as the batch size and *128* as the size of the hidden layer. The GRU unit includes *2* layers and the dropout layer has a probability of *70%* to forget the learned weights. Finally, the model is trained in *50* epoches with the learning rate of *1e−3*. The obtained results on detecting fake news and hate speech using the model are presented in the following section.

## 5  Results

In this section we present the overall performance of the mentioned architectures on two different tasks. All the experiments are done in a 5-fold cross validation setting. The reported results in this section are the average in the five folds.

To compare the impact of different embedding strategies on the performance of the model, we fixed all the parameters (e.g., hyper-parameters and the architecture), and tried a number of different embedding models as the only variable parameter in the experiment. This way, we tracked the impact of word embedding on the performance. We used HiggingFace's package [27] to implement the models. Moreover, for the training phase, we froze the weights from the embedding layer, so the model wouldn't update the pre-trained weights from different models.

As the embedding models, we tested random embedding, GloVe [21], fast-Text [2], BERT [5], RoBERTa [15], and XLNet [28]. They applied on a *Bi-GRU* architectures for both tasks. We used *bert-base-uncased*, *roberta-base*, and *xlnet-base-cased* for the BERT, RoBERTa, and XLNet models, respectively. The performance metrics of the models based on different embedding strategies are presented in Table 3.

**Table 3.** The overall performance of different embedding strategies on the tasks of fake news and hate speech detection

| Embedding | Task | | | | | |
|---|---|---|---|---|---|---|
| | Fake News | | | Hate Speech | | |
| | Precision | Recall | F1 | Precision | Recall | F1 |
| Random | 0.923 | 0.904 | 0.914 | 0.780 | 0.729 | 0.754 |
| GloVe | 0.946 | 0.891 | 0.918 | 0.756 | 0.822 | 0.787 |
| fastText | 0.936 | 0.887 | 0.911 | 0.775 | 0.755 | 0.765 |
| BERT | 0.944 | **0.946** | 0.945 | 0.773 | 0.867 | 0.817 |
| RoBERTa | 0.960 | 0.936 | 0.948 | **0.794** | 0.870 | 0.830 |
| XLNet | **0.973** | 0.941 | **0.957** | 0.793 | **0.873** | **0.831** |

As it is highlighted in the table, all the contextual embedding models could outperform the random and traditional embedding models. Also, the XLNet achieved the best result with respect to F1 for both tasks among the embedding models. However, BERT and RoBERTa embeddings have a competitive performance in both tasks.

In addition to compare different embedding models, we also tested different strategies to get the weights from hidden layers in the contextual embedding models. Unlike the previous experiments in which the embedding weights came from the last hidden layer of the models, here we tested averaging weights from the last hidden layers of the models (i.e., from 1 to 4 last layers). The performance of different strategies are tested against both fake news and hate speech detection tasks. The obtained results are presented in Fig. 1.

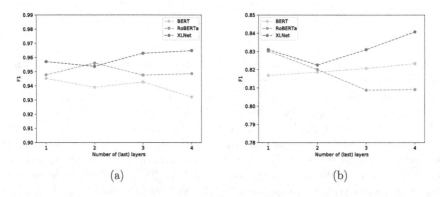

(a)                                              (b)

**Fig. 1.** The performance of the model with BERT, RoBERTa and XLNet contextual word embedding models, when the embedding weights come from the average of last $n$ hidden layers in **a)** Fake News detection, and **b)** Hate Speech detection, tasks

As depicted in the figure, in both tasks XLNet can achieve better results when more layers are used, not only compared to the other models, but also compared to when only the last layer is used. BERT and RoBERTa models show different patterns in using more than one layer for the embedding purpose. Using more layers of BERT could give better result in the hate speech detection task, while its performance decreases slightly in the fake news detection task. However, it works differently for RoBERTa when more layers are used for embedding, since the performance increases to a degree in the fake news task and fall down a bit in the hate speech detection task.

# 6    Conclusion and Future Works

In this paper, we analyzed the importance of word embedding in identification of harmful content in social media. Two tasks of fake news detection and hate speech detection have been used as the target tasks. We developed a deep neural network architecture for text classification and compared the impact of different embedding models on the overall performance of the classifier. Our results showed that XLNet pre-trained language model could better capture the concepts of the input text and the classifier achieve better results compared to the other word embedding models. Moreover, we tested the impact of using the average of last hidden layers in BERT, RoBERTa and XLNet models, and compared it with the common scenario in which the weights come from the very last layer. Our experiments show that averaging of last layers could leads to better overall results in all models.

As an open research question for the future works, we want to do the same experiments a more broad range of word embedding models. Moreover, the same experiments can be applied on different ML based text classifiers in order to better validate our findings in this paper.

**Acknowledgment.** This research was funded in part by the German Federal Ministry of Education and Research (BMBF) under grant number 01IS17043 (project ILSFAS).

# References

1. Asghari, H., Fatemi, O., Mohtaj, S., Faili, H., Rosso, P.: On the use of word embedding for cross language plagiarism detection. Intell. Data Anal. **23**(3), 661–680 (2019). https://doi.org/10.3233/IDA-183985
2. Bojanowski, P., Grave, E., Joulin, A., Mikolov, T.: Enriching word vectors with subword information. Trans. Assoc. Comput. Linguist. **5**, 135–146 (2017). https://transacl.org/ojs/index.php/tacl/article/view/999
3. Cho, K., van Merrienboer, B., Bahdanau, D., Bengio, Y.: On the properties of neural machine translation: Encoder-decoder approaches. In: Wu, D., Carpuat, M., Carreras, X., Vecchi, E.M. (eds.) Proceedings of SSST@EMNLP 2014, Eighth Workshop on Syntax, Semantics and Structure in Statistical Translation, Doha, Qatar, 25 October 2014, pp. 103–111. Association for Computational Linguistics (2014)
4. Demartini, G., Mizzaro, S., Spina, D.: Human-in-the-loop artificial intelligence for fighting online misinformation: challenges and opportunities. IEEE Data Eng. Bull. **43**(3), 65–74 (2020)
5. Devlin, J., Chang, M., Lee, K., Toutanova, K.: BERT: pre-training of deep bidirectional transformers for language understanding. In: Burstein, J., Doran, C., Solorio, T. (eds.) Proceedings of the 2019 Conference of the North American Chapter of the Association for Computational Linguistics: Human Language Technologies, NAACL-HLT 2019, Minneapolis, MN, USA, 2–7 June 2019, Volume 1 (Long and Short Papers), pp. 4171–4186. Association for Computational Linguistics (2019). https://doi.org/10.18653/v1/n19-1423

6. Ethayarajh, K.: How contextual are contextualized word representations? comparing the geometry of BERT, ELMO, and GPT-2 embeddings. In: Inui, K., Jiang, J., Ng, V., Wan, X. (eds.) Proceedings of the 2019 Conference on Empirical Methods in Natural Language Processing and the 9th International Joint Conference on Natural Language Processing, EMNLP-IJCNLP 2019, Hong Kong, China, 3–7 November 2019, pp. 55–65. Association for Computational Linguistics (2019). https://doi.org/10.18653/v1/D19-1006

7. Frenda, S., Ghanem, B., Montes-y-Gómez, M., Rosso, P.: Online hate speech against women: automatic identification of misogyny and sexism on twitter. J. Intell. Fuzzy Syst. **36**(5), 4743–4752 (2019). https://doi.org/10.3233/JIFS-179023

8. Ghanem, B., Ponzetto, S.P., Rosso, P., Rangel, F.: Fakeflow: fake news detection by modeling the flow of affective information. In: Merlo, P., Tiedemann, J., Tsarfaty, R. (eds.) Proceedings of the 16th Conference of the European Chapter of the Association for Computational Linguistics: Main Volume, EACL 2021, Online, 19–23 April 2021, pp. 679–689. Association for Computational Linguistics (2021). https://doi.org/10.18653/v1/2021.eacl-main.56

9. Giachanou, A., Rosso, P.: The battle against online harmful information: the cases of fake news and hate speech. In: d'Aquin, M., Dietze, S., Hauff, C., Curry, E., Cudré-Mauroux, P. (eds.) CIKM 2020: The 29th ACM International Conference on Information and Knowledge Management, Virtual Event, Ireland, 19–23 October 2020, pp. 3503–3504. ACM (2020). https://doi.org/10.1145/3340531.3412169

10. Gitari, N.D., Zhang, Z., Damien, H., Long, J.: A lexicon-based approach for hate speech detection. Int. J. Multimedia Ubiquit. Eng. **10**(4), 215–230 (2015). https://doi.org/10.14257/ijmue.2015.10.4.21

11. Haber, J., Poesio, M.: Word sense distance in human similarity judgements and contextualised word embeddings. In: Proceedings of the Probability and Meaning Conference (PaM 2020), pp. 128–145. Association for Computational Linguistics, Gothenburg, June 2020. https://aclanthology.org/2020.pam-1.17

12. Hu, L., et al.: Compare to the knowledge: graph neural fake news detection with external knowledge. In: Zong, C., Xia, F., Li, W., Navigli, R. (eds.) Proceedings of the 59th Annual Meeting of the Association for Computational Linguistics and the 11th International Joint Conference on Natural Language Processing, ACL/IJCNLP 2021, (Volume 1: Long Papers), Virtual Event, 1–6 August 2021, pp. 754–763. Association for Computational Linguistics (2021). https://doi.org/10.18653/v1/2021.acl-long.62

13. Jain, M., Goel, P., Singla, P., Tehlan, R.: Comparison of various word embeddings for hate-speech detection. In: Khanna, A., Gupta, D., Pólkowski, Z., Bhattacharyya, S., Castillo, O. (eds.) Data Analytics and Management. LNDECT, vol. 54, pp. 251–265. Springer, Singapore (2021). https://doi.org/10.1007/978-981-15-8335-3_21

14. Jhaver, S., Birman, I., Gilbert, E., Bruckman, A.S.: Human-machine collaboration for content regulation: the case of reddit automoderator. ACM Trans. Comput. Hum. Interact. **26**(5), 31:1–31:35 (2019). https://doi.org/10.1145/3338243

15. Liu, Y., et al.: RoBERTa: a robustly optimized BERT pretraining approach. CoRR abs/1907.11692 (2019). https://arxiv.org/abs/1907.11692

16. Modha, S., et al.: Overview of the HASOC subtrack at FIRE 2021: hate speech and offensive content identification in English and Indo-Aryan languages and conversational hate speech. In: Ganguly, D., Gangopadhyay, S., Mitra, M., Majumder, P. (eds.) FIRE 2021: Forum for Information Retrieval Evaluation, Virtual Event, India, 13–17 December 2021, pp. 1–3. ACM (2021). https://doi.org/10.1145/3503162.3503176

17. Mohtaj, S., Schmitt, V., Möller, S.: A feature extraction based model for hate speech identification. CoRR abs/2201.04227 (2022). https://arxiv.org/abs/2201.04227

18. Mohtaj, S., Woloszyn, V., Möller, S.: TUB at HASOC 2020: character based LSTM for hate speech detection in Indo-European languages. In: Mehta, P., Mandl, T., Majumder, P., Mitra, M. (eds.) Working Notes of FIRE 2020 - Forum for Information Retrieval Evaluation, Hyderabad, India, 16–20 December 2020. CEUR Workshop Proceedings, vol. 2826, pp. 298–303. CEUR-WS.org (2020). https://ceur-ws.org/Vol-2826/T2-26.pdf

19. Pan, J.Z., Pavlova, S., Li, C., Li, N., Li, Y., Liu, J.: Content based fake news detection using knowledge graphs. In: Vrandečić, D., et al. (eds.) ISWC 2018. LNCS, vol. 11136, pp. 669–683. Springer, Cham (2018). https://doi.org/10.1007/978-3-030-00671-6_39

20. Patwa, P., et al.: Fighting an infodemic: COVID-19 fake news dataset. In: Chakraborty, T., Shu, K., Bernard, H.R., Liu, H., Akhtar, M.S. (eds.) CONSTRAINT 2021. CCIS, vol. 1402, pp. 21–29. Springer, Cham (2021). https://doi.org/10.1007/978-3-030-73696-5_3

21. Pennington, J., Socher, R., Manning, C.D.: Glove: global vectors for word representation. In: Moschitti, A., Pang, B., Daelemans, W. (eds.) Proceedings of the 2014 Conference on Empirical Methods in Natural Language Processing, EMNLP 2014, 25–29 October 2014, Doha, Qatar, A meeting of SIGDAT, a Special Interest Group of the ACL, pp. 1532–1543. ACL (2014). https://doi.org/10.3115/v1/d14-1162

22. Peters, M.E., et al.: Deep contextualized word representations. In: Walker, M.A., Ji, H., Stent, A. (eds.) Proceedings of the 2018 Conference of the North American Chapter of the Association for Computational Linguistics: Human Language Technologies, NAACL-HLT 2018, New Orleans, Louisiana, USA, 1–6 June 2018, Volume 1 (Long Papers), pp. 2227–2237. Association for Computational Linguistics (2018). https://doi.org/10.18653/v1/n18-1202

23. Radford, A., Wu, J., Child, R., Luan, D., Amodei, D., Sutskever, I.: Language models are unsupervised multitask learners (2019)

24. Sharma, D.K., Garg, S.: IFND: a benchmark dataset for fake news detection. Complex Intell. Syst. 1–21 (2021)

25. Shu, K., Mahudeswaran, D., Liu, H.: FakeNewsTracker: a tool for fake news collection, detection, and visualization. Comput. Math. Organ. Theory **25**(1), 60–71 (2018). https://doi.org/10.1007/s10588-018-09280-3

26. Verma, P.K., Agrawal, P., Amorim, I., Prodan, R.: Welfake: word embedding over linguistic features for fake news detection. IEEE Trans. Comput. Soc. Syst. **8**(4), 881–893 (2021)

27. Wolf, T., et al.: Transformers: state-of-the-art natural language processing. In: Liu, Q., Schlangen, D. (eds.) Proceedings of the 2020 Conference on Empirical Methods in Natural Language Processing: System Demonstrations, EMNLP 2020 - Demos, Online, 16–20 November 2020, pp. 38–45. Association for Computational Linguistics (2020)

28. Yang, Z., Dai, Z., Yang, Y., Carbonell, J.G., Salakhutdinov, R., Le, Q.V.: XLNET: generalized autoregressive pretraining for language understanding. In: Wallach, H.M., Larochelle, H., Beygelzimer, A., d'Alché-Buc, F., Fox, E.B., Garnett, R. (eds.) Advances in Neural Information Processing Systems 32: Annual Conference on Neural Information Processing Systems 2019, NeurIPS 2019, 8–14 December 2019, Vancouver, BC, Canada, pp. 5754–5764 (2019). https://proceedings.neurips. cc/paper/2019/hash/dc6a7e655d7e5840e66733e9ee67cc69-Abstract.html

29. Zhang, X., Ghorbani, A.A.: An overview of online fake news: characterization, detection, and discussion. Inf. Process. Manag. **57**(2), 102025 (2020). https://doi. org/10.1016/j.ipm.2019.03.004

30. Zulqarnain, M., Ghazali, R., Hassim, Y.M.M., Rehan, M.: A comparative review on deep learning models for text classification. Indonesian J. Electr. Eng. Comput. Sci. **19**(1), 325–335 (2020)

# BERT-based Classifiers for Fake News Detection on Short and Long Texts with Noisy Data: A Comparative Analysis

Elena Shushkevich[1]([✉]), Mikhail Alexandrov[2], and John Cardiff[1]

[1] Technological University Dublin, Dublin, Ireland
elena.n.shushkevich@gmail.com, John.Cardiff@TUDublin.ie
[2] Autonomous University of Barcelona, Barcelona, Spain

**Abstract.** Free uncontrolled access to the Internet is the main reason for fake news propagation on the Internet both in social media and in regular Internet publications. In this paper we study the potential of several BERT-based models to detect fake news related to politics. Our contribution to the area consists of testing BERT, RoBERTa and MNLI RoBERTa models with (a) short and long texts; (b) ensembling with the best models; (c) noisy texts. To improve ensembling, we introduce an additional class 'Doubtful news'. To create noisy data we use cross-translation. For the experiments we consider the well-known FRN (Fake vs. Real News, long texts) and LIAR (short texts) datasets. The results we obtained on the long texts dataset are higher than the results we obtained on the short texts dataset. The proposed approach to ensembling provided significant improvement of the results. The experiments with noisy data demonstrated high noise immunity of the BERT model with long news and the RoBERTa model with short news.

**Keywords:** Fake News · BERT · RoBERTa · MNLI RoBERTa · Ensembling · Noise Immunity

## 1 Introduction

Today the Internet is a very important part of our lives, a place, where we spend a significant portion of the day, where we search for answers to our questions, meet new friends and communicate with old ones, where we study and work, where we watch movies and read news. Moreover, the Internet is a place where we want to be safe and be sure that the information we get is reliable, but nowadays with the growth of the Internet and with weak control of the validity of information that is published in it, the problem of fake news detection is as acute as never before.

Fake news is information hoaxes designed to deliberately mislead the reader in order to gain a financial or political advantage [1], and could harm users both mentally and physically, so the problem of fake news detection is important, and

© Springer Nature Switzerland AG 2022
P. Sojka et al. (Eds.): TSD 2022, LNAI 13502, pp. 263–274, 2022.
https://doi.org/10.1007/978-3-031-16270-1_22

the high quality of fake news identification tools could really help to make the Internet safer.

In our work we concentrate our efforts to analyze the quality of fake news detection using different BERT-based models. The topic under consideration is politics. Our focus is to explore the differences between analyzing long vs short news texts. To improve the quality of detection we propose ensembling based on the best models with an additional undefined class. We also study the noise immunity of the best models with the aim to see how resilient each approach is by introducing noise. This work is important as it helps to expand knowledge of the application of BERT-based models - models, which became more and more popular nowadays, and which allow researchers to obtain the highest results, in particular for classification tasks. Moreover, our work allows researchers to compare not only the different BERT-based models, but also the behavior of these models on the short and long texts, and also with noisy data.

The article consists of the following parts: in Sect. 1 we discuss the target of the research, Sect. 2 is devoted to literature review connected with the task. In Sect. 3 we present the datasets we chose for the research, and its preprocessing. Section 4 contains the description of models we use. In Sect. 5 we present the results of experiments. Section 6 is a conclusion with a discussion of the results, and plans of future work.

## 2   Literature Review

A large amount of research is devoted to the study of fake news detection, as an important task of binary classification. We divide this short review into several positions.

**Approaches and Relevant Methods.** We can highlight the three main approaches for fake news detection: 1) classical methods of machine learning, such as Logistic Regression, Support Vector Machines, Naive Bayes, and $K$-Nearest Neighbor Classifier [2,3]; 2) methods of Deep Learning based on deep neural networks, such as LSTM (Long short-term memory) (including [4] where the authors obtained 0.42 accuracy on the LIAR[1] dataset with multi-class classification, and [5] where the authors obtained 0.46 accuracy on the LIAR dataset with multi-class classification), CNN (convolutional neural network) ([6] where the authors obtained 0.96 accuracy on the LIAR dataset with 2-class label classification), HAN (Hierarchical Attention Network) [7–9]; and 3) advanced language models such as BERT (Bidirectional Encoder Representations from Transformers), ELMo (Embeddings from Language Models), ELECTRA (Efficiently Learning an Encoder that Classifies Token Replacements Accurately) etc., which demonstrated high results in various natural language processing tasks including text classification [10–12].

**Adversarial Machine Learning.** In [13] the authors formulated adversarial attacks that target compositional semantics, lexical relations, and sensitivity to

---

[1] https://metatext.io/datasets/liar-dataset.

modifiers. They then tested their benchmark using the BERT classifier, which was fine-tuned on the LIAR and Kaggle Fake-News[2] datasets. In [14] the authors made experiments on three different state-of-the-art datasets (LIAR, ISOT[3], and Kaggle Fake-News) under 4 different adversarial attacks (Text Bugger, Text Fooler, PWWS, and Deep Word Bugs) implemented using the state-of-the-art Text-Attack[4] NLP attack library, where they used CNN, RNN (recurrent neural network), and the hybrid CNN-RNN models for it. The authors of [15] conducted experiments on two multimedia datasets and improved fake news detection with domain-adversarial and graph-attention neural networks.

**Topics and Linguistic Resources.** We could mention works [16,17], where the authors researched emotional reactions and signals, and their role in fake news detection on the Twitter platform and Politifact[5] dataset. Fake news can reflect completely different topics. For example, the authors of [9] use neural networks to deal with fake news in political areas. The authors of [18] explore fake health information or misinformation related to social impact. The research presented in [19] is focused on Naive Bayes spam filtering using word-position-based attributes. The work [20] determines the contribution of different topics in dynamics to the publications of well-known media. The fuzzy definition of topics can be considered a consequence of reliable and unreliable (real and fake) information in publications. The approach taken in [21] could help to create a dataset for fake news detection, choosing articles for it using key phrases, the advantage of which is that there is no need for a priori information.

**Benchmarks.** As a benchmark for our experiments with BERT-based models on short and long texts we use the results from the work [22]. The authors used the same datasets - Fake vs. Real News [23] with long news (hereinafter FRN) and LIAR [24] with short news - as we used. As for benchmarks for the proposed procedure of ensembling and for testing noise immunity then by the moment we are not aware of corresponding publications.

## 3    Fake News Datasets

### 3.1    Description of Datasets

The objects of consideration are two mentioned datasets: FRN with long news and LIAR with short news. Our chosen datasets are both devoted to politics to be sure that our results are not affected by the fact that the datasets contain news devoted to different topics (in other words, to not compare results obtained on medical articles with results obtained on movie reviews).

The numerical features of the LIAR and FRN datasets, including the number of fake and real messages and an average length of messages, are presented in Table 1.

---

[2] https://www.kaggle.com/c/fake-news.
[3] https://www.uvic.ca/ecs/ece/isot/datasets/fake-news/.
[4] textattack.readthedocs.io/en/latest/.
[5] https://www.mpi-inf.mpg.de/dl-cred-analysis/.

**Table 1.** The numerical features of FRN and LIAR project datasets.

| Dataset | Number of messages | Fake Messages | Real Messages | Average length of messages |
|---------|--------------------|--------------|--------------|-----------------------------|
| FRN     | 6,335              | 3,164        | 3,171        | 765 words                   |
| LIAR    | 12,791             | 5,657        | 7,134        | 18 words                    |

The first dataset we chose, FRN, was developed by George McIntire, and contains more than 6,000 messages with a nearly equal number of fake and real messages. Fake news for the dataset was collected from a Kaggle fake news dataset[6], while the real news was collected from media organizations such as The New York Times, WSJ, Bloomberg, NPR, and The Guardian.

The LIAR dataset includes more than 12,000 short messages collected from POLITIFACT.COM, and all messages are labeled for six groups: pants-fire, false, barely-true, half-true, mostly-true, and true. As our target was to implement binary classification for fake and non-fake messages, we re-labeled these labels: pants-fire, false, and barely-true messages as fake messages, and half-true, mostly-true, and true messages as real messages. As a result, our dataset contains 56% real and 44% fake statements.

We created the standard splitting of the datasets into training/development/test with a 60/20/20 ratio.

## 3.2   Text Preprocessing

It is well-known that the preprocessing step is extremely important, as the correct text preprocessing could significantly improve the results of experiments, while careless preprocessing could similarly decrease the results. After a number of experiments, we settled on the following steps:

- converting all characters to lowercase;
- removing all characters except those of the English alphabet and numbers;
- removing stopwords;
- removing words that occur too often (in more than 50% of messages);
- removing words that occur too rarely (in less than 1% of messages);
- stemming.

In relation to the number of texts in which a word appears, we chose a threshold of 50% as we are applying binary classification: we indirectly associate words with their belonging to classes. However, the results remain practically the same with the thresholds of 40% and 60%.

For all preprocessing steps we used Python, NLTK - Porter Stemmer and Stopwords library.

---

[6] https://www.kaggle.com/mrisdal/fake-news.

### 3.3  Noisy Data

To study noise immunity of the selected models we need to generate noisy data with different levels of noise. For this purpose, we implemented the cross-translation of the original datasets for two different languages: Italian and Japanese. Our idea is based on the fact that a change of the number of original words may be considered as the action of a noise. With this operation the level of noise can be determined by the relative number of such words. This value is easily calculated by the Jaccard measure of similarity.

To obtain the first level of noise, we translated the datasets to Italian and back to English. To obtain the second level of noise, we translated the datasets to Japanese and back to English. We did the latter with the assumption that such translated datasets will be more different from the original ones in comparison with datasets translated from Italian. For translation we used Google Translate.

Jaccard Distances (the inverse values to Jaccard measures of similarity) for both datasets and both levels of noise are presented in Table 2.

**Table 2.** Jaccard Distance for translated datasets.

| Dataset/Noise level | 1st level (EN-IT) | 2nd level (EN-JA) |
| --- | --- | --- |
| FRN | 0.27 | 0.39 |
| LIAR | 0.25 | 0.46 |

Therefore we assume that the levels of noise for FRN dataset are equal 27% and 39% and the levels of noise for LIAR dataset are equal 25% and 46%.

**Note.** In order to present our results more clearly, in our experiments we interpolated the quality of fake news detection to the levels 25% and 50% of noise for both datasets (see Sect. 5.1).

## 4  Models and Their Combination

### 4.1  BERT-based Models

We consider the following three popular BERT-based models as the subject of consideration in this research:

**BERT** (Bidirectional Encoder Representations from Transformers) [25] is designed to pre-train deep bidirectional representations from unlabeled text by jointly conditioning on both left and right context in all layers. As a result, the pre-trained BERT model can be fine-tuned with just one additional output layer. We used the BERT-Base model for fine-tuning which has 12 layers, 12 attention heads and 110 million parameters.

**RoBERTa** (Robustly optimized BERT approach) [26] is based on the BERT model. RoBERTa obtains better performance using larger mini-batch sizes, spending more time to train the model and using more data. In comparison with BERT, RoBERTa uses longer sequences and removes NSP (next sentence prediction) loss. We used the RoBERTa-Base model for fine-tuning to perform the experiments.

**MNLI RoBERTa** (RoBERTa-Large-MNLI model) [26] is fine-tuned on the Multi-Genre NLI (Natural Language Inference) Corpus[7]. The idea of the model is to establish the relationship between two proposed sentences: neutral, contradiction or entailment. We used the pretrained MNLI RoBERTa model as follows: we chose all the fake messages from the train LIAR dataset and compared them with messages from the test LIAR dataset. If a message from the test dataset had an 'entailment' label with any message from the training dataset, we labeled this message as fake news. The same procedure was implemented for both the training and test subsets of the FRN dataset.

### 4.2    Ensembling with an Additional Class

It is well-known that in many cases ensembling (a collective of algorithms) may improve the results of classification. Such an effect is especially significant when we deal with diverse algorithms reflecting different parts of the same object of classification. In this research we have the contradictory situation that all the algorithms belong to the group of BERT-based algorithms. Under these circumstances we build an ensemble with two of the best algorithms and test two rules of decision-making:

**Rule-1.** The decision is 'False News' if both algorithms say 'False News'. The decision is 'Real News' if even one algorithm says 'Real News'. Here we take into account that the precision of Real News detection is slightly better than Fake News detection.

**Rule-2.** The decision is 'False News' or 'Real News' in case of consensus. Otherwise the decision is 'Doubtful News'. The latter means we use so-called delayed decision.

In case of the Rule-1 we calculate binary F1-measure having in view all the data. In case of the Rule-2 we calculate binary F1-measure twice: for all the data and for the certain classes except the class 'Doubtful news'.

## 5    Experiments

### 5.1    Options and Platforms

The full list of options of the experiments, including algorithms, experiments with noisy data, numbers of datasets and classes, are presented in Table 3.

---

[7] https://cims.nyu.edu/~sbowman/multinli/.

**Table 3.** Options for experiments.

| Experiments | Number | Description |
|---|---|---|
| Algorithms | 4 | 3 models (BERT, RoBERTa, MNLI RoBERTa), and ensemble (BERT, RoBERTa) |
| Experiments with noisy data | 8 | 2 models (BERT, RoBERTa) on 2 datasets with 2 levels of noise |
| Datasets | 2 | 2 datasets (FRN, LIAR) |
| Classes | 2 and (2+1) | 2 classes (Fake and Real news), 3 classes (Fake, Real and Doubtful news) |

We performed the experiments on the NVIDIA Tesla K80 GPU provided by Microsoft Azure. For the fine-tuning, we trained each model on the training sets for 2 epochs and evaluated on the validation sets. The models are optimized using AdamW [27] with a learning rate of 5e−5 and epsilon of 1e−8, and a batch size of 16. For the models' implementation we used Pytorch [28] and Huggingface Transformers [29] libraries.

## 5.2   Experiments with Different Models

The results of experiments with BERT, RoBERTa, MNLI RoBERTa models on FRN and LIAR datasets are presented in Table 4.

The results of experiments with an ensemble of BERT and RoBERTa models with 2 and 3 classes on FRN and LIAR datasets are presented in Table 5. The latter results refer only to certain classes 'Fake news' and 'Real news'. The size of 'Doubtful news' for FRN and LIAR datasets are equal to 9% and 32% respectively.

The results from Table 4 and Table 5 are presented also in graphical form in Fig. 1.

**Table 4.** Results of experiments with different models (F1-score).

| Dataset/Model | BERT | RoBERTa | MNLI RoBERTa |
|---|---|---|---|
| FRN | 0.91 | 0.89 | 0.66 |
| LIAR | 0.72 | 0.72 | 0.72 |

**Table 5.** Results of experiments with ensemble (F1-score).

| Dataset/Model | Ensemble of BERT and RoBERTa (2 classes) | Ensemble of BERT and RoBERTa (3 classes) |
|---|---|---|
| FRN | 0.92 | 0.94 |
| LIAR | 0.72 | 0.77 |

## 5.3 Experiments with Noisy Data

The results of the experiments with the BERT and RoBERTa models on FRN and LIAR datasets are presented in Table 6. Here the level of noise is presented in parentheses.

The data from the Table 6 were recalculated using the following 2 operations:

1) Normalization on F1-score without noise.
2) Smooth interpolation (using splines) on the levels 25% and 50%.

The results are presented in Table 7 and in Fig. 2.

## 5.4 Benchmark

We consider results [22] concerning two BERT-based models as baseline for our research. These results for BERT and RoBERTa models on FRN and LIAR datasets are presented in Table 8. The authors used the same FRN and LIAR datasets and the same ratio of 80/20 split of these datasets (train/test).

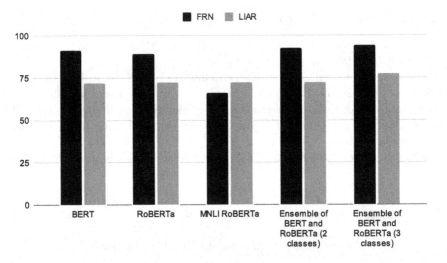

**Fig. 1.** Results of the experiments (F1-score, %).

**Table 6.** BERT and RoBERT with noisy data (F1-score).

| BERT/RoBERTa | BERT-FRN | BERT-LIAR | RoBERTa-FRN | RoBERTa-LIAR |
|---|---|---|---|---|
| Without noise | 0.91 (0%) | 0.72 (0%) | 0.89 (0%) | 0.72 (0%) |
| Noise(EN-IT) | 0.87 (27%) | 0.70 (25%) | 0.65 (27%) | 0.65 (25%) |
| Noise(EN-JA) | 0.86 (39%) | 0.59 (46%) | 0.60 (39%) | 0.66 (46%) |

**Table 7.** Normalized and aligned results for BERT and RoBERTa with noisy data (F1-score).

| BERT/RoBERTa | BERT-FRN | BERT-LIAR | RoBERTa-FRN | RoBERTa-LIAR |
|---|---|---|---|---|
| Without noise | 1.00 | 1.00 | 1.00 | 1.00 |
| Noise(EN-IT),25% | 0.96 | 0.97 | 0.75 | 0.91 |
| Noise(EN-JA),50% | 0.93 | 0.79 | 0.58 | 0.90 |

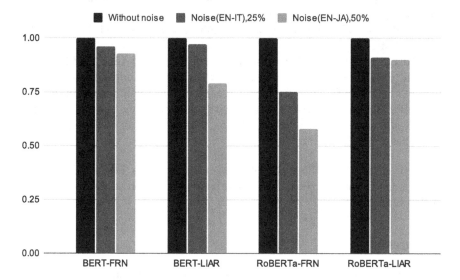

**Fig. 2.** Normalized and aligned results for BERT and RoBERTa with noisy data (F1-score).

**Table 8.** Benchmark results (F1-score).

| Dataset/Model | BERT | RoBERTa |
|---|---|---|
| FRN | 0.96 | 0.98 |
| LIAR | 0.62 | 0.62 |

## 6  Conclusion

The completed experiments showed the following results:

1. On short texts all the methods, BERT, RoBERTA and MNLI RoBERTa, provide the same results. These results, $F1 = 72\%$, essentially exceed the baseline of 62% (see Table 4 and Table 8).
2. On long texts BERT and RoBERTa show close results, which are essentially better than MNLI RoBERTa with their $F1 = 91\%$, 89%, 66% respectively, so we demonstrated that the idea of Natural Language Inference usage for long

texts classification is not good, as opposed to using this idea on short texts. The best result with BERT (F1 = 91%) yields slightly to that of the baseline of BERT and RoBERTa having F1 = 96%, 98% respectively (see Table 4 and Table 8).

3. Ensembling shows its significant advantages only when we include the additional 'Doubtful news' class. This improvement is reflected with F1 = 77%, 94% versus F1 = 72%, 92% for short and long texts, respectively (see Table 4 and Table 5), and this fact confirms the promise of using ensembles in future research.
   Note: Here the difference between 94% and 92% is statistically significant at the level of 5%.

4. The BERT model shows low noise immunity with short texts and high noise immunity with long texts. It is justified by the values of normalized F1 = 79%, 93% at the level of 50% noise for both cases, respectively (see Table 5).

5. RoBERTa shows the opposite results with short and long texts. It is justified by the values of normalized F1 = 90%, 58% on the level of 50% noise for both cases, respectively (see Table 5).

The ensembling and the study of noise immunity look like promising areas for further improvement. Here, it is worth paying attention to the works [30,31] respectively.

# References

1. Hunt, E.: What is fake news? How to spot it and what you can do to stop it. The Guardian (2016). https://www.theguardian.com/media/2016/dec/18/what-is-fake-news-pizzagate
2. Bandyopadhyay, S., Dutta, S.: Analysis of fake news in social medias for four months during lockdown in COVID-19 (2020). https://doi.org/10.20944/preprints202006.0243.v1
3. Gravanis, G., Vakali, A., Diamantaras, K., Karadais, P.: Behind the cues: a benchmarking study for fake news detection. Expert Syst. Appl. **128**, 201–213 (2019)
4. Long, Y., Lu, Q., Xiang, R., Li, M., Huang, C.-R.: Fake news detection through multi-perspective speaker profiles. In: Proceedings of the Eighth International Joint Conference on Natural Language Processing (Volume 2: Short Papers), vol. 2, pp. 252–256 (2017)
5. Kirilin, A., Strube, M.: Exploiting a speaker's credibility to detect fake news. In: Proceedings of Data Science, Journalism & Media Workshop at KDD (DSJM 2018) (2018)
6. Bhattacharjee, S.D., Talukder, A., Balantrapu, B.V.: Active learning based news veracity detection with feature weighting and deep-shallow fusion. In: 2017 IEEE International Conference on Big Data (Big Data), pp. 556–565. IEEE (2017)
7. Rashkin, H., Choi, E., Jang, J., Volkova, S., Choi, Y.: Truth of varying shades: analyzing language in fake news and political fact-checking. In: Proceedings of the 2017 Conference on Empirical Methods in Natural Language Processing, pp. 2931–2937 (2017)

8. Hamdi, T., Slimi, H., Bounhas, I., Slimani, Y.: A hybrid approach for fake news detection in twitter based on user features and graph embedding. In: Hung, D.V., D'Souza, M. (eds.) ICDCIT 2020. LNCS, vol. 11969, pp. 266–280. Springer, Cham (2020). https://doi.org/10.1007/978-3-030-36987-3_17

9. Oshikawa, R., Qian, J., and Wang., W.: A survey on natural language processing for fake news detection. arXiv preprint arXiv:1811.00770 (2018)

10. Akhtyamova, L.: Named entity recognition in Spanish biomedical literature: short review and BERT model. In: 26th Conference of Open Innovations Association (FRUCT), pp. 1–7. IEEE (2020)

11. Adhikari, A., Ram, A., Tang, R., and Lin, J.: Docbert: Bert for document classification. arXiv preprint arXiv:1904.08398 (2019)

12. Gonzalez-Carvajal S., Garrido-Merch E.: Comparing Bert against traditional machine learning text classification. arXiv preprint arXiv:2005.13012 (2020)

13. Flores, L.J., Yu, Hao, Y.: An adversarial benchmark for fake news detection models. arXiv:2201.00912v1 (2022)

14. Ali, H., et al.: All your fake detector are belong to us: evaluating adversarial robustness of fake-news detectors under black-box settings. IEEE Access **9**, 81678–81692 (2021)

15. Yuan, H., et al.: Improving fake news detection with domain-adversarial and graph-attention neural network. Decis. Support Syst. **151**, 113633 (2021)

16. Vosoughi, S., Roy, D., Aral, S.: The spread of true and false news online. Science **359**(6380), 1146–1151 (2018)

17. Giachanou, A., Rosso, P., Crestani, F.: Leveraging emotional signals for credibility detection. In: Proceedings of the 42nd International ACM SIGIR Conference on Research and Development in Information Retrieval (SIGIR 2019), Paris, France, 21–25 July (2019)

18. Pulido, C.M., Ruiz-Eugenio, L., Redondo-Sama, G., Villarejo-Carballido, B.: A new application of social impact in social media for overcoming fake news in health. Int. J. Environ. Res. Public Health **17**, 2430 (2020)

19. Hovold, J.: Naive Bayes spam filtering using word-position-based attributes. In: CEAS, pp. 41–48 (2005)

20. Petrov, A., Proncheva, O.: Identifying the topics of Russian political talk shows. In: Proceedings of the Conference on Modeling and Analysis of Complex Systems and Processes, 22–24 October (MACSPro 2020), pp. 79–86. CEUR-WS.org (2020). online. https://ceur-ws.org/Vol-2795/short1.pdf

21. Popova, S., Skitalinskaya, G.: Extended list of stop words: does it work for keyphrase extraction from short texts? In: Proceedings of 12th Intern Scientific and Technical Conference on Computing Sciences and Information Technologies (CSIT-2017), pp. 401–404. IEEE (2017)

22. Khan, J.Y., Khondaker, M.T.I., Afroz, S., Uddin, G., Iqbal, A.: A benchmark study of machine learning models for online fake news detection. Mach. Learn. Appl. 100032. https://arxiv.org/abs/1905.04749 (2021)

23. GitHub Repository. https://github.com/joolsa. Accessed 12 Mar 2022

24. Wang, W.Y.: "Liar, Liar Pants on Fire": a new benchmark dataset for fake news detection. ACL. https://arxiv.org/abs/1705.00648 (2017)

25. Devlin, J., Chang, M.-W., Lee, K., Toutanova, K.: Bert: pre-training of deep bidirectional transformers for language understanding. https://arxiv.org/abs/1810.04805 (2018)

26. Liu, Y., et al.: Roberta: a robustly optimized BERT pretraining approach. https://arxiv.org/abs/1907.11692 (2019)

27. Loshchilov, I., Hutter F.: Fixing weight decay regularization in ADAM. arXiv preprint arXiv:1711.05101 (2017)
28. Paszke, A., et al.: Pytorch: an imperative style, high-performance deep learning library. In: Advances in Neural Information Processing Systems, pp. 8026–8037 (2019)
29. Wolf, T. et al.: Transformers: state-of-the-art natural language processing. In: Proceedings of the 2020 Conference on Empirical Methods in Natural Language Processing: System Demonstrations, pp. 38–45 (2020)
30. Glazkova, A., Glazkov, M., Trifonov, T.: g2tmn at constraint@AAAI2021: exploiting CT-BERT and Ensembling learning for COVID-19 fake news detection. In: Combating Online Hostile Posts in Regional Languages during Emergency Situation, pp. 116–127 (2021)
31. Akhtyamova, L., Alexandrov, M., Cardiff, J., Koshulko, O.: Opinion mining on small and noisy samples of health-related texts. In: Shakhovska, N., Medykovskyy, M.O. (eds.) CSIT 2018. AISC, vol. 871, pp. 379–390. Springer, Cham (2019). https://doi.org/10.1007/978-3-030-01069-0_27

# Can a Machine Generate a Meta-Review?
# How Far Are We?

Prabhat Kumar Bharti[1]($\boxtimes$), Asheesh Kumar[1], Tirthankar Ghosal[2],
Mayank Agrawal[1], and Asif Ekbal[1]

[1] Department of Computer Science and Engineering,
Indian Institute of Technology Patna, Patna, India
{prabhat_1921cs32,mayank265,asif}@iitp.ac.in

[2] Institute of Formal and Applied Linguistics, Faculty of Mathematics and Physics,
Charles University, Prague, Czech Republic
ghosal@ufal.mff.cuni.cz

**Abstract.** A meta-review usually written by the editor of a journal or
the area/program chair in a conference is a summary of the peer-reviews
and a concise interpretation of the editors/chairs decision. Although the
task closely simulates a multi-document summarization problem, automatically writing reviews on top of human-generated reviews is something very less explored. In this paper, we investigate how current *state-
of-the-art* summarization techniques fare on this problem. We come up
with qualitative and quantitative evaluation of four radically different
summarization approaches on the current problem. We explore how the
summarization models perform on preserving aspects and sentiments in
original peer reviews and meta-reviews. Finally, we conclude with our
observations on why the task is challenging, different from simple summarization, and how one should approach to design a meta-review generation model. We have provided link for our git repository https://github.
com/PrabhatkrBharti/MetaGen.git so as to enable readers to replicate
the findings.

**Keywords:** Meta review generation · Text Summarization · Peer
reviews

## 1 Introduction

Editors write meta reviews of a journal or area-chairs of a conference to communicate peer review decisions to the authors. It is supposed to be a concise
description of the submission's main content, a summary of the discussions with
the reviewer or the original peer reviews, followed by the recommendation of
the meta-reviewer justifying their decision[1]. A critical difference between a peer

---

[1] https://iclr.cc/Conferences/2020/MetareviewGuide.

P. K. Bharti and A. Kumar—Equal Contribution.

P. Sojka et al. (Eds.): TSD 2022, LNAI 13502, pp. 275–287, 2022.
https://doi.org/10.1007/978-3-031-16270-1_23

review and a meta-review is that a meta-review has to recommend a decision and be not ambivalent about the paper. Hence meta-review is a crucial task in peer review usually performed by senior researchers in the community to craft the venue's content. Ideally, a meta-reviewer is expected to find the consensus of the reviewers to arrive at a decision, but there could be exceptions.

With the deluge of paper submissions in top-tier conferences nowadays, organizers are finding it difficult to hire experienced program committee as well as area-chairs. Here in this exploratory work, we investigate *what if we can automatically generate a meta-review and how would it look like?* We are intrigued to explore: *Is a meta-review a summary of the actual reviews or if is there something more? If meta-review is a summary of the reviews, is it an extractive or abstractive summary? How is the sentiment and aspects of the original reviews reflect in the generated meta-reviews?* We experiment with four *state-of-the-art* text-summarization models of different categories and seek answers to our questions. We evaluate the machine-generated reviews both qualitatively and quantitatively to understand where do the current text summarization models stand for this task. In this work, we also discuss that the generated meta-review should have the salient features of the peer reviews along with quantitatively scoring the aspect overlap and sentiment polarity. As we approach this problem as a summarization task we also experiment with some recently introduced automatic evaluation metrics.

## 2   Related Work

To our knowledge, this is a fairly new task to generate meta-review by peer reviews automatically. Therefore, metaGen [2] only work done in the direction of generating an assistive meta-review that will help speed up the review process, with conferences/journals having many submissions to be handled in the stipulated time. In this work authors first, generate the extractive draft and then uses fine-tuned UniLM Unified Language Model for the final decision of acceptance and making the final abstractive meta-review. Without data and associated code, we could not compare our approach with the one used by MetaGen [2]. Therefore, this paper compares SUPERT [10], PEGASUS [20], BART-based text summarization [15], and TextRank [14] models for mentioned task. Although we do not come across the same literature survey, here we mention some previous works in this direction. One of the first works done on opinion-based summarization is by Hu and Liu [11]. In this, they proposed ways to mine product features that expressed opinions from customer reviews. Based on features, they then summarize the customer reviews and determine whether opinions are positive or negative. Another prior work done in this direction by Li and Feng focuses on specific domain movie reviews [23]. They both also show that this task is different from traditional text summarization because the main goal of opinion summarization is to provide a feature-based summary. Opinosis [9] is a graph-based summarization framework generating concise abstractive summaries with highly redundant opinions. Evaluation results show that they agree better with human-generated summaries compared to the other baseline extractive models. As peer review can be very concise and rich in information, micro review-summarization with usual reviews are under 200 characters authors, formulate this as synthesizing a new "review" using snippets of full-text reviews [17]. Due to the lack of datasets with large paired documents and summaries, a recent focus on the unsupervised technique has included an unsupervised abstractive auto-encoder model for multi-document summarization over the documents that are only product and business reviews without example summaries given. Through human evaluation and automatic metrics, the author also shows that summaries are highly abstractive and fluent [4]. A generative model [3] is an extension of a vanilla text-variational auto encoder for end-to-end unsupervised abstractive summarization. The model is designed on the intuition that when generating a review for the product relying on the set of another review "amount of novelty" going into a new review can be controlled. At test time, it is forced to be minimal. Review summarization models discussed so far summarize mainly based on review content and neglect the author's attributes (e.g., gender, age, and occupation). So authors propose an attribute-aware sequence network that mainly uses attributes-specific vocabulary and uses four attribute-based strategies to build attribute aware encoder and summarise decoder [12].

## 3  Dataset Description

Peer reviews are hindered by confidentiality and proprietary metadata. However, a few venues have started publicizing peer review data, such as The International Conference on Learning Representations (ICLR). Such initiatives facilitate transparency and trust in the system and give rise to a recent interest in peer review studies.

**Data Collection:** We collect the required peer review data (reviews, meta-reviews, recommendations, and confidence score) from the OpenReview[2] platform along with the decision of acceptance/rejection in the top-tier ML conference ICLR for the years 2018, 2019, 2020, and 2021. After pre-processing and eliminating some unusable reviews/meta-reviews, we arrive at a total of 7,072 instances for our experiments. We use 15% of the data as the test set (1060), 75% as the training set (5304), and the remaining 10% as the validation set (708). A meta-review should contain key/deciding features along with the final decision. We remove the paper if the meta-review or reviews word token size is less than 10. We provide the total number of reviews, meta-reviews, and their length in terms of words in Table 1. The ground truth and generated meta-reviews statistics are shown in Table 2.

---

[2] https://openreview.net/.

**Table 1.** Statistics of the reviews and meta-review in our dataset across the year (2018 to 2021). Each value in the row corresponds to statistics for review/meta-review.

| Year | # Data | Max Length | Min Length | Avg Length |
|------|--------|------------|------------|------------|
| **ICLR 2018** | 2802/934 | 2557/458 | 23/11 | ~372.73/99.03 |
| **ICLR 2019** | 4239/1413 | 4540/839 | 14/10 | ~403.32/138.69 |
| **ICLR 2020** | 6390/2130 | 3970/810 | 15/11 | ~408.55/125.63 |
| **ICLR 2021** | 7785/2595 | 4110/1102 | 14/13 | ~455.65/177.45 |

**Table 2.** Details of ground truth and generated meta reviews.

| Data | # Data | Max Length | Min Length | Avg Length |
|------|--------|------------|------------|------------|
| Meta-review | 5304 | 1102 | 10 | 143.743 |
| Bert-extractive-summarizer | 5304 | 1647 | 70 | 313.672 |
| TEXTRANK | 5304 | 564 | 153 | 300.010 |
| SUPERT | 5304 | 330 | 79 | 119.001 |
| Pegasus | 708 | 243 | 17 | 61.374 |

# 4    Meta-Review Generation: A Text Summarization Struggle

For this task, we experiment with a model based on TextRank [14] and three state-of-the-art summarization models: SUPERT [10], PEGASUS [20], BART-based text summarization [15]. Further details on the hyperparameters are available in the our git repository.

## 4.1    Summarization Approaches

We experiment with the following supervised and unsupervised techniques for extractive and abstractive text summarization. We evaluate the performance of these techniques to generate a meta-review from the three official peer-reviews for each paper.

**SUPERT:** SUPERT [10] is an unsupervised multi-document summarization method using reinforcement learning, which requires neither human-written reference summaries nor human annotations. SUPERT rates the quality of a summary by measuring its semantic similarity with a pseudo reference summary, i.e. selected salient sentences from the source documents, using contextualized embeddings and soft token alignment techniques. Then SUPERT is used as a reward function to guide reinforcement learning based extractive summarizers.

**PEGASUS:** PEGASUS [20] is an abstractive method which uses self-supervised objective Gap Sentences Generation (GSG) to train a transformer-based encoder-decoder model. In PEGASUS, important sentences are removed/masked from an input document and are generated together as one output sequence from the remaining sentences, similar to an extractive summary. We fine-tune the pre-trained PEGASUS model on our peer review dataset.

**Bert-Extractive-Summarizer:** Bert-extractive-summarizer [15] is an extractive summarization technique built on top of BERT [8] language-representation model for text embeddings and uses K-Means clustering to identify sentences closest to the centroid for summary selection.

**TEXTRANK:** Textrank [14] is an extractive unsupervised summarizaton technique which uses a graph based ranking model to assign importance to each vertex which can build up the summary using "voting" or "recommendation".

## 4.2 Evaluation Metrics

The results of our analysis are analyzed quantitatively and qualitatively, and we conclude that quantitative text summarization metrics are unsuitable for evaluating the generated meta-reviews.

**Quantitative Analysis:** To evaluate the model generated meta-reviews, we use some popular automatic evaluation metrics applied to evaluate both text generation and summarization. We use multiple metrics ROUGE [13], S3 [19], BertScore [21], MoverScore [22], BLEU [18], METEOR [1], Sentence Mover's Similarity [5] since a single metric does not give the best evaluation for a generated summary.

**ROUGE:** [13] Widely adopted summarization metrics, Recall-Oriented Understudy for Gisting Evaluation, calculates n-gram recall (overlap) between the candidate and reference summary, while abstractive methods show less correlation with human scores in comparison to the extractive method. The intuition behind using ROUGE-2 and ROUGE-3 is to have more consecutive ordering which gives more information about fluency.

**BERTScore:** [21] Given candidate and reference sentences each token is represented by contextual embeddings and calculates matching using cosine similarity. BERTScore computes recall score by matching token in reference sentence x to token in candidate sentence $\hat{x}$ and precision vice-versa, F1 score is calculated by combining precision and recall. It also uses a greedy approach to match each token to the most similar token in the other sentence to maximize the similarity score.

**S3:** [19] This metrics create a regression model trained on human judgment datasets from TAC conferences, that uses existing automatic metric as features such as ROUGE, JS-divergence, and ROUGE-WE and predict the score. The model learns the combination exhibiting the best correlation with human judgments. Pyramid [16] measures how many important semantic content units in the reference summaries are covered by the system summary, while Responsiveness measures how well a summary responds to the overall quality combining both content and linguistic quality.

**BLEU:** [18] Stands for Bilingual Evaluation Understudy is precision-oriented metrics that calculate n-gram overlap between candidate and reference summary. Uses brevity penalty to penalize score wrt length of candidate summary.

**METEOR:** [1] The score is computed by aligning candidate and reference summary sentences such that every unigram in the generated summary maps to zero or one unigram in the reference summary. Unigrams can be matched based on exact, stem, synonym. Unlike BLEU which does not take recall into account directly, Meteor uses precision and recall reported as harmonic mean. METEOR 1.5 [7] weighs content and function words differently and also applies importance weighting to different matching types, phrases.

**MoverScore:** [22] Moverscore is a set-based similarity metric to measure the semantic distance between two sequences of n-gram words in candidate text to reference text. Uses contextual embeddings to encode each word of sentences (e.g. ELMO, BERT) and calculates Euclidean Distance Metric, flow transportation metric and sum up as transportation cost when moving embeddings from one set to other. The intuition of flow transportation metric is the effect of n-gram like those including function word (functors) can be downplayed by giving them lower weights e.g. using Inverse Document Frequency (IDF).

**Sentence Mover's Similarity:** [19] Extends word mover's distance to view documents as a bag of sentence embeddings to measure similarity, and to get sentence representation based on averaging or pooling word embeddings, they used the average of their word embeddings as they outperformed pooling. Word mover distance is transformed into similarity by taking negative exponent to match it in between 0 to 1. Based on their nature of usage, we can say ROUGE, S3, BLEU, METEOR are metrics which operate at the lexical level whereas BERTScore, MoverScore, SMS are intended for semantic evaluation.

Table 4 shows that Burt-extractive-summarizer and Textrank perform comparatively better in terms of ROUGE. ROUGE is based on $n$-gram similarity, and both Bert-extractive-summarizer and TextRank are extractive. The same goes for S3 and METEOR. Pegasus generated summaries do not perform well for either metric because they are small in length and do not exhibit good lexical overlap (abstracts). In the case of BLEU, SUPERT does better. However, as we can see, no one technique does justice to the given task and cannot serve as a baseline.

**Qualitative Analysis:** Table 4 shows an output of the four different techniques on a given paper review. Please note while SUPERT (reinforcement learning), TextRank (unsupervised) and Bert-extractive-summarizer (supervised) are extractive, PEGASUS (supervised) is abstractive. Please find the official reviews to this instance here[3].

The reinforcement learning-based technique SUPERT generated summary is extractive and not detailed. It lacked in-general meta-reviewing characteristics.

---

[3] https://openreview.net/forum?id=H1eH4n09KX.

**Table 3.** Automatically generated meta-review for a given paper

| Original Meta-Review |
| --- |
| *The paper presents an algorithm for audio super-resolution using adversarial models along with additional losses, e.g. using auto-encoders and reconstruction losses, to improve the generation process. Strengths- Proposes audio super resolution based on GANs, extending some of the techniques proposed for vision / image to audio. - The authors improved the paper during the review process by including results from a user study and ablation analysis. Weaknesses - Although the paper presents an interesting application of GANs for the audio task, overall novelty is limited since the setup closely follows what has been done for vision and related tasks, and the baseline system. This is also not the first application of GANs for audio tasks. - Performance improvement over previously proposed (U-Net) models is small. It would have been useful to also include UNet4 in user-study, as one of the reviewers' pointed out, since it sounds better in a few cases. - It is not entirely clear if the method would be an improvement of state-of-the-art audio generative models like Wavenet. Reviewers agree that the general direction of this work is interesting, but the results are not compelling enough at the moment for the paper to be accepted to ICLR. Given these review comments, the recommendation is to reject the paper.* |

| SUPERT generated meta-review |
| --- |
| *PRO's: +well-written +nice overall system: GAN framework for super-sampling audio incorporating features from an autoencoder +some good-sounding examples CON' s : some confusing/weakly-presented parts (admittedly covering lots of material in short space) -I am confused about the evaluation; would like additional qualitative/observational understanding of what works, including more on how the results differ from baseline SUMMARY : The task addressed in this work is : given a low-resolution audio signal, generate corresponding high-quality audio. This paper presents a GAN-based method to perform audio super-resolution. Fascinating problem & fair results. Ok but not good enough- rejection.* |

| Bert-extractive-summarizer |
| --- |
| *nice work, confused about evaluation-related aspects. Marginally above acceptance threshold. The training framework is basically that of a GAN, but where, rather than providing the generator with a low-dimensional noise signal input, they provide the generator with the subsampled audio signal. This is overall a nice problem and a nice approach! That said, I understand that there are page/space limitations. (more on this next) It's possible that there is something simple about it that I am not understanding. I'm open to being convinced. Otherwise, why not just write: or something along those lines, and leave it at that? Is this a result of careful selection of examples? I do believe what I hear, e.g. that the MU-GAN8 is clearly better on some examples than the U-net8. I guess I would like to get a better understanding of what is actually going on, even if qualitative. Is there any qualitative or anecdotal observation about which "types" of samples one system works better on than another? maybe I'm overgeneralizing from the few examples I heard. For example, are there visible but inaudible artifacts? A couple of typos: descriminator last sentence of 2nd par is actually not a sentence. "the reduction in convolutional kernels prior to the superpixel operation. something)– I would gladly consider revising my rating (which is currently somewhere between 6 and 7). . The reviewer is confident but not absolutely certain that the evaluation is correctOfficial review. From a technical perspective, I do not find the proposed approach very novel. This would be a good point for the paper. While this is an audio processing paper, it lacks domain insights (even the terminology feels borrowed from the image domain). Would a WaveNet decoder also be improved by including these auxiliary losses? The authors mention that not including it leads to audible artifacts. A van den Oord, Aaron, and Oriol Vinyals. Any nontrivial insight would be highly appreciated. Interesting idea and fascinating problem. The results are fair.* |

| PEGASUS |
| --- |
| *ICLR 2018 Conference Acceptance Decision. Pros: + well-written +nice overall system: GAN framework for super-sampling audio incorporating features from an autoencoder +some good- sounding examples Cons: - I am confused about the evaluation; would like additional qualitative/observational understanding of what works, including more on how the results differ from baseline . Accept (Poster)* |

| TEXTRANK |
| --- |
| *In this work, the authors avoid this auxiliary challenge by using unsupervised feature losses, taking advantage of the fact that any audio signal can be downsampled, and therefore one has the corresponding upsampled signal as well. In contrast to previous work, this work uses auto-encoder to obtain feature losses derived from unlabeled data. Would there be any info for the reader by doing an ablation removing the feature loss from the GAN framework? I think that more studies should be presented (including quantitative evaluations and audio samples). Working in raw sample-space (e.g. pixels) is known to be challenging, so a stabilizing solution is to incorporate a feature loss. GAN framework for super-sampling audio incorporating features from an autoencoder +some good-sounding examples CON. The paper presents a model to perform audio super resolution.. While the audio samples seem to be good, they are also a bit noisy even compared with the baseline.. My biggest confusion was with the evaluation & results: Since the most directly related work was (Kuleshov 2017), I compared the super resolution (U-net) samples on that website (https://kuleshov.github.io/audio-super-res/ ) to the samples provided for the present work ( https://sites.google.com/view/unsupervised-audiosr/home ). This paper presents a GAN-based method to perform audio super-resolution* |

The generated review highlights the merits and demerits of the paper with a short summary, and the decision of the human meta-reviewer is preserved.

We find that although PEGASUS generated meta-review manifests sentences with polarity, the output is not detailed. The significant aspects of concern in the human-generated review are not visible in the generated meta-review. The overall polarity and decision don't match with the original meta-review.

Bert-extractive-summarizer type extractive approach is not suitable for this task since a meta-review is written by another person in coherence with the existing peer reviews; it is not a combination of sentences from peer reviews. Secondly, a meta-review enforces the acceptance or rejection of a paper, which cannot be directly extracted as a combination of sentences from peer reviews.

Textrank outputs more details and extracts possibly the most important parts from the reviews; however, a meta-review is not a mere collection of critical reviewer comments. A meta-review is also a coherent text generated by the editor while considering the reviewer's judgment and consensus. Quite expected that the output from all these techniques does not appear that the meta-review is written by another person based on the original peer reviews. Hence fine-tuning on actual meta-reviews is required for such a system. Table 3 shows the automatically generated meta-reviews by Bert-extractive summarizer, Pegasus, SUPERT, and Textrank.

**Table 4.** Model scores for automatic evaluation metrics. The highest score of each metrics are in **Bold**. The output is the average of all the scores in the test set used for PEGASUS.

| Model | Bert-Extractive-Summ | TEXTRANK | SUPERT | Pegasus |
|---|---|---|---|---|
| ROUGE-1 | **0.49584** | 0.47599 | 0.31392 | 0.18842 |
| ROUGE-2 | 0.09987 | **0.10891** | 0.06159 | 0.03775 |
| ROUGE-3 | 0.02366 | **0.0336** | 0.01835 | 0.00812 |
| S3(pyr/resp) | **0.3977/0.4617** | 0.3894/0.4607 | 0.2170/0.3707 | 0.1046/0.3135 |
| BertScore(f1) | 0.5470 | **0.5508** | 0.5396 | 0.5350 |
| MoverScore | 0.0980 | 0.0927 | **0.1130** | 0.0783 |
| METEOR | **0.1633** | 0.1585 | 0.1100 | 0.0751 |
| BLEU | 2.3702 | 3.1684 | **3.5366** | 2.1358 |
| SMS | 0.08049 | **0.09911** | 0.09061 | 0.07464 |

## 5  How Sentiment Plays a Part?

With conferences and journals requesting reviewers to take a stand on the paper, it becomes important that the review bears certain polarity reflecting the overall attitude of the reviewer. This becomes even more important for the meta-reviews. We hypothesize three important characteristics that a generative model should manifest:

(a) *Sentiment Transfer*: Sentiment should be transferred from the peer reviews to the meta-review, i.e. the polarity of the meta-review should co-relate with the dominant sentiment from the peer reviews.

(b) *Sentiment Preservation*: While evaluating the performance of such a generative system, the sentiment of the generated meta-review should co-relate to the sentiment of the actual meta-review written by the editor.

(c) *Sentiment Polarity*: The meta-review should be decisive and indicate the acceptance or rejection of the paper. To evaluate sentiment empirically, we use generating reviews and Discovering Sentiment tool by OpenAI and extract out the sentiment scores for the peer reviews, actual meta-review and the generated meta-reviews. We calculate the average sentiment of the peer reviews and compare it with the sentiment score of meta-review. Our findings Table 5 suggest that the automatic methods lacked sentiment transfer and sentiment preservation. Most of the generated meta-reviews lacked in sentiment polarity. Though the extractive methods preserved the aspects, they were not able to transfer or preserve the sentiment. The mean polarity suggests that the automatically generated reviews do not manifest decisiveness which is an important characteristic of meta-reviews. Since a meta-review would ideally consist of a summary of peer reviews, and recommendation for acceptance and rejection[4], both of these are to be generated jointly; with one part of the model generating the aspect and sentiment preserved summary of the peer reviews, while the other part predicting the acceptance or rejection decision to maintain the polarity of the meta-review.

**Table 5.** Root Mean Square Deviation from sentiment of peer reviews (sentiment transfer) to meta-reviews, and sentiment of original meta-review to automatically generated meta-review (sentiment preservation). Mean polarity refers to the mean of absolute values of sentiment scores to show the polarity.

| Model | Transfer | Preservation | Mean Polarity |
|---|---|---|---|
| Bert-extractive-summarizer | 0.242 | 0.342 | 0.386 |
| Pegasus | 0.323 | 0.374 | 0.316 |
| SUPERT | 0.369 | 0.437 | 0.315 |
| Textrank | 0.304 | 0.401 | 0.264 |

## 6    How Aspect Plays a Part?

Here we investigate if the paper aspects highlighted in the meta-review are preserved in the automatically generated meta-reviews. We undertake manual annotation of 1300 peer reviews for two tasks: Section Identification (to which section of the paper does the review sentence correspond?) and Aspect Identification

---

[4] https://iclr.cc/Conferences/2020/MetareviewGuide.

(which aspect of the paper is highlighted in the given review sentence). We train a BERT-based Sequential Sentence Classification model [6] on the above data for the two tasks. The categories for Task 1 are

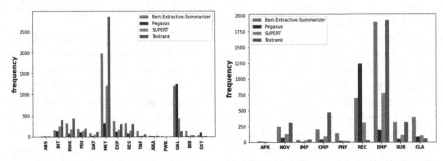

(a) Aspect identification labels distributions in the meta-review.

(b) Aspect identification labels distributions in the meta-review

**Fig. 1.** Section and aspect identification labels distributions in the automatically generated meta-reviews by Bert-extractive summarizer, Pegasus, SUPERT, and Textrank

**Task1:** [(ABS) Abstract, (INT) Introduction, (RWK) Related Works, (PDI) Problem Definition/Idea, (DAT) Datasets, (MET) Methodology, (EXP) Experiments, (RES) Results, (TNF) Tables & Figures, (ANA) Analysis, (FWK) Future Work, (OAL) Overall, (BIB) Bibliography, (EXT) External] while for **Task2:** [(APR) Appropriateness, (NOV) Originality/Novelty, (IMP) Significance/Impact, (CMP) Meaningful Comparison, (PNF) Presentation & Formatting, (REC) Recommendation, (EMP) Empirical/Theoretical Soundness, (SUB) Substance, (CLA) Clarity].

Figure 1 shows section and aspect labels distributions in the automatically generated meta-reviews by Bert-extractive summarizer, Pegasus, SUPERT, and Textrank. We predict the labels for Task 1 and Task 2 in both the human-generated meta-review and the automatically generated meta-review to calculate the overlap, signifying the degree of aspect preservation in Table 6. It shows Bert-extractive-summarizer much better than the others in terms of section and aspect identification coverage in the automatically generated meta-reviews. Because Bert-extractive-summarizer summaries are more extended, the model extracted basic sentences from the original reviews that could appear in the meta-review.

**Table 6.** Section (Task1) and Aspect (Task2) - overlap ratio for actual and generated meta-reviews

| Model | Task1 | Task2 |
|---|---|---|
| Bert-extractive-summarizer | **0.760** | **0.840** |
| Pegasus | 0.473 | 0.484 |
| SUPERT | 0.511 | 0.520 |
| Textrank | 0.458 | 0.487 |

## 7  Observation

We arrive at the following observations:

(1) Current *state-of-the-art* summarization techniques do not suffice the meta-review generation task.
(2) A meta-review generation system would need to manifest sentiment-aware aspect-based summarization from the reviews as well as conclude with the consensus polarity of the peer reviews to arrive at a decision.
(3) A supervised approach fine-tuned on the peer-reviews and corresponding meta-reviews (reference summary) could be an interesting direction to probe with considerations in (2).

## 8  Conclusion

Here in this work, we study a novel task of *meta-review generation*. We investigate different summarization techniques and their performance on the given task and also explore the differences of a meta-review from a simple summary. Finally, we arrive at some interesting observations and directions for the community to explore automatic approaches to generate a meta-review from the peer reviews. Our next step would be to investigate appropriate metrics for *meta-review generation* evaluation.

**Acknowledgement.** Prabhat Kumar Bharti acknowledges a fellowship grant from Quality Improvement Programme initiated by the All India Council for Technical Education (AICTE), Government of India. Asif Ekbal, the fourth author, has received the Visvesvaraya Young Faculty Award. The author acknowledges and thanks to Digital India Corporation, Ministry of Electronics and Information Technology, Government of India. Tirthankar Ghosal acknowledges and extends his thanks to Cactus Communications, India for funding him.

# References

1. Banerjee, S., Lavie, A.: METEOR: an automatic metric for MT evaluation with improved correlation with human judgments. In: Proceedings of the ACL Workshop on Intrinsic and Extrinsic Evaluation Measures for Machine Translation and/or Summarization, pp. 65–72. Association for Computational Linguistics, Ann Arbor, Michigan, June 2005. https://www.aclweb.org/anthology/W05-0909
2. Bhatia, C., Pradhan, T., Pal, S.: MetaGen: an academic meta-review generation system. In: Proceedings of the 43rd International ACM SIGIR Conference on Research and Development in Information Retrieval, pp. 1653–1656 (2020)
3. Bražinskas, A., Lapata, M., Titov, I.: Unsupervised opinion summarization as copycat-review generation. arXiv preprint arXiv:1911.02247 (2019)
4. Chu, E., Liu, P.: MeanSum: a neural model for unsupervised multi-document abstractive summarization. In: International Conference on Machine Learning, pp. 1223–1232. PMLR (2019)
5. Clark, E., Celikyilmaz, A., Smith, N.A.: Sentence mover's similarity: automatic evaluation for multi-sentence texts. In: Proceedings of the 57th Annual Meeting of the Association for Computational Linguistics, pp. 2748–2760. Association for Computational Linguistics, Florence, Italy, July 2019. https://doi.org/10.18653/v1/P19-1264, https://www.aclweb.org/anthology/P19-1264
6. Cohan, A., Beltagy, I., King, D., Dalvi, B., Weld, D.S.: Pretrained language models for sequential sentence classification. arXiv preprint arXiv:1909.04054 (2019)
7. Denkowski, M., Lavie, A.: Meteor universal: language specific translation evaluation for any target language. In: Proceedings of the Ninth Workshop on Statistical Machine Translation, pp. 376–380 (2014)
8. Devlin, J., Chang, M.W., Lee, K., Toutanova, K.: BERT: pre-training of deep bidirectional transformers for language understanding. In: Proceedings of the 2019 Conference of the North American Chapter of the Association for Computational Linguistics: Human Language Technologies, vol. 1 (Long and Short Papers), pp. 4171–4186. Association for Computational Linguistics, Minneapolis, Minnesota, June 2019. https://doi.org/10.18653/v1/N19-1423.https://www.aclweb.org/anthology/N19-1423
9. Ganesan, K., Zhai, C., Han, J.: Opinosis: a graph based approach to abstractive summarization of highly redundant opinions (2010)
10. Gao, Y., Zhao, W., Eger, S.: SUPERT: towards new frontiers in unsupervised evaluation metrics for multi-document summarization. In: Proceedings of the 58th Annual Meeting of the Association for Computational Linguistics, pp. 1347–1354. Association for Computational Linguistics, Online, July 2020. https://doi.org/10.18653/v1/2020.acl-main.124,https://www.aclweb.org/anthology/2020.acl-main.124
11. Hu, M., Liu, B.: Mining and summarizing customer reviews. In: Proceedings of the Tenth ACM SIGKDD International Conference on Knowledge Discovery and Data Mining, pp. 168–177 (2004)
12. Li, J., Wang, X., Yin, D., Zong, C.: Attribute-aware sequence network for review summarization. In: Proceedings of the 2019 Conference on Empirical Methods in Natural Language Processing and the 9th International Joint Conference on Natural Language Processing (EMNLP-IJCNLP), pp. 3000–3010 (2019)
13. Lin, C.Y.: ROUGE: a package for automatic evaluation of summaries. In: Text Summarization Branches Out, pp. 74–81. Association for Computational Linguistics, Barcelona, Spain, July 2004. https://www.aclweb.org/anthology/W04-1013

14. Mihalcea, R., Tarau, P.: TextRank: bringing order into text. In: Proceedings of the 2004 Conference on Empirical Methods in Natural Language Processing, pp. 404–411 (2004)
15. Miller, D.: Leveraging BERT for extractive text summarization on lectures (2019)
16. Nenkova, A., Passonneau, R., McKeown, K.: The pyramid method: incorporating human content selection variation in summarization evaluation. ACM Trans. Speech Lang. Process. (TSLP) 4(2), 4-es (2007)
17. Nguyen, T.S., Lauw, H.W., Tsaparas, P.: Review synthesis for micro-review summarization. In: Proceedings of the Eighth ACM International Conference on Web Search and Data Mining, pp. 169–178 (2015)
18. Papineni, K., Roukos, S., Ward, T., Zhu, W.J.: BLEU: a method for automatic evaluation of machine translation, October 2002. https://doi.org/10.3115/1073083.1073135
19. Peyrard, M., Botschen, T., Gurevych, I.: Learning to score system summaries for better content selection evaluation. In: Proceedings of the Workshop on New Frontiers in Summarization, pp. 74–84. Association for Computational Linguistics, Copenhagen, Denmark, September 2017. https://doi.org/10.18653/v1/W17-4510, https://www.aclweb.org/anthology/W17-4510
20. Zhang, J., Zhao, Y., Saleh, M., Liu, P.J.: PEGASUS: pre-training with extracted gap-sentences for abstractive summarization (2020)
21. Zhang, T., Kishore, V., Wu, F., Weinberger, K.Q., Artzi, Y.: BERTScore: evaluating text generation with BERT. CoRR abs/1904.09675 (2019), https://arxiv.org/abs/1904.09675
22. Zhao, W., Peyrard, M., Liu, F., Gao, Y., Meyer, C.M., Eger, S.: MoverScore: text generation evaluating with contextualized embeddings and earth mover distance. CoRR abs/1909.02622 (2019). https://arxiv.org/abs/1909.02622
23. Zhuang, L., Jing, F., Zhu, X.Y.: Movie review mining and summarization. In: Proceedings of the 15th ACM International Conference on Information and Knowledge Management, pp. 43–50 (2006)

# Speech

# Autoblog 2021: The Importance of Language Models for Spontaneous Lecture Speech

Abner Hernandez[1(✉)], Philipp Klumpp[1], Badhan Das[1], Andreas Maier[1], and Seung Hee Yang[2]

[1] Pattern Recognition Laboratory, Friedrich-Alexander Universität Erlangen-Nürnberg, Erlangen, Germany
{abner.hernandez,philipp.klumpp,badhan.das,andreas.maier}@fau.de
[2] Speech and Language Processing Laboratory, Friedrich-Alexander Universität Erlangen-Nürnberg, Erlangen, Germany
seung.hee.yang@fau.de

**Abstract.** The demand for both quantity and quality of online educational resources has skyrocketed during the last two years' pandemic. Entire course series had since been recorded and distributed online. To reach a broader audience, videos could be transcribed, combined with supplementary material (e.g. lecture slides) and published in the style of blog posts. This had been done previously for Autoblog 2020, a corpus of lecture recordings that had been converted to blog posts, using automated speech recognition (ASR) for subtitle creation. This work aims to introduce a second series of recorded and manually transcribed lecture videos. The corresponding data includes lecture videos, slides, and blog posts/transcripts with aligned slide images and is published under creative commons license. A state-of-the-art Wav2Vec ASR model was used for automatic transcription of the content, using different n-gram language models (LM). The results were compared to the human ground truth annotation. Findings indicated that the ASR performed well on spontaneous lecture speech. Furthermore, LMs trained on large amounts of data with fewer out-of-vocabulary words were outperformed by much smaller LMs estimated over in-domain language. Annotated lecture recordings were deemed helpful for the creation of task-specific ASR solutions as well as their validation against a human ground truth.

**Keywords:** Lecture video corpus · Speech recognition · Language model · Spontaneous lecture speech

## 1 Introduction

Teaching routines of educational institutions around the world had been severely impacted by the many restrictions that had been imposed during the early stages

---

A. Hernandez and P. Klumpp—Equal Contribution.

© Springer Nature Switzerland AG 2022
P. Sojka et al. (Eds.): TSD 2022, LNAI 13502, pp. 291–300, 2022.
https://doi.org/10.1007/978-3-031-16270-1_24

of the Covid-19 pandemic. Lectures had to be held online, students exchanged their real classrooms for virtual ones. To maintain an equally high teaching quality compared to on-site classes, supplementary material (on-demand recordings, slides,... ) could help increase the availability of online lecture resources. On the other hand, the creation of additional material often requires human experts to take action, it, therefore, does not scale well and can easily take too much time. Automated solutions could be of significant help, for example, to transcribe entire lecture series, making the content also available for reading. Such an approach had been introduced before with the Autoblog system [6], a sequence of routines to automatically convert lecture videos to blog posts. A more detailed description of Autoblog and the resulting dataset is given in Sect. 2.2.

Transcription of spontaneous speech is rather difficult for an ASR, as systems had commonly been optimized on vast amounts of read speech data. Furthermore, differences between the two types manifest in both the acoustic as well as the LM. This leads to a lower recognition performance on spontaneous speech samples [12]. The challenge of spontaneous speech recognition is further increased by the large amount of variety between speakers, different speaking styles and accents. If ASR is used to transcribe lecture recordings, the domain-specific vocabulary and semantic structures (e. g. spoken mathematical expressions) cause recognition rates to decline further. Lastly, recording conditions could yield challenging audio signals which are affected by reverberation, background noise or poor microphone configuration. Nevertheless, there could also be potential for improving ASR performance for a given setup. If a large number of recordings had to be transcribed for the same lecturer, better results are likely achieved with a system that had been fine-tuned on the particular speaker. Whilst this could be considered a violation of an elementary machine learning principle for speech processing (do not test on speakers seen during training), it could be justified by intentionally tailoring the application to that single speaker. Again, such speaker-adaption could be done on the level of the acoustic or language model.

The current study analyses the importance of LMs in the context of lecture video ASR. Specifically, we evaluate on lecture videos related to biomedical engineering, a growing field of research with a very technical vocabulary. We compare the performance of n-gram LMs built from large text corpora against smaller in-domain and lecture-style LMs. An intrinsic evaluation is conducted by measuring the perplexity of LMs with sentences from lecture transcripts. Furthermore, LMs are used as a decoder for the output of a pretrained Wav2Vec2 model. All data used in this paper will be made open access with the acceptance of the paper.

## 1.1   Related Works

The importance of language modelling in lecture videos is explored in [14] where researchers evaluated the language perplexity of computer sciences (CS) courses. Results showed that models with smaller vocabularies had lower perplexity and that using non-CS lectures along with smaller relevant text yielded lower perplexities. A perplexity of 160 was obtained when building an LM on non-CS lecture text with a CS textbook while building on the Switchboard [2] text and a CS textbook led to a perplexity of 265 (the lower the perplexity the better the LM). Results further indicate that spontaneous speech text generates more accurate transcriptions.

In a similar study with Japanese language lectures [9], researchers compared multiple LMs and their influence on ASR. They found that a smaller LM of 970 lectures and a vocabulary size of 20,000 had a better performance than a model built from 3,285 lectures and a vocabulary size of 20,000. However, this only applies when the content of the lecture is academically similar, otherwise, the model with a larger amount of lectures is better. They also showed that the rather small Corpus of Spontaneous Japanese [10] (CSJ) would produce more suitable LMs compared to two other, much larger corpora. To achieve improved results on lecture speech recognition, unsupervised LM adaption had been employed to perform speaker adaption from initial results yielded by an ASR [13]. Training data for successful LM estimation could also be generated by using the content of corresponding lecture slides, using a web-based resource gathering approach [11].

## 2    Materials and Methods

Bigram LMs are built using the KenLM toolkit [4] with a modified Kneser-Ney smoothing [5]. The data used for building LMs originate from multiple datasets reflecting in-domain, out-of-domain and lecture-style texts. For each LM we evaluate the number of out-of-vocabulary (OOV) words and the perplexity of all sentences in the biomedical engineering lecture transcripts.

For all video lectures, we extract the audio and split it into chunks based on silent segments using a audio detection toolkit[1]. The tool uses a simple energy detection algorithm on audio signals. Chunks contained a minimum of 2 s and maximum of 20 s of audio. A maximum silence duration of 1 s was chosen to split the files. We then run a Wav2vec2 model [1] on each chunk and evaluate the WER output of the model with different bigram LMs. Higher-order LMs made very little difference in improving WER. We utilise two Wav2Vec2 models: a base model pretrained and fine-tuned on 960 h of Librispeech, and a large model pretrained on 960 h of Librispeech along with 60,000 h from Libri-Light [16].

### 2.1    Acoustic Model

The acoustic model is trained by finetuning a Wav2Vec2 model with a Connectionist Temporal Classification (CTC) algorithm. Wav2Vec2.0 is transformer-based model that learns speech representations based on unlabelled data. Similar, to masked language modelling, Wav2Vec2 learns contextualized speech representations by randomly masking feature vectors before passing them to a transformer network. A contrastive loss function is then used to identify the true latent

---

[1] https://github.com/amsehili/auditok/.

speech representation. After training, a linear layer with C classes representing the vocabulary is attached for speech recognition finetuning. Optimization is done by minimizing the CTC loss [3]. For simplification, the CTC algorithm outputs a probability distribution over all possible characters given an acoustic feature vector (our Wav2Vec2 speech representations).

## 2.2  Autoblog Data

The Autoblog 2021 data[2] consists of 25 lectures from the biomedical Engineering course taught in the Summer of 2021 at Friedrich-Alexander Universität Erlangen-Nürnberg. In total, the lectures amount to nearly 10 h of audio, with an average duration of 37 min per lecture. Recording was conducted in a quiet room with an external microphone. The lecturer is a native German speaker and his speech contains German accented English. Some of the main topics covered can be seen in Table 1. The data comprises lecture videos, slides, and corresponding transcripts with aligned slide images as blog posts. The course give a comprehensive overview of different medical imaging modalities that are used in medicine to perform diagnoses. These include Endoscopy, Microscopy, X-Ray, Computed Tomography, Optical Coherence Tomography, Ultrasound, MRI, and PET/SPECT. The lectures provides an in-depth analysis of the different properties and sensitivities of all these modalities. It describes system theory, Fourier Transform, convolution, and sampling theorem to understand the trade-offs between spatial resolution and sensitivity. It also focuses on 2-D and 3-D image processing, non-linear filters, and non-linear image processing techniques. An LM generated by lectures transcripts from previous semesters is also built. This includes the 43 (11.4 h) pattern recognition lectures from an early version of the Autoblog corpus [6].

**Table 1.** AutoBlog 2021 biomedical engineering lecture topics.

| Lecture Topics | |
| --- | --- |
| Endoscopy | Microscopy |
| Magnetic Resonance Imaging | X-Ray |
| Computed Tomography | Emission Tomography |
| Phase Contrast Imaging | Ultrasound |
| Optical Coherence Tomography | System Theory |

## 2.3  Language Modelling

Without an LM, the Wav2Vec2 trained acoustic model still achieves state-of-the-art results as it makes use of the CTC algorithm for solving the problem of aligning varying audio lengths to output text length. In [16], a Wav2Vec2 model

---

[2] https://www.kaggle.com/datasets/abnerh/autoblog

acheived a WER of 1.9% without an LM on the LibriSpeech test-set. However, an LM can still be used to support the acoustic model output by predicting the next word given all previously transcribed words [8]. Specifically, the LM is a probabilistic model that can be defined as: $P(\mathrm{w}_n|\mathrm{w}_0^{t-1})$, where $\mathrm{w}_0^{t-1}$ refers to the sequence of all previous words in an utterance and $\mathrm{w}_n$ is the following word.

There are two main approaches to evaluating the quality of LM. First, we can evaluate the model extrinsically which measures how well the LM performs on real-world tasks. In our case, this is measured by the improvement of WER in an ASR system. Second, we can take an intrinsic evaluation of the model which purely considers the LM itself. Perplexity is a common metric for evaluating LMs and measures how well our probabilistic model predicts a sample. Perplexity can also be defined as the exponential of the cross-entropy as in Eq. 1 where $H(W)$ refers to the average number of bits needed to encode each word. Perplexity $2^H(W)$ is then the average number of words that can be encoded using $H(W)$ bits.

$$PP(W) = 2^{H(W)} = 2^{-\frac{1}{N}log_2 P(w_1, w_2, ..., w_N)} \tag{1}$$

Perplexity can also be simplified as the normalised inverse probability of the test set as in Eq. 2. In both cases, we want to lower the entropy and perplexity of the LM given a well-formed sentence.

$$PP(W) = n\sqrt{\frac{1}{P(w_1, w_2, ...w_N)}} \tag{2}$$

## 2.4  Datasets

**Out-of-Domain.** As seen in Table 2 the text used for building LMs range from large general datasets such as LibriSpeech to small in-domain datasets like Auto-Blog. The LibriSpeech LM is built on cleaned text from 14,500 public domain books. A second out of domain corpus is used by combining the monolingual used for the Workshop on Machine Translation (WMT). This corpus contains text from news articles, European parliament speeches, and text from Common Crawl [15]. The transcripts from the training set of TED-LIUM 3 [7] based on 2,351 TED talks are used to build a lecture-style LM. While this model is out-of-domain, it reflects a speaking style more similar to the lecture videos in the Autoblog dataset.

**In-Domain.** The Biomedical text (BMT) comes from datasets used in the 2021 EMNLP (Conference on Empirical Methods in Natural Language Processing) Biomedical Translation Task [17]. The datasets consist of titles and abstracts from Medline, SciELO, and EDP scientific publication databases[3]. While this represents in-domain information regarding medical terminology, these texts are based on formal journal-style language. The YouTube corpus consists of transcripts from math and computer science-related lectures. The information presented in these lectures is similar to the ones in the Medical Engineering dataset

---

[3] https://github.com/biomedical-translation-corpora/corpora.

and also represents lecture-style speech. Lastly, we build an LM on the transcripts of previous lectures in the AutoBlog corpus [6]. Specifically transcripts from Deep Learning, Pattern Recognition and Speech and Language Understanding courses. This model represent both domain-related information and speaker-dependent text as all lectures were given by the same professor.

# 3   Results

## 3.1   Intrinsic Language Model Evaluation

Perplexity and OOV for each LM is calculated on the full medical engineering lecture transcripts see Table 3. Perplexity is evaluated on all transcripts then normalized by length in words. The librispeech LM has a high perplexity of 595 but only 328 OOV words. This is in contrast to the AutoBlog LM which has 1,554 OOV words but a low perplexity of 138. We can balance the OOV and perplexity trade-off by combining datasets. When combining the YouTube, BMT and Ted3 datasets, we can decrease the OOV and perplexity to 205, and 182 respectively. Typically, the lower the perplexity, the better the language model,

**Table 2.** Language model information.

| Data | Number of Sentences | Vocab Size | LM Size |
|---|---|---|---|
| LibriSpeech | 40.4M | 9M | 1.1Gb |
| WMT | 12.8M | 3.8M | 498Mb |
| Tedlium3 | 254K | 200K | 24Mb |
| BMT | 325K | 247K | 34Mb |
| YouTube | 306K | 120K | 14Mb |
| AutoBlog | 15K | 16K | 1.7Mb |

**Table 3.** Intrinsic LM evaluation. Lower perplexity refers to a better language model.

| Language Model | OOV | Perplexity |
|---|---|---|
| LibriSpeech | 328 | 595 |
| WMT | 218 | 319 |
| Tedlium3 | 467 | 240 |
| BMT | 539 | 964 |
| YouTube | 778 | 213 |
| AutoBlog | 1,554 | **138** |
| Ted3+BMT | 261 | 247 |
| Ted3+YT | 330 | 181 |
| YT+BMT | 292 | 199 |
| YT+BMT+Ted3 | 205 | 182 |

but results from the extrinsic evaluation show that with enough in-domain and spontaneous lecture material, even a model with high perplexity can outperform a model with lower perplexity.

## 3.2 Extrinsic Language Model Evaluation

The results presented in Table 4 show the WERs when averaging across all 25 videos. As expected, in all cases an LM helps lower the WER but to varying degrees. Without an LM, the large Wav2Vec2 model can achieve a WER of 12.73%. The LMs built with out-of-domain text lowered the WER up to 1.25% for the large model and up to 4.08% with the base model. In both cases, the LM trained on the Tedlium3 text lead to the best results while the LM trained on LibriSpeech text led to the highest WER. Improvements are also seen with LMs trained on in-domain text and lecture-style text. In the base-model case, the Tedlium3 LM had the most impact on lowering WER followed by the AutoBlog, YouTube and BMT models respectively. In the large-model case, the AutoBlog model lowered the WER the most, followed by Tedlium3, BMT and YouTube models.

Figure 1 illustrates WER results observed for various fusions of training data. For easier comparison, the first set of bars represents the result of an LM estimated over the large LibriSpeech corpus. Any fusion of in-domain datasets leads to a further improvement of WER compared to the stand-alone results. Note that the AutoBlog dataset, which had been recorded from the same speaker as the one for AutoBlog 2021, had not been included in the combinations, as the intention was to purely observe the importance of domain on language modelling.

Table 5 summarizes the findings of the last experiment of combining in-domain and speaker-related language information. The table shows that a careful selection of domain-related data could outperform the speaker-adapted LM. A further speaker-adaption of already in-domain LMs would then improve the results even further, but these changes were found to be rather small.

**Table 4.** Word-error-rate results of Medical Engineering lectures with different language models.

| Language Model | Base-Model WER (%) | Large-Model WER (%) |
|:---:|:---:|:---:|
| No LM | 20.88 | 12.73 |
| LibriSpeech | 18.31 | 12.70 |
| WMT | 17.75 | 12.06 |
| Tedlium3 | 16.80 | 11.48 |
| BMT | 17.75 | 11.87 |
| YouTube | 16.82 | 11.68 |
| AutoBlog | 16.71 | 11.18 |

**Table 5.** WER results when combining in-domain and speaker-dependent autoblog texts.

| Language Model | Base-Model WER (%) | Large-Model WER (%) |
|---|---|---|
| Only Autoblog | 16.71 | 11.18 |
| Only Domain (YT&BMT) | 16.40 | 10.97 |
| Autoblog-25% & Domain | 16.29 | 10.92 |
| Autoblog-50% & Domain | 16.25 | 10.88 |
| Autoblog-75% & Domain | 16.21 | 10.85 |
| Autoblog-full & Domain | 16.20 | 10.85 |

## 4   Discussion

LMs are commonly estimated over a large amount of data to achieve decent generalization. Per definition, LMs model transitions between words on a statistical level and thus have to be shown *representative* data during training. The presented results clearly show the weaknesses of corpora like LibriSpeech when it comes to spontaneous speech. Whilst they are often quite large, and ultimately allow the LM to explore vast amounts of written (and read) language, they are limited to this semantic structure. Countless studies have already investigated the many differences between spontaneous and read speech. Consequently, a language model should ideally be estimated over data that is related to the final domain of application.

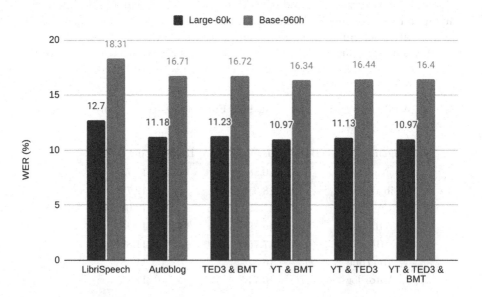

**Fig. 1.** WER results when combining in-domain and lecture style texts.

In our case, even small amounts of transcripts from spontaneous speech were sufficient to produce LMs superior to that from LibriSpeech. The observed improvements were even approaching the speaker-adapted LM. After fusing multiple domain-related datasets to increase the amount of data used for LM computation, the speaker model was outperformed. Despite all these fused models having a higher perplexity score, they still led to lower WERs in comparison to the speaker-adapted LM. This leads to the conclusion that domain information was of greater importance than speaker information for language modelling. At the same time, this could be different for another lecturer that employed a very unique language style.

## 5   Conclusion

The current study explores the importance of LMs for spontaneous lecture-style ASR. While recent state-of-the-art ASR systems perform well without LMs, spontaneous lectures still benefit from well-built LMs. Results from our experiments show that even with high OOV words, LMs built from lecture-style text outperform large models with few OOV words. Furthermore, an LM with high perplexity can still be useful as exemplified by the BMT LM which had a high perplexity of 1,624 but still reduced the WER of our base model. However, spontaneous lecture-style text is more important than in-domain text. Despite a smaller amount of OOV words in the BMT LM (539) compared to the YouTube (778) or Autoblog (1,554) LMs, higher WER improvement was seen in the lecture-style LMs. In the future, we would like to explore larger lecture-style corpora such as those available from online courses in Coursera, Udemy and others. The corpus data used for this study will be published with the acceptance of this paper.

## References

1. Baevski, A., Zhou, Y., Mohamed, A., Auli, M.: wav2vec 2.0: a framework for self-supervised learning of speech representations. Adv. Neural Inf. Process. Syst. **33**, 12449–12460 (2020)
2. Godfrey, J.J., Holliman, E.C., McDaniel, J.: Switchboard: telephone speech corpus for research and development. In: IEEE International Conference on Acoustics, Speech, and Signal Processing, vol. 1, pp. 517–520. IEEE Computer Society (1992)
3. Graves, A., Fernández, S., Gomez, F., Schmidhuber, J.: Connectionist temporal classification: labelling unsegmented sequence data with recurrent neural networks. In: Proceedings of the 23rd International Conference on Machine Learning, pp. 369–376 (2006)
4. Heafield, K.: KenLM: faster and smaller language model queries. In: Proceedings of the Sixth Workshop on Statistical Machine Translation, pp. 187–197. Association for Computational Linguistics, Edinburgh, Scotland, July 2011
5. Heafield, K., Pouzyrevsky, I., Clark, J.H., Koehn, P.: Scalable modified Kneser-Ney language model estimation. In: Proceedings of the 51st Annual Meeting of the Association for Computational Linguistics, vol. 2: Short Papers, pp. 690–696 (2013)

6. Hernandez, A., Yang, S.H.: Multimodal corpus analysis of Autoblog 2020: lecture videos in machine learning. In: Karpov, A., Potapova, R. (eds.) SPECOM 2021. LNCS (LNAI), vol. 12997, pp. 262–270. Springer, Cham (2021). https://doi.org/10.1007/978-3-030-87802-3_24

7. Hernandez, F., Nguyen, V., Ghannay, S., Tomashenko, N., Estève, Y.: TED-LIUM 3: twice as much data and corpus repartition for experiments on speaker adaptation. In: Karpov, A., Jokisch, O., Potapova, R. (eds.) SPECOM 2018. LNCS (LNAI), vol. 11096, pp. 198–208. Springer, Cham (2018). https://doi.org/10.1007/978-3-319-99579-3_21

8. Jurafsky, D., Martin, J.H.: Speech and language processing. chapter 3: N-gram language models (3rd ed. draft). Available from: https://web.stanford.edu/~jurafsky/slp3/3.pdf (2018)

9. Kogure, S., Nishizaki, H., Tsuchiya, M., Yamamoto, K., Togashi, S., Nakagawa, S.: Speech recognition performance of CJLC: corpus of Japanese lecture contents. In: Ninth Annual Conference of the International Speech Communication Association. Citeseer (2008)

10. Maekawa, K.: Corpus of spontaneous Japanese: its design and evaluation. In: ISCA & IEEE Workshop on Spontaneous Speech Processing and Recognition (2003)

11. Munteanu, C., Penn, G., Baecker, R.: Web-based language modelling for automatic lecture transcription. In: Eighth Annual Conference of the International Speech Communication Association (2007)

12. Nakamura, M., Iwano, K., Furui, S.: Differences between acoustic characteristics of spontaneous and read speech and their effects on speech recognition performance. Comput. Speech Lang. **22**(2), 171–184 (2008)

13. Nanjo, H., Kawahara, T.: Unsupervised language model adaptation for lecture speech recognition. In: ISCA & IEEE Workshop on Spontaneous Speech Processing and Recognition (2003)

14. Park, A., Hazen, T.J., Glass, J.R.: Automatic processing of audio lectures for information retrieval: vocabulary selection and language modeling. In: Proceedings. (ICASSP 2005). IEEE International Conference on Acoustics, Speech, and Signal Processing, 2005, vol. 1, pp. I-497. IEEE (2005)

15. Rousseau, A., Deléglise, P., Esteve, Y., et al.: Enhancing the TED-LIUM corpus with selected data for language modeling and more ted talks. In: LREC, pp. 3935–3939 (2014)

16. Xu, Q., et al.: Self-training and pre-training are complementary for speech recognition. In: ICASSP 2021–2021 IEEE International Conference on Acoustics, Speech and Signal Processing (ICASSP), pp. 3030–3034. IEEE (2021)

17. Yeganova, L., et al.: Findings of the WMT 2021 biomedical translation shared task: summaries of animal experiments as new test set. In: Proceedings of the Sixth Conference on Machine Translation, pp. 664–683. Association for Computational Linguistics, Online, November 2021

# Transformer-Based Automatic Speech Recognition of Formal and Colloquial Czech in MALACH Project

Jan Lehečka[(✉)] [iD], Josef V. Psutka [iD], and Josef Psutka [iD]

Department of Cybernetics, University of West Bohemia in Pilsen,
Pilsen, Czech Republic
{jlehecka,psutka_j,psutka}@kky.zcu.cz

**Abstract.** Czech is a very specific language due to its large differences between the formal and the colloquial form of speech. While the formal (written) form is used mainly in official documents, literature, and public speeches, the colloquial (spoken) form is used widely among people in casual speeches. This gap introduces serious problems for ASR systems, especially when training or evaluating ASR models on datasets containing a lot of colloquial speech, such as the MALACH project. In this paper, we are addressing this problem in the light of a new paradigm in end-to-end ASR systems – recently introduced self-supervised audio Transformers. Specifically, we are investigating the influence of colloquial speech on the performance of Wav2Vec 2.0 models and their ability to transcribe colloquial speech directly into formal transcripts. We are presenting results with both formal and colloquial forms in the training transcripts, language models, and evaluation transcripts.

**Keywords:** Wav2Vec 2.0 · Colloquial speech · ASR

## 1 Introduction

Formal Czech differs a lot from the colloquial Czech. Almost 20% of Czech words have different transcription in both varieties [17, p. 250]. This gap between the everyday, colloquial language, and the official codified formal language emerged during the Czech National Revival back in the 1830s when a group of Czech writers, poets, translators, editors, and teachers established new grammar rules and vocabularies independent of German influence. They took inspiration from other Slavic languages and outdated Czech Bible texts. However, common people did not adopt these new rules and words into their spoken language creating a very specific widely-spoken vernacular that persists to this day [7].

The gap between formal and colloquial Czech constitutes a serious problem for Automatic Speech Recognition (ASR) systems which automatically transcribe – possibly colloquial – spoken utterances into formal text [4]. The usual way how to deal with this phenomenon in a common Large-Vocabulary Continuous Speech Recognition (LVCSR) system is to train the acoustic model with

© Springer Nature Switzerland AG 2022
P. Sojka et al. (Eds.): TSD 2022, LNAI 13502, pp. 301–312, 2022.
https://doi.org/10.1007/978-3-031-16270-1_25

colloquial phonetic transcripts, define alternative (colloquial) pronunciations for formal words in the lexicon and finally use a formal language model to decode the speech into a formal transcript [14,16].

In the recent few years, self-supervised neural networks became a very popular alternative to LVCSR systems in speech recognition tasks. A significant milestone was the introduction of the Transformer architecture [18] into ASR systems [2,3,5,11,12]. The most studied transformer-based ASR model architecture is Wav2Vec 2.0 [3]. It is an end-to-end speech recognizer that alleviates the need for word pronunciation modeling and does not require any alignment of data. It is a single model converting the raw audio signal from the input into the sequence of tokens on the output, no meter whether these tokens are graphemes, phonemes, word pieces, or other speech units. Thus, the model has a very interesting ability: when the input audio data during fine-tuning contain colloquial speech and the target transcripts are in the formal Czech, it could internally learn the mapping between the two forms without any engineering or manual effort. In this paper, we are investigating the extent of this ability of Wav2Vec models.

## 2    MALACH Project

The whole story of the MALACH project began in 1994, when after the premiere of the film "Schindler's List", many survivors turned to Steven Spielberg to tell him their stories about the Holocaust. Inspired by these requests, Spielberg decided to establish the Shoah Visual History Foundation (VHF) so that as many survivors as possible could record their stories and save them for future generations. Nowadays are these video interviews located in the Shoah Foundation Institute at the University of Southern California (USC-SFI) along with another 54,000 video interviews with witnesses of the history of the entire 20th century.

The Shoah part of the archive contains testimonies in 32 languages of personal memories of survivors of the World War II Holocaust, in total it is 116,000 h of video. Interviews (in all languages) contain natural, unrestricted speech, full of disfluencies, emotional excitements, heavy accents, and are often influenced by the high age of speakers (problems with keeping ideas). More than 550 testimonies are in the Czech (almost 1000 h hours of video).

In 2014, the Linguistic Data Consortium (LDC) released the Czech part of the MALACH project [15]. There were published 420 testimonies along with their transcripts. The release contains 400 randomly selected testimonies for the purpose of acoustic model training. As only 15-min segments were transcribed for each testimony, the acoustic training part, therefore, consists of 100 h of Czech speech from theoretically up to 800 speakers (interviewer and interviewee). The rest of the Czech MALACH corpus consists of 20 testimonies, which have been completely transcribed and are intended for development (10 testimonies, i.e. 20 speakers) and testing (10 testimonies, i.e. 20 speakers) purposes. (see Table 1 for details).

# 3   Formal vs. Colloquial Czech

During the annotation process of the Czech Malach corpus, the transcribers were instructed to use the orthographic transcription of colloquial words (i.e., not to "formalize" them artificially) to bring the transcripts as close as possible to what was actually said. There were several reasons for this decision. Firstly, this procedure was very beneficial for classical acoustic modeling, because the resulting transcription is very close to the actual phonetic realization of the word. Secondly, transcribing colloquial sentences using formal words is not an easy task, especially for transcribers without a solid linguistic background. Another problem solved by the colloquial method of transcription was no need to unify the transcription of foreign words.

**Table 1.** Statistics of training and test data-sets of the Czech part of the MALACH project.

|                         | Train | Test  |
|-------------------------|-------|-------|
| # of speakers           | 776   | 20    |
| # of words              | 49k   | 10.3k |
| # of tokens             | 715k  | 63k   |
| dataset length [hours]  | 87.5  | 8.9   |

On the other hand, the effect of the abundance of colloquial words on the language model is rather negative. The orthographic transcription of colloquial words causes an unnecessary growth of the lexicon. There are often several different colloquial variants corresponding to one formal word form. Consequently, the already sparse language model training data became even sparser. To take advantage of formal word forms in language modeling, we decided to "formalize" the lexicon. We went through a lexicon built from the original (orthographic) transcriptions and added a corresponding standard form to each colloquial word form, but only in cases where it was unambiguous. The normalization of manual transcripts not only made the parameters of the estimated language model more robust but also brought this main and most useful source for language modeling much closer to other potential formal text sources. More details on this process can be found in [13].

A good example of the ambiguity of such a formalization is the word *sem*. While in formal Czech this word means *sem (here)*, in colloquial Czech it is also used instead of the correct form *jsem ((I) am)* which naturally occurs quite frequently (the fourth most frequent word in the corpus). To distinguish which formal variant of a word *sem* is the correct one, we would have to use a larger word context or better use a sophisticated method of text understanding. Nevertheless, by formalizing the lexicon, we found more than 13k unambiguous rules that reduced the number of colloquial words by almost 85%.

In order to illustrate that the number of colloquial forms for a single formal word form can be really high, we present a fragment from the "formalized" lexicon in Table 2. The new "formalized" text corpus was created by automatically replacing colloquial words in the original transcripts with their formal counterparts using the above-mentioned 2-column lexicon. Note that such a procedure does not take into account the word context, and therefore the formalization process is far from perfect.

## 4  Wav2Vec 2.0

Wav2Vec 2.0 model [3] is one of the current state-of-the-art models for ASR. It is a deep neural network pretrained to reconstruct the corrupted signals. The input raw audio signal is processed by a multi-layer convolutional neural network

Table 2. Example of formalization rules.

| formal | colloquial | in English |
|---|---|---|
| odjet | odejet odjec object vodjet vodejet vodject vodeject | to leave |
| odtamtud | odtamtad' odtamtud' vodtamtad' vodtamtud vodtamtud' votamtad' votamtud' | from there |
| bývalý | bejvalej bejvalý bývalej | former |

into a sequence of latent-speech representations which are fed into a multi-layer Transformer [18]. Only the encoder part of the full encoder-decoder Transformer architecture is used. The output of the Transformer is a sequence of frame-level contextualized speech representations encoding both the frame itself and its context in the signal. This approach is motivated by very successful self-supervised text-based Transformers solving Natural Language Processing (NLP) and Natural Language Understanding (NLU) tasks [8].

The training of Wav2Vec models consists of two phases: pretraining and fine-tuning. During the first self-supervised pretraining phase, the model learns contextualized speech representations from large-scale unlabeled audio datasets. This approach is motivated by the learning skills of infants, who do not learn to understand speech by reading its transcripts, but rather by listening to adults around them and trying to catch the meaning from the context. By masking latent representations of the raw waveform and solving a contrastive task over quantized speech representations, the model learns contextualized representations jointly with discrete speech units without the need for any annotations or labels.

Since labeled data could be very expensive and precious, the pretraining phase equips the model with deep knowledge about the speech signals mined out from tens of thousands of hours of unlabeled speech. This knowledge constitutes a great advantage over models trained from scratch using labeled data only. From this point of view, the pretrained weights of the Wav2Vec model could be seen as very clever initializations of the model weights for supervised training.

During the second supervised fine-tuning phase, the model transfers the pretrained knowledge into the ASR task. For input speech signals, the speech representations are fed into Connectionist Temporal Classification (CTC) layer [9] and the most probable sequences of graphemes are decoded. The model is fine-tuned with frozen feature-encoder weights from labeled data optimizing the CTC loss.

CTC is an alignment-free method for grouping audio frames belonging to the same output token in order to convert a sequence of speech representations (one per audio frame) into a much shorter sequence of output tokens. The CTC classification process can be described – in a simplified way – in 3 steps: (1) assign the most probable output token to each audio frame, (2) group sequences with the same tokens into a single token, and (3) remove blank tokens. Tokens are usually graphemes (i.e. characters including also a word delimiter) but could be any speech units.

## 5    Experimental Setup

### 5.1    Pretraining

Public monolingual Wav2Vec models for non-English languages are very rare. For the Czech language, there are none. However, there are several public multilingual pretrained models of sizes from large [6] to extremely large [1]. These models included also Czech in the pretraining datasets. The common practice with these models is to select the most suitable pretrained model and fine-tune it on the labeled ASR data from the target language. Since we were not satisfied with results from multilingual models and, at the same time, we had access to large unlabeled datasets and a high-performance GPU cluster, we decided to pretrain our own base-sized monolingual Wav2Vec model from scratch and released it to the public.

Self-supervised audio transformers are known to scale well with the size of pretraining data, even with extremely huge datasets [1]. Hence, we tried to gather as much public and in-house unlabeled audio data as possible. Together, we were able to collect more than 80 thousand hours of Czech speech. The collection includes recordings from radio (22 k h), unlabeled data from VoxPopuli dataset [19] (18.7 k h), TV shows (15 k h), shadow speakers (12 k h), sports (5 k h), telephone data (2 k h), and a smaller amount of data from several other domains. We included also raw unlabeled audio data from the MALACH project (1 k h).

Since the feature extraction of the input signal is limited by the memory of GPUs in use, we sliced all records not to exceed 30 s, which we found to be a reasonable input size for batching.

We followed the same pretraining setup as for the base Wav2Vec 2.0 model in [3]. We pretrained the model for 400 thousand steps with a batch size not exceeding 1.6 h, corresponding to more than 11 epochs over the dataset. The pretraining took about two weeks on a machine with four NVIDIA A100 GPUs. We released our pretrained model under the nickname *ClTRUS* (abbreviation for **C**zech language **TR**ransformer from **U**nlabeled **S**peech) for public non-commercial use[1]. We are not aware of any similar model for Czech mentioned in the literature so far.

## 5.2 Fine-tuning

When fine-tuning models, we used the same setup as in [3], i.e. we trained the pretrained model for 80 thousand update steps with the peak learning rate of $2 \times 10^{-5}$ and the batch size about 27 min of audio, resulting in 270 training epochs over the dataset. We removed non-speech events and punctuation from the transcripts and mapped texts into lowercase. We used implementation from the `Fairseq` tool[2] to fine-tune models.

First, we trained the colloquial model, denoted as $W2V_{colloq}$, from the original transcripts. Since annotators were instructed to transcribe the speech in the spoken form, i.e. exactly as it was spoken in the underlying speech, these transcripts are mainly in colloquial Czech. However, it is in fact a mix of both forms, because some people tend to speak more formally when giving an interview, and sometimes annotators were not able to distinguish between the two forms, especially in the strong emotional and heavily accented speeches. We left the formal words untouched as the rules from formal to colloquial form would be ambiguous.

After that, we transformed the original transcripts into formal Czech using the prepared set of rules (see Sect. 3) and fine-tuned the second model, denoted as $W2V_{formal}$. The whole fine-tuning process is depicted in the upper part of Fig. 1. The fine-tuning of each model took about 14 h on a machine with four NVIDIA A100 GPUs.

---

[1] Available at https://huggingface.co/fav-kky/wav2vec2-base-cs-80k-ClTRUS.
[2] https://github.com/pytorch/fairseq.

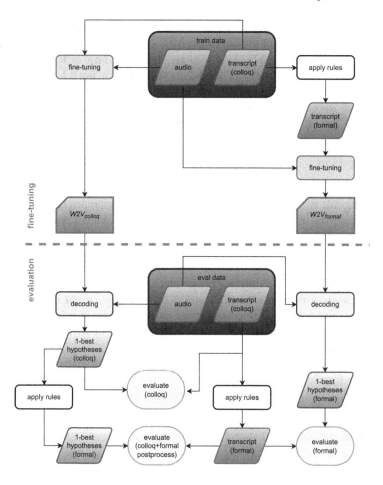

**Fig. 1.** Scheme of fine-tuning and evaluation.

## 5.3 Decoding

We studied two different decoding setups: (1) Connectionist Temporal Classification (CTC) [9], which is the training loss we used during fine-tuning of the models, and (2) CTC beam search decoder with a Language Model (LM). Decoding setup (1) is a grapheme-based lexicon-free speech recognition without any language constraints. The only orthography-related knowledge the model could learn is the training transcripts fed in during the fine-tuning. Wav2Vec with the CTC decoding setup (1) decodes also word delimiters, so it is an end-to-end ASR system, which can be evaluated using standard word-based metrics like word error rate.

Decoding setup (2) incorporates an LM into the CTC beam search decoder which usually improves the speech recognition accuracy by bringing useful language information into the decoding process and penalizing improbable outputs. For our experiments, we prepared 2 different word-based n-gram LMs: (a) $LM_{colloq}$ trained from all colloquial transcripts, and (b) $LM_{formal}$ trained from the formalized training transcripts, i.e. from the training data of $W2V_{formal}$ model. We limited the maximum order of models to 4-grams for both LMs.

We used implementation from `Transformers` [20] for CTC decoding and `pyctcdecode`[3] decoder for CTC beam search decoder with n-gram LM. To train LMs, we used `KenLM` [10] and mapped all texts into lowercase.

## 5.4   Evaluation

Both decoding setups described in Sect. 5.3 generated a 1-best hypothesis for each input signal. We aligned decoded hypotheses and reference transcripts using the minimum edit distance and evaluated the standard Word Error Rate (WER) and Character Error Rate (CER).

To evaluate colloquial models, we used the original reference transcripts processed in the same way as the training transcripts, i.e. we removed non-speech events and punctuation and mapped texts into lowercase. We denote test dataset with this colloquial reference as $TEST_{colloq}$. To evaluate formal models, we further converted the colloquial reference texts into formal texts using the prepared set of rules (see Sect. 3) and thus generated the test dataset with formal reference transcripts, denoted as $TEST_{formal}$.

We evaluated all combinations of formal and colloquial models and LMs against both formal and colloquial reference transcripts. From these combinations, we are particularly interested in three real-world scenarios:

1. Evaluation of the colloquial model, i.e. how well $W2V_{colloq}$ model with $LM_{colloq}$ transcribes the colloquial speech (thus evaluated against $TEST_{colloq}$ dataset).
2. Evaluation of the formal model, i.e. how well $W2V_{formal}$ model with $LM_{formal}$ transcribes the colloquial speech into formal Czech (thus evaluated against $TEST_{formal}$ dataset). This scenario is particularly interesting as it evaluates how well the Wav2Vec model internally learns the mapping between the two forms without any engineering or manual effort.
3. Transcripts generated from $W2V_{colloq}$ with $LM_{colloq}$ post-processed by rule-based formalization of texts evaluated against $TEST_{formal}$ dataset. This scenario shows how the Wav2Vec model can use data prepared with a great manual effort for a standard LVCSR system in order to generate formal transcripts. We denote this colloquial model with Formalization Post-processing as $W2V_{colloq} + FP$

These three scenarios are depicted in a flowchart diagram in the bottom part of Fig. 1 and corresponding error rates will be underlined in the results table.

Note, that the numbers of reference words in $TEST_{colloq}$ and $TEST_{formal}$ differ due to multi-word replacements in the rules. While the formal transcripts consist of 62 690 words, the colloquial has 62 918 words, so results evaluated against $TEST_{formal}$ and $TEST_{colloq}$ are not exactly comparable.

---

[3] https://github.com/kensho-technologies/pyctcdecode.

# 6    Results

Results of our experiments are tabulated in Table 3. First, we evaluated the existing LVCSR system developed specifically for MALACH dataset [16]. The system was a CNN-TDNN LF-MMI with iVectors, sMBR criterion, and system-specific 3-gram LM denoted as $LM_{LVCSR}$. The system was trained to transcribe colloquial speech into formal form, so we report only results evaluated against $TEST_{formal}$. A comparison of this system with the formal Wav2Vec model clearly reveals the superiority of transformer-based ASR systems.

**Table 3.** WER [%] and CER [%] of colloquial and formal models evaluated against colloquial and formal evaluation datasets ($TEST_{colloq}$ and $TEST_{formal}$). Each Wav2Vec model was decoded using three different decoding setups: as an end-to-end ASR with no LM and with the beam search CTC decoder with $LM_{formal}$ and $LM_{colloq}$ (see Sect. 5.3). Underlined values correspond to scenarios we are particularly interested in (see Sect. 5.4). Bold values are the best error rates for each model.

| model | LM | $TEST_{colloq}$ | | $TEST_{formal}$ | |
|---|---|---|---|---|---|
| | | WER | CER | WER | CER |
| LVCSR | $LM_{LVCSR}$ | – | – | 14.71 | 5.25 |
| $W2V_{colloq}$ | – | 12.24 | **3.58** | 19.73 | 5.28 |
| | $LM_{formal}$ | 13.85 | 4.05 | 15.96 | 4.68 |
| | $LM_{colloq}$ | **11.55** | <u>3.64</u> | 18.99 | 5.27 |
| $W2V_{formal}$ | – | 19.17 | 5.07 | 11.52 | 3.32 |
| | $LM_{formal}$ | 18.60 | 5.19 | <u>**10.48**</u> | <u>**3.31**</u> |
| | $LM_{colloq}$ | 18.60 | 5.16 | 10.85 | 3.37 |
| $W2V_{colloq} + FP$ | – | 19.02 | 5.05 | 11.18 | 3.33 |
| | $LM_{formal}$ | 18.47 | 5.07 | 11.09 | 3.53 |
| | $LM_{colloq}$ | 18.47 | 5.12 | <u>**10.43**</u> | <u>**3.30**</u> |

As for the Wav2Vec models, the best results evaluated against $TEST_{colloq}$ are significantly higher (i.e. worse) than best results evaluated against $TEST_{formal}$. It is mainly because the colloquial Czech does not have codified rules and one formal word could have many possible colloquial forms. Each speaker can use – based on his or her geographical background – a different set of colloquial words in the speech. Moreover, each annotator can perceive the spoken colloquial forms differently, especially in the strong emotional and heavily accented speeches. This ambiguity of transcribed speech leads to confusion when training and evaluating the colloquial models.

If we compare the underlined results of the last two Wav2Vec models in Table 3 (corresponding to scenarios 2. and 3. from Sect. 5.4), we see very similar error rates. The $W2V_{colloq} + FP$ is slightly better, which we found to be caused by an occasional incorrect exact match of formalized hypotheses with the formalized reference, as both were generated using the same rules. After analyzing errors from $W2V_{formal}$ model, we found that many recognition errors were actually errors in the reference as the rules were not covering all occurrences of colloquial form in the reference. For example, the formal reference contained (incorrectly) the word "německýho" (colloquial inflected form meaning "German"), because it was not covered by mapping rules due to its non-existence in training transcripts. Formalized output from $W2V_{colloq} + FP$ exactly matched the reference for the same reason, so there was no error counted. $W2V_{formal}$ predicted the correct formal form "německého", which was, however, wrongly counted as a recognition error due to an error in the reference. We didn't make more effort to clean the reference transcripts and fix these errors as they were infrequent and it would cost a lot of manual work with only a little effect on the error rates. Nevertheless, observing these types of errors was a clear sign of the generalization ability of the $W2V_{formal}$ model and we can conclude that $W2V_{formal}$ is – despite slightly higher error rates – a more useful model than rule-based $W2V_{colloq} + FP$ because of its generalization ability.

To sum up the results, Wav2Vec models are significantly better ASR systems for the MALACH project than LVCSR systems. They are able to learn the mapping from colloquial speech into a formal transcript and generalize this skill also to words not observed in training data, which is a more beneficial solution than limited rule-based formalization post-processing of the colloquial model. Moreover, the Wac2Vec's internal mapping from colloquial speech to formal transcripts could make the acquisition of training transcripts much simpler as the annotators could be instructed to transcribe the speech directly into formal Czech alleviating the problems with ambiguous colloquial transcripts and manual listing of rules.

## 7    Conclusion

In this paper, we showed that the new paradigm models in ASR – Transformer-based models with CTC decoder (specifically Wav2Vec 2.0) – have a very interesting ability to learn how to transcribe Czech colloquial speech directly into formal transcripts. Such models not only perform better than common LVCSR systems, but also alleviate the need for complicated and ambiguous colloquial annotations, data alignments, phonetic transcriptions, and pronunciation lexicons. When collecting training transcripts for a new ASR dataset, we can instruct annotators just to transcribe the speech directly into formal Czech sentences, which is codified and unambiguous form, and that's all that is needed for the Wav2Vec model to be fine-tuned. From the formal transcript and raw audio signal, the model is able to learn the alignment between the speech signal frames and graphemes, and also how to generalize the conversion between the colloquial speech and formal text. We believe our findings will simplify and accelerate the acquisition of training data for new challenging datasets containing a lot of colloquial speech.

**Acknowledgments.** This research was supported by the ITI project of the Ministry of Education of the Czech Republic CZ.02.1.01/0.0/0.0/17 048/0007267 InteCom. Computational resources were supplied by the project "e-Infrastruktura CZ" (e-INFRA CZ LM2018140) supported by the Ministry of Education, Youth and Sports of the Czech Republic.

# References

1. Babu, A., et al.: XLS-R: self-supervised cross-lingual speech representation learning at scale. arXiv preprint arXiv:2111.09296 (2021)
2. Baevski, A., Mohamed, A.: Effectiveness of self-supervised pre-training for ASR. In: ICASSP 2020–2020 IEEE International Conference on Acoustics, Speech and Signal Processing (ICASSP), pp. 7694–7698 (2020)
3. Baevski, A., Zhou, Y., Mohamed, A., Auli, M.: Wav2Vec 2.0: a framework for self-supervised learning of speech representations. Adv. Neural Inf. Process. Syst. **33**, 12449–12460 (2020)
4. Byrne, W., et al.: Automatic recognition of spontaneous speech for access to multilingual oral history archives. IEEE Trans. Speech Audio Process. **12**(4), 420–435 (2004). https://doi.org/10.1109/TSA.2004.828702
5. Chen, S., et al.: WavLM: large-scale self-supervised pre-training for full stack speech processing. arXiv preprint arXiv:2110.13900 (2021)
6. Conneau, A., Baevski, A., Collobert, R., Mohamed, A., Auli, M.: Unsupervised cross-lingual representation learning for speech recognition. In: Hermansky, H., Cernocký, H., Burget, L., Lamel, L., Scharenborg, O., Motlícek, P. (eds.) Interspeech 2021, 22nd Annual Conference of the International Speech Communication Association, Brno, Czechia, 30 August–3 September 2021, pp. 2426–2430. ISCA (2021). https://doi.org/10.21437/Interspeech. 2021–329. https://doi.org/10.21437/Interspeech.2021-329
7. Cummins, G.M.: Literary czech, common czech, and the instrumental plural. J. Slavic Linguist. **13**(2), 271–297 (2005), https://www.jstor.org/stable/24599659
8. Devlin, J., Chang, M.W., Lee, K., Toutanova, K.: BERT: pre-training of deep bidirectional transformers for language understanding. arXiv preprint arXiv:1810.04805 (2018)
9. Graves, A., Fernández, S., Gomez, F., Schmidhuber, J.: Connectionist temporal classification: labelling unsegmented sequence data with recurrent neural networks. In: Proceedings of the 23rd International Conference on Machine Learning, pp. 369–376 (2006)
10. Heafield, K.: KenLM: faster and smaller language model queries. In: Proceedings of the Sixth Workshop on Statistical Machine Translation, pp. 187–197. Association for Computational Linguistics, Edinburgh, Scotland, July 2011. https://aclanthology.org/W11-2123
11. Hsu, W.N., Bolte, B., Tsai, Y.H.H., Lakhotia, K., Salakhutdinov, R., Mohamed, A.: Hubert: self-supervised speech representation learning by masked prediction of hidden units. IEEE/ACM Trans. Audio Speech Lang. Process. **29**, 3451–3460 (2021)
12. Liu, A.T., Li, S.W., Lee, H.Y.: TERA: self-supervised learning of transformer encoder representation for speech. IEEE/ACM Trans. Audio Speech Lang. Process. **29**, 2351–2366 (2021)

13. Psutka, J., et al.: Issues in annotation of the Czech spontaneous speech corpus in the MALACH project. In: Proceedings of the Fourth International Conference on Language Resources and Evaluation (LREC 2004), pp. 607–610. European Language Resources Association, Lisbon (2004)

14. Psutka, J., Ircing, P., Psutka, J.V., Hajič, J., Byrne, W., Mírovský, J.: Automatic transcription of Czech, Russian and Slovak spontaneous speech in the MALACH project. In: Eurospeech 2005, pp. 1349–1352. ISCA (2005)

15. Psutka, J., Radová, V., Ircing, P., Matoušek, J., Müller, L.: USC-SFI MALACH Interviews and Transcripts Czech LDC2014S04 (2014). https://catalog.ldc.upenn.edu/LDC2014S04

16. Psutka, J.V., Pražák, A., Vaněk, J.: Recognition of heavily accented and emotional speech of English and Czech Holocaust survivors using various DNN architectures. In: Karpov, A., Potapova, R. (eds.) Speech and Computer, pp. 553–564. Springer International Publishing, Cham (2021). https://doi.org/10.1007/978-3-030-87802-3_50

17. Tahal, K.: A Grammar of Czech as a foreign language. FACTUM CZ, s.r.o. (2010)

18. Vaswani, A., et al.: Attention is all you need. In: Proceedings of the 31st International Conference on Neural Information Processing Systems, pp. 6000–6010. NIPS 2017. Curran Associates Inc., Red Hook, NY, USA (2017)

19. Wang, C., et al.: VoxPopuli: a large-scale multilingual speech corpus for representation learning, semi-supervised learning and interpretation. In: Proceedings of the 59th Annual Meeting of the Association for Computational Linguistics and the 11th International Joint Conference on Natural Language Processing, vol. 1: Long Papers, pp. 993–1003. Association for Computational Linguistics, Online, August 2021. https://aclanthology.org/2021.acl-long.80

20. Wolf, T., et al.: Transformers: state-of-the-art natural language processing. In: Proceedings of the 2020 Conference on Empirical Methods in Natural Language Processing: System Demonstrations, pp. 38–45. Association for Computational Linguistics, Online, October 2020. https://www.aclweb.org/anthology/2020.emnlp-demos.6

# Wakeword Detection Under Distribution Shifts

Sree Hari Krishnan Parthasarathi, Lu Zeng(✉), Christin Jose, and Joseph Wang

Alexa, Amazon, Seattle, USA
{sparta,luzeng,chrjse,wangjose}@amazon.com

**Abstract.** We propose a novel approach for semi-supervised learning (SSL) designed to overcome distribution shifts between training and real-world data arising in the keyword spotting (KWS) task. Shifts from training data distribution are a key challenge for real-world KWS tasks: when a new model is deployed on device, the gating of the accepted data undergoes a shift in distribution, making the problem of timely updates via subsequent deployments hard. Despite the shift, we assume that the marginal distributions on labels do not change. We utilize a modified teacher/student training framework, where labeled training data is augmented with unlabeled data. Note that the teacher does not have access to the new distribution as well. To train effectively with a mix of human and teacher labeled data, we develop a teacher labeling strategy based on confidence heuristics to reduce entropy on the label distribution from the teacher model; the data is then sampled to match the marginal distribution on the labels. Large scale experimental results show that a convolutional neural network (CNN) trained on far-field audio, and evaluated on far-field audio drawn from a different distribution, obtains a 14.3% relative improvement in false discovery rate (FDR) at equal false reject rate (FRR), while yielding a 5% improvement in FDR under no distribution shift. Under a more severe distribution shift from far-field to near-field audio with a smaller fully connected network (FCN) our approach achieves a 52% relative improvement in FDR at equal FRR, while yielding a 20% relative improvement in FDR on the original distribution.

**Keywords:** wakeword detection · distribution shifts · keyword spotting

## 1 Introduction

While deep learning models have a remarkable capacity to fit the training data distribution, fitting even random labels [26], distribution shifts from the training data can present challenges [12,19,23]. These challenges include covariate shifts, prior shifts, selection bias, domain shift etc. [18]. Such distribution shifts can cause a model to learn spurious structures in the data and generalize poorly [9].

© Springer Nature Switzerland AG 2022
P. Sojka et al. (Eds.): TSD 2022, LNAI 13502, pp. 313–325, 2022.
https://doi.org/10.1007/978-3-031-16270-1_26

Our work in this paper happens in this context and focuses on small footprint on-device wakeword detection[1] models [5,7,11,15,21,24,25].

Wakeword detection is a modeling area that is prone to distribution shifts. For wakeword detection models deployed on device, the data that is accepted or rejected is gated by the model, causing a tight coupling between the model on device and the data available for subsequent training and evaluations. However, continuously selecting and labeling data can be time consuming and expensive. Beyond distribution shifts associated with deployed models, shifts can also occur due to changes in devices, user populations, and usage patterns/applications. An extreme version of this shift is the introduction of devices that differ significantly from existing population. Generalizing annotated data collected for one such set of devices to another requires addressing distribution shifts introduced.

In this paper we investigate the problem of helping generalize an on-device wakeword detection model over a distribution shift caused by a model update and underlying temporal changes in data distributions. We propose a novel version of teacher/student training with two major deviations from the standard approach, where labeled training data is augmented with unlabeled data. First, since the teacher does not have access to the new distribution, our proposed labeling strategy reduces the entropy on the label distribution by using confidence heuristics, enabling student models to be trained from a combination of human and teacher labeled data. Second, assuming that the marginal distributions on labels do not change, we develop an approach to sampling unlabeled data to overcome both distribution shifts inherent to the KWS task as well as biases introduced by the proposed labeling scheme. To empirically validate the proposed approach we conducted two sets of large scale experiments (over 200K hours of unlabeled data) on de-identified production data. In these experiments, we demonstrate the ability to overcome both temporal distribution shifts as well as device-type distribution shifts.

**Related Work:** Research related to modeling under distribution shifts falls into three categories: a) without access to the shifted distribution, approached using robust optimization and meta-learning [1,12]; b) with access to shifted distribution and a small set of labeled data, approached using active learning [4]; c) with access to the shifted distribution, but without labels - our problem falls under the third category. Continual learning [16] is a related topic where the data is constrained to be processed online.

Learning from unlabeled data, especially under distribution or domain shifts, remains a challenge [6,20]. Zhao et al. [27] imposed similarity constraints on labeled and unlabeled distributions as a form of *consistency regularization* principle, proposed in [2,3,22]. Our algorithm falls under this category, imposing the assumption that the marginal distributions on labels do not change; however the previous approaches perturb the data in an unbiased fashion, whereas in our setting, the data distribution shifts. Another principle used in SSL, *entropy minimization*, encourages the pseudo-labels to be well-separated on the unlabeled

---

[1] Also known as keyword spotting; this is a task of detecting keywords of interest in a continuous audio stream.

data, through the use of regularizers [10,14]. Inspired by this principle, but to scale it to a large unlabeled dataset, our algorithm uses confidence thresholds to encourage separability of classes. Our approach combines these two principles to handle distribution shifts in a teacher/student framework where the teacher has not seen the new distribution too.

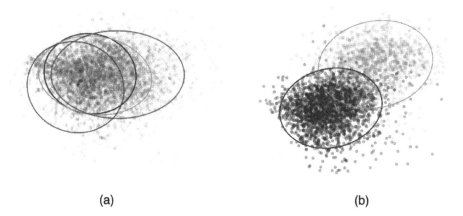

(a)                                          (b)

**Fig. 1.** *(a) Embeddings of wakeword data plotted with respect to year along with the first standard deviation contour of a Normal distribution approximation. Data from 2018 is represented by blue, from 2019 by red, 2020 by cyan, and 2021 by green; (b) Embeddings of random samples of wakeword data drawn from a far-field device (blue) and mobile devices (red) along with the first standard deviation contour of a Normal distribution approximation.* (Color figure online)

## 2    Distribution Shifts in Wakeword Data

We illustrate two shifts in data distributions below. First, Fig. 1(a) shows the temporal drift in the distribution of data the model observes due to factors such as the wakeword model gating behavior (as described in the introduction), physical changes to devices, introduction of newer versions of devices with differing hardware/software, growth and change in user population, and change in use of devices. This introduces the challenge of leveraging older annotated data that may not be representative of the current distribution.

A second major shift in wakeword data distributions occurs due to generalization to differing devices/use cases. An example of this is shown in Fig. 1(b), where data collected from mobile devices is compared to data collected on far-field devices. Mobile device data is fundamentally different for a wide range of factors. Differing customer usage leads to different acoustic and background noise conditions (e.g. use in automobiles, while walking around), generally is near-field, and has significantly differing microphones and audio front-end capabilities. In this setting, our goal is to build performant models for new device-types with limited annotated data by leveraging annotated data from different device-types.

## 3   On-device Wakeword Detection Models

We describe the two wakeword detection models, namely the CNN and FCN. Models are similar to [5, 21], with the difference being that the input window encompasses a larger audio context. The models are trained using a set of positive and negative examples (i.e. positive examples contain the wakeword, while the negatives do not). During training, the wakeword is consistently center aligned in the input window [11].

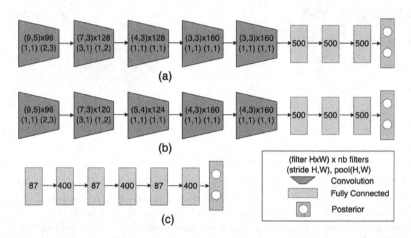

**Fig. 2.** *Model architectures: (a) CNN annotation model with 5 CNN layers and 3 fully-connected layers (4M parameters); (b) CNN on-device wakeword detection model with 5 CNN layers and 3 fully-connected layers (2M parameters); (c) FCN on-device wakeword detection model with 5 fully-connected layers (250k parameters).*

The CNN model architecture has 2M learnable parameters, and it operates on 64-dimensional log mel filter bank energy (LFBE) features, computed with analysis window size and shift of 25 ms and 10 ms respectively; the input to the model is 100 frames. The model has 5 CNN layers and 3 fully-connected layers, as shown in Fig. 2(b). Dropout and batch normalization are used in all the layers. The output is a binary classification layer trained with cross entropy loss, representing the probability of "wakeword" and "non-wakeword" [8].

The FCN model architecture has 250K learnable parameters, and it operates on 20-dimensional LFBE features computed over the same analysis window size and shift as the CNN; the input to the model is 81 frames, downsampled by a factor of 3. The architecture consists of five fully connected layers. Details of this model architecture is presented in Fig. 2(c). Dropout and batch normalization are used with all hidden layers. Similar to CNN, the output is a binary classification layer trained with cross entropy loss.

During inference, the posterior estimates, from CNN or FCN, corresponding to the wakeword are smoothed by an exponential moving average (EMA) or a windowed smoothing average (WMA) filter respectively; these are then thresholded to infer the wakeword hypothesis.

## 4   Proposed SSL Algorithm

The SSL algorithm consists of selection of an annotation model, selection of thresholds to compute pseudo-labels, distributing matching with subsampling, and the actual training. We describe each of these components in depth.

**Selecting and Annotating Data:** A critical aspect of model training to account for distribution shifts in the selection of unlabeled training data to be annotated with a teacher model. Let $z_s^o = (x_s^o, y_s^o)$ be the original supervised training data distribution. This supervised data is not drawn from the distribution of examples the model is exposed to due to both access to the data, as well as the imbalance of classes in the detection setting. Instead, the supervised data selection is more heavily drawn from "hard" examples that are close to the decision boundary of previous models. Note that an example can be "hard" due to a number of reasons beyond distribution shift; for example, features not being able to separate examples.

Under a distribution shift, we ideally would like to have access to $z_s^n = (x_s^n, y_s^n)$, the equivalent supervised training data distribution drawn heavily from "hard" examples from the new shifted distribution, with subsequent models then trained using $\{z_s^o \cup z_s^n\}$. Since manual labeling of hard examples is slow, we want some approximation of $z_s^n$ using an SSL algorithm. Let $(z_u^n, s_u^n) = (x_u^n, y_u^n, s_u^n)$ be the unsupervised distribution with score $s_u^n$ from a teacher model. We want to approximate $z_s^n$ with $z_u^n$. We make the assumption that the marginal distributions on labels (i.e. $y_s^o$ and $y_s^n$) share the same distributions, even under distribution shifts.

In the absence of distribution shifts, we could use a teacher model to derive soft or hard pseudo labels. However in the presence of distribution shifts, selecting data that is hard for the student will yield noisy labels since teacher model has not been trained on the shifted distribution. To ameliorate this issue, we design our algorithm so that the teacher is able to label well, applying thresholds $\tau_+$ and $\tau_-$ to obtain $z_{u_\tau}^n := (x_{u_\tau}^n, y_{u_\tau}^n) = f_\tau(x_u^n, y_u^n, s_u^n)$.

The thresholded scores on unlabeled examples from the annotation model are binarized to pseudo-labels: data above the accept threshold ($\tau_+$) have positive labels, while those below the reject threshold ($\tau_-$) have negative labels. Unlabeled data with scores between the two thresholds are then discarded.

The accept/reject thresholds are determined based on analysis done on held-out examples that have groundtruth. We investigated precision and false positive rate (FPR) as means to quantify the "purity" of positive labels. Since data is biased towards positive examples, precision does not capture purity with sufficient granularity: therefore, we choose an accept threshold value on FPR. Similarly, FRR and False Omission Rate (FOR) were considered as metrics for negative labels. Analysis on held-out data showed that both FOR and FRR are reasonable metrics; we choose a reject threshold value on FRR.

Applying the thresholds $\tau_+$ and $\tau_-$ can be viewed as a form of entropy minimization, however this strategy alone is not sufficient to approximate $z_s^n$ with $z_{u_\tau}^n$. Since we have access to $y_s^o$ (and we assume $y_s^o$ and $y_s^n$ share the same distribution), we subsample $z_{u_\tau}^n$ to yield $z_{u_{\tau,\theta}}^n := (x_{u_{\tau,\theta}}^n, y_{u_{\tau,\theta}}^n) = g_\theta(f_\tau(x_u^n, y_u^n, s_u^n))$. Subsampling of the data can be viewed as a form of consistency regularization, where the distributions of $y_s^o$ and $y_s^n$ are kept close through the selection of data.

**Training Method:** We use the verification model described in Fig. 2(a) as the annotation model: it has a similar architecture to the CNN model described earlier, with 64-dimensional LFBE feature input to 5 stacking CNN layers fed to 3 fully-connected layers; the last layer performs the binary classification task, however the input window context is larger (consisting of 195 frames) and the model is specifically trained for the verification task rather than general wake-word detection. The model parameters are optimized with the cross entropy loss, and the model outputs a posterior probability [13]. The posteriors from the annotation model are used to annotate unlabeled data with hard labels; we refer to these as scores.

---

**Algorithm 1:** SSL scheme to generate pseudo-labels on unlabeled data

---

**Data:** $\tau_+$, accept threshold
    $\tau_-$, reject threshold
    $\theta_+$, positive class subsampling
    $s \in \mathcal{S}$, unlabeled data
    $score$, annotation model posterior
**Result:** Pseudo-labeled data
initialization;
**for** $s \in \mathcal{S}$ **do**
    score = query_score(s);
    u = rand();
    **if** $score \geq \tau_+$ *and* $u \leq \theta_+$ **then**
      | label = "Wakeword";
    **else if** $score \leq \tau_-$ **then**
      | label = "Not Wakeword";
    **else**
      | return None;

---

Similar to [3,17], we interleave this teacher annotated data with human labeled data within a minibatch during training. We set a weight of $\lambda : (1 - \lambda)$ for labeled and pseudo-labeled data respectively.

## 5    Experimental Setup

All experiments in this paper were conducted on de-identified production datasets. We now describe the setup for the two sets of training and evaluation experiments: a) CNN trained on far-field audio, and evaluated on far-field audio with and without distribution shift; b) FCN trained on far-field audio, and evaluated on near and far-field audio. We also discuss the evaluation metric used in our experiments. For all datasets, pseudo-labels are generated using annotation models as described in Sect. 4; in the interest of space, we do not discuss these annotation models as the training has been described in [13].

**Datasets:** For the two sets of experiments, we created a labeled and a pseudo-labeled training dataset; the latter was constructed using the procedure described in Sect. 4. For CNN: a) the labeled data consisted of 8K hours of far-field audio; b) the pseudo-labeled data consisted of 200K hours of far-field audio. Note these datasets are drawn from different distributions, as discussed earlier. For FCN: a) the labeled data consisted of 12K hours of far-field audio; b) the pseudo-labeled data consisted of 16K hours of near-field mobile phone data.

We created evaluation datasets with and without distribution shifts for the two cases. For CNN: a) without distribution shift labeled data consisting of 3K hours of far-field audio drawn from the same distribution as the labeled training data; b) distribution shifted labeled data consisting of 1K hours of far-field audio drawn from the same distribution as the pseudo-labeled training data. For FCN: a) without distribution shift labeled data consisting of 33 h of far-field audio drawn from the same distribution as the labeled training data; b) distribution shifted labeled data consisting of 30 h of near-field mobile phone audio drawn from the same distribution as the pseudo-labeled training data.

**Training and Evaluation:** We select the accept/reject thresholds and the sub-sampling factor for the positive class for the two sets of model training based on held-out datasets. We tuned $\lambda$, the mixing factor, for CNN and FCN training, obtaining a smaller $\lambda$ for FCN training (reasonable given the extent of distribution shift). During model training, with each minibatch, we updated the model using the Adam optimizer to compute the error signal; 700K model updates were done for CNN, while 200K model updates were done for FCN. During inference, we tuned the EMA and WMA values for the models on held-out datasets.

We use DET curves to measure the performance of the models, using False Rejection Rate (FRR) and False Discovery Rate (FDR); DET curves for proposed models are plotted compared to their baselines. Similar to [8,11,13,24,25], we normalize the axes of the DET curves using the baseline model's operating point (OP). For certain results, in the interest of space, we only report the results in terms of relative FDR at the baseline model's OP.

## 6    Results

We now describe the results for two sets of experiments presented in Sect. 5: a) far-field to far-field distribution shifts with CNN; b) far-field to near-field distribution shifts with FCN. We discuss the first experiment in depth using an ablation study with respect to the size of pseudo-labeled datasets as well as an analysis using the reliability of annotations.

## 6.1 Far-field Distribution Shifts with CNN

The baseline and the proposed approach use the CNN model architecture discussed in Sect. 3, with results presented in Table 1. While the baseline model was trained on labeled data, the proposed model was trained on a mixture of labeled and pseudo-labeled data. As can be seen from the table, the proposed approach achieves a 14.3% relative improvement in FDR at FRR matching the baseline model on eval data with a distribution shift (matching the distribution of the pseudo-labeled data). Furthermore, it achieves a 5.0% relative improvement in FDR on eval data without a distribution shift (matching the distribution of the labeled data).

We also present the full DET curves for both the baseline and the proposed model in Fig. 3. Note that $(1.0, 1.0)$ on the DET curves correspond to the OP of the baseline model. It can be seen from Fig. 3 that the DET curves mirror the larger and smaller gains, respectively, on evaluation data sets observed in the table; these correspond to conditions with and without distribution shifts. This shows that the proposed approach generalizes well.

**Table 1.** *Rel. imp. in FDR at FRR matching the baseline model on eval data with and without distribution shifts. Baseline model was trained on only labeled data while the model using proposed approach was trained on both labeled and pseudo-labeled data.*

| Condition | Rel. FDR Imp. (%) |
|---|---|
| Distribution shift | 14.3 |
| No distribution shift | 5.0 |

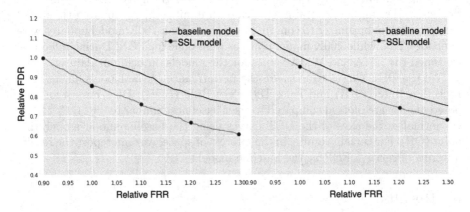

**Fig. 3.** *DET curves showing the baseline (blue) and the SSL (orange/with dots) models evaluated on a distribution shift (left) and no distribution shift (right).* (Color figure online)

**Table 2.** *Rel. imp. in FDR at FRR matching the baseline model on eval data with and without distribution shifts. The size of the pseudo-labeled training data is increased.*

| Data (hrs) | Relative FDR (Distr. Shift) | Relative FDR (No Distr. Shift) |
|---|---|---|
| 1K | −16.8 | −22.5 |
| 4K | −1.8 | −3.2 |
| 16K | 4.7 | 0.7 |
| 64K | 10.1 | 1.5 |
| 200K | 9.6 | 1.3 |

**Effect of Pseudo-Labeled Training Data Size.** Given the small model size, we wanted to understand how much pseudo-labeled data was useful. Table 2 presents performance of the CNN models in terms of increasing sizes of the pseudo-labeled data. To avoid the impact of imbalanced training set sizes, no labeled data was used. Results are reported on evaluation data (both with and without a distribution shift) in terms of relative improvement in FDR at equal FRR compared to the baseline model (from Table 1). We see a steady

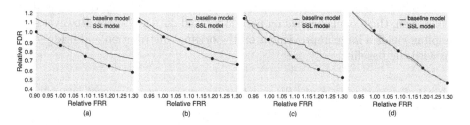

**Fig. 4.** *Baseline (blue) and the SSL (orange/with dots) models evaluated on: (a) easier examples with distribution shift; (b) easier examples with no distribution shift; (c) harder examples with distribution shift; (d) harder examples with no distribution shift.* (Color figure online)

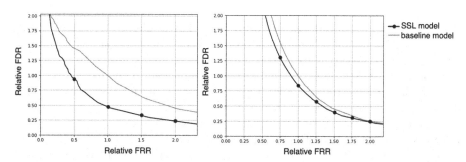

**Fig. 5.** *Comparing the baseline (orange) and the SSL (blue/with dots) models evaluated on a distribution shift (left) and no distribution shift (right).* (Color figure online)

improvement in performance on both eval data sets till the training data increases to 64K hours; thereafter the performance saturates indicating the capacity of the model.

**Table 3.** *Rel. imp. in FDR at FRR matching the baseline model on eval data with and without distribution shifts for models trained without (-) and with (+) subsampling.*

| Models | Rel. FDR Imp (%) (Dist. Shift) | Rel. FDR Imp (%) (No Dist. Shift) |
|---|---|---|
| − subsampling | 2.0 | −21.0 |
| + subsampling | 4.0 | −3.0 |

**Effect of Subsampling on Pseudo-Labeled Training Data.** For studying the effect of subsampling, we trained a baseline model only on 1K hours of labeled audio. Two models were trained only on 1K hours of pseudo-labeled audio using the approach in Sect. 4: a) a model that uses the best subsampling factor identified in Sect. 5; b) a model that uses no subsampling. Table 3 presents the results in terms of relative improvement in FDR at equal FRR compared to the baseline model. With distribution shift, the pseudo-labeled models are better, independent of the subsampling factor; not surprisingly, on the original distribution, the models trained on pseudo-labeled data are worse. However subsampling yields a large improvement on the original distribution and bridges the gap with the baseline.

**Table 4.** *Rel. imp. in FDR at FRR matching the baseline model on eval data with and without distribution shifts.*

| Condition | Rel. FDR Imp. (%) |
|---|---|
| Distribution shift | 52.0 |
| No distribution shift | 20.0 |

**Effect of Pseudo-Labeling on Easy and Hard Cases.** A risk of using pseudo-labeled examples the annotation model was confident on is whether the model performance generalized well over "hard" cases. We divided the eval data from both the shifted and unshifted distributions based on whether it was hard or easy for the annotator to label. Figure 4 presents the DET curves for those cases, with and without distribution shifts.

Figure 4(a, b) shows that for easier examples the proposed method yields improvements with and without distribution shifts. We see the same trend as in Fig. 3, where the gains were larger on the setting with distribution shift. For harder examples (Fig. 4(c, d)), the trend is similar, except that we observe no gains when there is no distribution shift, demonstrating the proposed method generalizes to "hard" examples.

## 6.2    Far and Near-Field Distribution Shifts with FCN

For the second set of experiments, the baseline and the proposed approach use the FCN model architecture discussed in Sect. 3. Table 4 presents the results. The proposed approach achieves a 52% relative improvement in FDR at FRR matching the baseline model on eval data with a distribution shift. Furthermore, it yields a 20.0% relative improvement in FDR without a distribution shift, showing that the proposed approach generalizes well even under a severe distribution shift even with models having much lower capacity. The gains observed in the table also reflects on Fig. 5 with DET curves corresponding to conditions with and without distribution shifts.

# 7    Conclusions

This paper characterizes distribution shifts in wakeword detection and proposes an approach to address it. Utilizing large scale unlabeled data from the shifted distribution, we use an annotation model with guidance from accept/reject confidence heuristics to generate pseudo-labels. We mitigate the over representation of subsets of data on which the annotation model does well by subsampling the positive class conditional distribution. Experiments on de-identified production data show that for a CNN model (2M parameters) trained on far-field audio and evaluated on far-field audio drawn from a different distribution, the proposed approach achieves a 14.3% relative improvement in FDR at equal FRR, while still yielding a 5% improvement in FDR under no distribution shift. We performed 3 ablation studies: a) size of pseudo-labeled data; b) with and without subsampling; c) easy and hard cases, confirming the viability of the proposed approach. As a second study, under a more severe distribution shift from far-field to near-field audio, with a smaller footprint FCN (250K parameters), our approach achieves a 52% relative improvement in FDR at equal FRR, while yielding a 20% relative improvement in FDR on the original far-field distribution.

# References

1. Arjovsky, M., Bottou, L., Gulrajani, I., Lopez-Paz, D.: Invariant risk minimization. arXiv preprint arXiv:1907.02893 (2019)
2. Bachman, P., Alsharif, O., Precup, D.: Learning with pseudo-ensembles. Adv. Neural Inf. Process. Syst. **27** (2014)
3. Berthelot, D., Carlini, N., Goodfellow, I., Papernot, N., Oliver, A., Raffel, C.: Mixmatch: a holistic approach to semi-supervised learning. In: NeurIPS (2019)
4. Chelba, C., Acero, A.: Adaptation of maximum entropy capitalizer: little data can help a lot. Comput. Speech Lang. **20**(4), 382–399 (2006)
5. Chen, G., Parada, C., Heigold, G.: Small-footprint keyword spotting using deep neural networks. In: 2014 IEEE International Conference on Acoustics, Speech and Signal Processing (ICASSP), pp. 4087–4091. IEEE (2014)

6. Elsahar, H., Gallé, M.: To annotate or not? Predicting performance drop under domain shift. In: Proceedings of the 2019 Conference on Empirical Methods in Natural Language Processing and the 9th International Joint Conference on Natural Language Processing (EMNLP-IJCNLP), pp. 2163–2173 (2019)

7. Fernndez, S., Graves, A., Schmidhuber, J.: An application of recurrent neural networks to discriminative keyword spotting. In: Artificial Neural Networks-ICANN, pp. 220–229 (2007)

8. Gao, Y., et al.: On front-end gain invariant modeling for wake word spotting. arXiv preprint arXiv:2010.06676 (2020)

9. Geirhos, R., Rubisch, P., Michaelis, C., Bethge, M., Wichmann, F.A., Brendel, W.: ImageNet-trained CNNs are biased towards texture; increasing shape bias improves accuracy and robustness. ICLR (2019)

10. Grandvalet, Y., Bengio, Y.: Semi-supervised learning by entropy minimization. Adv. Neural Inf. Process. Syst. **17** (2004)

11. Jose, C., Mishchenko, Y., Senechal, T., Shah, A., Escott, A., Vitaladevuni, S.: Accurate detection of wake word start and end using a CNN. In: Interspeech (2020)

12. Krueger, D., et al.: Out-of-distribution generalization via risk extrapolation (rex). arXiv preprint arXiv:2003.00688 (2020)

13. Kumar, R., Rodehorst, M., Wang, J., Gu, J., Kulis, B.: Building a robust word-level wakeword verification network. In: Interspeech (2020)

14. Lee, D.H., et al.: Pseudo-label: the simple and efficient semi-supervised learning method for deep neural networks. In: Workshop on Challenges in Representation Learning, ICML, vol. 3, p. 896 (2013)

15. Panchapagesan, S., et al.: Multi-task learning and weighted cross-entropy for DNN-based keyword spotting. In: Interspeech (2016)

16. Parisi, G.I., Kemker, R., Part, J.L., Kanan, C., Wermter, S.: Continual lifelong learning with neural networks: a review. Neural Netw. **113**, 54–71 (2019)

17. Parthasarathi, S.H.K., Strom, N.: Lessons from building acoustic models with a million hours of speech. In: ICASSP 2019–2019 IEEE International Conference on Acoustics, Speech and Signal Processing (ICASSP), pp. 6670–6674. IEEE (2019)

18. Quionero-Candela, J., Sugiyama, M., Schwaighofer, A., Lawrence, N.D.: Dataset Shift in Machine Learning. The MIT Press (2009)

19. Recht, B., Roelofs, R., Schmidt, L., Shankar, V.: Do ImageNet classifiers generalize to ImageNet? In: Proceedings of the 36th International Conference on Machine Learning, pp. 5389–5400 (2019)

20. Ruder, S., Plank, B.: Strong baselines for neural semi-supervised learning under domain shift. arXiv preprint arXiv:1804.09530 (2018)

21. Sainath, T.N., Parada, C.: Convolutional neural networks for small-footprint keyword spotting. In: Interspeech (2015)

22. Sajjadi, M., Javanmardi, M., Tasdizen, T.: Regularization with stochastic transformations and perturbations for deep semi-supervised learning. Adv. Neural Inf. Process. Syst. **29** (2016)

23. Shalev, G., Adi, Y., Keshet, J.: Out-of-distribution detection using multiple semantic label representations. In: Advances in Neural Information Processing Systems (NeurIPS) (2018)

24. Sun, M., et al.: Compressed time delay neural network for small-footprint keyword spotting. In: Interspeech (2017)

25. Tucker, G., Wu, M., Sun, M., Panchapagesan, S., Fu, G., Vitaladevuni, S.: Model compression applied to small-footprint keyword spotting. In: Proceedings of Interspeech (2016)

26. Zhang, C., Bengio, S., Hardt, M., Recht, B., Vinyals, O.: Understanding deep learning requires rethinking generalization. ICLR (2017)
27. Zhao, X., Krishnateja, K., Iyer, R., Chen, F.: Robust semi-supervised learning with out of distribution data. arXiv preprint arXiv:2010.03658 (2020)

# End-to-End Parkinson's Disease Detection Using a Deep Convolutional Recurrent Network

Cristian David Rios-Urrego[1]([✉]) [iD], Santiago Andres Moreno-Acevedo[1] [iD],
Elmar Nöth[2] [iD], and Juan Rafael Orozco-Arroyave[1,2] [iD]

[1] Faculty of Engineering, University of Antioquia UdeA, Medellín, Colombia
cdavid.rios@udea.edu.co
[2] Pattern Recognition Lab, Friedrich-Alexander-Universität Erlangen-Nürnberg,
Erlangen, Germany

**Abstract.** Deep Learning (DL) has enabled the development of accurate computational models to evaluate and monitor the neurological state of different disorders including Parkinson's Disease (PD). Although researchers have used different DL architectures including Convolutional Neural Networks (CNN), Recurrent Neural Networks (RNN) with Long Short-Term Memory (LSTM) units, fully connected networks, combinations of them, and others, but few works have correctly analyzed and optimized the input size of the network and how the network processes the information. This study proposes the classification of patients suffering from PD vs. healthy subjects using a 1D CNN followed by an LSTM. We show how the network behaves when its input and the kernel size in different layers are modified. In addition, we evaluate how the network discriminates between PD patients and healthy controls based on several speech tasks. The fusion of tasks yielded the best results in the classification experiments and showed promising results when classifying patients in different stages of the disease, which suggests the introduced approach is suitable to monitor the disease progression.

**Keywords:** Parkinson's Disease · Speech Processing · Convolutional Neural Networks · Long Short-Term Memory

## 1 Introduction

The automatic evaluation of pathological speech has captured the attention of the research community for many years. Among the benefits of using speech signals to diagnose and monitor different diseases are that it is non-invasive, and can be captured remotely at a very low cost. In the context of Parkinson's Disease (PD), different biomarkers have been studied for the development of computer-aided tools to support the diagnosis and monitoring of patients [11]. PD is a neurological disease characterized by resting tremor, rigidity, bradykinesia, postural instability, and other symptoms [9]. The disease is caused by a

P. Sojka et al. (Eds.): TSD 2022, LNAI 13502, pp. 326–338, 2022.
https://doi.org/10.1007/978-3-031-16270-1_27

progressive loss of dopaminergic neurons in the substantia nigra of the brain [6]. Most PD patients develop speech deficits which are grouped and called hypokinetic dysarthria where the speech is characterized by monotone intensity, low pitch variability, and poor prosody that tends to fade at the end of the utterance [12,14].

Several speech tasks are typically performed with the aim to model different pathologies. The most common tasks are read text, isolated words, the rapid repetition of diadochokinetic (DDK) tasks, sustained vowels, modulated vowels, and others. Each task brings different information that enables a better understanding of the pathology. Although there is significant progress in modeling pathological speech signals through classical methods mainly based on digital signal processing techniques, nowadays, Deep Learning (DL) has enabled different methodologies to speech traits processing in PD [1,3,17]. The main limitation of DL approaches is that it is typically considered as *black-box* because their interpretability is very limited or null, therefore it is not possible to know what happens inside the model.

In the last years, DL techniques have been implemented to classify PD patients vs. Healthy Control (HC) subjects, achieving promising results in the automatic assessment of speech in PD patients. Different techniques and architectures have been used to analyze speech data including Convolutional Neural Networks (CNNs) [15,17,18], 1D convolutional layers [3,7], Recurrent Neural Networks (RNNs) with Long Short-Term Memory (LSTM) units [1,13], fully-connected networks [2,3,13], and combinations of them [8]. However, to the best of our knowledge, there are no studies about the interpretation and understanding of the configuration of the networks. Different DL models used to predict pathologies work with the raw data, therefore their hyper-parameters should have a meaning or interpretation depending on the studied phenomenon.

Motivated by the above mentioned, the main objective of this study is to present different experiments using several speech tasks to find the best network configuration that allows the discrimination of pathological speech traits. In order to address this objective, we have created an architecture composed of two 1D convolutional layers, 2 LSTM layers, and a fully-connected neural network. The architecture was trained to classify PD patients vs. HC subjects by varying the input size of the architecture. Once the best input size is found, the kernel size of the 1D convolutional layers is varied to find the best kernel configuration. Afterwards, given the best input and kernel sizes, the architecture was tested upon different tasks and combinations. In addition, we evaluated the model in a multi-class experiment where ranges of the modified Frenchay Dysarthria Assessment (m-FDA) scale [16] are considered as threshold to create different groups of speakers. This experiment allows to evaluate the suitability of the proposed approach to classify patients in different stages of the disease. Finally, with the aim to perform a more realistic evaluation of the proposed model, an independent test set with 20 PD patients and 20 HC subjects was considered.

The rest of the paper is as follows: Sect. 2 describes the corpora considered for this study. Section 3, presents the methods used in the study and the final architecture created to identify which task and which hyper-parameters settings yield better results. Section 4 shows the results of the study, and finally, Sect. 5 contains the conclusions and future work.

# 2 Data

## 2.1 PC-GITA

This corpus contains speech recordings of 50 PD patients and 50 HC subjects sampled at 44.1 kHz [10]. All participants are native speakers of Colombian Spanish and are balanced in age and gender. Each patient was in ON-state during the recording session, i.e., under the effect of their medication and was evaluated by an expert neurologist who labeled the patients according to the Movement Disorder Society - Unified Parkinson's Disease Rating Scale (MDS-UPDRS-III) scale [5]. Additionally, the dysarthria level of each participant (patients and healthy controls) was evaluated by three phoniatricians according to the m-FDA scale. The median value over the three labels was considered as the dysarhtria level of each participant. Further details can be found in [16]. The speech signals were down-sampled to 16 kHz to standardize the sampling rate with the independent test set presented below. Table 1 shows demographic and clinical information of the speakers. The subjects produced a total of 21 speech tasks, including: 10 sentences, a monologue, a read text, 24 isolated words, rapid repetition of 6 DDK tasks, sustained vowels, and modulated vowels.

**Table 1.** Demographic and clinical information of the participants. [F/M]: Female/Male. Time since diagnosis and age are given in years. Values are reported as mean ± standard deviation.

|  | PD patients | HC subjects | Patients vs. Controls |
|---|---|---|---|
| Gender [F/M] | 25/25 | 25/25 | $^*p = 1.00$ |
| Age [F/M] | 60.7±7/61.3±11 | 61.4±7/60.5±12 | $^{**}p = 0.98$ |
| Range of age [F/M] | 49-75/33-81 | 49-76/31-86 | |
| Time since diagnosis [F/M] | 12.6±12/8.7±6 | | |
| MDS-UPDRS-III [F/M] | 37.6±14/37.8±22 | | |
| Speech item (MDS-UPDRS-III) [F/M] | 1.3±0.8/1.4±0.9 | | |
| m-FDA [F/M] | 28.3±8.5/29.2±8.5 | 7.3±7/6.7±7.8 | |

$^*p$-value calculated through Chi-square test.
$^{**}p$-value calculated through t-test.

## 2.2 Independent Test Set

This corpus is formed with 20 PD patients and 20 HC subjects. The patients group consisted of 9 males and 11 females with ages between 29 an 83 years (mean = 61.3 ± 14.3). All of them were evaluated by a neurologist expert according to the MDS-UPDRS-III scale. The scores of such evaluations ranged between 9 and 106 (mean = 40.1 ± 22.7). The healthy group is formed with 11 males and 9 females with ages between 49 and 78 years (mean = 62.6 ± 10). None of the participants of this group had symptoms of neurological or movement disorders. All participants are also native speakers of Colombian Spanish and are independent of the PC-GITA database. Each patient was captured at a sampling frequency of 16 kHz and performed 3 tasks: (1) read text, (2) monologue, and (3) /pa-ta-ka/ DDK.

## 3  Methods

Figure 1 summarizes the architecture proposed in this work. It consists of two 1D convolutional layers followed by an LSTM network. Finally, a fully-connected layer is in charge of the classification between PD patients and HC subjects. In addition to this, max pooling layers were added to down-sample the information after each convolutional layer. Details of each stage are presented below.

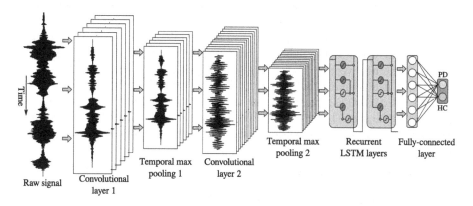

**Fig. 1.** Architecture proposed in this work to classify between PD patients and HC subjects.

### 3.1  1D Convolutional Layer

1D convolutional layer configurations are typically used to model sequential data, the main idea is to extract different representations based on the temporal domain. The layer consists of 2 main elements, number of channels and kernel. The kernel works as a filter upon the input data, it slides through the signal to extract information according to its weights and size. The layer has as many kernels as channels. The output data will have different representations from the same signal, as many as the number of channels. The weights of the kernel are learned during the training process and the size is given as a hyper-parameter. The output value of a convolutional layer with input size $(N, C_{in}, L)$

and output $(N, C_{out}, L)$ can be precisely described as Eq. 1[1].

$$out(N_i, C_{out_j}, L) = bias(C_{out_j}, L) + \sum_{k=0}^{C_{in}-1} weight(C_{out_j}, k, L) \star input(N_i, k, L)$$

(1)

where $\star$ is the valid cross-correlation operator, $N$ is a batch size, $C$ denotes a number of channels, and $L$ is the length of the signal sequence. Notice that in this type of layers, the kernel represents a temporal sliding window. Therefore, when a signal is represented by 16000 samples per second, a kernel size of 40 corresponds to an analysis window of 2.5 ms.

## 3.2   Temporal Max Pooling

Temporal max pooling is a down-sampling technique used to reduce the temporal size of the data. The pooling depends on the kernel size, which indicates how many samples of the input vector should be reduced. The max pooling procedure creates a new vector obtained from the input data with less samples. The kernel slides through the original data taking as many samples as its size and calculating the maximum value of the samples. Such a maximum will be the number of samples in the new vector. The sliding step is equal to the length of the kernel. In this way, if a temporal max pooling with a kernel size of 2 is applied to a 1 s signal with 16000 samples, the new vector will be temporally down-sampled representing the same 1 s of information with 8000 samples, where each sample is the maximum of a pair of consecutive values in the original data.

## 3.3   Recurrent LSTM Layer

RNNs have been proposed to model sequential data, inside its architecture, it has a hidden state $h_t$ that contains the information of the samples that have already passed through the network. These networks were improved when the storing process was introduced, resulting in the well-known LSTM networks. The LSTM is a cell that tries to remember sequential information for a longer time than the RNNs. The LSTM includes a status state that stores the long-term information, and also includes the following three new concepts: the input gate $I$ aims to determine what new information should be added to the network status state. The forget gate $F$ decides what information to keep for a long term and what information to forget from the status state. And finally, the output gate $S$ decides the new hidden state as a combination of the previous hidden state, the new input, and the status state.

---

[1] https://pytorch.org/docs/stable/generated/torch.nn.Conv1d.html.

## 3.4   Network's Topology

Figure 1 shows the architecture implemented in this work. It is composed of two 1D convolutional layers with 16 and 32 channels, respectively. Each layer is followed by a temporal max pooling with a kernel size of 2. Then, the characterization performed by the convolutional layers is the input to an LSTM that is responsible of performing the temporal analysis of the network. The recurrent network is composed of 2 LSTMs layers with 64 cells each. Finally, the output of the LSTMs feeds a fully-connected network to make the final decision. ReLu activations are considered in the convolutional layers, and a Softmax activation function is used at the output. For the training of the network, we used Pytorch with a cross-entropy loss function and an Adam optimizer. Batch normalization, dropout, and L2-regularization techniques are also used.

# 4   Experiments and Results

Motivated to know the best configuration of the network concerning the input and kernel sizes to classify PD patients vs. HC subjects, we performed two experiments: (1) we segmented the raw input waveform into different window sizes: 125 ms, 250 ms, 500 ms, 1 s, 2 s, and 4 s. The size that yielded the best result was considered for the next experiment. (2) Given the best input size, we changed the kernel size in the convolutional layers from 20 to 640 which corresponds to analysis windows from 2.5 ms to 40 ms. Once for the best input and kernel size configuration were found, we performed the classification experiments. In addition, we included a multi-class classification experiment to evaluate the dysarthria level of the speakers according to the m-FDA scale. Finally, we evaluated the model over an independent test set with 20 PD patients and 20 HC subjects. All experiments (except the independent test) are performed following a speaker-independent 10-fold cross-validation strategy. The results are reported in terms of mean and standard deviation computed along the folds.

## 4.1   Parameters Optimization

**Input Size:** The raw signals were segmented into different sizes to observe the behavior of the network at different lengths and to conclude which input size gives the best performance. Each sample was down-sampled to 16 kHz and pre-processed by removing its DC level and normalizing its amplitude. The results obtained are shown in Table 2. Notice that the best configuration is obtained with 1 s windows. This input size yielded an accuracy of 89.1% and 88.5% of F1-score. It is important to highlight that this result is balanced in sensitivity (86%) and specificity (91%).

**Table 2.** Classification of PD patients vs. HC subjects at different input sizes in the proposed architecture. Values are reported as mean ± standard deviation.

| Input size | Accuracy(%) | Sensitivity(%) | Specificity(%) | F1-score(%) |
|---|---|---|---|---|
| 125 ms | 83.6 ± 10.3 | 70.3 ± 19.6 | 94.3 ± 13.1 | 82.8 ± 10.9 |
| 250 ms | 85.1 ± 9.6 | 80.0 ± 23.0 | 91.3 ± 13.1 | 84.4 ± 10.4 |
| 500 ms | 86.4 ± 9.8 | 74.0 ± 23.2 | 96.0 ± 12.7 | 85.4 ± 10.9 |
| **1 s** | **89.1 ± 9.3** | **86.0 ± 21.1** | **91.0 ± 15.5** | **88.5 ± 10.2** |
| 2 s | 87.3 ± 10.6 | 81.0 ± 23.3 | 96.3 ± 14.1 | 86.6 ± 11.4 |
| 4 s | 83.6 ± 9.4 | 74.0 ± 23.1 | 90.7 ± 19.1 | 82.4 ± 10.6 |

A visual comparison was performed to analyze the behavior of each input size in terms of accuracy and also considering the Receiver Operating Characteristic (ROC) curves obtain in each case. The Area Under the ROC Curve (AUC) was also reported for each configuration. From Fig. 2, we conclude that the input size of 1 s is the best choice, with an AUC of 0.87 and the maximum accuracy. It is worth noting that this input size not only yielded the highest accuracy, but also provided the best balance between sensitivity and specificity.

**Kernel Size:** After obtaining the best configuration regarding the input size, we decided to evaluate different kernel sizes in the first and second convolutional layers, this allows determining the window of information that will be characterized

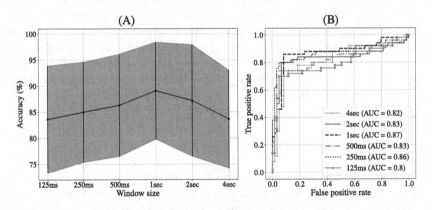

**Fig. 2.** (A). Mean accuracy and standard deviation (width of the gray stripe) with different input sizes. (B). ROC curves for different input sizes.

by the network as a response to the input signal. In the first convolutional layer, we performed kernel length variations between 40 and 640, corresponding to analysis windows of 2.5 ms and 40 ms, respectively (for a sample rate of 16 kHz). For the second layer, the kernel size was changed between 20 and 320, corresponding to 2.5 ms and 40 ms for a sample rate of 8 kHz, this is due to the temporal max pooling layer, which reduces the sampling rate of the sequence. The results are reported in Table 3.

**Table 3.** Classification of PD patients vs. HC subjects at different kernel sizes. Input length is fixed at 1 s. Values are reported as mean ± standard deviation.

| Kernel size | | Accuracy(%) | Sensitivity(%) | Specificity(%) | F1-score(%) |
|---|---|---|---|---|---|
| layer 1 | layer 2 | | | | |
| 40 | 20 | 89.1 ± 11.9 | 84.0 ± 22.7 | 92.6 ± 11.9 | 88.5 ± 12.7 |
| 80 | 40 | 89.1 ± 10.3 | 86.0 ± 21.2 | 91.0 ± 15.6 | 88.5 ± 11.1 |
| **160** | **80** | **89.1 ± 9.3** | **86.0 ± 21.2** | **91.0 ± 15.6** | **88.5 ± 10.2** |
| 320 | 160 | 80.8 ± 7.8 | 69.5 ± 21.4 | 89.0 ± 18.9 | 79.6 ± 8.9 |
| 640 | 320 | 80.6 ± 9.0 | 68.7 ± 19.1 | 91.3 ± 12.1 | 80.1 ± 9.7 |

The results show that a kernel size of 160 in the first convolutional layer and 80 in the second convolutional layer yield a classification accuracy of 89.1%. The corresponding AUC value is 0.87 (see Fig. 3.B). It is also possible to observe that for the first 3 combinations of kernel sizes, the results are very similar. The main difference is the standard deviation which is computed along the 10 folds considering in the cross-validation stage.

Figure 3 shows the plot with the average accuracies and the corresponding standard deviation. It can be observed a kind of saturation bend in the first three values, i.e., from 40–20 to 160–80 kernel sizes. A comparison of the ROC curves for each experiment is shown on the right side of Fig. 3. Notice that there are 2 groups of curves with similar trends. The group with larger areas corresponds

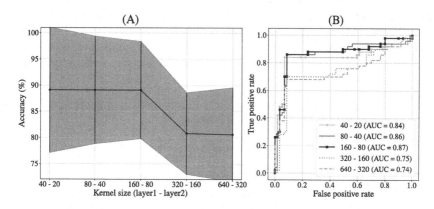

**Fig. 3.** (A). Mean accuracy and standard deviation (width of the gray stripe) with different kernel sizes. (B). ROC curves for different kernel sizes.

to the solid lines with an AUC values of 0.84, 0.86, and 0.87. And the group with smaller values correspond to the dashed lines with AUC of 0.75 and 0.74.

According to the results presented above, temporal and spectral in-deep analyses to find optimal parameters for the 1D CNN-LSTM architecture proposed in this study help in maximizing the classification performance to discriminate between PD patients and HC subjects.

## 4.2   Bi-class and Multi-class Classification

Previous experiments allowed to find the best configuration concerning input and kernel sizes. In this experiments, we want to validate how stable the network configuration is for different speech tasks. We also performed multi-class classification experiments to assess the dysarthria level of the participants according to the m-FDA scale [16].

**Bi-class Classification:** The neural network is trained and evaluated by using different tasks performed by each participant, including: (1) the DDK task consisting in the repetition of the syllables /pa-ta-ka/, (2) read text, (3) monologue, and (4) the fusion of the 21 tasks mentioned in the Sect. 2. Table 4 contains the results of each experiment. Notice that the fusion of all tasks yields the best classification result with an accuracy of 89.1%, which is comparable with state of the art when the same database is used.

Figure 4.B shows the ROC curves and the corresponding AUC values obtained in each experiment. It can be observed that the fusion of tasks yields the highest AUC value. Notice also that the monologue provides a similar result. Figure 4.A illustrates the histogram and the probability density distribution obtained from the best result (the fusion of speech tasks). It can be observed that the error for the discrimination of HC subjects is small (i.e., specificity = 91%), while the discrimination of PD patients is larger (i.e., sensitivity = 86%).

**Table 4.** Classification of PD patients vs. HC subjects based on different speech tasks. Values are reported as mean ± standard deviation.

| Task | Accuracy(%) | Sensitivity(%) | Specificity(%) | F1-score(%) |
|------|-------------|----------------|----------------|-------------|
| /pa-ta-ka/ | 65.8 ± 18.8 | 51.7 ± 25.5 | 79.0 ± 20.3 | 64.3 ± 19.6 |
| Read text | 77.9 ± 12.2 | 78.3 ± 17.6 | 76.5 ± 26.9 | 76.9 ± 13.3 |
| Monologue | 78.9 ± 14.4 | 86.3 ± 13.4 | 70.5 ± 26.1 | 78.1 ± 15.3 |
| **Fusion** | **89.1 ± 9.4** | **86.0 ± 21.2** | **91.0 ± 15.6** | **88.5 ± 10.2** |

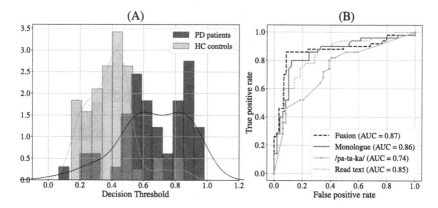

**Fig. 4.** (A). Histogram and the corresponding probability density distribution of the scores obtained from the classification of PD patients and HC subjects for the fusion of speech tasks. (B). ROC curves for several speech tasks performed by the participants.

**Multi-class Classification:** Besides the bi-class classification, we evaluated the dysarthria level of the speakers according to the m-FDA scale, which is a modified version of the Frenchay dysarthria assessment scale [4]. The m-FDA evaluates several aspects of speech, including: respiration, lips movement, palate/velum movement, larynx, tongue, monotonicity, and intelligibility. The participants are divided into four groups according to their m-FDA score. The distribution of the groups is illustrated in Fig. 5.A. Note that the white bars correspond to HC subjects while the others are for PD patients.

The result for the multi-class classification yielded an accuracy of $59.9 \pm 6.7$ and an F1-score of $55.7 \pm 13.1$. Figure 5.B shows the confusion matrix resulting from this experiment. Note that most speakers were correctly classified in the intermediate levels. Most of the errors occurred in groups 0 and 3, where the scores of the m-FDA are the smallest and the largest. To the best of our knowledge, this is one of the first works that includes an end-to-end architecture for the dysarthria level classification of PD patients.

## 4.3   Classification Using the Independent Test Set

This experiment is performed with the aim to evaluate the proposed approach in a more realistic scenario. This will provide a better impression regarding the generalization capability of the proposed models. We considered 20 independent

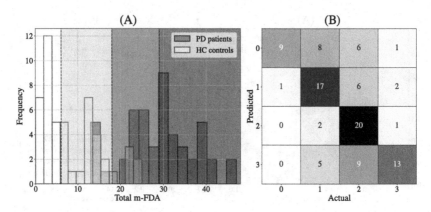

**Fig. 5.** (A). Distribution of the m-FDA scores for the participants of this study. The scores for the PD patients are grouped into three classes: low, intermediate, and severe according to the severity of the disease. The scores for the m-FDA scale also include HC subjects, represented with the white bars. (B). Confusion matrix for the multi-class classification.

PD patients and 20 HC subjects that were not included in the training and validation processes introduced before. Notice that this additional test set represents a group of subjects that arrived at the clinic and performed speech recordings to decide whether to continue with further tests to define their neurological condition.

The results are shown in Table 5. Note that the fusion of speech tasks yielded the best result with an accuracy of 77.5% and an F1-score of 75.3%. Furthermore, it can be observed that the same trend of the trained network is preserved with higher specificity (85%) than sensitivity (70%). These results confirm that it is possible to design deep neural network models to support the PD diagnosis and screening. We hypothesize that by adding more data in the training process, we could improve the stability and robustness of this classifier in order to obtain results closer to those reported with the cross-validation strategy (see Table 4).

**Table 5.** Classification of PD patients vs. HC subjects based on several tasks performed by the participants in the independent test set.

| Task | Accuracy(%) | Sensitivity(%) | Specificity(%) | F1-score(%) |
|---|---|---|---|---|
| /pa-ta-ka/ | 62.5 | 52.0 | 73.0 | 61.6 |
| Read text | 73.0 | 78.0 | 68.0 | 72.9 |
| Monologue | 71.0 | 78.5 | 63.5 | 69.1 |
| **Fusion** | **77.5** | **70.0** | **85.0** | **75.3** |

## 5   Conclusions

This paper proposes an end-to-end architecture of an 1D CNN-LSTM network for the classification of patients suffering from PD vs. HC subjects. We evaluated and determined the best configuration of the proposed architecture for different input and kernel sizes in the convolutional layer. The results showed that the best configuration with respect to the input is obtained from windows of 1 s. We noticed that a correct window analysis for the convolutional layers corresponds to a kernel size of 160 and 80 for the first and second layers, respectively. (i.e., windows of 10 ms for two layers). Then, we evaluated how the network classifies patients and controls based on several tasks performed by the participants. The fusion of speech tasks yielded the best results in the classification experiments with an accuracy of 89.1%. Motivated by this result, we included an experiment for the evaluation of the dysarthria level according to the m-FDA scale. We obtained an accuracy of up to 60%, and we could observe that the error in classification was mainly in the subjects with the smallest and largest m-FDA scores. Finally, we evaluated the robustness and generalization capability of the network with an independent test set of 20 PD patients and 20 HC subjects. For this last experiment, we observed that the fusion of speech tasks yielded also the best result, with an accuracy of 77.5%, which demonstrates that despite the small amount of data, it is possible to generate deep neural network models for the automatic diagnosis of PD.

Future experiments will include the training of architectures with larger amounts of data, as well as other pathologies in different languages. In addition, we will also address experiments for the interpretation of the hidden states of RNNs, preliminary results showed that in some cases, the hidden states of the network carry the same behavior as the fundamental frequency of the participant.

**Acknowledgements.** This work was financed by CODI from University of Antioquia grant # 2017-15530. This project received funding from the European Unions Horizon 2020 research and innovation programme under the Marie Sklodowska-Curie Grant Agreement # 766287.

## References

1. Arias-Vergara, T., et al.: Automatic detection of voice onset time in voiceless plosives using gated recurrent units. Digit. Signal Process. **104**, 102779 (2020)
2. Caliskan, A., et al.: Diagnosis of the Parkinson disease by using deep neural network classifier. IU J. Electr. Electron. Eng. **17**(2), 3311–3318 (2017)
3. El Maachi, I., Bilodeau, G.A., Bouachir, W.: Deep 1d-convnet for accurate Parkinson disease detection and severity prediction from gait. Expert Syst. Appl. **143**, 113075 (2020)
4. Enderby, P.: Frenchay dysarthria assessment. Br. J. Disord. Commun. **15**(3), 165–173 (1980)

5. Goetz, C.G., et al.: Movement disorder society-sponsored revision of the unified Parkinson's disease rating scale (MDS-UPDRS): scale presentation and clinimetric testing results. Mov. Disord. **23**(15), 2129–2170 (2008)
6. Jankovic, J.: Parkinson's disease: clinical features and diagnosis. J. Neurol. Neurosurg. Psychiatry **79**(4), 368–376 (2008)
7. Kim, H., et al.: Convolutional neural network classifies pathological voice change in laryngeal cancer with high accuracy. J. Clin. Med. **9**(11), 3415 (2020)
8. Mallela, J., et al.: Voice based classification of patients with amyotrophic lateral sclerosis, Parkinson's disease and healthy controls with CNN-LSTM using transfer learning. In: Proceedings of ICASSP, pp. 6784–6788. IEEE (2020)
9. McKinlay, A., et al.: A profile of neuropsychiatric problems and their relationship to quality of life for Parkinson's disease patients without dementia. Parkinsonism Relat. Disord. **14**(1), 37–42 (2008)
10. Orozco-Arroyave, J.R., et al.: New Spanish speech corpus database for the analysis of people suffering from Parkinson's disease. In: Proceedings of LREC, pp. 342–347 (2014)
11. Orozco-Arroyave, J.R., et al.: Apkinson: the smartphone application for telemonitoring Parkinson's patients through speech, gait and hands movement. Neurodegener. Dis. Manag. **10**(3), 137–157 (2020)
12. Pinto, S., et al.: Treatments for dysarthria in Parkinson's disease. Lancet Neurol. **3**(9), 547–556 (2004)
13. Rizvi, D.R., et al.: An LSTM based deep learning model for voice-based detection of Parkinson's disease. Int. J. Adv. Sci. Technol. **29**(8) (2020)
14. Spencer, K.A., Rogers, M.A.: Speech motor programming in hypokinetic and ataxic dysarthria. Brain Lang. **94**(3), 347–366 (2005)
15. Trinh, N.H., O'Brien, D.: Pathological speech classification using a convolutional neural network (2019)
16. Vásquez-Correa, J.C., et al.: Towards an automatic evaluation of the dysarthria level of patients with Parkinson's disease. J. Commun. Disord. **76**, 21–36 (2018)
17. Vavrek, L., et al.: Deep convolutional neural network for detection of pathological speech. In: Proceedings of the SAMI, pp. 000245–000250. IEEE (2021)
18. Wodzinski, M., et al.: Deep learning approach to Parkinson's disease detection using voice recordings and convolutional neural network dedicated to image classification. In: Proceedings of the EMBC, pp. 717–720. IEEE (2019)

# Lexical Bundle Variation in Business Actors' Public Communications

Brett Drury[1,2(✉)] [iD] and Samuel Morais Drury[3]

[1] Liverpool Hope University, Hope Campus, Liverpool, UK
druryb@hope.ac.uk
[2] LIAAD-INESC-TEC, R. Dr. Roberto Frias, Porto, Portugal
[3] Colégio Puríssimo, R. Sete, 881, Rio Claro, SP 13500-060, Brazil

**Abstract.** Business Actors communicate to audiences via the mass media through public statements or informal interviews with journalists. This information is directly quoted in news stories about financially significant events. The motivation for speaking to the mass media varies from job role to job role, and therefore the vocabulary of a job role and the delivery of the information to the press varies also. This paper provides a comprehensive analysis using lexical bundles and sentimental lexical bundles to discover the common vocabulary of four selected job roles: Analyst, CEO, CFO and Economist, and their similarity with other job roles. This work demonstrates that the CEO job role makes ample use of highly positive repetitive lexical bundles, whereas the Economist holds a unique role where it has a vocabulary with less of a positive skew and few shared lexical bundles with other job roles.

**Keywords:** Lexical Bundles · Corpus Linguistics · Business Actors

## 1 Introduction

Public business communication does influence the prospects of an organisation [6]. Business Actors who make unguarded or unvarnished statements can prejudice the organisation's share price and in some extreme cases bankrupt the company. The most famous example of this phenomenon is the case of Gerald Ratner, who stated: "People say to me, 'how can you sell this for such a low price?' And I say because it's total crap" [11]. His company, Ratners the Jewellers, promptly lost eighty per cent of its value and renamed itself Signet [11]. The reputational damage caused by "straight talking" has led to Business Actors developing their own method of communication with unique idioms and risk-averse language [4]. Finance Professionals, such as Economists and Analysts are not bound by such concerns, and can make objective and factual statements about a company, but do not have access to private information, and therefore may have to couch their statements with expressions of uncertainty.

Lexical bundles are a method of determining the vocabulary and the idioms of speakers [12]. This article uses the 500,000 public statements by Business

© Springer Nature Switzerland AG 2022
P. Sojka et al. (Eds.): TSD 2022, LNAI 13502, pp. 339–351, 2022.
https://doi.org/10.1007/978-3-031-16270-1_28

Actors and Finance Professionals from the 2007 Financial Crisis to determine the common language of each group, as well as the differences and similarities between each group. The article will adhere to the following structure: Literature Review, Lexical Bundle Methodology, Lexical Bundle Experiments, Sentiment Lexical Bundle Experiments, and Conclusion.

## 2   Literature Review

The literature review covers relevant business speech corpora and lexical bundles. The corpora research search limited itself to identifying corpora that contained day-to-day public communication by Business Actors, whereas the lexical bundle research was limited to the examination of diverse domains using lexical bundles.

The main corpus discovered in the literature review is the Minho Quotation Resource [2], which is a resource of 500,000 public statements from Business Actors during the Financial Crisis of 2007 to 2011. The statements contain the speaker's name, where possible a job title and the quote. The resource was updated in 2021 [5]. The update cleaned up the quotes to make sure that they had the same encoding and inferred missing job titles.

Lexical bundles are a technique that can be used to discover patterns within corpora. They are a sequence of words or Part of Speech Tags (POS) from the same sentence [10]. The most common sequences will represent the everyday language of the corpora. Lexical bundles can be of any length, however, the research literature suggests that a length of four words (tetragrams) is optimal [10]. The lexical bundle approach to determine common vocabularies has been applied to several domains including Wikipedia [7], spam emails [9], and historical English [13]. The literature review failed to discover the application of lexical bundles to the business speech domain.

## 3   Lexical Bundle Methodology

This paper seeks to explore the hypothesis that the employment status affects the vocabulary and style of public utterances of Business Actors. This paper asserts that Business Actors employed by an organisation will moderate their language, and use a style of delivery that will use risk-averse language to downplay uncertainty and exaggerated language to amplify success or rise a banal event to a positive achievement. Independent Business Actors will not have limitations imposed on their language, however, they will not have access to private information which is available to their employed counterparts and consequently will not communicate an accurate picture of the current financial situation.

### 3.1   Lexical Bundles

The experimental methodology collects tetragrams with a minimum of twenty occurrences per million words, as this is a common cut-off point in the research literature [1].

The speech of four job roles was chosen for comparison. They are Analyst, Chief Executive Officer (CEO), Chief Financial Officer (CFO) and Economist. These roles were chosen because they represent different roles in the business domain. The Analyst and Economist are typically independent of constraints of causing reputational damage as they are commenting on third-party organisations, whereas the CEO and CFO are subject to constraints as their utterances can affect share price and sales. The lexical bundle analysis will 1. analyse the most frequent lexical bundles and 2. compute the lexical bundle similarity between the job roles. Job roles with similar lexical bundle similarity will have a common motivation for public communication.

The common use of sentiment in the vocabulary of a speaker can be an indication of a manipulative role, where the speaker seeks to convince an audience to accept their point of view through the use of emotion [4]. The use of sentiment to manipulate opinion is known as framing [4]. The sentiment lexical bundle analysis will follow the lexical bundle analysis, but will exclude any lexical bundle that does not have a sentiment word.

# 4   Lexical Bundle Experiments

The lexical bundle analysis extracted tetragrams that had a relative frequency of twenty or above. The results for the four selected speakers are shown in Table 1, and because of space limits the most frequent ten lexical bundles for each speaker are displayed. The raw results data can be found here. Lexical bundles that are common to all speakers are in bold.

The lexical bundles for the Analyst job role clearly show that their vocabulary is dominated by forward-looking lexical bundles that imply a short-term prediction about a financial instrument. The forward-looking lexical bundles include "is going to be" and "in the short term". This is not unexpected, as the prediction or estimation of financial results is part of an analyst's job role.

The CEO lexical bundles show the language of manipulation, as there is frequent use of positive sentiment to frame a subject. The common sentiment terms are "pleased" and "excited", and the lexical bundles also reveal that a common sentiment phrase "look forward to" is frequently used.

The CFO lexical bundles are similar to both that of the Analyst and CEO role, as the lexical bundles have both the sentimental lexical bundles such as "we are pleased to" as well as the reporting type lexical bundles such as "in the first quarter" and "in the second half". These reporting and manipulation lexical bundles are expected as the CFO is employed directly by a company, but also has a reporting function where the CFO is legally mandated to provide a truthful account of the origination's financial position.

The Economist lexical bundles, except for the named entity, Bank of England, seem to be reporting bundles such as "in the fourth quarter" and "in the first quarter", which again is in line with the demands of the job role.

The most frequent lexical bundles as shown in Table 2 does not seem to have common bundles across each of the job roles. There is one, "the end of the", which is common to all job roles. However, the use of a lexical bundle may vary between job roles. A sample of the use of the lexical bundles is shown below.

- Analyst: Last Christmas was **the end of the** world, so we're seeing some quite good numbers
- CEO: he had not abdicated from his pledge to make an announcement on the post before **the end of the** year
- CFO: While Credit Suisse's Tier 1 ratio was 14.1 per cent at **the end of the** first quarter
- Economist: There are some who are **at the end of** their operating capital.

**Table 1.** The Most Frequent Lexical Bundles per Speaker Role, where L.B = Lexical Bundle and Rel. Freq. = Frequency Per Million Bundles

| Analyst | | CEO | | CFO | | Economist | |
|---|---|---|---|---|---|---|---|
| L.B | Rel. Freq. | L.B | Rel. Freq. | L.B | Rel. Freq. | L.B | Rel. Freq. |
| is going to be | 228 | we look forward to | 433 | in the first quarter | 523 | the bank of england | 511 |
| the end of the | 185 | we are pleased to | 365 | in the fourth quarter | 481 | in the third quarter | 468 |
| in the short term | 174 | we are very pleased | 272 | the end of the | 396 | the second half of | 373 |
| in the second half | 149 | the end of the | 178 | at the end of | 382 | in the fourth quarter | 347 |
| is likely to be | 145 | are very pleased to | 163 | in the third quarter | 382 | the end of the | 338 |
| at the end of | 141 | we are excited to | 160 | in the second quarter | 311 | in the second half | 303 |
| in the united states | 127 | as we continue to | 152 | by the end of | 283 | over the coming months | 286 |
| going to be a | 127 | look forward to working | 149 | we are pleased to | 283 | in the first quarter | 277 |
| the second half of | 123 | and look forward to | 145 | we look forward to | 269 | at the end of | 251 |
| per cent of the | 120 | we will continue to | 140 | in the second half | 255 | in the second quarter | 243 |

As demonstrated by the examples is that the lexical bundle **at the end of** can refer to different types of speech, such as time periods or idioms such as "the end of the world".

The relative frequency and variety of lexical bundles can indicate a type of vocabulary. A restricted number of lexical bundles with high relative frequency will indicate a repeated and frequently used vocabulary, whereas numerous lexical bundles with low relative frequency may indicate a richer vocabulary. A comparison was made where the lexical bundles were aggregated by their relative frequency, and the results are shown in Fig. 1, and it is clear from the results that the CEO job role has the most restricted vocabulary of all the job types as the most frequent lexical bundles represent a large amount of the total frequency of all lexical bundles when compared to other job roles.

The remaining speakers have similar profiles where the low-frequency bundles in combination make up the majority of the linguistic profile of each of the Analyst, CFO and Economist job roles. This suggests that these job roles have a richer vocabulary than the CEO, with less repetition. The research by [4] would suggest that this repetition would be used in framing and manipulative statements, and that the remaining job roles would indulge in this activity less often than the CEO job role.

The speakers from each job role will share lexical bundles, as they will have common functions when communicating with the mass media. It is possible to compute the similarity of lexical bundle profiles with a weighted

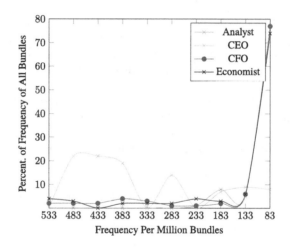

**Fig. 1.** A Comparison of The Distribution of Frequency of Use of Lexical Bundles with a minimum relative frequency of twenty

lexical bundle similarity, which can be represented as $weighted\_sim = \frac{sum\_of\_common\_bundles\_rel\_frequency}{sum\_of\_all\_bundles}$. The similarity results are in Table 2, and it is clear from the results that the two most similar job roles are the CEO and Analyst with a 0.40 weighted lexical bundle similarity score, and the most dissimilar job roles are the CFO and the Economist.

**Table 2.** Weighted Lexical Bundle Similarity by Job Role

| Job Role | Analyst | CEO | CFO | Economist |
|----------|---------|-----|-----|-----------|
| Analyst | N/A | **0.40** | 0.14 | 0.26 |
| CEO | **0.40** | N/A | 0.22 | 0.18 |
| CFO | 0.14 | **0.22** | N/A | 0.12 |
| Economist | **0.26** | 0.18 | 0.12 | N/A |

The shared vocabulary between Analysts and CEOs are forward-looking statements that include lexical bundles such as: "is expected to be", "in the coming years", "end of this year", "be one of the", "market share in the", and "in the next few". It is likely that because the CEO is obliged to manipulate various audiences, they will speculate positively about the prospects of the organisation, whereas the Analyst will also speculate, but objectively. It should be noted that the shared vocabulary between the CEO and the Analyst is objective lexical bundles, whereas the most common CEO lexical bundles have sentiment words such as "pleased" and "excited".

The average similarity of each job role to other job roles, can indicate the breadth of the job role when communicating through the mass media. Low average similarity indicates a unique communication function, whereas a high average similarity indicates a shared communication function with other job roles. The average similarity for each job role is: Analyst 0.26($\pm$0.11), CEO 0.26($\pm$0.09), CFO 0.16($\pm$0.04) and Economist 0.19($\pm$0.06). The Analyst and the CEO roles have the highest average similarity, but they are within one standard deviation of the lowest score. The Analyst and the CEO roles have the highest similarity score because of their mutual similarity. However, the similarity scores for the CFO and the Economist are relatively low due to their unique vocabulary and role when communicating with the mass media.

The Minho Quotation Resource contains additional job roles to the four that have been used thus far. This experiment used job roles that have more than two hundred quotes in the aforementioned resource. The similarity experiment was repeated with these new job roles. The results are in Table 3.

**Table 3.** Most Similar Job Roles by Weighted Lexical Bundle

| Job Roles | Similarity | | | |
|-----------|------|------|------|------|
| | Role | Role | Role | Role |
| Analyst | Head (0.54) | Director (0.42) | CEO (0.40) | Managing Director (0.31) |
| CEO | President (0.78) | Chairman (0.74) | Director (0.6) | Vice President (0.52) |
| CFO | CEO (0.22) | Chairman (0.19) | President (0.18) | Head (0.15) |
| Economist | Head (0.26) | Analyst (0.26) | Chief Economist (0.20) | CEO (0.18) |

In common with the previous experiments, the CFO and the Economist job roles have the least lexical bundle similarity with the other job roles, and therefore it is possible to assume that their lexical bundles are unique to their job role when communicating with the mass media. The Analyst and the CEO job roles have a shared lexical bundle across some job roles, which infers that they share similar communication functions with other job roles. For example, the CEO and President job roles share numerous highly frequent lexical bundles, such as "i am pleased to", "and we are confident" as well as reporting lexical bundles such as "in the second quarter", although the common lexical bundles did not reveal any lexical bundles that speculated about the financial future of the organisation. The Analyst and the Head roles in common share forward-looking lexical bundles, such as "is likely to be" and "the next six months".

The lexical bundle analysis reveals some characteristics of the vocabulary of the public utterances of each of the selected job roles. The Analyst role is preoccupied with forward-looking lexical bundles whereas the CEO, despite having the most restricted vocabulary, has the broadest role when communicating with the mass media. They have forward-looking, reporting and framing lexical bundles. The Economist and CFO job roles have very few frequent lexical bundles in common with other job roles. This paper claims that these job roles' communication with the mass media is very limited or specialised.

## 5    Sentiment Lexical Bundle Experiments

The previous section mentioned sentiment lexical bundles as lexical bundles that have sentimental words. Job roles that have a sentimental lexicon could be using sentiment to manipulate the audience that the quote was directed to [8]. The first experiment was to compute the percentage of the lexical bundles that have a sentiment orientation. Two measures were used: a simple percentage computation, $\frac{number\_sentimental\_lexical\_bundles}{total\_number\_lexical\_bundles}$, and a weighted percentage computation, which is computed by $\frac{frequency\_sentimental\_lexical\_bundles}{frequency\_all\_lexical\_bundles}$. These measures determine the percentage of the common vocabulary of a job role that uses sentiment. High use of sentiment is an indicator of manipulation [4].

**Table 4.** The Percentage of Sentimental Lexical Bundles

| Job Role | Percent. Sentiment | Weighted Percent. Sentiment |
|---|---|---|
| Analyst | 0.09 | 0.07 |
| CEO | 0.26 | 0.30 |
| CFO | 0.12 | 0.13 |
| Economist | 0.09 | 0.07 |

It is clear from results in Table 4 that the CEO job role relies more upon sentimental lexical bundles than the other job roles. The use of sentimental language is probably by design to portray their organisation and its achievements in a positive light. The most frequent lexical bundles are shown in Table 6, and it is clear from the results is that the relative frequency of the lexical bundles for the CEO and CFO roles is far higher than for the Analyst and Economist roles and that the CEO and CFO lexical bundles have a framing role. The bundles such as "we are pleased to" and "we are excited to" frame the event or action which is next in the sequence. For example, "We are excited to see a genuine transformation for insurance buyers, brokers and insurers"[1], which is a framing quote as it caries a high sentiment score, but little or no actionable information.

The sentiment bundles for the Analyst and Economist job roles are not framing an event or action to promote their organisation, but are bundles that provide an opinion or description about a third party. For example, "in the right direction" and "recovery will be slow", are non-manipulative lexical bundles as they are objective statements.

The type of sentiment that is used is an indicator of the function of the language in the mass media. An overly positive lexicon could be an indicator of a manipulative imperative when communicating with the public at large. The distribution of bundles across the sentiment categories could be found in Table 5, where the per cent measure is a simple intersection of lexical bundles with each sentiment category and the weighted per cent is where the relative frequency of the bundle is included in the calculation. It is calculated by $\frac{freq\_lb\_sent\_cat}{total\_frequency}$ where $freq\_lb\_sent\_cat$ is the relative frequency of all lexical bundles with a given sentiment direction, and $total\_frequency$ is the total frequency of all lexical bundles with a sentiment category.

**Table 5.** Sentiment Profile of Lexical Bundles by Job Role

| Job Role | Lexical Bundles | | | |
|---|---|---|---|---|
| | Positive | | Negative | |
| | Percent. Weighted | Percent. | Percent. Weighted | Percent |
| Analyst | 0.79 | 0.79 | 0.21 | 0.21 |
| CEO | 0.99 | 0.99 | 0.01 | 0.01 |
| CFO | 0.86 | 0.83 | 0.14 | 0.17 |
| Economist | 0.65 | 0.68 | 0.35 | 0.32 |

The results demonstrate that the CEO vocabulary is dominated by positive lexical bundles. This would imply that the CEO job role may be using framing [4] to manipulate audiences. A restricted vocabulary and frequent highly positive lexical bundles, indicates that CEOs communicate no useful information when using positive sentiment [4]. The CFO job role is also highly positive with 0.86 of lexical bundles being positive, and this would imply that a job role that has a

---

[1] https://archive.fo/aGN0g.

dependent employment role will have a highly positive lexicon. The Economist has the highest percentage of negative lexical bundles, and this would imply that they have a more balanced vocabulary, and this is not unexpected as the economist job role should provide balanced commentary on the economy.

In common with the lexical bundle section, an experiment was conducted to identify the distribution of sentiment lexical bundles by job role. And from the results, it is clear that the CEO and CFO have differing sentimental lexical profiles to that of the Economist and Analyst roles. The sentimental lexical bundles appear infrequently for the Analyst and Economist job roles. There are no sentimental lexical bundles that have a relative frequency higher than one thirty-three times per million lexical bundles for either job role. Conversely, the CEO job role uses very high frequently occurring sentimental lexical bundles in their vocabulary. The CFO role is almost equidistant between the profiles, as it demonstrates that the majority of its sentimental lexical bundles are low frequency, but not as many as the Analyst and Economist roles. And it has a higher use of more frequent sentimental lexical bundles than the Analyst and Economist roles, but lower than the CEO.

The distribution of sentimental lexical bundles is similar to that of lexical bundles in Fig. 1 for that of the Analyst, CEO, and Economist job roles. However, the CFO role uses sentimental lexical bundles differently from that of lexical bundles, as it has a heavier reliance on more frequent lexical bundles. It can be inferred that the CFO has a dual role, where they behave similarly to an Analyst or Economist with objective lexical bundles. However, the CFO behaves similar to a CEO when it comes to the use of sentiment lexical bundles.

The similarity of sentimental lexical bundles between job roles is an indicator of similar use of sentiment in their communication with the mass media. And from the results in the Table 7, it is clear that the use of sentiment is determined

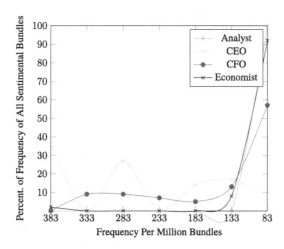

**Fig. 2.** A Comparison of The Distribution of Frequency of Use of Sentimental Lexical Bundles with a minimum relative frequency of twenty

by the type of employment, where the CFO and the CEO have the highest mutual common use of sentimental lexical bundles, whereas the Economist and Analyst job roles share a higher degree of common sentimental lexical bundles than with the CFO and CEO roles. This is different to the similarity experiments with all lexical bundles in Table 2 where the Analyst and the CEO shared the most lexical bundles. Therefore, it can be concluded that the Analyst and the CEO job roles have a common objective or neutral shared vocabulary, but a dissimilar sentimental lexicon. It can be also concluded that although similar information is being communicated to the mass media by both the Analyst and the CEO, the function of the communication is different due to the dissimilar use of sentiment. This characteristic justifies the approach taken by [3] who identified actionable quotes by CEOs when their quotes were similar to that of Economists and Analysts (Fig. 2).

The similarity of sentimental bundles can indicate a similar motivation when communicating through the mass media. This experiment repeated the experiment on page 322, where the job roles compared were expanded to all job roles in the Minho Quotation Resource that had more than two hundred quotes.

**Table 6.** The Most Frequent Sentimental Lexical Bundles Per Job Role, where L.B = Lexical Bundle and Rel. Freq. = Frequency Per Million

| Analyst | | CEO | | CFO | | Economist | |
|---|---|---|---|---|---|---|---|
| L.B | Rel. Freq. | L.B | Rel. Freq. | L.B | Rel. Freq. | L.B | Rel. Freq. |
| more than per cent | 72 | we are pleased to | 365 | we are pleased to | 283 | the worst of the | 121 |
| to be able to | 58 | we are very pleased | 272 | we are very pleased | 212 | in the right direction | 87 |
| at the top of | 51 | are very pleased to | 163 | one of the most | 170 | more than per cent | 78 |
| will be able to | 51 | we are excited to | 160 | for the full year | 127 | the worst is over | 61 |
| in the right direction | 47 | we are delighted to | 139 | we were able to | 113 | this is good news | 52 |
| would be able to | 43 | we are very excited | 129 | will be able to | 113 | is good news for | 52 |
| it will be difficult | 40 | to be able to | 127 | are very pleased with | 99 | that the worst is | 52 |
| is unlikely to be | 36 | one of the most | 119 | very pleased with our | 99 | it is hard to | 52 |
| not be able to | 36 | will be able to | 116 | would be able to | 85 | at the very least | 52 |
| the worst of the | 36 | we are pleased with | 103 | we are delighted to | 99 | it is important to | 43 |

**Table 7.** Weighted Sentimental Lexical Bundle Similarity by Job Role

| Job Role | Analyst | CEO | CFO | Economist |
|----------|---------|-----|-----|-----------|
| Analyst | N/A | 0.17 | 0.07 | **0.18** |
| CEO | 0.17 | N/A | **0.36** | 0.08 |
| CFO | 0.07 | **0.36** | N/A | 0.04 |
| Economist | **0.18** | 0.08 | 0.04 | N/A |

It is clear from the results in Table 8 that the CEO and CFO roles have a higher similarity with the nearest job roles when considering only sentimental bundles. This would imply that how these job roles communicate is more similar when communicating using sentiment than when communicating factual or objective information. The average increase in similarity for the four most similar job roles was $0.09 \pm 0.01$ for the CEO role and $0.19 \pm 0.05$ for the CFO role. Conversely, the Economist and the Analyst roles saw a decline in similarity when considering sentimental lexical bundles, with the Analyst similarity score declining by an average of $0.17 \pm 0.03$ and the Economist's similarity score declined by $0.12 \pm 0.02$. This infers that these job roles share more objective or neutral lexical bundles with other job roles than sentimental ones. It is possible to conclude that these job roles do not have a common function when communicating with the mass media, however, they do have a common subject.

The sentimental lexical bundle analysis clearly shows that sentiment is used frequently by the CEO job role, however, because the job role depends upon a limited number of high frequent lexical bundles, their sentimental vocabulary is limited. There is a sentimental vocabulary that is common between several job roles, which is demonstrated by the increase in weighted lexical bundle similarity between the CEO job role and the most similar job roles. The converse is true for the Economist and the Analyst, as there seems to be no common sentimental

**Table 8.** Most Similar Job Roles by Weighted Sentimental Lexical Bundle

| Job Roles | Similarity | | | |
|-----------|------|------|------|------|
| | Role | Role | Role | Role |
| Analyst | Head (0.37) | Director (0.26) | Managing Director (0.19) | Economist (0.18) |
| CEO | Chairman (0.86) | President (0.86) | Director (0.70) | Vice President (0.63) |
| CFO | CEO (0.36) | Chairman (0.33) | Vice President (0.26) | Director (0.23) |
| Economist | Analyst (0.18) | Head (0.13) | CEO (0.08) | Director (0.07) |

vocabulary. This is demonstrated by lexical bundle weighted similarity being lower for the most similar job role than for lexical bundle weighted similarity.

The common sentimental vocabulary is designed to manipulate, or at least to maintain, a positive perception of an organisation. This is demonstrated by the highly positive lexicon of the CEO and CFO job roles, despite the quotes being drawn from the Financial Crisis of the early two-thousands.

## 6    Conclusion

The analysis in this article provides a comparison of the vocabulary of four types of speakers from their public communication during the Financial Crisis of 2007. It is clear from the analysis that the CEO is a unique position that shares some common functions with other job roles, however, it does have a unique function which is to use sentiment to manipulate the various audiences that the public communication is aimed at. The CEO job role not only relies upon sentiment but also on a repetitive vocabulary where highly positive sentimental lexical bundles dominate public communication. This characteristic is shared by several leadership roles such as Chairman, President and Director. The inference that can be drawn from this characteristic is that sentiment analysis will not be successful in predicting the prospects of the CEO's organisation. The other job roles are not dominated by a few lexical bundles and have a richer lexicon than the CEO role, and the skew between positive and negative sentiment is not as pronounced as in the CEO job role.

The Economist job role in terms of lexical bundles is unique as their communication with the mass media has the least common lexical bundles with other job roles, and these lexical bundles are more likely to be negative than any other job role.

The differing lexical bundles and the varying reliance upon sentimental lexical bundles, as well as the disparate richness of vocabulary used by the selected job roles, imply that one form of analysis to infer future economic prospects will not be sufficient for Business Actors. Models will need to be generated for each type of speaker, and differing assumptions will have to be made.

## References

1. Biber, D., Conrad, S.: Lexical bundles in conversation and academic prose. Lang. Comput. **26**, 181–190 (1999)
2. Drury, B., Almeida, J.J.: The Minho quotation resource. In: LREC, pp. 2280–2285 (2012)
3. Drury, B., Dias, G., Torgo, L.: A contextual classification strategy for polarity analysis of direct quotations from financial news. In: Proceedings of the International Conference Recent Advances in Natural Language Processing 2011, pp. 434–440 (2011)
4. Drury, B., Drury, S.M.: The identification of framing language in business leaders' speech from the mass media. In: Lossio-Ventura, J.A., Valverde-Rebaza, J.C., Díaz, E., Alatrista-Salas, H. (eds.) SIMBig 2020. CCIS, vol. 1410, pp. 376–383. Springer, Cham (2021). https://doi.org/10.1007/978-3-030-76228-5_27

5. Drury, B., Morais-Drury, S.: An update to the Minho quotation resource. arXiv preprint arXiv:2104.06987 (2021)

6. Higgins, R.B., Bannister, B.D.: How corporate communication of strategy affects share price. Long Range Plan. **25**(3), 27–35 (1992)

7. Hiltunen, T.: Lexical bundles in Wikipedia articles and related texts. In: Applications of Pattern-Driven Methods in Corpus Linguistics, vol. 82, p. 189 (2018)

8. Lee, S.Y., Qiu, L., Whinston, A.: Sentiment manipulation in online platforms: an analysis of movie tweets. Prod. Oper. Manag. **27**(3), 393–416 (2018)

9. McVeigh, J.: lexical bundles and repetition in email marketing texts. In: Kopaczyk, J., Tyrkko, J. (eds.) Applications of Pattern-Driven Methods in Corpus Linguistics (chap. 9), pp. 213–250. John Benjamins (2018)

10. Pinna, A., Brett, D.: Constance and variability. In: Applications of Pattern-Driven Methods in Corpus Linguistics, vol. 82, p. 107 (2018)

11. Ratner, G.: Gerald Ratner: The Rise and Fall... and Rise Again. Wiley, Hoboken (2008)

12. Schneider, G., Grigonytė, G.: From lexical bundles to surprisal and language models. In: Applications of Pattern-Driven Methods in Corpus Linguistics, vol. 82, p. 15 (2018)

13. Tichỳ, O.: Lexical obsolescence and loss in English: 1700–2000. In: Applications of Pattern-Driven Methods in Corpus Linguistics, pp. 81–103 (2018)

# 50 Shades of Gray: Effect of the Color Scale for the Assessment of Speech Disorders

Paula Andrea Pérez-Toro[1,2]([✉]) [ID], Philipp Klumpp[1] [ID],
Juan Camilo Vasquez-Correa[2], Maria Schuster[3], Elmar Nöth[1] [ID],
Juan Rafael Orozco-Arroyave[1,2] [ID], and Tomás Arias-Vergara[1,2,3] [ID]

[1] Pattern Recognition Lab, Friedrich-Alexander-Universität Erlangen-Nürnberg,
Erlangen, Germany
`paula.andrea.perez@fau.de`
[2] GITA Lab, Faculty of Engineering, Universidad de Antioquia UdeA,
Medellín, Colombia
[3] Department of Otorhinolaryngology, Head and Neck Surgery, Ludwig-Maximilians
University, Munich, Germany

**Abstract.** Spectrograms provide a visual representation of the time-frequency variations of a speech signal. Furthermore, the color scales can be used as a pre-processing normalization step. In this study, we investigated the suitability of using different color scales for the reconstruction of spectrograms together with bottleneck features extracted from Convolutional AutoEncoders (CAEs). We trained several CAEs considering different parameters such as the number of channels, wide-band/narrowband spectrograms, and different color scales. Additionally, we tested the suitability of the proposed CAE architecture for the prediction of the severity of Parkinson's Disease (PD) and for the nasality level in children with Cleft Lip and Palate (CLP). The results showed that it is possible to estimate the neurological state for PD with Spearman's correlations of up to 0.71 using the Grayscale, and the nasality level in CLP with F-scores of up to 0.58 using the raw spectrogram. Although the color scales improved performance in some cases, it is not clear which color scale is the most suitable for the selected application, as we did not find significant differences in the results for each color scale.

**Keywords:** AutoEncoder · Grayscale · Color Scales · Cleft Lip and Palate, Parkinson's Disease · Speech Analysis

## 1 Introduction

Many deep learning approaches in speech analysis use 2D-representations such as spectrograms as input to a Convolutional Neural Network (CNN). Each raw

---

T. Arias-Vergara—Work done during Ph.D. studies.

© Springer Nature Switzerland AG 2022
P. Sojka et al. (Eds.): TSD 2022, LNAI 13502, pp. 352–363, 2022.
https://doi.org/10.1007/978-3-031-16270-1_29

value of a time-frequency representation is a frequency bin which can be transformed via a quantization (e.g., 8 bit grayscale) or a transformation into a color scale with a succeeding quantization, e.g., 8 bit for the Red, Green, and Blue channels (RGB). Other color scales such as Jet and Viridis are used as well. A color scale spectrogram can be considered as a sequence of three different, parallel quantizations. For the creation of the raw spectrogram, the length of the Short Time Fourier Transform window is crucial, leading for instance to a narrow or broad band spectrogram.

In [7], a method based on pseudo-color quantification for sound event classification was proposed. In this approach, the regular spectrogram is normalized into grayscale and then the dynamic range is quantized into regions according to the RGB scale. The obtained results indicate that this approach outperformed in most of the cases the equivalent grayscale features, where the separability between sound classes has increased using the proposed quantification to RGB. Several approaches use deep spectrum features extracted from color-spectrograms by using image processing methods based on CNN for the classification of different speech tasks [1,6]. The authors compared these features to state-of-the-art approaches for speech-based emotion recognition [6] and for the detection of several snoring types [1], obtaining significant improvement using the Viridis color map. These studies motivated the use of grayscale / color spectrograms in this paper for the assessment of different speech disorders in adults with Parkinson's Disease (PD) and in children with Cleft Lip and Palate (CLP).

PD is associated to the loss of common neurotransmitters in the midbrain, which causes progressive degeneration of physiological and cognitive capabilities [14]. It results in the appearance of motor disturbances such as muscle stiffness, bradykinesia, resting tremor, among others. Additionally, PD also affects the speech production of the patients. The most common symptoms include abnormal variation of pitch, decreased loudness, and hypokinetic dysarthria [9]. The standard scales to evaluate movement and speech impairments caused by PD are the third part of the Movement Disorders Society Unified Parkinson's Disease Rating Scale (U-III) [11], the Hoehn & Yahr (H&Y) scale [3], and the modified Frenchay Dysarthria Assessment (mFDA) [22]. The U-III and the H&Y scale aim at describing the neurological state of PD patients, while mFDA aims at evaluating the dysarthria level in diseases that involve speech disorders. In this study, we focused on the prediction of the neurological state and dysarthria level of PD patients according to the aforementioned scales.

We use the PC-GITA dataset [18], which was analyzed in previous works for the classification (healthy vs. PD) [21,26] and regression of the disease severity [5,10]. In [26] a transfer learning approach using CNN-based features extracted from spectrograms for the prediction of PD was proposed. The authors reported results of up to 99% on vowel based tasks. An approach based on convolutional (CAEs) and recurrent (RAEs) AutoEncoders was proposed in [21] to discriminate PD with accuracies of up to 84% for RAEs and of up to 80% for CAEs. Speaker embeddings were considered in [10] for the prediction of the U-III and mFDA score of PD patients, reporting Spearman's correlations ($\rho$) of .63

and .72, respectively. The prediction of the dysarthria level in PD patients was also performed in [5], where a $\rho$ of .57 was obtained by using phoneme posterior probabilities.

Speech disorders can also affect the communication ability of children. Common medical conditions that lead to speech impairments such as CLP, occurs 1 in every 700 live births [17]. Patients with CLP may experience feeding and swallowing difficulties, hearing loss, and different speech disorders associated to voice and articulatory impairments. Further, CLP can cause Velopharyngeal Dysfunction (VPD) resulting in hypernasality, which is characterized by excessive resonance in the nasal cavity during the production of vowels or voiced consonants, and significant nasal emission due to a large velopharyngeal opening, resulting in weak consonant production, short utterance length [15,24]. The speech of children with CLP is impaired (even after surgery) and shows abnormal characteristics such as hypernasality or hyponasality, glottal stops, backing, and weakening of consonants [23]. Resonance and VPD are evaluated by speech pathologist in different ways. A perceptual evaluation is performed to determine the type, severity, and cause of the speech disorder.

Different approaches have been considered to model speech disorders in children with CLP. In [16], different pronunciation and articulation features along are used to evaluate speech disorders in recordings of German children with CLP. An analysis of Malayalam children speech with Cleft Palate (CP) before and after surgery was presented in [8]. The authors considered the Voice Low tone to High tone Ratio (VLHR) as a measure of nasality, finding a significant decreasing in the VLHR index (at 95% confidence level) after surgery for the sustained phonation of vowels. Classical articulatory and spectral features were considered in [4,12] to classify between normal speech and hypernasal speech in children with CLP, achieving accuracies of up to 85% and 80%, respectively.

In this paper, we analyze the suitability of different color scales in the assessment of PD and CLP using a CAE approach, since several papers reported improved performance in speech disorder related tasks. We wanted to confirm the suitability of color scales (a.k.o normalization) and whether they improve consistently in a known dataset with standard tasks. We found inconsistent results and no significant differences in most predictions.

## 2   Methods

### 2.1   Data

**PC-GITA:** this corpus [18] consists of 50 PD patients and 50 Healthy Control subjects (HC). The participants are native Spanish speakers from Colombia. They were asked to perform different exercises. T1: a monologue, the participants described their daily routines, T2: the reading of a phonetically balanced text, and T3: a Diadochokinetic (DDK) task, i.e., the rapid repetition of /pa/-/ta/-/ka/. The patients were evaluated by an expert neurologist and labeled according to the U-III and H&Y scale, and by an expert phoniatrician according to the mFDA scale. In these scales, the higher the label the higher the severity, where the U-III ranges from 0 to 132, the H&Y from 0 to 5, and the mFDA from 0 to 52. The HC subjects were only included to add variability in the prediction of the mFDA score. Additional demographic information is displayed in Table 1.

**Children with Cleft Lip and Palate:** recordings of 81 Colombian children with CLP are considered. All of them native Spanish speakers. This dataset was recorded in Bogotá, Colombia in a controlled acoustic environment. The children were asked to read 3 sentences containing a combination of vowel, fricative, stop, nasal, and liquid speech sounds: *"Carlos coge su pelota"*, *"Susi come sopa"*, and *"Tomás toca tambor"*. All of them where evaluated by an expert phoniatricians according to four nasality levels: normal (18 subjects), mild (27 subjects), moderate (22 subjects), and severe (14 subjects).

**Table 1.** General information of the subjects in PC-GITA

|  | PD patients | HC subjects |
|---|---|---|
| Gender [f/m] | 25/25 | 25/25 |
| Age [f/m] | 60.7(7.3)/61.3(11.7) | 61.4(7.1)/60.5(11.6) |
| U-III [f/m] | 37.6(14.0)/37.8(22.1) | − |
| H&Y [f/m] | 2.2(0.6)/2.3(0.9) | − |
| mFDA [f/m] | 27.2(8.1)/29.0(8.2) | 6.6(6.9)/8.7(7.8) |

f: female. m: male. Values are expressed as mean(standard deviation). Age is given in years.

**Additional Datasets:** we combined the CIEMPIESS corpus [13] and the LibriSpeech dataset [19] to increase the robustness for the training process of the CAE (see Sect. 2.2). Both datasets were recorded in controlled conditions (e.g., no background noise) at 16 kHz. CIEMPIESS consists of 16717 audio recordings (17 h) of radio podcast from 141 Mexican Spanish speakers (45 f). The recordings were divided into 75% for training and 25% for validation. LibriSpeech is composed of read English speech. We used the 100 h of clean speech subset for training, which contains a total of 251 speakers (125 f). The average duration of each recording is 25 min. The validation set consisted of 5.4 h from 40 speakers (20 f).

### 2.2  Model Description

**Mel Spectrogram Representations:** In this paper, we considered two ways to extract information from the logarithmic Mel spectrogram. On the one hand, we computed the regular log-Mel spectrogram for three different resolution windows (15, 25, and 45 ms) with a hop size of 10 ms in order to capture different patterns related to articulation and prosody. Sequences of 500 ms (50 frames) were taken and the number of Mel filters was set to 128. These resolutions provide three different channels to be used in the proposed model.

On the other hand, in order to compare the suitability of using image representations, we also converted the spectrograms to RGB, i.e., different color scales were used as a pre-processing normalization, which has not been explored for the assessment of PD. Inspired by [1,6,7], the spectrograms were converted using a linear and non-linear color scale transformations. The color-spectrograms were obtained using different non-linear color maps ( *"Gray"*, *"Jet"*, and *"Viridis"*) extracted with the *"matplotlib library"* from Python [2]. Finally, they were converted to images with a resolution of 266 × 200 pixels. A grayscale transformation is performed by quantizing the spectrogram to 50 Shades of Gray (50SGray), while the Gray color map is obtained from a non-linear transformation (NL-Gray). This is performed to analyze the suitability of features extracted from spectrogram images as proposed in [1,6]. Jet scale ranges from blue via cyan, yellow, orange to red, while Viridis from blue via green to yellow.

**Multi-Resolution Convolutional AutoEncoder:** Generative Models aim to learn the data distribution by encoding the most relevant information. AEs are one of the most popular techniques regarding these models in deep learning, which aims to reconstruct a specific input starting from an encoded representation known as the latent-space. It allows the model to learn the optimal parameters that minimize the reconstruction loss, which in this study is defined by the Mean Squared Error (MSE). A variation of AEs which includes CNNs are the CAEs. Commonly, they are used in order to reproduce an image in the output layer. The image is passed through the encoder that in this case compresses the image by using Convolutional Layers (CLs). Then, the bottleneck representation is obtained with a linear layer. The decoder is composed by another set of CLs with the same structure and parameters as the encoder.

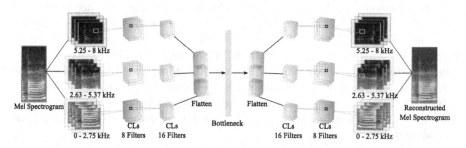

**Fig. 1.** General architecture of the CAE model. It consists of three parts for the encoder and the decoder: (1) three parallel CLs of 8 filters with a kernel size of (3,3), max pooling (2,2), a batch normalization layer, and an ELU activation, (2) three parallel CLs of 16 filters with a kernel size of (3,3), max pooling (2,2), a batch normalization layer, and an ELU activation, and (4) one linear layer of 128 units for the bottleneck representation

Figure 1 illustrates the proposed CAE model, which consists of a set of parallel CLs and a linear layer for the bottleneck vector. The input dimension will vary depending on whether it is the original or the color-spectrogram and also depending on the resolutions; however, the same architecture is used. We noted that the reconstruction of the harmonics in middle and higher frequencies seems more challenging. To handle this issue, we proposed a parallel CNN with three levels of abstraction to process different frequency bands separately with a shift of 125 Hz: (1) $0-2.75$ kHz, (2) $2.63-5.37$ kHz, and (3) $5.25-8$ kHz. This improved the reconstruction, noticeable in the error and by visual inspection. The bottleneck representation was used as feature vector for the prediction of the severity of PD. Furthermore, four functionals (mean, standard deviation, skewness, and kurtosis) were computed across the sequences to form a static vector of 512 elements.

## 2.3 Optimization and Regression

A Linear-Support Vector Regressor (L-SVR) was considered for the prediction of the U-III, mFDA, and H&Y in PD patients. The optimal parameters were found through a grid search where $C$ and $\epsilon \in \{10^{-5}, 10^{-4}, ..., 10^5\}$. Further, a Light Gradient Boosting Machine (LGBM) was used for classification of the nasality levels in children with CLP The optimal parameters of the LGBM were found through a grid search where *number of estimators* $\in \{10, 20, ..., 300\}$ and the *maximum depth* $\in \{5, 10, ..., 100\}$. The validation for all experiments followed a 5-Fold Cross-Validation strategy. For the classification and regression an early fusion strategy was applied by merging the different sets of bottleneck features before performing the classification/regression and making the final decision.

## 3 Experiments and Results

This study proposes to investigate the use of different parameters in CAEs for the assessment of PD and CLP. The reconstruction errors according to the MSE were computed, where on average, the lowest reconstruction error is obtained with 45 ms (.014), and the highest with 15 ms (.027). It may be an indicator that the proposed model is focused more on the frequency than on the temporal domain. For the color scales, Viridis achieved the lowest reconstruction error (.0042), while the highest was for Jet (.073). One reason may be that Viridis has a lower range of different color/values compared to the original spectrogram and Jet.

The following subsections describe different experiments according to the applied RGB scales for the spectrograms: (1) Raw, (2) 50SGray, (3) Gray, (4) Viridis, and (5) Jet. Moreover, two different experiments were performed: (1) the prediction of the dysarthria level (mFDA) and the neurological state (U-III, and H&Y score) of PD patients, and (2) the classification of the nasality level in children wih CLP.

## 3.1   Parkinson's Disease

Table 2 shows the results of different experiments according to the applied color scales for the spectrograms along several tasks that were described in Sect. 2.1. The performance is evaluated according to the average of $\rho$. The highest performance in the prediction of the mFDA ($\rho =.63$) is achieved using the NL-Gray and merging the bottleneck features from the all tasks. Regarding the prediction of the U-III score, the best result ($\rho =.52$) is achieved by using the Jet scale and the DDK task. The prediction of the H&Y score reported slightly more accurate results for the Jet ($\rho =.38$) compared to the other scales. Notice that the performance is similar for the different color scales.

For the analysis and to compare the performance of the different color scales and resolutions, Fig. 2 illustrates a heatmap visualization of the overall results, where 3D is the 3-channel spectrogram composed by the different resolution and used as input in the CAE. The value of the highest $\rho$ for each constellation is provided. In general, the best results were obtained for the prediction of the mFDA. This was expected since it evaluates directly impairments in speech. Although the U-III and the H&Y scale also aim at assessing the severity of the disease, these scores consider different factors related to movement disorders, not only speech. The low performance for the H&Y prediction could be explained due to the lower range of values and the low variability (See Table 1).

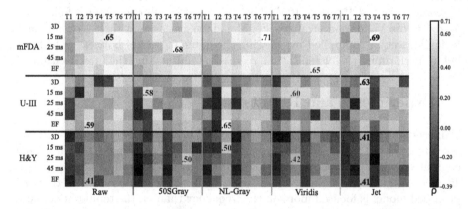

**Fig. 2.** Heatmap of the Spearman's correlation coefficients for the prediction mFDA, U-III, and H&Y score. T4: T1 & T2. T5: T1 & T3. T6: T2 & T3. T7: T1 & T2, & T3. EF: Early fusion of the resolution windows

**Table 2.** Top 3 of the average Spearman's correlation coefficients for the prediction mFDA, U-III, and H&Y score using the different color scales

| Task/Color scale | Raw | 50SGray | NL-Gray | Viridis | Jet |
|---|---|---|---|---|---|
| | | mFDA | | | |
| T5 | **0.61** | 0.54 | 0.58 | 0.59 | 0.58 |
| T6 | 0.59 | 0.58 | 0.59 | 0.57 | 0.57 |
| T7 | 0.60 | **0.60** | **0.63** | **0.60** | **0.61** |
| | | U–II | | | |
| T3 | 0.46 | **0.39** | **0.50** | 0.46 | **0.52** |
| T6 | **0.49** | 0.37 | 0.43 | **0.49** | 0.41 |
| T7 | 0.40 | **0.39** | 0.35 | 0.32 | 0.28 |
| | | H&Y | | | |
| T3 | 0.30 | 0.25 | 0.34 | **0.28** | **0.38** |
| T5 | 0.17 | 0.16 | 0.19 | 0.18 | 0.22 |
| T6 | **0.34** | **0.33** | **0.30** | 0.21 | 0.24 |

T5: T1 & T3. T6: T2 & T3. T7: T1 & T3 & T3

In the case of the resolutions, the 15 ms and the early fusion yielded the most accurate results, particularly for the prediction of the mFDA and U-III, while for H&Y there is not a clear trend w.r.t. the resolutions.

Notice from the figure that Raw spectrograms seem to be lighter and more consistent along the experiments, while the color scale has more variations specially in those values related to the prediction of the U-III and H&Y. As we expected and since NL-Gray is still grayscale, similar results were obtained for the two representations, where the NL-Gray was slightly better ($\rho = .71$) compared to the 50Sgray ($\rho = .68$). This may be due to when converting the spectrograms to a non-linear scale. In general, the DDK and its fusion with the other tasks report higher results.

However, there is no a clear tendency to state that one color scale could be more suitable than the other, since in several cases the results were close to each other, inconsistent, or varied according to the task, and resolution.

## 3.2  Cleft Lip and Palate

Two classification problems were addressed: (1) a 2-class system was trained for the discrimination of nasal speech, and (2) a 4-class system was trained considering the four nasality levels described in Sect. 2.1.

**Table 3.** Top 3 of the average F-scores for the 2-class (normal vs. nasal) and 4-class (nasality levels) classification in children with CLP using the different color scales

| Task/Color Scale | Raw | 50SGray | Gray | Viridis | Jet |
|---|---|---|---|---|---|
| 2-class | | | | | |
| T3 | 0.59 | **0.68** | **0.71** | **0.65** | **0.66** |
| T6 | **0.64** | 0.62 | 0.61 | 0.59 | 0.63 |
| T7 | **0.64** | 0.62 | 0.61 | 0.61 | 0.60 |
| 4-class | | | | | |
| T6 | 0.35 | 0.38 | **0.37** | 0.32 | **0.38** |
| T3 | 0.36 | **0.40** | 0.35 | 0.32 | 0.31 |
| T7 | **0.39** | 0.35 | 0.36 | **0.33** | 0.32 |

T5: T1 & T3. T6: T2 & T3. T7: T1 & T3 & T3

The performance of the classification was measured according to the unweighted average F-Score along the classes. The three best classification results according to the sentences (see Sect. 2.1) are displayed in Table 3, where the average of the F-scores along the resolutions was computed. For this case, T1 refers to *"Carlos coge su pelota"*, T2 to *"Susi come sopa"*, and T3 to *"Tomás toca tambor"*.

Notice that the overall results showed that grayscale (on average) was more suitable to classify nasality levels in CLP. For the 2-class case an average F-Score of up to 0.71 was achieved, while for the 4-class of up to 0.40. Moreover, the task providing more information to discriminate nasality was the task three, which only consider of reading the sentence *"Tomás toca tambor"*. Despite grayscale reporting the overall highest performance, no significant differences were found when using the raw spectrogram.

For a closer look at the best results, Fig. 3 illustrates a heatmap visualization of the performance considering the different resolution, tasks, and color scales.

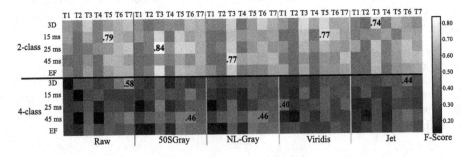

**Fig. 3.** Heatmap of the F-Scores for the 2-class (normal vs. nasal) and 4-class (nasality levels) classification in children with CLP. T4: T1 & T2. T5: T1 & T3. T6: T2 & T3. T7: T1 & T2, & T3. EF: Early fusion of the resolution windows

On the one hand, the best results of the 2-class problem were obtained with information from the 50SGray together with a 25 ms resolution window (F-Score = 0.84) and the raw spectrogram together with a 15 ms resolution (F-Score = 0.79). For this case, the highest F-scores are related to or a merger with task T3, while it seems that task T2 achieved the lowest performance. On the other hand, for the discrimination of the nasality levels (4-class), the fusion of different tasks was more suitable. The best classification was achieved by using raw spectrogram with 3-channel resolution (3D) for the combination of all tasks (F-Score = 0.58).

Similar to the prediction of the different scores in PD, it is difficult to state that one color scale is more suitable than the other. Nevertheless, the different color scales can be used as a normalization pre-processing step.

## 4    Discussion and Conclusions

A CAE-based approach was proposed in this study to analyze the suitability of compressed representations (bottleneck features) extracted from spectrogram images for the assessment of PD and CLP. In addition, we investigate the use of different time-frequency resolutions and color scales applied to several tasks such as spontaneous speech, reading text/sentence, and DDK exercises. The prediction of three disease severity scores related to the neurological state and dysarthria level in PD was performed. Compared to the state-of-the-art results, we showed that our approach outperformed the results of [5,10] for U-III and mFDA. Notice that from the results presented in this study, the DDK task was more suitable and consistent for predicting disease severity, while the spontaneous speech (monologue) obtained the lowest correlations. The DDK is commonly used for the assessment of speech disorders related to articulatory capabilities, which consists of the repetition of a simple and cyclic syllabic sequences. This allows the computation of the extracted functionals for the bottleneck static features [25].

The combinations of resolutions were not suitable in most of the cases for the prediction of the different scores in PD. It is not clear to us, whether this is due to training data size since the combination/muti-channel approach for the resolutions was considered due to good results for the emotional modeling and detection of depression in PD [20].

In the case of CLP, we considered two classification schemes: (1) normal vs. nasal speech and (2) estimation of the nasality level according to four categories (normal, mild, moderate and severe). In both tasks, we obtained the highest results using grayscale spectrograms. Furthermore, we found that the highest classification performance was obtained with the sentence *"Tomás toca tambor"*, which includes more stop sounds (/t/, /b/, /c/) than the other two sentences. These results indicate that children with CLP have more difficulties to produce stop sounds resulting in a lower speech intelligibility. Therefore, speech therapy should be focused on improving the accuracy of certain phoneme groups such as the stop sounds. In future work, we will focus on automatic methods to analyze phoneme accuracy of children with CLP.

In addition, different Kruskal Wallis tests were performed for the different color scales w.r.t. the raw spectrogram. No significant improvement was found in all cases ($p \gg 0.05$) for the prediction of mFDA and U-III in PD, and the classification of nasality levels in CLP. The H&Y prediction obtained significant improvement along all the scales ($p = 0.05$). This can be explained due to the small variation of the scale itself and in the dataset (see Sect. 2.1).

We are aware that one of the limitations of this study is the amount of data and the comparison to clinical scores that are based on perceptual estimations of motor competence or on several aspects of speech, which may not provide a precise evaluation. We are currently collecting and labeling more data for further research. Other fusion methods will be explored in future research to merge different resolutions. Therefore, we need to investigate other possible architectures and causes that influenced the results.

**Acknowledgements.** This work was funded by the European Union's Horizon 2020 research and innovation programme under Marie Sklodowska-Curie grant agreement No. 766287, and partially funded by CODI at UdeA grant # PRG2020-34068. T. Arias-Vergara is under grants of Convocatoria Doctorado Nacional-785 financed by COL-CIENCIAS.

# References

1. Amiriparian, S., et al.: Snore sound classification using image-based deep spectrum features. In: Proceedings of the Interspeech 2017, pp. 3512–3516 (2017). https://doi.org/10.21437/Interspeech.2017-434
2. Barrett, P., Hunter, J., Miller, J.T., Hsu, J.C., Greenfield, P.: matplotlib-a portable python plotting package. In: Astronomical Data Analysis Software and Systems XIV, vol. 347, p. 91 (2005)
3. Bhidayasiri, R., Tarsy, D.: Parkinson's disease: Hoehn and Yahr scale. In: Movement Disorders: a Video Atlas. CCN, pp. 4–5. Humana Press, Totowa, NJ (2012). https://doi.org/10.1007/978-1-60327-426-5_2
4. Carvajal-Castaño, H.A., Orozco-Arroyave, J.R.: Articulation analysis in the speech of children with cleft lip and palate. In: Nyström, I., Hernández Heredia, Y., Milián Núñez, V. (eds.) CIARP 2019. LNCS, vol. 11896, pp. 575–585. Springer, Cham (2019). https://doi.org/10.1007/978-3-030-33904-3_54
5. Cernak, M., Orozco-Arroyave, J.R., Rudzicz, F., Christensen, H., Vásquez-Correa, J.C., Nöth, E.: Characterisation of voice quality of Parkinson's disease using differential phonological posterior features. Comput. Speech Lang. **46**, 196–208 (2017)
6. Cummins, N., Amiriparian, S., Hagerer, G., Batliner, A., Steidl, S., Schuller, B.W.: An image-based deep spectrum feature representation for the recognition of emotional speech. In: Proceedings of the 25th ACM international conference on Multimedia, pp. 478–484 (2017)
7. Dennis, J., Tran, H.D., Li, H.: Spectrogram image feature for sound event classification in mismatched conditions. IEEE Signal Process. Lett. **18**(2), 130–133 (2010)
8. Dodderi, T., Narra, M., Varghese, S.M., et al.: Spectral analysis of hypernasality in cleft palate children: a pre-post surgery comparison. J. Clin. Diagn. Res. JCDR **10**(1), MC01 (2016)

9. Duffy, J.R.: Motor Speech Disorders: Substrates, Differential Diagnosis, and Management. Elsevier Health Science (2013)

10. Garcia, N., Orozco-Arroyave, J.R., D'Haro, L.F., Dehak, N., Nöth, E.: Evaluation of the neurological state of people with Parkinson's disease using i-vectors. In: Interspeech, pp. 299–303 (2017)

11. Goetz, C.G., et al.: Movement disorder society-sponsored revision of the unified Parkinson's disease rating scale (MDS-UPDRS): scale presentation and clinimetric testing results. Mov. Disord. **23**(15), 2129–2170 (2008)

12. Golabbakhsh, M., Abnavi, F., Kadkhodaei Elyaderani, M., et al.: Automatic identification of hypernasality in normal and cleft lip and palate patients with acoustic analysis of speech. J. Acoust. Soc. Am. **141**(2), 929–935 (2017)

13. Hernández-Mena, C.D., Herrera-Camacho, J.A.: CIEMPIESS: a new open-sourced mexican spanish radio corpus. In: LREC, vol. 14, pp. 371–375 (2014)

14. Hornykiewicz, O.: Biochemical aspects of Parkinson's disease. Neurology **51**(2 Suppl 2), S2–S9 (1998)

15. Kummer, A.W.: Cleft Palate and Craniofacial Anomalies: Effects on Speech and Resonance. Nelson Education (2013)

16. Maier, A., Hönig, F., Bocklet, T., et al.: Automatic detection of articulation disorders in children with cleft lip and palate. J. Acoust. Soc. Am. **126**(5), 2589–2602 (2009)

17. Mossey, P.A., Catilla, E.E., et al.: Global registry and database on craniofacial anomalies: report of a WHO registry meeting on craniofacial anomalies (2003)

18. Orozco-Arroyave, J.R., Arias-Londoño, J.D., Vargas-Bonilla, J.F., Gonzalez-Rátiva, M.C., Nöth, E.: New Spanish speech corpus database for the analysis of people suffering from Parkinson's disease. In: LREC, pp. 342–347 (2014)

19. Panayotov, V., Chen, G., Povey, D., Khudanpur, S.: Librispeech: an ASR corpus based on public domain audio books. In: 2015 IEEE International Conference on Acoustics, Speech and Signal Processing (ICASSP), pp. 5206–5210. IEEE (2015)

20. Pérez-Toro, P.A., et al.: Emotional state modeling for the assessment of depression in Parkinson's disease. In: Ekštein, K., Pártl, F., Konopík, M. (eds.) TSD 2021. LNCS (LNAI), vol. 12848, pp. 457–468. Springer, Cham (2021). https://doi.org/10.1007/978-3-030-83527-9_39

21. Vásquez-Correa, J.C., Arias-Vergara, T., Schuster, M., Orozco-Arroyave, J.R., Nöth, E.: Parallel representation learning for the classification of pathological speech: studies on Parkinson's disease and cleft lip and palate. Speech Commun. **122**, 56–67 (2020)

22. Vásquez-Correa, J.C., Orozco-Arroyave, J.R., Bocklet, T., Nöth, E.: Towards an automatic evaluation of the dysarthria level of patients with Parkinson's disease. J. Commun. Disord. **76**, 21–36 (2018)

23. Williams, A.C., Bearn, D., Mildinhall, S., et al.: Cleft lip and palate care in the United Kingdom-the Clinical Standards Advisory Group (CSAG) Study. Part 2: dentofacial outcomes and patient satisfaction. Cleft Palate-Craniofac. J. **38**(1), 24–29 (2001)

24. Wyatt, R., Sell, D., Russell, J., Harding, A., Harland, K., Albery, L.: Cleft palate speech dissected: a review of current knowledge and analysis. Br. J. Plast. Surg. **49**(3), 143–149 (1996)

25. Yang, C.C., Chung, Y.M., Chi, L.Y., Chen, H.H., Wang, Y.T.: Analysis of verbal diadochokinesis in normal speech using the diadochokinetic rate analysis program. J. Dent. Sci. **6**(4), 221–226 (2011)

26. Zahid, L., et al.: A spectrogram-based deep feature assisted computer-aided diagnostic system for Parkinson's disease. IEEE Access **8**, 35482–35495 (2020)

# Sub 8-Bit Quantization of Streaming Keyword Spotting Models for Embedded Chipsets

Lu Zeng$^{(\boxtimes)}$ (ID), Sree Hari Krishnan Parthasarathi (ID), Yuzong Liu (ID),
Alex Escott (ID), Santosh Cheekatmalla (ID), Nikko Strom (ID),
and Shiv Vitaladevuni (ID)

Alexa, Amazon, Seattle, USA
{luzeng,sparta,liuyuzon,escottal,cheekatm,nikko,
shivnaga}@amazon.com

**Abstract.** We propose a novel 2-stage sub 8-bit quantization aware training algorithm for all components of a 250K parameter feedforward, streaming, state-free keyword spotting model. For the first stage, we adapt a recently proposed quantization technique using a non-linear transformation with tanh(.) on dense layer weights. In the second stage, we use linear quantization methods on the rest of the network, including other parameters (bias, gain, batchnorm), inputs, and activations. We conduct large scale experiments, training on 26,000 h of de-identified production, far-field and near-field audio data (evaluating on 4,000 h of data). We organize our results in two embedded chipset settings: a) with commodity ARM NEON instruction set and 8-bit containers, we present accuracy, CPU, and memory results using sub 8-bit weights (4, 5, 8-bit) and 8-bit quantization of rest of the network; b) with off-the-shelf neural network accelerators, for a range of weight bit widths (1 and 5-bit), while presenting accuracy results, we project reduction in memory utilization. In both configurations, our results show that the proposed algorithm can achieve: a) parity with a full floating point model's operating point on a detection error tradeoff (DET) curve in terms of false detection rate (FDR) at false rejection rate (FRR); b) significant reduction in compute and memory, yielding up to 3 times improvement in CPU consumption and more than 4 times improvement in memory consumption.

**Index Terms:** 2-stage quantization, keyword spotting, embedded chipsets

## 1 Introduction

Wakeword detection, also known as keyword spotting (KWS), detects words or phrases of interest from streaming audio and plays a vital role in voice assistants [5,17]. KWS models are based on neural network architectures and are

L. Zeng and S. H. K. Parthasarathi—Equal contribution.

processed on device. A challenge for KWS systems is to attain high accuracy under tight resource constraints such as model size, runtime memory footprint, and power consumption. To address some of the constraints, previous work has explored knowledge distillation [24], low rank approximation [18,23], and computationally efficient architectures [4,13,15]. As an orthogonal direction, quantization has been applied to KWS, where the components of the model are converted from 32-bit floating points to lower bit width representations.

Quantization is often applied post-training, resulting in performance degradation [25]. To mitigate this, quantization aware training (QAT) is applied to reduce errors [14,20]. QAT, including very low bit width (even binary quantization), is an established technique [6,19]. Since the quantization function is discrete (and therefore the gradient is zero almost everywhere), a fake quantizer with straight through estimator (STE) [3] or a Gumbel-Softmax trick [11] are used to estimate the parameters. Since accuracy of 1-bit models is still a challenge, in the context of speech processing, 4 to 6-bit QAT has been studied for event detection [20], speech recognition [16], and KWS [14].

Furthermore, commercially realizable KWS models have additional challenges often ignored in research focused on "model size vs accuracy" tradeoff: a) sub 8-bit quantization requires hardware support[1]; b) need to run in streaming mode[2]; c) cannot use corruptible memory[3]. Our paper happens in the context of: a) using sub 8-bit representations to avoid overflow errors with 8-bit containers in commodity or off-the-shelf platforms; b) addressing accuracy challenges with sub 8-bit, including 1-bit representations.

**Contributions:** In this paper, we tackle the problem of sub 8-bit quantization of on-device, small footprint, streaming, state-free KWS models, that can execute on commodity or off-the-shelf hardware platforms. We propose a novel 2-stage QAT algorithm: for the first stage, we adapt a non-linear quantization method on weights [21], while for the second stage, we use linear quantization methods on other components of the network. We conduct large scale experiments, training on 26K hours of de-identified production audio, collected from a mix of far-field devices and mobile phones (evaluating on 4K hours of data). We show the efficacy of our methods by presenting accuracy and compute results (CPU[4], memory, and model size) for sub 8-bit models (4, 5, 8-bit) on ARM NEON chipset, while projecting memory gains for a range of weight bit widths (1 and 5-bit) on off-the-shelf neural network accelerators.

## 2    Small Footprint, Streaming, State-Free KWS Models

While QAT algorithm can be applied to convolutional models, we use a model that is a feedforward network (FFN) with 250k parameters using a bottleneck

---

[1] An instruction set that can efficiently carry out matrix-vector multiplications.
[2] Models have to run with low latency – i.e., cannot use large buffers.
[3] Since the models are running continuously, they cannot get into a "bad" state.
[4] We use CPU cycles as a proxy for power consumption.

architecture [8]. The full precision version of this model has been optimized for low power, small footprint, streaming and state-free setting and serves as our baseline. It is trained on a set of positive and negative examples (i.e. positive examples contain the wakeword, while negative examples do not).

The model architecture has 250K learnable parameters, and it operates on 20-dimensional log mel filter bank energy (LFBE) features, computed with an analysis window size and shift of 25 ms and 10 ms respectively; the input to the model is 81 frames, downsampled by a factor of 3. The architecture consists of five fully connected layers with batch normalization [10] and ReLU [1] being used with all hidden layers. The output is a binary classification layer trained with cross entropy loss, representing the posterior probability of "wakeword" and "non-wakeword" [8]. Later, to investigate quantized models with lower bit width, we explore two other model sizes with different layer sizes, keeping the other architectural aspects the same. During training, the wakeword is consistently center aligned in the input window [12]. Adam optimizer is used to update the model parameters during training. During inference, the posterior estimates corresponding to the wakeword are smoothed by a windowed smoothing average (WMA) filter and then thresholded to infer the wakeword hypothesis.

## 3    Relevant Embedded Chipsets

In this section, we describe hardware considerations in two settings: a) commodity ARM NEON instruction set; b) off-the-shelf neural network accelerators.

**Commodity ARM NEON Instruction Set Overview:** In 2021 over 90% of mobile phones use ARM-based chipsets[5]. The majority of these include a Single-Instruction-Multiple-Data (SIMD) extension known as NEON; this is available by default in ARM's chipsets for mobile phones (*armv8a, aarch64*[6]). The NEON instruction set is based on parallelizing arithmetic operations on vectors stored in 128-bit registers, allowing packing of multiple scalar values in the register - i.e. $4 \times 32$-bit floating point, $4 \times 32$-bit integer, $8 \times 16$ bit-integer, or $16 \times 8$-bit integer - then perform an arithmetic operation on every value in the register in a clock cycle. For NEON, 8-bit is the smallest supported container for Multiply-And-Accumulate (MAC) operations.

The compute requirement for a KWS model can be reduced by using lower bit widths for weights, input and activations. Our QAT algorithm produces a model that can utilize the SIMD instruction set available with NEON. While NEON uses 8-bit containers for MAC operations, using sub 8-bit weights can yield benefits: a) prevent overflow when performing computations; b) lower model size for over the network deployments.

**Off-the-Shelf Neural Network Accelerators:** The smallest container in ARM NEON architecture is 8-bit, so we do not observe a memory reduction with

---

[5] https://www.counterpointresearch.com/global-smartphone-ap-market-share/.

[6] https://www.arm.com/blogs/blueprint/android-64bit-future-mobile.

sub 8-bit weights. Some off-the-shelf accelerators can utilize sub 8-bit weights[7,8]. In this paper, we use data sheets from them to project memory savings for our QAT algorithm.

# 4    Proposed 2-Stage QAT Algorithm

In this section, we describe the design of our approach. Section 4.1 gives an overview of our second stage training algorithm. We provide detailed descriptions of the first and second stages in Sects. 4.2 and 4.3.

## 4.1    Quantization Overview

A layer in a feedforward neural network typically takes the following form:

$$\mathbf{y} = \psi_{bn}(\phi_{relu}(\mathbf{W}\mathbf{x} + \mathbf{b})) \tag{1}$$

where $\mathbf{x}$ is the input to the dense layer, $\mathbf{W}$ is the dense layer weight matrix, $\mathbf{b}$ is the bias, $\phi_{relu}$ and $\psi_{bn}$ represent ReLU and batch norm transformations. Using a gain $\alpha$ and a linear quantizer $(q_z(.))$ that discretizes the values to $z$ levels ($\log_2(z)$ bits), let $\mathbf{W_q}$, $\mathbf{x_q}$, $\alpha_\mathbf{q}$, $\mathbf{b_q}$ be the corresponding quantized representations. Quantization of such a layer can be done in the following steps:

$$\mathbf{y_q} \leftarrow \alpha_\mathbf{q}(\mathbf{W_q} \cdot \mathbf{x_q} + \mathbf{b_q})$$
$$\mathbf{y_q}^{(\phi_\mathbf{q})} \leftarrow q_z(\phi_{relu}(\mathbf{y_q}))$$
$$\mathbf{y_q}^{(\phi_\mathbf{q}, \psi_\mathbf{q})} \leftarrow q_z(\psi_{bn}(\mathbf{y_q}^{(\phi_\mathbf{q})}))$$

Our QAT algorithm for the layer follows a 2-stage procedure. During the first stage we adapt the tanh(.) based quantization technique introduced in [21], for obtaining $\mathbf{W_q}$. In the second stage of training, we propose specific linear quantization techniques for the remaining components: gain $(\alpha_\mathbf{q})$, bias $(\mathbf{b_q})$, batch normalization $(q_z(\psi_{bn}(.)))$, activations $(q_z(\phi_{relu}(.)))$, and inputs $(\mathbf{x_q})$.

## 4.2    First Stage: tanh(.) Quantization of Weights

Linear quantization [26] is widely used for model compression. However, the weights of a neural network are typically Gaussian distributed. Linear quantization is not efficient for Gaussian distributions. To mitigate this problem, we adopt [21]: it encourages the weights of a neural network to become more uniform distributed, by first applying tanh(.) on $\mathbf{W}$, and then applying a linear quantizer to obtain $\mathbf{W_q} \leftarrow q_z(\tanh(\mathbf{W}))$; here $\mathbf{W_q}$ is the quantized weight matrix.

Figure 1(a) shows an example on the original weight distribution $\mathbf{W} \sim \mathcal{N}(0, \sigma_w^2)$. In order to push the weight distribution towards $\mathcal{U}(-1, 1)$, the

---

[7] https://datasheets.maximintegrated.com/en/ds/MAX78000.pdf.

[8] https://www.syntiant.com/post/syntiant-introduces-second-generation-ndp120-deep-learning-processor-for-audio-and-sensor-apps.

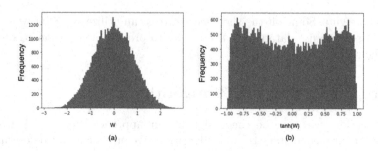

**Fig. 1.** *Distributions for (a) original dense layer weights with a nearly Gaussian distribution; (b) dense layer weights with a flatter distribution after* tanh(.).

weights are initialized with a target distribution $\mathcal{N}(0, \sigma_t^2)$ and a regularizer $\lambda_\sigma(\sigma_w - \sigma_t)^2 + \lambda_\mu \mu_w^2$ is added during training to penalize deviations from the target weight distribution, where $\sigma_w$ and $\mu_w$ are the standard deviation and mean of the weights. An example of the resultant distribution is shown in Fig. 1(b).

### 4.3 Second Stage: Linear Quantization of Full Network

In this section we describe the second stage, providing details on quantization of gain and bias, batch norm, activations, and lastly the inputs. We then perform one epoch of training to reestimate parameters.

**Quantization of BatchNorm.** Recall that BatchNorm (BN) has four sets of parameters, $\gamma$, $\beta$, $\mu_B$ and $\sigma_B^2$. While $\gamma$ and $\beta$ are trainable parameters, $\mu_B$ and $\sigma_B^2$ are the empirical estimates of means and variances. These are running estimates of mean and standard deviation during training, while they are replaced by global estimates during inference. In this work, we quantize all four sets of parameters.

From the first stage, we inherit floating point representations of the four sets of parameters. During this stage of training (i.e., second), we quantize these parameters. To quantize the BN parameters, given a preferred bit-width, we apply linear quantization on $\gamma$, $\beta$, $\mu_B$ and $\sigma_B^2$ separately. Following [2], BN parameters, especially $\mu_B$ and $\sigma_B^2$, tend to have large dynamic range. We also observe that the parameters continuously shift during training. We start with $\mu_B$ and $\sigma_B^2$: to reduce the dynamic range, we introduce a scale factor $C_{BN}$ and quantize $\mathbf{x}$, $\mu_B$ and $\sigma_B^2$ with a linear quantizer $(q_z(.))$:

$$\mathbf{x}^{\text{norm}} = \frac{\mathbf{x} - \mu_B}{\sqrt{\sigma_B^2}} = \frac{\frac{\mathbf{x}}{C_{BN}} - \frac{\mu_B}{C_{BN}}}{\sqrt{\frac{\sigma_B^2}{C_{BN}^2}}}$$

$$\mathbf{x_q^{\text{norm}}} \leftarrow \frac{q_z\left(\frac{\mathbf{x}}{C_{BN}}\right) - q_z\left(\frac{\mu_B}{C_{BN}}\right)}{\sqrt{q_z\left(\frac{\sigma_B^2}{C_{BN}^2}\right)}} \tag{2}$$

We then perform the remaining steps in quantizating a BN transformation, with the application of the $q_z(.)$ on $\gamma$ and $\beta$ to obtain $q_z(\psi_{bn}(\mathbf{x}))$:

$$\gamma_q \leftarrow q_z(\gamma)$$
$$\beta_q \leftarrow q_z(\beta)$$
$$q_z(\psi_{bn}(\mathbf{x_q^{norm}})) \leftarrow \gamma_q \cdot \mathbf{x_q^{norm}} + \beta_q$$

**Quantization of Gain and Bias.** We apply a linear quantizer on gain $(\alpha)$ and bias $(\mathbf{b})$ to obtain the respective quantized representations $\mathbf{b_q}$ and $\alpha_\mathbf{q}$.

**Quantization of Activation Functions.** A standard dense layer is typically followed by a non-linear activation function and a BN layer in order. Our initial experiments showed that a direct linear quanization of ReLU can lead to a large drop in accuracy. To mitigate this, since ReLU is unbounded on the positive domain, we experimented with bounded (clipped ReLU, sigmoid, and tanh) as well as with smoother activation functions (GeLU, SiLU) [7,9]. Clipped ReLU was the most promising activation function in our initial study; experiments with GeLU and SiLU did not yield conclusive results; while sigmoid and tanh yielded worse performance than with a direct quantization of ReLU (presumably require more training updates due to gradient saturation). The output of clipped ReLU is processed with the linear quantizer to obtain $q_z(\phi_{relu}(.))$. We also found that with quantization, the order of BN and the activation matters. Specifically, we switch the order of BN and clipped ReLU activations.

**Quantization of Inputs.** The input LFBE features are processed using global mean and variance normalization. Subsequent to this step, the normalized input is processed similar to Sect. 4.3, such that $\mathbf{x_q^{input}} \leftarrow q_z(\frac{\mathbf{x^{input}}}{C_{input}})$.

## 5   Experimental Setup

In this section we describe our training and test datasets; we also discuss the models and evaluation metrics. All experiments in this paper were conducted on de-identified production datasets.

**Datasets:** For our experiments we used a fully labeled training dataset consisted of 26K hours of audio. The training dataset contains both far-field audio and near-field mobile phone audio. We used two test sets in this work: (a) a validation test set (referred to as VAL), which consisted of about 4K hours of audio data, (b) an independent test set (referred to as TEST), which also consisted of about 4K hours of audio data. Both VAL and TEST data contain far-field audio and near-field mobile phone audio. TEST data was collected from a wider range of commodity devices.

**Evaluation Metrics:** During inference, we tuned the WMA values for the models on held-out datasets. We measure the model performance with DET curves having False Rejection Rate (FRR) on the x-axis and False Discovery Rate (FDR) on the y-axis. Similar to [8,12,22], we normalize the axes of DET curves and report relative FDR. In the interest of space, we do not present the full DET curves for all experiments; in such cases we only report relative degradation in FDR at the FRR of the baseline model's operating point (OP), where the chosen OP corresponds to the 1.0 in relative FRR.

**Table 1.** *Model architecture including hidden layer size, # param., # bits for weights, # bits for gain ($\alpha$), bias (b), and BN parameters ($\mu, \sigma, \gamma, \beta$), and input and activation.*

| ID | Layer Size | # Param. | # bits weight | # bits $(\alpha, b, BN)$ | # bits act. | # bits input |
|----|-----------|----------|---------------|--------------------------|-------------|--------------|
| M0 | {87, 400, 87, 400, 87, 400} | 250K | 32 | 32 | 32 | 32 |
| M1 | {87, 400, 87, 400, 87, 400} | 250K | 8 | 8 | 16 | 16 |
| M2 | {87, 400, 87, 400, 87, 400} | 250K | 8 | 8 | 8 | 8 |
| M3 | {87, 400, 87, 400, 87, 400} | 250K | 5 | 8 | 8 | 8 |
| M4 | {87, 400, 87, 400, 87, 400} | 250K | 4 | 8 | 8 | 8 |

**Models:** All our models use the architecture described in Sect. 2. The proposed QAT technique, presented in Sect. 4, is applied to different components of the model, and the results are described in Sect. 6. We also study the effect of number of bits for parameters (weights, biases, gain, BN parameters), input and activations. Details of the models are summarized in Table 1. M0 is a full precision model. M1 uses 8-bit parameters and 16-bit activation and input. M2, M3 and M4 use weights quantized to 8, 5, and 4 bits respectively, while the activations and input are quantized to 8-bits. Models M0 to M4 have 250K learnable parameters.

## 6  Results

In this section, we provide a detailed study of the proposed 2-stage QAT approach, against an unquantized full precision model in terms of (a) accuracy, (b) memory and computation. Our results are presented in 2 groups: a) Non-binary, sub 8-bit models in Sects. 6.1 and 6.2, for ARM NEON instruction set; b) Binary (1-bit) weight models in Sect. 6.3, for off-the-shelf accelerators.

### 6.1  Non-binary Sub-8 Bit Models: First Stage Training

To study the effectiveness of tanh(.), we train models with 5-bit dense layer weights for 100K updates, with and without tanh; note that other components are not quantized in this experiment, and that all trainable parameters are updated. Table 2 presents the results, comparing against an unquantized base-line model. The table also presents results with two quantizers for weights: a) the non-linear quantization with tanh(.); b) a linear quantizer without tanh(.). The model with tanh(.) achieves a 7.4% relative degradation in FDR, while the model without tanh(.) yields a 12.3% degradation in FDR.

## 6.2   Non-binary Sub-8 Bit Models: Second Stage Training

In this section, we compare the performance of the quantized models against the baseline unquantized model. The baseline model is trained for 500K model updates. For the proposed QAT approach, the models were trained for 500K and 35K updates in the first and second stage training respectively. Firstly, we discuss the accuracy implications, and then present results in terms of memory and CPU gains (for ARM NEON instruction set).

**Table 2.** *Relative degradation in FDR at baseline model's FRR on VAL. Models have 5-bit weights with or without tanh(.).*

| Quantization | Rel. FDR (%) |
|---|---|
| Unquantized model | 0.0 (Baseline) |
| With *tanh*(.) | 7.4 |
| Without *tanh*(.) | 12.3 |

**Evaluation of Accuracy.** From Table 3, M1 with the proposed 2-stage train-ing algorithm yields a 3.1% relative degradation in FDR. To study the effect of number of bits for weights, we quantized M2, M3 and M4 with 2-stage training. Notice that going from M0 to M1, there is a very small increase in relative degra-dation in FDR at FRR (3.1% increase). Here the changes include: 32 to 8-bit weights; 32 to 8-bit quantization of other parameters (bias, gain, BN parame-ters); and 32 to 16-bit input and activations. Further reducing the inputs and activations from 16-bit to 8-bit (i.e., M1 to M2) does not lead to an increase in FDR (3.1% to 3.5%). A further change in weights from 8 to 5 or 4-bits (i.e., M2 to M3 or M4) leads to a small increase in FDR (3.5% to 7.4% or 8.7%).

**CPU, Memory, and Model Size Gains.** Reduction in compute resources (memory, CPU) is dependent on hardware architecture. In Table 3, we present CPU, memory consumption on ARM NEON.

**CPU:** We observe a 45% reduction in CPU when using 8-bit activation and input versus 16-bit activation and input. This reduction in bandwidth is due to 8-bit SIMD processors achieving a throughput of 2x computation with $8 \times 8$ bit multiplications compared to $8 \times 16$ bit multiplications. Note that going from a full precision M0 model to M1 (a 8-bit parameters, 16-bit activations and input),

**Table 3.** *Performance of models in terms of rel. degradation in FDR at FRR against baseline full precision model on TEST data. CPU, memory consumption, and model size for ARM NEON in MCPS and KB (MCPS refers to Million Cycles Per Second).*

| ID | # bits weight | # bits act. | # bits input | Quant. Method | Rel. FDR Degrad. (%) | CPU (MCPS) | Memory (kb) | Model size (kb) |
|----|------|------|------|-----------|-----------------|------|-----|-----|
| M0 | 32 | 32 | 32 | No Quant. | 0.0 (Baseline) | 37.6 | 912 | 912 |
| M1 | 8 | 16 | 16 | 2-stage | 3.1 | 18.8 | 228 | 228 |
| M2 | 8 | 8 | 8 | 2-stage | 3.5 | 10.3 | 228 | 228 |
| M3 | 5 | 8 | 8 | 2-stage | 7.4 | 10.3 | 228 | 142 |
| M4 | 4 | 8 | 8 | 2-stage | 8.7 | 10.3 | 228 | 114 |

**Table 4.** *Relative degradation in FDR at FRR against baseline on TEST, compressing weights, other parameters, input and activations to 8-bit.*

| Quantization on | Rel. FDR Degrad. (%) |
|-----------------|----------------------|
| weight | 3.8 |
| weight + bias + gain | 4.7 |
| weight + input + activation | 5.2 |
| weight + $BN_1$ | 5.3 |
| weight + $BN_2$ | 9.0 |

lead to a 50% saving in CPU consumption. Also, since 8-bit containers are used, further reduction in bit widths (i.e. from M2 to M4), do not yield gains in MCPS.

**Memory and Model Size:** We observe a 75% reduction in memory by using 8-bit weights, input and activations when compared to non-quantized, 32-bit models. The smallest data type in ARM NEON is 8-bit, so we don't observe any memory reduction by using sub-8-bit weights. However, we study and use sub 8-bit weights because this effectively provides more headroom for accumulation of weights, input and activations – reducing the likelihood of overflow, and using a lower-precision accumulator. We also note the model size, which decreases linearly with bit width.

**Some Ablation Studies.** In this segment, we present 3 sets of ablation studies: 1) quantizing different components of the network to 8-bits; 2) quantizing inputs and activations from 8-bit to 5-bit; 3) quantizing other components of the network from 8-bit to 5-bit (bias, gain, batch norm parameters).

**1) 8-bit models:** Fixing 8-bit quantization for all components of the network, we perform an ablation study for accuracy implications in terms of quantizing bias, gain, BN parameters, input and activations. The unquantized baseline model and the quantized models in this section were trained for 100K updates. Table 4 presents the results in terms of relative degradation in FDR at equal FRR compared to the baseline model on TEST data. With $tanh(.)$ 8-bit weight

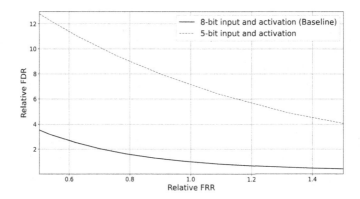

**Fig. 2.** *On TEST: DET curves showing performance of quantized model with 8-bit input and activation (Baseline, Blue) and 5-bit quantization (Orange)* (Color figure online)

quantization we obtain a 3.8 % relative degradation in FDR. With further quantization of input and activations (5.2%) or bias and gain (4.7%) or batch norm parameters (5.3%), we did not see a significant decrease in model performance. However, it is interesting to note from the Table 4 that the dynamic scaling of BN yields an improvement (i.e., from 9.0% to 5.3% relative FDR degradation).

**2) 8-bit to 5-bit change in input and activations**: While compressing input and activations from 16-bit to 8 bits (from M1 to M2 in Table 3) only results in a minor performance degradation, reducing further from 8-bit to 5-bit input and activations leads to a significant drop in performance (see Fig. 2).

**3) 8-bit to 5-bit change in parameters**: Similar to the small degradation in FDR in going from 8 bits to 5 bits for weights (Table 3), reducing the bit width from 8 to 5 for other parameters does not lead to a significant degradation in FDR (3.0% increase in relative FDR).

### 6.3    Binary Weight Models

In this section, we present results for models with 1-bit weights using 2-stage training; note that the other parameters, input and activations are non-binary (i.e., either quantized or full precision). The models were trained for 500K and 35K updates in the first and second stage training respectively.

We experimented with two quantized models, with 2-times and 6-times the number of parameters as the baseline model (250K parameters): a) M5 with 500K parameters – where the first, second, and the last layer weights are 5-bit, the other layer weights are 1-bit, and all other parameters, input and activations being 8-bit; b) M6 with 1.5M parameters – where all layer weights are 1-bit, and other parameters, input and activations being 8-bit. Results are reported in Table 5. In addition to FDR, we report the model size and project reduction in memory utilization with off-the-shelf neural network accelerators.

**Table 5.** *Performance of the models in terms of rel. degradation in FDR at FRR matching baseline full precision model on TEST. Hidden layer sizes of M5 are {123, 566, 123, 566, 123, 566}, while those of M6 are {1080, 566, 123, 566, 123, 566}.*

| ID | # Param. | Rel. FDR Degrad. (%) | Memory (kb) | Model size (kb) | Note |
|----|----------|----------------------|-------------|-----------------|------|
| M0 | 250K | 0.0 | 912 | 912 | Baseline |
| M5 | 500k | 14.0 | 128 | 128 | with large LR |
| M6 | 1.5M | 6.2 | 198 | 198 | with large LR |
| M5 | 500k | 0.4 | 128 | 128 | with LR change |
| M6 | 1.5M | -0.4 | 198 | 198 | with LR change |

In our experiments, models having binary weights are sensitive to learning rates. Although Adam optimizer is employed in model training, we find that manually changing learning rate to a smaller number for the last few model updates of the first stage improves the model performance for M5 and M6. In Table 5, we find that the learning rate change results in 13.6% and 6.6% reduction in relative degradation in FDR against baseline model (M0) for M5 and M6 respectively. With the LR change, M5 and M6 are able to achieve performance parity with M0. With off-the-shelf neural network accelerators, projected memory utilization is equivalent to the model size, with 86.0% and 78.3% reduction in memory consumption with M5 and M6.

## 7   Conclusions

We proposed a 2-stage algorithm for sub 8-bit quantization of 250K parameter KWS models. For the first stage, we adapted a recently proposed QAT technique using a non-linear transformation on weights. In the second stage, we used linear quantization methods on other parameters, input and activations. This paper happens in the setting of on-device, low footprint, streaming KWS models, that being explored on two embedded chipset settings, where we achieved parity in accuracy against a full precision model in terms of FDR at a chosen FRR. With sub 8-bit non-binary weight models, on an ARM NEON architecture, we match accuracy, and obtain up to 3 times improvement in CPU consumption and more than 4 times improvement in memory consumption. With a binary weight model (and other components being 8-bit), using off-the-shelf neural network accelerators, at accuracy parity with a full precision model, we project 4 to 7 times reduction in memory consumption and model size.

## References

1. Agarap, A.F.: Deep learning using rectified linear units (ReLU). arXiv preprint arXiv:1803.08375 (2018)

2. Banner, R., Hubara, I., Hoffer, E., Soudry, D.: Scalable methods for 8-bit training of neural networks. In: Advances in Neural Information Processing Systems, vol. 31 (2018)

3. Bengio, Y., Léonard, N., Courville, A.: Estimating or propagating gradients through stochastic neurons for conditional computation. arXiv preprint arXiv:1308.3432 (2013)

4. Blouw, P., Malik, G., Morcos, B., Voelker, A.R., Eliasmith, C.: Hardware aware training for efficient keyword spotting on general purpose and specialized hardware. arXiv preprint arXiv:2009.04465 (2020)

5. Chen, G., Parada, C., Heigold, G.: Small-footprint keyword spotting using deep neural networks. In: Proceedings of ICASSP (2014)

6. Courbariaux, M., Bengio, Y., David, J.P.: BinaryConnect: training deep neural networks with binary weights during propagations. In: Advances in Neural Information Processing Systems, pp. 3123–3131 (2015)

7. Elfwing, S., Uchibe, E., Doya, K.: Sigmoid-weighted linear units for neural network function approximation in reinforcement learning. Neural Netw. **107**, 3–11 (2018)

8. Gao, Y., et al.: On front-end gain invariant modeling for wake word spotting. arXiv preprint arXiv:2010.06676 (2020)

9. Hendrycks, D., Gimpel, K.: Gaussian error linear units (GELUS). arXiv preprint arXiv:1606.08415 (2016)

10. Ioffe, S., Szegedy, C.: Batch normalization: accelerating deep network training by reducing internal covariate shift. In: International Conference on Machine Learning, pp. 448–456 (2015)

11. Jang, E., Gu, S., Poole, B.: Categorical reparameterization with Gumbel-softmax. arXiv preprint arXiv:1611.01144 (2016)

12. Jose, C., Mishchenko, Y., Senechal, T., Shah, A., Escott, A., Vitaladevuni, S.: Accurate detection of wake word start and end using a CNN. In: InterSpeech (2020)

13. Li, X., Wei, X., Qin, X.: Small-footprint keyword spotting with multi-scale temporal convolution. arXiv preprint arXiv:2010.09960 (2020)

14. Mishchenko, Y., et al.: Low-bit quantization and quantization-aware training for small-footprint keyword spotting. In: Proceedings of IEEE International Conference On Machine Learning and Applications (ICMLA) (2019)

15. Mittermaier, S., Kürzinger, L., Waschneck, B., Rigoll, G.: Small-footprint keyword spotting on raw audio data with SINC-convolutions. In: Proceedings of ICASSP (2020)

16. Nguyen, H.D., Alexandridis, A., Mouchtaris, A.: Quantization aware training with absolute-cosine regularization for automatic speech recognition. In: Proceedings of InterSpeech (2020)

17. Panchapagesan, S., et al.: Multi-task learning and weighted cross-entropy for DNN-based keyword spotting. In: Proceedings of InterSpeech (2016)

18. Prabhavalkar, R., Alsharif, O., Bruguier, A., McGraw, L.: On the compression of recurrent neural networks with an application to LVCSR acoustic modeling for embedded speech recognition. In: 2016 IEEE International Conference on Acoustics, Speech and Signal Processing (ICASSP), pp. 5970–5974. IEEE (2016)

19. Rastegari, M., Ordonez, V., Redmon, J., Farhadi, A.: XNOR-net: imagenet classification using binary convolutional neural networks. In: Leibe, B., Matas, J., Sebe, N., Welling, M. (eds.) ECCV 2016. LNCS, vol. 9908, pp. 525–542. Springer, Cham (2016). https://doi.org/10.1007/978-3-319-46493-0_32

20. Shi, B., Sun, M., Kao, C.C., Rozgic, V., Matsoukas, S., Wang, C.: Compression of acoustic event detection models with low-rank matrix factorization and quantization training. arXiv preprint arXiv:1905.00855 (2019)
21. Strom, N., Khan, H., Hamza, W.: Squashed weight distribution for low bit quantization of deep models. In: Submitted to Proceedings of InterSpeech (2022)
22. Sun, M., et al.: Compressed time delay neural network for small-footprint keyword spotting. In: InterSpeech (2017)
23. Sun, M., et al.: Compressed time delay neural network for small-footprint keyword spotting. In: Proceedings of InterSpeech (2017)
24. Tucker, G., Wu, M., Sun, M., Panchapagesan, S., Fu, G., Vitaladevuni, S.: Model compression applied to small-footprint keyword spotting. In: Proceedings of InterSpeech (2016)
25. Vandersteegen, M., Van Beeck, K., Goedemé, T.: Integer-only CNNs with 4 bit weights and bit-shift quantization scales at full-precision accuracy. Electronics (2021)
26. Vanhoucke, V., Senior, A., Mao, M.Z.: Improving the speed of neural networks on CPUs. In: Deep Learning and Unsupervised Feature Learning Workshop, NIPS 2011 (2011)

# Detection of Prosodic Boundaries
# in Speech Using Wav2Vec 2.0

Marie Kunešová[(✉)] [ID] and Markéta Řezáčková [ID]

New Technologies for the Information Society and Department of Cybernetics,
Faculty of Applied Sciences, University of West Bohemia,
Pilsen, Czech Republic
{mkunes,juzova}@ntis.zcu.cz

**Abstract.** Prosodic boundaries in speech are of great relevance to both speech synthesis and audio annotation. In this paper, we apply the wav2vec 2.0 framework to the task of detecting these boundaries in speech signal, using only acoustic information. We test the approach on a set of recordings of Czech broadcast news, labeled by phonetic experts, and compare it to an existing text-based predictor, which uses the transcripts of the same data. Despite using a relatively small amount of labeled data, the wav2vec2 model achieves an accuracy of 94% and F1 measure of 83% on within-sentence prosodic boundaries (or 95% and 89% on all prosodic boundaries), outperforming the text-based approach. However, by combining the outputs of the two different models we can improve the results even further.

**Keywords:** Phrasing · Prosodic boundaries · Phrase boundary detection · wav2vec

## 1  Introduction

Prosodic phrasing is the division of fluent speech into *prosodic* (or *intonation* [2]) *phrases* – groups of words in a spoken sentence, typically featuring an intonation peak and often separated by pauses.

Prosodic phrasing not only plays an important role in the human understanding of spoken language [6] but is also highly relevant for many speech processing tasks, such as speech synthesis and audio annotation.

In text-to-speech (TTS) systems, information about prosodic boundaries in text helps improve the naturalness of synthesized speech, by allowing the system to insert pauses and modify intonation in a similar way to a human speaker. In audio, it can be used to enhance the training data, likewise leading to a more natural-sounding speech [17].

In speech recognition and spoken language understanding, phrase breaks also help distinguish between otherwise identical sentences with a different meaning (such as the popular example *"Let's eat, grandma!"* versus *"Let's eat grandma!"*).

© Springer Nature Switzerland AG 2022
P. Sojka et al. (Eds.): TSD 2022, LNAI 13502, pp. 377–388, 2022.
https://doi.org/10.1007/978-3-031-16270-1_31

There are two different scenarios for the automatic detection of prosodic boundaries: detection solely from text, most often for the purposes of speech synthesis [7,13,18,20,24], or detection from spoken utterances as a form of audio annotation. In the latter case, some approaches have been based solely on acoustic information (though sometimes with word or syllable boundaries derived from text transcripts) [11,14–16], while others have combined both lexical and acoustic information [4,8,9].

In this paper, our main goal is to obtain a detector which works solely in the audio modality, using only acoustic cues. However, its results will also be compared to an existing text-based model [20], evaluated on the transcripts of the same utterances.

## 2    Data

The experiments were performed on a set of recordings of Czech radio broadcast news (Channels 1 and 2 of the Czech Radio), previously used in [20] as the News-Reading Speech (NRS) corpus[1]. The dataset consists of 12 news bulletins presented by different speakers (six male and six female), each between 2.5 and 5 min long, for a total of 42 min of speech (486 sentences). The recordings have been annotated by phonetic experts, following the guidelines in [2].

The annotation conventions, as described in [2], include multiple levels of phrasing: most relevantly, prosodic (intonation) phrases can also be further divided into one of more *intermediate* phrases – smaller units with less discernible boundaries. These are also labeled in the NRS dataset. However, in our work, we are specifically interested in the detection of *prosodic* boundaries as the most important ones for most speech processing applications – we will explore the use of intermediate boundaries during *training*, but we ignore them during evaluation.

## 3    Model for Text-Based Detection

We compare the results of our audio-based prosodic boundary detection to those achieved by our existing text-based detector [20] on the same dataset.

This model remains as described in [20]: it is a Text-to-Text Transfer Transformer (T5) model [12], which transforms a given sequence of words into an output sequence with predicted phrase boundaries. It was pre-trained on large amounts of unlabeled Czech text in the CommonCrawl corpus and fine-tuned for the phrase detection task on what [20] referred to as The Laboratory Speech (LS) data – text sentences from 6 large-scale Czech speech corpora created for the purposes of speech synthesis in the TTS system ARTIC [19].

---

[1] Since the publication of [20], the NRS annotations have undergone a round of revisions and the model was updated accordingly. The text-based results in Sect. 5.3 will thus differ from those listed in the aforementioned paper.

The prosodic boundaries in the LS dataset were labeled only using automatic segmentation, but the fine-tuned model was subsequently adapted on the hand-annotated NRS data using a leave-one-out approach – 12 different models were trained, each adapted on 11 speakers and evaluated on the last speaker.

## 4  Model for Audio-Based Detection

Systems for audio-based prosodic boundary detection have traditionally utilized combinations of different features such as the duration of pauses and syllables, $F_0$ range and resets, intensity, or pitch movement [4,9,11,14,15]. Rather than use such handcrafted combinations of features, however, we chose to employ learned representations from raw audio data.

Wav2vec 2.0 [1] is a self-supervised framework for speech representation which has been used for a large variety of different speech-related tasks [5,22,23]. One of the main advantages of the wav2vec approach is that a generic pre-trained model can be fine-tuned for a specific purpose using only a small amount of labeled data.

We use the pre-trained wav2vec 2.0 base model "ClTRUS"[2], which is specifically trained for the Czech language using more than 80 thousand hours of Czech speech from various domains [10].

Using the HuggingFace Transformers library [21], we fine-tuned the model for an audio frame classification task ($Wav2Vec2ForAudioFrameClassification$) on the NRS data and evaluate it using a leave-one-out approach, similarly to the text-based T5 model (12 different models, each fine-tuned using 11 speakers and tested on the last speaker) (Fig. 1).

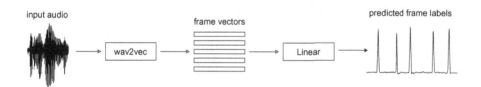

**Fig. 1.** Illustration of the wav2vec2-based prosodic boundary detector. The model outputs a label for each audio frame (every 20 ms).

During the fine-tuning of the wav2vec 2.0 model, the references are given in the form of a fuzzy labeling function, as depicted in Fig. 2 (top): prosodic boundaries are given the reference label 1, linearly decreasing to 0 in an interval $\pm 0.2$ s around each boundary.

The model was fine-tuned with MSE loss. The fine-tuning process is very fast – the model learns to predict the triangular shapes nearly perfectly within

---

[2] Czech language **TR**ransformer from **U**nlabeled **S**peech,
available from: https://huggingface.co/fav-kky/wav2vec2-base-cs-80k-ClTRUS.

several epochs, at which point the results do not improve further with additional training.

Due to the relatively high memory requirements of wav2vec, the audio is processed in chunks of 30 s, with a 15 s step – the chunks are partially overlapping. When the outputs are stitched back together for evaluation, the middle part of each chunk is used and the overlapping edges are discarded. This was originally meant to avoid potential issues near the beginning and end of each chunk (due to missing context on one side). However, in terms of the overall precision and recall, the difference appears to be minimal.

Finally, in order to improve the robustness and consistency of the results and limit the influence of random chance, each model (for each leave-one-out fold) was fine-tuned five times with identical settings and different random seeds, and the raw outputs were averaged. This does not substantially improve the results, but it reduces random fluctuations and allows for a more reliable comparison between models fine-tuned with different training labels or different amounts of data (e.g. in Figs. 3 and 5).

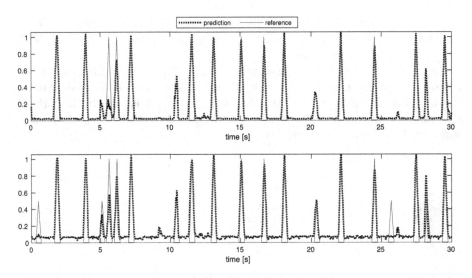

**Fig. 2.** Example of the reference labels and predictions for one audio segment. Training labels for the wav2vec2 model either include only prosodic phrase boundaries, with a peak value of 1 (top), or also intermediate phrase boundaries, with a smaller peak value of 0.5 (bottom).

## 4.1   Influence of Intermediate Phrase Boundaries

As previously stated, our targets for prediction are only the prosodic phrase boundaries. However, the less important intermediate boundaries may also convey useful information for training, particularly since the distinction between the two categories is not always clear.

In our initial experiments with a model fine-tuned solely on prosodic boundaries, we found that the majority of false positives (approximately two thirds, as seen in Fig. 3) were located in spots marked as *intermediate* phrase boundaries by the expert annotators. This is despite the fact that intermediate boundaries are present in less than 7% of all word boundaries in the NRS dataset.

This spurred us to question whether it is truly appropriate to label these boundaries as *zero* in the reference labels - they clearly exhibit similar acoustic features that the model is learning to detect, albeit perhaps to a less pronounced degree. Assigning them a label with a smaller, but non-zero value may have a positive effect on the resulting model.

Thus, we decided to test two options for the training data:

a) Only prosodic phrases are included in the reference labels.
b) Both prosodic and intermediate phrases are included in the reference labels, with different values. Prosodic boundaries are given the maximum value of 1 and intermediate boundaries are labeled as 0.5 – both with a linear decrease to zero over $\pm 0.2$ s, as previously described.

In both cases, the model is still evaluated on *prosodic* boundaries only.

### 4.2 Post-processing

The fine-tuned wav2vec2 model outputs predicted labels for each audio frame (every 20 ms, as per the base model). However, the text-based T5 model naturally predicts phrase breaks between words and is evaluated in terms of within-sentence word boundaries. Thus, it is necessary to convert the wav2vec2 predictions to a more comparable format:

First, we identify the peaks in the raw outputs. If the value of a peak is higher than a specific threshold and there is no higher peak within 0.25 s, the system marks this as a predicted boundary.

For the purposes of evaluation, these predicted boundaries are then aligned to the nearest end of a word within 100 ms, based on the reference annotations – this is because the ground truth phrase boundaries are likewise aligned to the ends of words. For the numeric results listed in this paper, we did not specifically tune the decision threshold – we simply chose the value 0.5 as the "middle ground". Similarly, for the model trained with added intermediate boundaries, the threshold was selected as 0.75 – as the average between the labels of prosodic boundaries (1.0) and intermediate boundaries (0.5).

## 5    Results

In this paper, we list two separate sets of results, evaluated under slightly different conditions: First, evaluation of the full outputs of the wav2vec2 models, given as time labels, and including all boundaries, even those between sentences.

However, for a fair comparison with the T5 model, we secondly convert our predictions into text form (using the transcripts to ensure identical sentences), with boundaries marked only between words and ignoring the ends of sentences – this is because the text-based T5 model worked with isolated sentences and only searched for prosodic boundaries *within* the sentence (i.e. not at the end).

## 5.1  Evaluation Measures

The standard evaluation metrics for phrase boundary detection are precision ($P$), recall ($R$), accuracy (Acc), and F1-score, given as

$$P = \frac{tp}{tp + fp} \tag{1}$$

$$R = \frac{tp}{tp + fn} \tag{2}$$

$$\text{Acc} = \frac{tp + tn}{tp + tn + fp + fn} \tag{3}$$

$$F1 = 2 \cdot \frac{P \cdot R}{P + R} \tag{4}$$

where $tp$ refers to the number of correctly detected phrase boundaries (*true positives*), $fp$ the number of *false positives*, $fn$ is the number of missed phrase boundaries (*false negatives*) and $tn$ is the number of *true negatives* - between-word boundaries that were correctly labeled as not being phrase breaks.

As the wav2vec2 model outputs per-frame predictions, not constrained to word boundaries, we decided to also perform frame-wise evaluation, in terms of segmentation of each audio file into prosodic phrases. For this, we chose segment purity and coverage (e.g. [3]) as the main metrics. These are obtained as

$$\text{purity}(S, R) = \frac{\sum_k \max_j |s_k \cap r_j|}{\sum_k |s_k|} \tag{5}$$

and

$$\text{coverage}(S, R) = \frac{\sum_j \max_k |s_k \cap r_j|}{\sum_j |r_j|} \tag{6}$$

where $S = \{s_1, \ldots, s_K\}$ is the set of segments (i.e. prosodic phrases) found by the system, $R = \{r_1, \ldots, r_J\}$ corresponds to the reference segments, $|r_j|$ is the duration of segment $r_j$, and $s_k \cap r_j$ denotes the intersection of segments $s_k$ and $r_j$.

## 5.2  Audio-Based Evaluation

Figure 3 shows the precision-recall and purity-coverage curves achieved by the two fine-tuned wav2vec2 models when evaluated on the entire audio data. Table 3 then lists the numeric results corresponding to the default thresholds.

From the results displayed in Fig. 3, it appears that the addition of intermediate boundaries to the training data has had a very minimal effect on the two curves, at least when evaluated only on prosodic boundaries. However, if we look at the false positives, a greater percentage of them now consists of intermediate boundaries as opposed to no-breaks. This could be considered an improvement by itself – in many use-cases, an intermediate boundary being incorrectly marked as a prosodic boundary is a less problematic mistake than if a location with *no* phrase boundary was marked as such.

**Table 1.** Results on the entire audio files, including boundaries at the ends of sentences, and with a wav2vec2 model fine-tuned a) only on prosodic boundaries (threshold 0.5) or b) also intermediate boundaries (threshold 0.75). "Pur" and "Cov" refers to purity and coverage, respectively.

| fine-tuning data | Pur | Cov | Acc | P | R | F1 | tp | fp | fn | tn |
|---|---|---|---|---|---|---|---|---|---|---|
| a) prosodic b. only | 93.82 | 92.94 | 94.87 | 88.22 | 88.90 | 88.56 | 1266 | 169 | 158 | 4781 |
| b) pros. & interm. b | 92.29 | 94.39 | 94.78 | 90.26 | 85.88 | 88.02 | 1223 | 132 | 201 | 4818 |

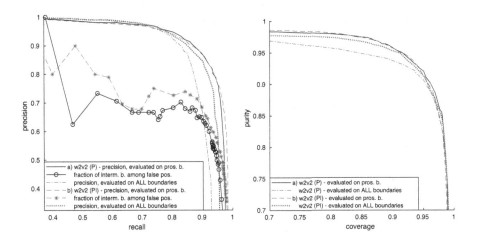

**Fig. 3.** Precision-recall (left) and purity-coverage (right) curves of models fine-tuned a) only on prosodic boundaries ("w2v2 (P)"), or b) on both prosodic and intermediate boundaries ("w2v2 (PI)"). The left plot additionally shows the fraction of false positives which correspond to intermediate boundaries, relative to the total number of false positives.

### 5.3   Text-Based Evaluation

In order to compare the results of the wav2vec2 model with the text-based T5 model, we convert the wav2vec2 predictions to the same format – sequences of words, separated by sentence, with marked prosodic boundaries.

Thus, for this second evaluation, we only consider the predicted phrase boundaries which were matched to word boundaries within the sentence during post-processing. Peaks in the wav2vec2 output which were more than 100 ms from the nearest end of a word are simply ignored. However, the number of such cases is minimal (3 out of 1435 predicted boundaries at threshold 0.5).

The text-based results are illustrated in Fig. 4, which compares the precision-recall curve of the wav2vec2 model (fine-tuned with prosodic boundaries only) with the results of the T5 model. The latter are shown only as a single point, as there is no threshold to change – the T5 model directly outputs a sequence of words and prosodic boundaries.

The graph additionally shows the precision-recall curves for two possible combinations of the two models:

a) prosodic boundaries are marked only where *both* the T5 model and the wav2vec2 model predict them ("T5 AND wav2vec"),
b) prosodic boundaries are marked where *at least one* of the models predicts them ("T5 OR wav2vec").

Finally, the numeric results are presented in Tables 2 and 3: Table 2 lists the individual results of the T5 model and one wav2vec2 model (fine-tuned only on prosodic boundaries) for separate speakers. Table 3 then shows the overall results for both wav2vec2 models and also for the combinations of T5 and wav2vec2.

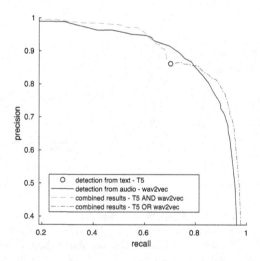

**Fig. 4.** Results evaluated on text - precision and recall of the text-based T5 model, audio-based wav2vec2 model, and their combinations (wav2vec2 fine-tuned only on prosodic boundaries)

We can see that in the terms of accuracy and F1, the listed "T5 OR wav2vec" variants score higher that the individual models alone. However, it is at the cost of slightly reduced precision. Conversely, the "T5 AND wav2vec" achieve a very high precision of ∼94%, but with a relatively low recall of ∼60%. Which one of these alternatives is best would depend on the specific application.

**Table 2.** Results on individual speakers, wav2vec2 fine-tuned only on prosodic boundaries and with a threshold of 0.5.

| model | speaker | # sent. | Acc | P | R | F1 | tp | fp | fn | tn |
|---|---|---|---|---|---|---|---|---|---|---|
| T5 | NRS01 | 36 | 91.42 | 85.25 | 64.20 | 73.24 | 52 | 9 | 29 | 353 |
| | NRS02 | 60 | 94.24 | 82.02 | 76.84 | 79.35 | 73 | 16 | 22 | 549 |
| | NRS03 | 38 | 95.74 | 86.36 | 83.82 | 85.07 | 57 | 9 | 11 | 393 |
| | NRS04 | 31 | 92.76 | 84.91 | 66.18 | 74.38 | 45 | 8 | 23 | 352 |
| | NRS05 | 48 | 92.56 | 87.67 | 66.67 | 75.74 | 64 | 9 | 32 | 446 |
| | NRS06 | 45 | 89.29 | 92.54 | 54.39 | 68.51 | 62 | 5 | 52 | 413 |
| | NRS07 | 33 | 94.66 | 87.04 | 77.05 | 81.74 | 47 | 7 | 14 | 325 |
| | NRS08 | 37 | 93.28 | 91.07 | 66.23 | 76.69 | 51 | 5 | 26 | 379 |
| | NRS09 | 50 | 94.4078 | 80.00 | 74.73 | 77.27 | 68 | 17 | 23 | 606 |
| | NRS10 | 34 | 94.57 | 90.00 | 73.77 | 81.08 | 45 | 5 | 16 | 321 |
| | NRS11 | 35 | 94.70 | 86.00 | 75.44 | 80.37 | 43 | 7 | 14 | 332 |
| | NRS12 | 39 | 93.96 | 85.71 | 75.00 | 80.00 | 54 | 9 | 18 | 366 |
| | all | 486 | 93.44 | 86.18 | 70.24 | 77.40 | 661 | 106 | 280 | 4835 |
| wav2vec2 | NRS01 | 36 | 92.55 | 81.58 | 76.54 | 78.98 | 62 | 14 | 19 | 348 |
| | NRS02 | 60 | 95.61 | 82.35 | 88.42 | 85.28 | 84 | 18 | 11 | 547 |
| | NRS03 | 38 | 94.68 | 77.92 | 88.24 | 82.76 | 60 | 17 | 8 | 385 |
| | NRS04 | 31 | 94.39 | 84.38 | 79.41 | 81.82 | 54 | 10 | 14 | 350 |
| | NRS05 | 48 | 92.01 | 80.23 | 71.88 | 75.82 | 69 | 17 | 27 | 438 |
| | NRS06 | 45 | 96.24 | 92.73 | 89.47 | 91.07 | 102 | 8 | 12 | 410 |
| | NRS07 | 33 | 95.67 | 85.48 | 86.89 | 86.18 | 53 | 9 | 8 | 323 |
| | NRS08 | 37 | 93.49 | 84.06 | 75.32 | 79.45 | 58 | 11 | 19 | 373 |
| | NRS09 | 50 | 94.12 | 76.34 | 78.02 | 77.17 | 71 | 22 | 20 | 601 |
| | NRS10 | 34 | 95.09 | 83.87 | 85.25 | 84.55 | 52 | 10 | 9 | 316 |
| | NRS11 | 35 | 95.20 | 76.39 | 96.49 | 85.27 | 55 | 17 | 2 | 322 |
| | NRS12 | 39 | 94.63 | 82.43 | 84.72 | 83.56 | 61 | 13 | 11 | 362 |
| | all | 486 | 94.46 | 82.47 | 83.00 | 82.73 | 781 | 166 | 160 | 4775 |

**Table 3.** Results on the entire NRS data, using a leave-one-out-approach. "T5 AND wav2vec2" places prosodic boundaries only where *both* models predicted them. "T5 OR wav2vec2" places them where *at least one* of the models did.

| model | Acc | P | R | F1 | tp | fp | fn | tn |
|---|---|---|---|---|---|---|---|---|
| T5 Model | 93.44 | 86.18 | 70.24 | 77.40 | 661 | 106 | 280 | 4835 |
| wav2vec2 - f.-t. on pros. b. only | 94.46 | 82.47 | 83.00 | 82.73 | 781 | 166 | 160 | 4775 |
| wav2vec2 - fine-tuned with int. b | 94.36 | 85.12 | 78.43 | 81.64 | 738 | 129 | 203 | 4812 |
| T5 AND wav2vec2 (pros. b.) | 93.35 | 93.38 | 62.91 | 75.17 | 592 | 42 | 349 | 4899 |
| T5 OR wav2vec2 (pros. b.) | 94.54 | 78.70 | **90.33** | **84.12** | 850 | 230 | 91 | 4711 |
| T5 AND wav2vec2 (with int. b.) | 93.15 | **94.39** | 60.79 | 73.95 | 572 | 34 | 369 | 4907 |
| T5 OR wav2vec2 (with int. b.) | **94.64** | 80.45 | 87.89 | 84.00 | 827 | 201 | 114 | 4740 |

One may also notice that the precision and recall values here are slightly lower than those in Table 1. This is because of the exclusion of end-of-sentence boundaries. These are naturally much more pronounced in speech, in terms of both intonation and pause, and so the wav2vec2 model can detect them with much greater accuracy than the within-sentence boundaries.

## 6    Discussion

We have shown that the results achieved by the wav2vec2 model surpass those of the text-based T5 model. However, it is important to note that this is still a somewhat "unfair" comparison: The ground truth labels (provided by phonetic experts) used in our experiments were based on the spoken sentences and therefore reflect the specific phrasing of the speaker. However, the locations of phrase breaks are partly subjective and different speakers may place them differently. Thus, the predictions made by the T5 model, which does not have access to acoustic information, may not necessarily be *less correct*, they simply do not match the specific speaker.

Another thing to consider is the relatively small amount of data which was available for fine-tuning and testing – approximately 42 min of speech or 486 sentences. Although the wav2vec2 framework is known for being able to achieve good results with small amounts of data, and the results achieved here do indeed look very promising, it is likely that the performance could be improved further if more data were available.

This is also suggested by Fig. 5, which compares wav2vec2 models fine-tuned with different amounts of training data: models fine-tuned using only one, three or six of the 12 speakers show a lower precision and recall, indicating that *increasing* the amount of training data could lead to further improvement.

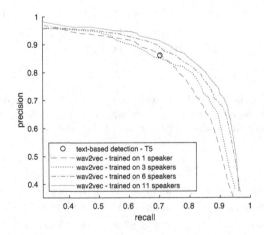

**Fig. 5.** Precision-recall curve for wav2vec2 models fine-tuned using different amounts of training data, evaluated on the text sentences and with the text-based results shown for comparison.

# 7  Conclusion and Future Work

In this paper, we explored the use of the wav2vec 2.0 framework for the detection of prosodic boundaries in speech.

We have found that the relatively straightforward and easy to use wav2vec 2.0 approach works surprisingly well: it does not require text annotation or knowledge of word boundaries (these were only used for evaluation), nor a handcrafted selection of features, yet it achieves very good results, surpassing the text-based T5 model which was used for comparison.

Still, this was, in its essence, only an initial experiment. In the future, we would like to test the approach on a larger amount of more varied data and also explore the possibilities of combining the audio and text modalities within a single model, rather than merely combining the outputs.

**Acknowledgements.** This research was supported by the Czech Science Foundation (GA CR), project No. GA21-14758S, and by the grant of the University of West Bohemia, project No. SGS-2022-017. Computational resources were supplied by the project "e-Infrastruktura CZ" (e-INFRA CZ LM2018140) supported by the Ministry of Education, Youth and Sports of the Czech Republic.

# References

1. Baevski, A., Zhou, Y., Mohamed, A., Auli, M.: wav2vec 2.0: A framework for self-supervised learning of speech representations. In: Advances in Neural Information Processing Systems, vol. 33, pp. 12449–12460 (2020)
2. Beckman, M.E., Ayers Elam, G.: Guidelines for ToBI Labelling, Version 3. The Ohio State University Research Foundation, Ohio State University (1997)
3. Bredin, H.: TristouNet: triplet loss for speaker turn embedding. In: Proceedings of ICASSP 2017, pp. 5430–5434 (2017)
4. Christodoulides, G., Avanzi, M., Simon, A.C.: Automatic labelling of prosodic prominence, phrasing and disfluencies in French speech by simulating the perception of Naïve and expert listeners. In: Proceedings of InterSpeech 2017, pp. 3936–3940 (2017)
5. Cooper, E., Huang, W.C., Toda, T., Yamagishi, J.: Generalization ability of MOS prediction networks. In: Proceedings of ICASSP 2022, pp. 8442–8446 (2022)
6. Frazier, L., Carlson, K., Clifton, C., Jr.: Prosodic phrasing is central to language comprehension. Trends Cogn. Sci. **10**(6), 244–249 (2006)
7. Futamata, K., Park, B., Yamamoto, R., Tachibana, K.: Phrase break prediction with bidirectional encoder representations in Japanese text-to-speech synthesis. In: Proceedings of InterSpeech 2021, pp. 3126–3130 (2021)
8. Gallwitz, F., Niemann, H., Nöth, E., Warnke, V.: Integrated recognition of words and prosodic phrase boundaries. Speech Commun. **36**(1), 81–95 (2002)
9. Kocharov, D., Kachkovskaia, T., Skrelin, P.: Prosodic boundary detection using syntactic and acoustic information. Comput. Speech Lang. **53**, 231–241 (2019)
10. Lehečka, J., Švec, J., Pražák, A., Psutka, J.: Exploring capabilities of monolingual audio transformers using large datasets in automatic speech recognition of Czech. In: To appear at Interspeech 2022 (2022)

11. Lin, B., Wang, L., Feng, X., Zhang, J.: Joint detection of sentence stress and phrase boundary for prosody. In: Proceedings of InterSpeech 2020, pp. 4392–4396 (2020)
12. Raffel, C., et al.: Exploring the limits of transfer learning with a unified text-to-text transformer. J. Mach. Learn. Res. **21**, 1–67 (2020)
13. Read, I., Cox, S.: Stochastic and syntactic techniques for predicting phrase breaks. Comput. Speech Lang. **21**(3), 519–542 (2007)
14. Rosenberg, A.: AuToBI - a tool for automatic ToBI annotation. In: Proceedings of InterSpeech 2010, pp. 146–149 (2010)
15. Schuppler, B., Ludusan, B.: An analysis of prosodic boundary detection in German and Austrian German read speech. In: Proceedings of Speech Prosody 2020, pp. 990–994 (2020)
16. Suni, A., Simko, J., Vainio, M.: Boundary detection using continuous wavelet analysis. In: Proceedings of Speech Prosody 2016, pp. 267–271 (2016)
17. Taylor, P.: Text-to-Speech Synthesis, 1st edn. Cambridge University Press, New York (2009)
18. Taylor, P., Black, A.W.: Assigning phrase breaks from part-of-speech sequences. Comput. Speech Lang. **12**(2), 99–117 (1998)
19. Tihelka, D., Hanzlíček, Z., Jůzová, M., Vít, J., Matoušek, J., Grůber, M.: Current state of text-to-speech system ARTIC: a decade of research on the field of speech technologies. In: Sojka, P., Horák, A., Kopeček, I., Pala, K. (eds.) TSD 2018. LNCS (LNAI), vol. 11107, pp. 369–378. Springer, Cham (2018). https://doi.org/10.1007/978-3-030-00794-2_40
20. Volín, J., Řezáčková, M., Matoušek, J.: Human and transformer-based prosodic phrasing in two speech genres. In: Karpov, A., Potapova, R. (eds.) SPECOM 2021. LNCS (LNAI), vol. 12997, pp. 761–772. Springer, Cham (2021). https://doi.org/10.1007/978-3-030-87802-3_68
21. Wolf, T., et al.: Transformers: state-of-the-art natural language processing. In: Proceedings of the 2020 Conference on Empirical Methods in Natural Language Processing: System Demonstrations, pp. 38–45 (2020)
22. Yang, S.W., et al.: SUPERB: speech processing Universal PERformance benchmark. In: Proceedings InterSpeech 2021, pp. 1194–1198 (2021)
23. Zhang, Y., et al.: Pushing the limits of semi-supervised learning for automatic speech recognition. arXiv preprint arXiv:2010.10504 (2020)
24. Zou, Y., et al.: Fine-grained prosody modeling in neural speech synthesis using ToBI representation. In: Proceedings of InterSpeech 2021, pp. 3146–3150 (2021)

# Text-to-Text Transfer Transformer Phrasing Model Using Enriched Text Input

Markéta Řezáčková$^{(\boxtimes)}$ and Jindřich Matoušek

New Technologies for the Information Society (NTIS)
and Department of Cybernetics, Faculty of Applied Sciences,
University of West Bohemia, Pilsen, Czech Republic
{juzova,jmatouse}@kky.zcu.cz

**Abstract.** Appropriate prosodic phrasing of the input text is crucial for natural speech synthesis outputs. The presented paper focuses on using a Text-to-Text Transfer Transformer for predicting phrase boundaries in text and inspects the possibility of enriching the input text with more detailed information to improve the success rate of the phrasing model trained on plain text. This idea came from our previous research on phrasing that showed that more detailed syntactic/semantic information might lead to more accurate predicting of phrase boundaries.

**Keywords:** Phrasing · Prosodic boundaries · T5 · Part-of-Speech tags · Syntactic categories

## 1 Introduction

Human speech is not monotonous but it expresses itself by variable intonation patterns which, together with the words themselves, help the speaker to manifest the meaning of the words and, thus, present his/her thoughts to the listeners. Longer sentences, for example, when read out, are usually divided into smaller units, *phrases* – groups of several words carrying a special meaning [3,4,24]. They are defined by a complex set of acoustic cues, e.g. the prosodic boundaries (PBs) between them (both with or without a pause) or a prosodic coherence within a phrase. The appropriate prosodic phrasing in speech is very important for the listeners so that they are able to understand and easily follow the thoughts of the speaker. On the other hand, inappropriate phrasing (i.e. making phrase boundaries and pauses in incorrect positions in the sentence) might cause misunderstanding or irritation.

In text-to-speech (TTS) systems, the correct phrasing increases the naturalness of the speech synthesis outputs – which includes both the correct phrase

This research was supported by the Czech Science Foundation (GA CR), project No. GA21-14758S, and by the grant of the University of West Bohemia, project No. SGS-2022-017.

P. Sojka et al. (Eds.): TSD 2022, LNAI 13502, pp. 389–400, 2022.
https://doi.org/10.1007/978-3-031-16270-1_32

boundary placement and adequate prosody within the phrase itself [19]. Nevertheless, this paper focuses only on the PBs prediction.

Many different approaches to phrase boundary detection task have been studied and published during the last decades, including deterministic approaches based on punctuation marks, classification-based approaches with different sets of features, HMM, and neural networks [5,10,17,18,20].

## 2    Data and Model Description

The main problem in the phrase boundary task usually lies in the difficulty of obtaining enough data for training. Moreover, the task is ambiguous – i.e. missing some PBs may not be such a mistake and, similarly, some extra predicted PBs could be correct, in fact [23].

In our study, we use two different sets of data – *Laboratory Speech* and *News-Reading Speech*. The *Laboratory Speech* (LS) data originated from 6 large-scale Czech speech corpora (3 male and 3 female speakers) created and recorded for our TTS system *ARTIC* [21] (following the approach described in [13]), more than 10,000 sentences each. The phrase boundaries in the audio were assigned automatically during the segmentation process [7,14] and then transformed to PBs labels in the original texts. The recording itself was carried out in a sentence-by-sentence manner (the sentences were isolated and did not interfere with each other) and the speakers were instructed to keep the same informative style and speed of speech during the whole recording process.

The News-Reading Speech (NRS), on the other hand, represents a set of sentences with phrases established by phonetic experts during the auditory analysis guided by [1][1]. These sentences originated from the transcriptions of authentic recordings of 3–4 min long news-bulletins from Czech Radio. In this paper, we experiment with 12 Czech Radio professional readers (6 male and 6 female), with only about 40 sentences each. Note that the same original audio data are used in [11] for detecting phrase boundaries in speech signal (using only acoustic information) and the results are compared to those presented in this paper.

### 2.1    T5 Phrasing Model

Neural network approaches (mostly with *encoder-decoder* architecture) represent *state-of-the-art* techniques for almost all tasks in natural language processing (NLP), including predicting phrase boundaries in text. *Transformer* [22] is a novel architecture of sequence-to-sequence model which uses the *attention mechanism* allowing the model to focus only on some parts of the input sequence, making the training much more efficient. In our experiments, we used the Text-to-Text Transfer Transformer (T5) model (following the architecture presented in [16,25]) pre-trained from a huge amount of unlabeled text from the Czech

---

[1] Note that only the level '4' phrases (*prosodic/intonational phrases*) were considered in our experiments; smaller ones (e.g. *intermediate phrases* were also labeled but not used).

CommonCrawl corpus [27]. For training the model itself, we used the Tensorflow implementation [25] and the framework of [26].

This paper presents our T5 phrasing model, firstly introduced in [23], and explores the possibilities of input text adjustments for obtaining better results of phrase boundary detection from text.

## 2.2 Evaluation Measures

From the machine learning point of view, the task of phrase boundary detection can be considered a binary classification into 2 classes. Thus we have 4 types of outputs: *true positives* (*tp*; correctly predicted phrase boundaries), *true negatives* (*tn*; correctly predicted no-breaks), *false positives* (*fp*; incorrectly (extra) predicted phrase boundaries) and *false negatives* (*fn*; missed phrase boundaries). To compare results, these four numbers are often recalculated to some measures.

*Accuracy* (*Acc*, Eq. (1)) is the proportion of correct predictions among the total number of all cases examined. This measure needs not necessarily be the best choice since it can be misleading for unbalanced classes and does not reflect the real "success rate" of the model on testing data. So while the accuracy measure can be used for tasks with similar class distribution, our phrase boundary detection issue, with definitely uneven class distribution (significantly larger number of negatives), requires a different approach for the evaluation.

To obtain more relevant results, other two measures and their combination are usually used instead: The measure called *precision* (*P*, Eq. (2)) is the fraction of correct positive predictions among all positive predictions, in other words, it tells us how much we can trust the positive results we detected, which means fewer false positives for higher precision value. The second one, *recall* (*R*, Eq. (3), also known as *sensitivity*), represents the fraction of positive instances that were detected. It is defined as the ratio of correct positive predictions to all positive instances in data and higher numbers signify fewer false negatives.

The harmonic mean of the two measures explained above is called *F1-measure* or *F1-score*, defined in Eq. (4). That gives a better measure of the incorrectly classified instances than the accuracy. Let us note that this measure will be the main indicator for us during the evaluation in Sect. 3.

$$R = \frac{tp}{tp + fn} \tag{3}$$

$$Acc = \frac{tp + tn}{tp + tn + fp + fn} \tag{1}$$

$$P = \frac{tp}{tp + fp} \tag{2}$$

$$F1 = 2 \cdot \frac{P \cdot R}{P + R} \tag{4}$$

## 3    Experiments and Results

The presented paper follows the paper [23] and compares the phrasing models from that study to the new, enriched phrasing models.

## 3.1   Former Experiment

In our preceding study [23], we trained a general T5 phrasing model on LS data, excluding 40 sentences for each speaker for testing. The training process lasted for 50 epochs (with 1000 steps per epoch) and we got the general phrasing model which was tested both on the LS and NRS data. When applied to LS data, the results were acceptable, yet, it would be better to train speaker-dependent models for each speaker in case we wanted to use the model predictions for TTS using these voices (similarly to [9,12,15])) – but that is beyond the scope of this paper. On the contrary, we wanted to train a general model which could be applied to data obtained from unseen speakers. On the NRS data, the model was less successful in predicting phrases compared to the application to LS data, the lower values of the measures were mostly caused by higher number of *false negatives* (i.e. missed PBs) – which was caused, as explained in the mentioned paper, by a different genre of those data.

So we, therefore, adapted the general model on NRS data to get a transferred phrasing model for news-reading speech and tested that on each of the 12 speakers' sentences. Because of a small amount of NSR data, we used a *leave-one-out* approach – we trained 12 transferred models, using data from 11 speakers for training and the sentences of the remaining speaker for testing. These adapted phrasing models provided better results compared to the general model (especially *fn* cases and the *Recall value*), even with the small amount of NRS data. The overall results are shown in Table 1[2].

Our previous paper also contained an in-depth syntactic-semantic analysis which showed the most common categories of errors in T5 phrasing (and also point to the fact that many *false positives* and *false negatives* are acceptable, yet the speaker used a different phrasing of the sentence). The detailed analysis is described in Sect. 3.4 in [23], let us just list the most well-represented categories:

- missed phrase boundary between subject and predicate part of the sentence
- missed phrase boundary before an attribute in post-position
- missed phrase boundary after an initial adverbial

Those categories (all together with the others) are connected with the syntactic/semantic description of the sentence. This led us to the idea of using other information in training the model, not just the text. And although the T5 model should be able to grasp the syntax (and part-of-speech tags) by itself (internally), we hoped that additional information explicitly added to the input text could increase the model's ability of correct phrase break prediction.

## 3.2   Phrasing Models with Enriched Text Input

As described before, in our former study we had used only a text input during the T5 model training process – that is also a common use of T5 networks. Nevertheless, we hoped that the enriched text input could help to train

---

[2] The numbers in the second and the third part of the table slightly differ from those in [23] since a couple of manual corrections and amendments had been made in NRS data during the last year.

**Table 1.** Overall results using plain text input (Acc, P, R, F1 in %).

|   | speaker | No. of sents | Acc | P | R | F1 | tp | fp | fn | tn |
|---|---|---|---|---|---|---|---|---|---|---|
| (a) General model, LS | LS01 | 40 | 99.20 | 100.00 | 95.24 | 97.56 | 60 | 0 | 3 | 312 |
| | LS02 | 40 | 97.38 | 87.50 | 96.55 | 91.80 | 56 | 8 | 2 | 316 |
| | LS03 | 40 | 96.63 | 89.39 | 90.77 | 90.08 | 59 | 7 | 6 | 314 |
| | LS04 | 40 | 96.86 | 94.12 | 85.71 | 89.72 | 48 | 3 | 8 | 291 |
| | LS05 | 40 | 96.63 | 85.71 | 93.75 | 89.55 | 60 | 10 | 4 | 342 |
| | LS06 | 40 | 95.42 | 94.23 | 77.78 | 85.22 | 49 | 3 | 14 | 305 |
| | all | 240 | 97.02 | 91.46 | 89.97 | 90.71 | 332 | 31 | 37 | 1880 |
| (b) General model, NRS | NSR01 | 36 | 89.35 | 89.47 | 41.98 | 57.14 | 34 | 4 | 47 | 394 |
| | NRS02 | 60 | 92.64 | 88.89 | 50.53 | 64.43 | 48 | 6 | 47 | 619 |
| | NRS03 | 38 | 93.11 | 83.67 | 60.29 | 70.09 | 41 | 8 | 27 | 432 |
| | NRS04 | 31 | 92.37 | 88.37 | 55.88 | 68.47 | 38 | 5 | 30 | 386 |
| | NRS05 | 48 | 90.48 | 86.79 | 47.91 | 61.74 | 46 | 7 | 50 | 496 |
| | NRS06 | 45 | 89.08 | 96.36 | 46.49 | 62.72 | 53 | 2 | 61 | 461 |
| | NRS07 | 33 | 93.66 | 90.48 | 62.30 | 73.79 | 38 | 4 | 23 | 361 |
| | NRS08 | 37 | 91.16 | 90.24 | 48.05 | 62.71 | 37 | 4 | 40 | 417 |
| | NRS09 | 50 | 92.02 | 72.73 | 52.75 | 61.15 | 48 | 18 | 43 | 655 |
| | NRS10 | 34 | 92.87 | 91.89 | 55.74 | 69.39 | 34 | 3 | 27 | 357 |
| | NRS11 | 35 | 92.34 | 83.33 | 52.63 | 64.52 | 30 | 6 | 27 | 368 |
| | NRS12 | 39 | 91.77 | 83.33 | 55.56 | 66.67 | 40 | 8 | 32 | 406 |
| | all | 486 | 91.69 | 86.65 | 51.75 | 64.80 | 487 | 75 | 454 | 5352 |
| (c) Adapted model, NRS | NSR01 | 36 | 92.07 | 85.25 | 64.20 | 73.24 | 52 | 9 | 29 | 389 |
| | NRS02 | 60 | 94.72 | 82.02 | 76.84 | 79.35 | 73 | 16 | 22 | 609 |
| | NRS03 | 38 | 96.06 | 86.36 | 83.82 | 85.07 | 57 | 9 | 11 | 431 |
| | NRS04 | 31 | 93.25 | 84.91 | 66.18 | 74.38 | 45 | 8 | 23 | 383 |
| | NRS05 | 48 | 93.16 | 87.67 | 66.67 | 75.74 | 64 | 9 | 32 | 494 |
| | NRS06 | 45 | 90.12 | 92.54 | 54.39 | 68.51 | 62 | 5 | 52 | 458 |
| | NRS07 | 33 | 95.07 | 87.04 | 77.05 | 81.74 | 47 | 7 | 14 | 358 |
| | NRS08 | 37 | 93.78 | 91.07 | 66.23 | 76.69 | 51 | 5 | 26 | 416 |
| | NRS09 | 50 | 94.76 | 80.00 | 74.73 | 77.27 | 68 | 17 | 23 | 656 |
| | NRS10 | 34 | 95.01 | 90.00 | 73.77 | 81.08 | 45 | 5 | 16 | 355 |
| | NRS11 | 35 | 95.13 | 86.00 | 75.44 | 80.37 | 43 | 7 | 14 | 367 |
| | NRS12 | 39 | 94.44 | 85.71 | 75.00 | 80.00 | 54 | 9 | 18 | 405 |
| | all | 486 | 93.94 | 86.18 | 70.24 | 77.40 | 661 | 106 | 280 | 5321 |

a T5 model predicting the phrase boundaries more precisely, so we prepared the training inputs supplemented with syntactic word categories (*analytic functions*, i.e. **afun** phrasing model). Besides that, we also used part-of-speech tags since those were used frequently and successfully in different phrasing approaches, usually as one of the features in classification-based ones, e.g. [8], (**POS** phrasing model). And finally, we add both syntactic categories and the part-of-speech tags (**afun+POS** model).

The text inputs (and the output) used for training the models are as follows:

- original text input (**plain**):
  - word1 word2 word3 ...
- analytic functions (**afun**):
  - word1/afun1 word2/afun2 word3/afun3 ...
- part-of-speech categories (**POS**):
  - word1/POS1 word2/POS2 word3/POS3 ...
- both  syntactic  (analytic)  functions  and  part-of-speech  categories (**afun+POS**):
  - word1/afun1/POS1 word2/afun2/POS2 word3/afun3/POS3 ...
- outputs (the same for all inputs) with a special symbol for marking the phrase boundary positions in the sentence:
  - word1 word2 | word3 ...

For tagging the training and testing data with syntactic and part-of-speech tags, we used our proprietary T5 taggers trained from the data in PDT corpus and its analytical and morphological annotation [2].

All the three new general models were trained in the same manner as the *plain* general model from [23] (50 epochs with 1000 steps per epoch, with 10 % of training data used for validation during the training process), and all transferred models (using a *leave-one-out* approach) were being adapted from the general model for 10 epochs.

### 3.3   Results

The results are listed in Table 2, Table 3 and Table 4; the overall results for each task are also shown in Fig. 1.

The results in the tables and Fig. 1 show that adding more information to the plain text input could lead to better results. That is especially true for enriching the input words with syntactic functions (**afun** model) which have resulted in obtaining more precise phrasing models – despite the fact that adding tags brought some errors in the input data, since the taggers were hardly error-free. Higher F1 values were mostly caused by higher *recall* numbers – i.e. there were less *false negatives* which means more phrase boundaries were set by the model in the testing sentences. It is also satisfactory that the *false positives* were about the same as for the **plain** model (and it should be noted that some of them are acceptable, as previously stated in [23]). A quick analysis also showed that some of these cases corresponded to other level of phrase boundaries (*intermediate phrases*, level '3' in ToBI [1]).

**Table 2.** Overall results using text input enriched with analytic functions (Acc, P, R, F1 in %).

| | speaker | No. of sents | Acc | P | R | F1 | tp | fp | fn | tn |
|---|---|---|---|---|---|---|---|---|---|---|
| (a) General model, LS | LS01 | 40 | 99.20 | 98.39 | 96.83 | 97.60 | 61 | 1 | 2 | 311 |
| | LS02 | 40 | 97.91 | 89.06 | 98.28 | 93.44 | 57 | 7 | 1 | 317 |
| | LS03 | 40 | 96.89 | 89.55 | 92.31 | 90.91 | 60 | 7 | 5 | 314 |
| | LS04 | 40 | 97.14 | 92.59 | 89.29 | 90.91 | 50 | 4 | 6 | 290 |
| | LS05 | 40 | 97.12 | 87.14 | 95.31 | 91.04 | 61 | 9 | 3 | 343 |
| | LS06 | 40 | 96.23 | 92.98 | 84.13 | 88.33 | 53 | 4 | 10 | 304 |
| | all | 240 | 97.41 | 91.44 | 92.68 | 92.06 | 342 | 32 | 27 | 1879 |
| (b) General model, NRS | NSR01 | 36 | 91.02 | 93.18 | 50.62 | 65.60 | 41 | 3 | 40 | 395 |
| | NRS02 | 60 | 93.19 | 91.07 | 53.68 | 67.55 | 51 | 5 | 44 | 620 |
| | NRS03 | 38 | 93.69 | 84.31 | 64.18 | 72.88 | 43 | 8 | 25 | 432 |
| | NRS04 | 31 | 93.25 | 87.76 | 63.24 | 73.50 | 43 | 6 | 25 | 385 |
| | NRS05 | 48 | 86.21 | 85.96 | 38.28 | 52.97 | 49 | 8 | 47 | 495 |
| | NRS06 | 45 | 89.77 | 96.61 | 50.50 | 65.90 | 57 | 2 | 57 | 461 |
| | NRS07 | 33 | 94.13 | 90.91 | 65.57 | 76.19 | 40 | 4 | 21 | 361 |
| | NRS08 | 37 | 91.97 | 89.36 | 54.55 | 67.74 | 42 | 5 | 35 | 416 |
| | NRS09 | 50 | 92.28 | 72.86 | 56.04 | 63.35 | 51 | 19 | 40 | 654 |
| | NRS10 | 34 | 92.87 | 91.89 | 55.74 | 69.39 | 34 | 3 | 27 | 357 |
| | NRS11 | 35 | 92.34 | 83.33 | 52.63 | 64.52 | 30 | 6 | 27 | 368 |
| | NRS12 | 39 | 92.36 | 85.71 | 58.33 | 69.42 | 42 | 7 | 30 | 405 |
| | all | 486 | 92.24 | 87.31 | 55.58 | 67.92 | 523 | 76 | 418 | 5349 |
| (c) Adapted model, NRS | NSR01 | 36 | 92.48 | 83.58 | 69.14 | 75.68 | 56 | 11 | 25 | 387 |
| | NRS02 | 60 | 95.00 | 82.42 | 78.95 | 80.65 | 75 | 16 | 20 | 609 |
| | NRS03 | 38 | 96.06 | 86.36 | 83.82 | 85.07 | 57 | 9 | 11 | 431 |
| | NRS04 | 31 | 93.25 | 82.46 | 69.12 | 75.20 | 47 | 10 | 21 | 381 |
| | NRS05 | 48 | 93.82 | 87.34 | 71.88 | 78.86 | 69 | 10 | 27 | 493 |
| | NRS06 | 45 | 90.47 | 91.55 | 57.02 | 70.27 | 65 | 6 | 49 | 457 |
| | NRS07 | 33 | 95.31 | 85.96 | 80.33 | 83.05 | 49 | 8 | 12 | 357 |
| | NRS08 | 37 | 94.38 | 91.53 | 70.13 | 79.41 | 54 | 5 | 23 | 416 |
| | NRS09 | 50 | 95.42 | 81.82 | 79.12 | 80.45 | 72 | 16 | 19 | 657 |
| | NRS10 | 34 | 96.20 | 90.91 | 81.97 | 86.21 | 50 | 5 | 11 | 355 |
| | NRS11 | 35 | 95.36 | 86.27 | 77.19 | 81.48 | 44 | 7 | 13 | 367 |
| | NRS12 | 39 | 94.86 | 85.07 | 79.17 | 82.01 | 57 | 10 | 15 | 404 |
| | all | 486 | 94.36 | 86.01 | 73.86 | 79.47 | 695 | 113 | 246 | 5314 |

The part-of-speech tags, representing the morphological layer of the sentences, did not improve the phrasing models considerably, except for the adapted models. The results of combined enriched models were very close to the **afun** models, but they predicted slightly worse results (however, the precision values were slightly higher in average). Nevertheless, the detailed analysis of the errors (both *false positives* and *false negatives*) is needed.

**Table 3.** Overall results using text input enriched with part-of-speech tags (Acc, P, R, F1 in %).

|   |   | speaker | No. of sents | Acc | P | R | F1 | tp | fp | fn | tn |
|---|---|---------|--------------|-----|---|---|----|----|----|----|----|
| (a) | General model, LS | LS01 | 40 | 99.20 | 100.00 | 95.24 | 97.56 | 60 | 0 | 3 | 312 |
|     |   | LS02 | 40 | 97.91 | 89.06 | 98.27 | 93.44 | 57 | 7 | 1 | 317 |
|     |   | LS03 | 40 | 96.63 | 89.39 | 90.77 | 90.08 | 59 | 7 | 6 | 314 |
|     |   | LS04 | 40 | 96.57 | 92.31 | 85.71 | 88.89 | 48 | 4 | 8 | 290 |
|     |   | LS05 | 40 | 96.88 | 86.96 | 93.75 | 90.23 | 60 | 9 | 4 | 343 |
|     |   | LS06 | 40 | 95.42 | 94.23 | 77.78 | 85.22 | 49 | 3 | 14 | 305 |
|     |   | all | 240 | 97.11 | 91.74 | 90.24 | 90.98 | 333 | 30 | 36 | 1881 |
| (b) | General model, NRS | NSR01 | 36 | 89.35 | 89.47 | 41.98 | 57.14 | 34 | 4 | 47 | 394 |
|     |   | NRS02 | 60 | 92.50 | 87.27 | 50.53 | 64.00 | 48 | 7 | 47 | 618 |
|     |   | NRS03 | 38 | 93.11 | 83.67 | 60.29 | 70.09 | 41 | 8 | 27 | 432 |
|     |   | NRS04 | 31 | 92.59 | 88.64 | 57.35 | 69.64 | 39 | 5 | 29 | 386 |
|     |   | NRS05 | 48 | 90.32 | 86.54 | 46.88 | 60.81 | 45 | 7 | 51 | 496 |
|     |   | NRS06 | 45 | 89.08 | 96.36 | 46.49 | 62.72 | 53 | 2 | 61 | 461 |
|     |   | NRS07 | 33 | 94.13 | 92.86 | 63.93 | 75.73 | 39 | 3 | 22 | 362 |
|     |   | NRS08 | 37 | 91.16 | 90.24 | 48.05 | 62.71 | 37 | 4 | 40 | 417 |
|     |   | NRS09 | 50 | 92.02 | 72.06 | 53.85 | 61.64 | 49 | 19 | 42 | 654 |
|     |   | NRS10 | 34 | 92.87 | 91.89 | 55.74 | 69.39 | 34 | 3 | 27 | 357 |
|     |   | NRS11 | 35 | 92.58 | 83.78 | 54.39 | 65.96 | 31 | 6 | 26 | 368 |
|     |   | NRS12 | 39 | 91.77 | 83.33 | 55.56 | 66.67 | 40 | 8 | 32 | 406 |
|     |   | all | 486 | 91.72 | 86.57 | 52.07 | 65.03 | 490 | 76 | 451 | 5351 |
| (c) | Adapted model, NRS | NSR01 | 36 | 92.48 | 82.61 | 70.37 | 76.00 | 57 | 12 | 24 | 386 |
|     |   | NRS02 | 60 | 95.28 | 83.52 | 80.00 | 81.72 | 76 | 15 | 19 | 610 |
|     |   | NRS03 | 38 | 96.26 | 86.57 | 85.29 | 85.93 | 58 | 9 | 10 | 431 |
|     |   | NRS04 | 31 | 93.25 | 83.64 | 67.65 | 74.80 | 46 | 9 | 22 | 382 |
|     |   | NRS05 | 48 | 93.99 | 87.50 | 72.92 | 79.55 | 70 | 10 | 26 | 493 |
|     |   | NRS06 | 45 | 89.95 | 90.00 | 55.26 | 68.48 | 63 | 7 | 51 | 456 |
|     |   | NRS07 | 33 | 95.07 | 87.04 | 77.05 | 81.74 | 47 | 7 | 14 | 358 |
|     |   | NRS08 | 37 | 94.38 | 90.16 | 71.43 | 79.71 | 55 | 6 | 22 | 415 |
|     |   | NRS09 | 50 | 95.42 | 81.82 | 79.12 | 80.45 | 72 | 16 | 19 | 657 |
|     |   | NRS10 | 34 | 95.72 | 89.09 | 80.33 | 84.48 | 49 | 6 | 12 | 354 |
|     |   | NRS11 | 35 | 95.13 | 86.00 | 75.44 | 80.37 | 43 | 7 | 14 | 367 |
|     |   | NRS12 | 39 | 94.65 | 83.82 | 79.17 | 81.43 | 57 | 11 | 15 | 403 |
|     |   | all | 486 | 94.30 | 85.77 | 73.65 | 79.25 | 693 | 115 | 248 | 5312 |

**Table 4.** Overall results using enriched text input, both analytic functions and part-of-speech tags (Acc, P, R, F1 in %).

| | | speaker | No. of sents | Acc | P | R | F1 | tp | fp | fn | tn |
|---|---|---|---|---|---|---|---|---|---|---|---|
| (a) | General model, LS | LS01 | 40 | 99.20 | 100.00 | 95.24 | 97.56 | 60 | 0 | 3 | 312 |
| | | LS02 | 40 | 97.91 | 89.06 | 98.27 | 93.44 | 57 | 7 | 1 | 317 |
| | | LS03 | 40 | 96.89 | 89.55 | 92.31 | 90.91 | 60 | 7 | 5 | 314 |
| | | LS04 | 40 | 97.14 | 94.23 | 87.50 | 90.74 | 49 | 3 | 7 | 291 |
| | | LS05 | 40 | 97.60 | 88.57 | 96.88 | 92.54 | 62 | 8 | 2 | 344 |
| | | LS06 | 40 | 95.69 | 92.73 | 80.95 | 86.44 | 51 | 4 | 12 | 304 |
| | | all | 240 | 97.52 | 92.12 | 91.87 | 91.99 | 339 | 29 | 30 | 1982 |
| (b) | General model, NRS | NSR01 | 36 | 90.40 | 90.70 | 48.15 | 62.90 | 39 | 4 | 42 | 394 |
| | | NRS02 | 60 | 92.92 | 89.29 | 52.63 | 66.23 | 50 | 6 | 45 | 619 |
| | | NRS03 | 38 | 93.11 | 83.67 | 60.29 | 70.09 | 41 | 8 | 27 | 432 |
| | | NRS04 | 31 | 93.03 | 89.13 | 60.29 | 71.93 | 41 | 5 | 27 | 386 |
| | | NRS05 | 48 | 90.48 | 86.79 | 47.91 | 61.74 | 46 | 7 | 50 | 496 |
| | | NRS06 | 45 | 89.77 | 96.61 | 50.00 | 65.90 | 57 | 2 | 57 | 461 |
| | | NRS07 | 33 | 94.13 | 92.86 | 63.93 | 75.73 | 39 | 3 | 22 | 362 |
| | | NRS08 | 37 | 91.77 | 89.13 | 53.25 | 66.67 | 41 | 5 | 36 | 416 |
| | | NRS09 | 50 | 92.02 | 72.06 | 53.85 | 61.64 | 49 | 19 | 42 | 654 |
| | | NRS10 | 34 | 92.87 | 91.89 | 55.74 | 69.39 | 34 | 3 | 27 | 357 |
| | | NRS11 | 35 | 92.58 | 83.78 | 54.39 | 65.96 | 31 | 6 | 26 | 368 |
| | | NRS12 | 39 | 92.18 | 84.00 | 58.33 | 68.85 | 42 | 8 | 30 | 406 |
| | | all | 486 | 92.04 | 87.03 | 54.20 | 66.80 | 510 | 76 | 431 | 5351 |
| (c) | Adapted model, NRS | NSR01 | 36 | 92.48 | 83.58 | 69.14 | 75.68 | 56 | 11 | 25 | 387 |
| | | NRS02 | 60 | 95.14 | 83.33 | 78.95 | 81.08 | 75 | 15 | 20 | 610 |
| | | NRS03 | 38 | 96.06 | 86.36 | 83.82 | 85.07 | 57 | 9 | 11 | 431 |
| | | NRS04 | 31 | 93.46 | 83.93 | 69.12 | 75.81 | 47 | 9 | 21 | 382 |
| | | NRS05 | 48 | 93.82 | 86.42 | 72.92 | 79.10 | 70 | 11 | 26 | 492 |
| | | NRS06 | 45 | 90.29 | 91.43 | 56.14 | 69.57 | 64 | 6 | 50 | 457 |
| | | NRS07 | 33 | 95.07 | 85.71 | 78.69 | 82.05 | 48 | 8 | 13 | 357 |
| | | NRS08 | 37 | 94.38 | 91.53 | 70.13 | 79.41 | 54 | 5 | 23 | 416 |
| | | NRS09 | 50 | 95.42 | 81.82 | 79.12 | 80.45 | 72 | 16 | 19 | 657 |
| | | NRS10 | 34 | 95.96 | 90.74 | 80.33 | 85.22 | 49 | 5 | 12 | 355 |
| | | NRS11 | 35 | 95.13 | 86.00 | 75.44 | 80.37 | 43 | 7 | 14 | 367 |
| | | NRS12 | 39 | 94.65 | 84.85 | 77.78 | 81.16 | 56 | 10 | 16 | 404 |
| | | all | 486 | 94.32 | 86.05 | 73.43 | 79.24 | 961 | 112 | 250 | 5315 |

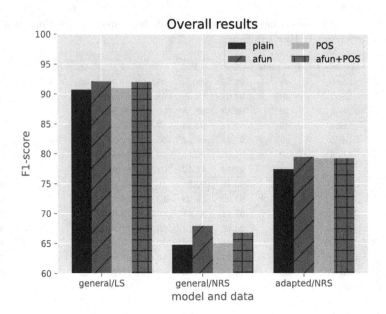

**Fig. 1.** Comparison of phrasing models – average results.

## 4   Conclusion

The presented paper explored the possibility of enriching the text input of the Text-to-Text Transfer Transformer model. We used part-of-speech tags and syntactic categories to adjust the plain text input and we trained phrasing models using these inputs. The comparison of the results showed that the phrasing models using enriched texts were able to yield more precise phrase boundary predictions compared to our previous study described in [23].

Anyway, the proposed approach has to be also verified for different languages (since all the presented results were obtained on Czech), and the in-depth analysis of the wrong predicted boundaries should be performed by phonetic experts to find out in which cases the additional information in the input text helped. The possibility of using the proposed enriched T5 phrasing models in the TTS system (to split the input text into phrases) must also be verified using a listening test (e.g. [6]), in which the listeners would evaluate the naturalness of the synthesized sentences with the suggested phrasing.

**Acknowledgements.** Computational resources were supplied by the project "e-Infrastruktura CZ" (e-INFRA CZ LM2018140) supported by the Ministry of Education, Youth and Sports of the Czech Republic.

## References

1. Beckman, M.E., Ayers Elam, G.: Guidelines for ToBI Labelling, Version 3. The Ohio State University Research Foundation, Ohio State University (1997)

2. Bejček, E., et al.: Prague dependency treebank 3.0 (2013). http://hdl.handle.net/11858/00-097C-0000-0023-1AAF-3, LINDAT/CLARIAH-CZ digital library at the Institute of Formal and Applied Linguistics (ÚFAL), Faculty of Mathematics and Physics, Charles University

3. Cruttenden, A.: Intonation. Cambridge Textbooks in Linguistics, 2nd edn. Cambridge University Press, Cambridge (1997)

4. Daneš, F.: Intonace a věta ve spisovné češtině. ČSAV, Praha (1957)

5. Fernandez, R., Rendel, A., Ramabhadran, B., Hoory, R.: Prosody contour prediction with long short-term memory, bi-directional, deep recurrent neural networks. In: Li, H., Meng, H.M., Ma, B., Chng, E., Xie, L. (eds.) INTERSPEECH, pp. 2268–2272. ISCA (2014)

6. Grůber, M., Matoušek, J.: Listening-test-based annotation of communicative functions for expressive speech synthesis. In: Sojka, P., Horák, A., Kopeček, I., Pala, K. (eds.) TSD 2010. LNCS (LNAI), vol. 6231, pp. 283–290. Springer, Heidelberg (2010). https://doi.org/10.1007/978-3-642-15760-8_36

7. Hanzlíček, Z., Vít, J., Tihelka, D.: LSTM-based speech segmentation for TTS synthesis. In: Ekštein, K. (ed.) TSD 2019. LNCS (LNAI), vol. 11697, pp. 361–372. Springer, Cham (2019). https://doi.org/10.1007/978-3-030-27947-9_31

8. Jůzová, M.: Prosodic phrase boundary classification based on Czech Speech Corpora. In: Ekštein, K., Matoušek, V. (eds.) TSD 2017. LNCS (LNAI), vol. 10415, pp. 165–173. Springer, Cham (2017). https://doi.org/10.1007/978-3-319-64206-2_19

9. Jůzová, M., Tihelka, D.: Speaker-dependent BiLSTM-based phrasing. In: Sojka, P., Kopeček, I., Pala, K., Horák, A. (eds.) TSD 2020. LNCS (LNAI), vol. 12284, pp. 340–347. Springer, Cham (2020). https://doi.org/10.1007/978-3-030-58323-1_37

10. Klimkov, V., et al.: Phrase break prediction for long-form reading TTS: exploiting text structure information. In: Proceedings of InterSpeech 2017, pp. 1064–1068 (2017)

11. Kunešová, M., Řezáčková, M.: Detection of prosodic boundaries in speech using Wav2Vec 2.0. In: Sojka, P., et al. (eds.) TSD 2022. LNCS. vol. 13502, pp. 376–387. Springer, Cham (2022)

12. Louw, J.A., Moodley, A.: Speaker specific phrase break modeling with conditional random fields for text-to-speech. In: 2016 Pattern Recognition Association of South Africa and Robotics and Mechatronics International Conference (PRASA-RobMech), pp. 1–6 (2016)

13. Matoušek, J., Romportl, J.: On building phonetically and prosodically rich speech corpus for text-to-speech synthesis. In: Proceedings of the 2nd IASTED international conference on Computational intelligence, pp. 442–447. ACTA Press, San Francisco (2006)

14. Matoušek, J., Tihelka, D., Psutka, J.: Experiments with automatic segmentation for Czech speech synthesis. In: Matoušek, V., Mautner, P. (eds.) TSD 2003. LNCS (LNAI), vol. 2807, pp. 287–294. Springer, Heidelberg (2003). https://doi.org/10.1007/978-3-540-39398-6_41

15. Prahallad, K., Raghavendra, E.V., Black, A.W.: Learning speaker-specific phrase breaks for text-to-speech systems. In: SSW (2010)

16. Raffel, C., et al.: Exploring the limits of transfer learning with a unified text-to-text transformer (2020). arXiv:1910.10683

17. Read, I., Cox, S.: Stochastic and syntactic techniques for predicting phrase breaks. Comput. Speech Lang. 21(3), 519–542 (2007)

18. Rosenberg, A., Fernandez, R., Ramabhadran, B.: Modeling phrasing and prominence using deep recurrent learning. In: InterSpeech 2015. pp. 3066–3070. ISCA (2015)

19. Taylor, P.: Text-to-Speech Synthesis, 1st edn. Cambridge University Press, New York (2009)
20. Taylor, P., Black, A.: Assigning phrase breaks from part-of-speech sequences. Comput. Speech Lang. **12**, 99–117 (1998)
21. Tihelka, D., Hanzlíček, Z., Jůzová, M., Vít, J., Matoušek, J., Grůber, M.: Current state of text-to-speech system ARTIC: a decade of research on the field of speech technologies. In: Sojka, P., Horák, A., Kopeček, I., Pala, K. (eds.) TSD 2018. LNCS (LNAI), vol. 11107, pp. 369–378. Springer, Cham (2018). https://doi.org/10.1007/978-3-030-00794-2_40
22. Vaswani, A., et al.: Attention is all you need (2017). arXiv:1706.03762
23. Volín, J., Řezáčková, M., Matouřek, J.: Human and transformer-based prosodic phrasing in two speech genres. In: Karpov, A., Potapova, R. (eds.) SPECOM 2021. LNCS (LNAI), vol. 12997, pp. 761–772. Springer, Cham (2021). https://doi.org/10.1007/978-3-030-87802-3_68
24. Volín, J.: The size of prosodic phrases in native and foreign-accented read-out monologues. Acta Universitatis Carolinae - Philologica **2**, 145–158 (2019)
25. Wolf, T., et al.: Transformers: state-of-the-art natural language processing. In: Proceedings of the 2020 Conference on Empirical Methods in Natural Language Processing: System Demonstrations, pp. 38–45. Association for Computational Linguistics, Online, October 2020
26. Švec, J.: t5s–T5 made simple. http://github.com/honzas83/t5s (2020). Accessed 02 April 2020
27. Švec, J., et al.: General framework for mining, processing and storing large amounts of electronic texts for language modeling purposes. Lang. Resour. Eval. **48**(2), 227–248 (2013). https://doi.org/10.1007/s10579-013-9246-z

# Lexicon-based vs. Lexicon-free ASR for Norwegian Parliament Speech Transcription

Jan Nouza$^{(\boxtimes)}$ , Petr Červa , and Jindřich Žd'ánský

Institute of Information Technologies and Electronics, Technical University
of Liberec, Studentská 2, 46117 Liberec, Czech Republic
{jan.nouza,petr.cerva}@tul.cz

**Abstract.** Norwegian is a challenging language for automatic speech recognition research because it has two written standards (Bokmål and Nynorsk) and a large number of distinct dialects, from which none has status of an official spoken norm. A traditional lexicon-based approach to ASR leads to a huge lexicon (because of the two standards and also due to compound words) with many spelling and pronunciation variants, and consequently to a large (and sparse) language model (LM). We have built a system with 601k-word lexicon and an acoustic model (AM) based on several types of neural networks and compare its performance with a lexicon-free end-to-end system developed in the ESPnet framework. For evaluation we use a publically available dataset of Norwegian parliament speeches that offers 100 h for training and 12 h for testing. In spite of this rather limited training resource, the lexicon-free approach yields significantly better results (13.0% word-error rate) compared to the best system with the lexicon, LM and neural network AM (that achieved 22.5% WER).

**Keywords:** automatic speech recognition · Norwegian · Bokmål · Nynorsk · Deep neural network · end-to-end speech recognition

## 1  Introduction

Norwegian, spoken by some 5.3 million people, belongs to the branch of North-Germanic languages, together with Swedish and Danish. All the three share some common features and to a certain extent they are mutually intelligible. Yet, Norwegian is unique as it utilizes 2 written standards, Bokmål (BK) and Nynorsk (NN). The former is historically older and has its roots in Danish, the latter was created in 19th century. Both are official languages of Norway, with equal rights, even though a large majority of people (about 85%) use Bokmål.

The choice between them is done mainly on the regional level (during school education) and later it follows personal preferences. As to the spoken form, there are many distinct dialects in Norway from which none has status of an official standard [1]. They are used both in informal and formal communication, such as

© Springer Nature Switzerland AG 2022
P. Sojka et al. (Eds.): TSD 2022, LNAI 13502, pp. 401–409, 2022.
https://doi.org/10.1007/978-3-031-16270-1_33

**Table 1.** Two examples of the same utterance transcribed either in Bokmål or Nynorsk. In English, the first means *"I come from Norway"*, the second *"In the report, the government points out how reparations can help . . . "*.

| BK | Jeg kommer fra Norge |
|----|---------------------|
| NN | Eg kjem frå Noreg |
| BK | I meldingen så peker regjeringen på hvordan reparasjon kan være med . . . |
| NN | I meldinga så peikar regjeringa på korleis reparasjon kan vere med . . . |

in public media, government institutions or in the parliament. When transcribing someone's speech, one must take into account his/her dialect and also his/her written preference, so technically it is a many-to-two mapping. This means that the same spoken utterance can be transcribed in (at least) two distinct ways, using different words (and sometimes also different grammar), as it is shown in Table 1.

This has a large impact on the development and evaluation of an ASR system that must cope with many spelling and pronunciation variants. Moreover, Norwegian morphology heavily uses compounding, which significantly increases lexical inventory. And even further, many compound words occur in more variants, e.g. *universitets-sykehus, universitets-sjukehus, universitetssykehus, universitetssjukehus* (university hospital, in English). Another challenging feature is Norwegian numbers that use alternative words for some digits and two different paradigms for constructing numbers in range of 21–99 (a direct one as in English, or a reversed one as in German) [2]. Hence, for example, year 2022 can be expressed in one of the following forms: *totusen og tjueto, totusen og toogtjue, totusen og tyveto, totusen og toogtyve, tjue tjueto, tyve toogtyve*, and even more.

All the above mentioned facts imply that a traditional general-purpose ASR system for Norwegian requires a very large lexicon with hundreds of thousands items and multiple pronunciations and, consequently a large and sparse language model

## 2    State-of-the-Art and Research Goals

There are not many publications aimed at automatic speech recognition in Norwegian. One can find some older papers that deal with simpler tasks, such as digit recognition [2], information retrieval over telephone in a limited application domain [3], or dictation of medical records [4]. Several recent publications focus on supplementary tasks, e.g., pronunciation variants and their modeling [5], or automatic grapheme-to-phoneme conversion [6].

There is no doubt that Norwegian ASR will be appreciated in many application fields as stated recently by the Language Council of Norway in [1]. A large effort has been devoted to collecting speech databases that cover various speaking styles, dialects and topics, and that are necessary both for research and practical development. Some of them have been made publicly available thanks to the National Library of Norway. Its webpage called Språkbanken[1] (the Language bank) offers open access to large text and speech resources. Some were collected in early 2000 s, such as a 540-hour set of prompted phonetically rich speech sentences (known as NST set), others have been compiled and uploaded recently. This is the case of the NPSC database that contains 126 h of recorded and transcribed plenary sessions in the Norwegian parliament [7]. In contrast to the previously mentioned NTS set, the NPSC data provides realistic and challenging resource for research and hence we used it this study.

Our project (supported by Norway funds) aims at developing an ASR system that could be used in practical on-line and off-line applications, such as automatic speech-to-text document conversion, meeting transcription, or broadcast monitoring. We can benefit from our previous research oriented mainly on multi-lingual ASR applications [8,9] where we often utilized data from public sources, such as parliament archives [10]. So far, we have been using our modular ASR system in which the language-specific components, i.e. a lexicon, a language model (LM) and an acoustic model (AM) had to be adapted to a target language. In this paper, we investigate an alternative approach, known as end-to-end (E2E) one, which is based on connectionist temporal classification (CTC) method introduced in [11]. We wanted to learn if it was applicable to Norwegian whose speech resources are significantly limited when compared to many other European languages.

## 3   Lexicon-based ASR System for Norwegian

Here, we briefly introduce our baseline large-vocabulary continuous-speech recognition (LVCSR) system. It utilizes a lexicon, whose size can go up to 1 million words with multiple pronunciations. Optionally, it can contain also frequent multi-word expressions and phrases to cover longer context in the corresponding N-gram LM. The AM is based on hidden Markov models (HMM) whose smallest units are triphone states. Their output probabilities can be represented by gaussian mixture models (GMM) or by deep neural nets (DNN). Recently, we use bidirectional feedforward sequential memory net (BFSMN) that proved to be a computational efficient alternative to recurrent NNs [13]. In our implementation, it has 11 layers, each covering 4 left and 4 right temporal contexts. Previously, we used also a 5-layer feedforward DNN with 512 neurons in a layer. When bootstrapping an AM for a new language, we usually start with the GMM that is more appropriate for smaller amounts of data. Later, after harvesting more data, we move to the more complex NN models [8]. For AM training, we utilize the open-source pytorch platform. In all cases, log mel-spectral coefficients serve as acoustic features.

In order to build the lexicon and the LM for Norwegian, we have collected a large amount of texts. The main sources were webpages of major and regional

---

[1] https://www.nb.no/sprakbanken/.

newspapers, broadcasters (mainly NRK TV and radio) and the Stortinget (Norwegian parliament). As to the last one, we downloaded the available official transcriptions of the plenary sessions, except of those from the 2017–2018 period (to avoid a potential conflict with the test set described in Sect. 5. After that, the texts were cleaned and repeated articles (occurring in regional editions of some newspapers) were removed. Numbers expressed as digits were replaced by their most frequent word equivalents, which was a compromise with regards to the variability mentioned in Sect. 1. Let us note that a large majority of the text sources in the corpus use Bokmål, except of the Parliament proceedings where official speech transcriptions respect the speakers' preferences. The complete cleaned corpus contains 1.4 GB text data.

The lexicon was built from all the words that occurred at least three times in the corpus. Next we added about 2500 most often occurring multi-word names and phrases. Pronunciations were generated according to major rules for spoken Norwegian, including some frequent variants. For foreign words and names, manual corrections were required. The recent lexicon contains 601k words (both Bokmål and Nynorsk) with 639k pronunciations. The LM is technically a bigram model, though it covers also many 3 to 4-word long sequences due to the multi-word lexicon items. This choice reflects the large lexicon size and also the decoder requirements for real-time performance.

During the development of a Norwegian ASR we have trained and tested various architectures using up to several hundred hours of training data. The system worked well but at some moment it reached a performance plateau and any further improvement required an immense load of additional work and data. The main reasons were: a) too many out-of-vocabulary (OOV) words, b) pronunciations not fitting some dialects, and c) the LM too rigid for informal and spontaneous speech.

## 4    Lexicon-free System

End-to-end systems have become very popular during the last 5 years. Instead of assembling a recognizer from separately optimized and trained modules (lexicons, AMs and LMs), they utilize a single (yet complex) neuron network based architecture that learns to convert a speech signal directly to text. It has been possible after the introduction of several key concepts, namely the connectionist temporal classification (CTC) [11] and its successful application to speech [13] and an attention-based encoder-decoder (AED) design [14]. The former utilizes a dynamic programming strategy (similar to that used in HMMs) to map speech frames to the output symbols, the latter tries to solve the same task via the encoder-decoder NN structure supported by an attention mechanism. Both the techniques have been implemented in an open-source toolkit ESPnet [15] and it is possible to combine them to get better results [16]. A slight improvement can be further achieved if the output symbols are not just single letters but word fragments derived from the most frequent words [17].

**Table 2.** Statistics of the Norwegian Parliament Speech Corpus (NPSC)

| | |
|---|---|
| Total duration (after removing long pauses) | 125.7 h |
| Word count | 1.17 million |
| Utterance count | 64,531 |
| Number of different speakers | 267 |
| Number of different words | 45,800 |
| Bokmål : Nynorsk distribution | 87 : 13 |
| Male : female distribution | 62 : 38 |

**Table 3.** Statistics of NPSC subsets

| | Train | Eval | Test |
|---|---|---|---|
| Hours of speech | 100.3 | 13.1 | 12.3 |
| Number of sessions | 32 | 5 | 4 |
| Utterance count | 51,342 | 6,844 | 6,355 |
| Word count | 942,102 | 120,834 | 112,312 |
| Unique words not in Train set | - | 2,786 | 2,747 |

We have been using the above mentioned ESPnet platform[2] for our experiments. Speech recordings in the train set had to be no longer than 25 s and their text annotations were filtered to keep only letters and spaces. For tests with sub-word units, we used Sentencepiece[3] to get the list of K most frequent tokens and to re-annotate the transcriptions. Speech files were parametrized to 80 mel-spectral features per frame (25 ms long). For training the neural net, we used the hybrid CTC/AED option (CTC weighting factor equal to 0.3). The other important parameters were set as follows: output size of the encoder: 256, encoder/decoder attention heads: 8, linear units in AED: 2048, Adam optimizer, max epochs: 120. In initial tests, we employed the provided decoder, later we wrote our own implementation of the CTC prefix beam search algorithm [18].

## 5   Experiments

### 5.1   Data

Our experiments are organized in a closed-set manner. This means that training, evaluation and testing is performed within the given dataset only. It is fairly large and, more importantly, it is publicly available. This will allow other researchers to compare their results with ours.

---

[2] https://github.com/espnet.
[3] https://github.com/google/sentencepiece.

We have been using a set of recordings from the Norwegian parliament known as the NPSC. It has been available since 2021[4] and its description can be found in [7]. It covers 41 plenary sessions from 2017–2018 years. The records have been cut into shorter sentence-like utterances (1 to 43 s long) and transcribed. This dataset represents most features of spoken Norwegian, namely all major dialects, transcriptions in Bokmål or Nynorsk, all types of speech (read, planned, spontaneous and emotional) and includes also some low quality records when speakers do not speak directly to the main microphone. Table 2 summarizes its basic statistics.

The dataset is officially split into 3 parts aimed at ASR training, evaluation (during development) and testing. The split has been done so that each part contains a subset of complete sessions. In Table 3, we present basic facts on the split. Let us admit that a small portion (3.6 h) had to be removed from the training part because our baseline recognizer detected notable mismatch between its output and provided annotations. A brief check unveiled that some of these utterances had been in English, the other had probably wrong transcriptions. Hence, the data really used for training had a size of 96.7 h.

### 5.2    Tests and Results

We have investigated various architectures and their parameters. All the systems were trained using the NPSC-Train set only and tests were conducted on the NPSC-Test data. The Eval part was applied for parameter optimizations if the training process required it. The most relevant results for this study are presented in Table 4 where we compare three lexicon-based recognizers with an E2E system. The former type shares the same 601k word lexicon and LM, and differs only in the deployed AM. As expected, the lowest word-error rate (22.46%) was achieved with the bidirectional feedforward sequential memory net (BFSMN), i.e. the model that operates with the longest temporal contexts (in a similar way as recurrent NNs). Let us note that even the large general-purpose 601k-word lexicon led to 1.09% out-of-vocabulary (OOV) rate in this test.

The E2E system was trained within the ESPnet framework and evaluated by our decoder. The training phase on the 100-hour set took about 20 h on a PC equipped with a GPU card. The recognition was much faster with real-time factor about 0.22. We investigated mainly the impact of the E2E output-symbol inventory, starting from characters only (all Norwegian letters + several letters from other major European languages + space and blank symbol) and going up to 5000 word-substrings proposed by the Sentencepiece tool. The best performance (12.97% WER) was achieved with the 1000-item inventory but the difference between the letters only and the biggest set was not that large, which is probably due to the rather small size of the training data. In any case, the E2E system significantly outperformed all the other ones.

In general, a large portion of the errors were just confusions between Bokmål and Nynorsk word forms. It is something hardly avoidable in Norwegian since

---

[4]  https://www.nb.no/sprakbanken/en/resource-catalogue/oai-nb-no-sbr-58/.

**Table 4.** Word-error rate (WER) achieved on NPSC-Test set for several investigated ASR architectures

| ASR system | Lexicon | LM | AM | WER [%] |
|---|---|---|---|---|
| GMM-HMM | 601k words | 2-gram | GMM | 35.77 |
| DNN-HMM | 601k words | 2-gram | DNN | 27.28 |
| BFSMN-HMM | 601k words | 2-gram | BFSMN | 22.46 |
| E2E | 42 chars | none | CTC/AED | 14.26 |
| E2E | 1k subwords | none | CTC/AED | 12.97 |
| E2E | 5k subwords | none | CTC/AED | 13.67 |

the choice of the written standard is given by speakers' personal preferences as explained in Sect. 1 and can be hardly predicted just from speech. Yet, the number of confusions was significantly smaller when compared to the lexicon-based system. This indicates that the E2E system was able to learn inter-word context better than the traditional language model. Also, we tried to analyse how the latter system coped with the words not seen in the training (2,747 unique words, see the last line in Table 3) and found that about 1/5 of them were recognized correctly. This was true mainly for those that were somehow acoustically and orthographically related to the seen ones. The system also seemed to learn at least some rules of word compounding. On the other side, a word like 'autisme' (autism in English) often used in one of the debates included in the test set, has never been recognized correctly and occurred in many misspelled or strange forms.

## 5.3   Discussions

We are aware of the fact that the rather low WER achieved by our best system is partly due to the tight match between the training and testing data (the same acoustic environment and the same group of speakers). Yet, the performance of the lexicon-free system (trained on 100 h only) is much better compared to the systems with a traditional architecture that can benefit from additional linguistic resources.

Our results can be directly compared to those published recently in [7]. Its authors utilize the same test and training set but their ASR system is based on DeepSpeech 2 platform [19] and equipped with a large lexicon (size not mentioned) and a 3-gram LM prepared from their large non-public text corpus that includes - in contrast to ours - also the NPSC-Train transcriptions. They report slightly worse 15.9% WER as their best result.

Besides experimenting with the NPSC data, the same authors tested their system on another (smaller) Norwegian dataset known as NB Tale[5], namely on its Part3. This subset consists of 2-min talks given by speakers representing 12

---

[5] https://www.nb.no/sprakbanken/en/resource-catalogue/oai-nb-no-sbr-31/.

major dialects. They were asked to speak freely about their own hobbies and professional interests, and they did it in a more or less spontaneous way. The authors report 37.3% WER. We conducted a similar experiment employing the best E2E system mentioned in the previous section. We used it as it was, without changing any of its parameters and received 38.9% WER. This result documents two aspects: The E2E system trained on a (small-size) data from a restricted domain performs significantly worse when tested in another (non-related) domain, which is obviously not surprise. Yet, our WER is still comparable to that of an established ASR system with a large lexicon and general LM used in [7].

# 6    Conclusions and Future Work

In spite of the large recent popularity of the E2E approach, we had not been sure whether it could be used for a language like Norwegian where both orthography and phonology had such complex nature and relation, and where speech resources were quite limited (especially when compared to other studies, e.g. [20]). That is why we decided to make a comparison between the traditional procedure to adapt an existing ASR platform to a new language, and the E2E method to build an ASR system in a more straightforward and efficient way. In our experiments we used data that represented many aspects of spoken Norwegian and the achieved results clearly confirmed the superiority of the modern E2E approach.

The next step will be incorporation of the other available data from Språkbanken into the training material. It should be done carefully, because, for example, the largest set (NST) consists of many identical (phonetically rich) sentences recorded by hundreds of speakers, which may be a drawback for the E2E training concept. After that we plan to run a data mining campaign that will allow us to harvest automatically additional training data from the Norwegian parliament archive and also from TV channel NRK whose news programs are equipped by subtitles. Our goal is to collect up to 1000 h hours to train a Norwegian E2E system suitable for the practical tasks mentioned in Sect. 2.

**Acknowledgements.** This work was supported by the Technology Agency of the Czech Republic (project No. TO01000027).

# References

1. Frostad, B.H., Schall, V., Holte, S.M.: Towards ASR that supports linguistic diversity in Norway. In: Proceedings of LT4All, Paris, pp. 328–331 (2019)
2. Kvale, K.: Norwegian numerals: a challenge to automatic speech recognition. In: Proceedings of ICSLP, Philadelphia, pp. 2028–2031 (1996)
3. Johnsen, M. H., Amble, T., Harborg, E.: A norwegian spoken dialogue system for bus travel information. In: SLT in Telecommunications, pp. 125–131 (2003)
4. Markhus, V., Gajic, B., Svarverud, J., Solbraa, L. E., Johnsen, M. H.: Annotation and automatic recognition of spontaneously dictated medical records for Norwegian. In: Proceedings of NORSIG, pp. 316–319 (2004)

5. Adde, L.: A discriminative approach to pronunciation variation modeling in speech recognition. PhD Thesis, NTNU Trondheim (2013)
6. Kristensen, T. S., Nilssen, M. S.: Grapheme to phoneme conversion of norwegian using hidden markov models. In: 2020 15th IEEE Conference on Industrial Electronics and Applications (ICIEA), pp. 1121–1126 IEEE (2020)
7. Solberg, P. E., Ortiz, P.: The norwegian parliamentary speech corpus. arXiv preprint arXiv:2201.10881 (2022)
8. Nouza, J., Safarik, R., Cerva, P.: ASR for south slavic languages developed in almost automated way. In: Proceedings of Interspeech, pp. 3868–3872 (2016)
9. Safarik, R., Nouza, J. Unified approach to development of ASR systems for East Slavic languages. In: Proceedings of International Conference on Statistical Language and Speech Processing, pp. 193–203 (2017)
10. Nouza, J., Safarik, R.: Parliament archives used for automatic training of multilingual automatic speech recognition systems. In: Ekštein, K., Matoušek, V. (eds.) TSD 2017. LNCS (LNAI), vol. 10415, pp. 174–182. Springer, Cham (2017). https://doi.org/10.1007/978-3-319-64206-2_20
11. Graves, A., Fernández, S., Gomez, F.: Connectionist temporal classification: labelling unsegmented sequence data with recurrent neural networks. In: Proceedings of ICML, pp. 369–376 (2006)
12. Zhang, S., Jiang, H., Xiong, S., Wei, S., Dai, L.: Compact feedforward sequential memory networks for large vocabulary continuous speech recognition, In: Proceedings of Interspeech, San Francisco, pp. 3389–3393 (2016)
13. Graves, A., Jaitly, N.: Towards end-to-end speech recognition with recurrent neural networks. In: Proceedings of ICML, pp. 1764–1772 (2014)
14. Chorowski, J. K., Bahdanau, D., Serdyuk, D., Cho, K., Bengio, Y.: Attention-based models for speech recognition. In: Advances in Neural Information Processing Systems, vol. 28 (2015)
15. Watanabe, S., Hori, T., Karita, S., Hayashi, T., Nishitoba, J., Unno, N., et al.: ESPnet: end-to-end speech processing toolkit, In: Proceedings Interspeech, pp. 2207–2211 (2018)
16. Watanabe, S., Hori, T., Kim, S., Hershey, J.R., Hayashi, T.: Hybrid CTC/attention architecture for end-to-end speech recognition. IEEE J. Sel. Top. Sign. Process. **11**(8), 1240–1253 (2017)
17. Sennrich, R., Haddow, B., Birch, A.: Neural machine translation of rare words with subword units. In: Proceedings of ACL, pp. 1715–1725 (2016)
18. Hannun, A. Sequence modeling with CTC, distill (2017). https://distill.pub/2017/ctc
19. Amodei, D., et al.: Deep speech 2: end-to-end speech recognition in English and Mandarin. In: Proceedings of PMLR, pp. 173–182 (2016)
20. Chen, G., et al.: Gigaspeech: an evolving, multi-domain ASR corpus with 10,000 hours of transcribed audio. In: Proceedings of Interspeech, pp. 3670–3674 (2021)

# On Comparison of Phonetic Representations for Czech Neural Speech Synthesis

Jindřich Matoušek[1,2]([✉])[iD] and Daniel Tihelka[2][iD]

[1] Department of Cybernetics, Faculty of Applied Sciences,
University of West Bohemia, Plzeň, Czech Republic
`jmatouse@kky.zcu.cz`
[2] New Technology for the Information Society (NTIS), Faculty of Applied Sciences,
University of West Bohemia, Plzeň, Czech Republic
`dtihelka@ntis.zcu.cz`

**Abstract.** In this paper, we investigate two research questions related to the phonetic representation of input text in Czech neural speech synthesis: 1) whether we can afford to reduce the phonetic alphabet, and 2) whether we can remove pauses from phonetic transcription and let the speech synthesis model predict the pause positions itself. In our experiments, three different modern speech synthesis models (FastSpeech 2 + Multi-band MelGAN, Glow-TTS + UnivNet, and VITS) were employed. We have found that the reduced phonetic alphabet outperforms the traditionally used full phonetic alphabet. On the other hand, removing pauses does not help. The presence of pauses (predicted by an external pause prediction tool) in phonetic transcription leads to a slightly better quality of synthetic speech.

**Keywords:** neural speech synthesis · phonetic representation · phonetic reductions · pause modeling · czech language

## 1 Introduction

Modern *neural speech synthesis* models can utilize raw text (i.e., *letters*) as the input representation. In that case, the explicit phonetic representation is omitted because the neural model maps the input letters (or *graphemes*) directly to their acoustic counterparts. Such an approach is called *end-to-end*. On the other hand, graphemes generally do not represent the pronunciation, and consequently, they need not correspond to the acoustic representation closely [2,27].

On contrary, *phonemes* (or *phones*) are often used as the input representation to a speech synthesizer in *text-to-speech* (TTS) systems. The advantage of using phonemes is that, for many languages, they have a more direct relationship to

This research was supported by the Technology Agency of the Czech Republic (TA CR), project No. TL05000546.

P. Sojka et al. (Eds.): TSD 2022, LNAI 13502, pp. 410–422, 2022.
https://doi.org/10.1007/978-3-031-16270-1_34

the acoustic signal than graphemes, and they approximate speech more closely than graphemes. This is especially true for *analytic languages* (like English) in which the written and pronunciation forms differ significantly. As a result, phonemes are expected to lead to improved quality of the resulting synthetic speech. The disadvantage of using phonemes is that an additional module, usually called *front-end*, is required. The front-end typically includes a pronunciation lexicon lookup and a *grapheme-to-phoneme* (G2P) model for dealing with out-of-vocabulary words (OOVs), phonetic disambiguation of non-standard words such as numbers, abbreviations, and homographs [3]. Development of these modules traditionally requires a large amount of manual expertise and effort. On the other hand, the textual material consisting of sequences of words/graphemes and the corresponding sequences of phonemes is usually more readily available and in much larger quantities (many times more than an end-to-end system that, given it also needs acoustic signals, has only a limited amount of data available). Then, the above-mentioned modules can be trained on such large textual data; for instance, the G2P model was successfully trained using sequence-to-sequence models like long short-time memory (LSTM) networks [7,21], or more recently, transformer-based models [32,33], obtaining very good results.

In this paper, we focus on phonetic representation and compare the effect of different phonetic representations on the quality of Czech synthetic speech generated by different neural speech synthesis models. Unlike Fong et al. [3] who investigated the differences between graphemic and phonetic representations and different levels of phonetic transcription imperfection, in this paper we assume perfect phonetic transcription on the input.

The paper is organized as follows. In Sect. 2, we introduce the research questions. In Sect. 3, we describe the data used for our experiments. Different phonetic representations are introduced in Sect. 4. In Sect. 5, we present neural speech synthesis models used to generate speech from the different phonetic representations in our experiments. Section 6 describes and discusses the results. Finally, conclusions are drawn in Sect. 7.

## 2   Research Questions

In this study, we explore two research questions related to input phonetic representation in neural-based speech synthesis of Czech speech.

Firstly (RQ1), we investigate the size of the phonetic inventory. Traditionally, relatively rich phonetic inventories are used in speech synthesis, distinguishing between some variants of a phoneme. For instance, in Czech, two variants of a vibrant [r̝] or non-syllabic/syllabic variants of [r, l, m] are distinguished. The question is if such a fine differentiation is really necessary for neural-based speech synthesis. Since neural speech synthesis models cope well even with orthographic input (typical for the end-to-end approach), we examine if a smaller inventory is not sufficient. Given the ability of modern neural speech synthesis models to capture speech contexts (using the attention mechanism [28]), the hypothesis is that less-frequent phones and/or phones occurring in very specific contexts can be omitted and a smaller phonetic inventory can be utilized.

**Table 1.** Phonetic transcription examples using three different phonetic alphabets (in Czech). The English translation would be *If there's time, my brother will drive to the bank, otherwise he'll take the tram.*

| | |
|---|---|
| **Text** | *Když bude čas, bratr pojede do banky autem, jinak půjde třeba na tramvaj.* |
| **Full** | \$ ɡdɪʒ bʊdɛ t͡ʃas, # bratr̝ pɔjɛdɛ dɔ baŋkɪ ʔautɛm, # jɪnak puːjdɛ tr̝ɛba na tram̩vaj. \$ |
| **Reduced** | # ɡdɪʒ bʊdɛ t͡ʃas, # bratr pɔjɛdɛ dɔ bankɪ autɛm, # jɪnak puːjdɛ tr̝ɛba na tramvaj. # |
| **Pause-free** | ɡdɪʒ bʊdɛ t͡ʃas, bratr̝ pɔjɛdɛ dɔ baŋkɪ ʔautɛm, jɪnak puːjdɛ tr̩ɛba na tram̩vaj. |

Secondly (RQ2), in speech synthesis, phonetic transcription is often accompanied by symbols of pauses, and pauses are treated like any other phone. Given punctuation is present in the input phonetic representation (see Sect. 4) and pauses often correspond to punctuation symbols, the question is whether pauses should be included in the phonetic representation at all.

## 3   Speech Data

For our experiments, we used a large corpus of Czech read speech recorded by a professional male speaker. The corpus was primarily designed for the use with *unit-selection* speech synthesis [15–17], but Vít et al. [29] showed that the corpus is also suitable for neural speech synthesis. It contains paired text-audio data with approximately 14 h of audio (including pauses) distributed over 12,240 utterances. For our purposes, the audio has been downsampled to 24 kHz, carefully annotated and the resulting text has been normalized to expand out numbers, dates, ordinals, monetary amounts, etc. Finally, the text of each audio was transcribed into a sequence of phones using a set of carefully designed Czech phonetic rules and a pronunciation dictionary with words that do not obey Czech pronunciation rules [33].

## 4   Phonetic Representations

In line with the research questions set out in Sect. 2, we defined three phonetic representations: *full phonetic alphabet* (see Sect. 4.1), *reduced phonetic alphabet* (Sect. 4.2), and *pause-free phonetic alphabet* (Sect. 4.3). Examples of phonetic transcription[1] using the different phonetic representations are shown in Table 1.

---

[1] For phonetic transcription we use *International Phonetic Alphabet* (IPA), https://www.internationalphoneticassociation.org/content/ipa-chart.

**Table 2.** Full phonetic alphabet.

| Phone group | Phones | Number (51) |
|---|---|---|
| Short vowels | a, ɛ, ɪ, ɔ, ʊ | 5 |
| Long vowels | aː, ɛː, iː, oː, uː | 5 |
| Diphthongs | o͡ʊ, a͡ʊ, e͡ʊ | 3 |
| Plosives | p, b, t, d, c, ɟ, k, g | 8 |
| Affricates | t͡s, t͡ʃ, d͡z, d͡ʒ | 4 |
| Fricatives | f, v, s, z, ʃ, ʒ, x, ɦ, l, r, r̝, j | 12 |
| Nasals | m, n, ɲ | 3 |
| Additional phones | ə, ʔ, ŋ, ɱ, ɣ, r̝, r̥, l̩, m̩ | 9 |
| Pauses | \$, # | 2 |

Note that all phonetic transcriptions contain punctuation symbols. This was done in purpose to help neural models to capture prosodic characteristics associated with the punctuation [23]. The full stop at the end of each transcription denotes a declarative sentence and thus should capture the falling intonation pattern typical for this kind of sentences. On the other hand, a comma inside a sentence indicates a prosodic boundary usually accompanied by a slightly rising intonation [23].

A detailed description of the phonetic representations is given in the following subsections.

## 4.1  Full Phonetic Alphabet

By the term *full phonetic alphabet* we denote a standard phonetic inventory[2] usually used in Czech speech-synthesis related research [18,20]. This phonetic alphabet was the one used to transcribe textual sentences in Sect. 3. The alphabet consists of "basic" phone groups like short/long *vowels* (containing 10 phones), *diphthongs* (3), *plosives* (8), *affricates* (4), *fricatives* (12), and *nasals* (3). The inventory also includes fine phonetic units denoted as "additional phones" in Table 2. From the phonetic point of view, these are *allophonic variants* of the "basic" phones [25]. Since the additional phones are mostly the phones to be considered for reduction, they are described in Sect. 4.2 in more detail.

In our phonetic description, we also use two symbols for a pause. Sentence leading and trailing pauses are denoted as [\$], while the sentence-internal (inter-

---

[2] Czech SAMPA, http://www.phon.ucl.ac.uk/home/sampa/czech-uni.htm.

word) pauses are denoted as [#]. The reason for distinguishing the two types of pauses is that [#] results from the natural phrasing of the speaker during speaking; thus it is related to temporal characteristics imposed by the speaker. On the other hand, [$] can be viewed as a longer "artificial" silence present at the beginning and end of the recording of each utterance. We use an external speech segmentation tool [5] as a pause predictor to add both kinds of pauses to the phonetic transcription of input text.

The total number of symbols in the full phonetic alphabet is 51 (see Table 2).

## 4.2   Reduced Phonetic Alphabet

As mentioned in Sect. 2, the idea behind phonetic reductions is that some phones occur less frequently and/or in very specific contexts in spoken Czech. Given the ability of modern neural speech synthesis models to capture speech contexts, the following phonetic reductions (corresponding mainly to additional phones in Table 2) were taken into account [25]:

- Velar nasals [ŋ] and [ɱ] are replaced by their "standard" nasal variants [n], or [m], respectively.
- Syllabic consonants [r̩, l̩], and [m̩] are replaced by their non-syllabic versions [r, l, m].
- Since the difference between unvoiced and voiced variants of [r̝] is rather small, the unvoiced vibrant [r̝̊] is replaced by its voiced variant [r̝].
- The status of voiced [ɣ] is relatively unclear and in phonetic descriptions it is sometimes replaced by voiced [ɦ] or unvoiced [x]. In this study, we replace [ɣ] by [x].
- Low-frequency affricates [d͡z, d͡ʒ] are replaced by a combination of the two corresponding consonants [dz, dʒ].
- Diphthongs [a͡ʊ, o͡ʊ, e͡ʊ] are replaced by a combination of the two corresponding vowels [au, ou, eu].
- Since glottal stop [ʔ] occurs in very specific contexts (usually after a pause and before a vowel or diphthong) [14,30], it is ignored, i.e. deleted without replacement.
- Schwa [ə] occurs very rarely in standard Czech pronunciation, limiting itself primarily to a certain form of spelling, like in ČR [t͡ʃərə]. Therefore, schwa is ignored in this study.
- As part of the phonetic reductions, both types of pauses were combined into one and denoted as [#].

The number of phones after the reduction decreased to 36. A summary of the phonetic reductions is given in Table 3. More general phonetic reductions were introduced by Hanzlíček et al. [5] to cope with the modeling and segmentation of different foreign languages.

**Table 3.** Phonetic reductions.

| Full alphabet | | Reduced alphabet | | |
|---|---|---|---|---|
| Phone | Example | Phone | Example | Word |
| ŋ | baŋka | n | banka | *banka* |
| ɱ | traɱvaj | m | tramvaj | *tramvaj* |
| r̩ | bratr̩ | r | bratr | *bratr* |
| l̩ | vl̩k | l | vlk | *vlk* |
| m̩ | ʔosm̩ | m | osm | *osm* |
| r̩̊ | tr̩̊i | r̩ | tr̩i | *tři* |
| ɣ | abɪɣ bɪl | x | abɪx bɪl | *abych byl* |
| d͡z | lɛd͡zgdo | dz | lɛdzgdo | *leckdo* |
| d͡ʒ | d͡ʒʊs | dʒ | dʒʊs | *džus* |
| o͡ʊ | bo͡ʊda | ɔʊ | boʊda | *bouda* |
| a͡ʊ | ʔa͡ʊtɔ | aʊ | aʊto | *auto* |
| e͡ʊ | ʔe͡ʊrɔ | eʊ | eʊro | *euro* |
| ʔ | ʔʊʃɪ | ∅ | ʊʃɪ | *uši* |
| ə | t͡ʃərə | ∅ | t͡ʃ r | *ČR* |
| $ | $ ʔano # rɔzumiːm $ | # | # ano # rɔzumiːm # | *Ano, rozumím.* |

### 4.3  Pause-free Phonetic Alphabet

The pause-free phonetic alphabet is almost identical to the full phonetic alphabet. The only difference is that it includes no pauses. In this case, the neural speech synthesis models are left to train pauses implicitly from the pause-free input phonetic representation and the punctuation present in the input representation. The advantage of the pause-free alphabet is that it does not need an external pause predictor to add pauses.

## 5  Speech Synthesis Models

For the evaluation of the effect of different phonetic representations on the quality of Czech synthetic speech, we employed three modern neural speech synthesis models. Two of them follow the most widely used scheme today: they employ an *acoustic model* (also called *text-to-spectrogram* or *text-to-mel*), which generates *acoustic* features (usually mel-spectrograms) from either text (graphemes) or phonemes, and a *vocoder* to generate waveform from acoustic features. In our study, we used (a) FastSpeech 2 [22] as an acoustic model and Multi-band MelGAN [31] as a vocoder (see Sect. 5.1), and (b) Glow-TTS [8] as an acoustic model and UnivNet [6] as a vocoder (see Sect. 5.2).

As the third neural model, we employed VITS [9], which could be viewed as a full end-to-end model in that it directly converts graphemes/phonemes into waveform. For an excellent overview of neural speech synthesis models, please see [26].

## 5.1   FastSpeech2 + Multi-band MelGAN

FastSpeech 2 [22] is a fast and robust Transformer-based acoustic model proposed to solve issues typical for autoregressive models (such as Tacotron 2 [24]) by adopting feed-forward Transformer network to generate mel-spectrograms from an input phone sequence in parallel and replacing the error-prone attention mechanism by an explicit phone duration predictor to match the length of mel-spectrograms. In our experiments, FastSpeech 2 models were trained using the AdamW optimizer [13] with $\beta_1 = 0.9$, $\beta_2 = 0.98$ and weight decay $\lambda = 0.001$. The initial and end learning rates were set to $10^{-3}$ and $5 \times 10^{-5}$ respectively, with 4k warm-up steps. The batch size was set to 16 and the models were trained up to 200k steps on a single GeForce GTX 1080 Ti GPU.

Multi-band MelGAN [31] is a vocoder based on *generative adversarial networks* (GANs). GAN consists of a generator for data (audio) generation, and a discriminator to judge the authenticity of the generated audio. MelGAN uses multiple discriminators to judge audios in different scales; thus in each scale, it can focus on the characteristics in different frequency ranges. Multi-band modeling divides the waveform into multiple sub-bands and enables the parallel generation and fast inference. The Multi-band MelGAN vocoders were trained with the Adam optimizer [10] for both generator and discriminator with $\beta_1 = 0.9$, $\beta_2 = 0.999$, using piece-wise learning rate decay starting at $5 \times 10^{-4}$ going to $10^{-6}$ for generator and $2.5 \times 10^{-4}$ to $10^{-6}$ for discriminator, both stepping down to half after each 100k steps. The batch size was set to 64, and the models have been trained up to 2.7M steps, with the discriminator employed after 200k training steps.

Both FastSpeech 2 and Multi-band MelGAN models were trained using the TensorFlowTTS project [19].

## 5.2   Glow-TTS + UnivNet

Glow-TTS is a flow-based acoustic model that leverages generative flow for non-autoregressive mel-spectrogram generation [8]. It applies a novel *monotonic alignment search* (MAS) to perform internal alignment between graphemes/phonemes and mel-spectrograms and to predict the duration. In our experiments, Glow-TTS models were trained using the RAdam optimizer [12] with $\beta_1 = 0.9$, $\beta_2 = 0.998$, weight decay $\lambda = 10^{-6}$, and with the Noam learning rate schedule [28]. The batch size was set to 48 and the models were trained up to 570k steps on a single NVIDIA A100 GPU.

UnivNet is a neural GAN-based vocoder that uses *full-band* mel-spectrograms input to generate high-fidelity waveforms in real-time [6]. Similar to Multiband MelGAN, it utilizes a multi-resolution spectrogram discriminator that uses multiple linear spectrogram magnitudes computed using various parameter sets (including spectral and temporal domains). In our experiments, UnivNet vocoders were trained using the Adam optimizer [10] with $\beta_1 = 0.5$, $\beta_2 = 0.9$, and under a $10^{-4}$ learning rate. The batch size was set to 32 and the models were trained up to 2.72M steps on a single GeForce GTX 1080 Ti GPU. The generator was trained with only auxiliary loss without discriminators in the first 200k steps [6].

Both Glow-TTS and UnivNet models were trained using the Coqui-TTS project [4].

## 5.3   VITS

VITS is a conditional variational autoencoder with adversarial learning [9]. It employs different deep-learning techniques together (adversarial learning, normalizing flows, variational autoencoders, transformers) to achieve high-quality natural-sounding output. VITS is mainly built on the Glow-TTS model but it updates on Glow-TTS by introducing the following updates. First, it replaces the duration predictor with a stochastic duration predictor that better models the variability in speech. Then, it connects a HiFiGAN vocoder [11] to the decoder's output and joins the two with a variational autoencoder (VAE). That allows the model one-stage training in an end-to-end fashion and finds a better intermediate representation than traditionally used mel-spectrograms. This results in high fidelity and more precise prosody [1,8].

In our experiments, VITS models were trained using the AdamW optimizer [13] with $\beta_1 = 0.8$, $\beta_2 = 0.99$, and weight decay $\lambda = 0.01$. The learning rate decay was scheduled by a $0.999^{1/8}$ factor in every epoch with an initial learning rate of $2 \times 10^{-4}$. The batch size was set to 16 and the models were trained up to 1.3M steps using mixed precision training on a single GeForce GTX 1080 Ti GPU.

VITS models were trained using the Coqui-TTS project [4].

## 6   Results and Discussion

### 6.1   Listening Tests

Two preference listening tests were conducted for a direct comparison of the investigated phenomena. The first listening test concerned RQ1 (see Sect. 2), i.e., it answers the question of whether it is possible/advantageous to reduce the phonetic alphabet (full vs reduced). The second listening test concerned RQ2 and answers the question of whether it is necessary to add pauses (by an external predictor) to phonetic transcription (full vs pause-free).

Each listening test contained the same 18 sentences that were synthesized by each of the three synthesis models described in Sect. 5. The sentences were chosen to differ in the phenomena under study and were 4–12 words long. Of course, we used sentences not included in the training data. The longer sentences were compound/complex sentences that contained internal pauses. The listeners then listened to two versions of the same sentence: (a) one with a full phonetic alphabet and one with the reduced phonetic alphabet (full vs reduced), and (b) one with external pauses and one without pauses (full vs pause-free). In each test, 54 comparisons were made.

12 listeners participated in both listening tests. They were instructed to evaluate each pair of the synthesized sentences on a three-point scale (better/same/worse) concerning the overall quality of synthesized speech. The synthetic sentences were presented in the same order to all listeners. As a result, 648 comparisons (216 for each synthesis model) were made in each test. All the listeners were native Czech speakers (some of them had no knowledge of speech synthesis) and had no hearing problems.

## 6.2   Full vs Reduced Phonetic Alphabet (RQ1)

The results in Table 4 show a clear preference for the reduced phonetic alphabet. The reduced alphabet was preferred consistently across all the synthesis models examined. The total preference rate for the reduced alphabet was 43.67%, only 22.38% of all comparisons preferred the full alphabet, and 33.95% were without preference. Addressing RQ1 introduced in Sect. 2, we can see that (at least for the Czech language and the male voice under investigation) a smaller phonetic inventory (with 36 phones, as opposed to 51 phones in the full phonetic inventory) that does not use less frequent and overspecified phones leads to better synthetic speech in neural-based speech synthesis. This may be considered a surprising finding since there has always been a tendency in speech synthesis (as opposed to, for example, speech recognition) to use a rather finer phonetic alphabet and thus larger inventories. Of course, we would like to repeat this experiment on more voices (including female ones) and more languages.

**Table 4.** Results of the preference listening test: full phonetic alphabet vs reduced phonetic alphabet.

| | Preference [%] | | |
|---|---|---|---|
| Model | Full | Same | Reduced |
| FastSpeech2 + Multi-band MelGAN | 28.24 | 33.80 | **37.96** |
| Glow-TTS + UnivNet | 11.57 | 35.19 | **53.24** |
| VITS | 27.32 | 32.87 | **39.82** |
| Overall preference | 22.38 | 33.95 | **43.67** |

**Table 5.** Results of the preference listening test: full phonetic alphabet vs pause-free alphabet.

| | Preference [%] | | |
|---|---|---|---|
| Model | Full | Same | Pause-free |
| FastSpeech2 + Multi-band MelGAN | 31.02 | **42.13** | 26.85 |
| Glow-TTS + UnivNet | **38.89** | **38.89** | 22.22 |
| VITS | **35.19** | 30.56 | 34.26 |
| Overall preference | 35.03 | **37.19** | 27.78 |

### 6.3  Full vs Pause-free Alphabet (RQ2)

The results of this experiment are not as clear as they were in the "full vs reduced" experiment described in the previous section (Table 5). Yet, the results are consistent across all the synthesis models examined and show that listeners tend to prefer the full phonetic alphabet including pauses (35.03%) or they prefer neither option (37.19%). Only 27.78% of all comparisons preferred the pause-free version. Addressing RQ2 introduced in Sect. 2, it seems that explicit usage of pause symbols in neural-based speech synthesis slightly helps. But again, additional experiments with other voices and languages are needed to confirm this finding.

## 7  Conclusions and Future Work

In this paper, we investigated two research questions related to the phonetic representation of input text in Czech neural speech synthesis. In our experiments, three different modern speech synthesis models were employed. Two of them are two-stage models, employing both an acoustic model and a vocoder, and the other is a fully end-to-end model. In the first experiment, we showed that the reduced phonetic alphabet with 36 phonetic symbols outperformed the traditionally used full phonetic alphabet with 51 phonetic symbols. The second experiment concerned the explicit use of pauses in the phonetic representation. We have found that removing pauses from phonetic transcription and letting the synthesis model predict the position of the pauses on its own does not help – slightly better results were obtained when pauses (predicted by an external speech segmentation tool [5]) were included in phonetic transcription of input text.

In our future work, in addition to extending the experiments to more voices and languages, we also plan to investigate other levels of phonetic alphabet reduction – for example, ignoring phenomena such as voicing or articulatory assimilation. It would also be interesting to see what would happen if we reduced the phonetic inventory even further.

**Acknowledgements.** Computational resources were supplied by the project "e-Infrastruktura CZ" (e-INFRA CZ LM2018140) supported by the Ministry of Education, Youth and Sports of the Czech Republic.

# References

1. Casanova, E., Weber, J., Shulby, C., Junior, A.C., Gölge, E., Ponti, M.A.: YourTTS: towards zero-shot multi-speaker TTS and zero-shot voice conversion for everyone. CoRR abs/2112.0 (2021), http://arxiv.org/abs/2112.02418
2. Fong, J., Gallegos, P.O., Hodari, Z., King, S.: Investigating the robustness of sequence-to-sequence text-to-speech models to imperfectly-transcribed training data. In: INTERSPEECH, pp. 1546–1550. Graz, Austria (2019). https://doi.org/10.21437/Interspeech.2019-1824
3. Fong, J., Taylor, J., Richmond, K., King, S.: A comparison of letters and phones as input to sequence-to-sequence models for speech synthesis. In: Speech Synthesis Workshop, pp. 223–227. Vienna, Austria (2019). https://doi.org/10.21437/SSW.2019-40
4. Gölge, E., The coqui TTS team: coqui TTS (2021). https://doi.org/10.5281/zenodo.6334862, https://github.com/coqui-ai/TTS
5. Hanzlíček, Z., Vít, J.: LSTM-based speech segmentation trained on different foreign languages. In: Sojka, P., Kopeček, I., Pala, K., Horák, A. (eds.) TSD 2020. LNCS (LNAI), vol. 12284, pp. 456–464. Springer, Cham (2020). https://doi.org/10.1007/978-3-030-58323-1_49
6. Jang, W., Lim, D., Yoon, J., Kim, B., Kim, J.: UnivNet: a neural vocoder with multi-resolution spectrogram discriminators for high-fidelity waveform generation. In: INTERSPEECH, pp. 2207–2211. Brno, Czechia (2021). https://doi.org/10.21437/Interspeech.2021-1016
7. Jůzová, M., Tihelka, D., Vít, J.: Unified language-independent DNN-based G2P converter. In: INTERSPEECH, pp. 2085–2089. Graz, Austria (2019). https://doi.org/10.21437/Interspeech.2019-2335
8. Kim, J., Kim, S., Kong, J., Yoon, S.: Glow-TTS: a generative flow for text-to-speech via monotonic alignment search. In: Neural Information Processing Systems. Vancouver, Canada (2020)

9.  Kim, J., Kong, J., Son, J.: Conditional variational autoencoder with adversarial learning for end-to-end text-to-speech. In: International Conference on Machine Learning, pp. 5530–5540 (2021)

10. Kingma, D.P., Ba, J.L.: Adam: a method for stochastic optimization. In: International Conference on Learning Representations, San Diego, USA (2015)

11. Kong, J., Kim, J., Bae, J.: HiFi-GAN: generative adversarial networks for efficient and high fidelity speech synthesis. In: Conference on Neural Information Processing Systems, Vancouver, Canada (2020). http://arxiv.org/abs/2010.05646

12. Liu, L., et al.: On the variance of the adaptive learning rate and beyond. In: International Conference on Learning Representations, Addis Ababa, Ethiopia (2020). http://arxiv.org/abs/1908.03265

13. Loshchilov, I., Hutter, F.: Decoupled weight decay regularization. In: International Conference on Learning Representations, New Orleans, USA (2019)

14. Matoušek, J., Kala, J.: On modelling glottal stop in Czech text-to-speech synthesis. In: Matoušek, V., Mautner, P., Pavelka, T. (eds.) TSD 2005. LNCS (LNAI), vol. 3658, pp. 257–264. Springer, Heidelberg (2005). https://doi.org/10.1007/11551874_33

15. Matoušek, J., Romportl, J.: On building phonetically and prosodically rich speech corpus for text-to-speech synthesis. In: IASTED International Conference on Computational Intelligence, pp. 442–447. San Francisco, USA (2006)

16. Matoušek, J., Tihelka, D.: Annotation errors detection in TTS corpora. In: INTERSPEECH, pp. 1511–1515. Lyon, France (2013)

17. Matoušek, J., Tihelka, D., Romportl, J.: Building of a speech corpus optimised for unit selection TTS synthesis. In: Language Resources and Evaluation Conference, pp. 1296–1299. Marrakech, Morocco (2008)

18. Matoušek, J., Tihelka, D., Romportl, J., Psutka, J.: Slovak unit-selection speech synthesis: creating a new Slovak voice within a Czech TTS system ARTIC. IAENG Int. J. Comput. Sci. **39**(2), 147–154 (2012)

19. Nguyen, M., et al.: TensorflowTTS (2020). https://github.com/TensorSpeech/TensorFlowTTS

20. Nouza, J., Psutka, J., Uhlíř, J.: Phonetic alphabet for speech recognition of Czech. Radioengineering **6**(4), 16–20 (1997)

21. Rao, K., Peng, F., Sak, H., Beaufays, F.: Grapheme-to-phoneme conversion using long short-term memory recurrent neural networks. In: IEEE International Conference on Acoustics Speech and Signal Processing, pp. 4225–4229 (2015). https://doi.org/10.1109/ICASSP.2015.7178767

22. Ren, Y., et al.: FastSpeech 2: fast and high-quality end-to-end text to speech. In: International Conference on Learning Representations (2021)

23. Romportl, J., Matoušek, J.: Formal prosodic structures and their application in NLP. In: Matoušek, V., Mautner, P., Pavelka, T. (eds.) TSD 2005. LNCS (LNAI), vol. 3658, pp. 371–378. Springer, Heidelberg (2005). https://doi.org/10.1007/11551874_48

24. Shen, J., et a;.: Natural TTS synthesis by conditioning WaveNet on mel spectrogram predictions. In: IEEE International Conference on Acoustics Speech and Signal Processing, pp. 4779–4783. Calgary, Canada (2018)

25. Skarnitzl, R.: Allophonic variability in Czech from the perspective of speech synthesis. Akustické listy **24**(1–2), 15–20 (2018)

26. Tan, X., Qin, T., Soong, F.K., Liu, T.Y.: A survey on neural speech synthesis. CoRR abs/2106.1 (2021), https://arxiv.org/abs/2106.15561

27. Tihelka, D., Matoušek, J., Tihelková, A.: How much end-to-end is Tacotron 2 end-to-end TTS system. In: Ekštein, K., Pártl, F., Konopík, M. (eds.) TSD 2021. LNCS (LNAI), vol. 12848, pp. 511–522. Springer, Cham (2021). https://doi.org/10.1007/978-3-030-83527-9_44

28. Vaswani, A., et al.: Attention is all you need. In: Advances in Neural Information Processing Systems, pp. 6000–6010. Long Beach, CA, USA (2017)

29. Vít, J., Hanzlíček, Z., Matoušek, J.: On the analysis of training data for Wavenet-based speech synthesis. In: IEEE International Conference on Acoustics Speech and Signal Processing, pp. 5684–5688. Calgary, Canada (2018). https://doi.org/10.1109/ICASSP.2018.8461960

30. Volín, J., Uhrinová, M., Skarnitzl, R.: The effect of word-initial glottalization on word monitoring in Slovak speakers of English. Res. Lang. **10**(2), 173–181 (2012). https://doi.org/10.2478/v10015-011-0030-0

31. Yang, G., Yang, S., Liu, K., Fang, P., Chen, W., Xie, L.: Multi-band MelGAN: faster waveform generation for high-quality text-to-speech. CoRR abs/2005.0 (2020), https://arxiv.org/abs/2005.05106

32. Yolchuyeva, S., Németh, G., Gyires-Tóth, B.: Transformer based grapheme-to-phoneme conversion. In: INTERSPEECH, pp. 2095–2099. Graz, Austria (2019). https://doi.org/10.21437/Interspeech.2019-1954

33. Řezáčková, M., Švec, J., Tihelka, D.: T5G2P: using text-to-text transfer transformer for grapheme-to-phoneme conversion. In: INTERSPEECH, pp. 6–10. Brno, Czechia (2021). https://doi.org/10.21437/Interspeech.2021-546

# The Influence of Dataset Partitioning on Dysfluency Detection Systems

Sebastian P. Bayerl[1]([⊠]) [ID], Dominik Wagner[1], Elmar Nöth[2][ID], Tobias Bocklet[2], and Korbinian Riedhammer[1][ID]

[1] Technische Hochschule Nürnberg Georg Simon Ohm, Nürnberg, Germany
sebastian.bayerl@ieee.org
[2] Friedrich Alexander Universität Erlangen-Nürnberg, Nürnberg, Germany

**Abstract.** This paper empirically investigates the influence of different data splits and splitting strategies on the performance of dysfluency detection systems. For this, we perform experiments using *wav2vec 2.0* models with a classification head as well as support vector machines (SVM) in conjunction with the features extracted from the *wav2vec 2.0* model to detect dysfluencies. We train and evaluate the systems with different non-speaker-exclusive and speaker-exclusive splits of the Stuttering Events in Podcasts (SEP-28k) dataset to shed some light on the variability of results w.r.t. to the partition method used. Furthermore, we show that the SEP-28k dataset is dominated by only a few speakers, making it difficult to evaluate. To remedy this problem, we created SEP-28k-Extended (SEP-28k-E), containing semi-automatically generated speaker and gender information for the SEP-28k corpus, and suggest different data splits, each useful for evaluating other aspects of methods for dysfluency detection.

**Keywords:** stuttering · dysfluencies · pathological speech · SEP-28k

## 1 Introduction

Stuttering is a speech disorder that negatively affects a person's ability to communicate. Detecting if speech is dysfluent has implications for stuttering self-help applications, monitoring of stuttering behaviour, therapy applications, and enabling speech recognition systems to be more inclusive. Stuttering is highly individual and has a huge inter and intra-person variance w.r.t. the occurrence of symptoms, which among other things, depends on psychological factors, the communication situation, or the linguistic complexity of an utterance [6]. Those properties make the detection of stuttering a very hard problem.

Data scarcity has always been a problem for research on pathological speech in general, even more so with the rise of neural networks, which typically need large amounts of labeled training data. Datasets containing pathological speech are often small, inconsistently labeled, and rarely publicly available. The same was true for stuttering in the past, but recent efforts by various research groups

© Springer Nature Switzerland AG 2022
P. Sojka et al. (Eds.): TSD 2022, LNAI 13502, pp. 423–436, 2022.
https://doi.org/10.1007/978-3-031-16270-1_35

are a step towards resolving the problem of data scarcity and being able to focus on detection methods.

Kourkounakis et al. released LibriStutter, a dataset containing artificially generated stuttered speech with word-level stuttering annotations [10]. Stuttering Events in Podcasts (SEP-28k) is a large corpus consisting of some 28000 clips ($\sim$23 h) annotated with five stuttering event types [11]. The authors also released a relabeled version of the *adults who stutter* subset of FluencyBank using the same annotation scheme, adding another 4000 clips [3,11]. Using a similar labeling approach, Bayerl et al. introduced a therapy-centric dataset of stuttered speech containing data taken from stuttering therapy with an additional label for modified speech, indicating the use of speech technique as it is taught in stuttering therapy [2].

It is good practice to use speaker-exclusive data partitioning when training and testing machine learning systems on pathological speech and paralinguistic tasks (e.g., splits in [18–20]). This data partitioning method prevents that systems learn speaker-specific traits instead of the targeted behaviour. Even when using this data partitioning method, there are many possible combinations of speakers. Ideally, the distributions of classes, the speakers' gender, and age are similar among the train, test, and development sets. If this cannot be guaranteed, $N$-fold cross-validation is a possible way of partitioning the data but will increase the number of experiments necessary $N$ times. Even with cross-validation, speakers in the train and development partition of a fold should not appear in the test partition of the same fold. To be able to compare the performance of different machine learning systems on such a problem, it must be ensured that the data-partitioning can be reproduced [18]. If this is not the case, it is impossible to compare different methods' results. Results reported on unknown, arbitrary splits are not representative and are of little use to other researchers.

In the initial release of SEP-28k, the authors suggest several baseline systems and hint at their data partitioning [11], but unfortunately did not include the splits. There is little metadata available besides the podcast name and episode number the clips were taken from, making it hard to create an ideal speaker-exclusive data split. Using this information only allows for leave-one-podcast out validation, to not include speakers in the test fold that were in the training or development partition. This metadata is available for the relabeled FluencyBank portion of their data, but unfortunately, the baseline results were not reported with the split used.

In this paper, we evaluate the influence of different non-speaker and speaker-exclusive data partitioning methods using a frozen wav2vec 2.0 model with a classification head and use the same features in conjunction with Support Vector Machine (SVM) classifiers. We provide additional insights into the composition of the SEP-28k dataset and describe a process to generate per-episode speaker labels based on manually collected metadata and ECAPA-TDNN embeddings. The additional metadata is made available to the scientific community in an updated release called SEP-28k-Extended. Furthermore, we report baseline results for newly created splits which consider the retrieved metadata.

## 2   Data

In this paper, we use and extend data from the SEP-28k dataset. The dataset consists of 385 podcast episodes taken from eight podcasts revolving around the topic of stuttering. It contains ~28000 3 s long clips extracted from the episodes and labeled with five dysfluency types; blocks, sound repetitions, interjections, word repetitions, and prolongations [11]. The labels are non-exclusive, meaning a clip can be labeled as belonging to more than one class. The initial release of the dataset also contains ~4000 clips extracted from the *adults who stutter* portion of FluencyBank, that were labeled similarly [3,11].

**Table 1.** Distribution of stuttering-related labels in SEP-28k per podcast, total number of clips, and share of the complete dataset.

|  | HVSA | ISW | MSL | SV | ST | SIC | WWS | HS | total |
|---|---|---|---|---|---|---|---|---|---|
| Block | 12.23 | 14.71 | 10.09 | 15.16 | 10.78 | 8.80 | 13.59 | 11.45 | 12.10 |
| Interjection | 33.70 | 20.00 | 13.51 | 6.76 | 23.72 | 22.43 | 21.96 | 26.22 | 21.04 |
| Prolongation | 11.96 | 11.84 | 7.87 | 14.99 | 8.33 | 7.87 | 9.89 | 12.13 | 10.61 |
| Sound repetition | 11.41 | 29.08 | 6.71 | 1.60 | 8.04 | 5.18 | 8.07 | 12.40 | 10.31 |
| Word repetition | 6.66 | 6.32 | 6.46 | 1.95 | 11.45 | 8.35 | 11.38 | 13.90 | 8.31 |
| No stuttered words | 51.49 | 42.41 | 64.77 | 62.52 | 59.46 | 65.94 | 53.34 | 48.72 | 56.08 |
| Total # | 736 | 870 | 2339 | 2308 | 5064 | 4013 | 9163 | 3684 | 28177 |
| % of total | 2.61 | 3.09 | 8.30 | 8.19 | 17.97 | 14.24 | 32.52 | 13.07 | 100.00 |

For this paper, we researched missing metadata from all 385 episode descriptions to extract the number of speakers per episode, i.e., the maximum number of speakers that can be expected in the extracted clips of each episode. A closer examination of the label distribution (see Table 1) of each podcast and the statistics for the whole dataset reveals a large imbalance w.r.t. the distribution of labels between the individual podcasts and the number of clips in the total dataset. A substantial share of clips was extracted from the podcast Women Who Stutter (WWS), about 33% of total clips, followed by three other podcasts that each add ≥10% of total clips. Analysis of the retrieved metadata reveals that the He Stutters (HS) podcast is hosted by the same women as WWS, interviewing men instead of women. Aggregating those two podcasts shows an even greater imbalance, which means that one female speaker could be in up to 46% of total clips. This has a potentially negative effect on the generalisation ability of detection systems trained on this data, even though the dataset is rather big. For experiments in this paper, we will therefore treat the two podcasts as one.

# 3   Methods

## 3.1   Classification Experiments

We chose a simple experimental design based on the *wav2vec 2.0* (W2V2) model to evaluate the influence of data partitioning on the detection of atypical speech patterns. W2V2 features have shown robust performance in several speech tasks, such as speech recognition, speech emotion recognition, and mispronunciation detection [1,15,25].

We use a W2V2 model that was pre-trained in an unsupervised manner on 960 h of unlabeled speech data from the LibriSpeech corpus [13] and later fine-tuned for automatic speech recognition (ASR) on the transcripts of the same data. The weights for the model were published by [1]. The model yields different hidden representations after each of the models' twelve transformer blocks. Depending on the location in the processing hierarchy, the model has encoded different information into the representations, with embeddings from lower layers having basic speech information encoded and higher layers encoding information closer to phonemic information. The W2V2 model uses the self-attention mechanism that helps the model focus on relevant parts of the input sequence, w.r.t. the learning objective [23]. The hidden representations have information about their relationship to other vectors in the extraction context encoded. The model takes the raw wave-form audio as its inputs and yields 768-dimensional speech representations for roughly every 0.02s of audio, yielding 149 vectors for every 3s long clip in the dataset.

For our experiments, we used pre-trained W2V2 models with a classification head equivalent to the implementation from the Transformers library [24]. The classification head consists of a mean-pooling operation, pooling model outputs over the time dimension, yielding a single 768-dimensional vector for every audio clip. The pooling operation is followed by a 256-dimensional dense projection layer and a classification layer.

The same model is also used to extract the contextual W2V2 embeddings as input features for training Support Vector Machine (SVM) classifiers, as they allow quick experimentation and can learn from only a few samples. We extract W2V2 features for each audio clip and, similar to the mean-pooling operation in the classification head described previously, take the mean over the time dimension, yielding one 768-dimensional vector for every 3s long audio clip.

## 3.2   ECAPA-TDNN

The Emphasized Channel Attention, Propagation, and Aggregation - Time Delay Neural Network (ECAPA-TDNN) architecture builds on the x-vector architecture for speaker identification and proposes several enhancements [5,21]. The two main modifications are 1-dimensional Res2Net [7] modules with skip connections and squeeze-and-excitation (SE) [8] blocks to capture channel interdependencies. Furthermore, features are aggregated and propagated across multiple layers.

We use the ECAPA-TDNN implementation from [16]. The model was trained on the VoxCeleb dataset [12]. The training data is augmented with additive noises from the MUSAN corpus [22] and reverberation using a collection of room impulse responses [9]. It uses 80-dimensional Mel Frequency Cepstral Coefficients (MFCC) with a frame width of 25 ms and a frame-shift of 10 ms as its' inputs. Additionally, the data is speed-perturbed at 95% and 105% of the normal utterance speed, and the SpecAugment [14] method is applied in the time domain.

### 3.3   Metadata Retrieval

We use the ECAPA-TDNN embeddings to automatically generate speaker labels for each of the clips in the SEP-28k dataset, allowing more granular speaker exclusive splits than on the podcast. The assignment of a speaker to individual audio clips is accomplished in an unsupervised manner using K-Means clustering and silhouette analysis [17].

We employ silhouette analysis to assess the distance of separation between clusters without ground truth labels being available. The silhouette coefficient $s$ for an individual data point $x$ is given by $s_x = (b-a)(\max(a,b))^{-1}$. The variable $a$ represents the average distance between the sample and all other points in the same cluster. The variable $b$ is the mean distance between the sample and all other points in the nearest cluster.

The measure has a value range of $[-1, 1]$. Silhouette coefficients close to $+1$ indicate that the sample is far away from neighboring clusters and therefore likely assigned correctly. A value of 0 indicates that the sample is close to the decision boundary between two neighboring clusters and negative values indicate that those samples might have been assigned to the wrong cluster.

Silhouette analysis can also be used to determine the optimal number of clusters. For a set of cluster values $k \in \{m, \ldots, n\} \subset \mathbb{N}_{>0}$, the optimal number of clusters $k_{opt}$ can be chosen as the one that maximizes the global average silhouette coefficient. We employ this method to episodes where the number of guests could not be determined.

The process of generating speaker labels and determining podcast hosts starts with the extraction of high-dimensional ($\mathbb{R}^{192}$) speaker embeddings from the trained ECAPA-TDNN model. We collect all embeddings belonging to one podcast, preprocess the embeddings, and subsequently cluster them using the K-Means algorithm. The preprocessing pipeline involves removing the mean, scaling to unit variance, and dimensionality reduction using Principal Component Analysis (PCA). We reduce the embedding dimensionality to $\mathbb{R}^4$, since it led to more robust distance computations, while the principal components still explained ~33% of total variance.

We assume that the largest cluster for each podcast belongs to the podcast's host. This assumption is reasonable as most podcasts have the same host, who speaks across multiple episodes, while the guests and co-hosts vary across different episodes. After preprocessing and clustering, we obtain the cluster centroids and select the one belonging to the largest cluster. The centroid of the host cluster serves as a prototype vector, against which other clip-level representations are compared to determine whether they belong to the host.

We also fit individual cluster models for each podcast episode. The preprocessing and clustering steps are equivalent to the host centroid creation. In this case, the K-Means algorithm is applied to embeddings representing clips from a the same podcast episode. The resulting cluster labels serve as labels for the different speakers in an episode. The cluster centroids obtained on the episode-level are then compared to the global host centroids to determine which cluster label belongs to the host speaker. We compute the cosine distance between the global host centroid of the podcast and each centroid representing a cluster in a specific podcast episode. The smallest cosine distance indicates which cluster label is the best candidate for the host speaker.

### 3.4  Quality Criteria

We analyze the quality of the automatically generated speaker labels based on the sample-specific silhouette score, average per-episode silhouette score, and the variance ratio criterion [4]. An overview of those quality measures can be found in Table 2. The measures and their respective per clip and episode values are included in the metadata published with this work. Depending on the desired quality level of the speaker labels, it is possible to exclude clips for stricter evaluation.

**Table 2.** Statistics for cluster quality measures aggregated across all podcast episodes in SEP-28k containing more than one speaker.

| Model | Measure | Mean | Standard Deviation | Minimum | Maximum |
|---|---|---|---|---|---|
| | Silhouette Score | 0.46 | 0.09 | 0.17 | 0.68 |
| K-Means | Variance Ratio | 69.50 | 83.06 | 8.52 | 406.21 |
| | Cosine Distance | 0.34 | 0.46 | 0.00 | 1.96 |

Higher sample-specific silhouette scores indicate that the speaker label is more likely to be assigned correctly. The average silhouette score can be used to assess the assignment quality within full podcast episodes. The absence of clusters where all sample-specific scores are below the average silhouette score for the cluster, can be a quality indicator. For instance, clips belonging to an episode could be excluded if not all $k$ clusters contain at least one sample with an above-average silhouette score.

The variance ratio criterion defined in [4] measures how well-defined clusters are. For a dataset $D$ with $n_D$ elements, which has been divided into $k$ clusters, the variance ratio criterion $v$ is defined as the ratio of the between-cluster dispersion and the within-cluster dispersion for all clusters. A threshold could be set to filter out episodes with less well-defined clusters. The score is higher when clusters are dense and well separated.

We chose to use K-Means for clustering instead of Gaussian Mixture Models (GMM), as we found the slightly better quality criteria (e.g., average silhouette score of 0.46 vs. 0.44). The impact of setting different thresholds for silhouette score and variance ratio is illustrated in Table 3. The two columns under *Combined Fulfilled* show the number of podcast episodes in which *all three* quality criteria are fulfilled, and their share of the total number of episodes. The three criteria are also shown individually under *Standalone Fulfilled*. The first criterion measures the number of episodes in which at least one sample silhouette score in each of the episodes' clusters is above the average silhouette score. The criterion is independent of the thresholds of the other criteria and therefore remains constant. The second and third criteria measure the number of episodes where the average silhouette score and the variance ratio are above the threshold displayed below the *Threshold* columns.

## 4  SEP-28k-Extended

The extended data set created for this paper, SEP-28k-Extended (SEP-28k-E), is available online.[1] It contains information about the gender and number of speakers to expect in the clips taken from each episode, and a label, identifying the podcast hosts. The dataset repository contains the original content of SEP-28k with the additional metadata and instructions for using the data.

**Table 3.** Impact of varying silhouette score and variance ratio thresholds on the quality of speaker labels obtained using K-Means clustering. Thirty-three episodes were excluded from the analysis since they contained only one speaker. The numbers below indicate the number of episodes meeting the specified quality criterion thresholds.

| Threshold | | Standalone Fulfilled | | | Combined Fulfilled | |
|---|---|---|---|---|---|---|
| Silhouette Score | Variance Ratio | 1. All Above Average | 2. Silhouette Score | 3. Variance Ratio | Episodes | % of Total |
| 0.20 | 10 | 278 | 332 | 331 | 270 | 76.7% |
| 0.30 | 20 | 278 | 317 | 281 | 234 | 66.5% |
| 0.40 | 30 | 278 | 272 | 197 | 166 | 47.2% |
| 0.50 | 40 | 278 | 123 | 135 | 72 | 20.5% |

---

[1] https://github.com/th-nuernberg/ml-stuttering-events-dataset-extended.

**Table 4.** Shares of clips that belong to podcast hosts in the SEP-28k dataset.

| Podcast | Host | Clips | Host Share | % of total clips | Cumulative |
|---|---|---|---|---|---|
| WomenWhoStutter | Pamela Mertz | 9163 | 69.2% | 22.63% | 22.63% |
| HeStutters | Pamela Mertz | 3684 | 71.5% | 9.40% | 32.02% |
| StutterTalk | Peter Reitzes | 5064 | 63.2% | 11.42% | 43.45% |
| StutteringIsCool | Daniele Rossi | 3853 | 66.6% | 9.16% | 52.60% |
| MyStutteringLife | Pedro Peña | 2339 | 79.4% | 6.63% | 59.23% |
| HVSA | TJ Travor | 736 | 53.0% | 1.39% | 60.62% |
| IStutterSoWhat | Evan Sherman | 870 | 43.8% | 1.36% | 61.98% |

## 4.1 Speaker Imbalance

Across all 385 podcast episodes, there are 42 (11%) episodes in which the estimated speaking time of a single speaker (most likely the host) is above 90% and 92 (24%) episodes in which the estimated speaking time is above 80%. This indicates that the dataset is dominated by a few speakers, which possibly has a detrimental influence on the generalisation ability and validity of evaluation results. Table 4 shows the share of clips belonging to various podcast hosts relative to the total number of clips in a podcast. The StrongVoices (SV) podcast has two hosts, which makes the automatic assignment of a cluster label to the host speaker more difficult, so we excluded it from the analysis. There are about 500 unique speakers in the dataset, but Table 4 displays the strong dominance of only four speakers, which are in 59% of all clips (see column *Cumulative*). This makes it very difficult to split the dataset so that it does not introduce a strong bias w.r.t. the dominant speakers.

## 4.2 Data Partitioning Considering Metadata

This section briefly describes four different speaker-exclusive dataset splits, that were created considering the peculiarities of SEP-28k. Each split has its purpose and tests another facet of a detection method. The priorities for creating test, development, and training set, in order, where speaker-exclusiveness, label distribution, and gender distribution; statistics for the newly created splits can be viewed in Table 5.

The **SEP-12k** split consists of about 12,000 clips taken from the original dataset. These are all clips that are not associated with the top-four dominant speakers. We suggest evaluating the split using five-fold cross-validation without overlapping speakers between the folds. The use of this split tests a method's ability to use many speakers with only few samples for training while also evaluating the method on many unseen speakers.

The **SEP-28k-E** split is partitioned into training, development, and test. The training partition contains only clips belonging to the top-four dominant speakers. The split can be used to test a method's ability to learn from many examples provided by few speakers.

The **SEP-28k-T** and **SEP-28k-D** splits are similar to each other as well as to SEP-28k-E. They can be used to evaluate a model's capability to train on

**Table 5.** Composition of train, test and development set of SEP-28k-E and SEP-12k

|  | SEP-28k-E train | SEP-28k-E dev | SEP-28k-E test | SEP-12k |
|---|---|---|---|---|
| Block | 11.57 % | 12.84 % | 12.01 % | 12.48 % |
| Interjection | 22.94 % | 18.79 % | 19.51 % | 19.10 % |
| Prolongation | 9.87 % | 10.07 % | 10.13 % | 10.15 % |
| Sound repetition | 8.13 % | 10.40 % | 6.69 % | 8.57 % |
| Word repetitions | 9.98 % | 8.79 % | 10.48 % | 9.67 % |
| No stuttered words | 56.92 % | 55.78 % | 58.15 % | 56.81 % |
| Total # | 15213 | 6402 | 6562 | 12804 |

relatively few samples by many different speakers and review its performance on only a few speakers with many samples. The test partition consists of the four dominant speakers, and the development and training set are an equal size split of the remaining clips. SEP-28k-D uses the same partitioning as SEP-28k-T but switches the test and development partitions.

## 5 Experiments

The experiments described in this section are formulated as binary classification tasks that vary mostly w.r.t. the data partitioning used. To evaluate the influence of different data partitioning strategies on classification results, we performed experiments using a classification head on top of a frozen W2V2 feature extractor, and SVM classifiers with radial basis function (rbf) kernels on seven different data-partitioning strategies; a leave-one-podcast-out strategy, speaker agnostic five- and ten-fold cross-validation, three different balanced, speaker separated train/validation/test splits considering the additional metadata from SEP-28k-E, and five-fold speaker-separated cross-validation on the SEP-12k subset. All results reported are F1-scores for the dysfluency classes, which is the harmonic mean of precision and recall and was also used for evaluation of the baseline systems by the original authors of SEP-28k [11].

The leave-one-podcast-out strategy uses data from all podcasts for training and validation and uses data from the podcast that was left out for testing. Both podcasts, He Stutters and Women Who Stutter, have the same host; we, therefore treat them as one podcast labeled as HeShe in the classification experiments. Both cross-validation splits are performed completely agnostic to the speaker and podcast label. All cross-validation experiments were performed five times. We report the mean and the respective standard deviation of these results.

The training uses a single weighted cross-entropy loss term with an initial learning rate of 0.001, a batch size of 200, training for up to 200 epochs using the adam optimizer, with early stopping if the development loss is not decreasing for 10 epochs. The optimal position of the classification head after W2V2 transformer layer $L$ was determined from $L \in \{1, 2, \ldots, 12\}$ using cross-validation on the respective development partition.

**Table 6.** Results (F1-Scores) for experiments with leave-one-podcast-out evaluation. Column headers are indicating the podcast name used as test-set.

|  |  | HVSA | ISW | MSL | SV | ST | SIC | HeShe | Mean (std) |
|---|---|---|---|---|---|---|---|---|---|
| | Blocks | 0.34 | 0.37 | 0.32 | 0.40 | 0.33 | 0.29 | 0.36 | 0.34 (0.03) |
| | Interjections | 0.73 | 0.68 | 0.62 | 0.48 | 0.73 | 0.71 | 0.70 | 0.66 (0.08) |
| SVM | Prolongations | 0.53 | 0.50 | 0.46 | 0.54 | 0.45 | 0.44 | 0.44 | 0.48 (0.04) |
| | Sound repetitions | 0.39 | 0.70 | 0.38 | 0.19 | 0.45 | 0.36 | 0.41 | 0.41 (0.14) |
| | Word repetitions | 0.34 | 0.35 | 0.43 | 0.31 | 0.50 | 0.42 | 0.49 | 0.41 (0.07) |
| | Blocks | 0.19 | 0.21 | 0.16 | 0.23 | 0.19 | 0.15 | 0.17 | 0.19 (0.03) |
| | Interjections | 0.65 | 0.63 | 0.58 | 0.44 | 0.71 | 0.68 | 0.68 | 0.62 (0.09) |
| NN | Prolongations | 0.42 | 0.37 | 0.44 | 0.45 | 0.31 | 0.40 | 0.39 | 0.40 (0.05) |
| | Sound Repetitions | 0.27 | 0.62 | 0.40 | 0.14 | 0.38 | 0.36 | 0.37 | 0.36 (0.14) |
| | Word Repetitions | 0.25 | 0.26 | 0.42 | 0.34 | 0.42 | 0.37 | 0.40 | 0.35 (0.07) |

The optimal hyperparameters and input features for the SVM classifiers were determined using grid search in five-fold cross-validation on the respective development sets described in Sect. 2. The kernel parameter $\gamma$ was selected from the set $\gamma \in \{10^{-k} \mid k = 1, \ldots, 4\} \subset \mathbb{R}_{>0}$, the regularisation parameter $C$ was selected from $C \in \{1, 10, 100\} \subset \mathbb{N}_{>0}$, and the W2V2 extraction layer $L$ was selected from $L \in \{1, 2, \ldots, 12\}$.

## 5.1  Results

We observed that across most experiments, using the SVM on the extracted W2V2 features outperforms the simple mean-pooling based classification head (NN). Analyzing results on the podcast level, as done in Table 6, reveals a wide spread of results, with relative differences of up to 37% for blocks, 52% for interjections, 20% for prolongations, 268% for sound repetitions, and 61% for word repetitions.

Table 7 contrasts the results for the speaker agnostic splits (5/10-fold-cv), the average results over the leave-one-podcast-out (LOPO) cross-validation(CV), SEP12k-CV results, and the three train-development-test splits described in Sect. 4.2. Results on the speaker agnostic CV splits are slightly more optimistic than the LOPO results except in one case. The effect is more pronounced in the experiments using the neural network classification head on top of the W2V2 model. Each CV result reported, is to be interpreted as the mean of five unique CV runs, each using different random seeds for splitting. Results for ten-fold CV and five-fold CV are very similar and vary only slightly across multiple validation runs, which is indicated by the small standard deviation of the results, and also shows that results are converging after multiple runs. Experimental results of prolongations are an outlier, being the only time LOPO results are greater than 5- and ten-fold CV.

Results for NN on the SEP-28k-E split are among the best for word repetitions and prolongations and are overall slightly optimistic compared to LOPO, SEP28k-T, SEP-28k-D, and SEP-12k results. SVMs achieve decent performance

**Table 7.** Results (F1-scores) for non-speaker exclusive cross-validation experiments, leave-one-podcast-out (LOPO), five-fold CV results on SEP-12k, and three different speaker exclusive splits from SEP-28k-E, omitting "SEP" in the interest of brevity. LOPO and CV results are reported in the formant mean (std).(Bl=block, Pro=prolongation, Wd=word repetition, In=interjection)

| | | 5-fold CV | 10-fold CV | LOPO | SEP-12k | 28k-E | 28k-T | 28k-D |
|---|---|---|---|---|---|---|---|---|
| | **Bl** | **0.36** (0.03) | **0.36** (0.03) | 0.34 (0.03) | 0.34 (0.02) | 0.33 | 0.33 | 0.33 |
| | **In** | **0.71** (0.01) | **0.71** (0.01) | 0.66 (0.08) | 0.64 (0.03) | 0.68 | 0.70 | 0.70 |
| SVM | **Pro** | 0.46 (0.02) | 0.47 (0.02) | **0.48** (0.04) | 0.44 (0.03) | 0.46 | 0.43 | 0.44 |
| | **Snd** | 0.46 (0.05) | **0.47** (0.03) | 0.41 (0.14) | 0.41 (0.06) | 0.39 | 0.41 | 0.42 |
| | **Wd** | 0.51 (0.03) | **0.52** (0.03) | 0.41 (0.07) | 0.42 (0.05) | 0.51 | 0.45 | 0.45 |
| | **Bl** | **0.22** (0.02) | **0.22** (0.02) | 0.19 (0.03) | 0.22 (0.05) | 0.19 | 0.19 | 0.21 |
| | **In** | **0.69** (0.01) | **0.69** (0.02) | 0.62 (0.09) | 0.66 (0.02) | 0.65 | 0.69 | 0.70 |
| NN | **Pro** | **0.41** (0.02) | **0.41** (0.02) | 0.40 (0.05) | 0.40 (0.04) | **0.41** | 0.39 | 0.39 |
| | **Snd** | **0.43** (0.02) | 0.42 (0.03) | 0.36 (0.14) | 0.38 (0.03) | 0.39 | 0.37 | 0.38 |
| | **Wd** | 0.44 (0.02) | 0.44 (0.03) | 0.35 (0.07) | 0.40 (0.01) | **0.46** | 0.39 | 0.40 |

on SEP-28k-E, with overall results slightly less optimistic than the speaker agnostic CV experiments. Compared to the SEP-12k evaluation scenario, results on SEP-28k-E are slightly better for interjections and prolongations, substantially better for word repetitions, and slightly worse for sound repetitions and blocks, but within the expected deviation.

## 5.2 Discussion

It is hard to directly compare the results of all splits and strategies introduced in this paper, as they vary greatly w.r.t. the amount of training data and their speaker composition. Results from the experiments utilizing the LOPO strategy reveal that evaluation results on unique splits can vary considerably, and there is potential for cherry-picking particularly favourable subsets for reporting results. There are many possible splits and there will never be only one perfect evaluation strategy. Despite this, common ground has to be established; otherwise, it is not possible to compare methods. For a fair evaluation that makes sure that systems detect dysfluencies reliably and independent of the speaker, it is paramount to avoid having audio samples of speakers in the test set that are either in the development or training set. In scenarios such as long-term monitoring, it might be advisable to adapt models to a speaker, but this requires different methods, datasets, and evaluation scenarios. This is supported by the slightly optimistic results on the speaker agnostic CV splits.

Keeping in mind what gets evaluated using a certain data split or evaluation method is important when comparing the results of different methods for dysfluency detection. The five-fold CV experiments on the SEP-12k subset, consisting of speech from many speakers, consistently yield lower F1-scores across most experiments. Even though less training data was used for training and testing, these experiments indicate that speaker-independent splits can lead to worse results. SVMs can learn solid decision boundaries from only a few good representatives, which at least makes the SVM results a fair comparison.

The problem of the speaker imbalance in the dataset cannot be solved for the whole dataset, no matter which speaker-exclusive split is used, as the dominant speakers, almost certainly bias the training process, no matter in which data partition they are. An ideal speaker-independent evaluation would be a leave-one-speaker-out evaluation, but this is not feasible for large datasets with many unique speakers and would probably harm overall progress in the interest of supposed maximum fairness.

Therefore, we suggest using the SEP-28k-E split for swift and easy development with a fixed train-test-validation split. Still, this does not guarantee perfect generalisation, as it is only trained on a few speakers, but the development- and test-set vary considerably and can hopefully provide realistic results. When adapting the weights of a neural network pre-trained on data from a few speakers with transfer learning, we expect that even a few out-of-domain samples from multiple speakers will lead to greater generalisation.

The approach in this paper is limited w.r.t. the classification methods used, that was not specifically tailored for each dysfluency type. Therefore results vary greatly for different dysfluency types. Especially those that need longer temporal context or a higher temporal-resolution, such as word-repetitions, and blocks suffer from the method employed. Still, all experiments achieve above chance-level results [11], making the demonstrated differences based on multiple data partitionings meaningful. Even though, we strongly believe that the semi-automatically generated speaker labels are valid, there are limitations. The splits created and used here did use the least restrictive clustering criteria in order to keep all training data. Some episodes have hosts from other podcasts appearing as guests, or episodes of, e.g., StutterTalk feature former guests as hosts for some episodes. We tried to account for this with manual rules but are aware that this speaker separation will not be perfect. If one seeks maximum speaker independence, the meta data and quality metrics provided allow the exclusion of such clips.

## 6    Conclusion

SEP-28k is a very valuable resource when working on new methods and applications for dysfluency detection systems because it significantly increases the amount of training data available, but one has to be aware of peculiarities that might lead to problems. This paper contributed important insights into working with the SEP-28k dataset. We created and published SEP-28k-Extended, as an addition to one of the largest freely available resources containing labeled stuttered speech. It provides semi-automatically generated speaker labels obtained using K-Means clustering on ECAPA-TDNN speaker representations. The speaker labels are accompanied by quality metrics for these automatically generated speaker labels, enabling the creation of new speaker-independent splits with different levels of strictness. We hope to raise awareness about potential problems when working with SEP-28k and provide potential remedies to a few.

Based on the generated and retrieved metadata, we suggest five different possible splits, each with a different evaluation goal alongside baseline results. Thus, establishing common ground for the future evaluation of dysfluency detection methods using the SEP-28k dataset.

# References

1. Baevski, A., Zhou, Y., Mohamed, A., Auli, M.: Wav2Vec 2.0: a framework for self-supervised learning of speech representations. In: Larochelle, H., et al. (eds.) Advances in Neural Information Processing Systems, vol. 33, pp. 12449–12460. Curran Associates, Inc. (2020)
2. Bayerl, S.P., von Gudenberg, A.W., Hönig, F., Nöth, E., Riedhammer, K.: KSoF: the Kassel state of fluency dataset - a therapy centered dataset of stuttering. arXiv:2203.05383 [cs, eess] (2022)
3. Bernstein Ratner, N., MacWhinney, B.: Fluency bank: a new resource for fluency research and practice. J. Fluency Disord. **56**, 69–80 (2018)
4. Caliński, T., Harabasz, J.: A dendrite method for cluster analysis. Commun. Stat. **3**(1), 1–27 (1974). https://doi.org/10.1080/03610927408827101
5. Desplanques, B., Thienpondt, J., Demuynck, K.: ECAPA-TDNN: emphasized channel attention, propagation and aggregation in TDNN based speaker verification. In: Proceedings of INTERSPEECH 2020, pp. 3830–3834 (2020)
6. Ellis, J.B., Ramig, P.R.: A handbook on stuttering. J. Fluency Disord. **34**(4), 295–299 (2009). https://doi.org/10.1016/j.jfludis.2009.10.004
7. Gao, S., Cheng, M., Zhao, K., Zhang, X., Yang, M., Torr, P.: Res2net: a new multi-scale backbone architecture. IEEE Trans. Pattern Anal. Mach. Intell. **43**(02), 652–662 (2021)
8. Hu, J., Shen, L., Sun, G.: Squeeze-and-excitation networks. In: 2018 IEEE/CVF Conference on Computer Vision and Pattern Recognition, pp. 7132–7141 (2018)
9. Ko, T., Peddinti, V., Povey, D., Seltzer, M.L., Khudanpur, S.: A study on data augmentation of reverberant speech for robust speech recognition. In: 2017 IEEE International Conference on Acoustics, Speech and Signal Processing (ICASSP), pp. 5220–5224 (2017). https://doi.org/10.1109/ICASSP.2017.7953152
10. Kourkounakis, T.: LibriStutter (2021). https://doi.org/10.5683/SP3/NKVOGQ
11. Lea, C., Mitra, V., Joshi, A., Kajarekar, S., Bigham, J.P.: SEP-28k: a dataset for stuttering event detection from podcasts with people who stutter. In: ICASSP 2021 - 2021 IEEE International Conference on Acoustics, Speech and Signal Processing (ICASSP), pp. 6798–6802. IEEE, Toronto (2021)
12. Nagrani, A., Chung, J.S., Zisserman, A.: Voxceleb: a large-scale speaker identification dataset. In: INTERSPEECH (2017)
13. Panayotov, V., Chen, G., Povey, D., Khudanpur, S.: Librispeech: an ASR corpus based on public domain audio books. In: 2015 IEEE International Conference on Acoustics, Speech and Signal Processing (ICASSP). IEEE (2015)
14. Park, D.S., et al.: SpecAugment: a simple data augmentation method for automatic speech recognition. In: INTERSPEECH 2019 (2019). https://doi.org/10.21437/interspeech.2019-2680

15. Pepino, L., Riera, P., Ferrer, L.: Emotion recognition from speech using Wav2Vec 2.0 embeddings. In: INTERSPEECH 2021, pp. 3400–3404. ISCA (2021)

16. Ravanelli, M., Parcollet, T., Plantinga, P., et al., A.R.: SpeechBrain: a general-purpose speech toolkit (2021). arXiv preprint arXiv:2106.04624

17. Rousseeuw, P.J.: Silhouettes: a graphical aid to the interpretation and validation of cluster analysis. J. Comput. Appl. Math. **20**, 53–65 (1987)

18. Schuller, B., Batliner, A.: Computational Paralinguistics: Emotion, Affect and Personality in Speech and Language Processing, 1st edn. Wiley, Hoboken (2014)

19. Schuller, B., Steidl, S., Batliner, A., et al.: The INTERSPEECH 2018 computational paralinguistics challenge: atypical and self-assessed affect, crying and heart beats. In: INTERSPEECH 2018. ISCA (2018)

20. Schuller, B., et al.: The INTERSPEECH 2016 computational paralinguistics challenge: deception, sincerity and native language. In: Proceedings of INTERSPEECH 2016, pp. 2001–2005 (2016)

21. Snyder, D., Garcia-Romero, D., Sell, G., Povey, D., Khudanpur, S.: X-Vectors: robust DNN embeddings for speaker recognition. In: 2018 IEEE International Conference on Acoustics, Speech and Signal Processing (ICASSP), pp. 5329–5333 (2018). https://doi.org/10.1109/ICASSP.2018.8461375

22. Snyder, D., Chen, G., Povey, D.: MUSAN: a music, speech, and noise corpus (2015). arXiv preprint arXiv: 1510.08484v1

23. Vaswani, A., Shazeer, N., et al.: Attention is all you need. In: Guyon, I., et al. (eds.) Advances in Neural Information Processing Systems, vol. 30 (2017)

24. Wolf, T., Debut, L., Sanh, V., et al.: Transformers: state-of-the-art natural language processing. In: Proceedings of the 2020 Conference on Empirical Methods in Natural Language Processing: System Demonstrations, pp. 38–45. Association for Computational Linguistics (2020)

25. Xu, X., Kang, Y., Cao, S., Lin, B., Ma, L.: Explore wav2vec 2.0 for Mispronunciation Detection. In: INTERSPEECH 2021, pp. 4428–4432. ISCA (2021)

# Going Beyond the Cookie Theft Picture Test: Detecting Cognitive Impairments Using Acoustic Features

Franziska Braun[1]([✉]), Andreas Erzigkeit[2], Hartmut Lehfeld[3],
Thomas Hillemacher[3], Korbinian Riedhammer[1], and Sebastian P. Bayerl[1]

[1] Technische Hochschule Nürnberg Georg Simon Ohm, Nuremberg, Germany
`franziska.braun@th-nuernberg.de`
[2] Psychiatrische Klinik und Psychotherapie, Universitätsklinikum Erlangen,
Erlangen, Germany
[3] Klinik für Psychiatrie und Psychotherapie, Universitätsklinik der Paracelsus
Medizinischen Privatuniversität, Klinikum Nürnberg, Nuremberg, Germany

**Abstract.** Standardized tests play a crucial role in the detection of cognitive impairment. Previous work demonstrated that automatic detection of cognitive impairment is possible using audio data from a standardized picture description task. The presented study goes beyond that, evaluating our methods on data taken from two standardized neuropsychological tests, namely the German SKT and a German version of the CERAD-NB, and a semi-structured clinical interview between a patient and a psychologist. For the tests, we focus on speech recordings of three subtests: reading numbers (SKT 3), interference (SKT 7), and verbal fluency (CERAD-NB 1). We show that acoustic features from standardized tests can be used to reliably discriminate cognitively impaired individuals from non-impaired ones. Furthermore, we provide evidence that even features extracted from random speech samples of the interview can be a discriminator of cognitive impairment. In our baseline experiments, we use OpenSMILE features and Support Vector Machine classifiers. In an improved setup, we show that using wav2vec 2.0 features instead, we can achieve an accuracy of up to 85%.

**Keywords:** dementia screening · pathological speech · paralinguistics · neuropsychological tests

## 1 Introduction

In geriatric patients, dementia represents one of the most common condition seen in the psychiatric consultation service of a general hospital. According to the WHO, over 55 million people worldwide were living with dementia in 2020 [28]. This number will nearly double every 20 years, reaching 78 million in 2030 and 139 million in 2050. The estimated annual global cost of dementia currently

© Springer Nature Switzerland AG 2022
P. Sojka et al. (Eds.): TSD 2022, LNAI 13502, pp. 437–448, 2022.
https://doi.org/10.1007/978-3-031-16270-1_36

exceeds US\$ 1.3 trillion and is expected to rise to US\$ 2.8 trillion by 2050, of which more than half is care costs.

Dementia is characterized by a loss or decline of function; in addition to memory impairments, patients exhibit one or more of aphasia, apraxia, agnosia or impairments of executive function. These symptoms can relate to different neurological conditions (e.g., Alzheimer's). Due to its typically insidious onset, dementia is in many cases detected too late. Early diagnostic clarification with the resulting possibility of a rapid start of treatment is key to slowing the progression of dementia and thus achieving a gain in quality of life for the patient and their family caregivers. Dementia screening and monitoring enable early detection, classification and tracking of cognitive decline.

In addition to medical examinations (e.g., brain imaging), a combination of medical and psychological history taking, cognitive testing, and the use of rating scales is the gold standard for dementia screening in clinical or research settings [9]. To that end, standardized tests play a key role in clinical routine since they aim at minimizing subjectivity by measuring performance on a variety of cognitive tasks. Tests typically target both short- and long-term memory and cover tasks such as naming, memorizing, counting and recalling objects, or general situational awareness. The widely used Mini Mental State Examination (MMSE), the Clock Drawing Test (CDT), the Mini-Cog test, the German SKT [26], among other cognitive scales have gained acceptance since they are brief while still showing good sensitivity and specificity [25]. Neuropsychological test batteries such as the Boston Diagnostic Aphasia Exam (BDAE) [7]) and the CERAD-NB [18] evaluate various perceptual modalities (auditory, visual, gestural), processing functions (comprehension, analysis, problem-solving), and response modalities (writing, articulation, manipulation). They include common sub-tests such as the Cookie Theft Picture Test (CTP), the Boston Naming Test (BNT), and the Verbal Fluency Test (VFT). Additionally, history taking interviews assist in looking for further dementia indicators related to activities of daily living (ADL), mood, physical activity and more. Such interviews and tests are administered by trained physicians or psychologists who spend about 30–60 min with the patient. With waiting times for appointments frequently exceeding six months, automated dementia screening could help to monitor patients closely and prioritize urgent cases for in-person appointments.

The automation of dementia screening based on speech is an area of high interest; it was previously covered by the ADReSS and ADReSSo challenges [16,17]. Previous work shows strong evidence for the effectiveness of speech-based screening in dementia patients, even at early stages, and focuses primarily on the publicly available DementiaBank [5]. [2,13,15,16,20] obtained convincing results on spontaneous speech of the CTP from the BDAE. Free recall tasks of visual material, such as the CTP, have the advantage of eliciting speech on a common topic, making it more self-contained and thus easier to process. The same is true for elicited speech based on free recall tasks from moving images, such as short films [27]. Most work uses either fluency [12,14] or deep speech markers [17] for classification, as these show high selectivity for discriminating patients with cognitive impairment from healthy controls.

This paper describes and reports the results of baseline experiments on the automated evaluation of a semi-structured clinical interview and three standardized sub-tests from the Syndrom-Kurz-Test (SKT, translates to "Syndrome Short Test") and the Consortium to Establish a Register for Alzheimer's Disease Neuropsychological Battery (CERAD-NB). The speech data used in the experiments comprise 101 recordings of conversations between patients and psychologists collected during dementia screening sessions at the Memory Clinic of the Department of Psychiatry and Psychotherapy, Nuremberg Hospital in Germany. In our experiments, Support Vector Machine (SVM) classifiers are used in conjunction with openSMILE (OS) and wav2vec 2.0 (W2V2) features to test the feasibility of using speech data to automatically evaluate three sub-tests and categorize patients into cognitively impaired and non-impaired. In addition, we investigate whether this classification is possible using short segments of spontaneous speech extracted from the clinical interview.

## 2   Data

All dementia screenings were carried out at the Memory Clinic ("Gedächtnissprechstunde") of the Department of Psychiatry and Psychotherapy, Nuremberg Hospital, Germany.[1] From an ongoing recording effort, to date, a total of 101 recordings of German-speaking subjects aged 55 to 88 years ($\mu = 73.9 \pm 8.5$) have been acquired (40 male, 61 female). Their medical diagnoses range from no or mild cognitive impairment to mild and moderate dementia. The fact that the data includes patients with no cognitive impairment despite being referred to the Memory Clinic makes this data set somewhat unique: typically, such "healthy controls" would be recruited separately.

All participants underwent a three-part screening procedure: clinical interview (cf. Sect. 2.2); SKT and CERAD-NB tests; two questionnaires for self-assessment of mood (GDS-K: Geriatric Depression Scale Short Form) and activities of daily living (B-ADL: Bayer-Activities of Daily Living Scale).

Data includes labels for SKT and CERAD-NB sub- and total scores, both as raw and normalized values, as well as coded medical and psychological diagnoses (work in progress). Metadata includes sex, age, smoker/non-smoker, medication (antidementives, antidepressants, analgesics), GDS-K, B-ADL (self and informant assessment), NPI (Neuropsychiatric Inventory, informant assessment), IQ-range (below average, <90; average, 90–110; above average, >110), and years of education. Furthermore, we labeled the data with start and end times for each of the sub-tests.

The audio recordings consist of 83.3 h of speech and were performed with a Zoom H2n Handy Recorder in XY stereophonic mode, positioned between the patient and the psychologist in such a way that level differences between the

---

[1] Research approved by the Ethics Committee of the Nuremberg Hospital under File No. IRB-2021-021; each subject gave informed consent prior to recording.

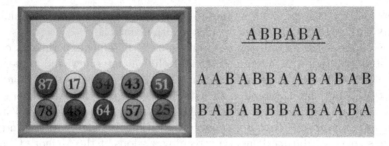

**Fig. 1.** Example templates of the sub-tests SKT 3 (left) and SKT 7 (right) from the original SKT Manual [26].

left (psychologist) and right (patient) channels could be used to separate the speakers. The audio samples were recorded in 16-bit stereo wav format with a sampling rate of 48 kHz and later converted to uncompressed PCM mono wav format with a sampling rate of 16 kHz. Both psychologists and patients reported that they were not affected by the presence of the device. Due to the Corona pandemic, psychologists and patients wore surgical or KN95 masks that affect the speech signal according to [19]. The speech of some subjects exhibits strong forms of local accents and dialects.

## 2.1   Standardized Sub-Tests

The dataset contains recordings from screening sessions, including time-labeled segments with speech from subjects performing the standardized sub-tests of SKT and CERAD-NB. We selected recordings from three sub-tests that we considered particularly suitable for classification experiments using only acoustic features; the time limit of all three tasks is one minute. The following section provides a brief description of the sub-tests and the data.

**SKT 3 (reading numbers).** Sub-test SKT 3 starts with the psychologist asking the patient to read the two-digit numbers written on the colored game pieces (Fig. 1, left) out loud in the direction of reading; this should be done as quickly as possible. We chose this reading task because of its simplicity compared to the other sub-tests; patients with mild impairments usually still perform well in it. The time needed to complete the task is converted into norm values from 0 (no impairment) to 3 (severe impairment). These values are normalized according to age and IQ-group (below average, average, above average) [26]. With a cut-off value of 1 (mild impairment), we separate the subjects into impaired (1–3) and non-impaired (0) and observe an almost balanced class distribution of 47/54 respectively.

**SKT 7 (interference test).** Sub-test 7 is an interference test (Fig. 1, right). It measures the "disposition rigidity" according to R.B. Cattell [8], i.e., the mental ability to switch. The aim is to learn to quickly break through intensively learned responses (here: the alphabet). A sequence consisting of two repeating letters (e.g., "A" and "B") is to be read as quickly and accurately as possible. The particular challenge is that the subject has to read one letter but say the other (i.e., read "A" but say "B" and vice versa). The underlined letters serve to explain the task and are not to be worked on by the patient and thus are not included in the temporal evaluation. We chose this interference test because it is comparatively the most demanding in terms of subjects' cognitive performance. It happens that more severely impaired patients do not understand the task or achieve only very low performance. The merit of this task lies in its sensitivity to mental performance impairment: Especially in the range of questionable or very mild impairments, it can differentiate best. As in sub-test 3, the time required is converted into norm values from 0 to 3 and a cutoff value of 1 is set, resulting in a balanced class distribution of 50/51 for non-impaired and impaired subjects, respectively.

**CERAD-NB 1 (verbal fluency test).** The CERAD-NB 1 is used to examine the speed and ease of verbal production ability, semantic memory, linguistic ability, executive functions, and cognitive flexibility. The psychologist conducting the sub-test asks the patient to name as many different animals as possible within one minute; the number of correctly named animals forms the basis for the test score. We choose this verbal fluency test (VFT) because it has already been shown to be suitable for our purpose in related work [12,14]. The CERAD-NB 1 raw values (number of named animals) are normalized taking into account the influence of age, education level, and sex according to [6] and then converted to z-scores. The z-score indicates by how many standard deviations a found value deviates from the mean of the population. Statistics of the studied healthy norm population from [1] are used as reference. However, there are inherent selection biases in the overall (Memory Clinic) and study (mildly impaired) populations, and at the time of writing there is no compensating healthy control group, making class separation considerably more difficult. While SKT 3 and SKT 7 address the patient's mental attention, CEARD-NB 1 differs in execution and examines mental production. To obtain a conclusive class division despite these limitations and differences, we calculate the z-score threshold for CERAD-NB 1 based on the individuals matched in the classes for SKT 3 and SKT 7 (73%), i.e., between the two groups for true-positive (impaired) and true-negative (non-impaired). The resulting z-score of $-1.2$ leads to a balanced distribution of 50/51 for the non-impaired ($> -1.2$) and impaired ($\leq -1.2$) classes in our data set.

## 2.2 Clinical Interview

The semi-structured clinical interview includes questions on memory, orientation, attention, activities of daily living, mood, sleep quality, appetite, physical activity, and medication of the patient. It also includes an intro (greeting and introduction of the interview part) at the beginning and a final part (introduction of the testing part) by the psychologist. For this reason, we extracted samples (4×30 sec) from the middle (at 30%, 40%, 50% and 60%) of the interview to capture as much patient speech as possible; ground truth diarization was available from manual transcriptions of 30 patients.

For the interview samples, we use the CERAD-NB 1 labels as targets since speech of the VFT is inherently more similar to the spontaneous speech from the interview and also allows for more deep speech markers than the other two tasks (more in Sect. 5).

## 3    Methods

This section briefly describes the features used for the machine learning experiments conducted.

### 3.1    openSMILE

OpenSMILE is a popular toolkit that is used for the extraction of audio features [11]. The toolkit computes several functionals over low-level descriptor (LLD) contours in a brute-force approach. In our experiments, we use the ComParE 2016 feature set, which consists of 6373 static features. OpenSMILE features are widely used in baseline experiments. The features have been shown to achieve proper baseline performance in numerous paralinguistic applications such as gender detection, age detection, or speech emotion recognition [23,24].

### 3.2    wav2vec 2.0

Models based on transformer architectures achieve state-of-the-art performance in various areas. Early breakthrough results have been achieved in the natural language processing domain [10]. Wav2vec 2.0 (W2V2) is a neural network model based on the transformer architecture designed for learning speech representations from raw audio data. The model is usually pre-trained with large amounts of unlabeled audio data [4]. The W2V2 model takes raw waveform audio data as inputs, which are processed by a Convolutional Neural Network (CNN) encoder, followed by a contextualized transformer network and a quantization module. The CNN generates latent representations directly from the waveform inputs, which are then discretized by the quantization module. The convolutional feature extractor is followed by twelve contextualized transformer blocks that use self-attention to make the model focus on the parts of the audio relevant to respective tasks. The model can be used as a feature extractor with or without adaptation.

W2V2 features are contextualized audio representations that encode information about a vector's relationship at time step $t$ to other vectors inside the extraction window [4]. Due to the way transformer models are trained, they are capable of extracting many aspects of the underlying data. The W2V2 model yields different speech representations after every transformer block, encoding the audio depending on the position in the processing hierarchy. Thus, the representations after each layer focus on different aspects of the encoded audio, making them more or less useful for a particular task [3]. Features extracted from the model have been successfully applied to tasks such as phoneme recognition, speech emotion detection, and mispronunciation detection [4,21,29].

The W2V2 features used in our experiments were extracted from models pre-trained unsupervised on 960 h of speech from the LibriSpeech corpus. We hypothesize that features extracted using only the weights obtained with unsupervised training will emphasize fine-grained differences in speech, as opposed to features that were fine-tuned for speech recognition, since these must reduce differences to be more robust w.r.t. articulation and speech production in order to increase robustness of speech recognition. The model takes the raw waveform audio data as inputs and returns 768-dimensional speech representations after each transformer block, representing roughly 0.02 s of audio. This yields $N = T/0.02 - 1$ vectors for the extraction context of T, i.e. 449 vectors with the extraction context of 10 s used. For the speech data of each sub-test, we extract features and, analogous to mean pooling along the time dimension, compute a mean vector over all extracted feature vectors of a sample. As a result, we obtain one vector representing the audio of the respective sub-test. For the interview audio data, we take the mean for the samples extracted at the specified relative duration and perform the same processing, yielding four vectors for each subject.

## 4 Experiments

Our experiments aim to differentiate the speech of individuals who are cognitively impaired from the speech of individuals who are not cognitively impaired in the context of their performance on neuropsychological tests. The experiments are conducted with speech data from the three sub-tests described in Sect. 2.1 and with speech data extracted at specific points in the semi-structured interview described in Sect. 2.2, relative to the duration of the interview.

The experiments using speech data from the standardized sub-tests are similar to experiments conducted with data from the ADReSSo challenge, which includes recordings of patients and healthy control speakers performing the CTP. Since subjects are asked to perform a standardized task in a given time, the speech samples should be inherently comparable, making them ideal for experimentation. There are however some limitations to our experiments: At the time of writing, we do not have an independent healthy control group, which is why we relate the labels for cognitive impairment to performance on the three sub-tests. Thus, performance on the sub-tests is not necessarily equivalent to the subject's diagnostic cognitive state. We choose labels for impaired and non-impaired for SKT 3, SKT 7, CERAD-NB 1 according to Sect. 2.1 and for the interview speech samples according to Sect. 2.2.

We use Support Vector Machine (SVM) classifiers with radial basis function kernels (rbf) as they allow for quick experiment turnaround and are able to learn from only a few samples. The optimal hyperparameters for the SVM and

**Table 1.** Average classification accuracy and standard deviation (in %) over the five test folds using OpenSMILE (OS) and wav2vec 2.0 (W2V2) features for SKT 3, SKT 7, CERAD-NB 1, and the interview (predicted on CERAD-NB 1 label). For W2V2, the best numbers after investigating the classification performance of features taken from the 12 different layers of the model are shown.

| Method | SKT 3 | SKT 7 | CERAD-NB 1 | Interview |
|:------:|:-----:|:-----:|:----------:|:---------:|
| OS | $78.1 \pm 5.4$ | $84.8 \pm 2.1$ | $67.6 \pm 7.1$ | $53.5 \pm 3.3$ |
| W2V2 | $82.9 \pm 4.3$ | $84.8 \pm 7.1$ | $77.1 \pm 8.5$ | $67.3 \pm 4.4$ |

the respective input features for the SVM classifiers were determined using grid search in stratified five-fold cross-validation on the respective training portion of the data.

We use five-fold cross-validation of disjoint speakers. For the sub-tests, the data was split into five distinct training sets comprising 80% of the data and test sets comprising the remaining 20%. The training test partitioning of the interview segment data (4 segments/speaker) uses stratified group partitioning for speaker-exclusive folds considering label distribution. Each training portion is then split again into five folds to determine the best hyperparameters in a stratified five-fold cross-validation. The kernel parameter $\gamma$ was selected from the set $\gamma \in \{10^{-k} \mid k = 1, \ldots, 5\} \subset \mathbb{R}_{>0}$, the regularization parameter $C$ was selected from $C \in \{10^k \mid k = -1, \ldots, 3\} \subset \mathbb{N}$, and specific to the experiments conducted using W2V2 features, the W2V2 extraction layer $L$ was selected from $L \in \{1, 2, \ldots, 12\}$.

We evaluate our models' performance by accuracy, which is a good indicator of model performance since the data set is mostly balanced between the classes.

## 4.1   Results

Table 1 contains the experimental results. We report the average classification accuracy over all five test folds using OS and W2V2 features.

With OS features, we observe solid classification results on the sub-tests SKT 3, SKT 7 and CERAD-NB 1 with accuracies of 78.1%, 84.8% and 67.6%, respectively. Using the speech samples taken from the interview, OS features do not seem to provide any discriminatory power, leading to results at chance level.

Table 1 contains the best results using W2V2 features. We investigated the classification performance w.r.t. the features taken from the 12 different layers of the W2V2 model. To that end, Fig. 2 depicts the performance of classifiers utilizing W2V2 features taken from each of the 12 layers for each task. Experiments on the constrained tasks of reading numbers (SKT 3) and the interference test (SKT 7) achieve adequate to high accuracies on all W2V2 layers, with both reaching their maximum accuracy of 82.9% (SKT 3) and 84.8% (SKT 7) on layer 8. This suggests that markers of cognitive status for constrained speech tasks are amplified in the upper-middle layers of the processing hierarchy. The VFT

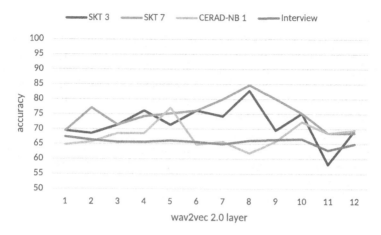

**Fig. 2.** Average classification accuracy over the five test folds for features taken from each of the 12 wav2vec 2.0 layers for SKT 3, SKT 7, CERAD-NB 1, and the interview.

is the task of naming animals (CERAD-NB 1), which is intrinsically more open-ended than the other two tasks focusing on production instead of attention; the speech and content will therefore vary more from patient to patient. Nevertheless, experiments on CERAD-NB 1 are promising, yielding an accuracy of up to 77.1% using features extracted from W2V2 layer 5. For the selected speech segments from the interview, the average accuracy does not vary much across the layers, ranging around 66%. Here, we obtain the best classification result on layer 1 with 67.3% accuracy. We therefore hypothesize that spontaneous speech taken from a semi-structured interview may be sufficient to extract discriminating speech features that can help with the detection of cognitive impairment.

## 5   Discussion

Even though we achieve partly high accuracies on the SKT 3 and SKT 7, it is important to question whether the features represent "deep speech markers" that lead to these results or whether they rather capture basic features such as delays and rate of speech. It is noticeable that OS features perform as well as W2V2 features on the SKT 7. This could be due to the fact that this sub-test has a high sensitivity for mental performance impairment, which in turn is reflected in basic acoustic features, such as the ones extracted with OS. It is becoming clear that there will be no one-fits-all method for automating the entire SKT and CERAD-NB test inventories. This may be well suited for the CTP, as it captures both attention (timing constraints) and production (picture description) in one test and thus allows screening for dementia in general. However, we focus on test inventories that intentionally cover a number of different neuropsychological domains with specific tests in order to obtain a detailed diagnostic picture of the patient, which therefore will also require a differentiated investigation in methodology. Thus, an important finding for us is the question of which sub-tests are actually suitable for acoustic evaluation and which sub-tests should rather be evaluated at a textual or even semantic level. All the more we would like to emphasize the result that the classification on the spontaneous speech of the interview already worked in our basic experiment with random samples. Manual transcriptions for all patients, which are in progress, will allow the targeted selection of patient speech in the interview and thus a more accurate interpretation of the results. Once the medical and psychological diagnoses are finalized, a detailed analysis of the diagnoses, e.g., Alzheimer's dementia (AD) or mild cognitive impairment (MCI), of the misclassified individuals could be helpful in understanding and improving the results. For example, AD patients are presumably more likely to be identified in language production, whereas MCI patients should be evaluated semantically.

## 6    Conclusion

We successfully classified cognitive impairments in three neuropsychological sub-tests, namely the SKT 3, SKT 7, and CERAD-NB 1, by using OS and W2V2 features from the elicited speech of these standardized tests to train SVM classifiers. Using OS features, we demonstrated high accuracies of 78.1% (SKT 3), 84.8% (SKT 7), and 67.6% (CERAD-NB 1), which remained the same for SKT 7 but improved to 82.9% and 77.1% for SKT 3 and CERAD-NB 1, respectively, when using W2V2 features. We found that constrained speech (SKT 3 and 7) performed best at level 8, while speech from a fluency task (CERAD-NB 1) performed best at level 5. Spontaneous speech (interview), on the other hand, showed similar performance on all layers, with layer 1 performing slightly better than the others. In addition, we provided conclusive evidence that spontaneous speech from the interview can be used to extract discriminating features for the detection of cognitive impairment.

The task of automating test inventories such as the SKT and the CERAD-NB is difficult, and there will probably never be just one universal method to accomplish this. Just as the original tests are an ensemble of specialized sub-tests that target different neuropsychological domains, tailored methods will be needed to automatically evaluate the sub-tests. In the future, the analysis of completed diagnoses and the inclusion of a healthy control group will help to define more distinct classes. For the experiments on the spontaneous speech of the interview, automatic as well as manual transcriptions including speaker diarization will help to target patient speech only and factor out the potential influence of the interviewer [22].

## References

1. Aebi, C.: Validierung der neuropsychologischen Testbatterie CERAD-NP?: eine Multi-Center Studie (2002). https://doi.org/10.5451/UNIBAS-002728525

2. Al-Hameed, S., Benaissa, M., Christensen, H.: Simple and robust audio-based detection of biomarkers for Alzheimer's disease. In: Proceedings of the 7th Workshop on Speech and Language Processing for Assistive Technologies (SLPAT 2016), pp. 32–36 (2016). https://doi.org/10.21437/SLPAT.2016-6

3. Baevski, A., Hsu, W.N., Conneau, A., Auli, M.: Unsupervised speech recognition. In: Ranzato, M., Beygelzimer, A., Dauphin, Y., Liang, P., Vaughan, J.W. (eds.) Advances in Neural Information Processing Systems, vol. 34, pp. 27826–27839. Curran Associates, Inc. (2021)

4. Baevski, A., Zhou, Y., Mohamed, A., Auli, M.: wav2vec 2.0: a framework for self-supervised learning of speech representations. In: Larochelle, H., Ranzato, M., Hadsell, R., Balcan, M.F., Lin, H. (eds.) Advances in Neural Information Processing Systems, vol. 33, pp. 12449–12460. Curran Associates, Inc. (2020)

5. Becker, J.T., Boller, F., Lopez, O.L., Saxton, J., McGonigle, K.L.: The natural history of Alzheimer's disease: description of study cohort and accuracy of diagnosis. Arch. Neurol. 51(6), 585–594 (1994)

6. Berres, M., Monsch, A.U., Bernasconi, F., Thalmann, B., Stähelin, H.B.: Normal ranges of neuropsychological tests for the diagnosis of Alzheimer's disease. Stud. Health Technol. Inf. 77, 195–199 (2000)

7. Borod, J.C., Goodglass, H., Kaplan, E.: Normative data on the Boston diagnostic aphasia examination, parietal lobe battery, and the Boston naming test. J. Clin. Neuropsychol. 2(3), 209–215 (1980). https://doi.org/10.1080/01688638008403793

8. Cattell, R.B., Tiner, L.G.: The varieties of structural rigidity. J. Pers. 17(3), 321–341 (1949). https://doi.org/10.1111/j.1467-6494.1949.tb01217.x

9. Cooper, S.: The clinical assessment of the patient with early dementia. J. Neurol. Neurosurg. Psychiatry 76(suppl_5), v15–v24 (2005). https://doi.org/10.1136/jnnp.2005.081133

10. Devlin, J., Chang, M.W., Lee, K., Toutanova, K.: Bert: pre-training of deep bidirectional transformers for language understanding. In: NAACL (2019)

11. Eyben, F., Wöllmer, M., Schuller, B.: Opensmile: the munich versatile and fast open-source audio feature extractor. In: Proceedings of the International Conference on Multimedia - MM 2010, p. 1459. ACM Press, Firenze, Italy (2010). https://doi.org/10.1145/1873951.1874246

12. Frankenberg, C., et al.: Verbal fluency in normal aging and cognitive decline: results of a longitudinal study. Comput. Speech Lang. 68, 101195 (2021). https://doi.org/10.1016/j.csl.2021.101195

13. Fraser, K.C., Meltzer, J.A., Rudzicz, F.: Linguistic features identify Alzheimer's disease in narrative speech. J. Alzheimer's disease: JAD 49(2), 407–422 (2016). https://doi.org/10.3233/JAD-150520

14. König, A., Linz, N., Tröger, J., Wolters, M., Alexandersson, J., Robert, P.: Fully automatic speech-based analysis of the semantic verbal fluency task. Dement. Geriatr. Cogn. Disord. 45(3–4), 198–209 (2018). https://doi.org/10.1159/000487852

15. König, A., Satt, A., Sorin, A., Hoory, R., Toledo-Ronen, O., Derreumaux, A., Manera, V., Verhey, F., Aalten, P., Robert, P.H., David, R.: Automatic speech analysis for the assessment of patients with predementia and Alzheimer's disease. Alzheimer's Dement. Diagn. Assess. Dis. Monit. 1(1), 112–124 (2015). https://doi.org/10.1016/j.dadm.2014.11.012

16. Luz, S., Haider, F., de la Fuente, S., Fromm, D., MacWhinney, B.: Alzheimer's dementia recognition through spontaneous speech: the ADReSS challenge. In: Interspeech 2020, pp. 2172–2176. ISCA (2020). https://doi.org/10.21437/Interspeech.2020-2571

17. Luz, S., Haider, F., de la Fuente, S., Fromm, D., MacWhinney, B.: Detecting cognitive decline using speech only: the ADReSSo challenge. In: Interspeech 2021, pp. 3780–3784. ISCA, August 2021. https://doi.org/10.21437/Interspeech.2021-1220

18. Morris, J.C., et al.: The consortium to establish a registry for Alzheimer's disease (CERAD). Part I. Clinical and neuropsychological assesment of Alzheimer's disease. Neurology **39**(9), 1159–1165 (1989). https://doi.org/10.1212/WNL.39.9.1159

19. Nguyen, D.D., et al.: Acoustic voice characteristics with and without wearing a facemask. Sci. Rep. **11**(1), 5651 (2021). https://doi.org/10.1038/s41598-021-85130-8

20. Orimaye, S.O., Wong, J.S.M., Golden, K.J., Wong, C.P., Soyiri, I.N.: Predicting probable Alzheimer's disease using linguistic deficits and biomarkers. BMC Bioinf. **18**(1), 34 (2017). https://doi.org/10.1186/s12859-016-1456-0

21. Pepino, L., Riera, P., Ferrer, L.: Emotion recognition from speech using wav2vec 2.0 embeddings. In: Interspeech 2021, pp. 3400–3404. ISCA, August 2021. https://doi.org/10.21437/Interspeech.2021-703

22. Pérez-Toro, P., et al.: Influence of the interviewer on the automatic assessment of Alzheimer's disease in the context of the ADReSSo challenge. In: Proceedings of the Interspeech 2021, pp. 3785–3789 (2021)

23. Schuller, B.W., et al.: The INTERSPEECH 2021 computational paralinguistics challenge: COVID-19 cough, COVID-19 speech, escalation and primates. In: Proceedings INTERSPEECH 2021, 22nd Annual Conference of the International Speech Communication Association. ISCA, Brno, Czechia, September 2021

24. Schuller, B., et al.: The INTERSPEECH 2016 computational paralinguistics challenge: deception, sincerity and native language. In: Proceedings of the Interspeech 2016, pp. 2001–2005 (2016). https://doi.org/10.21437/Interspeech.2016-129

25. Sheehan, B.: Assessment scales in dementia. Ther. Adv. Neurol. Disord. **5**(6), 349–358 (2012). https://doi.org/10.1177/1756285612455733

26. Stemmler, M., Lehfeld, H., Horn, R.: SKT nach Erzigkeit - SKT Manual Edition 2015, vol. 1. Universität Erlangen-Nürnberg, Erlangen, Germany (2015)

27. Vincze, V., et al.: Linguistic parameters of spontaneous speech for identifying mild cognitive impairment and Alzheimer disease. Comput. Linguist. **48**, 119–153 (2022)

28. World Health Organization: Global status report on the public health response to dementia. World Health Organization, Geneva (2021)

29. Xu, X., Kang, Y., Cao, S., Lin, B., Ma, L.: Explore wav2vec 2.0 for mispronunciation detection. In: Interspeech 2021, pp. 4428–4432. ISCA, August 2021. https://doi.org/10.21437/Interspeech.2021-777

# Dialogue

# Federated Learning in Heterogeneous Data Settings for Virtual Assistants – A Case Study

Paweł Pardela[1,2] (ID), Anna Fajfer[1] (ID), Mateusz Góra[1(✉)] (ID), and Artur Janicki[2] (ID)

[1] Samsung R&D Institute Poland, Warsaw, Poland
anna@fajfer.org, m.gora2@samsung.com
[2] Warsaw University of Technology, Warsaw, Poland
artur.janicki@pw.edu.pl

**Abstract.** Due to recent increased interest in data privacy, it is important to consider how personal virtual assistants (VA) handle data. The established design of VAs makes data sharing mandatory. Federated learning (FL) appears to be the most optimal way of increasing data privacy of data processed by VAs, as in FL, models are trained directly on users' devices, without sending them to a centralized server. However, VAs operate in a heterogeneous environment – they are installed on various devices and acquire various quantities of data. In our work, we check how FL performs in such heterogeneous settings. We compare the performance of several optimizers for data of various levels of heterogeneity and various percentages of stragglers. As a FL algorithm, we used FedProx, proposed by Sahu et al. in 2018. For a test database, we use a publicly available *Leyzer* corpus, dedicated to VA-related experiments. We show that skewed quantity and label distributions affect the quality of VA models trained to solve intent classification problems. We conclude by showing that a carefully selected local optimizer can successfully mitigate this effect, yielding 99% accuracy for the ADAM and RMSProp optimizers even for highly skewed distributions and a high share of stragglers.

**Keywords:** federated learning · FedProx · natural language understanding · virtual assistants · ADAM · PGD

## 1 Introduction

Virtual assistants (VA) were proposed in the early 60s [23]. With the rapid increase of computational power on consumer electronics it has become possible to implement and distribute personal VAs that reach millions of users [11,20].

Modern VAs can provide weather information, play music, control IoT devices, make recommendations or even answer complex questions. They have become an interface to many digital services. Major tech companies, like Amazon, Apple, Google, Microsoft and Samsung, compete to come up with the best

© Springer Nature Switzerland AG 2022
P. Sojka et al. (Eds.): TSD 2022, LNAI 13502, pp. 451–463, 2022.
https://doi.org/10.1007/978-3-031-16270-1_37

solution. Their VAs are powered by complex deep learning models that can recognize speech, analyze it, and then process it according to user needs. Currently, the most common way to train the model is to aggregate the data on a server and train a centralized model, often in an iterative process of updating the training set and fine-tuning the model.

The data used for the training comes from multiple sources, such as webcrawling, dictionaries, crowd-sourcing and logs collected from end user devices. The latter source raises questions about data privacy and relevant regulations [5]. VAs are usually available all around the globe and there might be legal barriers to the transfer of data across national borders. Many additional VA-related privacy concerns have been recently raised [2,4,16]. The main question that emerges is: how can one conduct effective machine learning (ML) without exposing users' data?

Federated learning (FL), originally proposed by [12], tries to answer to this question. It has been proven to increase data privacy, both in research studies and practical applications [3,7]. The federated approach keeps the data decentralized and only the local models' weights are transferred to update the global model. However, there is one frequent challenge that comes with distributed data environments: the data on local devices is non-independently and identically distributed (the so called *non-IID data*). FedProx is one of the frameworks that aims to tackle this issue. To our knowledge, so far there have been no studies that investigate its performance in real-life applications.

We want to bring focus to the problems we faced while improving our VA. Non-IID data is a significant issue, that has been raised by [19] – the authors of the FedProx framework. We seek to further research the issue of non-IID data by comparing the end results on differently distributed data.

In this work we describe a case study using the Leyzer corpus [22], the largest open-source dataset for VA-oriented intent and domain utterance classification. We show that the performance of FedProx can be seriously affected by heterogeneous data settings in the context of natural language understanding (NLU). We also demonstrate that proper selection of the local optimizer improves the overall performance even for significantly skewed label distribution.

## 2   Related Work

### 2.1   Federated Learning

FL is a distributed learning paradigm whereby as in edge computing, models are retrained locally and only then shared with the central server to be aggregated and redistributed as an improved, consolidated model.

The classical way of improving the model is to:

1. distribute the server trained model to users' devices;
2. collect the data on how the VA is used by the user;
3. pack the data and send to the main server;
4. use the data both to retrain the model and to improve the test set.

However, in FL the steps are slightly different:

1. distribute the pretrained model;
2. periodically retrain the local model on users' devices;
3. send extracted weights from local models to the main server;
4. the main server aggregates the local weights and uses them to update the main model.

The main advantages of the FL approach over edge computing or standard ML methods are as follows:

– data is never merged into one dataset; the handling of missing data and uneven distribution is built into the algorithm;
– the training data is kept on devices and never sent over the network, thus strengthening data security;
– models on end devices can be improved and (in some cases) also personalized without forfeiting privacy.

However, FL introduces some challenges. One of them is expensive communication between the server and user devices. Another one is the impact of system and statistical heterogeneity on the FL effectiveness [14].

Over recent years research on FL has yielded variations on its conceptualization in order to overcome such challenges [1,18]. One of them is Federated Averaging (FedAvg), proposed by [17]. In this method, the stochastic gradient descent (SGD) is used as the local optimizer. In each iteration, $K \ll N$ clients are picked and SGD is run locally for $E$ epochs. After each iteration only the model weights are shared with the server and then averaged.

The authors point out that in FedAvg it is very important to set the hyperparameters properly. Increasing the number of local epochs boosts the amount of computation done on local devices. This, in turn, potentially decreases the number of connections between the server and end devices. However, setting local epochs too high in highly heterogeneous environments may cause the end devices to find only the local optima, which hurts convergence. The increased load may prevent some devices from finishing their local computation and only the partial solutions will be dropped during the aggregation phase.

In the Federated Proximity (FedProx) version [19] introduce small modifications to FedAvg. Firstly, FedProx allows for partial solutions to be aggregated, meaning that devices with less resources can execute fewer epochs and their partial solutions will still be counted instead of dropped. Secondly, it allows one to use a local solver of choice. [19] suggest that too many local updates may still have a negative impact on convergence. To further deal with the problem of statistical and systems heterogeneity, it is recommended by [19] to add a proximal term to the local sub-problem.

## 2.2 Tackling Heterogeneity in Federated Learning

In a federated setting each device creates a local dataset based on user's interactions. This leads to *statistical heterogeneity*. It is a common issue when data is non-independently and identically distributed (non-IID) between clients. In recent years it has become a subject of research [8,13,24]. Both the quantity of data and label (or feature) distribution might differ on different devices. This is often caused by real-world data imbalance, as some users generate more data than others. Some functionalities might be limited to certain groups of users, which may result in label distribution skew.

Many studies [9,15] suggest that non-IID data settings may degrade the effectiveness of the trained model. [10] address statistical heterogeneity by sharing local device data. However, those methods might turn out to be insufficient, due to the data privacy validation and the increased strain on the network bandwidth. As previously mentioned, [19] tackle the issue of system heterogeneity, and (for synthetic datasets) statistical heterogeneity with one data distribution for each dataset.

## 3    Materials and Methods

### 3.1    Our Case Study

In this article we focus on a case of distributed VAs, i.e., VA instances installed on various end devices (e.g., smartphones, tablets etc.). To provide high quality of service, we need to update VA models systematically. What is more, we would like to ensure the privacy of users' data, therefore we should not transfer users' data to a central server. Even though FL appears to be a solution to our problems, we need to stress that the FL performance can be seriously influenced by the following factors:

- devices with VAs installed differ significantly in processing power and internet accessibility;
- data gathered on each device ranges from a few to thousands of samples.

Both problems – system and statistical heterogeneity – have been partially addressed in [19]. In our work we would like to perform a deeper study on heterogeneity, using the VA context and a relevant dataset. We will also check if (and to what extent) the performance of FedProx can be improved by the choice of local optimization algorithm.

### 3.2    Datasets Used

To provide a broad benchmark we use the same corpora as [19]. In addition, we use a VA-dedicated Leyzer dataset. We briefly characterize these datasets below.

**Synthetic Data.** In [19] synthetic data were generated using the formula proposed in [21], with two variables added:

$\alpha$ – to control how much local models differ from each other

$\beta$ – to control how much the local data on each device differs from that of other devices

In Eq. 1, $\alpha$ and $\beta$ scale the width (or spread) of normal distribution for $W$ and $b$ respectively when drawing samples.

$$y = argmax(softmax(\alpha W x + \beta b)), \tag{1}$$

where $x \in R^{60}$, $W \in R^{10 \times 60}$, $b \in R^{10}$.

In [19] $\alpha$ and $\beta$ are set to $(0,0), (0.5, 0.5), (1, 1)$. This way three distinctive non-IID datasets are generated. They contain 30 devices in total, and the number of samples on each device is decided by the rules of the power law.

The **Leyzer** dataset consists of 20 domains and 186 intents with a wide variety of utterance samples. We only use the English subset of the corpus. We distributed the samples among 1000 devices using several different distributions. Our goal was to utilize this dataset for intent classification. The dataset was preprocessed by expanding the set to size of 156,772 utterances, using the slots provided by the authors. The generated utterances were encoded with uncased BERT Base 12/768 [6].

**Table 1.** Statistics for three synthetic datasets with various $\sigma$.

| Dataset | $\sigma$ | Devices | Samples | Samples/device | |
| --- | --- | --- | --- | --- | --- |
| | | | | Mean | Stddev |
| | 0.2 | 1,000 | 156,772 | 156 | 67 |
| Leyzer | 0.5 | 1,000 | 90,034 | 90 | 57 |
| | 0.9 | 1,000 | 17,357 | 17 | 24 |

**Real Data.** In [19] FedProx was tested on four real datasets (MNIST, FEM-NIST, Sent140 and Shakespeare). We used the same datasets with exception for the Shakespeare, which we had to skip due to memory limitations.

**Table 2.** Statistics for three datasets with real data.

| Dataset | Devices | Samples | Samples/device | |
| --- | --- | --- | --- | --- |
| | | | Mean | Stddev |
| MNIST | 1,000 | 69,035 | 69 | 106 |
| FEMNIST | 200 | 18,345 | 92 | 159 |
| Sent140 | 772 | 40,783 | 53 | 32 |

**Table 3.** Parameters used in experiments.

| Parameter | Value |
|---|---|
| No. of rounds | 200 |
| No. of epochs | 20 |
| Learning rate | 0.01 |
| Batch size | 10 |
| No. of clients | 20 |
| Drop | 0.01, 0.2, 0.5, 0.9 |
| $\mu$ | 0.1, 0.5, 1 |
| Optimizer | PGD, SGD, ADAM, RMSProp, AdaGrad |

### 3.3 Emulating Heterogeneous Condition

To simulate different heterogeneous data settings we used normal and skewed distributions of labels and quantity of data to simulate the real world imbalance in data distribution (described in Subsect. 2.2). For comparison, we also prepared an IID homogeneous data setting.

It bears mentioning that for this set of experiments we use the expanded Leyzer dataset with focus on cross-domain intent detection. We use log-normal distribution to create various skewed distributions. For parametrization, we change $\sigma$ – a standard deviation of the normally distributed random variable, which is commonly used for parametrization of log-normal distribution.

**Skewed Data Quantity Distribution.** In this case, we shuffle and split the main dataset into local datasets according to the skewed normal distribution. Each device is assigned one dataset that is unique in content and number of samples.

We test several cases of similar distributions with different $\sigma$ parameter, which affects the skewness of the distribution. We test the FedProx method on 1,000 devices.

**Skewed Label Distribution.** For this part of experiment our goal is to simulate the label imbalance. We opted for quantity-based label imbalance, where a fixed number of labels is allocated to each device, so only a part of all labels is included in each local dataset. The quantity of labels assigned to a device is decided by applying the skewed normal distribution to the label set. In the case of Leyzer, we use intents as labels and utterances as samples.

### 3.4 Evaluation of Local Optimizers

The choice of optimizer usually depends on the problem that is being solved. We decided to compare the PGD, SGD, ADAM, RMSProp, and AdaGrad optimizers in the FedProx framework on several problems, to find the best suit for the VA case. We conducted tests for all optimizers on all the datasets described in Subsect. 3.2. The number of devices, rounds and epochs is presented in Table 3. The drop value in the latter table is a share of devices with uncompleted computations (the so called stragglers), that would be dropped in the FedAvg procedure.

## 4  Results

### 4.1  Results on Non-IID Data Distributions

Below we present the results of the skewed data distribution impact on the accuracy of intent classification on the Leyzer dataset.

**Table 4.** Highest accuracy for homogeneous and skewed data quantity distributions ($drop = 0.9$) for Leyzer dataset.

| Optimizer | Homogeneous | $\sigma$ | | | |
|---|---|---|---|---|---|
| | | 0.01 | 0.2 | 0.5 | 0.9 |
| ADAM | 1.00 | **0.99** | **0.99** | **0.99** | **0.98** |
| AdaGrad | 1.00 | 0.87 | 0.86 | 0.84 | 0.83 |
| PGD $\mu$0.1 | 0.89 | 0.95 | 0.94 | 0.92 | 0.90 |
| PGD $\mu$0.5 | 0.73 | 0.92 | 0.91 | 0.89 | 0.87 |
| PGD $\mu$1 | 0.65 | 0.90 | 0.88 | 0.86 | 0.85 |
| RMSProp | 1.00 | **0.99** | **0.99** | **0.98** | **0.98** |
| SGD | 1.00 | 0.95 | 0.94 | 0.92 | 0.91 |
| FedAvg – SGD | 1.00 | 0.96 | 0.95 | 0.92 | 0.88 |

**Skewed Data Quantity Distribution.** In Table 4 we compare the accuracy of the model trained with different optimizers on the Leyzer data, distributed among devices with various skewness. These results show that non-uniform distribution affects accuracy. For example, even for a low $\sigma = 0.01$ and the AdaGrad optimizer, accuracy drops from 1.00 down to 0.87. However, the negative impact can be amortized with proper choice of the local optimizer. For the RMSProp and ADAM optimizers, the accuracy drop is minor (by 2% relative); they achieve the highest accuracy regardless of the skewness of the distribution.

With the inclusion of the partial results, FedProx was more successful when compared to the original FedAvg algorithm. As expected, the PGD optimizer with higher $\mu$ values performed worse in the homogeneous setting. The learning curves in Fig. 1 additionally indicate that FedProx combined with ADAM or RMSProp achieved the convergence in a smaller number of rounds than the FedAvg.

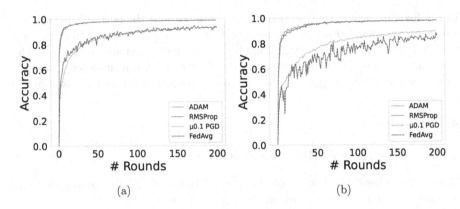

(a)

(b)

**Fig. 1.** Testing accuracy for FL with *drop* = 0.9 and Leyzer dataset, for skewed data quantity distribution with: **(a)** $\sigma = 0.2$ and **(b)** $\sigma = 0.9$.

**Skewed Label Distribution.** Table 5 shows the results of experiments conducted on data with the skewed label distribution. All the results were severely impacted. ADAM and RMSProp once again outperformed all other choices for training using the Leyzer data. However, the accuracy of RMSProp with $\sigma = 0.9$ declined, while ADAM yields better results in this case.

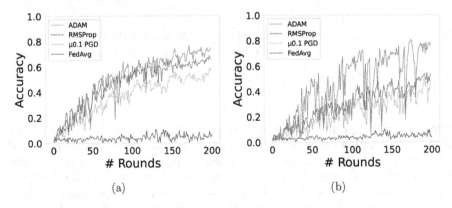

(a)

(b)

**Fig. 2.** Testing accuracy for FL with *drop* = 0.9 and Leyzer dataset, for skewed label distribution with: **(a)** $\sigma = 0.2$ and **(b)** $\sigma = 0.9$.

**Table 5.** Highest accuracy for skewed label distribution classification on Leyzer with $drop = 0.9$.

| Optimizer | $\sigma$ | | |
|---|---|---|---|
| | 0.2 | 0.5 | 0.9 |
| ADAM | **0.77** | **0.76** | **0.81** |
| AdaGrad | 0.62 | 0.55 | 0.45 |
| PGD $\mu$0.1 | 0.59 | 0.53 | 0.51 |
| PGD $\mu$0.5 | 0.56 | 0.51 | 0.51 |
| PGD $\mu$1 | 0.53 | 0.48 | 0.50 |
| RMSProp | **0.69** | **0.66** | **0.55** |
| SGD | 0.60 | 0.53 | 0.51 |
| FedAvg – SGD | 0.11 | 0.13 | 0.10 |

ADAM also achieved the highest accuracy more quickly than other local solvers, which might also suggest the need for an increase in the total number of rounds for training with other local solvers in order to achieve similar results. Especially intriguing here was, for the ADAM optimizer, when the skewness increased from $\sigma = 0.5$ to $\sigma = 0.9$, results seem to improve (Table 5). Once again using PGD with lower $\mu$ value yielded better results. However, in this setting, FedAvg performs worse than any other local optimizer used with FedProx. Especially with higher percentage of stragglers the solver shows to be largely ineffective.

Figure 2 illustrates the learning curves for the case of 90% of stragglers and skewed label distribution. The FedProx algorithm manages to converge scoring the accuracy of 0.81, whereas FedAvg in the same setting does not get past 0.1 accuracy score.

### 4.2 Choosing the Best Local Optimizer

In Fig. 3 we present the learning curves for FedAvg, FedProx with PGD, and FedProx with RMSProp. The combination of FedProx with PGD as a local solver seems to be the most stable, though it is not always the fastest one to reach convergence. The learning process for FEMNIST seems most monotonous for all optimizers. In contrast, while the learning curve for MNIST looks rather monotone for PGD, it is very hectic for FedAvg and RMSProp.

**Table 6.** Accuracy for different datasets and optimizers ($drop = 0.01$). Best results for each column are shown in bold.

| Optimizer | Real Datasets | | | Synthetic Datasets | | | Mean |
|---|---|---|---|---|---|---|---|
| | MNIST | FEMNIST | Sent140 | Synthetic 0_0 | Synthetic 0.5_0.5 | Synthetic 1_1 | |
| ADAM | 0.85 | **0.71** | **0.72** | 0.67 | 0.62 | 0.64 | 0.70 |
| AdaGrad | **0.90** | 0.55 | 0.70 | 0.68 | 0.73 | 0.62 | 0.70 |
| PGD $\mu$0.1 | **0.90** | 0.67 | 0.71 | 0.73 | 0.74 | 0.68 | 0.74 |
| PGD $\mu$0.5 | **0.90** | 0.65 | 0.71 | 0.76 | **0.80** | **0.72** | **0.76** |
| PGD $\mu$1 | **0.90** | 0.63 | 0.71 | **0.78** | **0.80** | **0.72** | **0.76** |
| RMSProp | 0.76 | 0.69 | **0.72** | 0.64 | 0.59 | 0.62 | 0.67 |
| SGD | 0.89 | 0.68 | 0.71 | 0.71 | 0.68 | 0.68 | 0.73 |
| FedAvg – SGD | 0.89 | 0.68 | 0.71 | 0.71 | 0.68 | 0.68 | 0.73 |

Table 6 also shows that the PGD algorithm with $\mu = 1$ is the best performing local optimizer in our tests when it comes to accuracy. PGD achieves the highest training accuracy on MNIST and the synthetic corpora. ADAM, on the other hand, has the best results in terms of accuracy on FEMNIST and Sent140, with RMSProp also scoring high on the latter. We find that RMSProp paired with FedProx scores the lowest when it comes to mean accuracy for all problems, but it outperforms other algorithms in the Sent140 set.

It appears no single optimizer can be claimed to be universally superior to the others. The disparities in their performance in different contexts suggest the suitability of each optimizer is by and large defined by the problem at hand.

The experiment shows that the solution proposed by the authors of FedProx is the best choice in most cases. However, we also point out examples where other local solvers perform significantly better, e.g., ADAM for the FEMNIST dataset.

When investigating various straggler percentages (i.e., drop values), the algorithms achieve similar results when paired with FedProx. For FedAvg the accuracy drops with higher drop percentages. Table 6 shows the best case for FedAvg with $drop = 0.01$.

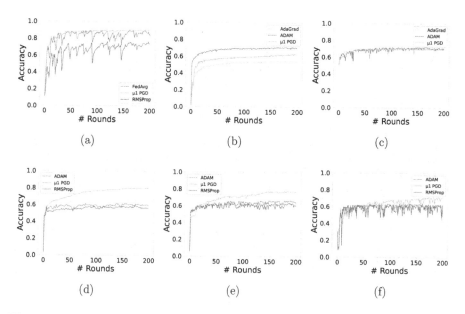

**Fig. 3.** Testing accuracy in local optimizer benchmark. The results are shown for different datasets: **(a)** MNIST, **(b)** FEMNIST, **(c)** sent140, **(d)** synthetic(0,0), **(e)** synthetic(0.5,0.5), and **(f)** synthetic(1,1).

## 5    Conclusions

In this study we present a case study of using FL in the VA context, which is characterized by non-uniform distribution of data samples and labels, as well as various shares of stragglers. We use the FedProx framework to compare how various local optimizers handle such non-IID data. We compare the results on several different datasets and ML models, with the main focus on the Leyzer dataset, as it was best suited for the intent classification problem, crucial for VAs.

The main conclusion of our study is that skewed label distribution can drastically affect overall federated model performance – we show the accuracy drops to be up to 17% relative. We find the performance to be the worst for the skewed label distribution with the highest $\sigma$ value. For the data quantity distribution the effect was not as severe.

We also show that the selection of the proper local optimizer improves the overall performance. We achieve 99% accuracy on the Leyzer dataset (with ADAM and RMSProp optimizers) even in the worst case scenario of 90% stragglers. We find that the right choice of a local optimizer, in addition to improving the results, also decreases the time needed to train the models on end devices. Based on our experiments, we can recommend the choice of RMSProp for intent classification and PGD for tasks such as digit classification.

# References

1. Amiri, M.M., Gündüz, D.: Federated learning over wireless fading channels. IEEE Trans. Wireless Commun. **19**(5), 3546–3557 (2020). https://doi.org/10.1109/TWC.2020.2974748

2. Ammari, T., Kaye, J., Tsai, J., Bentley, F.: Music, search, and IoT: how people (really) use voice assistants. ACM Trans. Comput.-Hum. Interact. **26**, 1–28 (2019). https://doi.org/10.1145/3311956

3. Bonawitz, K., et al.: Towards federated learning at scale: system design (2019)

4. Chung, H., Iorga, M., Voas, J., Lee, S.: Alexa, can I trust you? Computer **50**, 100–104 (2017). https://doi.org/10.1109/MC.2017.3571053

5. European_Commission: 2018 reform of EU data protection rules (2018). https://ec.europa.eu/commission/sites/beta-political/files/data-protection-factsheet-changes_en.pdf

6. Google: BERT model: uncased_l-12_h-768_a-12 (2018). https://storage.googleapis.com/bert_models/2018_10_18/uncased_L-12_H-768_A-12.zip

7. Hard, A., et al.: Federated learning for mobile keyboard prediction (2019)

8. Hsieh, K., Phanishayee, A., Mutlu, O., Gibbons, P.: The non-IID data quagmire of decentralized machine learning. In: Daumé, H., Singh, A. (eds.) Proceedings of the 37th International Conference on Machine Learning. Proceedings of Machine Learning Research, vol. 119, pp. 4387–4398. PMLR, 13–18 July 2020. https://proceedings.mlr.press/v119/hsieh20a.html

9. Hsu, T.M.H., Qi, H., Brown, M.: Measuring the effects of non-identical data distribution for federated visual classification (2019)

10. Jiang, P., Agrawal, G.: A linear speedup analysis of distributed deep learning with sparse and quantized communication. In: Bengio, S., Wallach, H., Larochelle, H., Grauman, K., Cesa-Bianchi, N., Garnett, R. (eds.) Advances in Neural Information Processing Systems, vol. 31. Curran Associates, Inc. (2018). https://proceedings.neurips.cc/paper/2018/file/17326d10d511828f6b34fa6d751739e2-Paper.pdf

11. Kinsella, B.: Samsung Bixby has 10 million active users globally, October 2017. https://voicebot.ai/2017/10/19/samsung-bixby-10-million-active-users-globally

12. Konečný, J., McMahan, H.B., Yu, F.X., Richtarik, P., Suresh, A.T., Bacon, D.: Federated learning: strategies for improving communication efficiency. In: NIPS Workshop on Private Multi-Party Machine Learning (2016). https://arxiv.org/abs/1610.05492

13. Li, Q., Diao, Y., Chen, Q., He, B.: Federated learning on Non-IID data silos: an experimental study. ArXiv:abs/2102.02079 (2021)

14. Li, T., Sahu, A.K., Talwalkar, A., Smith, V.: Federated learning: challenges, methods, and future directions. IEEE Signal Process. Mag. **37**(3), 50–60 (2020). https://doi.org/10.1109/msp.2020.2975749

15. Li, X., Huang, K., Yang, W., Wang, S., Zhang, Z.: On the convergence of FedAvg on non-IID data (2020)

16. Malkin, N., Deatrick, J., Tong, A., Wijesekera, P., Egelman, S., Wagner, D.: Privacy attitudes of smart speaker users. In: Proceedings on Privacy Enhancing Technologies 2019, pp. 250–271, October 2019. https://doi.org/10.2478/popets-2019-0068

17. McMahan, H.B., Moore, E., Ramage, D., Hampson, S., y Arcas, B.A.: Communication-efficient learning of deep networks from decentralized data. In: AISTATS (2017)

18. Reddi, S.J., et al.: Adaptive federated optimization. CoRR abs/2003.00295 (2020). https://arxiv.org/abs/2003.00295
19. Sahu, A.K., Li, T., Sanjabi, M., Zaheer, M., Talwalkar, A., Smith, V.: On the convergence of federated optimization in heterogeneous networks. CoRR abs/1812.06127 (2018). http://arxiv.org/abs/1812.06127
20. Schwartz, E.H.: Samsung Bixby Lives! New features quash premature demise rumors, October 2021. https://voicebot.ai/2021/10/26/samsung-bixby-lives-new-features-quash-premature-demise-rumors/
21. Shamir, O., Srebro, N., Zhang, T.: Communication-efficient distributed optimization using an approximate newton-type method. In: Xing, E.P., Jebara, T. (eds.) Proceedings of the 31st International Conference on Machine Learning. Proceedings of Machine Learning Research, vol. 32(2), pp. 1000–1008. PMLR, Beijing, China, 22–24 June 2014. https://proceedings.mlr.press/v32/shamir14.html
22. Sowański, M., Janicki, A.: Leyzer: a dataset for multilingual virtual assistants. In: Sojka, P., Kopeček, I., Pala, K., Horák, A. (eds.) TSD 2020. LNCS (LNAI), vol. 12284, pp. 477–486. Springer, Cham (2020). https://doi.org/10.1007/978-3-030-58323-1_51
23. Zemčík, T.: A brief history of chatbots. DEStech Trans. Comput. Sci. Eng. (2019). https://doi.org/10.12783/dtcse/aicae2019/31439, https://www.dpi-proceedings.com/index.php/dtcse/article/view/31439
24. Zhao, Y., Li, M., Lai, L., Suda, N., Civin, D., Chandra, V.: Federated learning with non-IID data (2018)

# PoCaP Corpus: A Multimodal Dataset for Smart Operating Room Speech Assistant Using Interventional Radiology Workflow Analysis

Kubilay Can Demir[1] , Matthias May[2], Axel Schmid[2], Michael Uder[2],
Katharina Breininger[3] , Tobias Weise[1,4] , Andreas Maier[4] ,
and Seung Hee Yang[1(✉)]

[1] Speech and Language Processing Laboratory,
Friedrich-Alexander-Universität Erlangen-Nürnberg, Erlangen, Germany
{kubilay.c.demir,seung.hee.yang}@fau.de
[2] Radiologisches Institut Universitätsklinikum Erlangen, Erlangen, Germany
[3] Artificial Intelligence in Medical Imaging Laboratory,
Friedrich-Alexander-Universität Erlangen-Nürnberg, Erlangen, Germany
[4] Pattern Recognition Laboratory,
Friedrich-Alexander-Universität Erlangen-Nürnberg, Erlangen, Germany

**Abstract.** This paper presents a new multimodal interventional radiology dataset, called PoCaP (Port Catheter Placement) Corpus. This corpus consists of speech and audio signals in German, X-ray images, and system commands collected from 31 PoCaP interventions by six surgeons with average duration of $81.4 \pm 41.0$ min. The corpus aims to provide a resource for developing a smart speech assistant in operating rooms. In particular, it may be used to develop a speech-controlled system that enables surgeons to control the operation parameters such as C-arm movements and table positions. In order to record the dataset, we acquired consent by the institutional review board and workers' council in the University Hospital Erlangen and by the patients for data privacy. We describe the recording set-up, data structure, workflow and preprocessing steps, and report the first PoCaP Corpus speech recognition analysis results with 11.52% word error rate using pretrained models. The findings suggest that the data has the potential to build a robust command recognition system and will allow the development of a novel intervention support systems using speech and image processing in the medical domain.

**Keywords:** Multimodal interventional corpus · Interventional radiology · Surgical data science · Automatic speech recognition · Operating room smart assistant · Port catheter placement

## 1 Introduction

Modern operating rooms (OR) are adapting advancing technologies rapidly and becoming more digitalized environments [9]. Necessary medical devices are collecting and visualizing large amounts of data required for an improved execution

© Springer Nature Switzerland AG 2022
P. Sojka et al. (Eds.): TSD 2022, LNAI 13502, pp. 464–475, 2022.
https://doi.org/10.1007/978-3-031-16270-1_38

of an operation. This allows physicians to do more intricate and successful procedures, improving patient safety and OR efficiency. However, the quantity of data and the complexity of an operation cannot be expanded indefinitely. Therefore, intelligent systems which can follow the execution of an operation and assist physicians are proposed [5]. These systems can process available data in the OR and present it in the correct time and format, follow the operation semantically, and take over some routine tasks.

A major approach in the creation of an intelligent workflow assistance system is surgical workflow analysis, which is often done by hierarchically decomposing an operation into smaller meaningful activities on different semantic levels [8]. In this approach, an operation is typically defined by *phases*, *steps* or *actions*. Phases are highest-level actions such as preparation, cutting, or sterilization. Steps are necessary activities to perform phases, such as table positioning, instrument setting, or putting covers. Actions are generally the lowest-level activities in an analysis. They include basic activities such as grabbing an instrument or turning on a device.

The available corpora for surgical workflow analysis vary considerably in size, quality, coverage, and depth of linguistic and structural characteristics. However, the vast majority of corpora only contains endoscopic video data, while some include additional instrument usage information. Other possible data modalities in OR such as speech are mostly under-investigated. We claim that a corpus for surgical workflow analysis can benefit from multimodal data, including not only images and videos, but also speech uttered by the surgeons in their language. This will allow development of a smart OR speech assistant, which is able to understand the different phases of a surgery and identify surgeons' command words during operations.

To this end, we construct a new kind of multimodal German dataset in the domain of interventional radiology workflow. We describe the design, collection, and development of our 31 PoCaP (Port-catheter Placement) Corpus. It consists of X-ray images, RGB ambient videos, speech uttered by the surgeons, and system commands given by medical personnel to operate devices in the OR. The dataset is annotated with different levels of structural and descriptive meta-information, as well as linguistic information. All speech samples are automatically transcribed using an Automatic Speech Recognition (ASR) engine, and surgical phases are manually annotated with the help of surgeons in the Radiology Department at the University Hospital of Erlangen in Germany. Unfortunately, this dataset cannot be made publicly available to ensure patients' and personal's data privacy.

The following section of this paper summarizes the related works on biomedical corpus collection and processing. Section 3 and 4 describe our PoCaP data and preprocessing results, respectively. In Sect. 5, we discuss surgery-specific and surgery-independent challenges regarding annotation and data processing. Finally, we end with the potential use of the corpus, future research direction, and concluding remarks.

## 2   Related Works

Similar to other medical fields, publicly available data for surgical phase recognition are not abundant. Firstly, collecting and annotating data from OR is a costly procedure. Acquiring any sort of data requires the implementation of new hardware or software in the OR and maintenance during the whole procedure. Annotation is a time-intensive step in the data collection and needs to be performed or validated by medical experts. Secondly, local legal requirements have to be followed in order to ensure the security of the medical data. This factor may also limit the public sharing of collected datasets.

*Cholec80* is a endoscopic video dataset of 80 laparoscopic cholecystectomy surgeries, including phase annotations for seven distinctive phases and seven tools [15]. *m2cai16-workflow* dataset contains 41 endoscopic videos of laparoscopic cholecystectomy and phase annotations for eight phases [14,15]. *HeiChole* is another endoscopic video dataset of laparoscopic cholecystectomy containing 33 surgeries with phase, action and tool annotations [16]. In HeiChole, phase annotations are provided similar to Cholec80. In [3], authors created a private dataset of 1243 endoscopic videos for laparoscopic cholecystectomy from multiple medical centers. *CATARACTS* is a microscopic video dataset of 50 cataracts surgery, which contains annotations consisting of 14 phases [17]. Another dataset of cataract surgery is *Cataract-101*, which has 101 operations and annotations with ten phases [13]. *Kitaguchi et al.* collected 300 laparoscopic colorectal surgery videos from multiple institutions and annotated them with nine phases [6]. *Bypass40* is an private dataset of 40 endoscopic videos of gastric bypass surgical procedures annotated with both phases and steps [11].

## 3     Data Collection Procedure and Setup

As described in the previous section, datasets on the workflow analysis are mostly concentrated on video signals, either endoscopic or microscopic. Some datasets include additional tool annotations. However, other possible data sources are mostly under-investigated. In this paper, we propose a multimodal dataset consisting of three-channel speech and audio signals, X-ray images, and system commands collected during PoCaP interventions in the Radiology Department of University Hospital Erlangen, Germany. Before data collection, we obtained approvals from the institutional review board and workers' council. Additionally, we asked every patient for their consent in a written form. Operations are performed by six different surgeons with different levels of expertise. The average duration of an intervention is $81.4 \pm 41.0$ min. Additionally, we have captured ambient videos to help the annotation procedure, see Fig. 1. Our dataset includes 31 operations. We defined 31 surgical steps and eight surgical phases for the PoCaP intervention, to use in surgical phase and step recognition tasks, which are shown in Table 1.

### 3.1     Port-Catheter Placement

Port-catheter placement is a frequently executed intervention in the radiology department. It is often applied to patients who require frequent infusions, e.g. during chemotherapy. A port-catheter is a device consisting of a port, an access

**Table 1.** Definitions of surgical phases and steps of port-catheter placement surgery in the PoCaP Corpus.

| Phases | Steps |
| --- | --- |
| 1. Preparation | 1.1 Patient positioning on the table |
| | 1.2 Table moves up |
| | 1.3 Radiologist in sterile |
| | 1.5 Preparation of sterile material |
| | 1.6 Patient in sterile |
| 2. Puncture | 2.1 Local anesthesia |
| | 2.2 Ultrasound guided puncture |
| 3. Positioning of the Guide Wire | 3.1 C-Arm moves in |
| | 3.2 Fluoroscopy on the subclavian area |
| | 3.3 Fluoroscopy on the vena cava inferior (VCI) area |
| | 3.4 C-Arm moves out |
| 4. Pouch Preparation and Catheter Placement | 4.1 Local anaesthesia |
| | 4.2 Incision |
| | 4.3 Pouch preparation |
| | 4.4 Sheath |
| 5. Catheter Positioning | 5.1 C-Arm moves in |
| | 5.2 Fluoroscopy on the VCI area |
| | 5.3 Positioning of the catheter |
| 6. Catheter Adjustment | 6.1 Shortening of the catheter |
| | 6.2 C-Arm moves out |
| | 6.3 Connection of the catheter to the port capsule |
| | 6.4 Positioning of the port capsule in the pouch |
| | 6.5 Surgical suture |
| | 6.6 Puncture of the port capsule |
| 7. Catheter Control | 7.1 C-Arm moves in |
| | 7.2 Digital subtraction angiography of the chest |
| | 7.3 C-Arm moves out to parking position |
| 8. Closing | 8.1 Sterile patch |
| | 8.2 Table moves down |

point to use for infusions during treatment, and a thin flexible tube called a catheter. During an intervention, the port is placed approximately two centimetres under the skin on either side of the chest and the catheter is connected to a large vein emptying into the heart. The placement of a port makes it possible to avoid repeated injuries to small vessels and chemotherapy-related inflammation of peripheral veins during chemotherapy [4].

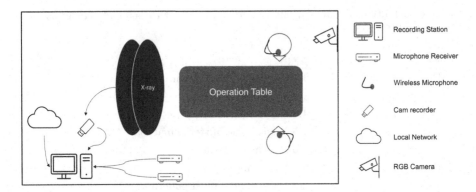

**Fig. 1.** The data recording setup of our corpus. During an intervention, X-ray images are recorded with a C-Arm machine and displayed on a screen in the OR. X-ray images were captured from this display. The surgeon and the assistant were equipped with personal microphones to record their speech signals. System commands were recorded from a local network utilizing a monitoring software. An RGB camera with an embedded microphone recorded the interventions. Audio data from this camera were added to our corpus and recorded videos are used solely for aiding with the annotation process.

## 3.2    Data Collection Setup

A PoCaP intervention is commonly performed by a surgeon and an assistant. While the surgeon is in the sterile area, the assistant controls the table, lights, C-Arm X-ray machine, or other medical equipment in accordance with commands given by the surgeon. Therefore, it is meaningful to capture all verbal conversations between the surgeon and the assistant, in order to capture rich contextual information for the surgical workflow analysis. Additionally, speech is the sole data source that appears in every type of surgery, and it is therefore important to analyze for the design of scalable systems. In order to record these speech signals, the surgeon and the assistant were equipped with personal microphones during surgeries. For this task, we used two sets of Sennheiser XSW 2 ME3-E wireless headsets. With this configuration, we were able to obtain two-channel high-quality speech signals uttered by the surgeon and the assistant individually. In some cases, a second surgeon or assistant was necessary in the OR, however, that personnel didn't wear a microphone. The necessity is generally due to complications during the operation.

X-ray images are another highly useful data source, especially for a PoCaP intervention. For example, the subclavian area and VCI area are monitored before catheter placement, using fluoroscopy during the intervention. Furthermore, the catheter is guided into the patients' body and controlled similarly by X-ray images. These activities are represented in phases 3,5 and 7 in Table 1. For those reasons, it is a very rich complementary data source for the surgical workflow analysis in this case. In the OR, X-ray images are shown on a widescreen located on the other side of the surgical table for immediate assessment. To record X-ray data, we utilized the input signal going into this display, see Fig. 2. We duplicated the input signal and recorded it with the Open Broadcaster Software (OBS) [1]. We also utilized OBS to concurrently capture audio and speech input from the configuration described in the previous paragraph.

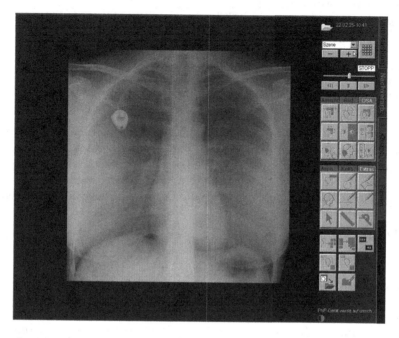

**Fig. 2.** An illustration of the screen capture with an X-ray image from a port-catheter placement intervention captured with OBS. For data privacy purposes, the X-ray image is replaced by an open-source image from [10].

Modern ORs have many digital sensors providing information about the status and activities of medical devices. We included such data from the C-Arm machine in our corpus as system commands. System commands refer to status and activity logs and they are created when the device is utilized, which is typically done by the assistant during a PoCaP intervention. In our case, the C-Arm machine is connected to a local network and can be monitored by a local PC and a monitoring software called *ACSOS*. ACSOS generates a *ticket* when a function of a medical device in the OR is used and logs all related variables. It can display a total of 393 different variables in total. An example of a ticket is shown in Fig. 3. This information can be regarded as similar to tool usage information and as a relevant source for the workflow analysis. We manually copied this data from the local computer for each operation.

In order to ease the annotation procedure, we recorded ambient videos with a single GoPro Hero 8 camera. Depending on the patients' choice, intervention can be done on the left or right side of their chest. We positioned the camera on the

| Ticket: C-Arm Machine Status | | | |
|---|---|---|---|
| Variable | Min - Max Range | Dimension | Value |
| Longitudinal position | [-5000, 5000] | mm | 0 |
| Height from floor | [-1000, 5000] | mm | 1100 |
| Physical rotation angle | [-3600, 3600] | 0.1 Degree | 510 |
| Acquisition and fluro mode | [1, 20] | none | 5 |
| X-ray pulse rate | [0, 32767] | 0.01 Frame / second | 7100 |

**Fig. 3.** When the C-Arm machine is utilized, a respective ticket containing all necessary variables is created. The exemplary ticket variables in this table show the current position of the C-arm machine and mode settings with arbitrary values.

left or right side of the OR to cover the operation table and the sterile area. We utilized ambient videos solely to annotate our corpus accurately. However, these ambient videos include also speech and audio signals recorded with an embedded microphone. We integrated these signals as a third channel to our dataset. When compared to personal microphones, this data channel is noisy and reverberant.

## 4   Dataset

### 4.1   Data Structure

After the data collection process, we created a data structure with different modalities. We extracted two-channel audio signals from OBS captures and single-channel audio from ambient videos. We saved this audio data separately. As shown in Fig. 2, OBS recordings include software tool section on the right side. We cropped this section and converted videos to frames at $1fps$. The cropped section did not include relevant information about the intervention. Finally, we included system commands in our corpus. We used extracted audio and video frames for the alignment of the data sources. Moreover, we used the audio signals to obtain transcriptions of the conversations as explained in Sect. 4.3. The data structure of our corpus is shown in Fig. 4.

### 4.2   Alignment

In our data collection protocol, three different recording devices are used. X-ray images and audio signals are recorded with OBS on a laptop, system commands are recorded on a local computer, and ambient videos are recorded with a single camera. Each recording is started from the relative source manually in the following order: ambient video recording, X-ray and audio capture with OBS, and system commands recording with ACSOS. Thus, it is necessary to align these data sources before continuing with the preprocessing and data annotation steps.

We used the audio channels to align the ambient videos and OBS video captures. First, we randomly chose a reference channel from the personal microphones. Next, we computed the autocorrelation function of the reference channel and the third channel from the ambient videos. We used the position of the

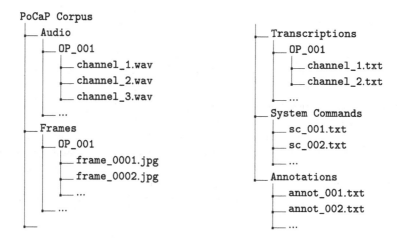

**Fig. 4.** The multimodal data structure of the PoCaP Corpus, consisting of speech, transcriptions, X-ray images, system commands, and workflow annotations.

maximum correlation point to find the time difference between these sources. We padded the microphone signals at the beginning with zeros to align them with the third channel from the ambient videos. Additionally, due to limitations of the battery capacity of the ambient camera, we could not capture the last parts of every operation, if the intervention took longer than approximately one and a half hours. For these operations, we padded the audio signals with zeros at the end as well, in order to have the same length as the microphone signals.

Finally, systems commands are aligned utilizing the OBS video captures. When the monitoring software ACSOS is started from the local computer, it is displayed on the same screen as the X-ray images. Therefore, the launch scene of ACSOS is also captured in the OBS videos. Lastly, since the OBS video capture started before the system command recording with ACSOS, we are also able to observe it's starting time on the OBS video captures.

### 4.3   Transcription

After the alignment step, we used Voice Activity Detection (VAD) and ASR algorithms to convert speech signals to corresponding transcriptions.

Personal microphones are always placed closely to the talkers and have low background noise. In this case, the VAD task is close to a signal activity detection task. Therefore, we used simple energy and correlation-based thresholding to detect voice activities [2]. Initially, we applied *30* ms length Hann Window with *50%* overlap. For each window, we calculated signal energy $\sigma^2$ and autocorrelation $c_k$ at *lag* = 1 of microphone signal $x$ as:

$$\sigma^2(x) = ||x||^2 = \Sigma_{k=0}^{N-1} x_k^2 \tag{1}$$

and

$$c_k = \frac{E\{x_k x_{k-1}\}}{E\{x_k^2\}},\tag{2}$$

where $k \in \{0, ..., N-1\}$ is the time index and $E$ is the expectation operator. Afterwards, we applied a threshold to detect voice activities.

After the voice detection, we used publicly available, pre-trained German ASR models to transcribe the speech. To find the best performing ASR model for our case, we manually transcribed a total of six minutes of speech data from different operations with different surgeons and tested six different models. We compared models with our transcriptions using the basic Word Error Rate (WER) as a metric. After the evaluation of the results, we chose *stt_de_conformer_transducer_large* model for the preprocessing pipeline. All results are shown in Table 2.

**Table 2.** Performance of different ASR models on a short clip from our dataset.

| ASR Model | PoCaP Corpus WER (%) |
|---|---|
| *asr-crdnn-commonvoice-de* [12] | 85.80 |
| *stt_de_quartznet15x5* [7] | 56.46 |
| *stt_de_citrinet_1024* [7] | 29.87 |
| *stt_de_contextnet_1024* [7] | 26.96 |
| *stt_de_conformer_ctc_large* [7] | 29.37 |
| *stt_de_conformer_transducer_large* [7] | 11.52 |

## 5    Discussion

In this section, we discuss the challenges in our data collection process and considerations in terms of future machine learning approaches with our corpus. In Sect. 3, the average duration and standard deviation of PoCaP intervention in our dataset were reported. The execution of an intervention can be affected naturally by many different variables. Some actions can be repeated several times or may require a longer time period due to complications. The expertise of surgeons is another noteworthy factor. The duration of an intervention is significantly affected by the experience level of the surgeon.

Since speech and audio data are the main components of the PoCaP Corpus, the performance of an ASR algorithm is crucial for any application. This performance is significantly affected by the use of medical words and dialect. Even with correct transcriptions, speech dialects can pose additional challenges for the following steps. It may be necessary to consider translating these transcriptions to standard language before employing a language model or extracting word vectors. It would be challenging to train such a translation model, similar to difficulties in low-resource language processing.

Moreover, for the development of a smart operating room speech assistant, it is necessary to classify surgery-related conversations and understand synonyms in the speech. Some conversations recorded with personal microphones may not be related to the intervention. These conversations can occur between the surgeons, the assistant, or other medical personnel in the OR. These conversations should be classified and removed as they carry information not related to the procedure and could rather be seen as noisy observations at the semantic level. After this removal, synonyms should be processed next. Here, different surgeons or the same surgeon at different time points, may use synonyms to refer to the same underlying meaning. These commands should be recognized accordingly as having the same meaning.

As depicted in Table 1, X-Ray images are used in three phases and are typically utilized for a short duration in order to emit a minimal radiation dose to the patient. This also highlights that X-ray images are only taken a few times during a single operation especially considering the overall duration of the intervention. This fact makes them a very valuable source of information for the task of phase recognition of an intervention since they can be used as distinct landmarks for the identification of specific phases. However, this aspect should be further investigated in future works.

In order to develop robust machine learning algorithms, a large dataset with a large variety of variables is necessary. In our case, the number of operations, the number of medical institutions, and the number of surgeons are important. Currently, our corpus includes 31 interventions performed by six surgeons in a single medical center. For these reasons, we plan to expand our corpus with recordings of more interventions in the future.

## 6   Conclusion

In this paper, we presented the PoCaP Corpus, which consists of speech and audio signals, X-ray images, and system commands collected from 31 PoCaP interventions in the Radiology Department of University Hospital Erlangen, Germany. With this unique dataset, we aim to contribute to the development of a smart speech assistant in the operating room of the future. When compared to previous corpora for workflow analysis, the PoCaP Corpus differs in data types and multi-modality. To best of our knowledge, the PoCaP Corpus is the first dataset that includes speech and audio signals and X-ray images for the development of a Smart Speech Assistant.

We described the data collection procedure, used systems, and preprocessing stages. Furthermore, we described the alignment process of the three different sources using audio signals and screen recordings. Later, we extracted X-ray images from screen recordings and transcriptions from speech signals, recorded by two personal microphones equipped to medical personnel in the OR and reported the ASR results. Finally, we reported challenges and possible future directions. Speech recognition is a more challenging task due to the terminology in a medical environment and speech dialects when compared to the standard

ASR tasks. Therefore, the performance of ASR algorithms is worse than in the usual settings. These challenges may also manifest in the feature extraction tasks of future work. In addition to ASR performance improvements, correctly recognized dialect words should be translated into the standard German language. Synonymous medical terms will be also included in the training of feature extraction algorithms.

In the future, we plan to expand our dataset with more recordings. In the development of a Smart Speech Assistant, the PoCaP Corpus can be used for workflow analysis, recognition of commands given by surgeons, optimization of operation parameters, remaining surgery time estimation, or similar tasks. In that sense, the PoCaP Corpus enables the development of a wide variety of applications and thereby has the potential of making significant contributions to surgical data science.

**Acknowledgement.** We greatfully acknowledge funding for this study by Friedrich-Alexander-University Erlangen-Nuremberg, Medical Valley e.V. and Siemens Healthineers AG within the framework of d.hip campus.

# References

1. Obs project. https://github.com/obsproject/obs-studio (2022)
2. Bäckström, T.: Speech coding: with code-excited linear prediction. Springer (2017)
3. Bar, O., et al.: Impact of data on generalization of AI for surgical intelligence applications. Scient. Rep. **10**(1), 1–12 (2020)
4. Gonda, S.J., Li, R.: Principles of subcutaneous port placement. Tech. Vasc. Interv. Radiol. **14**(4), 198–203 (2011)
5. Herfarth, C.: Lean surgery through changes in surgical work flow. J. Br. Surg. **90**(5), 513–514 (2003)
6. Kitaguchi, D., et al.: Automated laparoscopic colorectal surgery workflow recognition using artificial intelligence: experimental research. Int. J. Surg. **79**, 88–94 (2020)
7. Kuchaiev, O., et al.: Nemo: a toolkit for building AI applications using neural modules. arXiv preprint arXiv:1909.09577 (2019)
8. Lalys, F., Jannin, P.: Surgical process modelling: a review. Int. J. Comput. Assist. Radiol. Surg. **9**(3), 495–511 (2013). https://doi.org/10.1007/s11548-013-0940-5
9. Maier-Hein, L., et al.: Surgical data science for next-generation interventions. Nat. Biomed. Eng. **1**(9), 691–696 (2017)
10. Radiopaedia.org: Case courtesy of Dr Henry Knipe, rID: 26966
11. Ramesh, S., et al.: Multi-task temporal convolutional networks for joint recognition of surgical phases and steps in gastric bypass procedures. Int. J. Comput. Assist. Radiol. Surg. **16**(7), 1111–1119 (2021). https://doi.org/10.1007/s11548-021-02388-z
12. Ravanelli, M., et al.: SpeechBrain: a general-purpose speech toolkit. arXiv preprint arXiv:2106.04624 (2021)
13. Schoeffmann, K., Taschwer, M., Sarny, S., Münzer, B., Primus, M.J., Putzgruber, D.: Cataract-101: video dataset of 101 cataract surgeries. In: Proceedings of the 9th ACM Multimedia Systems Conference, pp. 421–425 (2018)

14. Stauder, R., Ostler, D., Kranzfelder, M., Koller, S., Feußner, H., Navab, N.: The TUM LapChole dataset for the M2CAI 2016 workflow challenge. arXiv preprint arXiv:1610.09278 (2016)
15. Twinanda, A.P., Shehata, S., Mutter, D., Marescaux, J., De Mathelin, M., Padoy, N.: EndoNet: a deep architecture for recognition tasks on laparoscopic videos. IEEE Trans. Med. Imaging **36**(1), 86–97 (2016)
16. Wagner, M., et al.: Comparative validation of machine learning algorithms for surgical workflow and skill analysis with the HeiChole benchmark. arXiv preprint arXiv:2109.14956 (2021)
17. Zisimopoulos, O., et al.: DeepPhase: surgical phase recognition in cataracts videos. In: International Conference on Medical Image Computing and Computer-Assisted Intervention, pp. 265–272. Springer (2018). https://doi.org/10.1007/978-3-030-00937-3_31

# Investigating Paraphrasing-Based Data Augmentation for Task-Oriented Dialogue Systems

Liane Vogel[1]([✉])[iD] and Lucie Flek[2][iD]

[1] Data and AI Systems, Department of Computer Science,
Technical University of Darmstadt, Darmstadt, Germany
`liane.vogel@cs.tu-darmstadt.de`
[2] Conversational AI and Social Analytics (CAISA) Lab,
Department of Mathematics and Computer Science, University of Marburg,
Marburg, Germany
`lucie.flek@uni-marburg.de`

**Abstract.** With synthetic data generation, the required amount of human-generated training data can be reduced significantly. In this work, we explore the usage of automatic paraphrasing models such as GPT-2 and CVAE to augment template phrases for task-oriented dialogue systems while preserving the slots. Additionally, we systematically analyze how far manually annotated training data can be reduced. We extrinsically evaluate the performance of a natural language understanding system on augmented data on various levels of data availability, reducing manually written templates by up to 75% while preserving the same level of accuracy. We further point out that the typical NLG quality metrics such as BLEU or utterance similarity are not suitable to assess the intrinsic quality of NLU paraphrases, and that public task-oriented NLU datasets such as ATIS and SNIPS have severe limitations.

**Keywords:** Paraphrasing · Synthetic Data Generation · Conversational Assistants · NLU

## 1 Introduction

Task-oriented conversational assistants are designed to perform certain tasks to accomplish a user goal, such as booking a table at a restaurant or playing a specific song. Natural Language Understanding (NLU) components are part of such assistants to perform the tasks of intent classification (IC) and slot filling (SF) [28].

Training data for NLU systems are user utterances such as "I want to book a table in an Italian restaurant", annotated with the intent (here *book a restaurant*) and slots (here *cuisine* = "Italian"). To reduce the immense manual effort needed to conduct such annotations, we explore automatic augmentation possibilities using paraphrasing techniques. Our starting point are template phrases in

© Springer Nature Switzerland AG 2022
P. Sojka et al. (Eds.): TSD 2022, LNAI 13502, pp. 476–488, 2022.
https://doi.org/10.1007/978-3-031-16270-1_39

natural language, such as "Play *[song]* by *[artist]*", that contain slot type place-holders. These template phrases can be specified by developers and are automatically populated from database entries. Our strategy is to directly generate a larger and more varied number of these templates rather than first generating and then paraphrasing example sentences.

Comparing two different paraphrasing techniques, namely a Conditional Variational Autoencoder (CVAE) [27] and the language model GPT-2 [25], we conduct several experiments with different ratios of original and generated data to analyze:

- Under which circumstances does paraphrasing template phrases increase the performance of an NLU system? What are the limitations of this approach?
- How far we can reduce the amount of manually annotated data without a significant loss in NLU performance?
- Which role does the quality of the generated paraphrases in terms of diversity, grammatical correctness and preservation of the intent play in downstream tasks?

## 2   Related Work

Data augmentation for task-oriented dialogue systems has been explored in multiple directions. Similar to our approach, Malandrakis et al. [22] explore variants of variational autoencoders to generate template phrases and Sahu et al. [26] explore the usage of GPT-3 [2] for data augmentation. However, they both focus only on the task of intent classification, disregarding the often more challenging tasks of slot filling and slot preservation. Yu et al. [31] augment data for new Alexa skills by generating template phrases with a transformer-based encoder-decoder sequence-to-sequence model. They only evaluate their approach on internal data that is not publicly available. D'Ascoli et al. [8] augment data from the SNIPS dataset [6] by creating intent embeddings and extracting relevant information from large unlabeled datasets with CVAEs.

Some approaches use simple solutions for data augmentation. Louvan et al. [21] present a lightweight non-machine-learning approach including methods like slot substitution and cropping and rotating parts of phrases based on dependency parse trees. Andreas et al. [1] introduce a rule-based approach for data augmentation. It is based on replacing fragments in training examples with other fragments that appear in the same context. They propose this method for a variety of tasks as it is model-agnostic. However, the approach is different from paraphrasing methods, as it focuses on rewriting phrases but is not necessarily concerned with preserving the meaning of phrases. Gaspers et al. [11] use machine translation to leverage existing datasets while manually replacing slots. Recent approaches explore the usage of GPT-2 or other language models to generate paraphrases [17]. Witteveen et al. [29] use a supervised approach to paraphrase sentences by fine-tuning GPT-2 on pairs of phrases that are separated with a delimiter. They filter the phrases generated by GPT-2 based on several scores (USE [3], Rouge-L [19], BLEU [23]). They do not evaluate their methods in an extrinsic task. Hedge et al. [13] explore generating paraphrases with GPT-2 in an unsupervised setting. They fine-tune GPT-2 for reconstructing phrases from corrupted input in which all stopwords were removed. The reconstructed phrases are paraphrases of the input phrases. They evaluate their approach on a downstream classification task. However, none of these approaches was applied to the domain of task-oriented dialogue systems, which faces particular challenges due to its slot preservation and intent disambiguation needs.

## 3    Datasets

The number of annotated, publicly available datasets for natural language understanding is limited [20]. We conduct our experiments on the frequently used benchmark datasets ATIS [14] and SNIPS [6]. The Airline Travel Information System (ATIS) dataset contains user utterances in the domain of airline travel, categorized into 17 intents and labeled with 67 different slot types[1]. It is an unbalanced dataset where about 75% of the datapoints are from the *atis_flight* intent with a variety of slots. The SNIPS dataset contains utterances for seven intents from different domains, such as booking a restaurant or playing music. It is a balanced dataset with about 2000 datapoints per intent class, the utterances are annotated with 39 different slot types.

## 4    Methodology

### 4.1    Generating Paraphrases

In this section we describe how we generate the paraphrases. To simulate the industry development bootstrapping scenario on publicly available datasets, we automatically construct template phrases by replacing slot values in every utterance with generic slot tokens, and sample fixed volumes of the most frequent ones.

*GPT-2.* We start with a pre-trained GPT-2 model from Huggingface [30], which we further fine-tune for the task of template phrase generation, treating the slot placeholders as words. We then sample from the fine-tuned model to obtain paraphrases. The fine-tuning is done on un-paired template phrases, and only for a small number of epochs to avoid overfitting on the limited training data. The embedding layer of GPT-2, which is shared between the input and output layer, is kept fixed from the pre-training and is not set to be trainable during fine-tuning. We observe that not adapting the previously learned embeddings leads to more diverse paraphrases, as more of the knowledge acquired during pre-training can be incorporated. We train one model for each intent in a dataset separately. The training data is the set of template phrases from that intent.

At inference time, the model receives only the Beginning-Of-Sentence token *[BOS]* as input. When sampling from the predicted distribution, it generates phrases that are similar to the training data. Some input template phrases and generated phrases from GPT-2 are shown in Table 1.

---

[1] Dataset Source: https://www.kaggle.com/siddhadev/atis-dataset-clean.

**Table 1.** Example input and output template phrases finetuning GPT-2 on single template phrases

| Intent | Example utterance | Input | Generated |
|---|---|---|---|
| GetWeather | What's the weather going to be in <city> <state> at <timeRange> | x | |
| GetWeather | Will it be getting <condition_description> on <timeRange> in <country> | x | |
| GetWeather | Is there any chance to change your forecast for <timeRange> in <country> | | x |
| GetWeather | Will the temperature be going to be <condition_temperature> in <timeRange> | | x |
| GetWeather | You can forecast the weather for <timerange> in <country> | | x |
| PlayMusic | I would like to hear <track> | x | |
| PlayMusic | Please play a <music_item> off the <artist> <music_item> <album> | x | |
| PlayMusic | I would love to hear some <sort> <music> | | x |
| PlayMusic | Play some <artist> music that we think people will enjoy | | x |
| PlayMusic | Play <music_item> by <artist> | | x |

*Conditional Variational Autoencoder (CVAE).* Additionally to GPT-2 we generate paraphrases using a CVAE, trained to reconstruct input templates from the latent representation. As conditional input for the encoder and decoder we construct a vector with size of the available slots per template. Elements in the vector are 1 if the slot is present in the corresponding template and 0 otherwise. We sample from the trained models using a mixture of sampling strategies, namely random sampling with temperature, top-k sampling [9] and nucleus sampling [16]. We observed that combining diverse sampling strategies and parameter values outperformed single-approach scenarios in the extrinsic evaluation. All sampled phrases that duplicate the training data or reoccur in the generation are discarded. We also discard paraphrases without slots. We automatically fill the generated templates with specific slot values from a database to obtain user utterances. For each slot type, we randomly pick a slot value to substitute the placeholder in the template phrase (e.g. *date* = "tomorrow evening").

### 4.2   Intrinsic Evaluation – Utterance Quality

We compute intrinsic metrics in order to assess diversity and grammatical correctness of the generated phrases. As metrics we explore BLEU-2 score [23] and sentence embedding cosine similarity between the generated and the original template phrases, using a pre-trained Universal Sentence Encoder [3]. We save the maximum cosine similarity score encountered for each generated template, average all of those maximum scores and report the mean to obtain a similarity value for a set of generated phrases. We also considered utterance perplexity [5], but discarded it as it is unsuitable to properly measure grammaticality [18].

### 4.3   Extrinsic Evaluation – NLU System

Our NLU model for the extrinsic evaluation of the data augmentation techniques consists of a combined LSTM-based [15] NLU system similar to [12] that jointly performs IC and SF. The architecture is shown in Fig. 1. In order to focus on improvements through data augmentation, we intentionally decided to use a fairly simple NLU system. State-of-the-art NLU systems such as [4] are optimized for large datasets, and are therefore unlikely to work optimally in low-resource environments. As preprocessing, all utterances are padded or cropped to a length of 25 tokens as 99% of the utterances are shorter. The tokenizer is constructed with a vocabulary size of 75% of the most frequent words occurring in the training data. This ensures that the model is confronted with out of vocabulary words in the training process, and is intended to better generalize to out-of-vocabulary words encountered during inference. We split the data into 70% for the training and 30% for the validation. An unseen test set is already provided in the datasets. The hyperparameters used during training are listed in Table 2. We evaluate the NLU model on both ATIS and SNIPS datasets and report intent classification accuracy and slot filling F1 scores on unseen test data. In line with previous work, only slots where all tokens are correctly labeled are considered correct.

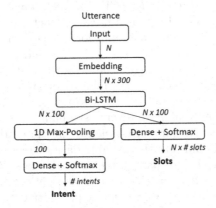

**Fig. 1.** NLU Bi-LSTM model architecture. Blocks represent layers in the model, arrows indicate intermediate values and are marked with the corresponding dimensionality. $N$ is the length of the input utterance.

**Table 2.** Hyperparameters for training the NLU model

| Parameter | Value |
|---|---|
| Tokenizer Vocabulary Size | 75% of train set words |
| Embeddings | GloVe [24] 300d |
| Train / Validation Split | 70% / 30% |
| Epochs | 200 |
| Batch Size | 16 |
| Layer Dimension | 100 units |
| Regularization Strength | 5e−4 |
| Optimizer | Nadam [7] |
| Learning Rate | 4e−4 |

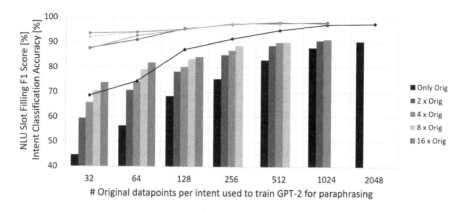

(a) SNIPS original data augmented with GPT-2

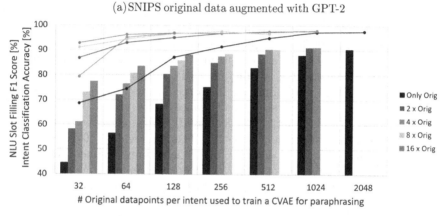

(b) SNIPS original data augmented with CVAE

**Fig. 2.** Scores for Slot filling (bar chart) and Intent classification (line chart) on the SNIPS test data augmented using GPT-2 and CVAE models. The x-axis shows the number of original utterances per intent used to create templates to train paraphrasing models. The y-axis shows the performance of NLU models trained on each (augmented) split. Different colored lines represent different augmentation multipliers for the initial data. (Color figure online)

## 5    Results

In the following subsections we address the individual research questions by reporting and discussing the results of our experiments.

### 5.1    NLU Performance with Augmented Data

In this set of experiments, we explore if augmenting template phrases by paraphrasing increases NLU performance, and if so, until when. Figure 2a shows that the performance of the NLU system increases for all used splits when adding data generated using GPT-2 to the SNIPS dataset. As intuitively expected, the increase of slot filling performance is highest for experiments with a low number of datapoints. Starting with a higher number of manually produced examples, the improvement is smaller, indicating a saturation behavior at around 1,000–2,000 utterances per intent. Figure 2b shows similar trends as Fig. 2a, indicating that both, the CVAE and GPT-2 models are suitable approaches for generating data that helps the NLU system compared to non-augmented data.

## 5.2   Reduction of Manually Annotated Training Data

In these experiments, we explore how far we can reduce the volume of manually annotated training data, i.e. what loss in performance is expected when replacing a part of original utterances with generated ones. In contrast to the previous set of experiments, where we ask how far can we increase the performance by augmenting, here the aim is to minimize the manual efforts. Figure 3 shows the intent classification and slot filling results over varying amounts and proportions of original and generated data. For instance, using 64 original datapoints per intent, the intent classification accuracy on SNIPS is 68.6% (see Fig. 3a, black bar in first column). When fine-tuning GPT-2 on templates from only 32 randomly selected utterances, and generating 32 utterances more, the NLU model trained on the combined 64 datapoints (50% generated) reaches an intent classification accuracy of 87.7% (same column, red bar). This represents a 50% reduction in annotations, with not only no decrease, but an actual improvement in accuracy. We can see that a reduction of over 75% of manual annotations is feasible on SNIPS without a notable performance impact. Overall, the results using GPT-2 and CVAE models to obtain paraphrases are very similar. Compared to the results on the SNIPS dataset, a more noticeable decrease in intent classification performance is observed on the ATIS dataset. We hypothesize that this is due to the shared airline travel domain of all intents, which are more difficult to distinguish for the NLU model. ATIS is an imbalanced dataset, where around 75% of the data belongs to the intent *atis_flight*. In order to estimate how many template phrases per intent class are required to use the data augmentation approach, we use a manually balanced (downsampled) version. For intents with fewer utterances than the specified threshold on x-axis, all utterances are used.

## 5.3   Comparison Between GPT-2 and CVAE Models

The results in Fig. 4a show that both the CVAE and GPT-2 are suitable approaches to augment the SNIPS training data. In direct comparison, for both tasks, the NLU performance trained on data generated by the CVAE (blue) is always slightly higher than the results for data generated using GPT-2 (red). Further research is needed to fully understand why the phrases generated by the CVAE are better in this scenario.

Figure 4b shows that on ATIS, for the task of intent classification, the data generated by GPT-2 outperforms the model trained on data generated by the CVAE. For the task of slot filling, it is the other way around and the CVAE

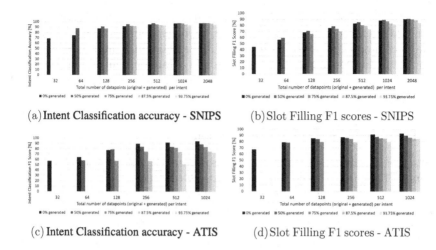

(a) Intent Classification accuracy - SNIPS      (b) Slot Filling F1 scores - SNIPS

(c) Intent Classification accuracy - ATIS       (d) Slot Filling F1 scores - ATIS

**Fig. 3.** How far can we reduce original annotated data and replace it with generated paraphrases? Different utterance sample volumes and proportions of original training data per intent were paraphrased using GPT-2. Each column shows the NLU test data performance values from using only original to using mostly generated training utterance mix for that total volume, indicating a replacement of over 75% of the utterances is feasible.

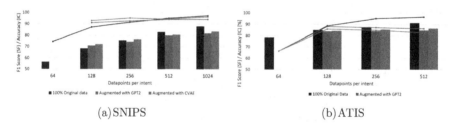

(a) SNIPS                                        (b) ATIS

**Fig. 4.** NLU performance with GPT-2 (red) and CVAE (blue) paraphrasing models trained on 64 original datapoints per intent. Lines show the Intent Classification Accuracy, bars the Slot Filling F1. (Color figure online)

outperforms GPT-2 in this case. One possible reason why the data generated by GPT-2 is less helpful for the slot filling task is that GPT-2 often paraphrases the slot placeholders. For example the input template phrase "Show me the flights from *[fromloc.city_name]* to *[toloc.city_name]*" can be paraphrased by GPT-2 to the template phrase "I want to see flights from *[from.city_name]* to *[toloc.city_name]*". The slot placeholder *[fromloc.city_name]* has been converted by GPT-2 to the placeholder *[from.city_name]*, which is not a valid annotation tag in the ATIS dataset and therefore cannot be correctly filled up with a real value. This modification of slot placeholders cannot occur with the CVAE approach, because a different strategy for word embeddings is used. GPT-2 makes use of byte-pair-encodings [10], where depending on the frequency of occurrence, each character, syllable or word receives an embedding. For the CVAE approach, we use GloVe embeddings [24]. The CVAE predicts words over a vocabulary of the most common 20,000 words in the GloVe embeddings, and uses an out-of-vocabulary token for unknown words. We add a random embedding vector for each of the occurring slot placeholders. Thus, there is no possibility for the CVAE to modify slot placeholders as GPT-2 does.

## 5.4   Limitations on Intent Preservation

We observe that the generated data contains phrases that do not perfectly preserve the intent. Therefore, this section investigates if conflicts occur, and whether the NLU performance for intent classification suffers from noisy, possibly mis-labeled paraphrases. We report F1 scores for intent classification as accuracy values are not suitable for a per-class comparison. The reported values are the mean ± standard deviation of three different runs. When a generated paraphrase does not clearly belong to the intent it was generated for, its semantic content can conflict with the assigned intent label. If the content of a paraphrase is more similar to a different intent from the dataset, this may affect the intent classification accuracy of the NLU system. For example, when training GPT-2 on phrases of the intent *AddToPlaylist*, one of the generated phrases was "Remove this *[music_item]* to my playlist", even though all training phrases only concerned adding songs to playlists. This phrase inherits the intent label *AddToPlaylist*, because it was generated by the model trained for this class. The SNIPS dataset does not contain an intent for removing songs from playlists. However, in a real-world scenario this intent would likely be present, leading to conflicts and a decrease in the NLU system's performance. Figure 5 shows NLU intent classification F1 scores for intents from the SNIPS and ATIS datasets, for ATIS only the 7 intents with the most examples are shown. For the SNIPS dataset, the generated data appears to preserve the intent sufficiently. On ATIS data, especially for the intent *atis_aircraft*, the NLU system has difficulties to classify unseen test data correctly. This suggests that on ATIS, the generated paraphrases do create conflicts between the

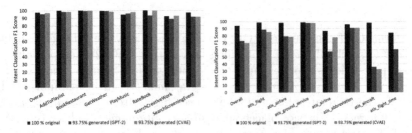

(a) SNIPS, generated data mostly preserves the intent sufficiently (experiment done with 2048 datapoints per intent)

(b) **ATIS, generated data creates conflicts be-** tween the intents (experiment done with 1024 datapoints per intent)

**Fig. 5.** Intent classification performance per intent for both datasets

intents. One possible explanation for this decrease in performance on ATIS is that the intents in this dataset are closer related than those in the SNIPS dataset. Therefore, we assume that it is more common on ATIS that generated paraphrases would actually belong to a different intent, because the intents are more similar and errors can happen more easily.

A selection of example utterances generated by a GPT-2 model trained on ATIS are shown in Table 3, labeled manually according to whether or not they preserve intent for which they were generated. The examples in this table are illustrative and not representative of the overall distribution of generated paraphrases. Based on our results, we conclude that in "easy" datasets such as SNIPS, preservation of intent is not an issue for data augmentation, as the NLU model can still learn to distinguish between the different intents based on generated data. Supposedly, this is because the similarity between intents in the SNIPS data is not very high. However, on datasets with many intents from similar domains, such as ATIS, more care must be taken to preserve the initial intent of the generated paraphrases. More open-access NLU data is needed to draw quantifiable findings.

**Table 3.** Example utterances generated by GPT-2 trained on 128 original datapoints per intent from ATIS (manually balanced dataset). Some of the generated utterances do not belong to the intent they were generated for.

| Model | Generated Utterance | Intent to be generated | Belongs to intent? |
|-------|---------------------|------------------------|--------------------|
| GPT-2 | what's the fare from detroit to chicago on april second | atis_airfare | ✓ |
| GPT-2 | how many passengers are allowed the tampa dc from denver dc | atis_airfare | x |
| GPT-2 | where is the ticket for the flight from westchester county to bay area tuesdays | atis_airfare | x |
| GPT-2 | please let me know about ground transportation in denver | atis_ground_service | ✓ |
| GPT-2 | can you help pittsburgh in dc | atis_ground_service | x |
| GPT-2 | show me the airlines with flights between Pumwani and san diego | atis_airline | ✓ |
| GPT-2 | is it possible to fly to nashville and check flights from new york to miami | atis_airline | x |
| GPT-2 | what type of aircraft is used on flights from newark to tampa | atis_aircraft | ✓ |
| GPT-2 | why does least aircraft not fly eastern flying from new york to new york | atis_aircraft | x |

## 5.5 Qualitative Analysis

Additionally to the extrinsic evaluation of the generated paraphrases for the NLU task, we perform an intrinsic evaluation to assess the internal quality of the generated phrases. On one hand, the generated paraphrases should be semantically close to the original phrases, especially the intent needs to stay the same in order to inherit the intent annotation. On the other hand, the generated phrases should be syntactically diverse and differ in choice of words, to represent a variety of possibilities for expressing an intention such as booking a restaurant. Simultaneously measuring these two desired properties with automated intrinsic metrics is challenging, since the sentences with subpar scores can be both plausibly diverse or undesirably misleading. We do not observe a clear correlation between the extrinsic intent classification performance and either of the intrinsic metrics (Table 4).

**Table 4.** BLEU-2 Scores to measure similarity of generated template phrases data and template phrases of the original data. BLEU between 0 and 1, higher scores = higher similarity. Cosine similarity scores between −1 and 1, 0 = no correlation, 1 = perfect match.

| Intent | Intent Classification F1 Score [%] 64 datapoints (50% generated) | BLEU-2 Score Generated vs. "unseen" 32 | BLEU-2 Score 32 orig vs. other 32 orig | Cosine similarity USE Generated vs. unseen | Cosine similarity USE 32 orig vs. other 32 orig |
|---|---|---|---|---|---|
| GetWeather | 83.26 | 0.6352 | 0.8064 | 0.7139 | 0.7820 |
| AddToPlaylist | 90.91 | 0.6703 | 0.8015 | 0.8504 | 0.8721 |
| PlayMusic | 88.05 | 0.7823 | 0.7048 | 0.8101 | 0.7745 |
| BookRestaurant | 85.29 | 0.7050 | 0.7990 | 0.6596 | 0.7176 |
| SearchCreativeWork | 82.63 | 0.5722 | 0.8021 | 0.6171 | 0.7664 |
| SearchScreeningEvent | 81.21 | 0.4995 | 0.5876 | 0.6550 | 0.6713 |
| RateBook | 97.54 | 0.7429 | 0.8707 | 0.7325 | 0.8125 |

**Slot Refilling.** As the output of the paraphrasing models are template phrases, we automatically fill up the generated slot placeholders with random slot values from a database to obtain utterances. This process is simple in theory but often yields unsatisfactory results especially for time information, where already in the original datasets phrases such as "The weather on Sunday" are sometimes labeled as "The weather on *[timeRange]*" and sometimes as "The weather *[timeRange]*". Such inconsistencies in preposition annotations as part of the slot value result in syntactically incorrect utterances. For example the template "I want to book a hotel on *[timeRange]*" sometimes results in utterances such as "I want to book a hotel on in 2 weeks" or "I want to book a hotel on at 3 pm". More syntactically and semantically informed heuristics could be attempted in the future to further improve results.

## 6    Conclusions and Future Work

In this paper, we investigate the paraphrasing of template phrases as a data augmentation method for task-oriented conversational assistants. Our results show that both used models, the CVAE and GPT-2, are suitable for generating useful paraphrases, improving the performance on downstream tasks. We further point out that we cannot properly assess the intrinsic quality of NLU paraphrases with traditional NLG quality metrics such as BLEU or utterance embedding similarity, and show that these metrics do not correlate with downstream performance improvements. The main limitation for further improving the proposed approach is a lack of diversity in publicly available task-oriented NLU datasets. As future work, it would be interesting to investigate whether our findings are also applicable to state-of-the-art transformer-based NLU models.

# References

1. Andreas, J.: Good-enough compositional data augmentation. In: Proceedings of the 58th Annual Meeting of the ACL, pp. 7556–7566 (2020)
2. Brown, T., Mann, B., Ryder, N., Subbiah, M., Kaplan, J.D., et al.: Language models are few-shot learners. Adv. Neural. Inf. Process. Syst. **33**, 1877–1901 (2020)
3. Cer, D., et al.: Universal sentence encoder for English. In: Proceedings of the 2018 EMNLP Conference: System Demonstrations, pp. 169–174 (2018)
4. Chen, Q., Zhuo, Z., Wang, W.: BERT for joint intent classification and slot filling. CoRR (2019). http://arxiv.org/abs/1902.10909
5. Chen, S.F., Beeferman, D., Rosenfeld, R.: Evaluation metrics for language models (1998)
6. Coucke, A., et al.: Snips voice platform: an embedded spoken language understanding system for private-by-design voice interfaces. arXiv preprint arXiv:1805.10190 (2018)
7. Dozat, T.: Incorporating Nesterov momentum into Adam. In: Proceedings of 4th International Conference on Learning Representations, Workshop Track (2016)
8. d'Ascoli, S., Coucke, A., Caltagirone, F., Caulier, A., Lelarge, M.: Conditioned text generation with transfer for closed-domain dialogue systems. In: Espinosa-Anke, L., Martín-Vide, C., Spasić, I. (eds.) SLSP 2020. LNCS (LNAI), vol. 12379, pp. 23–34. Springer, Cham (2020). https://doi.org/10.1007/978-3-030-59430-5_2
9. Fan, A., Lewis, M., Dauphin, Y.: Hierarchical Neural Story Generation. In: Proceedings of the 56th Annual Meeting of the ACL (Volume 1: Long Papers), pp. 889–898 (2018)
10. Gage, P.: A new algorithm for data compression. C Users J. **12**(2), 23–38 (1994)
11. Gaspers, J., Karanasou, P., Chatterjee, R.: Selecting machine-translated data for quick bootstrapping of a natural language understanding system. In: Proceedings of NAACL-HLT, pp. 137–144 (2018)
12. Hakkani-Tür, D., et al.: Multi-domain joint semantic frame parsing using bi-directional RNN-LSTM. In: InterSpeech 2016, pp. 715–719 (2016)
13. Hegde, C., Patil, S.: Unsupervised paraphrase generation using pre-trained language models. arXiv preprint arXiv:2006.05477 (2020)
14. Hemphill, C.T., Godfrey, J.J., Doddington, G.R.: The ATIS spoken language systems pilot corpus. In: Speech and Natural Language: Proceedings of a Workshop Held at Hidden Valley, Pennsylvania, 24–27 June 1990 (1990)
15. Hochreiter, S., Schmidhuber, J.: Long short-term memory. Neural Comput. **9**(8), 1735–1780 (1997)
16. Holtzman, A., Buys, J., Du, L., Forbes, M., Choi, Y.: The curious case of neural text degeneration. In: 8th International Conference on Learning Representations, ICLR (2020)
17. Kumar, V., Choudhary, A., Cho, E.: Data augmentation using pre-trained transformer models. CoRR (2020). https://arxiv.org/abs/2003.02245
18. Lau, J.H., Clark, A., Lappin, S.: Grammaticality, acceptability, and probability: a probabilistic view of linguistic knowledge. Cogn. Sci. **41**(5), 1202–1241 (2017)
19. Lin, C.Y.: Rouge: A package for automatic evaluation of summaries. In: Text Summarization Branches Out, pp. 74–81 (2004)
20. Louvan, S., Magnini, B.: Recent neural methods on slot filling and intent classification for task-oriented dialogue systems: a survey. In: 28th COLING, pp. 480–496 (2020)

21. Louvan, S., Magnini, B.: Simple is better! Lightweight data augmentation for low resource slot filling and intent classification. In: Proceedings of the 34th PACLIC, pp. 167–177 (2020)

22. Malandrakis, N., et al.: Controlled text generation for data augmentation in intelligent artificial agents. In: EMNLP-IJCNLP 2019, p. 90 (2019)

23. Papineni, K., Roukos, S., Ward, T., Zhu, W.J.: Bleu: a method for automatic evaluation of machine translation. In: Proceedings of the 40th ACL Meeting, pp. 311–318 (2002)

24. Pennington, J., Socher, R., Manning, C.D.: Glove: global vectors for word representation. In: Proceedings of the 2014 EMNLP Conference, pp. 1532–1543 (2014)

25. Radford, A., Wu, J., Child, R., Luan, D., Amodei, D., Sutskever, I.: Language models are unsupervised multitask learners (2019)

26. Sahu, G., Rodríguez, P., Laradji, I.H., Atighehchian, P., Vázquez, D., Bahdanau, D.: Data augmentation for intent classification with off-the-shelf large language models. CoRR (2022). https://doi.org/10.48550/arXiv.2204.01959

27. Sohn, K., Lee, H., Yan, X.: Learning structured output representation using deep conditional generative models. Adv. Neural. Inf. Process. Syst. **28**, 3483–3491 (2015)

28. Tur, G., De Mori, R.: Spoken Language Understanding: Systems for Extracting Semantic Information from Speech. Wiley, Hoboken (2011)

29. Witteveen, S., AI, R.D., Andrews, M.: Paraphrasing with large language models. In: EMNLP-IJCNLP 2019, p. 215 (2019)

30. Wolf, T., et al.: Transformers: state-of-the-art natural language processing. In: Proceedings of the 2020 EMNLP Conference: System Demonstrations, pp. 38–45 (2020)

31. Yu, B., Arkoudas, K., Hamza, W.: Delexicalized paraphrase generation. In: Proceedings of the 28th COLING: Industry Track, pp. 102–112 (2020)

# Transfer Learning of Transformers for Spoken Language Understanding

Jan Švec[(⊠)][ID], Adam Frémund[ID], Martin Bulín[ID], and Jan Lehečka[ID]

Department of Cybernetics, University of West Bohemia, Pilsen, Czech Republic
{honzas,afremund,bulinm,jlehecka}@kky.zcu.cz

**Abstract.** Pre-trained models used in the transfer-learning scenario are recently becoming very popular. Such models benefit from the availability of large sets of unlabeled data. Two kinds of such models include the Wav2Vec 2.0 speech recognizer and T5 text-to-text transformer. In this paper, we describe a novel application of such models for dialog systems, where both the speech recognizer and the spoken language understanding modules are represented as Transformer models. Such composition outperforms the baseline based on the DNN-HMM speech recognizer and CNN understanding.

**Keywords:** Wav2Vec model · Speech recognition · T5 model · Spoken language understanding

## 1   Introduction

Speech processing techniques historically relied on the noisy channel model and the generative paradigm. In automatic speech recognition (ASR), this class of models was represented by the GMM-HMM type of speech recognizers [3]. The same generative paradigm was followed also in the downstream tasks of speech processing in spoken dialog systems, especially in the spoken language understanding module (SLU) [5]. The rise of deep neural networks together with the massive popularity of automatic differentiation toolkits such as TensorFlow or PyTorch introduced the discriminative model paradigm first into the field of SLU [6]. The advent of deep neural networks emerged as a hybrid DNN-HMM architecture, where only the Gaussian mixtures were replaced by the deep neural networks keeping the rest of the decoder stack the same (pronunciation lexicon, language model, and decoding strategy).

The research was accelerated with the publication of the Transformer architecture [12], which was introduced first for the high-level linguistic tasks such as machine translation. The Transformer architecture is capable to capture the inherent knowledge present in large datasets. But for many tasks, including ASR

This research was supported by the Czech Science Foundation (GA CR), project No. GA22-27800S and by the grant of the University of West Bohemia, project No. SGS-2022–017.

P. Sojka et al. (Eds.): TSD 2022, LNAI 13502, pp. 489–500, 2022.
https://doi.org/10.1007/978-3-031-16270-1_40

and SLU, the number of available labeled data is always insufficient for training the powerful parameter-rich Transformer model. The problem was solved by using a transfer learning approach, that uses models trained on large unlabelled data in a self-supervised manner as a base for subsequent training of the parameters on small labeled data. The representatives of this class of models are BERT (Bidirectional Encoder Representations from Transformers) [4] or T5 (Text-To-Text Transfer Transformer) [10] models. The use of the Transformer architecture has also spread to the field of ASR, changing the modeling paradigm from generative models to discriminative models. The end-to-end training of ASR has started to become the state-of-the-art [9]. The recently published Wav2Vec 2.0 combines the Transformer architecture with the transfer learning approach and with the direct processing of a speech signal using convolutional layers [2].

In this paper, we present the results of using the transfer learning approach both in the ASR and the SLU modules of the Czech spoken dialog system. We use the Wav2Vec 2.0 speech recognizer instead of the traditional DNN-HMM hybrid ASR and the fine-tuned T5 model as a replacement for the discriminative SLU module based on carefully designed convolutional architecture.

## 2    Transfer Learning for Spoken Dialog Systems

The Transformer architecture is a building block of many modern approaches in speech and language processing. The rise of transfer-learning techniques leads to novel methods with state-of-the-art performance. The training process consists of two steps: (1) pre-training a generic model and (2) fine-tuning the pre-trained model on in-domain data. We used these paradigms for both models involved in spoken language understanding. We choose the Wav2Vec 2.0 model as a speech recognizer and the Text-To-Text Transfer Transformer (T5) as an SLU module. In this section, the pre-training procedure of the generic models is described. The fine-tuning step of speech recognizer is then described in Sect. 3.2 and fine-tuning of the SLU in Sect. 4.2.

### 2.1    Wav2Vec 2.0 Transformer

One of the most studied self-supervised end-to-end automatic speech recognition (ASR) model architectures is Wav2Vec 2.0 [2]. It is a deep neural network pre-trained to reconstruct the corrupted signals. The input raw audio signal is processed by a multi-layer convolutional neural network into a sequence of latent-speech representations which are fed into a multi-layer Transformer [12] (Fig. 1). The output of the Transformer is a sequence of frame-level contextualized speech representations which are then processed by the connectionist temporal classification (CTC) layer [1] decoding the most probable sequence of graphemes.

Because there is no Wav2Vec 2.0 model available for Czech language, which we are experimenting with, we decided to pre-train our own model. We gathered as much public and in-house unlabeled audio data as possible. Together, we collected more than 80 thousand hours of Czech speech. The collection includes recordings from radio (22k hours), unlabeled data from VoxPopuli dataset [13] (18.7k hours), TV shows (15k hours), shadow speakers (12k hours), sports (5k hours), telephone data (2k hours), and a smaller amount of data from several other domains.

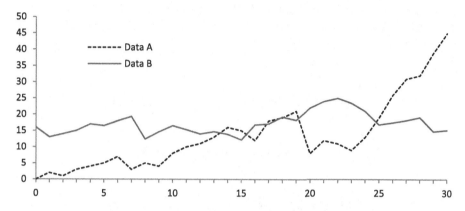

**Fig. 1.** Architecture of the Wav2Vec 2.0 model. Figure taken from [2].

Since the feature extraction of the input signal is limited by the memory of GPUs in use, we sliced all records not to exceed 30 s, which we found to be a reasonable input size for batching.

We followed the same pre-training steps as for the base Wav2Vec 2.0 model in [2]. We pre-trained the model for 400 thousand steps with a batch size of about 1.6 h, corresponding to more than 11 epochs over the dataset. We released our pre-trained model under the nickname *CITRUS* (abbreviation for **C**zech language **TR**ransformer from **U**nlabeled **S**peech) for public non-commercial use[1].

## 2.2    Text-to-Text Transfer Transformer

The Text-to-Text Transfer Transformer (T5) model is a self-supervised trained variant of the generic textual Transformer architecture [10]. The T5 model is able to construct the internal representation of input on many linguistic layers: starting from phonetic and syntactic through semantic to the pragmatic layer. The T5 model is pre-trained in a self-supervised manner by generating a text restoration task from unlabelled training data. An example of the pre-training input/output text pair is shown in Fig. 2.

The T5 model tries to recover missing tokens in the input sentence masked with sentinel tokens <X> and <Y>. The masked tokens are used as training targets and the output sentence is terminated using another sentinel token <Z>.

---

[1] Available at https://huggingface.co/fav-kky/wav2vec2-base-cs-80k-CITRUS.

This way, the T5 learns not only the knowledge required to understand the input sentence but also the knowledge necessary to generate meaningful output sentences.

The original Google's T5-base English model[2] was trained from Common Crawl data[3]. We replicated the same pre-processing procedure to obtain the Czech data and we pre-trained our own T5 model for Czech language. The pre-processing steps correspond with the steps presented in [11] for building the Colossal Clean Crawled Corpus (C4) on which Google's T5 model was pre-trained. Such rules are generally applied while processing web text:

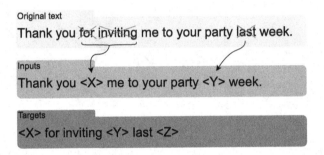

**Fig. 2.** Example of processing the original text and creating input/output text pairs. Figure taken from [10].

- Only lines ending in terminal punctuation are retained. Short pages and lines are discarded.
- Pages with dirty and obscene words are removed.
- Lines with the word "JavaScript" and the curly braces { } are removed (remains of incorrect crawling of the webpage).
- The pages in the corpus were de-duplicated. The resulting corpus contains each three-sentence span just once.

For the Czech language, we have collected the CommonCrawl corpus at the end of August 2020. It contains 47.9 GB of clean text, 20.5 M unique URLs and 6.7 B running words. The Czech T5 training procedure followed the original procedure described in [11].

We used the `t5-base` architecture consisting of 220M parameters, $2 \times 12$ transformer block in the encoder and the decoder. The dimensionality of hidden layers and embeddings was 768. The attention mechanism uses 12 attention heads with inner dimensionality 64.

---

[2] https://github.com/google-research/text-to-text-transfer-transformer.

[3] https://commoncrawl.org/.

# 3   Speech Recognition

Speech recognition is the first module in a dialog system that transforms an
input audio signal into a textual representation usable in the SLU module. The
accuracy of speech recognition is the key metric of the dialog system because the
entities which are not recognizable in this module cannot be used in downstream
dialog processing. In this paper, we compare the performance of the DNN-HMM
baseline speech recognizer and the Transformer-based Wav2Vec 2.0 (W2V) recognizer.

## 3.1   DNN-HMM Baseline

The traditional DNN-HMM baseline speech recognizer consists of a set of different models, esp. an acoustic model, pronunciation lexicon, and language model.
We used two separated class-based languages models for the HHTT and TIA
corpora trained from the training set with classes populated by the related
entities (names, station names, etc.). The acoustic model was a generic hybrid
DNN-HMM model with PLP parameterization. The pronunciation lexicon was
generated by the Czech phonetic rules. The DNN-HMM system allows generating of not only the 1-best word hypothesis but also the word-lattice of multiple
hypotheses. This allows the SLU module to compensate for the lower recognition
accuracy if it is designed to process such input structure.

## 3.2   Wav2Vec 2.0 Recognizer

The W2V recognizer consists of a stack of convolutional layers transforming the
raw input waveform into a latent speech representation. The latent speech representation is then processed in the Transformer model to obtain a contextual
representation of the speech. This representation is then classified using a single
dense multi-class classification layer with softmax activation and trained using
the CTC loss. In this paper, we used an unsupervised scenario where the recognizer was not trained on the in-domain data. The fine-tuning data consisted of
5k hours of labeled data including approximately 430 h of telephone speech with
no overlap with the in-domain data.

The W2V recognizer is a grapheme-based recognizer containing no recognition lexicon nor language model. The W2V recognizer generates an orthographic
transcription of the input audio. It is able to generate grapheme posterior probabilities, but the conversion of the output into the form of word-lattice is complicated. We, therefore, use only the 1-best hypothesis.

When analyzing the output of the W2V recognizer, the confusion tables
revealed that a significant number of errors were caused by wrong word forms,
while the meaning was fully kept. It was caused mainly by the use of Czech
colloquial word forms. Therefore, we decided to apply an output normalization
method mapping all possible word variants having the same semantic meaning
into one correct form.

## 4    Spoken Language Understanding

The spoken language understanding (SLU) module of a dialog system converts the output of the speech recognizer into a semantic representation, which encodes the meaning of the utterance. In this work, we used the abstract semantic trees. Such trees consist of nodes labeled with semantic concepts. The trees are abstract because they do not encode an alignment between the words of the recognized hypothesis and the nodes of the tree. The abstract semantic trees could be represented in the textual parenthesized form (for examples, see Table 1).

### 4.1    CNN SLU Baseline

The baseline SLU method used in this paper is a hierarchical discriminative model based on a convolutional neural network (CNN SLU) [15]. This model is able to cope with the multiple hypotheses output from the speech recognizer in the form of a word lattice. The convolution is performed directly on the word lattice, where each convolution region is represented as a bag-of-word vector with the corresponding lattice score assigned to this region. The output of the convolutional layer is max-pooled to obtain a fixed-size vector representation of the input word lattice. Then, this vector representation is transformed using a stack of fully connected layers to obtain expansion probabilities of the semantic grammar.

The semantic grammar is parameterized by the utterance $u$ and consists of a tuple $G_u = (\Theta, R_u, S)$, where $\Theta$ is a set of semantic concepts, $R_u$ is a set of grammar rules dependent on the utterance $u$ and $S \in \Theta$ is a root concept (starting symbol of the parsing algorithm). The rules $R_u$ are in the form $A \to \beta\ [p]$, where $A \in \Theta$, $\beta \subseteq \{\nu\} \cup \Theta$, $\nu$ is a special symbol representing rules without lexical realization in the utterance $u$ (see below) and $p$ is the probability of concept $A$ having a set of child nodes $\beta$:

$$p = P(A \to \beta|u) = P(\beta|A, u) \tag{1}$$

A standard best-first search algorithm is used to decode the most probable unordered semantic tree assigned to the utterance $u$ by iteratively expanding the nodes of the semantic tree starting with the root symbol $S_0$ and using the rules from $R_u$. In the CNN reimplementation of the HDM, the output layer contains multiple softmax units (one unit for each concept $A$ prediction posterior probability distribution $P(\beta|A, u)$). The parameters of the neural network are then optimized using the categorical cross-entropy loss function.

### 4.2    T5 SLU

For fine-tuning the T5-based SLU model we used the Tensorflow implementation of HuggingFace Transformers library [14] together with the t5s[4] library. This

---

[4] https://github.com/honzas83/t5s.

library simplifies the process of fine-tuning, predicting, and evaluating the model to easy-to-use Python modules. The input files (train, eval, test data sets) for fine-tuning are the tab-separated files (TSV) containing two columns: *input text* and *output text*. For training, it is also necessary to prepare a simple YAML configuration file, which specifies the name of the pre-trained T5 model, the SentencePiece model, the names of TSV files for fine-tuning and hyperparameters settings such as the number of epochs, batch sizes, and learning rate. The `t5s` library uses a variable sequence length and a variable batch size to fully utilize the underlying GPU used for training. In the experiments, we used the ADAM optimization with learning rate decay proportional to the inverse square root of the number of learning epochs.

As the T5 model allows to transfer the task of spoken language understanding into the text-to-text transformation, we used for fine-tuning pairs consisting of speech recognition outputs and relevant parenthesized abstract semantic trees. During the fine-tuning procedure, we tried many combinations of hyperparameter values (number of epochs, steps per epoch, and learning rate). We also experimented with training from ground-truth transcriptions only, recognized data only, and from the mixture of ground-truth and recognized data. The best combination of such hyperparameters was determined using the development set and subsequently, the test data were processed using these settings. The best results were obtained using the following values: the number of epochs: 2, steps per epoch: 1800, learning rate: $5 \cdot 10^{-4}$ and training from the mixture of ground-truth and recognized data.

**Table 1.** Examples of training pairs consisting of speech recognition output (input text) and relevant parenthesized abstract semantic trees (expected output). The first three examples come from the TIA corpus and the other three examples are from the HHTT corpus.

| Utterance transcription | Abstract semantic tree |
|---|---|
| dobrý den mám čas pozítří od jedný do půl druhý | HELLO, ZJISTI(KALENDAR(TIME)) |
| Lit. *hello I have time tomorrow from one to half past one* | |
| nejlepší by to bylo zítra od půl druhé do čtyř hodin | VYTVOR(SCHUZKY(TIME)) |
| Lit. *it would be best tomorrow from half past one to four o'clock* | |
| je volno v zasedačce dnes od čtyř do sedmi | ZJISTI(KALENDAR(SUBJECT, TIME, VEC)) |
| Lit. *is the meeting room available today from four to seven?* | |
| v kolik jedou vlaky na prahu kolem páté a šesté hodiny | DEPARTURE(TO(STATION), TIME) |
| Lit. *what time do the trains go to Prague around five or six o'clock?* | |
| no tak potom v šest sedmnáct s přestupem v chomutově | TIME, TRANSFER(STATION) |
| Lit. *well, then at six-seventeen with a transfer in Chomutov* | |
| ano dvacet jedna deset staví v rokycanech | ACCEPT(ARRIVAL(TIME, TO(STATION))) |
| Lit. *yes (the train) at ten past nine stops in Rokycany* | |

# 5  Dataset Description

In the experiments, we use two Czech semantically annotated corpora: a Human-Human Train Timetable (HHTT) corpus [8] which contains inquiries and answers about train connections; and an Intelligent Telephone Assistant (TIA) [16] corpus containing utterances about meeting planning, corporate resources sharing and conference call management. These corpora contain unaligned semantic trees together with word-level transcriptions (for examples, see Table 1). We have split the corpora into train, development, and test data sets (72:8:20) at the dialog level so that the speakers do not overlap (Table 2). To perform the multi-task training experiment, we had to unify some semantic concepts. In the HHTT corpus, all time and date information was annotated as TIME. On the opposite side the TIA corpus contained more granular annotation of dates and times include concepts like TIME, INTERVAL, RELATIVE-DATE etc. To avoid re-annotation of the first corpus, we have merged all time- and date-related concepts into a TIME concept. We have also unified the concepts for agreement and disagreement so that the resulting corpus contains ACCEPT and REJECT concepts.

To evaluate the SLU performance we use the *concept accuracy* measure [17] defined as $cAcc = \frac{N-S-D-I}{N} = \frac{H-I}{N}$ where $H$ is the number of correctly recognized concepts, $N$ is the number of concepts in reference and $S$, $D$, $I$ are the numbers of substituted, deleted and inserted concepts. The concept accuracy can measure the similarity of partially matching semantic trees. We also evaluate the *sentence accuracy* measure ($sAcc$), which measures the ratio of sentences with the predicted semantic tree exactly matching the reference semantic tree.

# 6  Experimental Evaluation

The comparison of the recognition word accuracy of the speech recognizers is presented in Table 3. First, we present the performance of two different DNN-HMM recognizers on the HHTT and TIA datasets. In this case, the recognizer

**Table 2.** Corpora characteristics.

|                                  | HHTT | TIA   | multi-task |
|----------------------------------|------|-------|------------|
| # different concepts             | 28   | 19    | 46         |
| # different semantic trees (train) | 380  | 253   | 630        |
| # train sentences                | 5240 | 6425  | 11665      |
| # train concepts                 | 8967 | 13499 | 22466      |
| # dev. sentences                 | 570  | 519   | 1089       |
| # dev. concepts                  | 989  | 1106  | 2095       |
| # test sentences                 | 1439 | 1256  | 2695       |
| # test concepts                  | 2546 | 2833  | 5379       |

is tailored for the specific task by using a domain-dependent language model. Then, we recognized the same data using the W2V recognizer. Although the Wav2Vec recognizer does not use domain knowledge, we report the recognition accuracy for TIA and HHTT datasets separately. The comparison of W2V with the DNN-HMM shows that the W2V provides a significant performance boost on the TIA dataset but no improvement on the HHTT dataset. The error analysis on the HHTT dataset showed that a large number of errors come from the orthographic transcription produced by the W2V recognizer scored against a normalized ground-truth reference. Therefore, we applied the rule-based normalization mentioned in Sect. 3.2. We defined a set of 91 normalization rules in total, for example:

- na shledanou ← nashledanou, naschledanou, na schledanou (**Lit.** *good bye*)
- tři čtvrtě ← tvičtvrtě, tvištvrtě, tvi štvrtě (**Lit.** *three quarters*)
- děkuji ← děkuju (**Lit.** *thanks*)

Using these rules, we normalized the recognizer output as well as the ground truth transcription. The vocabulary size was reduced by 31 words in the case of the HHTT corpus and by 47 words for the TIA corpus respectively. The normalized outputs from the W2V recognizer have a significantly higher recognition accuracy than the DNN-HMM baseline.

Since we train a single SLU model using multi-task conditions, we also report the recognition accuracy on the union of HHTT and TIA datasets. Under the multi-task condition, the recognition accuracy on test data increased from 76.23% (DNN-HMM baseline) to 85.01% (normalized W2V recognizer). The lower accuracy on development data is caused by the selection of utterances which are probably more challenging to recognize.

In the next set of experiments, we compared the CNN SLU baseline with the T5 SLU model. We have to note, that the CNN SLU baseline is a special model designed for the SLU task and is able to process the input in the form

**Table 3.** Speech recognition word-level accuracy.

|  | % Acc | |
| --- | --- | --- |
|  | devel | test |
| DNN-HMM TIA | 71.31 | 77.88 |
| DNN-HMM HHTT | 70.40 | 74.05 |
| W2V TIA | 83.70 | 86.08 |
| W2V HHTT | 68.93 | 73.66 |
| W2V TIA normalized | 86.39 | 89.14 |
| W2V HHTT normalized | 73.80 | 79.48 |
| DNN-HMM TIA+HHTT | 70.92 | 76.23 |
| W2V TIA+HHTT | 77.30 | 80.72 |
| **W2V TIA+HHTT normalized** | 80.96 | 85.01 |

**Table 4.** Spoken language understanding performance.

|  | % cAcc | | % sAcc | |
| --- | --- | --- | --- | --- |
|  | devel | test | devel | test |
| DNN-HMM ASR + CNN SLU (baseline) | 76.04 | 80.24 | 69.70 | 74.51 |
| DNN-HMM ASR + T5 SLU | 76.09 | 81.50 | 70.98 | 74.84 |
| W2V ASR + T5 SLU | 80.81 | 84.29 | 73.09 | 79.04 |
| **W2V ASR normalized + T5 SLU** | 81.19 | 85.37 | 73.55 | 79.33 |
| Ground truth transcription + T5 SLU | 87.54 | 87.69 | 81.27 | 83.41 |

of word lattice and also generate the probabilistic distribution over the set of semantic trees. In addition, we used ensembling of multiple models to filter-out different random initializations [16]. By contrast, the T5 SLU model is a text-to-text transformer working only with the 1-best input and 1-best output. From this point of view, the results shown in Table 4 are very promising – the much simpler fine-tuning and prediction of the T5 model is fully compensated by the knowledge extracted during self-supervised pre-training. The T5 SLU model provides better performance on the test data in both the *cAcc* and *sAcc* metrics when using the DNN-HMM speech recognizer in comparison with the baseline CNN SLU.

Since the T5 model is a generative model, the correctness of the generated parenthesized semantic trees is not guaranteed. The T5 generates its output in an autoregressive manner and therefore a small number of predicted semantic trees have an incorrect number of closing parentheses. We, therefore, perform a simple post-processing in which we add the missing parentheses to obtain valid semantic trees. The T5 model also does not have a fixed set of output semantic concepts and therefore it is able to generate semantic concepts not seen in the training data. We treat such concepts as erroneous predictions and count them as an insertion or substitution errors.

By moving from the DNN-HMM speech recognizer to the W2V recognizer, the performance of the T5 SLU significantly improves in both metrics (Table 4). The impact of W2V recognition output normalization is less obvious than in the speech recognition experiment. This is expected because the normalization rules only merge the semantically equivalent words.

The last row of Table 4 shows the ceiling for the *cAcc* and *sAcc* metrics obtained by using the ground-truth transcriptions instead of the speech recognizer. There is only a 2.32% margin in *cAcc* which indicates that the W2V speech recognizer graphemic hypotheses are semantically close to the human-made transcriptions. At the same time, the speech recognition accuracy is around 85% and we can state that the errors are not changing the semantics of the utterances.

# 7   Conclusion

In this paper, we presented the application of Transformer-based models in the spoken dialog systems. We combined the speech recognizer represented by the Wav2Vec 2.0 recognizer with CTC output and spoken language understanding implemented as the fine-tuned T5 model. The overall performance of the ASR/SLU pipeline outperforms the baseline method based on the traditional approach of DNN-HMM hybrid ASR and SLU based on convolutional networks.

The results presented in this paper are very promising and outline future research in the applications of transfer-learning Transformers in spoken dialog systems. First of all, the Wav2Vec 2.0 speech recognizer with the current architecture is not suitable for real-time usage required by natural speech interaction. The causes are mainly the full attention mechanisms used in the Transformer as well as the computational costs of the Wav2Vec model. Another open question is the composability of the Transformer models. In the current setup, the utterances are processed step-wise (speech $\rightarrow$ text $\rightarrow$ semantics). Future research should focus on the composition of multiple transformers (e.g. by using adapters [7]) and the joint end-to-end training. This way, the limitation on only the 1-best text hypothesis would be eliminated. Also, the text normalization process could be implicitly modeled in the composed model.

**Acknowledgement.** Computational resources were supplied by the project "e-Infrastruktura CZ" (e-INFRA CZ LM2018140) supported by the Ministry of Education, Youth and Sports of the Czech Republic.

# References

1. Baevski, A., Rahman Mohamed, A.: Effectiveness of self-supervised pre-training for ASR. In: ICASSP 2020–2020 IEEE International Conference on Acoustics, Speech and Signal Processing (ICASSP), pp. 7694–7698 (2020)
2. Baevski, A., Zhou, Y., Mohamed, A., Auli, M.: Wav2Vec 2.0: a framework for self-supervised learning of speech representations. Adv. Neural Inf. Process. Syst. **33**, 12449–12460 (2020)
3. Deng, L., Li, X.: Machine learning paradigms for speech recognition: an overview. IEEE Trans. Audio Speech Lang. Process. **21**(5), 1060–1089 (2013). https://doi.org/10.1109/TASL.2013.2244083
4. Devlin, J., Chang, M.W., Lee, K., Toutanova, K.: BERT: pre-training of deep bidirectional transformers for language understanding. In: Proceedings of the 2019 Conference of the NAACL: HLT, Vol. 1, pp. 4171–4186. ACL, Minneapolis, Minnesota (2019)
5. He, Y., Young, S.: Spoken language understanding using the hidden vector state model. Speech Commun. **48**(3), 262–275 (2006). https://doi.org/10.1016/j.specom.2005.06.002. www.sciencedirect.com/science/article/pii/S0167639305001421. Spoken Language Understanding in Conversational Systems
6. Henderson, M., Gašić, M., Thomson, B., Tsiakoulis, P., Yu, K., Young, S.: Discriminative spoken language understanding using word confusion networks. In: 2012 IEEE Spoken Language Technology Workshop (SLT), pp. 176–181 (2012). https://doi.org/10.1109/SLT.2012.6424218

7. Houlsby, N., et al.: Parameter-efficient transfer learning for NLP. In: International Conference on Machine Learning, pp. 2790–2799. PMLR (2019)

8. Jurčíček, F., Zahradil, J., Jelínek, L.: A human-human train timetable dialogue corpus. In: Proceedings of EUROSPEECH, Lisboa, pp. 1525–1528 (2005). ftp:// ftp.cs.pitt.edu/web/projects/nlp/conf/interspeech2005/IS2005/PDF/AUTHOR/ IS051430.PDF

9. Karita, S., Soplin, N.E.Y., Watanabe, S., Delcroix, M., Ogawa, A., Nakatani, T.: Improving transformer-based end-to-end speech recognition with connectionist temporal classification and language model integration. In: Proceedings Interspeech 2019, pp. 1408–1412 (2019). https://doi.org/10.21437/Interspeech.2019-1938

10. Raffel, C., et al.: Exploring the limits of transfer learning with a unified text-to-text transformer. J. Mach. Learn. Res. **21**(140), 1–67 (2020)

11. Raffel, C., et al.: Exploring the limits of transfer learning with a unified text-to-text transformer (2020). arXiv preprint arXiv:1910.10683

12. Vaswani, A., et al.: Attention is all you need. In: Advances in Neural Information Processing Systems, vol. 30 (2017)

13. Wang, C., et al.: VoxPopuli: a large-scale multilingual speech corpus for representation learning, semi-supervised learning and interpretation. In: Proceedings of the 59th Annual Meeting of the Association for Computational Linguistics and the 11th International Joint Conference on Natural Language Processing (Volume 1: Long Papers), pp. 993–1003. Association for Computational Linguistics (2021). https://aclanthology.org/2021.acl-long.80

14. Wolf, T., et al.: Transformers: state-of-the-art natural language processing. In: Proceedings of the 2020 Conference on Empirical Methods in Natural Language Processing: System Demonstrations, pp. 38–45. Association for Computational Linguistics (2020)

15. Švec, J., Chýlek, A., Šmídl, L.: Hierarchical discriminative model for spoken language understanding based on convolutional neural network. In: Proceedings Interspeech 2015, pp. 1864–1868 (2015). https://doi.org/10.21437/Interspeech.2015-72

16. Švec, J., Chýlek, A., Šmídl, L., Ircing, P.: A study of different weighting schemes for spoken language understanding based on convolutional neural networks. In: 2016 IEEE International Conference on Acoustics, Speech and Signal Processing (ICASSP), pp. 6065–6069 (2016). https://doi.org/10.1109/ICASSP.2016.7472842

17. Švec, J., Šmídl, L., Ircing, P.: Hierarchical discriminative model for spoken language understanding. In: 2013 IEEE International Conference on Acoustics, Speech and Signal Processing, pp. 8322–8326 (2013). https://doi.org/10.1109/ICASSP.2013. 6639288

# Evaluation of Wav2Vec Speech Recognition for Speakers with Cognitive Disorders

Jan Švec[1]([⊠])(iD), Filip Polák[1], Aleš Bartoš[2](iD), Michaela Zapletalová[3](iD), and Martin Víta[4](iD)

[1] Faculty of Applied Sciences, New Technologies for the Information Society, University of West Bohemia, Pilsen, Czech Republic
{honzas,polakf}@kky.zcu.cz

[2] Charles University, Third Faculty of Medicine, University Hospital Královské Vinohrady, Department of Neurology, AD Center, Prague, Czech Republic
ales.bartos@fnkv.cz

[3] Faculty of Education, Palacký University in Olomouc, Olomouc, Czech Republic
michaela.zapletalova01@upol.cz

[4] Department of Mathematics, Faculty of Informatics and Statistics, Prague University of Economics and Business, Prague, Czech Republic
martin.vita@vse.cz

**Abstract.** In this paper, we present a spoken dialog system used for collecting data for future research in the field of dementia prediction from speech. The dialog system was used to collect the speech data of patients with mild cognitive deficits. The core task solved by the dialog system was the spoken description of the vivid shore picture for one minute. The patients also performed other simple speech-based tasks. All utterances were recorded and manually transcribed to obtain a ground-truth reference. We describe the architecture of the dialog system as well as the results of the first speech recognition experiments. The zero-shot Wav2Vec 2.0 speech recognizer was used and the recognition accuracy on word- and character-level was evaluated.

**Keywords:** Spoken dialog systems · Degenerative diseases · Dementia · Tests

## 1 Introduction

Recent research in the interdisciplinary field between medicine and computer science leads to big advances in the development of technological tools that help doctors in the common medical practice. Other tools are available for the broad

The work has been supported by the grant of the University of West Bohemia, project No. SGS-2022-017 and by the programme Cooperatio, Neuroscience Charles University in Prague. Research of selected physiological and pathological mechanisms of voice, language and speech, their evaluation and intervention in the context of speech-language therapy, special education and neurodevelopmental research conducted at the Faculty of Education, Palacký University in Olomouc (IGA_PdF_2022_014).

P. Sojka et al. (Eds.): TSD 2022, LNAI 13502, pp. 501–512, 2022.
https://doi.org/10.1007/978-3-031-16270-1_41

public to perform self-assessments and to provide a recommendation about further medical examination under a specialist's supervision. The nature of human speech allows observing the first symptoms of many diseases in the changes in the speaker's speech characteristics. Such characteristics could change at all levels of human speech production, ranging from changes in phonetic and prosodic features to syntactic and semantic features to the pragmatic level of human interaction.

Current goals in terms of machine learning include two major branches of research: (1) automatic speech recognition of disordered speech and (2) automatic classification of diseases from speech. The first branch could be used as the compensation tool for patients with dysarthria [14] or recognition of the electrolaryngeal speech [15]. The second branch involves the classification of many degenerative diseases from speech, including Parkinson's disease [17] and Alzheimer's dementia [22] or other diseases such as dysarthria [1].

Alzheimer's disease (AD) and its research is a very broad field in medicinal research [7,21]. The importance of early recognition of dementia is also clearly visible in speech and NLP research. The research has shown that speech can be used to distinguish between a healthy population and AD patients [12] according to non-verbal features, such as length of segments and the amount of silence [9]. Researches for English speech [13] and German speech [20] were conducted. One of the most recent contributions was the *2021 ADReSSo Challenge* (Alzheimer's Dementia Recognition through Spontaneous Speech only) which targets three difficult automatic prediction problems of societal and medical relevance, namely: detection of Alzheimer's Dementia, inference of cognitive testing scores, and prediction of cognitive decline [10].

This paper describes our initial experiments with implementing the dialog system for patients with Alzheimer's dementia speaking Czech. The initial usecase of the dialog system is to collect speech data from real-world dialog scenarios. In the future, we plan to expand the usability of the dialog system to more interactive scenarios by re-implementing the current pen-and-paper standardized cognitive tests. The goal of this paper is to evaluate the modern, state-of-the-art Wav2Vec 2.0 technique for speech recognition of disordered Czech speech.

To the best of our knowledge, our work is the first attempt to deal with the Czech language in the context of dementia and speech recognition – this includes also the development of a corresponding speech corpus in Czech. In this paper, we provide also a comparison of recognition accuracies on word- and character-level between the group of people with cognitive disorders and the control group.

The paper is organized in the following way: Sect. 2 describes the implementation of the dialog system and dialog scenarios, Sect. 3 presents the Wav2Vec 2.0 recognizer used in experiments, Sect. 4 provides description of datasets used in the experimental evaluation in Sect. 5. Finally, Sect. 6 concludes the paper and describes possible future work.

## 2    Spoken Dialog System

Since the real-quality datasets are necessary for almost every machine learning task (excluding zero-shot scenarios), we designed a dialog system that can

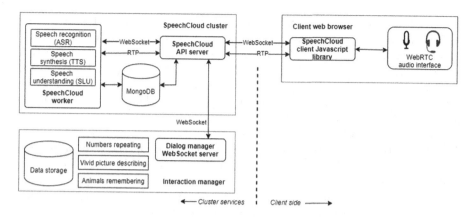

**Fig. 1.** SpeechCloud architecture

perform a set of pre-defined tasks with a person having potentially some kind of neurodegenerative disorder. The dialog system should be also able to store the metadata required for further machine-learning-based processing, such as automatic classification or detection of disorders.

The dialog system was implemented using the distributed platform called SpeechCloud. This platform provides a unified real-time interface between a dialog manager (which has to be implemented as part of the dialog system) and the speech modules such as automatic speech recognition (ASR), text-to-speech synthesis (TTS), and spoken language understanding (SLU) (such modules could be reusable across different dialog systems).

## 2.1   SpeechCloud

The SpeechCloud is a cluster-based technology [23], which allows to easily develop a dialog system and the corresponding dialog manager from scratch. During this development, the ASR, TTS, and SLU modules could be easily reused in a new system. The architecture divides into three parts (see Fig. 1): (1) the SpeechCloud cluster running all the shared services (2) the client system providing an audio interface, and (3) the dialog manager running separated from the SpeechCloud cluster. The communication between these parts is provided using the standardized WebSocket protocol and the SpeechCloud cluster serves as an interconnecting hub. The audio data are transferred between the client system and the SpeechCloud cluster using the RTP protocol. The dialog manager does not use directly the audio, instead, it uses the services provided by speech modules (ASR, SLU, TTS) to perform conversions between machine-readable structures and speech audio.

The client system can be implemented in many ways. One of the most flexible ways is the use of a standard modern web browser implementing the WebRTC protocol. WebRTC is a set of standards enabling the use of audio interfaces in the web browser and allowing the acquisition of an audio recorder (microphone) and audio player (loudspeakers) from the JavaScript code together with the session maintaining protocols like SDP (Session Description Protocol). On the server side, the SIP (Session Initiation Protocol) is used to connect the web browser with the speech engines and RTP (Real-time Transport Protocol) for the transmission of the audio packets. The FreeSwitch software was used as the telecommunication stack, which interconnects the SpeechCloud clients with the allocated speech engines.

SpeechCloud workers instantiate the speech recognizer and speech synthesizer. We used our in-house large vocabulary continuous speech recognition system, [11] and also the in-house speech synthesis, [16]. Typically, 2 CPU cores are used for each worker, but the nature of spoken dialog allows to overprovision the workers because the humans are not talking the whole time during the dialog and the CPU load interleaves across simultaneous sessions [23].

## 2.2 Spoken Dialog

Because the main goal of the spoken dialog at this stage of research was to collect the speech data and evaluate the speech recognizer, the dialog manager only carried out the set of predefined tasks.

The session with the human subject (potential patient) starts with filling in the textual form with the session metadata (subject's anonymized identification, date of birth, place where the subject lives, the scores of the subject in the cognitive tests etc.).

Then, the spoken dialog starts and mainly the text-to-speech synthesis is used to guide the subject through the dialog session consisting of a set of dialog scenarios (see Sect. 2.3). At the same time, the speech recognizer is used to recognize and store the subject's utterances. The dialog itself consists of a set of simple cognitive tests and the time to complete the test is indicated using a timer.

Although the feedback from the speech recognizer to the state of the dialog is not currently used, the overall framework and implementation of the dialog manager allows a simple modification and extension of the testing procedure in the future.

The dialog is executed from a multimodal web application, which uses the visual feedback to guide the subject through dialog, to present the visual stimulus to the subject and to measure the time remaining in the current dialog scenario. The web forms are used as the metadata input form. The audio output of the web page is generated using TTS and the utterances of the subjects are streamed to the SpeechCloud server. The web application alone is implemented using HTML, JavaScript and CSS code. For interfacing with the SpeechCloud platform, the SpeechCloud.js library was used.

## 2.3 Dialog Scenarios

The sequence of dialog scenarios is started after the dialog session is initiated by filling in the subject's metadata. Each dialog scenario is introduced using the prompt synthesized in TTS module. The prompt describes the goal of the scenario and its time constraints. After the time measured by the visible counter runs out, the next dialog scenario is automatically executed. It is supposed that the subject fulfills the scenario using his own voice. The speech data are recorded and together with the automatically recognized speech transcript are stored in the data storage of the dialog manager.

In the following paragraphs we will shortly describe the currently deployed dialog scenarios used to collect the data for this paper:

**Repeating Numbers.** The first test is meant to be more of a warm-up test for the patient. They are required to repeat numbers said to them by the application to test whether the application is working properly but more importantly to test the patient's hearing.

**Remembering Animals.** The patient has thirty seconds to name as many animals as he/she can remember, which is evaluated at the end of the test and cross-referenced with the number of animals remembered by a healthy population.

**Picture Description.** The core dialog scenario of the dialog system was the description of the vivid shore picture (Fig. 2). The picture was carefully designed by the members of our team. The picture takes into account all the effects that accompany cognitive disorders like dementia. The disorder not only affects

**Fig. 2.** Black and white vivid shore picture

memory, and thus remembering individual words, but also significantly impairs the patient's ability to sustain the flow of thought and the ability to describe interconnected events present in the picture.

The picture is divided into three layers of interest: (1) the water of the lake in the foreground (2) the grassy shoreline in the middleground, and (3) the sky and trees in the background. There are several events taking place in each layer so that the subject always has something to describe and talk about. This division of planes and distribution of events in each layer was specifically designed so that the flow of thoughts of the patient could be analyzed:

1. Where do patients start and where do patients end in describing the picture?
2. Do they go through the picture horizontally/vertically?
3. Do they notice all the events?
4. Do they use only single words to describe events?
5. Do they see the overall big picture – "sunny day at the river"?
6. Do they remember the right words (e.g., squirrel)?
7. Does the described story follow some story line or does the subject only repeat a few words describing the most obvious activities?

The description of the flow of thoughts must still be done by hand, however, the preparation of a new approach to automatic evaluation is an ongoing process, see Sect. 6.

## 3   Wav2Vec 2.0 Speech Recognition

The recorded audio data are very hard to recognize using traditional DNN-HMM hybrid speech recognizer for many reasons, we will mention the following: (1) hard acoustic conditions caused by the use of web browser and distant microphone recording (2) speech influenced by cognitive deficits (3) almost arbitrary language of utterances that is hard to model using language modeling (4) specific, open and probably large recognition lexicon.

Therefore, we looked for a new promising end-to-end method for speech recognition. The evaluation of available methods lead us to the use of the Wav2Vec 2.0 recognizer with the CTC trained output grapheme classification layer. The method uses a transfer learning approach consisting of pretraining on large unlabelled datasets and subsequent fine-tuning on a smaller labeled dataset.

We hope that such kind of recognizer could tackle the mentioned limitations of traditional hybrid recognizers. The adaptation to acoustic conditions is performed during the pretraining phase where many audios are recorded in other situations than the close-talk microphone. The remaining problems are solved inherently by the grapheme nature of the Wav2Vec 2.0 recognizer – it uses no recognition lexicon nor language model and therefore can recognize non-standard words or just fragments of words pronounced by people with cognitive deficits.

The Wav2Vec 2.0 [3] is a deep neural network pre-trained to reconstruct the corrupted signals. The input raw audio signal is processed by a multi-layer convolutional neural network into a sequence of latent-speech representations which are fed into a multi-layer Transformer [18]. The output of the Transformer is a sequence of frame-level contextualized speech representations which are then processed by the connectionist temporal classification (CTC) layer [2] decoding the most probable sequence of graphemes.

Public model repositories contain a large number of pretrained or even fune-tuned Wav2Vec models for many languages. Unfortunately, for Czech, the set of available models is limited. We used the pre-trained model nicknamed *ClTRUS* [8] (**C**zech language **TR**ransformer from **U**nlabeled **S**peech)[1]. The model was pretrained from more than 80 thousand hours of Czech speech. The collection includes recordings from radio (22k hours), unlabeled data from VoxPopuli dataset [19] (18.7k hours), TV shows (15k hours), shadow speakers (12k hours), sports (5k hours), telephone data (2k hours), and a smaller amount of data from several other domains. For fine-tuning, the model was trained using the labeled data which were out-of-domain from the point of view of the cognitive disordered speech evaluated in this paper.

Because the Wav2Vec model is a kind of Transformer model, the self-attention layers present in the Transformer blocks impose a quadratic computational and memory complexity with respect to the input sequence length. Therefore a manageable length of input waveforms is in the order of tens of seconds. To overcome this limitation, we used the sliding window approach to obtain the grapheme posteriors. In particular, we used the window length of 18 s with a 3-s overlap. The overlaps are split in half and the posteriors for the first 1.5 s are taken from the left window and the posteriors for the remaining 1.5 s from the right window. This way, we can decode input utterances of an arbitrary length, because the CTC decoding step is applied to the whole composite matrix of posterior probabilities.

## 4   Datasets (Participants and Their Inclusion Criteria)

We collected the evaluation data in two phases. The first phase consisted of recording the subjects using the vivid shore picture (Fig. 2) and recording the utterances using the smartphone laid on the top of the desk. At the same time, we developed the dialog system and the description of the picture was one of the implemented dialog scenarios. The dialog system was used in the second phase of recordings.

### 4.1   Mobile Phone Recordings

Data collection took place at the Memory Center at the University Hospital Kralovske Vinohrady Third Faculty of Medicine, Charles University, Prague in the Czech Republic in 2022. Participants were asked to describe a submitted picture for one minute. All the participants were informed about an audio record

---

[1] Available at https://huggingface.co/fav-kky/wav2vec2-base-cs-80k-ClTRUS.

being made during the examination. A mobile phone with a running dictaphone was laid on the table in front of the participants. There were total of 17 mild cognitive disorder (MCD) patients (*Dataset1*) and 11 normal elderly (NE) people (*Control Group*).

## 4.2 Dialog System Recordings

Black and white vivid shore picture (2) was described for one minute by patients with mild cognitive deficits individuals at Memory Center at the University Hospital Kralovske Vinohrady Third Faculty of Medicine, Charles University, Prague in the Czech Republic in 2022. There was a total of 16 recorded MCD patients using the presented dialog system. We denote this dataset as *Dataset2*.

The inclusion and exclusion criteria of normal elderly people were assessed during a brief interview based on a questionnaire. Inclusion criteria were age over 45 years, Czech native language, and independent living in the community. Exclusion criteria were psychiatric or neurological brain disorders (e.g., stroke, trauma, tumor, alcohol abuse, and psychoactive medications) and depression with a Geriatric Depression Scale score of more than six points.

Patients with MCD were recruited consecutively if they met the following inclusion criteria: long-term follow-ups at the Memory Center of the Department of Neurology, University Hospital Kralovske Vinohrady, Prague, Czech Republic, a neurocognitive disorder based on criteria from the Diagnostic and Statistical Manual of Mental Disorders 5 (DSM 5), which was determined by an experienced cognitive neurologist, and mild cognitive deficits based on scores of our in-house cognitive tests Amnesia Light and Brief Assessment (ALBA test) and PICture Naming and Immediate Recall (PICNIR test). These two innovative and original Czech tests are easy to perform and evaluate, but at the same time challenging for the subject, are very short, lasting up to five minutes, and are used to detect mild cognitive deficits, especially short-term episodic or long-term semantic memory. The ALBA test consists of repeating a sentence of six words, performing and then recall of six gestures, and finally recall of the words of the original sentence. In the PICNIR test, the first task is to write down the names of 20 black and white pictures and then to recall and write as many picture names as possible in one minute [4,5].

One-minute description of the picture was recorded using a smartphone during an in-person examination (normal elderly people, dataset *Control group*: 11 speakers, 1117 transcribed words, patients with MCD, dataset *Dataset1*: 17 speakers, 1960 transcribed words). The second type of data was recorded using the presented dialog system (patients with MCD during an in-person examination or online, dataset *Dataset2*: 16 speakers, 1593 transcribed words).

## 5   Experimental Evaluation

For experimental evaluation, we manually transcribed all three datasets. Then, we used the fine-tuned Czech Wav2Vec 2.0 speech recognizer to automatically transcribe all the utterances. Our goal in the evaluation was to estimate the expected recognition accuracy of the untrained Wav2Vec recognizer. We evaluated the accuracy on the character- and word-level, because the Wav2Vec recognizer is grapheme-based and can produce an exact transcription of the utterance not influenced by the recognition vocabulary. To compute the recognition accuracy, we computed a Levenshtein alignment of the reference and hypothesis, and then the accuracy is computed as $Acc = \frac{N-I-D-S}{N}$, where $N$ is the total number of tokens in reference, and $I/D/S$ are the counts of insertion/deletion/substitution errors.

The results of the evaluation are summarized in Table 1. The accuracy means and standard deviations are computed over the set of different speakers in a given dataset. We can see that the character-level and word-level accuracy are correlated. But, the same character-level accuracy of 90% for *Dataset2* and *Control group* is not mirrored in the word-level accuracy for those datasets. We suppose that this is influenced by the basic principle of the Wav2Vec recognizer – the recognition of graphemes. This leads to high character-level accuracy, but it can cause a drop in the word-level accuracy because the human transcriber naturally tends to transcribe the utterance into a readable form. Therefore, the transcriber sometimes inserts some characters, which are not audible in the utterance and are not recognized by the Wav2Vec recognizer.

The word accuracy of around 70% indicates a good baseline for subsequent machine-learning-based methods applied to the automatic transcriptions. The difference between character-level and word-level accuracy suggests, that further data collection and retraining of the Wav2Vec recognizer could improve the recognition performance. By training the Wav2Vec on the in-domain data, the model will be aware of the entities occurring in the vivid shore picture and also in the utterances (such as a swimmer, a fisherman, or a parasol).

**Table 1.** Character-level and word-level accuracy per dataset in percents. *avg* means the average accuracy over the speakers and *std* its standard deviation.

|  | Char-level Acc | | | Word-level Acc | | |
|---|---|---|---|---|---|---|
| Groups | avg | ± | std | avg | ± | std |
| *Dataset1* | 83.5 | ± | 10.2 | 64.6 | ± | 11.9 |
| *Dataset2* | 90.0 | ± | 7.8 | 67.4 | ± | 13.3 |
| *Control group* | 90.1 | ± | 5.7 | 74.1 | ± | 11.6 |

Finally, we plotted the scattered plot of the character accuracy versus the word accuracy (Fig. 3). Each data point in the scattered plot indicates an individual speaker. The majority of speakers are located inside a rectangle with the center designed with the mean accuracy and width and height of two standard deviations of the accuracy. But for all three datasets, the outliers are present. Again, we can hypothesize that the number of outliers will be reduced after retraining on the in-domain data.

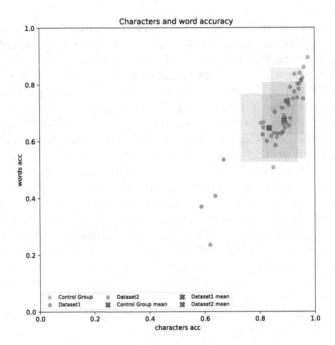

**Fig. 3.** Scattered plot of word-level accuracy vs. character-level accuracy for individual speakers.

# 6   Conclusion and Future Work

In this paper, we presented our initial effort toward the automatic processing (and in the future classification and prediction) of Czech speech data of people with cognitive disorders such as Alzheimer's dementia. We outlined the design and architecture of the baseline spoken dialog system. The system uses a modular architecture called SpeechCloud, which provides multiplatform access to speech modules such as speech synthesis and recognition.

We also evaluated the performance of the Wav2Vec 2.0 speech recognizer on a data sample containing the speech of people with cognitive disorders. A large portion of such data comprise the spoken description of the vivid shore picture. In evaluation, we observed that even the untrained speech recognizer provides high character-level accuracy. The lower word-level accuracy is caused by the fact that the words used in the utterances are not well-modeled in the speech recognizer. We hope that further data collection can lead to a sufficiently large dataset suitable for fine-tuning the Wav2Vec speech recognizer. We also plan to use the adaptation techniques for Wav2Vec models, for example, based on Transformer adapters and x-vectors [6].

The future of our research is not only in recognition of the utterances but also in understanding them. Our goal is to map the flow of spoken concepts related to the described vivid shore picture with the spatial position of the concept in the picture. We plan to model and visualize the flow of such concepts with respect to a particular group of people (normal elderly/patients with cognitive deficits). We would like also to include the linguistic and phonetic features present in the utterance, such as the timing of phonemes, mispronounced words, repeated phonemes, and words. The results presented in this paper suggest a good starting point for this research.

# References

1. Al-Qatab, B.A., Mustafa, M.B.: Classification of dysarthric speech according to the severity of impairment: an analysis of acoustic features. IEEE Access **9**, 18183–18194 (2021). https://doi.org/10.1109/ACCESS.2021.3053335
2. Baevski, A., Rahman Mohamed, A.: Effectiveness of self-supervised pre-training for ASR. In: ICASSP 2020–2020 IEEE International Conference on Acoustics, Speech and Signal Processing (ICASSP), pp. 7694–7698 (2020)
3. Baevski, A., Zhou, Y., Mohamed, A., Auli, M.: Wav2Vec 2.0: a framework for self-supervised learning of speech representations. In: Advances in Neural Information Processing Systems, **33**, pp. 12449–12460 (2020)
4. Bartoš, A.: Netestuj, ale pobav - písemné záměrné pojmenování obrázků a jejich vybavení jako krátká kognitivní zkouška. Cesko Slov Neurol N. **112**(6), 671–679 (2016)
5. Bartoš, A.: Netestuj, ale pobav - písemné zámšrné pojmenování obrázků a jejich vybavení jako krátká kognitivní zkouška. Cesko Slov Neurol N. **82**(4), 369–378 (2019)
6. Baskar, M.K., Herzig, T., Nguyen, D., Diez, M., Polzehl, T., Burget, L., Černocký, J.H.: Speaker adaptation for wav2vec2 based dysarthric ASR (2022). arXiv preprint arXiv: 2204.00770
7. De Roeck, E.E., De Deyn, P.P., Dierckx, E., Engelborghs, S.: Brief cognitive screening instruments for early detection of Alzheimer's disease: a systematic review. Alzheimer's Res. Ther. **11**(1), 21 (2019). https://doi.org/10.1186/s13195-019-0474-3
8. Lehečka, J., Švec, J., A.P., Psutka, J.: Exploring capabilities of monolingual audio transformers using large datasets in automatic speech recognition of Czech. In: Proceedings Interspeech (2022)
9. König, A., et al.: Automatic speech analysis for the assessment of patients with pre-dementia and alzheimer's disease. Alzheimer's Dementia Diagn. Assessment Dis. Monit. **1**(1), 112–124 (2015). https://doi.org/10.1016/j.dadm.2014.11.012, https://www.sciencedirect.com/science/article/pii/S2352872915000160
10. Luz, S., Haider, F., de la Fuente, S., Fromm, D., MacWhinney, B.: Detecting cognitive decline using speech only: the ADReSSo challenge. In: Proceedings Interspeech 2021, pp. 3780–3784 (2021). https://doi.org/10.21437/Interspeech.2021-1220
11. Pražák, A., Loose, Z., Psutka, J.V., Radová, V., Psutka, J., Švec, J.: Live tv subtitling through respeaking. In: INTERSPEECH 2021, pp. 2339–2340 (2021)
12. Pulido, M.L.B., et al.: Alzheimer's disease and automatic speech analysis: a review. Expert Syst. Appl. **150**, 113213 (2020). https://doi.org/10.1016/j.eswa.2020.113213, https://www.sciencedirect.com/science/article/pii/S0957417420300397
13. Qiao, Y.: Computer-assisted speech analysis in mild cognitive impairment and alzheimer's disease: a pilot study from shanghai, China. J. Alzheimer's Dis. **75**, 211–221 (2020). https://doi.org/10.3233/JAD-191056

14. Ren, J., Liu, M.: An automatic dysarthric speech recognition approach using deep neural networks. Int. J. Adv. Comput. Sci. Appl. **8**(12) (2017). https://doi.org/10.14569/IJACSA.2017.081207

15. Stanislav, P., Psutka, J.V., Psutka, J.: Recognition of the electrolaryngeal speech: comparison between human and machine. In: Ekštein, K., Matoušek, V. (eds.) TSD 2017. LNCS (LNAI), vol. 10415, pp. 509–517. Springer, Cham (2017). https://doi.org/10.1007/978-3-319-64206-2_57

16. Tihelka, D., Hanzlíček, Z., Jůzová, M., Vít, J., Matoušek, J., Grůber, M.: Current state of text-to-speech system ARTIC: a decade of research on the field of speech technologies. In: Sojka, P., Horák, A., Kopeček, I., Pala, K. (eds.) TSD 2018. LNCS (LNAI), vol. 11107, pp. 369–378. Springer, Cham (2018). https://doi.org/10.1007/978-3-030-00794-2_40

17. Vásquez-Correa, J., et al.: Convolutional neural networks and a transfer learning strategy to classify Parkinson's disease from speech in three different languages. In: Nyström, I., Hernández Heredia, Y., Milián Núñez, V. (eds.) CIARP 2019. LNCS, vol. 11896, pp. 697–706. Springer, Cham (2019). https://doi.org/10.1007/978-3-030-33904-3_66

18. Vaswani, A., et al.: Attention is all you need. In: Advances in Neural Information Processing Systems, vol. 30 (2017)

19. Wang, C., et al.: VoxPopuli: a large-scale multilingual speech corpus for representation learning, semi-supervised learning and interpretation. In: Proceedings of ACL (Volume 1: Long Papers), pp. 993–1003. Association for Computational Linguistics, (2021). https://aclanthology.org/2021.acl-long.80

20. Weiner, J., Herff, C., Schultz, T.: Speech-based detection of Alzheimer's disease in conversational German. In: Interspeech, pp. 1938–1942 (2016)

21. Yadav, V.G.: The hunt for a cure for Alzheimer's disease receives a timely boost. Sci. Transl. Med. **11**(509), eaaz0311 (2019). https://doi.org/10.1126/scitranslmed.aaz0311, https://www.science.org/doi/abs/10.1126/scitranslmed.aaz0311

22. Zhu, Y., Obyat, A., Liang, X., Batsis, J.A., Roth, R.M.: WavBERT: exploiting semantic and non-semantic speech using Wav2vec and BERT for dementia detection. In: Proceedings Interspeech 2021, pp. 3790–3794 (2021). https://doi.org/10.21437/Interspeech.2021-332

23. Švec, J., Neduchal, P., Hrúz, M.: Multi-modal communication system for mobile robot. In: Proceedings of 17th International Conference on Programmable Devices and Embedded Systems, PDeS 2022 (2022)

# Fine-Tuning BERT for Generative Dialogue Domain Adaptation

Tiziano Labruna[1,2]([✉])[iD] and Bernardo Magnini[1]([✉])[iD]

[1] Fondazione Bruno Kessler, Via Sommarive 18, Povo, Trento, Italy
{tlabruna,magnini}@fbk.eu
[2] Free University of Bozen-Bolzano, Piazza Università 1, Bozen-Bolzano, Italy

**Abstract.** Current data-driven Dialogue State Tracking (DST) models exhibit a poor capacity to adapt themselves to domain changes, resulting in a significant degradation in performance. We propose a methodology, called *Generative Dialogue Domain Adaptation*, which significantly simplifies the creation of training data when a number of changes (e.g., new slot-values or new instances) occur in a domain Knowledge Base. We start from dialogues for a source domain and apply generative methods based on language models such as BERT, fine-tuned on task-related data and generate slot-values substitutions for a target domain. We have experimented dialogue domain adaptation in a few-shot setting showing promising results, although the task is still very challenging. We provide a deep analysis of the quality of the generated data and of the features that affect this task, and we emphasise that DST models are very sensitive to the distribution of slot-values in the corpus.

**Keywords:** Dialogue State Tracking · Task-oriented Dialogue · Domain Adaptation

## 1 Introduction

Dialogue State Tracking (DST) [7] is a core component of task-oriented dialogue systems and conversational agents [11,12,15]. The goal of a DST model is to keep track of the information that is provided by the user during the whole conversation. Recent DST models (see [3] for a survey) are trained on annotated dialogues, and they learn how to detect slot-value pairs (mostly pre-defined in a domain ontology) in a certain user utterance. Recent research has focused on models that are robust to *unseen* slot-values, i.e., slot-values that are present in the test set but not in the training data [2,13], and on approaches that are able to manage substantial changes in the domain knowledge [8].

In this paper, we deal with the situation where we have a conversational dataset, i.e., a collection of annotated dialogues, for a source domain and we need to create new dialogues that are consistent with a target domain, where a number of the changes has occurred in the domain knowledge. We propose *Generative Dialogue Domain Adaptation* (G-DDA) as a methodology for facing dialogue

P. Sojka et al. (Eds.): TSD 2022, LNAI 13502, pp. 513–524, 2022.
https://doi.org/10.1007/978-3-031-16270-1_42

| Dialogue Source | Dialogue Target |
|---|---|
| USER: I am seeking a restaurant that serves **British** food in the **centre**. SYS: I have **about 7** different options for you. Do you have a certain price range in mind ? USER: I 'd like a **cheap** one. | USER: I am seeking a restaurant that serves **Tuscan** food in the **Lungarno area**. SYS: I have **several** different options for you. Do you have a certain price range in mind ? USER: I 'd like a **moderately priced** one. |

**Fig. 1.** Example of dialogue domain adaptation. Slot-values in the dialogues (indicated in bold) are generated by a fine-tuned Language Model.

adaptation. G-DDA consists in fine-tuning a Language Model on the target domain related data, and using the fine-tuned model for generating appropriate slot-values substitutions. Figure 1 shows an example of some utterances taken from the source dialogue, and corresponding utterances after undergoing the process of G-DDA. Slot-values (marked in bold) refer to a certain Source Domain (restaurants from Cambridge - left part of the figure), have been substituted in order to be adherent to a new target domain (restaurants from Pisa - in the right part of the figure).

Taking advantage of the capacity of the language model to generate several variants for a slot-value, we experimented with different configurations, and have obtained significant improvements with respect to the NO-ADAPTATION setting over the MultiWOZ dataset.

The main contributions of the paper are the following: (i) we propose *Generative DDA*, a strategy for generating slot-values substitutions based on the use of large pre-trained language models; (ii) we define a reproducible methodology for fine-tuning a language model given a target Knowledge Base, with four parameters that can be adjusted to optimize slot-value substitutions; (iii) we introduce new evaluation metrics for assessing the quality of automatically generated conversational dataset without the need for training a DST model.

## 2   Generative Dialogue Domain Adaptation

The objective of our research is to perform Dialogue Domain Adaptation (DDA), a process through which slot-values in a source conversational dataset are substituted with new values consistent to a target Knowledge Base (KB). For instance, the goal of DDA is to substitute the slot-value BRITISH, consistent with the Cambridge source domain, with the slot-value TUSCAN, which is consistent with the Pisa target domain (see Fig. 1). Such substitutions are challenging for several reasons: (i) slot substitutions need to consider morpho-syntactic constraints, e.g., in case the source dialogue list more than one options (*I have seven different options*, while there is only one for the target domain, then the sentence has to be modified (*I have only one option*; (ii) we need to preserve linguistic variability of slot-values, i.e., a certain slot-value (TUSCAN, can be expressed in several ways, like *Tuscan food*, *food from Tuscany*, or *Tuscanian food*; (iii) substitutions need to be consistent with the target KB, e.g., if there is only one

TUSCAN restaurant in Pisa with moderate price, then the source dialogue need to be adjusted accordingly; (iv) substitutions need to maintain dialogue internal coherence, e.g., if a certain substitution has been done at the beginning of the dialogue, then all substitutions that refer back to it (i.e., coreference) have to be coherent.

Given the above mentioned challenges, slot-substitutions can hardly been carried out using simple rule-based approaches. Rather, in this paper we propose a generative method (called *G-DDA*) based on masking a source slot-value (de-lexicalization phase) in an utterance and making a language model generate a target text (re-lexicalization phase) to be substituted to the mask. The generation is influenced both by the context (the text around the mask) and by the prior knowledge of the model.

Figure 2 depicts the process that has been followed for implementing G-DDA. At step 1) we use the slot-values from a target KB (cfr. Sect. 3.1) and the utterances from the source dialogues, to create the training utterances (cfr. Sect. 2.1). We then use these utterances to fine-tune a language model (cfr. Sect. 2.2). Finally, we use this fine-tuned model to generate slot-values (cfr. Sect. 2.3 and substituting them to the original ones in the source dialogues.

The choice of generating the new slot-values with a fine-tuned Language Model, instead of picking them from the Knowledge Base using some rule-based strategy (as already done in previous works [8,9]) is motivated by the fact that the generative approach produces benefits like language variability (the same concept can be expressed with different words, similarly to natural language), and linguistic agreement (e.g., singular-plural agreement is respected).

## 2.1   Training Utterances for Fine-Tuning

Within the DDA task, the training data required for performing fine-tuning consists of a list of utterances containing information on the target slot-values, namely the ones that are in the target KB.

To obtain new training utterances, we select a certain number of *patterns*, i.e., representative source domain sentences with masks in place of slot-values, and iteratively substitute all possible values in the target KB to the correspondent masks. For example, if we select the slot-values CHEAP, EXPENSIVE for the slot RESTAURANT-PRICE, and ITALIAN, INDIAN for RESTAURANT-FOOD, and we take the **pattern**:

[I want a RESTAURANT-PRICE restaurant that serves RESTAURANT-FOOD food]

we would create the following **training utterances**:

I want a cheap restaurant that serves Italian food.
I want an expensive restaurant that serves Italian food.
I want a cheap restaurant that serves Indian food.
I want an expensive restaurant that serves Indian food.

Increasing the number of patterns and slot-values produces exponential growth in the total number of different utterances.

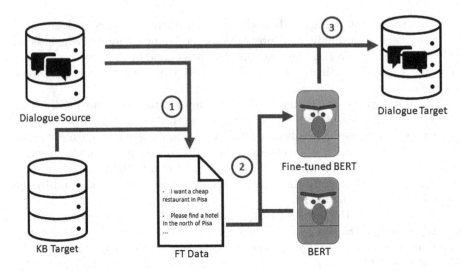

**Fig. 2.** Illustration of the *Generative DDA* approach. (1) Some utterances are selected from the Dialogue Source and the slot-values are substituted with values from KB target instances, in order to create a list of new utterances to be used as fine-tuning data (FT data); (2) BERT is fine-tuned on the FT Data, and a new model is created (Finetuned BERT); (3) the new fine-tuned model is used for generating the slot-values that substitute the ones in the Dialogue source, and a new dataset (Dialogue Target) is created.

## 2.2   Fine-Tuning: Choice of BERT

Starting from the patterns that have been created, as explained in Sect. 2.1, we then implemented fine-tuning of the pre-trained language model.

The fine-tuning process allows us to reap the benefits of large language models, and at the same time to specialize the model on a specific task with a very fast training phase. The choice of the language model to use fell on BERT.

BERT [4] is a language representation model presented by Google in 2018, which has rapidly become prominent for many tasks in NLP. Unlike previous language models, which use left-to-right or right-to-left approaches, BERT uses a bidirectional pre-training, meaning that all tokens in the input contribute to influencing the prediction. One feature of BERT that is particularly relevant for our purpose is that of using a masked language model (MLM) pre-trained objective: some random tokens are masked from the input, and the model has to predict the original word understanding it from the context. This is very well suited for the task of slot-values substitution, where the new value to be generated depends both on previous and subsequent context in the utterance. In addition to that, a second approach based on next sentence prediction (NSP) is used. NSP consist in predicting whether a given sentence A is followed by a sentence B. BERT has reached a new state-of-the-art on eleven NLP tasks including GLUE, SQuAD, and question answering Test F1.

Despite BERT is already 4 years old, we therefore considered it to best suite the requirements of our task. The fine-tuning process took around 30 min using an NVIDIA GeForce GPU. We used 12 hidden layers, a batch size of 8 and a dropout rate of 0.1.

## 2.3  Slot-Values Generation

Once we have a language model fine-tuned on our target domain, we can use it to generate the new slot-values. In order to do that, we select one by one each utterance in the source dialogues. If the utterance contains some slot-values, we mask them and we ask the language model to predict the word (or group of words) that should take the place of the mask.

We then take the prediction that has been generated and substitute it back to replace the mask. Figure 1 shows an example of original utterances that went through this process and corresponding target utterances with the slot-values generated by the language model.

After a generation has been substituted to an original slot-value, this substitution will be remembered throughout the whole dialogue, and the next time that the same slot-value is found, instead of asking the model to generate a new value, we use the same value that was generated before. This allows us to maintain a coherence throughout the dialogue.

## 2.4  Slot-Value Substitution Parameters

The methodology discussed so far can be put into practice with different implementation choices. In order to formalise them, we introduce four parameters, which we describe in the following paragraphs.

*Pattern Selection Method - M.* This parameter specifies the way in which the patterns are collected. It is a boolean value and corresponds to 1 if the patterns are created manually (*ad-hoc patterns*), 0 if they are automatically extracted from the source dialogues. In both cases, particular attention is paid to including the names of domains and slots explicitly in the pattern, so to help the model disambiguate between one slot and another.

*Number of Patterns - P.* This parameter refers to the number of patterns that are created for every [domain/slot-name] pair. It takes 1 as the minimum value so that the fine-tuning is performed on all the slots. With a higher value, we have an increment in the variety of training utterances.

*Number of Slot Masks - S.* It represents the number of slot-name masks for each pattern. The higher this number, the higher will be the total amount of training utterances, since more combinations of slot-values are possible. It takes 1 as the minimum value and MAX as the maximum. MAX means that every pattern has as many masks as is the total number of slot-names for the specific domain.

*Number of Generation Candidates - C.* This parameter indicates the number of generation candidates to choose from for performing the substitution. When the fine-tuned model is asked for generating a substitution to a given mask in an utterance, it proposes a list of possible candidates, ordered by prediction confidence. If this parameter is equal to 1, the first prediction is always picked. If the value is higher, any of the N candidates can be chosen by a conditioned probability, which means that the first values are selected with a higher probability than the last ones.

## 3    Experimental Setting

Following recent literature on DST [5,10,16], we use the MultiWOZ 2.3 dataset [6]. The dataset has been collected through the Wizard of OZ technique and it contains a total of more than ten thousand dialogues, each with an average of around 13 turns, spanning over 7 domains. The context of the dialogues relates to a user asking for information about activities to do in Cambridge and the system provides responses following the setting of a task-oriented dialogue system.

Starting from MultiWOZ 2.3 as source domain dialogues, the dialogue domain adaptation task that we intend to experiment consists in obtaining a new dialogue dataset that is no longer related to the Cambridge domain but relates instead to a Pisa domain (which is a city with similar characteristics), having at disposal only a KB of this target domain.

### 3.1    Source and Target KBs

The target Knowledge Base related to Pisa has been manually built, applying limited variations with respect to the source MultiWoz KB: specifically, the Pisa KB has the same [domain/slot-name] pairs, i.e., the schema of the domain ontology is shared, and it has the same number of instances for each domain (e.g., same number of restaurants), a constraint which is useful to keep under control the complexity of the task. Differences between source and target KB are due to different slot-values used in the Pisa context. For example, TRAIN-DAY has exactly the same slot-values in both KBs, since both have the same English names for the days of the week, while Train-Depart has zero overlaps since there are no train stations in common between Cambridge and Pisa.

The choices for matching a source instance to a target instance have been made following a frequency distribution strategy, meaning that an instance with characteristics that have a certain degree of rarity in the Cambridge KB has been substituted with an instance that has a similar degree of rarity in the Pisa KB. For example, instances of Indian restaurants have been substituted with instances of Italian restaurants, since Indian is the most common food in Cambridge, and Italian is the most common in Pisa.

The information for building the Pisa KB has been taken from an open-source database[1].

---

[1] http://www.datiopen.it/.

## 3.2  Datasets Implementation

Following the G-DDA procedure illustrated in Sect. 2, we have come to create an adaptation of MWOZ with dialogues that are adherent to the Pisa domain. We have produced different versions of Pisa dialogues, using various combinations of values of the parameters presented in Sect. 2.4. In order to find the best values for the parameters (according to an evaluation strategy described in Sect. 4), we used a Grid Search strategy. We report here only a limited number of relevant experiments:

– **BERT (no fine-tuning)** - original language model BERT without any fine-tuning;
– **BERT-M1.P1.S1.C1** - patterns created manually, 1 pattern per domain/slot-name couple, 1 slot-values masked for every pattern, only first generation is selected;
– **BERT-M1.P1.S3.C50** - patterns created manually, 1 pattern per domain/slot-name couple, 3 slot-values masked for every pattern, generation selected over first 50 predictions;
– **BERT-M1.P4.SMAX.C50** - patterns created manually, 4 patterns per domain/slot-name couple, maximum possible number of slot-values masked for every pattern, generation selected over first 50 predictions;
– **BERT-M0.P4.SMAX.C50** - patterns selected automatically, 4 patterns per domain/slot-name couple, maximum possible number of slot-values masked for every pattern, generation selected over first 50 predictions;
– **BERT-M0.P8.SMAX.C50** - patterns selected automatically, 8 patterns per domain/slot-name couple, maximum possible number of slot-values masked for every pattern, generation selected over first 50 predictions.

Each one of these configurations has been evaluated, as described in Sect. 4, and has been used as training set for a DST model, as described in Sect. 5.

## 3.3  Target Test Set

In order to evaluate the quality of our DDA techniques, we need a test set consisting of dialogues whose structure is similar to the ones in MultiWOZ, but related to the Pisa domains. We manually collected a total of 1,000 dialogues, using utterances in MWOZ, and changing the slot-values and their annotations so as to be consistent with the target Pisa KB. Utterances from both user and system have been modified, in order to maintain a coherence throughout the dialogue.

# 4  Evaluation

Table 1 shows the target dialogue datasets obtained using different configurations of slot-value generation parameters, as discussed in Sect. 3.2. For all configurations, DDA has made 78,264 slot-value substitutions. In order to estimate the quality of the substitutions, we consider four features of the resulting datasets.

**Table 1.** Training data obtained using different configurations of generative DDA applied on the MultiWoz 2.3 source dialogues. First line (Cam) is for reference, and reports the characteristics of the MultiWoz 2.3 training data.

| Training Data | rank@100 | correct@100 | # slot-values | st. dev. | KB adh. |
|---|---|---|---|---|---|
| CAM-MWOZ (TRAINING) | 1.00 | 0.97 | 1680 | 241.51 | 0.61 |
| BERT (NO FINE-TUNING) | 0.68 | 0.65 | 4323 | 106.79 | 0.18 |
| BERT-M1.P1.S1.C1 | 0.62 | 0.59 | 3183 | 115.21 | 0.27 |
| BERT-M1.P1.S3.C50 | 0.92 | 0.65 | 1313 | 221.53 | 0.65 |
| BERT-M1.P4.SMAX.C50 | 0.95 | 0.69 | 1475 | 207.03 | 0.67 |
| BERT-M0.P4.SMAX.C50 | 0.96 | 0.74 | 1679 | 215.08 | 0.72 |
| BERT-M0.P8.SMAX.C50 | 0.98 | 0.70 | 1841 | 202.20 | 0.74 |

*Correct@100 and Rank@100.* This is a human evaluation of the correctness of the slot-values generated by G-DDA. Given a triple [DOMAIN, SLOT-NAME, SLOT-VALUE], this is considered correct (scored 1) if the generated slot-value is appropriate for the corresponding domain and slot, otherwise it is considered as wrong (scored -1). As an example:

[HOTEL, PRICE, EXPENSIVE] = correct

[TRAIN, DAY, DAY] = wrong

In fact, the slot-value EXPENSIVE is an appropriate value for HOTEL-PRICE, but the slot-value DAY is not appropriate for TRAIN-DAY (it should instead be a week-day).

We manually assessed the first one hundred slot-values generated by different DDA configurations. In Table 1 we report two measures: correct@100 is the proportion of correct generations (percentage of correct slot-values), while rank@100 scores slot-values assigning higher scores to those that are correct in higher positions, using a Geometrical Series [1] (correct values with high ranking have a higher weight with respect to correct values with low ranking).

*# Slot-Values.* This is the number of unique slot-values generated by a certain DDA configuration. Intuitively, a high number of slot-values is an indication of a good generative capacity of the model, which is somehow expected by the BERT masked language approach. However, the goal is to generate correct slot-values, which are captured by correctness@100. Furthermore, different [DOMAIN, SLOT] pairs have different generative capacities, which are, to a large extent, inherent to domain knowledge. As an example, we may think that there are many more [TRAIN, DESTINATION] from Cambridge, than different [HOTEL, STARS].

*St. Dev.* This is the standard deviation over the occurrences of all slot-values generated by a certain DDA configuration. We consider standard deviation as useful information related to the distribution of the slot-values in the training data. While the slot-value distribution in test data of the target domain is not known, we can expect the standard deviation of the source training data (i.e., MultiWOZ 2.3) to be a good approximation.

*KB Adherence.* This is the proportion of slot-values generated by DDA that are present in the target Knowledge Base. Basically, KB Adherence measures the capacity of a DDA configuration to constrain slot-value generations to the target domain (i.e., the Pisa domain described in Sect. 3). We expect that a good trade-off between target slot values (i.e., used in the target KB), and *unseen* slot-values (not used in the target KB, although consistent with it), would allow best predictions by the dialogue state tracking model (see Sect. 5).

Several considerations can be extrapolated from Table 1. First, it is evident that the size of fine-tuning data used by DDA configurations has a relevant impact on the generated slot-values. In fact, both the correctness@100, the number of generated slot-values, and the KB Adherence increase as the number of patterns used by the DDA model (indicated with P1, P4 and P8) grows. However, correct@100 slightly decreases with the largest number of patterns (line 7 in Table 1), which indicates that the DDA model starts introducing noisy slot-values. This issue is also reflected in the high number of slot-values generated by the P8 model (1841, last line).

We also notice that the DDA configuration based on automatic extraction of patterns (lines 6 and 7 in Table 1) from the source training data has better quality results than the corresponding configuration with manually selected patterns. This is very significant, as it shows that the whole DDA process can be automatized, without losing the quality of data. Finally, we notice that the standard deviation of all DDA configurations is lower than in the MWoZ training data. This might mean that the DDA distribution is still not optimal, which may affect the performance of dialogue state tracking. Specifically, the MWoZ distribution is significantly more polarized than DDA.

**Table 2.** Results obtained with different DDA configurations on dialogue state tracking using the TRADE model.

| Training Data | Test Data | JGA | JGA (test) | F1 (test) | SA (test) |
|---|---|---|---|---|---|
| CAM-MWOZ (TRAINING) | CAM-MWOZ | 0.521 | 0.489 | 0.900 | 0.970 |
| CAM-MWOZ (TRAINING) | PISA-MWOZ | 0.521 | 0.131 | 0.632 | 0.918 |
| BERT (NO FINE TUNING) | PISA-MWOZ | 0.381 | 0.094 | 0.582 | 0.906 |
| BERT-M1.P1.S1.C1 | PISA-MWOZ | 0.400 | 0.074 | 0.551 | 0.902 |
| BERT-M1.P1.S3.C50 | PISA-MWOZ | 0.406 | 0.175 | 0.698 | 0.929 |
| BERT -M1.P4.SMAX.C50 | PISA-MWOZ | 0.404 | 0.190 | 0.705 | 0.930 |
| BERT-M0.P4.SMAX.C50 | PISA-MWOZ | 0.401 | 0.195 | 0.708 | 0.931 |
| BERT-M0.P8.SMAX.C50 | PISA-MWOZ | 0.389 | 0.192 | 0.710 | 0.931 |

## 5    Results

Table 2 shows how the training data generated by different DDA configurations performs in dialogue state tracking. For all experiments, we used a manually built test set for the Pisa domain, described in Sect. 3. As for the DST model we used TRADE [14], a model able to consider multiple domains and intensively experimented over several MultiWOZ versions. We used standard evaluation metrics for DST. Slot Accuracy (SA) indicates the average of single slot-values that have been correctly predicted; the Joint F1 score reflects the accuracy of the model, considering both precision and recall; finally, the Joint Goal Accuracy measures the percentage of correct predictions of dialogue states for every dialogue turn, where a prediction is considered correct if all the slot values in the dialogue turn are correctly predicted. We report both JGA at training time and JGA after evaluating the model on the Test Data. We notice that the performance of all the DDA configurations is low, if compared with the performance of the model trained on the MWoZ source dialogues and tested on the MWoZ source test data (line 1 in Table 2).

Although this was somehow expected, the gap with the best DDA model (line 7) indicates that automatic adaptation of source training dialogues is still very challenging. A relevant outcome so far is that there is a strong correlation between the indicators that we used in Table 1 to assess the quality of the DDA generations and the performance on the DST task. This is important for two reasons: (i) knowing which are the properties of the training set that affect DST performance allows to focus on improving DDA in those aspects; (ii) working on the DDA generation significantly shortens the developing cycle.

## 6   Conclusion

We have investigated a new task, Generative Dialogue Domain Adaptation, aiming at automatically developing new training dialogues when such dialogues become obsolete due to changes that occurred in the domain knowledge. We propose a generative DDA approach based on a large pre-trained language model such as BERT, fine-tuned on the target domain. We have defined a granular methodology for performing this kind of adaptation, by setting four parameters that can be adjusted for obtaining different target dialogue datasets. In addition to that, we have formulated new evaluation metrics for DDA generated datasets, which can be used for assessing the quality of the dataset in a very cost-effective way. The experiments that we conducted indicate that the DDA task is still very challenging, although we have shown evidence that, even with these first attempts, it can be possible to obtain strong improvements if compared to the No-adaptation setting, especially with patterns collected automatically from data and with larger sets of training utterances used for implementing fine-tuning.

## References

1. Andrews, G.E.: The geometric series in calculus. Am. Math. Mon. **105**(1), 36–40 (1998). https://doi.org/10.1080/00029890.1998.12004846

2. Balaraman, V., Magnini, B.: Domain-aware dialogue state tracker for multi-domain dialogue systems. IEEE/ACM Trans. Audio Speech Lang. Process. **29**, 866–873 (2021). https://doi.org/10.1109/TASLP.2021.3054309

3. Balaraman, V., Sheikhalishahi, S., Magnini, B.: Recent neural methods on dialogue state tracking for task-oriented dialogue systems: a survey. In: Li, H., et al. (eds.) Proceedings of the 22nd Annual Meeting of the Special Interest Group on Discourse and Dialogue, SIGdial 2021, Singapore and Online, 29–31 July 2021, pp. 239–251. Association for Computational Linguistics (2021). https://aclanthology.org/2021.sigdial-1.25

4. Devlin, J., Chang, M.W., Lee, K., Toutanova, K.: BERT: pre-training of deep bidirectional transformers for language understanding. In: Proceedings of the 2019 Conference of the North American Chapter of the Association for Computational Linguistics: Human Language Technologies, Volume 1 (Long and Short Papers), pp. 4171–4186. Association for Computational Linguistics, Minneapolis, June 2019. https://doi.org/10.18653/v1/N19-1423, https://www.aclweb.org/anthology/N19-1423

5. Feng, Y., Wang, Y., Li, H.: A sequence-to-sequence approach to dialogue state tracking. arXiv preprint arXiv:2011.09553 (2020)

6. Han, T., et al.: Multiwoz 2.3: a multi-domain task-oriented dataset enhanced with annotation corrections and co-reference annotation. arXiv preprint arXiv:2010.05594 (2020)

7. Henderson, M., Thomson, B., Williams, J.D.: The second dialog state tracking challenge. In: Proceedings of the 15th Annual Meeting of the Special Interest Group on Discourse and Dialogue (SIGDIAL), pp. 263–272. Association for Computational Linguistics, Philadelphia, June 2014. https://doi.org/10.3115/v1/W14-4337, https://www.aclweb.org/anthology/W14-4337

8. Labruna, T., Magnini, B.: Addressing slot-value changes in task-oriented dialogue systems through dialogue domain adaptation. In: Proceedings of RANLP 2021 (2021)

9. Labruna, T., Magnini, B.: From Cambridge to Pisa: a journey into cross-lingual dialogue domain adaptation for conversational agents (2021)

10. Madotto, A., Liu, Z., Lin, Z., Fung, P.: Language models as few-shot learner for task-oriented dialogue systems. arXiv preprint arXiv:2008.06239 (2020)

11. Magnini, B., Louvan, S.: Understanding Dialogue for Human Communication, pp. 1–43. Springer, Cham (2021). https://doi.org/10.1007/978-3-030-44982-7_20-1

12. McTear, M.: Conversational AI: Dialogue Systems, Conversational Agents, and Chatbots. Morgan and Claypool Publishers, San Rafael (2020). https://doi.org/10.2200/S01060ED1V01Y202010HLT048

13. Rastogi, A., Zang, X., Sunkara, S., Gupta, R., Khaitan, P.: Towards scalable multi-domain conversational agents: the schema-guided dialogue dataset. In: The Thirty-Fourth AAAI Conference on Artificial Intelligence, AAAI 2020, The Thirty-Second Innovative Applications of Artificial Intelligence Conference, IAAI 2020, The Tenth AAAI Symposium on Educational Advances in Artificial Intelligence, EAAI 2020, New York, NY, USA, 7–12 February 2020, pp. 8689–8696. AAAI Press (2020). https://aaai.org/ojs/index.php/AAAI/article/view/6394

14. Wu, C.S., Madotto, A., Hosseini-Asl, E., Xiong, C., Socher, R., Fung, P.: Transferable multi-domain state generator for task-oriented dialogue systems. In: Proceedings of the 57th Annual Meeting of the Association for Computational Linguistics, pp. 808–819. Association for Computational Linguistics, Florence, Italy, July 2019. https://doi.org/10.18653/v1/P19-1078, https://www.aclweb.org/anthology/P19-1078

15. Young, S., et al.: The hidden information state model: a practical framework for POMDP-based spoken dialogue management. Comput. Speech Lang. **24**(2), 150–174 (2010)
16. Zhao, J., Mahdieh, M., Zhang, Y., Cao, Y., Wu, Y.: Effective sequence-to-sequence dialogue state tracking. arXiv preprint arXiv:2108.13990 (2021)

# Empathy and Persona of English vs. Arabic Chatbots: A Survey and Future Directions

Omama Hamad[1]([✉])(iD), Ali Hamdi[2], and Khaled Shaban[1]

[1] Computer Science and Engineering Department, Qatar University, Doha, Qatar
{omama.hamad,khaled.shaban}@qu.edu.qa
[2] Computer Science School, University of Adelaide, Adelaide, Australia
alihamdi.ali@adelaide.edu.au

**Abstract.** There is a high demand for chatbots across a wide range of sectors. Human-like chatbots engage meaningfully in dialogues while interpreting and expressing emotions and being consistent through understanding the user's personality. Though substantial progress has been achieved in developing empathetic chatbots for English, work on Arabic chatbots is still in its early stages due to various challenges associated with the language constructs and dialects. This survey reviews recent literature on approaches to empathetic response generation, persona modelling and datasets for developing chatbots in the English language. In addition, it presents the challenges of applying these approaches to Arabic and outlines some solutions. We focus on open-domain chatbots developed as end-to-end generative systems due to their capabilities to learn and infer language and emotions. Accordingly, we create four open problems pertaining to gaps in Arabic and English work; namely, (1) feature representation learning based on multiple dialects; (2) modelling the various facets of a persona and emotions; (3) datasets; and (4) evaluation metrics.

**Keywords:** Chatbots · Deep learning · Empathetic dialogue · Natural language generation

## 1 Introduction

Chatbot systems have attracted increasing attention in recent years. These chatbots should exhibit empathy, which is the capacity to share another's emotional states. Additionally, tailoring the chatbot responses based on general or specific knowledge about the user increases the chatbot's adaptability and engagement. According to several psychological studies, empathy is associated with certain aspects of the persona [14,41]. Therefore, different types of interlocutors require an adaptable chatbot, capable of grasping several aspects of their personality based on the context of the conversation. Researchers have classified empathy into multiple levels: 'affective empathy', which is the ability to understand

© Springer Nature Switzerland AG 2022
P. Sojka et al. (Eds.): TSD 2022, LNAI 13502, pp. 525–537, 2022.
https://doi.org/10.1007/978-3-031-16270-1_43

another person's emotions and respond appropriately; and 'cognitive empathy', which is the ability to understand another person's mental state [33]. By incorporating this level of empathy into a humanoid chatbot, user engagement might be increased and the dialogue enriched rather than generating generic responses devoid of consistency, empathy or relevancy.

The sole survey on Arabic chatbots [3] focused exclusively on retrieval-based techniques. [8] conducted an analysis of dialogue systems that employed a variety of deep learning algorithms, datasets, and evaluation frameworks. They highlighted empathetic datasets, but they didn't focus on methods for analysing emotions and personas. Contemporary surveys [13, 42] reviewed recent techniques for text generation that capture emotions and personalities. [35] focused on generative adversarial networks for implementing empathetic chatbots. Due to the advancements in empathetic chatbots occurring at a breakneck pace, there is an ongoing need for up-to-date surveys. The reset of the article is organised as follows: Sect. 2 discusses two issues: (a) emotion versus sentiment response generation, as recent works have grouped emotions into sentiments, which generate a response with general feelings. (b) the research challenges associated with interpreting emotions in Arabic chatbots and preprocessing. Section 3 provides an overview of emotion-based chatbots and persona-based chatbots, highlighting the importance of personality understanding in empathetic chatbots. Section 4 presents various proposed chatbots that use deep learning and reinforcement learning techniques. Section 5 is to lay the ground work for future research into Arabic gaps and language-independent works. To the best of our knowledge, none of the recent surveys addressed these issues.

## 2    Research Challenges

This section highlights the challenges associated with recently proposed empathetic chatbots, as well as the difficulties related with preprocessing the Arabic language.

### 2.1    Emotion vs Sentiment

Some studies have focused on addressing the issue of conversing empathetically by sentiment or emotion modelling [25, 43]. In practice, user emotion modelling is much more challenging than sentiment analysis. Emotion analysis is based on a more in-depth analysis of the intensities associated with each emotion, which enables a chatbot to identify the user's thoughts and state. The sentiment is used to understand how individuals feel and has limited number of classes, such as positive, negative, or neutral. Still, the emotional analysis is broad and have been identified into eight bipolar emotions with varied intensities: joy, sadness, anger, fear, trust, disgust, surprise and anticipation [31]. As shown in Table 1, the sentiment analysis captures the general feeling of the user's statement. Yet, it does not focus on the nuances of feelings that the emotion analysis captures, which makes the sentiment-based model giving a generic answer. In contrast, the emotion-based response looks for specific positive emotions like surprise, which validates what the user is feeling. Complex colloquial expressions like sarcasm and negation continue to confound sentiment and emotion models. The negation might cause the emotion to change in the opposite direction, causing difficulties in determining the emotion and, as a result, generating inappropriate responses. To the best of our knowledge, this issue has not yet been addressed for Arabic chatbots due to limited resources for data-driven models.

**Table 1.** Emotional vs sentimental response

| Context | Response Sentiment analysis | Response Emotion analysis |
|---|---|---|
| It was my birthday last week, and I thought everyone forgot about it. | Sentiment: Positive I'm happy to hear that. | Emotion: Surprise That's cool... Did you have a surprise party? |

## 2.2 Arabic Preprocessing Challenges

Arabic is the fourth most spoken language in the world, and it comes in two forms: standard Arabic (MSA) and dialectal Arabic (DA). MSA is the standard form of Arabic, and DA is more common for everyday speaking and writing and has simpler grammar rules [4]. Arabic chatbots have fallen behind their English counterparts in terms of limited datasets and non-learning approaches. Some of the challenges in preprocessing the Arabic language are: (1) In Arabic writing, vowels are omitted, causing ambiguity [29], (2) clitics can be attached to a root word without orthographic markers and can be up to four clitics before a stem and three after [29], (3) Because Arabic does not support capital letters, it is difficult to recognise names [5], (4) There is a high degree of lexical sparsity, implying that words can take various forms while still communicating the same meaning, and (5) different dialect words may have the same spelling but an entirely different meaning, which affects a chatbot's ability to identify emotions and personas in written text without extra input.

## 3  Emotion- and Persona-Based Chatbots

Humans chat with someone who understands their feelings and personality. And, chatbots should reflect this skill. The chatbot system must first understand the emotion and topic of the written text, which entails dealing with the language linguistic issues. Through the application of empathy, three distinct machine learning-based approaches have been used to generate human-like responses to a user's statements: training a model for response generation while fixing it to a certain emotion; a multi-tasking approach that trained a model to predict the user's present emotional state and to generate an appropriate response based on that state [24]; and an end-to-end approach in which the model learned both the language and the emotional state required to generate an empathetic response. On the other hand, Zhong et al. [45] argued that personas are critical in empathetic conversations and presented a dataset for persona-based empathetic conversations. A persona is an abstract depiction of a large number of people who share certain traits, such as age, gender or a general or specific self-description of their personalities [38]. Learning the persona in chatbot systems ensures the consistency of generated responses and avoids giving out generic responses. Traits were grouped into what the 'Big Five personality traits', which reflect human temperament and identity [36]. For instance, neurotic people often feel anxious and sad and are more likely to be described as 'angry' or 'depressed'. Thus, personality and emotions are tightly correlated [26].

Conversational systems are composed of interconnected components, each of which affects overall system performance. Figure 1 depicts a framework that can be used to develop an end-to-end empathetic chatbot. It consists of the following four modules: (1) NLU consists of preprocessing and semantic analysis. The preprocessing includes standard tokenisation, stemming, normalisation and segmentation. Segmentation is especially needed for languages such as Arabic, as Arabic nouns can take on a variety of forms when prefixed with the definite article 'Al', (equivalent to the English 'the'). Thus, it is necessary to remove this portion from words before proceeding with further processing, otherwise the process will result in the term appearing multiple times [1]. The semantic analysis includes sentiment and/or emotion detection, named entity recognition, intent recognition and persona understanding. (2) Dialogue management tracks emotion-state changes by managing a conversation history, the user's emotion state and topic transition. (3) NLG generates an empathetic response. (4) knowledge access to produce useful responses [34]; however, the majority of end-to-end systems employ the first and third modules using data-driven techniques to understand the language's structure. Various datasets are used to train NLU and NLG models, including parallel data labelled with emotion, sentiment and persona [32]. The performance of the chatbot and the quality of the answers it generates are measured both automatically and by humans. Popular metrics based on word-overlapping are BLEU [30] and ROUGE [17]. There are other trained metrics, such as the automatic dialogue evaluation model, which is a hierarchical recurrent neural network trained to predict human scores [23].

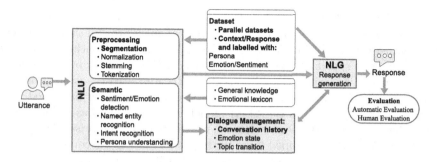

**Fig. 1.** Empathetic chatbot architecture.

# 4   Learning Models for Chatbots

This section surveys the recent work on empathetic and persona-based chatbots by employing deep learning and reinforcement learning techniques.

## 4.1   Deep Learning Models

Neural networks, such as seq2seq and Generative Adversarial Networks (GANs) [16], are commonly used in current generative-based models. They learn the language structure and syntax to generate a sequence based on the input [27]. Using pretrained, finetuned models can generate an appropriate sequence because the models have been trained on vast amounts of conversational open-domain data [7,27]. However, It is not a guarantee that using pretrained models will lead to an empathetic, consistent and relevant response. Empathy requires a thorough understanding of the current conversation and its preceding threads. Recent research papers employ end-to-end models for generative-based conversations by utilising encoder-decoder architectures or a mixture of experts [18]. This type of model takes user input at the $t-th$ dialogue turn and dialogue context $C_t$ to generate a response $Y_t$.

$$Y_t = \arg\max_{Y \in \alpha} \mathrm{P}_\theta(Y|X_t, C_t) \tag{1}$$

Typically, in the case of generation-based approaches, the search space $\alpha$ is quite big, specifically $Y \in V^m$, where $V$ represents the size of vocabulary, $m$ the length of the response and $\mathrm{P}_\theta(Y|X_t, C_t)$ creates a sentence word by word. A single-turn conversation is modelled when $C_t = \phi$. $C_t$ can also encode other contexts, such as personas and emotion labels [15].

According to Rashkin et al. [32], training the model over an empathetic conversation dataset can boost the effectiveness of an end-to-end chatbot system on empathetic conversation. Therefore, they released a new benchmark dataset with empathetic speech. This dataset was translated into Arabic by Naous et al. [28] to train the Arabic chatbot. Naous et al. [27] addressed the issue of limited Arabic datasets by introducing an encoder-decoder transformer initialised with AraBERT parameters [6] (a Bert2Bert model [9]). The model was trained using the Arabic Empathetic Dialogues dataset, which originally comprised 32 emotion labels, but the authors mapped them to the six core labels. As compared to the Bi-LSTM model [28], this model outperforms it with a perplexity score of 17.0, proving its high ability to exhibit empathy while generating relevant responses in open-domain scenarios. However, this approach is coarse-grained and has issues when applying the model to other dataset.

There are a handful of studies that take both persona and emotion into account by employing encoder-decoder framework. Zhong et al. [45] developed a method based on a BERT for response selection engine, to retrieve empathetic responses based on personas. However, they annotated 200 randomly selected conversations in order to determine their emotions, which are not enough to train a model. Firdaus et al. [11] suggested a transformer model for generating an emotional response in accordance with the user's persona by encoding both of them. However, this approach relies on sentiment, which does not always deliver the desired emotion. An empathetic neural chatbot called CAiRE was pretrained on the PersonaChat dataset [44] and fine-tuned on empathetic dialogues. This allowed CAiRE to have a more consistent persona. Detecting the interlocutor's emotions was implemented by taking the summary of the recent state of dialogue and passing it to a linear projection layer [19]. RoBERTa [22] was employed as an encoder and GPT-2 as a decoder to generate an empathetic response. This response generation decoder was supported by external knowledge, where keywords were extracted from sentences and emotional concepts [21]. However, empathy was not evaluated by a human. These chatbots would achieve good performance when trained on English datasets, but data-driven models would face difficulty in inferring the emotions and personas in Arabic text since the same word could convey multiple meanings and the same word could have at least 16 different nouns and verbs. Table 2 summaries some of the recent work.

**Table 2.** Empathetic and persona-based chatbots using RL and DL technique

| Objective | models | Challenges | Open Problems |
|---|---|---|---|
| **DL models** | | | |
| Generating an empathetic response [18] | • Mixture of standard decoders<br>• Meta listener<br>• Standard encoder | Additional inductive bias and interpretability | considering only the coarse-grained emotional classes |
| Empathetic Arabic chatbot [28] | • Seq2seq model using LSTM units and attention | Inferring emotions from the user's statement | There is some deviance from the topic in the response, as indicated by the relevance score |
| Personalising response generation [12] | • GRU<br>• persona-aware attention | lack of a dataset annotated with both emotions and personas | The followed strategy is susceptible to repetition and its relevance is not measured |
| **RL models** | | | |
| Rewriting conversations with low empathy to higher empathy [37] | • Policy model (GPT-2)<br>• Position classifier<br>• Sentence generator<br>• Empathy classification model<br>• Language model for English (GPT-2)<br>• Text-classification model (BERT)<br>• Reward functions: change in empathy from the original to the rewritten response | Language fluency must be maintained while converting low empathetic text to high empathetic text | This approach supposed that the responses are available which is not customised to the user's statement. |
| Making the chatbot learn from and be guided by the user's statements to influence its interlocutor with intentions [39] | • Interlocutor model<br>• Guiding Chatbot (DialoGPT)<br>• Emotion classifier (BERT)<br>• Reward function: conveying a specific emotion and speaking specific words | Understanding the impact of the chatbot's statements on the interlocutor | Response generation based on controlled emotions that do not empathize with the user's words but rather aim to influence the user |
| Incorporating mutual-persona perception [20] | • Pretrained model (GPT)<br>• Next Utterance Predictor<br>• Reward function: Characterising mutual-persona perception | Have a dialogue generation that is naturally focused on understanding | Used predefined personas, which limits the chabot's adaptability |
| A model learns to ask personalised questions to identify its partner's underlying persona [40] | • Identifier model<br>• Verifier network (PersonaGPT)<br>• Deep Q-learning<br>Reward function: loss function of the previous turns and the input agent's personality | Understanding of sentences is not always the goal of supervised dialogue generation | Only considers direct persona expressions, not indirect ones. |

## 4.2   Reinforcement Learning (RL) Models

Deep learning approaches have yielded outstanding results, however these models do not learn from their actions and do not measure the impact of those actions. This style of dynamic learning is achieved by RL, which learns through trial and error, allowing the system to self-improve and adapt to changes in the user's state. The reward functions at the core of RL provide feedback on the model's performance in relation to the chatbot's purpose. Even though the purpose of the chatbot is to understand the emotion in a user's statement and generate an empathetic response, other components are integral parts of the conversational system, such as sentence fluency and relevancy. Based on the motivation, research in RL may be broken into two categories: first, improving the response based on how the user would feel about the generated response, and, second, evaluating the empathy of the generated response. This first issue is critical because, if the response had been as intended, the user would have engaged more actively in the dialogue. Many studies have proposed combining the encoder-decoder model with RL to preserve emotion changes, fluency and relevance of responses [37,39]. Table 2, shows various works have proposed distinct reward functions for developing an emotion-based and persona-based chatbots.

## 5   Open Problems

This section outlines open problems related to gaps in Arabic and English work that could serve as future directions for developing empathetic and persona-based chatbots. These problems can be classified into four broad groups as follows:

**Modelling the Various Facets of a Persona and Emotions.** According to psychological studies, emotions can be confusing and they are classified into varying degrees of intensity. There are certain emotions that are a composite of two basic emotions. For instance, combining joy and trust creates love [31]. Due to the complexity of emotions, models will have a limited capacity to recognise them. Additionally, some emotions are close to one another, causing the model to have difficulties identifying them. For instance, with surprise and fear, the former may convey a positive sentiment while the latter may convey a negative sentiment. One possible solution is to layer sentiment analysis on top of fine-grained emotion analysis to generate appropriate responses with the relevant feelings. Another potential solution is to combine persona and emotion in order to boost engagement and make the model generate a more empathetic response based on the character being conversed with since most recent models are hindered by repeated and generic responses. All of these aspects require a paradigm shift in a variety of dimensions to construct an emotional-intelligence model.

**Feature Representations Learning Based on Multiple Dialects.** The proposed approaches for DA are limited to a single Arabic dialect or based on retrieval approaches employing artificial intelligence markup language (AIML)

[2]. So the proposed chatbots are limited in their capacity to respond to statements that are based on different dialects. Since there is no work on empathetic generative-based chatbots for multiple dialects, more study is needed. The difficulty with DA is that various countries share some words with distinct meanings and different emotions, so the model must understand which dialect is being used in the context in order to reply accordingly. For example, most dialects use the expression "May God give you strength" to indicate appreciation يعطيك العافية, in the Moroccan dialect, it represents anger and insult, and means "You wish him to burn with the fire". Moreover, diacritics are used to distinguish between the meanings of words that have the same form. For example, أَكِفَأ، أَكْفَاء the first one indicates praise, while the second means blindness and if they aren't understood appropriately, the model could be misled into producing incorrect embeddings, which affect the performance of the NLP tasks.

**Evaluation Metrics.** Automation can be achieved to some extent with open domain text generation, but it can be improved by developing a metric that is highly correlated with human judgments. The unstructured nature of the conversation makes evaluating an open-domain chatbot tricky, and it is challenging to determine whether the response is human-like. Since the majority of current evaluation measures are coarse-grained, it is necessary to create fine-grained techniques to have a better understanding of the model's various behaviours and the impact of token-level performance on the overall performance. One solution is to construct a dataset with multiple possible responses and compare the generated responses against them using the BLEU metric [30].

**Datasets.** Conversational datasets are a valuable resource for the development of end-to-end chatbots. In English, datasets are either annotated with emotions or personas, as shown in Table 3, but no Arabic dataset is annotated with personas. Hence, a dataset annotated with both is needed. These datasets will enable the generative-based model to learn complicated semantic associations. However, effective approaches to be suggested in the future may rely on the development of a model that learns from a small number of samples. More advancement could eventually lead to the creation of a parallel dialogue dataset that contains many different dialects of the Arabic language.

**Table 3.** Open-domain empathetic and persona-based datasets.

| Dataset | Dialogues | Dataset description | Multi-turn | Persona | Emotion | Public |
|---------|-----------|---------------------|:----------:|:-------:|:-------:|:------:|
| Persona-Based Empathetic Conversational [45] | Dialogues: 355k<br>Utter: 833k<br>Persona: 250k | -Source: social media (Reddit)<br>- 100 randomly sampled conversations annotated from each domain | ✓ | ✓ | ✗ | ✓ |
| PERSONA-CHAT [44] | Dialogues: 11,981<br>Utter:164,356<br>Persona: 1,155 | -Source: Crowd-sourced | ✓ | ✓ | ✗ | ✓ |
| ConvAI2 [10] | Dialogues: 19,893<br>Utter: 145,873<br>Personas: 1,355 | -Source: Crowd-source<br>- Extended version (with a new test set) of the persona-chat dataset | ✓ | ✓ | ✗ | ✓ |
| EMPATHETIC DIALOGUES [32] | Dialogues: 24,850<br>Emotions:<br>24,850/32 labels | -Source: Crowd-source | ✓ | ✓ | ✓ | ✓ |
| Arabic EMPATHETICDIALOGUES [28] | Dialogues: 24,850<br>Emotions:<br>24,850/32 labels | -Source: Crowd-source<br>-Translated from ED dataset [32] | ✗ | ✗ | ✓ | ✓ |

# 6    Conclusion

Empathy-based chatbots have been the focus of considerable research in recent years and this paper provides a survey of the state-of-the-art studies in this area in terms of approaches for empathetic response generation, datasets and persona modelling. Furthermore, it provides insights into the future directions for this field, such as understanding the persona from the emotions expressed in sentences and modelling both emotions and persona, which will improve engagement and consistency. In addition, it outlines the challenges associated with the Arabic language, as well as proposes some solutions. Despite extensive research on empathetic chatbots, this study found that most models do not capture the intensity of emotions, which opens the door to future directions for understanding the intensities of complex emotions.

**Acknowledgments.** This work was made possible by NPRP13S-0112-200037 grant from Qatar National Research Fund (a member of Qatar Foundation). The statements made herein are solely the responsibility of the authors.

# References

1. Abdelali, A., Darwish, K., Durrani, N., Mubarak, H.: Farasa: a fast and furious segmenter for Arabic. In: Proceedings of the 2016 conference of the North American Chapter of the Association for Computational Linguistics: Demonstrations, pp. 11–16 (2016)
2. Abu Ali, D., Habash, N.: Botta: an Arabic dialect chatbot. In: Proceedings of COLING 2016, the 26th International Conference on Computational Linguistics: System Demonstrations, pp. 208–212. The COLING 2016 Organizing Committee, Osaka, Japan, December 2016

3. AlHumoud, S., Al Wazrah, A., Aldamegh, W.: Arabic chatbots: a survey. Int. J. Adv. Comput. Sci. Appl. 535–541 (2018)
4. Aliwy, A., Taher, H., AboAltaheen, Z.: Arabic dialects identification for all Arabic countries. In: Proceedings of the Fifth Arabic Natural Language Processing Workshop, pp. 302–307. Association for Computational Linguistics, Barcelona, Spain (Online), December 2020
5. Almiman, A., Osman, N., Torki, M.: Deep neural network approach for Arabic community question answering. Alex. Eng. J. **59**(6), 4427–4434 (2020)
6. Antoun, W., Baly, F., Hajj, H.: AraBERT: transformer-based model for Arabic language understanding. In: LREC 2020 Workshop Language Resources and Evaluation Conference, 11–16 May 2020, p. 9 (2020)
7. Beredo, J., Bautista, C.M., Cordel, M., Ong, E.: Generating empathetic responses with a pre-trained conversational model. In: Ekštein, K., Pártl, F., Konopík, M. (eds.) TSD 2021. LNCS (LNAI), vol. 12848, pp. 147–158. Springer, Cham (2021). https://doi.org/10.1007/978-3-030-83527-9_13
8. Caldarini, G., Jaf, S., McGarry, K.: A literature survey of recent advances in chatbots. Information **13**(1), 41 (2022)
9. Devlin, J., Chang, M.W., Lee, K., Toutanova, K.: BERT: pre-training of deep bidirectional transformers for language understanding. In: Proceedings of the 2019 Conference of the North American Chapter of the Association for Computational Linguistics: Human Language Technologies, Volume 1 (Long and Short Papers), pp. 4171–4186. Association for Computational Linguistics, Minneapolis, June 2019
10. Dinan, E., et al.: The second conversational intelligence challenge (ConvAI2). In: Escalera, S., Herbrich, R. (eds.) The NeurIPS '18 Competition. TSSCML, pp. 187–208. Springer, Cham (2020). https://doi.org/10.1007/978-3-030-29135-8_7
11. Firdaus, M., Jain, U., Ekbal, A., Bhattacharyya, P.: SEPRG: sentiment aware emotion controlled personalized response generation. In: Proceedings of the 14th International Conference on Natural Language Generation, pp. 353–363. Association for Computational Linguistics, Aberdeen, August 2021
12. Firdaus, M., Thangavelu, N., Ekba, A., Bhattacharyya, P.: Persona aware response generation with emotions. In: 2020 International Joint Conference on Neural Networks (IJCNN), pp. 1–8 (2020)
13. Fu, T., Gao, S., Zhao, X., Wen, J.R., Yan, R.: Learning towards conversational AI: a survey. AI Open (2022)
14. Guilera, T., Batalla, I., Forné, C., Soler-González, J.: Empathy and big five personality model in medical students and its relationship to gender and specialty preference: a cross-sectional study. BMC Med. Educ. **19**(1), 1–8 (2019)
15. Huang, M., Zhu, X., Gao, J.: Challenges in building intelligent open-domain dialog systems. ACM Trans. Inf. Syst. (TOIS) **38**(3), 1–32 (2020)
16. Kusner, M.J., Hernández-Lobato, J.M.: GANs for sequences of discrete elements with the Gumbel-softmax distribution. arXiv preprint arXiv:1611.04051 (2016)
17. Lin, C.Y.: Rouge: a package for automatic evaluation of summaries. In: Text Summarization Branches Out, pp. 74–81 (2004)
18. Lin, Z., Madotto, A., Shin, J., Xu, P., Fung, P.: Moel: mixture of empathetic listeners. arXiv preprint arXiv:1908.07687 (2019)
19. Lin, Z., et al.: Caire: an end-to-end empathetic chatbot. In: Proceedings of the AAAI Conference on Artificial Intelligence, vol. 34, pp. 13622–13623 (2020)
20. Liu, Q., et al.: You impress me: dialogue generation via mutual persona perception. In: Proceedings of the 58th Annual Meeting of the Association for Computational Linguistics, pp. 1417–1427. Association for Computational Linguistics, Online, July 2020

21. Liu, Y., Maier, W., Minker, W., Ultes, S.: Empathetic dialogue generation with pretrained RobERTa-GPT2 and external knowledge. arXiv preprint arXiv:2109.03004 (2021)

22. Liu, Y., et al.: RoBERTa: a robustly optimized BERT pretraining approach. arXiv preprint arXiv:1907.11692 (2019)

23. Lowe, R., Noseworthy, M., Serban, I.V., Angelard-Gontier, N., Bengio, Y., Pineau, J.: Towards an automatic turing test: learning to evaluate dialogue responses. arXiv preprint arXiv:1708.07149 (2017)

24. Lubis, N., Sakti, S., Yoshino, K., Nakamura, S.: Eliciting positive emotion through affect-sensitive dialogue response generation: a neural network approach. In: Proceedings of the AAAI Conference on Artificial Intelligence, vol. 32 (2018)

25. Majumder, N., et al.: Mime: mimicking emotions for empathetic response generation. arXiv preprint arXiv:2010.01454 (2020)

26. Miller, T., Pedell, S., Lopez-Lorca, A.A., Mendoza, A., Sterling, L., Keirnan, A.: Emotion-led modelling for people-oriented requirements engineering: the case study of emergency systems. J. Syst. Softw. **105**, 54–71 (2015)

27. Naous, T., Antoun, W., Mahmoud, R., Hajj, H.: Empathetic BERT2BERT conversational model: learning Arabic language generation with little data. In: Proceedings of the Sixth Arabic Natural Language Processing Workshop, pp. 164–172. Association for Computational Linguistics, Kyiv, Ukraine (Virtual), April 2021

28. Naous, T., Hokayem, C., Hajj, H.: Empathy-driven Arabic conversational chatbot. In: Proceedings of the Fifth Arabic Natural Language Processing Workshop, pp. 58–68. Association for Computational Linguistics, Barcelona, Spain (Online), December 2020

29. Neme, A.A., Paumier, S.: Restoring Arabic vowels through omission-tolerant dictionary lookup. Lang. Resour. Eval. **54**(2), 487–551 (2020)

30. Papineni, K., Roukos, S., Ward, T., Zhu, W.J.: BLEU: a method for automatic evaluation of machine translation. In: Proceedings of the 40th Annual Meeting of the Association for Computational Linguistics, pp. 311–318 (2002)

31. Plutchik, R., Kellerman, H.: Emotion, Theory, Research, and Experience. Academic Press, Cambridge (1980)

32. Rashkin, H., Smith, E.M., Li, M., Boureau, Y.L.: Towards empathetic open-domain conversation models: a new benchmark and dataset. In: Proceedings of the 57th Annual Meeting of the Association for Computational Linguistics, pp. 5370–5381. Association for Computational Linguistics, Florence, Italy, July 2019

33. Reniers, R.L., Corcoran, R., Drake, R., Shryane, N.M., Völlm, B.A.: The QCAE: a questionnaire of cognitive and affective empathy. J. Pers. Assess. **93**(1), 84–95 (2011)

34. Roller, S., et al.: Recipes for building an open-domain chatbot. arXiv preprint arXiv:2004.13637 (2020)

35. de Rosa, G.H., Papa, J.P.: A survey on text generation using generative adversarial networks. Pattern Recogn. **119**, 108098 (2021)

36. Salminen, J., Rao, R.G., Jung, S., Chowdhury, S.A., Jansen, B.J.: Enriching social media personas with personality traits: a deep learning approach using the big five classes. In: Degen, H., Reinerman-Jones, L. (eds.) HCII 2020. LNCS, vol. 12217, pp. 101–120. Springer, Cham (2020). https://doi.org/10.1007/978-3-030-50334-5_7

37. Sharma, A., Lin, I.W., Miner, A.S., Atkins, D.C., Althoff, T.: Towards facilitating empathic conversations in online mental health support: a reinforcement learning approach. In: Proceedings of the Web Conference 2021, pp. 194–205 (2021)

38. Song, H., Wang, Y., Zhang, K., Zhang, W.N., Liu, T.: BoB: BERT over BERT for training persona-based dialogue models from limited personalized data. In: Proceedings of the 59th Annual Meeting of the Association for Computational Linguistics and the 11th International Joint Conference on Natural Language Processing (Volume 1: Long Papers), pp. 167–177. Association for Computational Linguistics, Online, August 2021

39. Su, H., Jhan, J.H., Sun, F.Y., Sahay, S., Lee, H.Y.: Put chatbot into its interlocutor's shoes: new framework to learn chatbot responding with intention. In: Proceedings of the 2021 Conference of the North American Chapter of the Association for Computational Linguistics: Human Language Technologies, pp. 1559–1569. Association for Computational Linguistics, Online, June 2021

40. Tang, F., Zeng, L., Wang, F., Zhou, J.: Persona authentication through generative dialogue. arXiv preprint arXiv:2110.12949 (2021)

41. Toussaint, L., Webb, J.R.: Gender differences in the relationship between empathy and forgiveness. J. Soc. Psychol. **145**(6), 673–685 (2005)

42. Yang, D., Flek, L.: Towards user-centric text-to-text generation: a survey. In: Ekštein, K., Pártl, F., Konopík, M. (eds.) TSD 2021. LNCS (LNAI), vol. 12848, pp. 3–22. Springer, Cham (2021). https://doi.org/10.1007/978-3-030-83527-9_1

43. Zaranis, E., Paraskevopoulos, G., Katsamanis, A., Potamianos, A.: EmpBot: a t5-based empathetic chatbot focusing on sentiments. arXiv preprint arXiv:2111.00310 (2021)

44. Zhang, S., Dinan, E., Urbanek, J., Szlam, A., Kiela, D., Weston, J.: Personalizing dialogue agents: I have a dog, do you have pets too? In: Proceedings of the 56th Annual Meeting of the Association for Computational Linguistics (Volume 1: Long Papers), pp. 2204–2213. Association for Computational Linguistics, Melbourne, Australia, July 2018

45. Zhong, P., Zhang, C., Wang, H., Liu, Y., Miao, C.: Towards persona-based empathetic conversational models. In: Proceedings of the 2020 Conference on Empirical Methods in Natural Language Processing (EMNLP), pp. 6556–6566. Association for Computational Linguistics, Online, November 2020

# Author Index

Printed in the United States
by Baker & Taylor Publisher Services